A Biographical Dictionary
of Psychologists, Psychiatrists
and Psychotherapists

WILLIAM STEWART

Foreword by Stan Gilmore

McFarland & Company, Inc., Publishers
Jefferson, North Carolina, and London

LIBRARY OF CONGRESS CATALOGUING-IN-PUBLICATION DATA

Stewart, William, 1927–
A biographical dictionary of psychologists, psychiatrists
and psychotherapists / William Stewart.
p.   cm.
Includes bibliographical references and index.

ISBN 978-0-7864-3292-9
(illustrated case binding: 50# alkaline paper) ∞

1. Psychologists — Biography — Dictionaries.   2. Psychiatrists — Biography —
Dictionaries.   3. Psychotherapists — Biography — Dictionaries.   I. Title.
BF109.A1S76   2008
150.92'2 — dc22   [B]   2007049399

British Library cataloguing data are available

Cover photograph ©2008 Shutterstock

Manufactured in the United States of America

*McFarland & Company, Inc., Publishers
Box 611, Jefferson, North Carolina 28640
www.mcfarlandpub.com*

Contents

Foreword

William Stewart is one of the most prolific authors in the field of counselling in the United Kingdom. He combines an encyclopedic knowledge and clinical experience derived from hospital contexts in both military and civilian settings.

This is demonstrated by his understanding of people in crisis or confronting the aching questions of the human heart when they are at their most vulnerable. This subtle blend of theory and practice of theory underpinned by an underlying warm humanity adds an authoritative tone to his writing.

However, as an extended professional, William possesses the gift of the born teacher. This gives a distinctive quality to this publication. Students and practitioners alike will find this book an easily accessible work of reference which will add to and consolidate their knowledge base. Devoid of troublesome jargon, William's writing style is characterized by clarity of expression and meticulous attention to the accurate rendition of the facts.

Each major figure in the history of psychiatry and psychology is presented with sufficient biographical detail and a concise elucidation of core concepts to provide the reader with an overview of the subject's place in the development of this comparative recent field of knowledge. At the same time, sufficient information is provided for the reader to engage in critical reflection. Students and lecturers will find the book a boon in the writing of essays and the preparation of lectures.

The general reader will also find it a thoroughly good read that can be dipped in for specific items of information or to engage in intelligent and meaningful browsing.

I warmly recommend this book to both professionals and the reading public.

Stan Gilmore, Ph.D.
External Examiner
Institute of Counselling
Glasgow
U.K.

Preface

I have been in the fields of psychiatry, nursing, social work and teaching since I was seventeen, so in many ways this book represents a lifetime interest.

More recently the idea for it took root when, as a student counsellor and lecturer, I would be asked details about specific people in the field of therapy, or details of the life of one of the theorists. I was sometimes able to give answers; more often I had to do some research. About two years ago, a comment by a reviewer of the fourth edition of my *A–Z of Counselling Theory and Practice* suggested an A to Z on key figures in counselling and their theories. This comment spurred my research and writing of a reasonably compact reference book that introduces readers to many of the main theorists and practitioners.

The book covers two major groups: psychologists and psychiatrists. A third group is psychotherapists whose training is either psychology or psychiatry or both.

Each entry is limited to 500 words and includes personal details, career highlights, contributions to the field and any important writings produced. Keeping to 500 words was essential; otherwise the book would run to several volumes, for there is so much material available for most of the people profiled.

I consider it a privilege to have been able to compile this book, and researching the lives of the people herein has enriched my own professional body of knowledge. My hope is that you will find the book both interesting and stimulating as you read about the men and women (some well-known, others not so well-known) who have all contributed to the body the knowledge of psychology, psychiatry and related fields.

William Stewart
Bishopstoke
Eastleigh
Hampshire, England

Dictionary of Psychologists, Psychiatrists and Psychotherapists

Abraham, Karl (1877–1925)

INFANT SEXUALITY

Karl Abraham was a German psychoanalyst, born in Bremen. Abraham served under psychiatrist Eugen Bleuler (see entry) at the Burghölzi Mental Hospital in Zürich (1904–1907), where he met Carl Jung (see entry) and became acquainted with the likes of Sigmund Freud (see entry). Entering psychoanalytic practice at Berlin (1907), he helped to establish the first branch of the International Psychoanalytic Institute (1910).

Major Contributions

Abraham devoted himself chiefly to pioneering efforts in the psychoanalytic treatment of manic-depressive psychosis. He agreed with Freud that anger (aggression) turned inward leads to depression. He also linked depression to early fixations at the anal and oral level stages of psychosexual development, with oral-sadistic tendencies as the primary source of self-punishment in depressed people. He inferred that inadequate mothering during the oral stage was involved.

While most theories of mania view such episodes as a defense or a reaction against depression, Abraham believed that manic episodes could relate to reaction to childhood depression caused by an event such as loss of a parent or other significant figure. Whereas in the depressive state the person is subjected to a tyrannical super-ego, in mania the tyranny is temporarily overruled, and self-criticism and low self-worth are replaced with self-praise and self-exaltation.

Abraham's stages of libido development are earlier oral, oral-sadistic, anal expulsion, retentive, phallic, and adult genital.

His thesis was that arrested development (nongratification) results in fixation of libido at that level and gives rise to mental disorder. Gratification at stage 1 is associated with the positive traits of curiosity, accessibility to new ideas, and sociability. Fixation at the anal stage results in the traits of reticence, moroseness, hesitation, procrastination, and inaccessibility to new ideas. He proposed that the dependent personality results from arrested psychosexual development at the oral stage, obsessive-compulsive personality at the anal stage, and hysterical personality at the phallic stage.

A person who is fixated at the oral stage of psychosexual development (Freud's oral character type), according to Abraham, is dominated by the belief that there will always be some kind person who will care for them, a substitute mother. This belief leads the person to adopt a passive attitude toward life and living. Such characters, according to Abraham, always seem to be asking for something; they dislike being alone, even for a short time. Further, in the obsessive-compulsive personality disorder, Abraham drew attention to the trait of finding pleasure in creating lists, superficial fastidiousness, preoccupation with preserving correct social appearances, and unproductive perseverance — the tendency to produce the same verbal or motor responses over and over to different stimuli.

Major Literature

Abraham, Karl. *Clinical Papers and Essays on Psychoanalysis*. Translated by H.C. Abraham. London: Karnac Books, 1979.
___. *Selected Papers on Psychoanalysis*. Translated by D. Bryan and A. Strachey. New York: Basic Books, Inc., 1953. London: Karnac Books, 1988.

Ackerman, Nathan Ward (1908–1971)

FAMILY THERAPY

Nathan Ward Ackerman, a Soviet-born Jew, immigrated to the United States in 1912 and studied medicine and psychiatry. He was a founding member of the American Academy of Psychoanalysis and a pioneer of family therapy. Ackerman joined the Menninger Clinic in Topeka, Kansas, and became the chief psychiatrist of the Child Guidance Clinic in 1937.

Major Contributions

Ackerman's belief in the influences of society and culture led him toward the treatment of the family as a group. His idea is that families are divided into factions by conflict within their minds. His provocative style of intervening uncovered the family's defenses and allowed their feelings, hopes, and desires to surface. He moved away from the traditional approach to child guidance — where the psychiatrist works with the child and a social worker with the mother or parents — to working with the whole family. He suggested that family therapy be used as the primary form of treatment in child guidance clinics. Therapy sessions focus on aiding families in developing more effective, less stressful patterns of living.

In 1955 Ackerman organized the first discussion on family diagnosis at a meeting of the American Orthopsychiatric Association to facilitate communication in the developing field of family therapy. In 1957 he established the Family Mental Health Clinic in New York City and began teaching at Columbia University. He opened in 1960 the Family Institute, which was renamed the Ackerman Institute after his death; it was the foremost of its kind in the U.S. Family therapists from throughout the world are trained there. He co-founded *Family Process*, which is still the leading journal of ideas in the field.

The Ackerman Institute is a not-for-profit agency devoted to the treatment and study of families and to the training of family therapists. One of the first training institutions in the United States, it is committed to promoting family functioning and family mental health, and to helping all families at all stages of life. Ackerman family therapists try to understand individuals' thoughts, feelings and behavior, not only as a personal expression, but within the context of their families. The goal is to harness and strengthen existing resources and help family members work collaboratively toward inventive solutions of their problems.

Family therapists help with a broad spectrum of problems, including, but not limited to, school difficulties, childhood and adolescent troubles, marital issues, divorce, life cycle changes, bereavement, learning disabilities, family violence, substance abuse, child abuse and incest, chronic medical illness, including AIDS, and infertility. The Ackerman Institute for the Family is located in a townhouse on a residential street, 149 East 78th Street, near Lexington Avenue, New York.

Major Literature

Ackerman, Nathan Ward. *The Psychodynamics of Family Life*. New York: Basic Books, 1958.
___. *Treating the Troubled Family*. New York: Basic Books, 1966.

Adler, Alfred (1870–1937)

INDIVIDUAL PSYCHOLOGY

Alfred Adler, an Austrian doctor and psychologist who exerted a profound influence on psychiatry, was one of the neo-Freudians and the first to break with Freud. He resigned as president of the Vienna Psychoanalytic Society in 1911 and formed a society that later became the Society for Individual Psychology.

Major Contributions

Adler established many child guidance centers in schools in Vienna and is credited with being the pioneer psychiatrist of group counseling. He disagreed with Freud over the libido theory, the sexual origin of neurosis and the importance of infantile wishes. Individual psychology is a broad, socially oriented, humanistic and holistic personality theory of psychology and psychotherapy. Adler's system is invested with a great deal of common sense, for it makes sense to the average reader.

According to Adler, people are guided by values and goals of which they may be aware, not driven by unconscious instincts. Adler believed that the main motives of human thought and behavior lie in the individual's striving for superiority and power, partly in compensation for feelings of inferiority. The individual moves from a sense of inferiority to a sense of mastery. The individual cannot be considered apart from society, for all human problems — relationships, occupation and love — are social. Adler coined the term "inferiority complex." The neurotically disposed person is characterized by increased inferiority feelings, underdeveloped social interest and an exaggerated, uncooperative goal of superiority. These characteristics express themselves as anxiety and aggression.

Individual psychology emphasizes:

- Social relationships, rather than biological factors
- Self, rather than the id and the superego
- Striving for self-actualization, rather than the sex instinct
- The present, rather than early, experiences
- Equality and co-operation between the sexes
- The person moves away from situations that make her or him feel inferior and toward goals of success and superiority.

Adler's "masculine protest" describes the drive for superiority or completeness arising out of a felt inferiority or incompleteness, femininity being regarded as incomplete and inferior. Adler also developed a birth order theory, where children's position in their family — their birth order — was seen as determining significant character traits.

Adlerian therapy goals include the following:

- To establish and maintain a therapeutic relationship in which there is equality, trust and acceptance and which does not reflect differences but sameness
- To uncover the uniqueness of the client
- To give insight
- To encourage redirection and reorientation.

Major Literature

Adler, Alfred. *The Practice and Theory of Individual Psychology*. Totowa, New Jersey: Adams, Littlefield, 1924.
___. *Social Interest: A Challenge to Mankind*. London, England: George Allen and Unwin, 1933.
___. *Understanding Human Nature*. London, England: George Allen and Unwin, 1937.
___. *What Life Should Mean to You*. New York: Capricorn Books, 1958.

Aichhorn, August (1878–1949)
PSYCHOLOGICAL CRIMINOLOGY

August Aichhorn was born in Austria, where he spent his entire life. One of twin boys, the sons of a well-to-do Viennese family, he became a teacher in 1898, the year his twin died. In 1907 he campaigned against the setting up of military settlements for boys, thus preventing the inculcation of the military spirit into the educational system.

Major Contributions

From 1908 to 1918 Aichhorn was chairman of a new board that was officially assigned the duty of organizing boys' settlements. In 1918, in Oberhollabrunn, Austria, with a group of like-minded people, he organized an institution for delinquent boys who had been severely deprived and brutally abused. He made the environment as enjoyable as possible, and the staff was encouraged to be affectionate, permissive and non-aggressive, even in the face of aggression from the boys. The rationale was that when aggression is not met with counter-aggression it ceases to be satisfying.

Aichhorn dabbled in many different approaches to delinquency, but it was in psychoanalysis that he eventually found his working model. He believed that the personality structure of the delinquent was not so different from the neurotic personality proposed by Freud. In psychoanalytic terms, deviant behavior is due to the faulty development of the superego. He not only worked with disturbed boys but also with their families; thus he was one of the pioneers of the therapeutic group.

Anna Freud encouraged Aichhorn to enter psychoanalytic training at the Vienna Psychoanalytic Institute in 1922 at age 44. He later organized a child guidance service for the Vienna Psychoanalytic Society. After his retirement from the municipal service he was made chairman of the child guidance clinic of the Viennese Psychoanalytic Society. He soon became one of the foremost teachers of that society, and when Germany occupied Austria, as a non–Jew, he remained at his post.

His experience of handling aggression provided him with first-hand experience for dealing with the Nazis. He quietly trained a number of young psychiatrists for future work in psychoanalysis, and after the liberation he was elected president of the Viennese Psychoanalytic Society, which was renamed the August Aichhorn Gesellschaft. In 1991, the August Aichhorn Center for Adolescent Residential Care, a residential treatment facility in Manhattan, New York, opened to provide an extensive array of services to its adolescent residents. The center's policy is to accept all referred youths who are 12 to 16 years of age and who have been certified by the New York City preadmission certification committee, without further screening except for Medicaid-required documentation.

Major Literature

Aichhorn, August. *Delinquency and Child Guidance*. Madison, Connecticut: International Universities Press, Inc., 1965.

___. *Wayward Youth*. New York: G.P. Putnam's Sons, 1936. Evanston, Illinois: Northwestern University Press, 1984.

Ainsworth, Mary Dinsmore Salter (1913–1999)
EARLY EMOTIONAL ATTACHMENT

Mary Dinsmore Salter was born in Glendale, Ohio. At the end of World War I the family moved to Toronto, Canada. At the University of Toronto she gained a B.A. (1935), M.A. (1936), Ph.D. (1939) and honrary D.Sc. (1990). In 1942, she joined the Canadian Women's Army Corps, attained the rank of major, and was a consultant to the director of personnel selection. She was superintendent of women's rehabilitation in the Department of Veteran Affairs, Ottawa, Canada (1945–1946), and assistant professor and research fellow at the Institute of Child Study, University of Toronto (1945–1950).

In 1950 she married Leonard H. Ainsworth and moved with him to England, where she was senior research psychologist, Tavistock Clinic, London (1950–1954), and senior research fellow, Makrere College, Kampala, Uganda (1954–1955). From 1956 to 1977 Ainsworth worked at Johns Hopkins University, Baltimore, Maryland, as a lecturer (1956 to 1958); associate professor (1958–1963); professor in psychology (1963–1975); and fellow, Center for Advanced Studies (1957–1977). She moved to the University of Virginia, Charlottesville, as professor (1975–1976), Commonwealth professor in psychology (1976–1984) and professor emeritus (1984–1999). Ainsworth was the recipient of seven Distinguished Scientific Contribution awards.

Major Contributions

In London, Ainsworth joined John Bowlby (see entry) at the Tavistock Clinic and was involved in investigating the effects of maternal separation on children's personality development. Ainsworth and Bowlby found evidence that a child's lack of a mother figure leads to adverse developmental effects. In 1954 her husband accepted a position at the East African Institute of Social Research in Uganda. Ainsworth accompanied him and was funded for a short-term longitudinal study of twenty-six Ganda village families with young infants.

Her work with mothers and children may have been sparked by her undergraduate studies with William Blatz (founder and first director of the Institute of Child Study, Toronto), whose "security theory" stated that the family is the secure base from which a developing individual can move out to develop new skills and interests. Bowlby and Ainsworth continued to work as partners in attachment research and theory. Ainsworth was included in the Tavistock Mother-Infant Interaction Study Group, which communicated with various developmental scientists of different nationalities and disciplines.

As professor in developmental psychology at Johns Hopkins University, she engaged in a sequel to the Ganda Study of monthly home observations on twenty-six families, from birth to twelve months, working with what became known as the "Strange Situation"—a procedure to assess differences in infants' reactions to a series of separations and reunions with their mothers.

Major Literature

Ainsworth, Mary Dinsmore Salter. *Infancy in Uganda: Infant Care and the Growth of Love*. Baltimore, Maryland: Johns Hopkins University Press, 1967.
___, Silvia Bell, and D. Stayton. "Infant-Mother Attachment and Social Development." In M.P. Richards (Ed.), *The Introduction of the Child into a Social World*. Cambridge, England: Cambridge University Press, 1974.
___, Mary C. Blehar, Evertt Waters, and Sally Wall. *Patterns of Attachment: A Psychological Study of the Strange Situation*. Mahwah, New Jersey: Lawrence Erlbaum Associates, Inc., 1978.

Ajzen, Icek (1942–)
CONSUMER HEALTH

Born in Chelm, Poland, Icek Ajzen gained a B.A. from the Hebrew University, Jerusalem (1966), and a Ph.D. (1969) from the University of Illinois, Urbana, Champaign, where he was professor of psychology (1969–1971). Since 1971 he has been professor of psychology; head, Division of Personality and Social Psychology; and associate chair, Department of Psychology, University of Massachusetts, Amherst. He was visiting professor of psychology at Tel-Aviv University in Israel in 1972–1973, 1978–1979, 1985–1986, 1993–1994, and 1999. He received a Fulbright Travel Award to Bulgaria (1995) and a Christiansen Memorial Award in Psychology, University of Bergen, Norway (2002). He is associate editor or consulting editor for *Personality and Social Psychology*, *Journal of Applied Social Psychology*, and *Basic and Applied Social Psychology*.

Major Contributions

Ajzen made contributions in the theory of measurement of attitude and the relationship between attitude and behavior. With Martin Fishbein, Ajzen developed the theory of reasoned action (TRA) in 1975 to examine the relationship between attitudes and behavior. It was later called the theory of planned behavior, which holds that human action is guided by the following considerations:

- Behavioral beliefs: beliefs about the likely outcomes of the behavior and the evaluations of these outcomes.
- Normative beliefs: beliefs about the standard expectations of others and motivation to comply with these expectations.
- Control beliefs: beliefs about the presence of factors that may facilitate or impede performance of the behavior and the perceived power of these factors.
- Beliefs lead to intentions, which lead to behavior.

Thus planned behavior looks at behavioral intentions rather than attitudes as the main predictors of behavior. According to this theory, attitudes toward a behavior (or more precisely, attitudes toward the expected outcome or result of a behavior) and subjective norms (the influence other people have on a person's attitudes and behavior) are the major predictors of behavioral intention. Planned behavior — which also looks at the relation between verbal attitudes and overt behavior — works most successfully when applied to behaviors that are under a person's volitional control.

Attitudes and subjective norms can explain why a person decides to behave or not to behave in a certain way. One limit of this model is that it does not include the importance of affect (mood and emotion). This model would fit with, for example, cognitive behavioral therapy; cognition is the focus, not feelings. The health education implications of this theory allow one to identify how and where to target strategies for changing behavior (e.g., prevention of sexually-transmitted diseases, smoking, binge drinking, healthy eating, dental care and family planning).

Major Literature

Ajzen, Icek, and M. Fishbein. *Belief, Attitude, Intention, and Behavior: An Introduction to Theory and Research.* Reading, Massachusetts: Addison-Wesley, 1975.
___, and M. Fishbein. *Understanding Attitudes and Predicting Social Behavior.* Englewood Cliffs, New Jersey: Prentice-Hall, 1980.
Ajzen, Icek. *Attitudes, Personality, and Behavior.* Milton-Keynes, England: Open University Press. Chicago, Illinois: Dorsey Press, 1988.

Alexander, Franz Gabriel (1891–1964)
Psychosomatic Medicine

Born in Hungary, Franz Gabriel Alexander was the first student in the Berlin Psychoanalytic Institute and was one of the most important members of the group often referred to as "the second generation of psychoanalysts." He is sometimes referred to as the father of psychosomatic medicine because of his leading role in identifying emotional tension as a significant cause of physical illness.

In 1932 he founded the Chicago Psychoanalytic Institute, which he directed until 1956. Under his leadership the institute attracted many analysts and students who conducted extensive research on emotional disturbance and psychosomatic disease, identifying various disorders with particular unconscious conflicts. From 1956 he was involved on a new research program in psychotherapy and psychosomatic medicine at Mount Sinai Hospital, Los Angeles, where he explored the effect of the therapist's personality in the treatment process.

Major Contributions

Although Alexander did not develop a theory of personality, he was the first to study mind-body interaction in any systematic way, and this led him to formulate the principles of psychosomatics, behavioral medicine, and psychophysiology. He postulated that certain illnesses are the products of the interaction between constitution, unconscious conflicts and specific stressors. The diseases Alexander studied were:

1. *Peptic ulcer.* The postulation is that the core conflict of hyper-independence is a defense against unacceptable dependency needs.
2. *Ulcerative colitis.* This is also related to dependency; the postulation is that the core conflict is rage at unmet needs.
3. *Essential hypertension.* The postulation is that the core conflict is inhibited anger and suspiciousness in an outwardly compliant, cooperative person.
4. *Rheumatoid arthritis.* Here the proposition is that the core conflict is rebellion against overprotective parents.

5. *Bronchial asthma.* The proposition is that the wheeze of bronchial asthma represents a symbolic cry and the core conflict is the wish for protection versus the fear of envelopment, and issues of separation.
6. *Neuro-dermatitis.* Alexander's proposal that early deprivation leads to wishes for closeness is now not accepted, although the role of conflicts remain widely accepted.

The reasoning is that if patients can be helped to resolve their core conflicts, leaving other parts of the personality alone, the medical condition will improve. In addition to his work on psychosomatics, he worked to shorten the duration of psychotherapy. His premise was that it is not intellectual insight that brings a cure, but correcting faulty emotions. His concept of "corrective emotional experience" is a technique in which the analyst purposely behaves in the transference in a corrective manner toward the patient. This view was not well received by the psychoanalytic fraternity.

Major Literature

Alexander, Franz Gabriel, and Helen Ross (Eds.). *Dynamic Psychiatry.* Chicago, Illinois: University of Chicago Press, 1952.
___, and Helen Ross. *Impact of Freudian Psychiatry.* Chicago, Illinois: University of Chicago Press, 1964.
___. *Psychosomatic Specificity: Experimental Study and Results.* Chicago, Illinois: University of Chicago Press, 1968.
___, and Thomas Morton French. *Psychoanalytic Therapy: Principles and Application.* Lincoln, Nebraska: University of Nebraska Press, 1980.
___. *The Medical Value of Psychoanalysis.* Madison, Connecticut: International Universities Press Inc., 1984.

Allen, Doris Twitchell (1901–2002)
PSYCHODRAMA

Born in Augusta, Maine, Doris Twitchell Allen graduated in chemistry and biology from the University of Maine. Her Ph.D. in psychology was from the University of Michigan. She then did post-graduate study at the Psychological Institute, University of Berlin, in 1932. Her career in psychology started with becoming director of the Field Laboratory at the Child Education Foundation in New York City (1932–1935). She was chief psychologist at the Longview State Hospital, Cincinnati, from 1944 to 1957, and associate professor of clinical psychology at the University of Cincinnati from 1949 to 1962.

In 1956 she was appointed a member of the White House Conference of 100, which organized an international people-to-people program. From 1962 until her retirement, she was professor of psychology at the University of Cincinnati and professor of psychology (psychodrama) at the University of Maine. Allen was a fellow of the American Association for the Advancement of Science and of the American Board of Professional Psychology, and served on the boards of the Ohio Psychological Association, American Society of Group Psychotherapy and Psychodrama, and the International Council of Psychologists.

Allen received the Gold Medal Award from the City of Stockholm (1953), Les Palmes Academiques from the French government (1961), and Orden del Quetzal from the government of Guatemala (1976). She was also nominated for the Freedom Medal (1999), an honor awarded by the president of the United States, and the Hague Appeal for Peace Prize (2001).

Major Contributions

Soon after World War II, Allen conceived the idea of an organization that would foster intercultural knowledge and understanding as the cornerstone for creating peace in a world that had seen too much war. Her premise was to start with children from several countries who could come together and explore the differences and similarities in the lives and cultures of their peers across the world. Allen also recognized that the village experience should be fully studied and documented so that it could contribute to global research and dialogue in the field. Children's International Summer Villages (CISV) was registered as a nonprofit corporation in Ohio in 1950.

Before she died Allen saw CISV grow from the first Children's International Village camp held in Cincinnati in 1951 to a worldwide organization that has reached over 125,000 participants, helping them learn to live and work together in peace and friendship. Close to 200 world-wide international activities now take place each year, bringing intercultural sensitivity and training to multi-cultural local communities. She also founded the International School to School Experience in 1971 to broaden the base of CISV by reaching more children through elementary school exchanges. There is a Doris Twitchell Allen Village for upperclassmen on the University of Maine campus.

Allik, Jüri (1949–)
VISUAL PSYCHOPHYSICS

Born in Tallinn, Jüri Allik is one of Estonia's eminent psychologists. His primary field of research is visual psychophysics (the branch of psychology that deals with the relationships between physical stimuli and sensory response), especially perception of visual motion. Allik holds Ph.D. degrees in psychology from the University of Moscow, Russia (1976), and University of Tampere, Finland (1991). He was appointed professor of psychophysics in 1992. Since 2002 he has been professor of experimental psychology and the head of the University of Tartu's Department of Psychology and the chairman of the Estonian Science Foundation, as well as an editor of Estonia's most important social science and humanities journal in English, *Trames*. In 1998 and again in 2005, he received the Estonian National Science Award, Social Sciences category.

Major Contributions

Allik's major contributions to international psychology involve visual perception and eye movement, and critical publications (in his own language) on Sigmund Freud, on the history of psychology, and on the measuring of science productivity, the transition of science, and quality control. Allik, with Anu Realo (2004), analyzed available data on the relationship between individualism-collectivism and social capital within one country (the United States) and across 42 other countries.

In America, the states with a high level of social capital (higher degree of civic engagement in political activity, where people spend more time with their friends and believe that most people can be trusted) were, paradoxically, found to be more individualistic. A correspondingly strong association between individualism and social capital was observed in the comparison of different countries. These results support Durkheim's view that when individuals become more autonomous and seemingly liberated from social bonds, they actually become even more dependent on society.

In addition Allik has done research on suicide. He proposes a link between the psychological variables of individualism-collectivism, locus of control, and subjective well-being, and the suicide rate. It was found that with regard to the suicide rate, a moderate individualism is more dangerous than an extreme one; the external locus of control is a risk factor, especially in the association with

the low individualism; and satisfaction with different aspects of life has an opposite effect on the suicide rate. In some instances, satisfaction with the status quo increases the risk of suicide. These findings suggest that the sociological theory of suicide needs to be supplemented by both psychological and cultural theories in order to explain by which psychological and cultural mechanisms the mind of an individual is programmed.

Major Literature

Allik, Jüri, and A. Realo. "Psychological and Cultural Mechanisms of Suicide." *Trames* 1 (1997): 306–321.
Kreegipuu, K., and J. Allik. "Perceived Onset Time and Position of a Moving Stimulus." *Vision Research* 43 (2003) 1625–1635.
Allik, Jüri, and R.R. McCrae. "Towards a Geography of Personality Traits: Patterns of Profiles Across 36 Cultures." *Journal of Cross-Cultural Psychology* 35 (2004): 13–28.
Allik, Jüri, and A. Realo. "Individualism-Collectivism and Social Capital." *Journal of Cross-Cultural Psychology* 35 (2004) 29–49.

Allport, Floyd Henry (1890–1978)
EXPERIMENTAL SOCIAL PSYCHOLOGY

Born in Milwaukee, Wisconsin, the elder brother of Gordon Willard Allport (see entry), Floyd Henry Allport gained his A.B. (1914) from Harvard University, Cambridge, Massachusetts. He was second lieutenant in the field artillery, U.S. Army Expeditionary Forces at the French Front (1917–1918), and was awarded the Croix de Guerre and citation from the French Corps d'Armée. Allport gained a Ph.D. (1919) from Harvard and was instructor in psychology at Harvard and Radcliffe College, Cambridge, Massachusetts (1919–1922); associate professor, University of North Carolina, Chapel Hill (1922–1924); and professor of social and political psychology, Maxwell School of Citizenship and Public Affairs, Syracuse University, New York (1924–1956). He was a visiting professor, University of California, Berkeley, and he retired from teaching in 1974. Syracuse University awarded him an honorary doctorate (1957). He received the Distinguished Scientific Contribution Award and Gold Medal from the American Psychological Association.

Major Contributions

Floyd Allport edited the *Journal of Abnormal and Social Psychology*. The lead article in the first issue of the expanded journal was a joint article with his brother Gordon—"Personality Traits:

Their Classification and Measurement." The article had a profound influence on the early development of personality psychology.

During his career he directed the first doctoral program in social psychology and played a key role in bringing about the acceptance of social psychology as a scientific field. From his studies of the effects of the group on the individual, he coined the phrase "social facilitation," a theoretical concept that he described as a tendency or *set* to perform with greater energy or intensity in the presence of others who are working at the same task. He also found that when asked to judge, for example, a weight, groups were more likely to avoid the extremes at either end of the scale than when the weight was judged individually.

He rejected the mythical idea of some super "group mind" where groups were endowed with personality attributes or "collective unconscious." He also made serious attempts to apply some Freudian mechanisms to social problems. It is from Floyd Allport that we get such social psychology concepts as social increment and decrement, prepotent reflexes and habits, circular and linear social behavior, co-acting and interacting groups, and attitudes of conformity. The "father of experimental social psychology" left a legacy of meticulous research, which still influences social psychology research three decades later.

Major Literature

Allport, Floyd Henry. *Social Psychology*. Boston, Massachusetts: Houghton Mifflin, 1924.
___. *Institutional Behavior: Essays Toward a Re-Interpretation of Contemporary Social Organization*. Chapel Hill: University of North Carolina Press, 1933.
___. *Theories of Perception and the Concept of Structure*. New York: Wiley, 1955.
___. "A Structuronomic Conception of Behavior: Individual and Collective. I: Structural Theory and the Master Problem of Social Psychology." *Journal of Abnormal and Social Psychology* 64 (1962): 3–30.

Allport, Gordon Willard (1897–1967)
THEORY OF PERSONALITY

Born in Montezuma, Indiana, Gordon Willard Allport gained a B.A. in psychology (1919) from Harvard University, Cambridge, Massachusetts. He taught English and sociology at Robert College, Constantinople (Istanbul), from 1919 to 1920 and gained a Ph.D. in psychology from Harvard in 1922. He was awarded a Sheldon Traveling Scholarship to Germany and Cambridge Univer-

sity, U.K. (1922–1924). From 1924 to 1926 he was lecturer in social ethics at Harvard, where he taught "Personality: Its Psychological and Social Aspects," possibly the first offered in the U.S. He was assistant professor of psychology at Dartmouth College, Hanover, North Hampshire (1926–1930). He was then at Harvard from 1930 to 1967 as assistant professor, associate professor, professor, and chair of the Psychology Department (1936–1946).

Allport was editor of the *Journal of Abnormal and Social Psychology* (1937–1948). He was president of the American Psychological Association (APA) in 1939 and the Society for the Psychological Study of Social Issues in 1944. He co-founded the Department of Social Relations at Harvard (1946) and in 1964 received from the APA the Distinguished Scientific Contribution to Psychology Award.

Major Contributions

Following a meeting with Freud in 1919, Gordon Allport concluded that depth psychology sometimes digs too deeply, in the same way that he had earlier realized that behaviorism often doesn't dig deeply enough. His career was spent examining such social issues as prejudice and in developing personality tests.

Allport's trait theory of personality has remained virtually unchanged. Allport considered that the personality functioning is essentially rational, organized, and directed by conscious goals, plans of action and philosophies of life. He put a strong emphasis on each person's uniqueness; thus the task of psychology is to understand the individual. This means understanding the person's past, present and how the person thinks he will function in the future. He suggests this through the use of a case history and a content analysis of personal documents. (Here one can see a similarity with the work of Adolf Meyer [see entry] and with person-centered counseling, where the emphasis is on working with the individual rather than trying to fit the individual into a model.)

Allport identifies the seven functions of the self as:

1. Sense of body, which develops in the first two years of life
2. Self-identity, which also develops in the first two years
3. Self-esteem, which develops between two and four years old
4. Self-extension, which develops between four

and six, where the child recognizes the identities of other people

5. Self-image, which also develops between four and six
6. Rational coping, learned predominantly in the years from six to twelve
7. Propriate functioning — the individual's goals, ideal, plans, vocations, callings, a sense of direction, a sense of purpose — doesn't usually begin till after twelve years old.

Major Literature

Allport, Gordon Willard. *Personality: A Psychological Interpretation.* New York: Holt, Rinehart and Winston, 1937.
___. *The Nature of Prejudice.* Upper Saddle River, New Jersey: Addison Wesley, 1954.
___. *Pattern and Growth in Personality.* New York: Holt, Rinehart and Winston, 1961.
___. *The Person in Psychology: Selected Essays.* Boston, Massachusetts: Beacon Press, 1968.

Altman, Irwin (1930–)
CLOSE RELATIONSHIPS

Born in New York City, Irwin Altman earned a B.A. from New York University (1951), an M.A. (1954), and a Ph.D. (1957) from the University of Maryland, College Park, Maryland. From 1976 to the present he is vice-president for academic affairs at the University of Utah, Salt Lake City. He received a David P. Gardner Research Fellowship at the University of Utah in 1976 and the Distinguished Research Award, University of Utah, in 1978. He was president of Division 8, American Psychological Association (APA), in 1979–1980 and president of Division 34 in 1981–1982. Altman received Distinguished Service Award in the Social Sciences, Utah Academy of Sciences, Arts and Letters (1981); Career Award, Environmental Design Research Association (1982); and the APA Award for Distinguished Education and Training Contributions (1994). He is distinguished professor of psychology, University of Utah. Altman served on the editorial boards of several distinguished psychology journals, including the *International Journal of Applied Social Psychology*, and is co-editor of the monograph series in environmental psychology. (Environmental psychology is an interdisciplinary approach that focuses on the interplay between humans and their surroundings.)

Major Contributions

Altman's studies of close relationships of friends, intimates and family members examine how relationships develop, how physical environments are used in relationships (e.g., homes), and the roles of social contexts (e.g., families) in interpersonal processes. This work is based on the transactions between people and what brings them together and holds them together. Added to this is what contributes to the ending of a relationship. Unstable relationships tend to throw all other aspects of life off balance.

Altman and Dalmas Taylor's *Social Penetration Theory*— on the nature of personality — states that humans are like onions, with many layers. As you proceed further through the onion the characteristics of the personality — the values and emotions that make up their true identity — become more explicit. Before the traits are unveiled, a strong relationship has to be formed. At the start of a relationship, basic information is revealed about each person. The inner layers are more difficult to reach and require a deeply intimate relationship to be formed. The deepest and most personal information define a person's self.

Breadth and depth are equally important in the social penetration process. People tend to disclose more information that is increasingly more personal as the relationship develops, and there is a point where the relationship can stabilize. Penetration begins to slow down when the inner layers are touched upon; growth ceases and "depenetration" or disengagement begins and reticence replaces openness.

Major Literature

Stokols, Daniel, and Irwin Altman (Eds.). *Handbook of Environmental Psychology.* Volume 1 and 2. New York: Wiley, 1987. Malabar, Florida: Krieger Publishing Company, 1991.
Altman, Irwin, and A. Churchman (Eds.). *Women and the Environment: Human Behavior and the Environment: Advances in Theory and Research. Volume 13.* New York: Plenum (1994).
Brown, B.B., C.M. Werner, and Irwin Altman. "Choicepoints for Dialecticians: A Dialectical/ Transactional Perspective on Close Relationships." In L. Baxter and B. Montgomery (Eds.), *Dialectical Approaches to Studying Personal Relationships.* Mahwah, New Jersey: Lawrence Erlbaum Associates, Inc., 1996.

Alzheimer, Aloysius, "Alois" (1864–1915)
PRE-SENILE DEMENTIA

Born in Marktbreit, Bavaria, Alois Alzheimer studied medicine at the German universities of Aschaffenburg, Tübingen, Berlin, and Würzburg.

He received his medical degree at Würzburg in 1887, then worked for a few months in the histological laboratory at Würzburg University. From 1888 to 1903 he was assistant, then second physician, at the city mental asylum for lunatics and epileptics in Frankfurt-Main. During his fourteen years at Frankfurt, he contributed to the development of a modern clinical service while setting up a scientific patient database. In addition, he built an archive of autopsy cases from which he could draw during the rest of his scientific career.

From 1903 to 1912, he was scientific assistant to Professor Emil Kraepelin (see entry) in his clinic in Munich. Soon after moving to Munich, Alzheimer published his habilitation thesis, "Progressive Paralysis," the histopathology of general paralysis of the insane (GPI), the third stage of syphilis, which was common in Alzheimer's time (see entry, Wagner-Jauregg).

Major Contributions

In 1901 at the Frankfurt Asylum, Alzheimer observed the strange behavior of a 51-year-old-patient named Mrs. Auguste D., who also suffered from a loss of short-term memory. In April 1906, Frau Auguste died and Alzheimer had the patient records and her brain sent to Munich. Together with two Italian physicians, he used staining techniques — developed by Franz Nissl, also at Munich — to identify plaques of waxy protein and tangled neurons in the brain. A speech Alzheimer delivered on November 3, 1906, was the first time the pathology and the clinical symptoms of presenile dementia would be presented together. Kraepelin used the term "Alzheimer's disease" in one of his textbooks, thus making Alzheimer's name famous. By 1911, the term was being used by European and American physicians to diagnose patients.

Alzheimer's microscopic study of the brain and his studies of the disorder of the nervous system marked him as one of the significant figures of psychiatry, and his legacy remains. In 1912, he was appointed professor of psychiatry at the University of Breslau (now Wroclaw, Poland). Alzheimer's newly founded "neuro-anatomical laboratory" in Munich won international acclaim, resulting in a large number of international visitors. One of Alzheimer's visiting researchers was the German neurologist F.H. Lewy (1885–1950), who discovered in 1912 the Lewy bodies in Parkinson's disease. Alzheimer invited Lewy to run his laboratory at Breslau, but Alzheimer died of heart failure at Breslau before Lewy could make the move.

Alzheimer was the co-founder and co-publisher of the journal *Zeitschrift für die gesamte Neurologie und Psychiatrie*. There are no known books by Alzheimer. (For a description of Alzheimer's disease, see the *Diagnostic and Statistical Manual of Mental Disorders [DSM IV]*, Washington, D.C.: American Psychiatric Association, 1994, pp. 142–143).

Ames, Adelbert, Jr. (1880–1955)
VISUAL PERCEPTION

Adelbert Ames, Jr., a man of many parts — an ophthalmologist and perceptual psychologist — was born in Lowell, Massachusetts. He attended Phillips Academy at Andover and earned his undergraduate and law degrees at Harvard in 1903 and 1906 respectively. He left law and worked for a time with his artist sister, and together they developed a system of color theory. From that he moved into how the human eye perceives color and worked with professor Wallace Baird at Worcester, Massachusetts. After World War I, in which he served as an observer, he moved to Dartmouth College, Hanover, New Hampshire, to work with Charles Proctor. There he was created professor of physiological optics and devoted himself entirely to research.

Major Contributions

An important discovery was the medical condition aniseikonia, where the lens of one eye sees an image that differs in size and shape from the image seen by the other eye; the consequence was severe headaches in certain people. The Dartmouth Eye Institute was subsequently founded.

He invented the Ames Demonstrations in Perception, the most famous of which is a full-sized room that looks normal but in which people appear to shrink as they walk across it. The trick behind an Ames room is that it appears cubic but its true shape is actually trapezoidal. Another trapezoid device is the Ames window, which produces a similar illusion as the Ames room. Another of Ames' illusions is the Ames chair. On looking through the front viewing holes, you see three identical chairs made by the apparent placement of fine threads. When viewed from the top, however, you can see that the threads don't form chairs, but an intricate, disconnected maze.

In 1954, Ames was awarded an honorary doctor of laws by Dartmouth College, and in 1955 he won the Tillyer Medal, awarded by the Optical Society of America. In the address given on the presentation of the Tillyer Medal, the president of the society listed 38 books and scientific papers Ames wrote and 21 patents awarded to him. Although not trained as a psychologist, he is included as one of the sensory-perceptual psychologists. His contributions make a valuable addition to the whole field of perception in psychology and psychiatry, particularly in illusions and misperceptions.

Major References to Ames's Work

Behrens, Roy R. "The Life and Unusual Ideas of Adelbert Ames, Jr." *Leonardo: Journal of the International Society of Arts, Sciences and Technology* 20 (1987): 273–279.
___. "Adelbert Ames and the Cockeyed Room." *Print* 48: 2 (1994): 92–97.
___. "The Artistic and Scientific Collaboration of Blanche Ames and Adelbert Ames II." *Leonardo: Journal of the International Society of Arts, Sciences and Technology* 31 (1998): 47–54.
___. "Eyed Awry: The Ingenuity of Del Ames." *North American Review,* 282 :2 (1997): 26–33.
___. "Adelbert Ames, Fritz Heider, and the Chair Demonstration." *Gestalt Theory* 21 (1999): 184–190.

Anastasi, Anne (1908–2001)
INTELLIGENCE TESTING

Anne Anastasi is usually associated with the terms "psychometrics" or the "test guru." Born in New York, her father died when she was one year old and she lost contact with her paternal family. She graduated with an A.B. in psychology from Barnard College, New York (1928), and a Ph.D. in general and experimental psychology from Columbia University, New York (1930). In 1933 she married John Porter Foley, Jr. (1910–1994), and a year after her marriage she was diagnosed with cervical cancer. The treatment left her unable to have children.

From 1930 on she had a distinguished academic career and was the third female president of the American Psychological Association. At one stage she was assistant professor of the new Department of Psychology at Queens College of the City University of New York. From 1947 until she retired in 1979 she was at Fordham University, rising to professor of psychology in the Graduate School of Arts. On retirement she was awarded an honorary D.Sc. and became professor emeritus.

Major Contributions

Anastasi's research focused on understanding and measuring the factors underlying the development of individual differences in psychological traits. She argued against the heredity over environment position, emphasizing instead that experience and environment had a strong influence on psychological development and on intelligence test scores, that test scores are not just a measure of innate ability. She refuted the claims by many others that tests are totally objective and free from cultural influences; different cultures have different ideas of what intelligence means and what an intelligent person is.

Psychometric tests, she argued, invariably measure only what is considered desirable for a particular industry or society. She emphasized that psychometric tests can be easily misused and should never be used to label anyone for the rest of their lives, for tests results can be improved with practice. Her books — particularly *Psychological Testing*— show that properly constructed and validated psychological tests can prove valuable. She also researched language development among black and Puerto Rican children, intelligence and family size, age changes in adult test performance, sex differences in psychological traits, and role experiential factors in the development of creative thinking in children and adolescents.

Major Literature

Anastasi, Anne. *Marriage: A Psychological and Moral Approach, Male vs. Female Attitudes.* New York: Fordham University Press, 1965.
___. *Testing Problems in Perspective.* Washington, D.C.: American Council of Education, 1966.
___. *Differential Psychology.* New York: Macmillan, 1937, 4th edition, 1981.
___. "Psychological Testing: Basic Concepts and Common Misconceptions." In A.M. Rogers and C.J. Scheirer (Eds.), *The G. Stanley Hall Lecture Series* (Vol. 5, pp. 87–120). Washington, D.C.: American Psychological Association, 1985.
___. *Psychological Testing.* New York: Macmillan, 1954, 7th edition, 1996.

Anderson, John Robert (1947–)
ARTIFICIAL INTELLIGENCE

Born in Vancouver, Canada, John Robert Anderson gained a B.A. and B.Sc. (1968) from the University of British Columbia, Vancouver, and a Ph.D. (1972) from Stanford University, California. At Yale University, New Haven, Connecticut, he was assistant professor, Department of Psychology (1972–1973), and associate professor and professor, Department of Psychology (1976–1978). From 1973 to 1976 Anderson was a junior fellow, University of Michigan, and member of the Human Performance Center. Since 2002 he has been Richard King Mellon professor of psychology and computer science, Carnegie Mellon University, Pittsburgh, Pennsylvania.

He received the American Psychological Association's Early Career Award (1978); the Research Scientist Award, National Institute of Mental Health (1989–1994); the David E. Rumelhart Prize for Contributions to the Formal Analysis of Human Cognition (2004); Howard Crosby Warren Medal for Outstanding Achievement in Experimental Psychology in the United States and Canada, Society of Experimental Psychology (2005); and Dr. A.H. Heineken Prize for Cognitive Science awarded by the Royal Netherlands Academy of Arts and Sciences (2006). Anderson was president of the Cognitive Science Society from 1988 to 1989.

Major Contributions

Anderson's research goal is to understand how people organize knowledge that they acquire from their different experiences to produce intelligent behavior. His current research involves two related enterprises. The first is concerned with modeling how we acquire intellectual competences, with the major foci being problem-solving skills, such as in air traffic control and mathematical problem solving skills. The second is concerned with using brain imaging (functional magnetic resonance imaging [fMRI]) to track different components of the cognitive processes in how we complete complex tasks.

The theory he and his colleagues have developed is called ACT-R (adaptive control of thought; the R stands for rational) and takes the form of a computer simulation capable of performing and learning from the same tasks that subjects perform in laboratories. Another area of research relates to modeling the cognitive competences that are taught in the domains of mathematics, computer programming, and cognitive psychology. They have built ACT-R simulations that are capable of solving problems in these domains and have developed computer-based instruction around these cognitive models.

Many of these computer-based instructional systems have the cognitive models as a component and attempt to understand student behavior by actually simulating what the student is doing in real time. These are called cognitive tutors and are currently being used to help teach courses in schools around the country. Much of this research has gone beyond the original goal of understanding human cognition and now is part of a major effort

to produce a significant improvement in American mathematics education.

Major Literature

Anderson, John Robert, and G.H. Bower. *Human Associative Memory.* Washington, D.C.: Winston and Sons, 1973.

Anderson, John Robert. *The Adaptive Character of Thought.* Mahwah, New Jersey: Lawrence Erlbaum Associates, Inc., 1990.

___. *Rules of the Mind.* Mahwah, New Jersey: Lawrence Erlbaum Associates, Inc., 1993.

___. *Learning and Memory.* New Jersey: John Wiley and Sons, Inc., 1995.

___. *Language, Memory, and Thought.* Mahwah, New Jersey: Lawrence Erlbaum Associates, Inc., 1976, 2006.

Angell, James Rowland (1869–1949)
FUNCTIONAL PSYCHOLOGY

Born in Burlington, Vermont, James Rowland Angell graduated from Michigan University in 1891 and studied for a year at Harvard with William James, gaining his M.A. in 1892. After a short spell of study abroad at the universities of Berlin and Halle, he taught from 1894 to 1920 at the University of Michigan under John Dewey. Then he became professor and head of the psychology department at Chicago University, Illinois, in 1905, dean of the university faculties in 1911, and acting president, 1918–1919.

From 1917 to 1918 Angell worked with the wartime Adjutant General's Committee on Classification of Personnel, developing means of integrating military and civilian training programs. This work led to the establishment of the Student Army Training Corps. In 1919–1920 he was chairman of the National Research Council. In 1920 Angell became president of the Carnegie Corporation, and from 1921 until 1937 he was the 14th president of Yale University, New Haven, Connecticut, the first non–Yale man to be president since the Harvard-trained rectors in the 18th century. He helped to establish its Institute of Human Relations.

In 1937 he became educational counselor of the National Broadcasting Company. His writings include several standard psychology textbooks. Two of Angell's famous students are Harvey Carr and John B. Watson (see entries).

Major Contributions

Angell is the first person to figure in the debate

of functionalism versus structuralism. Structuralism, a systematic movement founded in Germany by Wilhelm Wundt and mainly identified with Edward B. Titchener (see entries), is more concerned with the nuts and bolts of the conscious mind. Functionalism, associated with such people as John Dewey and William James (see entries), is more concerned with how the mind works and how the individual adapts to his environment.

Angell was at the forefront of the debate between structuralism and popular functionalism. An analogy could be drawn from the automobile. A structuralist would seek to know and understand what is under the hood and how the car works; a functionalist would be more concerned with driving the car and being aware of how the car is performing. In his 1906 presidential address to American Psychological Association, titled "The Province of Functional Psychology," Angell highlighted three major points about functional psychology:

1. Functionalism studies mental operations, not mental elements.
2. Functionalism views consciousness in terms of its use, mediating between an individual's needs and the pressures from the environment.
3. Functionalism regards mind and body as an inseparable unit.

Major Literature

Angell, James Rowland. *Psychology: An Introductory Study of Structure and Functions of Human Consciousness*. New York: Henry Holt and Company, 1904, 4th Ed., 1908.
___. "The Evolution of Intelligence." In G.A. Baitsell (Ed.), *The Evolution of Man* (pp. 103–125). New Haven, Connecticut: Yale University Press, 1922.
___. *American Education*. New Haven, Connecticut: Yale University Press, 1937.

Appelle, Stuart (1944–)
Sensory Perception

Stuart Appelle is a professor of psychology at the State University of New York (SUNY), Brockport, and a writer with an interest in topics dealing with abnormal perception, including hypnotic experience and reports of unidentified flying objects and alien abduction. His graduate work in experimental psychology was at Pennsylvania State University. He received his Ph.D. in experimental psychology from George Washington University in 1972.

In addition to teaching at SUNY, he has held teaching or research positions at George Washington University, Mount Vernon College, and the University of Rochester School of Medicine and Dentistry (Department of Pediatrics) and is currently professor of psychology at SUNY. A former chairman of the Department of Psychology, he has also served as interim dean of the School of Letters and Sciences. He now serves as associate dean of the School of Letters and Sciences, and as the director of the SUNY graduate program in liberal studies, where he teaches a course called "The Science of Consciousness."

Major Contributions

Appelle is author of more than 40 articles and book chapters, more than 80 entries in the reference text *Engineering Data Compendium: Human Perception and Performance*, and has presented papers at more than 20 professional meetings. His research focuses on perception and the nature of conscious experience.

His work has been widely published. His work and commentary optical illusions and on reports of unidentified flying objects and alien abduction appeared in publications of the American Psychological Association, the University Press of Kansas, the internationally recognized journal *Science*, several other publications and in a nationally televised documentary. He has hypnotized people who have claimed to have had encounters with aliens, including abduction. He is also editor of the *Journal of UFO Studies*, an academic journal dedicated to UFO-related phenomena.

Major Literature

Appelle, Stuart. "Reflections on Reports of Being Abducted by UFOs." *Journal of UFO Studies* 1 (1980): 127–129.
___. "Should We Discount the Extraterrestrial Hypothesis for UFOs?" *Mercury: The Journal of the Astronomical Society of the Pacific* 24(1) (1995): 9.
___. "The Abduction Experience: A Critical Evaluation of Theory and Evidence." *Journal of UFO Studies* 6 (1995–96): 29–78.

Apter, Michael John (1939–)
Reversal Theory

Born in Stockton on Tees, Cleveland, England, Michael John Apter graduated with a B.Sc. (1960) and Ph.D. (1964) from Bristol University. Much of his career has been in the academic world. He was for many years at the University of Wales in Cardiff and has held visiting professorships across the world, including Norway, Spain and Canada, and in the U.S. at Yale University, New Haven, Connecticut. His career has also included a spell in industry and a period as director of a residential home for the elderly. He is currently a visiting researcher at Georgetown University in Washington, D.C., and a director of Apter International, a management consultancy company based in the U.K. and affiliated with Georgetown.

Major Contributions

Although reversal theory is at the heart of this body of work, Apter has written on such topics as biological development, educational technology, computer simulation, humor, aesthetic experience, religion and crime. Reversal theory is a psychological theory addressing the inconsistency and changeability of individuals. It focuses on motivational styles, proposing that people regularly shift between different psychological states, depending upon the meaning and motives felt by an individual in different situations at different times. These reversals are healthy and necessary, both to ensure that one's motivations are being met, and to appropriately match personal style to the needs of a specific situation or other person. Reversal theory proposes that key emotions (such as anger and fear) and values (such as achievement and control) can be traced to four domains of experience, each with two opposing motivational states. We reverse between states based upon personal meaning and whether the values of the state are being fulfilled.

The four domains and their opposing states:

Domain	Opposing States	
Means-Ends Focus is on the intention of an activity and whether motivation comes from achieving goals (ends) or experiencing the process itself (means).	**Serious** Future goals, achievement	**Playful** Process, passion and fun
Rules Focus is on rules and norms and whether we perceive rules, belonging, and conformity as either supportive or restrictive.	**Conforming** Belonging, rules	**Rebellious** Freedom, change
Transactions Focus is on interactions and exchanges between people and whether motives are based in power, ability, and control or in care and emotional support.	**Mastery** Power, ability	**Sympathy** Relationship, care
Relationships Focus is upon whether one is motivated by fulfilling one's own needs or another's.	**Self** Self-oriented	**Other** Other-oriented

Major Literature

Apter, Michael John. *Computer Simulation of Behavior.* London: Random House Group, Hutchinson, 1970.
___. *Reversal Theory: Motivation, Emotion and Personality.* London: Taylor and Francis, Inc., 1989.
Svebak, Sven, and Michael John Apter (Eds.). *Stress and Health: A Reversal Theory Perspective.* London: Taylor and Francis, Inc., 1997.
Apter, Michael John (Ed.). *Motivational Styles in Everyday Life: A Guide to Reversal Theory.* Washington, D.C.: American Psychological Association, 2001.
___ (Ed.). *Reversal Theory: The Dynamics of Motivation, Emotion and Personality.* Oxford, England: Oneworld Publications, 2006.

Argyle, John Michael (1925–2002)

BODY LANGUAGE

Born in Nottingham, England, John Michael Argyle was a navigator in the Royal Air Force during World War II. He gained a B.A. (1950) and an M.A. in moral science and experimental psychology (1952) from the University of Cambridge, and an M.A. (1952) from the University of Oxford. He was fellow, Center for Advanced Study in the Behavioral Sciences at Cambridge (1958–1959) and at Wolfson College, Oxford (1965). He was fellow, member of council, and chairman of social psychology section, 1964–1967 and 1972–1974, of the British Psychological Society.

He received honorary degrees of D.Sc. at University of Oxford (1979), D.Litt. from the University of Adelaide, South Australia (1982), and D.Sc., University of Brussels (1982). In 1990, he received the Distinguished Career Contribution Award, International Society for the Study of Personal Relationships. In 1992 was made emeritus reader, University of Oxford. He was emeritus professor, Oxford Brookes University, and joint founder and editor of the *British Journal of Social and Clinical Psychology*, the first British journal with dedicated space for social psychology. He was editor of several other journals, including *Journal of Social and Personal Relationships*.

Major Contributions

Argyle opened up a whole new field of inquiry into non-verbal communication and social skills. His widely translated *The Penguin Psychology of Interpersonal Behaviour* is reputed to be the best-selling psychology paperback, with sales probably exceeding half a million. He started the social psychology section of the British Psychological Society. The first major research area to benefit from his attentions was non-verbal communication. He subsequently constructed and tested a model of social skills and their operation. He and his colleagues applied their findings into training programs for the workplace and everyday living.

The phrase "social skills" is now commonplace in everyday speech, and the issues have gained a central place in educational curricula, employment and clinical psychology. The United States Library of Congress catalog lists 44 titles of books authored, co-authored, edited, or co-edited by Argyle on a wide variety of topics. Most focus on the positives of human existence: cooperation, happiness, leisure, social interaction, social relationships and, for him, religious faith.

At noon on the third of June 2004, at County Hall, Exeter, England, a Lucombe oak tree was planted in memory of Michael Argyle. A speech was given by Professor Jim Kennedy. Michael Argyle's widow was present with two daughters and four grandchildren.

Major Literature

Argyle, Michael John. *The Psychology of Interpersonal Behaviour*. London: Penguin Books, Ltd., 1967.
___. *The Social Psychology of Work*. London: Penguin Books, Ltd., 1989.
___. *The Anatomy of Relationships*. London: Penguin Books, Ltd., 1990.
___. *The Social Psychology of Everyday Life*. Taylor and Francis Books, Ltd., Routledge, 1992.
___. *The Psychology of Social Class*. Taylor and Francis Books, Ltd., Routledge, 1993.
___. *The Social Psychology of Leisure*. London: Penguin Books Ltd, 1996.
___. *The Psychology of Religious Experience*. Taylor and Francis Books, Ltd., Routledge, 1997.
___. *The Psychology of Money*. Taylor and Francis Books, Ltd., Routledge, 1998.
___. *Psychology and Religion*. Taylor and Francis Books, Ltd., Routledge, 1999.
___. *The Psychology of Happiness*. Taylor and Francis Books, Ltd., Routledge, 2001.

Argyris, Chris (1923–)
INDUSTRIAL PSYCHOLOGY

Born in Newark, New Jersey, Chris Argyris served as an officer in the U.S. Army Signal Corps during the Second World War. In 1947 he gained an A.B. in psychology at Clark University, Worcester, Massachusetts. He received an M.A. in psychology and economics (1949), University of Kansas, Lawrence, and a Ph.D. in organizational behavior (1951) from Cornell University, Ithaca, New York. He worked at Yale University, New Haven, Connecticut, in 1951–1971. Since 1971 he has been James Bryant Conant Professor of Education and Organizational Behavior at Harvard University, Soldiers Field, Boston, Massachusetts.

He received the Distinguished Contribution Award, American Board of Professional Psychology (1977), and the McKinsey Prize, Distinguished Lifetime Contributions to Management (1994). Argyris is currently a director of the Monitor Company in Cambridge, Massachusetts. He has received honorary degrees from America, Belgium, Canada, Singapore, and Sweden. He is on the editorial boards of several journals, including *British Journal of Management* and *Journal of Applied Social Sociology*. In 1994, Yale University established the Chris Argyris Chair in the Social Psychology of Organizations.

Major Contributions

Argyris' research has focused on:

1. The impact of formal organizational structures, control systems and leadership on individuals, particularly at the middle and lower levels of organization;
2. The study of senior executives, his argument being that without commitment at this level there could be little change;
3. The role of the social scientist as both researcher and actor; and
4. Research and theorizing around individual and organizational learning, not just behavior, as a basis for diagnosis and action.

Arygis is also a renowned and influential teacher with the ability to demonstrate his ideas, beliefs and principles. Some of his key concepts:

A. LADDER OF INFERENCE
  Level 1. Data and experiences
  Level 2. Select data
  Level 3. Make assumptions based on meanings
  Level 4. Draw conclusions
  Level 5. Adopt beliefs
  Level 6. Take action.

This is not a linear model. It consists of a "Reflexive Loop" from Level 5 back to Level 2 as the person's beliefs act to modify the learning process.

B. SINGLE-LOOP AND DOUBLE-LOOP LEARNING
Single-loop learning — action and consequences — seems to be present when goals, values, frameworks and, to a significant extent, strategies are taken for granted. Double-loop learning involves the third factor of questioning the underlying values and assumptions.

C. ORGANIZATIONAL LEARNING
  Phase 1. Mapping the problem as clients see it.
  Phase 2. The internalization of the map by clients.
  Phase 3. Test the model, modify the map.
  Phase 4. Invent solutions to the problem and simulate them to explore their possible impact.
  Phase 5. Produce the intervention.
  Phase 6. Study the impact.

Adapted from Infed: The Encyclopaedia of Informal Education

Major Literature

Argyris, Chris. *Increasing Leadership Effectiveness.* New York: Wiley, 1976.
___. *Reasoning, Learning and Action: Individual and Organizational.* San Francisco: Jossey-Bass, 1982.
___. *Organizational Learning.* Cambridge, Massachusetts: Blackwell, 1993.
___. *On Organizational Learning.* Cambridge, Massachusetts: Blackwell, 1999.
___ (Ed.). *Reasons and Rationalizations: The Limits to Organizational Knowledge.* New York: Oxford University Press, 2006.

Arnheim, Rudolf (1904–2007)
VISUAL PERCEPTION

Rudolf Arnheim was born in Berlin, where his father owned a small piano factory. He studied psychology and philosophy, with secondary emphasis in the histories of art and music, at the University of Berlin. Part of his study was with the Gestalt psychologists Max Wertheimer, Wolfgang Köhler, and Kurt Lewin. From 1928 to 1933, following his Ph.D. dissertation — a study of expression in human faces and handwriting — he was assistant editor of a cultural affairs magazine, in which he wrote about films. Arnheim's book *Film als Kunst* (*Film as Art*) (1932) was banned by the Nazis because he was Jewish.

From 1933 to 1938 he worked for the International Institute for Educational Film, League of Nations, in Rome, then worked as a translator for the Overseas Service of the BBC in London. He emigrated from London to America in 1940 and became an American citizen in 1946. He was awarded a fellowship from the Rockefeller Foundation, in which he worked with the Office of Radio Research at Columbia University, analyzing soap operas and their effects on American radio audiences. A second award was a Guggenheim Fellowship in 1942 to study the role of perception in art and thereafter to write a book about the application of Gestalt psychology of perception to the visual arts.

From 1943 to 1968 he was on the psychology faculty of Sarah Lawrence College in Bronxville, New York, and was lecturer and visiting professor on the graduate faculty at the New School for Social Research, New York. From 1968 until his retirement in 1974 he was professor of psychology at the Department of Visual and Environmental Studies at Harvard University and visiting professor at the University of Michigan.

Major Contributions

Arnheim's three main contributions are art, art therapy, and visual cognition and problem-solving. He explored the perception of shape and color, asking the fundamental Gestalt question about why we see things as we do, why art exists, and how artistic work comes about. In his psychology of art, Arnheim provided a framework for understanding theory and practice of expressive art therapies, drawing freely from Gestalt psychology. He thus provided an alternative to, for example, behavioral and psychoanalytic approaches to art. His Gestalt background also influenced his approach to problem solving.

Major Literature

Arnheim, Rudolf. "Gestalt and Art." *Journal of Aesthetics and Art Criticism* 2 (1943): 71–5.
___. *Toward a Psychology of Art.* Berkeley: University of California Press, 1949, 1966.
___. *Visual Thinking.* Berkeley: University of California Press, 1969.

___. *Art and Visual Perception: A Psychology of the Creative Eye*. Berkeley and Los Angeles: University of California Press, 1954, 1966, 1974.

___. *Thoughts on Art Education*. Los Angeles: Getty Center for Education, 1990.

___. *Film Essays and Criticism*. Berkeley: University of California Press, 1997.

Aronson, Elliot (1932–)
MEDIA PSYCHOLOGY

Born in Revere, Massachusetts, Elliot Aronson graduated with a B.A. from Brandeis University, Waltham, Massachusetts (1954), an M.A. from Wesleyan University, Middletown, Connecticut (1956), and a Ph.D. from Stanford University, California (1959), where his doctoral advisor and mentor was Leon Festinger (see entry). He has taught at Harvard University, the University of Minnesota, the University of Texas, and the University of California, Santa Cruz.

In 1999, he won the Distinguished Scientific Contribution Award of the American Psychological Association (APA), making him the only psychologist to have won APA's highest awards in all three major academic categories: distinguished writing (1973), distinguished teaching (1980), and distinguished research. APA also awarded him the Gordon Allport prize for his contributions to the reduction of prejudice and the betterment of inter-group relations. In 1981, he was named Professor of the Year by the American Council for the Advancement and Support of Education. He is currently professor emeritus at the University of California in Santa Cruz.

Major Contributions

Aronson has long-standing research interests in social influence and attitude change, cognitive dissonance, research methodology, and interpersonal attraction. His experiments have been aimed both at testing theory and at improving the human condition by influencing people to change their dysfunctional attitudes and behavior (e.g., prejudice, bullying, wasting of water, energy and other environmental resources). He developed Festinger's work on cognitive dissonance, one of his major interests.

Aronson's revolutionary work on reducing classroom prejudice is known as "the jigsaw classroom experiment" conducted in 1971, aimed at identifying methods of reducing prejudice in the newly desegregated Austin, Texas, school system by having cooperation replace competition in the classroom. Jigsaw classroom students had lower levels of prejudicial attitudes and negative stereotyping. Group participants demonstrated higher self-confidence, lower absenteeism, and higher academic achievement than students in the competitive classrooms.

Following the 1999 Columbine High School massacre, Aronson published the powerfully influential book *Nobody Left to Hate: Teaching Compassion after Columbine* (New York: Henry Holt, 2000). In Chapter 1, Aronson draws a distinction between peripheral remedies and root cause remedies, and states that peripheral remedies are "not based on solid evidence — but rest on emotion, wishful thinking, bias, and political expediency."

Major Literature

Aronson, Elliot, and G. Lindzey. *The Handbook of Social Psychology* (3rd ed.). New York: Random House, 1985.

___, and S. Patnoe. *The Jigsaw Classroom: Building Cooperation in the Classroom* (2nd ed.). New York: Longman, 1997.

___. "Adventures in Experimental Social Psychology: Roots, Branches, and Sticky New Leaves." In A. Rodrigues and R. Levine (Eds.), *Reflections on 100 Years of Experimental Social Psychology*. Los Angeles, California: Westview, 1999.

___. "Drifting My Own Way: Following My Nose and My Heart." In R. Sternberg (Ed.), *Psychologists Defying the Crowd: Stories of Those Who Battled the Establishment and Won*. Washington, D.C.: American Psychological Association Books, 2002.

___. *The Social Animal* (9th ed.). New York: Worth/Freeman, 2003.

Asch, Solomon Elliot (1907–1996)
GESTALT PSYCHOLOGY

Solomon Elliot Asch was born in Warsaw, Poland, immigrated to the United States in 1920, graduated with a B.S. from City College, New York (1928), an M.A. from Columbia University (1930), and a Ph.D. from Columbia University, New York City (1932). His mentor at Columbia was the Gestalt psychologist Max Wertheimer (see entry). He joined Swarthmore College, Pennsylvania, and spent the next 19 years working with another notable Gestalt psychologist, Wolfgang Kohler (see entry).

Asch became famous in the 1950s following experiments that showed how the effect of social pressure can make a person believe an obviously wrong opinion is correct. Asch was assisted in his work into conformity by a young Stanley Milgram (see entry), who himself was later to achieve worldwide fame with his studies into obedience to authority.

The American Psychological Association (APA) gave Asch a Distinguished Scientific Contributions Award in 1967. The Solomon Asch Center, University of Pennsylvania, was created in 1998 to advance research, education, practice, and policy-relevant study in ethnic group conflict and political violence.

Major Contributions

1. *Conformity experiments.* Conformity is any change in a person's behavior or opinions as a result of real or imagined pressure from a person or group of people. In a series of studies (1955) Asch found that three out of four people tested agreed with a group of people giving false answers on some comparisons of the lengths of lines. Asch said that conformity should be measured in terms of our tendency to give the wrong answer on a task where the solution is obvious or unambiguous. Asch's work is not without its critics; a culture change has taken place in the student population, so students in the 21st century are likely to be less compliant, although there is little doubt that Asch's studies were a child of the time.

2. *Prestige suggestion.* An example would be: a suggestion from a doctor is more likely to be acted upon than the same suggestion by a lay person. Asch's conclusion was that behavior is not a response to the world as it is, but to the world as perceived.

3. *Halo effect.* This is a tendency to allow an overall impression of a person or one particular outstanding trait to influence the total impression of that person. "All nuns are kind" would be a positive statement to demonstrate the halo effect. "No politician ever speaks the truth" would be a negative application. Both are stereotypes and would not stand up to close scrutiny.

4. *Primacy effect.* Given a list of items to remember, we will tend to remember the first few things more than those things in the middle. On TV game shows where people can win everything in a list of items they see, they usually at least remember the first few items.

Major Literature

Asch's classic textbook, *Social Psychology* (Prentice-Hall, 1952, Oxford University Press, 1987), ranks among the great works in psychology. It influenced a whole generation of psychologists.

Assagioli, Roberto (1888–1974)
PSYCHOSYNTHESIS

Born in Venice, Roberto Assagioli graduated in medicine at the University of Florence, specializing in neurology and psychiatry. While studying psychoanalysis with Eugen Bleuler (see entry) in Zurich, Assagioli met with Carl Jung (see entry). He completed his doctoral dissertation on psychoanalysis in 1909.

Around 1910 he broke away from Freudian orthodoxy and developed psychosynthesis, an integrated approach to psychiatry. In 1928, he founded the Institute of Psychosynthesis in Rome. In 1938, Mussolini's fascist government, critical of Assagioli's Jewish background, his humanitarianism, and his internationalism, closed the Institute. In 1940, he was arrested, jailed, and eventually placed in solitary confinement. The Institute of Psychosynthesis was re-established in Florence after the war and it is still in operation. He traveled to the United States for the opening of the Psychosynthesis Research Foundation in New York in 1948.

Major Contributions

Psychosynthesis is a synonym for human growth, the ongoing process of integrating all the parts, aspects and energies of the individual into a harmonious, powerful whole. As distinct from Freud's "depth psychology," Assagioli speaks of "height psychology." Psychology, he said, must embrace the soul as well as the libido, the imagination as well as the complexes, the will as well as the instincts. Assagioli drew upon psychoanalysis, Jungian and existential psychology, Buddhism and yoga and Christian traditions and philosophies, and affirms the spiritual dimension of the person, i.e., the "higher" or "transpersonal" self. Unlike Freud, who considered religion to be irrational, Assagioli incorporated religion and spirituality into an overall view of the human psyche.

Assagioli's map of the human psyche has seven areas:

1. The lower (infra) unconsciousness — here are stored all our unconscious drives and instincts.
2. The middle unconsciousness — which we have access to during our waking state.
3. The higher unconsciousness — from where all our higher feelings and thoughts enter consciousness.
4. The field of consciousness — accessible to us during the waking state.

5. The conscious self or ego — the center of our consciousness.
6. The higher self— the self that keeps our consciousness alive, when we cannot control it.
7. The collective unconsciousness — where there is a constant exchange going on between the world inside individual consciousness and consciousness surrounding it.

Assagioli wanted in therapy to build up the whole structure of the personality around the concept of the higher self and use all its potentials in unifying individual consciousness. But a true synthesis is only brought about when we also make use of all the energies of the higher self. That was his major objective and that's the reason he called his new psychology *psychosynthesis*.

Major Literature

Assagioli, Roberto. *Psychosynthesis: A Manual of Principles and Techniques*. Wellingborough, England: Turnstone Press, 1965.
___. *Symbols of Transpersonal Experiences*. London, England: Institute of Psychosynthesis.
___. *The Act of Will*. London: Wildwood House, 1969.
___. *Transpersonal Inspiration and Psychological Mountain Climbing*. London, England: Institute of Psychosynthesis, 1976.
___. *Psychosynthesis Typology*. England: Institute of Psychosynthesis, 1983.

Bailey, Marian Breland (1920–2001)
Operant Conditioning

After high school, Marian Kruse studied psychology at the University of Minnesota under B.F. Skinner (see entry), worked as an undergraduate laboratory assistant, and proofread Skinner's work for publication. In 1941, she graduated with honors and became Skinner's second graduate student. Later in the year she married Keller Breland, who also became Skinner's student. Together the two began to work with operant conditioning and started to see how they could apply it in different settings.

When World War II began, Skinner was working on ways to train pigeons to guide bombs to their targets for use by the Navy; the Brelands were invited to be assistants on the project. The effort was a success but it was never installed. Marian Breland completed her studies several years later and received her Ph.D. in 1978. In 1981 she became a professor at Henderson State University, Arkansas, and retired from teaching in 1998 with the rank of full professor.

Major Contributions

With the success of the pigeon project, the Brelands began to develop a commercial enterprise to train a variety of animals using operant conditioning. In 1943, they formed their own company, Animal Behavior Enterprises (ABE). To develop their business the couple left their graduate program in 1942, and by the early 1950s they had trained many animals for shows across the United States. They moved to Hot Springs, Arkansas, where they had larger premises. They were the first to train animals for dolphin and bird shows and for commercial advertising.

In 1955 ABE opened the IQ Zoo where the trained animals played baseball and musical instruments and danced to music, all based on operant conditioning techniques. In the course of their work they discovered that animal instincts also played an important part in behavior and could not be discounted. In the 1960s the Navy hired the Brelands to teach skills to trainers to use with dolphins. They formed a partnership with Bob Bailey, the Navy's first director of training, and went on to study dolphin communication.

When Keller Breland died in 1965, Bailey became managing director of ABE, which continued to grow. At one stage they were working with 150 different species of animals (Bob and Marian married in 1976). Marian Bailey contributed a chapter to *Teaching the Mentally Retarded* (Gillaspy and Bihm, 2002), expounding on the values of behavior modification in teaching people self-care skills. In 1990, Marian and Bob closed ABE and went into a very short retirement before Marian began using the Internet to teach dog handling.

Major Literature

Breland, K., and Marian Breland. A New Field of Applied Animal Psychology. *American Psychologist* 6 (1951): 202–204.
___. The Misbehavior of Organisms. *American Psychologist* 16 (1961): 681–684.
___. *Animal Behavior*. New York: Macmillan, 1966.
See http://www.behavior.org/animals/animals_bailey. cfm for a tribute by Bob Bailey to his wife.

Baillarger, Jules-Gabriel-François (1815–1890)
Manic-Depression

Born at Montbazon, central France, Jules Baillarger studied medicine at Paris under Jean Etienne Dominique Esquirol (see entry), and while still in training he worked as an intern at the

Charenton asylum for the mentally ill, Paris. He gained his medical degree in 1837. In 1840, he was appointed to the Salpêtrière Hospital in Paris and soon became one of the directors of a mental asylum in Ivry, Paris, established by Esquirol.

In 1842 the Académie Royale de Médecine awarded him a prize for his outstanding work on hallucinations. In 1843 he co-founded the journal *Annales médico-psychologiques du système nerveux*, in which he published many of his papers. This is still published and is therefore the oldest journal of psychiatry in the world. In 1875 he declined the offer of the first chair of psychiatry in France, considering himself to be too old for the job.

Major Contributions

In 1840 Baillarger presented a paper before the Académie Royale de Médecine on the structure of the gray matter of the cortex. He demonstrated that the white lines previously observed in the occipital area could be traced in all parts of the cortex, although they were far less conspicuous at the front than at the back. This continuation of the line has come to be known as the "external line or white stripe of Baillarger." He also showed that fibers connected the cortex with the internal white matter. Baillarger also demonstrated that the surface of the volume of the human brain is less than the volume of animal brains, but that the human brain compensates by having many more fissures.

On January 31, 1854, Baillarger described to the Académie Impériale de Médecine a recurring two-phase mental illness swinging between mania and depression, which came to be known as manic-depression, and later bi-polar disorders. In 1865 Baillarger pointed out that patients who had had lost the power of voluntary speech nevertheless retained the ability to express themselves in ways that needed to be understood. This contribution was recognized by John Hughlings Jackson (see entry), who called it *Baillarger's principle*. Baillarger also studied the role of the intermediary state between being asleep and being awake, at which time normal people have hallucinatory experiences, now called "hypnagogic hallucinations."

Bain, Alexander (1818–1903)
PRAGMATISM AND EMPIRICISM

Scottish philosopher and psychologist Alexander Bain left school at age 11 and attended evening classes at the Aberdeen Mechanics Institute. He studied classics, mathematics, science, and philos-

ophy at Marischal College, Aberdeen, and graduated with an M.A. in 1840. He taught three years at Marischal and one year at Glasgow University, then moved to London, there to join a brilliant circle that included George Grote and John Stuart Mill, with whom he already had close literary relationships.

Bain's acquaintance with John Stuart Mill, who was a fellow advocate of pragmatism and empiricism, began when Bain began contributing to *The Westminster Review* after his university graduation. From 1848 to 1850 Bain served as secretary of the Board of Health and for the next 10 years was employed in the civil service and as an educator, including three years lecturing on psychology and geography at Bedford College, London.

From 1860 to 1880 he held the chair of logic at the University of Aberdeen, which involved teaching grammar, composition and rhetoric as well as mental and moral philosophy. During this period he wrote several books on grammar and rhetoric and a two-volume work titled *Logic* (1870) containing a detailed account of the application of logic to the natural sciences. After his retirement he was twice elected lord rector of Aberdeen University.

Major Contributions

With James Mill and his son, John Stuart Mill, Bain was a major advocate of the British school of empiricism, a theory that based all knowledge on basic sensory experiences and not on introspection. He worked for the reform of teaching methods in Scotland and devoted himself to a rigorous study of psychology. Not satisfied with such abstract concepts as "idea" and "mind," he sought to find physical correlations and pushed for further investigation of the brain and nervous system. Bain founded the first journal devoted to psychology, *Mind*, in 1876. His *The Senses and the Intellect* (1855) and *The Emotions and the Will* (1859) (later combined into one volume) became the recommended textbook of half a century.

Bain broadened the definition of "feeling" beyond emotions to incorporate sensation, and attributed volition to both feeling and intellect. He argued that action was independent of sensation and could exist independent of any external stimulus. In what would later be known as the law of effect, Bain studied the mechanisms by which movement was associated with feeling. He contributed greatly to the development of scientific psychology by demonstrating the relevance of anatomical and physiological data to psychological study. By emphasizing the importance of (conscious) movement, he blazed a trail for subsequent studies in functionalist psychology of adaptive behavior.

Major Literature

Bain, Alexander. *On the Study of Character*. London: Parker Publishing, 1861.
___. *Mental and Moral Science: A Compendium of Psychology and Ethics*. London: Longman, Green, 1868.
___. *Mind and Body: The Theories of Their Relation*. London: Henry King, 1873.
___. *Education as a Science*. London: Kegan Paul, 1879.

Baldwin, James Mark (1861–1934)
EDUCATIONAL PSYCHOLOGY

Born in Columbia, South Carolina, James Mark Baldwin gained a B.A. (1884), an M.A. (1887), and a Ph.D. (1889) from Princeton University, New Jersey. With a Green Fellowship in Mental Science awarded to him at Princeton, he studied at the University of Leipzig, Germany, with Wilhelm Wundt (see entry) and with the philosopher Friedrich Paulsen (1846–1908) at Berlin (1884–1885).

He was instructor in French and German at Princeton (1886–1887); professor of philosophy, Lake Forest University, Lake Forest, Illinois (1878–1889); and professor of philosophy, University of Toronto, Ontario, Canada, where he established the first psychological laboratory in the British Empire (1889–1892). He was professor of psychology at Princeton, where he established another laboratory (1893–1903). In 1896 Baldwin was honorary president of the International Congress of Criminal Anthropology held in Geneva. He was professor of philosophy and psychology, Johns Hopkins University, Baltimore, Maryland (1903–1909), and advisor, National University of Mexico, Mexico City (1909–1913). In 1897 he was awarded a gold medal from the Royal Academy of Arts and Sciences of Denmark, and from 1900 to 1905 he was awarded honorary doctorates from the universities of Oxford, Geneva, Glasgow and South Carolina.

Major Contributions

Baldwin was known internationally as a philosopher and psychologist; he was the author of numerous works in these fields, many of which were translated into European languages. To bring the "new psychology" to a wider English-speaking audience, he wrote *Handbook of Psychology: Senses and Intellect* (2 vols. New York: Henry Holt and Co.).

A key figure in North American psychology, Baldwin is also significant in the development of social psychology, developmental psychology and the psychology of individual differences. He was a founding member of the American Psychological Association (APA) in 1892 and its sixth president in 1897, and one of the founders of the *Psychological Review*, the journal of the APA.

In 1893, Baldwin organized the psychology exhibit at the World's Columbian Exposition at Chicago. His landmark work on mental development in children included, for the first time in psychology, experiments with children (namely, his own daughter Elizabeth). Baldwin was one of the first experimental psychologists to apply Darwin's theory of evolution to his theories of development. He also gave psychology the Baldwin illusion.

In 1902, he published the *Dictionary of Philosophy and Psychology: Including Many of the Principal Conceptions of Ethics, Logic, Aesthetics, Philosophy of Religion, Mental Pathology, Anthropology, Biology, Neurology, Physiology, Etc.* (republished by Thoemmes Press, 1998), which contained contributions from the leading figures in psychology and philosophy at the turn of the century.

Major Literature

Baldwin, James Mark. *Mental Development in the Child and the Race: Methods and Processes*. New York: Macmillan and Co., 1895.
___. *Social and Ethical Interpretations in Mental Development*. New York: Macmillan and Co., 1897. Manchester, New Hampshire: Ayer Co. Publishers, 1990.
___. *The Story of the Mind*. New York: D. Appleton and Company, 1905.
___. *History of Psychology: A Sketch and An Interpretation*. London: Watts, 1913.
___. *Between Two Wars: 1861–1921* (2 vols.). Boston: Stratford Co., 1926.

Bales, Robert Freed (1916–2004)
EVALUATION AND MEASUREMENT

Born in Ellington, Missouri, Robert Freed Bales gained a B.A. in 1938 and an M.S. in 1941, both in sociology, from University of Oregon, Eugene, and an M.A. (1943) and Ph.D. (1945) from Harvard University in Cambridge, Massachusetts.

He was research associate in alcohol studies at Yale University, New Haven, Connecticut (1944–1945). Between 1945 and 1986 he was instructor in sociology, assistant professor of sociology, lecturer on sociology, associate professor of social relations, professor of social relations, and emeritus professor at Harvard University. He was an affiliate of Boston Psychoanalytic Society and Institute in 1956, and president, Eastern Sociological Society, Social Psychology Section (1962–1963).

Bales received the Distinguished Career Award of the American Association of Specialists in Group Work (1982), Cooley-Mead Award of the American Sociological Association (1983), and the Distinguished Teaching Award of the American Psychological Foundation (1984).

Major Contributions

Bales' main work in social psychology focused on the nature of interpersonal interaction in small groups. His first book, *Interaction Process Analysis: A Method for the Study of Small Groups*, was published by Addison-Wesley in 1950, the culmination of a series of early studies on interactions in therapeutic group settings for alcohol addicts.

Interaction process analysis (IPA) looks at the interaction in groups of 12 to 16 people. Bales produced a grid for charting 16 different functions under three main headings: tasks, relationships and individual needs. For many years, Bales taught a popular undergraduate course on group psychology. Students were divided into two self-analytic groups that explored their own interactions as a basis for learning about the problems faced in groups by members and leaders. Furthermore, each group made systematic observations of the other group's interaction and fed back to that group the results of their observations.

His work was influenced by the field theory of Kurt Lewin (see entry) where the behavior of individuals *in* a group was influenced *by* the group, and could only be understood by examining the group processes. He developed the SYMLOG system (an acronym for systematic multilevel observation of groups). SYMLOG is a computerized system used in managerial settings in the assessment and training for team effectiveness and individual leadership potential in industrial management, classroom management, social work and many other areas. Both IPA and SYMLOG are easily understood and offer two models for understanding group processes.

Major Literature

Bales, Robert Freed. *Personality and Interpersonal Behavior.* Holt, Rinehart and Winston, 1970.

___. *Interaction Process Analysis.* Chicago, Illinois: University of Chicago Press, 1976.

___. *SYMLOG: Case Study Kit with Instructions for Group Self Study.* New York, Simon and Schuster, Inc., The Free Press, 1980.

Parsons, Talcot, and Robert Freed Bales. *Family: Socialization and Interaction Process.* London: Taylor and Francis Books, Ltd., Routledge, 1998.

Bales, Robert Freed. *Social Interaction Systems: Theory and Measurement.* New Jersey: Transaction Publishers, 2001.

Balint, Michael (1896–1970)
THE BASIC FAULT

Mihály Maurice Bergmann, born the son of a Jewish physician in Budapest, changed his name to Michael Balint and his religion to Christian. He saw service during World War I and completed his medical study in Budapest in 1918. He attended the lectures of Sándor Ferenczi, who in 1919 became the world's first university professor of psychoanalysis.

Around 1920 he and his wife moved to Berlin, where he worked part time at the Berlin Institute of psychoanalysis while studying for his doctorate in biochemistry. They returned to Hungary in 1924 but by the 1930s the political situation made the teaching of psychotherapy difficult, so they immigrated to England. His wife died; his parents, back in Hungary, in 1945, about to be arrested by the Nazis, committed suicide.

Balint moved to London, where he continued his group work with practicing physicians and obtained a master of science degree in psychology. Balint became involved with the Tavistock Institute of Human Relations, and with Enid Flora Eichholz, who would become his new wife; they formed what is now known as the Balint Group. In 1968 Balint became president of the British Psychoanalytical Society.

Major Contributions

Balint's premise is that the search for the primary love object underlies virtually all psychological phenomena. The failure to find the lost love object leads to a split and the development of a true self and a false self with a tendency to escape into over-idealizations. Balint described the feeling in many people that something is missing as *the basic fault,* the title of one of his books. He viewed all psychological motivations as stemming from that failure to receive adequate maternal love. Therapy with such clients is difficult, and the view is that at best it can help the patient to function while containing such a basic fault, but it cannot heal it completely.

Balint groups are small experiential training groups in which general practitioners develop effective methods of using the short consultations they have with their patients to help them not only in a strictly medical but also in a psychotherapeutic way. They learn some skills and techniques of counseling. The Balint Society, with branches in America, Germany, Finland, Sweden and Switzerland (with its own journal, now in volume 34), was founded in 1969 to continue the work begun by Michael and Enid Balint. The Balint method consists of regular case discussion in small groups under the guidance of a qualified group leader. The work of the group involves both training and research.

Major Literature

Balint, Michael. *The Doctor, His Patient and the Illness.* London: Churchill Livingstone, 1964, 2000.
___, and E. Balint. *The Basic Fault: Therapeutic Aspects of Regression.* London: Taylor and Francis Books Ltd., Routledge, 1984.
___(Ed.). *A Study of Doctors: Mutual Selection and the Evaluation of Results in a Training Programme for Family Doctors.* London: Tavistock Publications, 1966, 2001.

Baltes, Paul B. (1939–)
LIFESPAN DEVELOPMENT

Born in Saarlouis, Germany, Paul B. Baltes gained a B.A. in psychology with minors in biology and physiology in 1961 from the University of Saarland, Germany, and a diploma in psychology in 1963. From 1963 to 1964 he was an exchange student at the University of Nebraska, Lincoln. He was scientific assistant (1964–1967) at University of Saarland, from where he gained a D.Phil. in psychology with minors in physiology and psychopathology (1967). From 1968 to 1972 he was assistant to associate professor of psychology, West Virginia University, Morgantown, West Virginia, and from 1972 to 1979, associate to full professor of human development, Pennsylvania State University, Philadelphia, College of Human Development.

He was honorary professor of psychology, Free University of Berlin (1980), and since 1980, senior fellow of the Max Planck Society and institute director, Max Planck Institute of Lifespan Psychology Development in Berlin (dedicated to the study of human development and education, and their evolutionary, social, historical, and institutional contexts).

Since 2004 he has been distinguished professor of psychology (part-time) at the University of Virginia, Charlottesville, Virginia. Baltes received the Award for Distinguished Contributions to the International Advancement of Psychology (1995) and the German order Pour le Mérite of Science and the Arts (2000). He is active in various national and international organizations, including the U.S. Social Science Research Council (where from 1996 until 2000 he served as chair of the board of directors), the German-American Academy Council, the Berlin-Brandenburg Academy of Sciences, and the European Academy of Science.

Major Contributions

Baltes' areas of expertise include the following.

- creating the field of lifespan development, the goals of which are growth, maintenance, and regulation of loss, considering behavioral and cognitive functioning from childhood into old age
- the psychological study of wisdom
- research on cognitive aging and the plasticity of the aging mind
- developing Raymond B. Cattell's (see entry) idea of "fluid intelligence," the ability to perform novel tasks well
- social scenarios concerning the future of old age and an aging society
- the articulation and testing of models of successful development and aging
- cross-cultural comparative study of child development and school performance.

Major Literature

Baltes, Margaret M., and Paul B. Baltes (Eds.). *The Psychology of Control and Aging.* Mahwah, New Jersey: Lawrence Erlbaum Associates, Inc., 1986.
Baltes, Paul B., David L. Featherman, and Richard M. Lerner (Eds.). *Life Span Development and Behavior: Vol. 8.* Mahwah, New Jersey: Lawrence Erlbaum Associates, Inc., 1987.
Baltes, Paul B., and Margaret M. Baltes (Eds.). *Successful Aging: Perspectives from the Behavioral Sciences (European Network on Longitudinal Studies on Individual Development).* New York: Cambridge University Press, 1993.
Baltes, Paul B., and Ursula M. Staudinger (Eds.). *Interactive Minds: Life-span Perspectives on the Social Foundation of Cognition.* New York: Cambridge University Press, 1996.
Baltes, Paul B., and Karl Ulrich Mayer (Eds.). *The Berlin Aging Study: Aging from 70 to 100.* New York: Cambridge University Press, 1998.

Bandler, Richard (1950–)
NEUROLINGUISTIC PROGRAMMING

Richard Bandler, one of the developers of neurolinguistic programming, holds a B.A. (1973) in philosophy and psychology from the University of California, Santa Cruz, and an M.A. (1975) in psychology from Lone Mountain College in San Francisco. While studying mathematics at Santa Cruz, Bandler met John Grinder (see entry), a linguistics professor. In 1974 Bandler and Grinder began to make a model of the language patterns used by Fritz Perls, Virginia Satir and hypnotherapist Milton Erickson (see entries), which formed the foundation of the field of neurolinguistic programming (NLP).

Major Contributions

Bandler invented "brief therapy" type techniques that are said to cure severe phobias or get schizophrenics back to social life. His recent work is based on the combination of these techniques and hypnosis. Bandler's background as a musician and his interest in sound theory and the neurological impact of sound led him to develop the area of neuro-sonics, which utilizes qualities of music and sound to create specific internal states.

Bandler is also the founder of the model and techniques of design human engineering (DHE). NLP describes how the brain works with language, how language relates to other brain functions, and how this knowledge may enable people to achieve more satisfaction in their behavior. Although the study of eye movements is only a small part of NLP, it is a useful introduction to the model. Eye movements indicate whether we are making pictures, listening to internal tapes or concentrating on feelings.

Following a person's eye movements gives lots of information about that person's mental processes at the moment, but not the content. When reference is made to "right," "left," or "down," it means the person who is being studied, not the observer.

Visual: eyes up and right, up and left, or eyes straight ahead and out of focus.

Auditory: eyes level right, level left, eyes down left.

Kinesthetic (bodily sensations): eyes down right.

Matching language systems. Using the same primary language system as someone else helps to build rapport, and people will learn best when we present something to them in their primary representational systems — visual, auditory, or kines-

thetic. By paying attention to the words used by people, we can determine the systems they use most.

Major Literature

Bandler, Richard, and John Grinder. *Frogs into Princes.* Moab, Utah: Real People Press, 1981.
___. *Reframing: Neurolinguistic Programming and the Transformation of Meaning.* Moab, Utah: Real People Press, 1982.
___. *Structure of Magic* (Vols. 1 and 2). Palo Alto, California: Science and Behavior Books, 1989.
Bandler, Richard. *Insider's Guide to Submodalities.* Capitola, California: Meta Publications, 1989.
___, and J. Grinder. *Patterns of the Hypnotic Techniques of Milton H. Erickson, M.D.* Volume 1. Portland, Oregon: Metamorphous Press, 1997.
___. *Design Human Engineering.* Capitola, California: Meta Publications, 1996.

Bandura, Albert (1925–)
SOCIAL LEARNING THEORY

Born in Mundane, Alberta, Canada, Albert Bandura earned a B.A. at the University of British Columbia in Vancouver in 1949 and a Ph.D. in 1952 from the University of Iowa, Ames. He gained postdoctoral experience at Wichita Guidance Center in Wichita, Kansas. Since 1953 he has been at Stanford University, California, and is now Davis Storr Jordan Professor of Social Sciences. He received a Guggenheim Fellowship Award (1972); Distinguished Scientific Achievement Award, Canadian Psychological Association (1973); honorary doctorate, University of British Columbia (1979); Distinguished Contribution Award, International Society for Research on Aggression (1980); Distinguished Scientific Contributions Award (1980); William James Award, American Psychological Association (APA) (1989). Bandura was president of the APA in 1974; member, Institute of Medicine of the National Academy of Sciences in 1989, and fellow, American Academy of Arts and Sciences.

Major Contributions

Bandura is the leading exponent of the concept of social learning, often called modeling. Social learning theory (SLT) is concerned with the processes by which social influences alter human thought, feeling and action, as distinct from trait theory, which focuses on how traits predispose the individual to respond consistently in different situations. He has undertaken innumerable studies showing that children will mimic the aggressive responses they see performed by adults. Also, his studies showed that when children watch others they learn many positive forms of behavior, such as sharing, cooperation, social interaction, and delay of gratification. Environment causes behavior, but behavior causes environment as well.

Broadening his approach, he began to look at personality as an interaction among the environment, behavior, and the person's psychological processes. These psychological processes consist of our ability to entertain images in our minds, and language. By introducing imagery, Bandura moves away from strict behaviorism toward social cognitive theory. Psychologists following Bandura have stated that social learning based on observation is a complex process that involves three stages: exposure to the responses of others; acquisition of what an individual sees; and subsequent acceptance of the modeled acts as a guide for one's own behavior.

Bandura's straightforward, behaviorist-like style, where he has successfully blended behavior with cognition, makes good sense to most people. His approach focuses on getting things done.

Major Literature

Bandura, Albert, and Richard Haig Walters. *Adolescent Aggression.* New York: Ronald Press, 1959.
Bandura, Albert. *Principles of Behavior Modification.* New York: Henry Holt and Company, Inc., 1969.
___, and Richard Haig Walters. *Social Learning and Personality Development.* New York: Henry Holt and Company, Inc., 1970.
Bandura, Albert. *Aggression: A Social Learning Analysis.* Upper Saddle River, New Jersey: Prentice-Hall, 1971.
___. *Social Foundations of Thought and Action: A Social Cognitive Theory.* Upper Saddle River, New Jersey: Prentice-Hall, 1986.
___. *Self-efficacy: The Exercise of Control.* New York: W.H. Freeman and Co. Ltd., 1997.
___(Ed.). *Self-Efficacy in Changing Societies.* New York: Cambridge University Press, 1997.
___(Ed.). *Psychological Modeling: Conflicting Theories.* Somerset, New Jersey: Aldine Transaction, 2006.

Barber, Theodore Xenophon (1927–2005)

HYPNOSIS

Born in Martins Ferry, Ohio, Theodore Xenophon "Ted" Barber received his bachelor's degree and his doctoral degree in social psychology (1956) from American University, Washington, D.C. After a period of research at Harvard, in 1961 he joined the Medfield Foundation in Massachusetts, a private psychiatric research center, where he became chief psychologist. There he conducted in-

tensive research into hypnosis, and in 1973 was appointed director of research. From 1978 to 1986 he was chief psychologist at Cushing Hospital in Framingham, Massachusetts. He died of a ruptured aorta at a hospital in Framingham. At the time of his death he was still active in research and will be remembered as one of the most prolific and influential researchers in the field of hypnosis.

Major Contributions

Barber developed what became a career-long study of hypnosis in the 1960s, when the general opinion was that hypnosis worked by inducing a deep trance-like state. What Barber and his colleagues discovered was that they could induce sleepiness by suggestion alone, without swinging watches or formal protocols used by hypnotists. Power of suggestion worked effectively on about 20 percent of people tested, although another 25 percent had no reaction. The results stimulated Dr. Barber's interest in the hypnotic state, and he examined people who could be *easily* or *deeply* hypnotized.

Later Barber identified a small minority — 2 to 4 percent — and found that people who were most susceptible to hypnosis were those who were high users of fantasy; such people were also likely to have had paranormal interest and experience. Further, people who responded well to the hypnotist's suggestions were already motivated to respond and had a positive attitude and expectation toward hypnosis. Hypnotic behavior could thus be understood in ordinary, cognitive and social terms such as "thinking" and "imagining." Barber's ideas led to the cognitive-behavioral approach to hypnosis. The Barber Suggestibility Scale is a method of evaluating patients and measuring their responsiveness to a range of suggestions.

Major Literature

Barber, Theodore Xenophon. Physiologic Effects of Hypnotic Suggestions: A Critical Review of Recent Research (1960–64). *Psychological Bulletin* 63 (1965): 201–222.
___. *Pitfalls in Human Research: Ten Pivotal Points,* Philadelphia, Pennsylvania: Franklin Book Co., 1976.
___. "Changing 'Unchangeable' Bodily Processes by (Hypnotic) Suggestions: A New Look at Hypnosis Cognitions, Imagining, and the Mind-Body Problem." In *Imagination and Healing,* Anees A. Sheikh (Ed.). New York: Baywood Publishing Co., 1984.
___. *The Human Nature of Birds: A Scientific Discovery With Startling Implications.* Baltimore, Maryland: Bookman, 1993.
Straus, Roger A., and Theodore Xenophon Barber. *Stra-*

tegic Self-hypnosis: How to Overcome Stress, Improve Performance, and Live to Your Fullest Potential. iUniverse.com, U.S., 2000.

Gibbons, Don E., and Theodore Xenophon Barber. *Applied Hypnosis and Hyperempiria.* iUniverse.com, U.S., 2000. [Hyperempiria is a new "altered state of consciousness" induced by suggestion].

Bar-Tal, Daniel (1946–)
DEVELOPMENTAL PSYCHOLOGY

Born in Stalinbad, USSR, Daniel Bar-Tal gained a B.A. in psychology and sociology at Tel Aviv University, Ramat Aviv, Israel (1970). At the University of Pittsburgh, Pennsylvania, he gained an M.S. in social psychology (1973); a Ph.D. in social psychology (1974); and was post-doctoral fellow and research associate at the Learning Research and Development Center (1974–1975). Since 1975 he has been at Tel-Aviv University. He is currently professor of psychology at the School of Education, and a director of the Walter Lebach Research Institute for Jewish-Arab Coexistence through Education.

Between 1981 and 2001 Bar-Tel was visiting professor at seven universities in America, France, Poland, and Germany. He was academic director of in-service training of high school teachers in Jewish-Arab relations and of high school principals in Education for Democracy (1984–1987) and member of the executive committee of the Political Psychology Division of the International Association of Applied Psychology (1989–1994). He was vice president of the International Society of Political Psychology (1994–1996) and Golestan Fellowship, Netherlands Institute for Advanced Study in the Humanities and Social Sciences (2000–2001). He is co-director of the European Summer Institute in Political Psychology; co-editor-in-chief of the *Palestine Israel Journal*, and editor, co-editor and on the editorial board of ten other journals in social psychology, counseling and education. He has published over one hundred articles and chapters in major social and political psychological journals and books.

Major Contributions

In his early career Bar-Tal focused on attribution theory — how we explain things — and on the cognitive factors of helping behavior and how values and beliefs affected the successful outcome or failure of achievement behavior. His research highlighted the effectiveness of external rewards in encouraging helping behavior in younger children. For the past twenty years his interest shifted

to political psychology, where his focus was on shared beliefs in groups and societies in general. He then moved on to examining the psychological foundations of intractable conflicts and their resolution, including reconciliation. This research included shared societal beliefs of the ethos of conflict, of collective memory, and emotional collective orientations, how such beliefs are born, maintained and institutionalized, and the identity that emerges. His paper "The Israeli-Palestinian Conflict: A Cognitive Analysis" won the 1991 Otto Klineberg Intercultural and International Prize of the Society for the Psychological Study of Social Issues. In 2002 his paper "Why Does Fear Override Hope" won second place in the same competition.

Major Literature

Bar-Tal, Daniel. *Prosocial Behavior: Theory and Research.* New York: Halsted Press, 1976.

___, and L. Saxe (Eds.). *Social Psychology of Education: Theory and Research.* New York: Halsted, 1978.

Bar-Tal, Daniel. *Group Beliefs: A Conception for Analyzing Group Structure, Processes and Behavior.* New York: Springer-Verlag, 1990.

___. *Shared Beliefs in a Society: Social Psychological Analysis.* Thousand Oaks, California: Sage, 2000.

___, Teichman Y. *Stereotypes and Prejudice in Conflict: Representations of Arabs in Israeli Jewish Society.* New York: Cambridge University Press, 2005.

Bartlett, Sir Frederic Charles (1886–1969)
COGNITIVE PSYCHOLOGY

Born in Stow on the Wold, Gloucestershire, England, Frederic Charles Bartlett graduated with a B.A. in philosophy (1909) with first class honors from the University Correspondence College, London University, and MA (1914) in moral sciences from St. John's College, Cambridge. Cambridge at that time was in the forefront of the movement to make experimental psychology a recognized branch of science in the British university system. From 1914 to 1922 Bartlett was "relief director" of the Psychology Laboratory at Cambridge, then director. From 1924 to 1946 he was editor of the *British Journal of Psychology*. In 1931 he was appointed the first professor of experimental psychology, Cambridge University, and was made a fellow of the Royal Society in 1932.

From 1945 until his retirement in 1952 (when he became professor emeritus), on the death of Kenneth Craik at age 31, Bartlett was director of the Medical Research Council's Applied Psychology Unit at Cambridge. He received honorary doctorates from seven universities in England, Scotland and America. He was appointed to the order of Commanders of the British Empire in 1941; and was knighted in 1948 for services to the Royal Air Force on the basis of his wartime work in applied psychology. The U.K. Ergonomics Society awards a Bartlett medal in his honor, and the Experimental Psychology Society holds an annual Bartlett lecture.

Major Contributions

The work for which Bartlett is best known is *Remembering: A Study in Experimental and Social Psychology* (London: Cambridge University Press, 1932, republished 1967), although he wrote many other books and scientific papers. In *Remembering* Bartlett puts forward the concept that memories of past events and experiences are actually mental reconstructions that are colored by cultural attitudes and personal habits, rather than being direct recollections of observations made at the time. In experiments beginning in 1914, Bartlett showed that very little of an event is actually perceived at the time of its occurrence but that in reconstructing the memory, gaps in observation or perception are filled in with the aid of previous experiences.

On the outbreak of World War II, the Cambridge laboratory was turned over to applied work, and problems were brought to him in ever-increasing numbers by the armed services and by various government bodies — problems such as equipment design, training methods, fatigue, and personnel selection. Through his long association with Cambridge University, Bartlett strongly influenced British psychological method, emphasizing a descriptive, or case study, approach over more statistical techniques.

Major Literature

Bartlett, Frederic Charles. *Psychology and Primitive Culture.* London: Cambridge University Press, 1923.

___. *Psychology and the Soldier.* London: Cambridge University Press, 1927.

___. *Remembering: A Study in Experimental and Social Psychology.* London: Cambridge University Press, 1932, 1995.

___. *The Problem of Noise.* London: Cambridge University Press, 1934.

___. *The Mind at Work and Play.* London: Allen and Unwin, 1951.

___. *Thinking: An Experimental and Social Study.* London: Allen and Unwin, 1958.

Bateson, Gregory (1904–1980)
DOUBLE-BIND

Born in Grantchester, Cambridgeshire, England, Gregory Bateson gained a B.Sc. in biology (1924) and an M.A. in anthropology (1930) from the University of Cambridge, England. He was engaged in anthropological fieldwork in New Britain, Papua, New Guinea (1927–1928), was a lecturer in linguistics at the University of Sydney, Australia (1928), did fieldwork in New Guinea (1929–1930), and was a fellow at St. John's College, Cambridge (1931–1937). In 1934 he was lecturer at Columbia University, New York City, and the University of Chicago, Illinois. Then he did more fieldwork in New Guinea (1932), where he met the American anthropologist Margaret Mead. They married in 1936 and from 1936 to 1938, Bateson and Mead conducted fieldwork together in Bali, Indonesia. They moved to the USA (1939); Bateson became an American citizen in 1956.

From 1942 to 1943, Bateson worked as anthropological film analyst at the Museum of Modern Art in New York, analyzing German propaganda films, and was lecturer at Columbia University (1943–1944) when he worked for the United States Office of Strategic Services in Southeast Asia (1944–1947). In 1946, Bates went on a Guggenheim Fellowship to China, Burma, Sri Lanka, and India; he was visiting professor of anthropology at the New School for Social Research in New York (1946–1947). He was at Harvard University, Cambridge, Massachusetts, in 1947–1948 and at the University of California in San Francisco in 1948–1949. From 1949 to 1951, he was research associate in psychiatry and communications at the Langley-Porter Clinic in San Francisco, and visiting professor of anthropology at Stanford University, California (1951–1962).

He won the Freida Fromm-Reichmann Award for Research in Schizophrenia (1962). He was associate research director in ethnology; worked for the Communications Research Institute, Virgin Islands (1963–1964), and won the Career Development Award from the National Institute of Mental Health (1964). He was chief of the Biological Relations Division at the Oceanic Institute, Waimanalo, Hawaii (1964–1972); professor of anthropology and ethnology at the University of California, Santa Cruz (1972–1978); scholar-in-residence, Esalen Institute in California (1978–1980); and fellow of the American Association for the Advancement of Science.

Major Contributions

Although Bateson was an anthropologist, he played a major role in the early formulation of cybernetics and helped introduce systems theory into the work of social and natural scientists. His influence is most strongly felt in the fields of education, family therapy and ecology, with particular reference to his concept of the "double-bind," which made an impact on psychiatry with particular reference to communication in schizophrenia.

Major Literature

Bateson, G., D.D. Jackson, J. Haley, and J.H. Weakland. "Toward a Theory of Schizophrenia." *Behavioral Science* 1 (1956): 251–264.

___. "A Note on the Double Bind." *Family Process* 2 (1962): 154–161.

Bateson, Gregory. *Steps to an Ecology of Mind: Collected Essays in Anthropology, Psychiatry, Evolution, and Epistemology.* University of Chicago Press, 1972, republished by Mary Catherine Bateson in 2000.

___. *Mind and Nature: A Necessary Unity. Advances in Systems Theory, Complexity and the Human Sciences.* Cresskill, New Jersey: Hampton Press, 1979 and 2002.

Baumrind, Diana Blumberg (1927–)
FAMILY SOCIALIZATION

Born in New York, Diana Blumberg Baumrind graduated A.B. in psychology and philosophy from Hunter College, New York (1948), and M.A. (1951) and Ph.D. in psychology (clinical, social and developmental) (1955) both from the University of California, Berkeley. Baumrind was influenced by the research of Theodor Adorno and Else Frenkel-Brunswik on anti–Semitism and the authoritarian personality, the teaching of Egon Brunswik (see entry), and by the conformity research of David Krech.

Baumrind completed a clinical residency at the Cowell Hospital, University of California (1955–1958), and was a fellow under the National Institute of Mental Health (1984–1988), which funded her research into therapeutic change, extending her leadership research to families and therapy groups. In 1988 she received the G. Stanley Hall Award, American Psychological Association, Division 7. She is a fellow, American Psychological Association, American Psychological Society, Society for Research in Child Development, and Society for Research on Adolescence.

Major Contributions

Baumrind's later research on family socialization focused on a structured (authoritative, not authoritarian) parental leadership style, a mixture of authority and democratic styles. Her focus has been concerned with accounting for individual differences in two areas: competence (defined as socially responsible self-assertive behavior); moral outlook and behavior. She has published a large body of work on parent-child socialization throughout childhood. She concluded that child-rearing works best where there is both authority and mutual respect. She argues that the primary cause of child maltreatment is poverty rather than psychological factors. The principles that underpin all of Baumrind's work are that individual rights and responsibilities are inseparable, and that moral actions are determined by conscious choice.

She directs the longitudinal database of the Family Socialization and Developmental Competence Project, Institute of Human Development, University of California, Berkeley, which also supports studies the socialization effects of gender differences and the causes and consequences of adolescent drug abuse. In 2001 Baumrind was involved in controversy over "mild spanking" of children. *The New York Times*, on August 25, 2001, reported, "Baumrind of the University of California, asserted that social scientists had overstepped the evidence in claiming that spanking caused lasting harm to the child.... Dr. Baumrind, a psychologist known for her classic studies of authoritative, authoritarian and permissive styles of child-rearing, said she did not advocate spanking. But she argued that an occasional swat, when delivered in the context of good child-rearing, had not been shown to do any harm."

Major Literature

Baumrind, Diana Blumberg. "Some Thoughts on Ethics of Research: After Reading Milgram's 'Behavioral Study of Obedience.'" *American Psychologist,* 19(6) (1964): 421–423.

___. "Child Care Practices Anteceding Three Patterns of Preschool Behavior." *Genetic Psychology Monographs,* 75 (1967): 43–88.

___. "Current Patterns of Parental Authority." *Developmental Psychology Monographs,* Part 2, 4(1) (1971): 1–103.

___. *Child Maltreatment and Optimal Caregiving in Social Contexts.* New York: Garland Publishing, Inc., 1995.

Bayley, Nancy (1899–1994)
INFANT DEVELOPMENT

Born in The Dalles, Oregon, Nancy Bayley gained a B.S. (1922) and M.S. (1924) from the University of Washington, Seattle, and a Ph.D. (1926) from the University of Iowa, Ames. She became associate (1928), fellow (1937), president of Division 7 (1953–1954), and president of Division 20 (1957–1958) of the American Psychological Association (APA). She was president of the Western Psychological Association in 1953–1954, and received the Distinguished Scientific Contribution Award from the APA in 1966. She also received the Distinguished Contributions Award, Institute of Human Development, University of California at Berkeley (1967); the G. Stanley Hall Award, APA division 7, for outstanding contributions to knowledge in the field of development psychology (1971); the Distinguished Contributions to Psychology Award, California State Psychological Association (the first woman to be so honored) (1976); and the Gold Medal Award, American Psychological Foundation (APF) (1982).

Major Contributions

Bayley concentrated most of her work around the mental and motor development of children. During her time at Washington, she served as a research assistant at the university's Gatzert Foundation for Child Welfare, and her master's thesis involved the construction of performance tests for preschool children. For her doctoral dissertation she accomplished one of the first studies of children's fears utilizing the psychogalvanic skin response. She held fellow status in the American Association for the Advancement of Science and contributed to the Society for Research in Child Development, of which she was president for a period of time.

Bayley's contributions concentrated on mental and physical growth, psychomotor development, the earliest mental functions that predict later intelligence, and how environment influences intelligence. She was the first to publish correlations that related infant size to adult size. She carried out a number of well-known studies not only on developmental regularities but on handicapping conditions as well. This is known today as the Berkeley Growth Study. She was also associated with and helped design the National Collaborative Perinatal Project (NCPP) (1959–1974) for the study of cerebral palsy, mental retardation, and other neurological and psychological disorders. She developed the widely used Bayley Scales of Mental and Motor Development, which measure the cognitive development, motor development and tests the behavioral development of infants from one to 42 months of age. Nancy Bayley was one of the most influential psychologists in her time and her influence is still felt.

Major Literature

Bayley, Nancy. "The Development of Motor Abilities During the First Three Years of Life: A Study of Sixty-One Infants Tested Repeatedly." *Monographs of the Society for Research in Child Development*, 1 (1935): 26–27.
___. *Bayley Scales of Infant Development (BSID-I: Additional Mental Scale Record Forms)*. San Antonio, Texas: Harcourt Assessment, Inc., The Psychological Corporation, 1969, 1999.
___. *Bayley Scales of Infant Development (BSID-II: Additional Motor Scale Record Forms With Tracing Design Sheet)*. San Antonio, Texas: Harcourt Assessment, Inc., The Psychological Corporation, 1999.
Bayerm, Leona M., and Nancy Bayley. *Growth Diagnosis: Selected Methods for Interpreting and Predicting Physical Development from One Year to Maturity*. Chicago, Illinois: University of Chicago Press, 1976.

Beach, Frank Ambrose (1911–1988)
BEHAVIORAL ENDOCRINOLOGY

Born in Emporia, Kansas, the son of a distinguished professor of music at the Teachers College in Emporia, Frank Ambrose Beach received a B.A. from Emporia Teachers College (1932) and a Ph.D. on cortical control of maternal behavior in rats from the University of Chicago (1940). His adherence to strict experimental research earned him the title of "The Conscience of Comparative Psychology." He became assistant curator in the Department of Experimental Biology of the American Museum of Natural History in New York in 1937–38, and in 1940, when he was made the new chairman and curator, he changed the name to the Department of Animal Behavior. The department provided a home for numerous very active comparative psychologists for many years.

In 1946 Beach left the museum for a position in the Department of Psychology at Yale University in New Haven, Connecticut, and in 1952 he was named a Sterling professor of psychology at Yale. He was elected president of the Eastern Psychological Association and was selected as a charter member of the psychobiology panel of the National Science Foundation. In 1955 he became a member of the National Research Council's Committee for the Study of Problems of Sex, and two years later was made chairman. In 1958, Beach was appointed professor of psychology at the University of California, Berkeley. He was elected to the American Philosophical Society and the American Academy of Arts and Sciences, and was awarded the Distinguished Scientific Award and the Howard Crosby Warren Medal from the Society of Experimental Psychologists.

Major Contributions

Behavioral endocrinology, sexual behavior, and animal behavior were his three major scientific contributions. Beach was the first American to integrate the study of animal behavior (ethnology) with comparative psychology. Within his research, he provided valuable knowledge in the behaviors of rats, hamsters, guinea pigs, chinchillas, cats, dogs, alligators, Japanese quail, pouchless marsupials, and hyenas. Behavioral endocrinology was developed to establish that behavior is decreasingly dependent on hormones and increasingly affected by experience.

Beach was committed to the scientific study of sexual behavior, and worked with and influenced several sex researchers. In analyzing the importance of female sexual behavior, Beach helped destroy the myth that females were passive in sexual interactions; he coined the term "proceptivity" to refer to the female's strong sexual appetites. Many other words were coined by him, such as "ramstergig" (a hypothetical blend between rats, hamsters, and guinea pigs) and "thunch" (theory-hunch).

Major Literature

Beach, Frank A. *Hormones and Behavior*. New York: Paul B. Hoeber, Inc., 1948.

Ford, Clellan S., and Frank A. Beach. *Patterns of Sexual Behavior*. New York: Harper and Brothers, 1951.

Beach, Frank A. *Human Sexuality in Four Perspectives*. Baltimore: Johns Hopkins University Press (1980); Westport, Connecticut: Greenwood Press, 1977.

Beach, Frank A. "Historical Origins of Modern Research on Hormones and Behavior." *Hormones and Behavior*. 15 (1981): 325–76.

Beck, Aaron T. (1921–)
COGNITIVE THERAPY

Born in Providence, Rhode Island, Aaron T. Beck graduated from Brown University in Providence, Rhode Island and was a member of Phi Beta Kappa and a Francis Wayland Scholar (1942).

He gained an M.D. in psychiatry at Yale Medical School, New Haven, Connecticut, in 1946 and received the Rhode Island Medical Society Award for Research in 1948. During the Korean War (1950–1953), Beck was assistant chief of neuropsychiatry at the Valley Forge Army Hospital, Pennsylvania, and in 1954 was at the Department of Psychiatry of the University of Pennsylvania, where he is currently professor emeritus of psychiatry.

He was a fellow, Royal College of Psychiatrists, London, England (1987). He received the Distinguished Scientific Award for the Applications of Psychology from the American Psychological Association (1989), and was made honorary doctor of humane letters, Assumption College, Massachusetts (1995). In 1997, he became senior member of the Institute of Medicine of the National Academy of Sciences. In 2002, he received the Cherlin Lectureship at Yale University. Between 1948 and 2006, Beck received over thirty more awards, including research awards from the American Psychological Association and the American Psychiatric Association. He is president of the non-profit Beck Institute for Cognitive Therapy and Research. He was a visiting scientist of the Medical Research Council, Oxford, England, and is a visiting fellow of Wolfson College, Oxford, England, and a visiting Professor at several American universities.

Major Contributions

Trained in psychoanalysis, Dr. Beck designed and carried out a number of experiments to test psychoanalytic concepts of depression, but he was disappointed with the results. He found that by helping patients identify their negative ideas about themselves, the world and the future, the patients were able to think more realistically, which led them to feel better emotionally and behave more functionally. This led the development of cognitive therapy, which has been used in a wide range of disorders. Some of his most recent work has focused on cognitive therapy for schizophrenia, borderline personality disorder and for patients who repeatedly attempt suicide.

His cognitive therapy is based on the view that behavior is primarily determined by what that person thinks and that thoughts of low self-worth are incorrect and are due to faulty learning. Cognitive therapy is particularly relevant in treating depression, where thoughts of low self-worth and low self-esteem are a common feature. Beck has developed scales to assess anxiety, hopelessness, mania, self-esteem, panic, dysfunctional attitudes, substance abuse, insight, obsessive compulsion, depression and suicide intent.

Major Literature

Beck, Aaron Temkin. *Depression: Causes and Treatment.* Philadelphia: University of Pennsylvania Press, 1972.
___. *Cognitive Therapy and Emotional Disorders.* New York: International Universities Press, 1976.
___, and G. Emery. *Anxiety Disorders and Phobias: A Cognitive Perspective.* New York: Basic Books, 1985.
Beck, Aaron Temkin. "Cognitive Therapy: A 30 Year Retrospective." *American Psychologist* 46 (1991): 368–375.
___. *Prisoners of Hate: The Cognitive Basis of Anger, Hostility, and Violence.* New York: Harper Collins, Publishers, Inc., 2000.
___, Gary Emery, and Ruth L. Greenberg. *Anxiety Disorders and Phobias: A Cognitive Perspective.* New York: Basic Books, 2005.

Beers, Clifford Whittingham (1876–1943)
MENTAL HEALTH EDUCATOR

Clifford Beers was not a great philosopher, psychologist or psychiatrist. He has not contributed any great theory of personality, yet his name is renowned as a pioneer in the revolution of the care of mentally ill people.

Beers was born into privilege. After graduating from Yale University and beginning a promising career in business, subsequent to the death of a brother from epilepsy, Beers developed an obsessive fear of insanity. His despair became so great that he attempted suicide. He spent three terrible years in private, voluntary and state hospitals in Connecticut. There he experienced, first hand, the unenlightened treatment of mental illness so typical of earlier times. Following his recovery he was determined to reform the treatment of people with mental illnesses. His book *A Mind That Found Itself* is an account of his three years in hospitals.

Major Contributions

At the age of 32, five years after he had emerged from his harrowing experience, Beers took the first step toward realizing a grand vision and founded the Connecticut Society for Mental Hygiene. His idea was supported by William James and Adolf Meyer (see entries), both of whom had great concerns about the way mentally ill people were treated. Not only did he expose cruelty (something that other people had done), he personalized his account by relating his inner suffering and

confusion about the behavior to which he and others were subjected and the lack of supervision by the doctors.

Through his struggles, suffering and rebirth, Beers was able to shed light on a process that treated human beings as less than human. His revelations appealed to the conscience of America, and major reforms were initiated. He imagined an advocacy organization that would spread from local to international levels, an organization that would:

- Fight to improve care and treatment of people in mental hospitals;
- Work to correct the misconception that one cannot recover from mental illness; and
- Help to prevent mental disability and the need for hospitalization.

Beers founded the National Committee for Mental Hygiene (later called the National Mental Health Association, of which he was executive director). In 1913, he started the Clifford Beers Clinic — the first outpatient mental health clinic in America. Beers fought the ignorance of his times. He fought relentlessly, with truth and compassion as his only weapons. From Beers' work came the child-guidance movement in America. The aim was to help juvenile delinquents and reduce problems with good child rearing and treatment. Later the movement spread to the fields of education, family service and child development.

Major Literature

Beers, Clifford. *A Mind That Found Itself: An Autobiography.* Whitefish, Montana: R.A. Kessinger Publishing Co., 1917. Pittsburgh: University of Pittsburgh Press, 1980.

Related Literature

Grob, Gerald. The Mad Among Us: A History of the Care of America's Mentally Ill. The Free Press: New York, 1994.

Bejerot, Nils (1921–1988)
STOCKHOLM SYNDROME

Nils Bejerot, Swedish psychiatrist and criminologist, was born in Stockholm. He gained his higher school certificate at evening school, and after qualifying as a doctor at the Karolinska Institute, Stockholm, he started working as social medical officer in Stockholm in 1962. He was consulting psychiatrist to the Stockholm Police Department from 1958 and consulting physician to the Stockholm Remand Prison from 1965. He was then research fellow in drug dependence at the Swedish National Medical Research Council and reader in social medicine at the Karolinska Institute. Made associate professor in 1974, he was appointed full professor in 1979. In the early 1980s, he became one of the "top 10 opinion molders" in Sweden. He wrote several books on drug control. His bibliography, published in 1986, contains over 600 works.

Major Contributions

Bejerot is best known for several things:

1. His role as a psychiatric advisor during the Norrmalmstorg robbery and coining the term *Stockholm syndrome.*
2. His strong opposition against any legalization or prescription programs for narcotic drugs; he advocated zero tolerance.
3. His strong opposition to violence in comic books, which was the subject of his book, *Barn, Serie, Samhälle* (*Children, Comics, Society*), itself largely an adaptation of *Seduction of the Innocent* by Fredric Wertham (see entry).

In 1954, while serving as deputy social medical officer at the Child and Youth Welfare Board of the City of Stockholm, Bejerot diagnosed the first case of juvenile intravenous drug abuse ever seen by any public authority in Europe. In spite of his alarming report to the board, the incident did not lead to any official intervention. When the Swedish Drug Control System (SDCS) was introduced in 1965 (a liberalization of the use of drugs by proving prescriptions), Bejerot started the Injection Mark Study (looking for evidence of scarring) at the Remand Prison to monitor the spread of intravenous drug abuse in Stockholm. His two year study showed that rather than a decrease in drug abuse, there was a rapid rise; any hopes that the SDCS would stop the spread of drugs were dashed.

Bejerot was a leading critic of the Swedish drug control system, using epidemiological principles to argue for comprehensive measures to prevent, detect and stop drug abuse. He was one of the first to warn that the modern drug epidemics could become serious threats to public health. The nation-wide "Police Offensive" that started 1969 did produce results.

Major Literature

Bejerot, Nils. *Addiction: An Artificially Induced Drive.* Springfield, Illinois: Charles C. Thomas Pub., Ltd., 1972.
___. "Drug Abuse and Drug Policy: An Epidemiolog-ical and Methodological Study of Drug Abuse of Intravenous Type in the Stockholm Police Arrest Population 1965–1970, In Relation to Changes in Drug Policy." Copenhagen: Munksgaard: Acta Psychiatrica Scandinavica, Supplementum 256, 1975.
___. "The Swedish Addiction Epidemic in Global Perspective." Speech given in France, the Soviet Union and USA, Stockholm, the Carnegie Institute, 1988.

Békésy, Georg Von (1889–1972)
INDUSTRIAL PSYCHOLOGY

Born in Budapest, Hungary, the son of Alexander von Békésy, a diplomat, Georg von Békésy received his education in various cities around Europe. He studied chemistry at the University of Berne, Switzerland, and after a short military service, graduated Ph.D. in physics in 1923 from the University of Budapest, where from 1939 to 1946 he was professor of experimental physics. He spent 1946–1947 in Sweden at the Karolinska Institute and did research at the Technical Institute in Stockholm. Békésy immigrated to the USA and taught at Harvard University from 1947 to 1966, when he became professor of sensory sciences at the University of Hawaii.

He was awarded the 1961 Nobel Prize in Physiology and Medicine for his work on the physical mechanism of stimulation within the cochlea, a snail-shaped cavity of the inner ear. He bequeathed all of his various collections of art to the Nobel Foundation in gratitude for the honor it had bestowed upon him. He received many other prizes and awards, including the Howard Crosby Warren Medal of the Society of Experimental Psychologists (1955) and the Gold Medals of the American Otological Society (1957) and the Acoustical Society of America (1961). Honorary doctorates (M.D.) were conferred on him by the universities of Munster (1955) and Berne (1959).

Major Contributions

Békésy was director of the Hungarian Telephone System Research Laboratory (1923–46), where he worked on problems of long-distance communication, and became interested in the mechanics of human hearing. The Hungarian telephone lines often broke and it would take hours or days to locate the sites of disruption. Békésy reasoned that, like musicians tuning their violins by plucking on the strings, the way to locate the sites of disruption in the telephone lines should be possible by "plucking" on the lines. By transmitting "clicks" over the telephones, he refined a method of locating the sites of line disruptions.

At the telephone laboratory at the University of Budapest and at the Karolinska Institute, Stockholm, he conducted intensive research that led to the construction of two cochlea models and highly sensitive instruments that made it possible to understand the hearing process, differentiate between certain forms of deafness, and select proper treatment more accurately. At Harvard he developed a mechanical model of the inner ear. His research in Hawaii was partially sponsored by Hawaiian Telephone and was concerned with the general properties of all the senses.

Major Literature

Békésy, Georg von. "Sensations on the Skin Similar to Directional Hearing, Beats and Harmonics of the Ear." *Journal of the Acoustical Society of America* 29 (4) (1957): 489–501.
___. "Hearing Theories and Complex Sounds." *Journal of the Acoustical Society of America* 35 (4) (1965): 588–601.
___. *Sensory Inhibition.* Princeton, New Jersey: Princeton University Press, 1967.
___. *Sensory Inhibition* (The Herbert Sidney Langfeld Memorial Lectures). Princeton University Press, 1967.
___. *Experiments in Hearing.* Columbus, Ohio: McGraw-Hill, 1989. College Park, Maryland: American Institute of Physics, 1960.

Bem, Daryl J. (1938–)
SELF-PERCEPTION

Born in Denver, Colorado, Daryl J. Bem gained a B.A. in physics from Reed College in Portland, Oregon, in 1960 and a Ph.D. in social psychology from the University of Michigan, Ann Arbor, in 1964. He was assistant professor of psychology and industrial administration at Carnegie-Mellon University, Pittsburgh, Pennsylvania (1964–1971), and professor of psychology at Stanford University, California (1971–1978). From 1972 to 1973, he was a member of the Secretary's Advisory Commission on Women, United States Department of Health, Education and Welfare, and since 1978, he has been professor of psychology at Cornell University in Ithaca, New York.

He was visiting professor of psychology at Harvard University, Cambridge, Massachusetts (1987–1988); member-at-large, Division of Behavioral Sciences, National Research Council; member of Phi Beta Kappa; fellow, American Psychological Association; and charter fellow, American Psychological Society and National Academy of Sciences.

Major Contributions

Bem's inspiration to switch from physics to social psychology for his Ph.D. was the changing attitudes toward desegregation in the American South. Bem has presented testimony to a subcommittee of the United States Senate on the psychological effects of police interrogation and has served as an expert witness in several court cases involving sex discrimination. He is perhaps best known for his theory of "self-perception," which asserts that we come to know our own attitudes, emotions and other internal states partly through observing how our behavior influences other people. Sometimes we judge how we feel by how we act. We therefore develop our attitudes by observing our own behavior and concluding what attitudes must have caused them.

Bem proposes that sexual orientation results primarily (though not exclusively) from a social and psychological process rather than genetic one. Thus his theory incorporates both the nature and nurture views. The core concept of his "Exotic Becomes Erotic" (EBE) theory is that adults are erotically attracted to the gender-based class of peers (males or females) who were dissimilar or unfamiliar to them in childhood. However, other researchers point out that many homosexuals had leanings toward the same sex long before they had explicit sexual experiences. Bem is also known in parapsychology for his defense of the ganzfeld experiment, which uses audio and visual sensory deprivation to test for extra-sensory perception (ESP), where one person acts "sender" and another as "receiver."

Major Literature

Bem, Daryl J. "Self-Perception: The Dependent Variable of Human Performance." *Organizational Behavior and Human Performance* 2 (1967): 105–121.
___. *Beliefs, Attitudes and Human Affairs.* St. Paul, Minnesota: Brooks-Cole Publishing Co., 1970.
___. "Self-Perception Theory." In L. Berkowitz (Ed.), *Advances in Experimental Social Psychology, 6,* pp. 1–62. New York: Academic Press, 1972.
Bem, S.L., and Daryl J. Bem. "Does Sex-Biased Job Advertising 'Aid and Abet' Sex Discrimination?" *Journal of Applied Social Psychology* 1 (1973): 6–18.
Bem, D.J. "Exotic Becomes Erotic: A Developmental Theory of Sexual Orientation." *Psychological Review* 103 (1996): 320–335.
Nolen-Hoeksema, Susan, and Daryl J. Bem. *Fundamentals of Psychology.* London, England: Thomson Learning, Inc., 2000.

Bem, Sandra Lipsitz (1944–)
BEM SEX ROLE INVENTORY

Sandra Lipsitz was born in Pittsburgh, Pennsylvania, and earned a B.A. from Carnegie Mellon University, Pittsburgh, in 1965 and a Ph.D. from the University of Michigan, Ann Arbor, in 1968. She received the Distinguished Scientific Award for an Early Career Contribution to Psychology from the American Psychological Association (APA) (1976); Distinguished Publication Award from the Association for Women in Psychology (1977); Young Scholar Award from the American Association of University Women (1980); and an honorary doctor of science, Wilson College in Chambersburg, Pennsylvania (1985). She is professor of psychology and women's studies, Cornell University, Ithaca, New York.

Major Contributions

For her Ph.D. Bem worked in developmental psychology, particularly the cognitive processing and problem-solving of young children. She soon turned to women's liberation and feminist research. While at Mellon, she worked with Daryl Bem, whom she married in 1965. Bem's research into gender began in the early 1970s; the BEM Sex-Role Inventory (BSRI), published in 1977, introduced the concept of psychological androgyny, moving away from sex typing. Psychological tests of masculinity and femininity generally do not allow a person to say that he or she is both masculine and feminine.

The concept of androgyny refers specifically to the blending of the behaviors and personality characteristics that have traditionally been thought of as masculine and feminine. The androgynous individual is someone who is both independent and tender, both aggressive and gentle, both assertive and yielding, both masculine and feminine, appropriate to the situation. Androgynous does not mean bisexual, asexual, or homosexual. An androgynous person has integrated certain characteristics or qualities that society has stereotyped as belonging to one gender or the other. One way of looking at this is that such a person does not conform to the stereotype, but is comfortable using these qualities in living a well-balanced life.

The discussion supports the view that apart from obvious biological differences, many of the so-called gender differences are determined by society and not by our genes. The whole area of the cognitive processes linked to sex typing and androgyny is now termed gender schema theory, a set of beliefs about gender. The theory proposes that children become sex typed in part as a result of their perception of what other people expect and the culture in which they live. They learn that to be categorized by whether they are male or female influences all other aspects of culture. For example, is a particular toy not only age-appropriate but is it sex-appropriate? Children, therefore, view the world through the lens of the gender schema.

Major Literature

Bem, Sandra Lipsitz. "Sex Role Adaptability: One Consequence of Psychological Androgyny." *Journal of Personality and Social Psychology,* 31 (1975): 634–643.
___. "BEM Sex-Role Inventory (BSRI)." *The 1977 Annual Handbook for Group Facilitators.* San Diego, California: University Associates, 1977.
___. *The Lenses of Gender: Transforming the Debate on Sexual Inequality.* New Haven, Connecticut: Yale University Press, 1993.
___. *An Unconventional Family.* New Haven, Connecticut: Yale University Press, 2001.

Bender, Lauretta (1897–1987)
CHILD PSYCHIATRY

Lauretta Bender was born in Butte, Montana, and as a child was thought to be mentally retarded, in large part because of her tendency to reverse letters in reading and writing. However, by the time she completed grammar school, such fears were proved groundless. She graduated with a B.S. and M.A. from at the University of Chicago and qualified for an M.D. in 1926 from the State University of Iowa Medical School. She then studied overseas and served an internship at the University of Chicago, a residency at Boston Psychopathic Hospital, and a research appointment at the Henry Phipps Psychiatric Clinic of Johns Hopkins Hospital in Baltimore, Maryland. In 1930 she moved to the Bellevue Hospital, New York, with the psychoanalyst Paul Schilder. After Schilder's divorce, the two were married in November of 1936. In 1940 after visiting his wife in the hospital with their third child, Schilder was killed by an automobile.

Major Contributions

Bender served on the psychiatric staff at Bellevue Hospital from 1930 through 1956 and was appointed head of the Children's Psychiatric Division in 1934. She also held numerous other positions, including a professorship at New York University and a faculty position at New York State

Psychiatric Institute. In 1936 Bender used group therapy with hospitalized children, and in 1940 she described childhood schizophrenia as a disorder of early onset, caused by central nervous system (CNS) abnormality and characterized by behaviors such as anxiety, unusual language and disturbances of movement.

Bender may be best remembered for the Bender Visual Motor Gestalt Test, also called the Bender Gestalt Test, first published in 1938. The test is a psychological assessment used to evaluate visual-motor functioning, visual-perceptual skills, neurological impairment, and emotional disturbances in children age three and older and adults. Gestalt psychology teaches that whatever we see or perceive we experience immediately as a global organized whole or gestalt. This organized whole is more immediately experienced than any of its parts or details, which are recognized later as we take in the differences. Max Wertheimer (see entry) presented adults with line drawings, configurations, and gestalten, asking them to describe what they saw. Bender adapted his work, putting her drawings on cards and asking her subjects to copy the drawings.

Lauretta Bender's accomplishments have been acknowledged by numerous professional organizations, and she has had many honors and awards bestowed upon her. In retirement in Maryland, Bender served as a consultant to various organizations, including the Anne Arundel County Board of Education, Maryland.

Major Literature

Bender, Lauretta. "A Visual-Motor Gestalt Test and Its Clinical Use." *American Orthopsychiatric Association Research Monographs* (1938): No. 3.
___. *Child Psychiatric Techniques.* Springfield, Illinois: Charles C. Thomas Pub., Ltd., 1952.
___. *Aggression, Hostility and Anxiety in Children.* Springfield, Illinois: Charles C. Thomas Pub., Ltd., 1953.
Schilder, Paul, and Lauretta Bender. *Contributions to Developmental Neuropsychiatry.* Madison, Connecticut: International Universities Press, Inc., 1964.
Bender, Lauretta. "The Visual-Motor Gestalt Test in the Diagnosis of Learning Disabilities." *Journal of Special Education* 4 (1970): 29–39.

Bentall, Richard P. (1956–)
FORENSIC CLINICAL PSYCHOLOGY

Born in Sheffield, Yorkshire, England, Richard P. Bentall gained his B.Sc. in psychology and his Ph.D. in experimental psychology (1983) from University College of North Wales, Bangor. After qualifying in clinical psychology at the University of Liverpool in 1984, he obtained an M.A. in philosophy applied to health care from University College Swansea in 1989. After briefly working as a forensic clinical psychologist in the National Health Service, he was appointed to a lectureship at the University of Liverpool in 1986 and became professor of clinical psychology in 1994. He was appointed professor of experimental clinical psychology at the University of Manchester in 1999. He is a fellow of the British Psychological Society. In 1989 he was awarded the society's May Davidson Award for contributions to the field of clinical psychology.

Major Contributions

Bentall's research focuses on five main areas:

1. He argues that the current classifications of mental illness, such as DSM-IV, have very little scientific value. He advocates research targeted at specific psychological symptoms.
2. In studies of auditory hallucinations he has explored cognitive failures that lead the hallucinating individual to misattribute their inner speech to an external source. Hallucinations and delusions may be understandable reactions to life events and circumstances rather than symptoms of a mental illness.
3. He is one of a team funded by the Medical Research Council, London, investigating cognitive behavioral therapy (CBT) as in intervention in schizophrenia, for patients with a diagnosis of bipolar disorder (formerly manic depression), and for individuals at high risk of psychosis, the aim of which is to determine whether vulnerable individuals can be prevented from becoming ill.
4. Studying the effects of neuroleptic (anti-psychotic) drugs, the medical treatment most often given to schizophrenia patients.
5. He directs a clinical trial of a psychosocial intervention (CBT plus graded exercises and support) for people suffering from chronic fatigue syndrome, funded by the Lindbury Trust. Bentall's approach is to assume that the symptoms that chronic fatigue patients experience are very real ones, and they're caused by a disruption of body rhythms, such as circadian rhythms that regulate sleeping and waking. The study looks at the factors that maintain the fatigue rather than factors which cause the fatigue.

Major Literature

Slade, Peter D., and Richard P. Bentall. *Sensory Deception: Scientific Analysis of Hallucinations*. London, England: Croom Helm, 1988.

Bentall, Richard P. (Ed.). *Reconstructing Schizophrenia*. London: Taylor and Francis Books Ltd., Routledge, 1992.

___, and Aaron T. Beck. *Madness Explained: Psychosis and Human Nature*. London, England: Penguin Books Ltd., 2004.

Bentall, Richard P. (Ed.). *Models of Madness: Psychological, Social and Biological Approaches to Schizophrenia*. London: Taylor and Francis Books Ltd., Brunner-Routledge, 2004.

Jones, Steven, and Richard P. Bentall (Eds.). *The Psychology of Bipolar Disorder: New Developments and Research Strategies*. Oxford, England: Oxford University Press, 2006.

Berkowitz, Leonard (1926–)

HUMAN AGGRESSION

Born in New York City, Leonard Berkowitz gained a B.A. from New York University in 1948 and a Ph.D. in social psychology from the University of Michigan, Ann Arbor, in 1951. He was a research psychologist at the U.S. Air Force Human Resources Center in San Antonio, Texas (1951–1955). At University of Wisconsin, Madison, he was assistant professor (1955–1959), associate professor (1959–1962), professor (1962), Vilas research professor (1969–1993), then Vilas research professor emeritus. From 1964 to 1989 he was editor of the social psychology series *Advances in Experimental Social Psychology*.

He was a fellow, Center for the Advanced Study in Behavioral Sciences, Stanford, California (1970–1971). From 1971 to 1972 he was president of the American Psychological Association (APA) Division 8. In 1977, he received an honorary doctorate from the University of Louvain-la-Neuve, Belgium. He also received the APA Distinguished Scientific Award for the Application of Psychology (1988), Distinguished Scientific Award from the Society of Experimental Social Psychology (1989), and the James McKeen Cattell Fellow Award (1993). He was chair of the APA Publications Board (1981–1982) and the International Society for Research on Aggression (1981–1983). He held visiting appointments at the universities of Western Australia, Perth; Mannheim, Germany; and Cambridge and Oxford, England. He is the author of about 170 articles and books, mostly concerned with aggression, and has been president of the American Psychological Association's Division of Personality and Social Psychology and the International Society for Research on Aggression.

Major Contributions

Berkowitz is well known for his studies of human aggression and situational influences on aggressive behavior, including the effects of movie and television depictions of violence. He was one of the first social psychologists to study prosocial behavior (voluntary behavior that is intended to help or benefit another individual or group). From his work with group dynamics, he observed that some people worked hard on behalf of other people, without any apparent desire for reward. This ties in with the concept of altruism — the tendency to see the needs of others as more important than one's own.

At Wisconsin he led a seventeen-year program of research on aggression (in Europe as well as in the United States) funded by the National Institute of Mental Health. Berkowitz's view of aggression is that particular feelings, ideas, memories, and expressive-motor reactions are linked together in an emotion-state network. Focusing on one activates the other components in the same network. In the case of anger, it is presumed that any unpleasant feeling will tend to activate rudimentary anger feelings as well as aggression-related ideas, memories, and expressive-motor reactions. Berkowitz's work suggests that violence can be controlled by strengthening social norms that promote non-aggressive actions and reducing exposure to aggressive models.

Major Literature

Berkowitz, Leonard. *Aggression: A Social Psychological Analysis*. Columbus, Ohio: McGraw-Hill Education, 1962.

___(Ed.). *Roots of Aggression: A Re-examination of the Frustration-Aggression Hypothesis*. Oxford, England, Atheron, 1969.

___, and J. Macaulay. *Altruism and Helping Behavior*. London, England: Reed Elsevier Group, Academic Press, Inc., 1970.

Berkowitz, Leonard. *Social Psychology*. Glenview, Illinois: Scott Foreman, 1972.

___. *Aggression: Its Causes, Consequences and Control*. New York: McGraw-Hill Companies, Inc., 1993.

___. "Frustration-Aggression Hypothesis: Examination And Reformulation." *Psychological Bulletin* 106 (1993): 59–73.

Berlyne, Daniel Ellis (1924–1976)

COMPARATIVE PSYCHOLOGY

Born in Salford, Lancashire, England, Daniel Ellis Berlyne was educated at Manchester Grammar School and graduated with a B.A. (1947) and M.A. (1949) from Cambridge University. He earned his Ph.D. at Yale University, Connecticut (1953). He was professor of psychology at the University of Toronto from 1947 until he died in Toronto. He held teaching posts at Brooklyn College, New York; St. Andrews University and Aberdeen University, Scotland; and Boston University, along with several visiting posts in Europe and North America. He was fellow of the Royal Society of Canada and president of the Canadian Psychological Association from 1971 to 1972.

During his comparatively short life Berlyne wrote or co-edited seven books and about 150 articles and chapters, which have been translated into several languages. The impact of his ideas is felt internationally. He lectured in eight languages on five continents and carried on his research in North and South America, Europe, Africa, and Japan.

Major Contributions

Berlyne's main contribution to psychology is in the concept of curiosity, a subject that received scant interest before 1960, when his first book, *Conflict, Arousal and Curiosity* (McGraw-Hill), was published. Fifteen years later *Psychological Abstracts* listed 78 references to curiosity. (Even in some modern psychology textbooks this topic is not mentioned.) Berlyne's view is that curiosity motivates exploratory behavior. He did not study the state of curiosity but looked at the behavior it led to, for example, why animals and humans explore their environment.

Early in his professional career Berlyne recognized that the impact of objects and events can be measured along three dimensions — psychophysical, ecological, and collative. He defined collation as the examination of similarities and differences, the compatibilities and incompatibilities among elements of an object or event. He started to develop a theory he called "collative motivation," and the potential motivators he identified as information seeking — uncertainty, variety, and novelty.

He was also drawn to aesthetics, exploring the role of art in society and the attractions of the arts. He was concerned with the understanding and appreciation of the arts and what it is that creates an interest and pleasure in them. He helped establish in Toronto what was possibly the only study circle on aesthetics, composed of scientists, philosophers, and practitioners of the arts.

Major Literature

Berlyne, Daniel Ellis. "'Interest' as a Psychological Concept." *British Journal of Psychology* 39 (1949): 186–195.

___. "Motivational Problems Raised by Exploratory and Epistemic Behavior." In S. Koch (Ed.), *Psychology: A Study of Science*. Vol. 5. New York: McGraw-Hill, 1963.

___. "Curiosity and Education." In J.D. Krumboltz (Ed.), *Learning and the Educational Process*. Chicago: Rand McNally, 1965, pp. 67–89.

___. *Structure and Direction in Thinking*. New Jersey: John Wiley and Sons Inc., 1965.

___. *Aesthetics and Psychobiology*. New York: Appleton-Century-Crofts, 1971.

___. "Humor and Its Kin." In J.H. Goldstein and P.E. McGhee (Eds.), *The Psychology of Humor*. New York: Academic Press, 1972, pp. 43–60.

Bernal, Martha (1931–2001)
Racism and Sexism

Martha Bernal was born in San Antonio and raised in El Paso, Texas. Her Mexican parents had come to the U.S. in the 1920s as political refugees. When Bernal started school she was punished because she did not speak English, just one of the injustices she experienced as a Mexican-American child. She felt that the discrimination she experienced was compounded by the fact that she was female. At first her father did not agree that his daughters should have a college education; this did not fit with his traditional view of what a Mexican woman should do. Bernal gained her M.A. in 1955 at Syracuse University and her Ph.D. in clinical psychology in 1962 from Indiana University, Bloomington. She was the first woman of Mexican descent to receive a doctorate in psychology in the United States.

Major Contributions

Bernal obtained a two-year U.S. Public Health Service postdoctoral fellowship at UCLA (University of California, Los Angeles) researching human psychophysiology. In 1969 she was appointed assistant professor at the University of Arizona at Tucson. She returned to the Neuropsychiatric Institute at UCLA, where, in 1965, the National Institute of Mental Health (NIMH) gave Bernal her first grant to study the use of classical conditioning on autistic children.

A second project was the training of parents using television feedback. From the feedback she created lesson plans, based on learning principles, for the parents to follow when trying to change their children's conduct problems. Her research led her to conclude that children with behavioral problems were not internally damaged but had learned maladaptive behavior and were influenced by the different social systems within which children are expected to function.

In the 1970s, at the University of Denver, Bernal turned her attention to minority groups. One of her goals was to try to work within the American Psychological Association to improve minorities' status. In 1979 she received a National Research Service Award from NIMH that allowed her to study the preparation of psychologists to work with multicultural populations. Further grants enabled her to continue and extend her research into minority groups.

In 1994 she was appointed to the Commission on Ethnic Minority Recruitment, Retention and Training. At the first National Multicultural Conference and Summit in 1999 she was honored as one of four "Pioneer Senior Women of Color" and received the Carolyn Attneave Award for lifelong contributions to ethnic minorities psychology. At the American Psychological Association 2001 convention, the Public Interest Directorate awarded Bernal the 2001 Contributions to Psychology Award. She died of cancer.

Major Literature

Bernal, Martha, and G.P. Knight (Eds.). *Ethnic Identity: Formation and Transmission Among Hispanics and Other Minorities.* Albany: State University of New York Press, 1993.

Bernal, Martha, and F.G. Castro. "Are Clinical Psychologists Prepared for Service and Research with Ethnic Minorities? Report of a Decade of Progress." *American Psychologist* 49 (1994): 797–805.

Bernal, Martha, Phylis C. Martinelli, and John Cise (Eds.). *Mexican American Identity.* Mountain View, California: Floricanto Press, 2005.

Berne, Eric (1910–1970)
Transactional Analysis

Eric Berne was born Leonard Bernstein in Montreal, Quebec, Canada, the son of Polish-Russian immigrants. Some time around 1938–1939, he became an American citizen and shortened his name to Eric Berne. He graduated in medicine from McGill University Medical School, Montreal, Canada, in 1935, studied psychiatry at Yale University School of Medicine, Connecticut, and was appointed clinical assistant in psychiatry at Mt. Zion Hospital, New York City. His training as a psychoanalyst at the New York Psychoanalytic Institute was interrupted by the war, and when discharged from the Medical Corps in 1946, Berne resumed his psychoanalytic training at the San Francisco Psychoanalytic Institute. He broke with psychoanalysis in the 1950s to concentrate on a shorter form of treatment, transactional analysis (TA).

Major Contributions

Berne's *Games People Play* assumed almost cult status and contributed to what is known as pop psychology. However, behind that is a very useful way of relating to people.

There are four forms of hunger or need:

- *Tactile*— intimacy and physical closeness.
- *Recognition*— "I cannot physically touch you, but I will verbally *stroke* you." (The stroke is a basic unit of social interaction.) A *transaction* is an exchange of strokes.
- *Structure*—"I must fill my time to prevent boredom."
- *Excitement*—"I must fill my life in interesting and exciting ways." Many of us are brought up to believe that seeking excitement is bad and should be shunned.

The personality structure has three ego states:

- Parent (critical and nurturing). The "Taught" concept of life.
- Adult (rational). The "Thought" concept of life.
- Child (free or adapted). The "Felt" concept of life.

The aim of TA is to become aware of the intent behind the individual's communications, to eliminate subterfuge and deceit so that the individual can interpret his or her behavior accurately. The method is therapy in a group setting. Communications between married couples or group members are analyzed based on which part of the personality is speaking—"Parent," "Child," or "Adult"—and the intent of the message. Destructive social interactions or "games" are exposed for what they are.

Transactional analysis posits four life positions:

- I'm OK, You're not OK
- I'm not OK, You're OK
- I'm not OK, You're not OK
- I'm OK, You're OK

TA helps clients to become aware of how they hurt themselves, the changes they need to make, and the inner forces that hinder change. Therapeutic change is based on decisions and action. If clients do not decide to act, no one can do it for them.

Major Literature

Berne, Eric. *The Mind in Action*. New York, Simon and Schuster, 1947.
___. *Transactional Analysis in Psychotherapy*. New York: Grove Press, 1961. London, England: Souvenir Press Ltd., 2001.
___. *Sex in Human Loving*. Beverly Hills, California: City National Bank, 1963.
___. *Games People Play*. London, England: Penguin Books Ltd., 1970.
___. *What Do You Say After You Say Hello*. New York: Random House Inc., Corgi, 1971.
___. *A Layman's Guide to Psychiatry and Psychoanalysis*. London, England: Random House Group: Ballantine Books, 1979.

Bettelheim, Bruno (1903–1990)
EMOTIONALLY DISTURBED CHILDREN

Bruno Bettelheim, an Austrian-born Jew, gained his Ph.D. from the University of Vienna in 1938, then spent one year in Nazi concentration camps. When he immigrated to the United States he became a research associate with the Progressive Education Association at the University of Chicago. When he was an associate professor at Rockford College, Illinois, he wrote "Individual and Mass Behavior in Extreme Situations" (*Journal of Abnormal and Social Psychology*, 38, 1943, pp. 417–452). This article, based on his observations and experiences at Dachau and Buchenwald, won wide and immediate recognition. By 1944 he was both assistant professor of psychology at the University of Chicago in Illinois and head of the university's Sonia Shankman Orthogenic School, a residential laboratory school for 6- to 14-year-old children with serious emotional problems, which became the center of his work with autistic children.

Major Contributions

Bettelheim set out to apply psychoanalytic principles to relieve emotional suffering and turmoil of disturbed children and to help them function socially and usefully. Although his theories on autism have been largely discredited, he authored a number of influential works on child development. Autism was once believed to be a psychiatric disorder but is now known to be neurological, even though many of its characteristic traits appear psychological. Typical characteristics include problems with social relationships and emotional communication. Bettelheim avowed that autism was caused entirely by mothers — whom he dubbed "refrigerator mothers" — and absent fathers. He said that all his life he had been working with children whose lives had been destroyed because their mothers hated them. Other Freudian analysts, as well as scientists who were not psychiatrists, followed Bettelheim in blaming mothers for their child's autism.

Bettelheim, depressed after the death of his wife in 1984, and after suffering a stroke in 1987, committed suicide. Although many of his counselors at the Orthogenic School considered him brilliant and admirable, others began to openly question his work and to call him a cruel tyrant. His reputation was subsequently clouded by revelations that he had invented his Viennese academic credentials and that he had abused and misdiagnosed a number of the children under his care at the Orthogenic School. In an affidavit, dated 10th day of July 1945, and signed in the presence of notary public Edward L. Davis, Bettelheim swore on oath that the details of his education and interment were accurate. (See http://www.ess.uwe.ac.uk/genocide/conentration%20camps1.htm.)

Major Literature

Bettelheim, Bruno. *Love Is Not Enough*. New York: Macmillan, 1959.
___. *Empty Fortress: Infantile Autism and the Birth of Self*. New York: The Free Press, 1967.
___. *The Informed Heart: Autonomy in Mass Age*. New York: Penguin Group (USA), Inc., 1991.
___. *The Uses of Enchantment: The Meaning and Importance of Fairy Tales*. New York: Penguin Group (USA), Inc., 1991.
___. *Good Enough Parent: Guide to Bringing Up Your Child*. London, England: Thames and Hudson Ltd., 1995.
___. *Freud and Man's Soul*. New York: Random House, Inc., Pimlico, 2001.

Bickhard, Mark H. (1945–)
DEVELOPMENTAL PSYCHOLOGY

Born in Fort Wayne, Indiana, Mark H. Bickhard grew up in Wichita, Kansas, and earned a B.S. in mathematics (1966), an M.S. in statistics, developmental and clinical psychology (1970), and a Ph.D. in human development (1973) from University of Chicago, Illinois. He did a clinical internship at the University of Chicago Counseling Center, 1969–1971, and went on to the Department of Educational Psychology, University of Texas at Austin (1972–1990), moving up to full professor. He was a research consultant at the National Opinion Research Center, University of Chicago, from 1973 to 1977 and then at the Center for Psychosocial Studies, Chicago Lehigh University, Bethlehem, Pennsylvania (1977–1980). He has been a Henry R. Luce professor of cognitive robotics (since 1990); philosophy of knowledge director, Complex Systems Research Group (1999–2005); and director of the Institute for Interactivist Studies (since 2000).

Major Contributions

As part of his Ph.D. thesis, Bickhard extended Jean Piaget's (see entry) theories of human development; he has written extensively on Piaget's theories, on James Jerome Gibson's work on visual perception, and on the individual psychology of Alfred Adler (see entries). From 1975 to 1990 he practiced as a psychotherapist.

Bickhard argues that many of the psychological models in use are false because they depend on another model for verification. This, he says, is a remnant from false and outdated metaphysics that he calls "substance metaphysics." The old view was that new phenomena were attributed to substances; for example, heat was attributed to the substance called caloric, whereas modern physics shows that heat is a process — kinetic energy. So "process metaphysics" replaces "substance metaphysics." However, as Bickhard points out, "substance metaphysics" persists; for example, mind is still commonly regarded as substance rather than as a process. Bickhard advocates process metaphysics and has offered models of various psychological functions, including perception, rationality and language.

Major Literature

Bickhard, Mark H. *Cognition, Convention, and Communication.* New York: Praeger Publishers, 1980.

___, and D.M. Richie. *On the Nature of Representation: A Case Study of James Gibson's Theory of Perception.* New York: Praeger Publishers, 1983.

Campbell, R.L., and M.H. Bickhard. *Knowing Levels and Developmental Stages: Contributions to Human Development.* Basel, Switzerland: Karger, 1986.

Bickhard, Mark H., and L. Terveen. *Foundational Issues in Artificial Intelligence and Cognitive Science: Impasse and Solution.* London, England: Reed Elsevier Group Scientific, 1995.

Bickhard, Mark H. "The "Social Ontology of Persons." In J.I.M. Carpendale and U. Muller (Eds.), *Social Interaction and the Development of Knowledge* (111–132). Mahwah, New Jersey: Erlbaum, 2004.

___. "Consciousness and Reflective Consciousness." *Philosophical Psychology* 18 (2) (2005): 205–218.

___. "Anticipation and Representation." In C. Castelfranchi (Ed.), *From Reactive to Anticipatory Cognitive Embodied Systems* (1–7). American Association for Artificial Intelligence (Fall Symposium), Technical Report FS-05-05. Menlo Park, California: AAAI Press, 2005.

Binet, Alfred (1857–1911)
MEASUREMENT OF INTELLIGENCE

Born in Nice, France, Alfred Binet joined the Laboratory of Physiological Psychology at the Sorbonne in Paris (1891), gained his doctorate and became the director at the Sorbonne and director of laboratory of experimental psychology (1894). He co-founded *L'Année psychologique*, a major psychology journal (1894), and became a member of the newly founded Société Libre pour l'Etude Psychologique de l'Enfant (the Free Society for the Psychological Study of the Child) (1899). He was appointed to the Commission for the Retarded in 1903, developed the first intelligence tests with the help of Theodore Simon (1873–1961) in 1903, and in 1908, issued the second version of the revised Binet-Simon scale.

Major Contributions

Binet studied law and natural sciences at the Sorbonne and taught himself psychology. He studied under Jean-Martin Charcot at the neurological clinic, Salpêtrière Hospital, Paris, before setting out on his distinguished career at the Sorbonne. Binet was interested in the workings of the normal mind rather than the pathology of mental illness. He wanted to find a way to measure the ability to think and reason. His interest in the study of development is linked with the relationship with his two daughters. He asked them questions and queried how they solved them. This led to an understanding of individual differences in mental performance, and most importantly, that not all thought processes followed the same course.

He published more than 200 books, articles, and reviews in what now would be called experimental, developmental, educational, social, and differential psychology. It is likely that his writings influenced Jean Piaget's (see entry) work with children. In 1881, the French government asked Binet to create a test that would detect children who were too slow intellectually to benefit from a regular school curriculum. Binet, with the French psychologist Theodore Simon, developed the Binet-Simon scale, published in 1905 and revised several times. From this the Stanford-Binet intelligence scale was developed in America by Lewis Terman at Stanford University, California, in 1916. The Stanford, the Herring, and the Kuhlmann are important revisions.

Binet assumed that intelligence should be measured by tasks that required reasoning and problem solving abilities rather than perceptual-motor skills. The test Binet developed measured what he called intelligence quotient (IQ). The pioneering work by Binet has led to the development of many tests that measure intelligence; they are used in many different occupations, including the armed services. Binet died only five years after the first use of his test, and the necessary revisions and refinements were left largely to others.

Major Literature

Binet, Alfred. *L'Etude experimentale de l'intelligence.* Paris, 1903.

Binet, Alfred, and Theodore Simon. *The Development of Intelligence in Children.* Baltimore: Williams and Wilkins, 1916. New York: Arno Press, 1983. Salem, New Hampshire: Ayer Company, 1973. The 1973 volume includes reprints of many of Binet's articles on testing.

Binet, Alfred. *Significant Contributions to the History of Psychology: 1750–1920.* Westport, Connecticut: University Publications of America, 1978.

Bingham, Walter Van Dyke (1880–1952)

INDUSTRIAL PSYCHOLOGY

Born in Swan Lake City, Iowa, Walter Van Dyke Bingham graduated from Beloit College, Wisconsin, in 1901. He received a master's degree in 1907 from Harvard and doctorates from both Harvard University, Cambridge, Massachusetts, and the University of Chicago, Illinois, in 1908. Bingham founded the Division of Applied Psychology at the Carnegie Institute of Technology in 1915 and was its first director, and remained in the role until 1924. (The Carnegie Institute of Technology is the predecessor to Carnegie Mellon University, Pittsburgh, Pennsylvania, founded in 1900 by Andrew Carnegie, Scottish-born businessman and philanthropist.)

The role of the Division of Applied Psychology was to devise and supervise entrance testing and vocational guidance, as well as provide courses in psychology and education. Between 1908 and 1924, in addition to his work at the Carnegie Institute, Bingham taught at several universities, including the University of Chicago, Teachers' College of Columbia University, and Dartmouth College, Hanover, New Hampshire. He was at one time president of the American Association of Applied Psychology, Secretary of the American Psychological Association, and editor of the *Personnel Journal*.

Major Contributions

When America entered World War I, Bingham and his colleagues became involved with the War Department as the Committee for Classification of Personnel in the Army, headed by Robert Mearns Yerkes (see entry) with Bingham as executive secretary. Their task was to develop and revise a series of tests to determine the suitability of enlisted men and recruits for certain ranks, with particular reference to selecting men for officer rank. These intelligence and personality tests are forerunners of the familiar Scholastic Aptitude Tests. The final forms of the Army Alpha and Beta tests were published in January of 1919, and by the end of the war they had been administered to around two million men.

The Division of Applied Psychology adapted the tests for use in business, looking specifically at the ideal traits for workers and managers. This led to standardization of retail training and testing methods used by personnel departments. This research reflected the growing support for the field of industrial psychology.

Bingham was recalled by the War Department when World War II broke out to serve on the Army's National Research Council on Classification of Military Personnel, and was chief psychologist at the adjutant general's office, where again he helped to design aptitude tests. Bingham believed that heredity is the most important factor in intellectual development, and that environmental influences serve only to modify what is already present within the individual, but he warned against placing blind faith in intelligence test scores alone.

Major Literature

Bingham, Walter Van Dyke. "Army Personnel Work." *Journal of Applied Psychology* 3 (1919): 1–12.

Bingham, Walter Van Dyke, and B.V. Moore. *How to Interview.* New York: Harper and Brothers, 1931. Harper and Row, 1966.

Bingham, W.V. *Aptitudes and Aptitude Testing.* New York: Harper and Brothers, 1937.

———. "Psychological Services in the United States Army." *Journal of Consulting Psychology* 5 (1941): 221–224.

Binswanger, Ludwig (1881–1966)

EXISTENTIAL PSYCHOTHERAPY

Ludwig Binswanger, considered the founder of existential psychology, was born in Kreuzlingen, Switzerland, into a family well established in medicine and psychiatric studies. His grandfather, also named Ludwig, founded Bellevue Sanatorium in Kreuzlingen in 1857. His uncle, Otto Binswanger, discovered an Alzheimer's-like disease called Binswanger's Disease and was one of Friedrich Nietzsche's doctors. After Ludwig Binswanger received his medical degree in 1907, he studied under Eugen Bleuler and Carl Jung (see entries), who introduced Binswanger to Freud in 1907.

In 1911, like his father and grandfather before him, Binswanger was appointed chief medical director at Bellevue Sanatorium in Kreuzlingen. Binswanger became interested in the work of Edmund Husserl, Martin Heidegger and Martin Buber, and turned increasingly toward an existential rather than Freudian perspective, so that by the 1920s, he had become the first existential. In 1943, he published his major work *Grundformen und Erkenntnis menschlichen Daseins*, which remains untranslated into English. Binswanger stepped down from his position at Bellevue after 45 years as its chief medical director. He continued to study and write until his death.

Major Contributions

Binswanger formed the theory that certain psychic abnormalities — such as elation fixation, eccentricity, and mannerism — are the effect of the person's distorted self-image and his inadequate relation to the world. He developed a form of psychoanalysis to establish the patient's consciousness of self as a total person, uniquely existing in and communicating with the concrete world as it is. Existential therapy is a psychodynamic approach within psychotherapy influenced by existentialism, rather than a distinct school of therapy. The existential therapy movement was not founded by one person or by a singular group of people. It grew out of the need to help people resolve such issues as isolation, alienation, and meaninglessness. The key figures of the existentialist movement are:

- Viktor Frankl (see entry), who developed logotherapy, which means therapy through meaning.
- Rollo May (see entry), who was instrumental in bringing existentialism from Europe to the U.S.
- James Bugental, who views therapy as a journey undertaken by the therapist and the client, where the focus is the client's inner world. This relationship demands of counselors a willingness to be in contact with their own inner world.

- Irvin Yalom, whose approach focuses on death, freedom, existential isolation, and meaninglessness.

Enshrined in Binswanger's approach is a belief in the individual's capacity to become healthy and fully functional, to rise above self through self-consciousness and self-reflection. This is achieved as the person concentrates on what is happening in the present, accepting that what happens in life is partly his or her personal responsibility and influenced by decisions. Existentially oriented psychotherapists concern themselves with how the client experiences life rather than with diagnosis and cause. Psychoanalysis, conversely, concentrates on cause and effect and on trying to reduce complicated patterns to individual parts.

Major Literature

Binswanger, Ludwig. Translated by J. Needleman. *Being-in-the-World: Selected Papers of Ludwig Binswanger.* New York: Basic Books, 1963.

Bion, Wilfred Ruprecht (1897–1979)
GROUP PSYCHOTHERAPY

Born in India, Wilfred Ruprecht Bion was educated in England, served in France during WWI and was awarded the Distinguished Service Order and the Legion of Honor. After the war he read history at Oxford and studied medicine at University College, London. He achieved the Gold Medal for Clinical Surgery in 1930. A growing interest in psychoanalysis led him to undergo training analysis with John Rickman and, later, Melanie Klein. During the 1940s he directed his attention to the study of group processes, his research culminating in the publication of a series of influential papers later produced in book form as *Experiences in Groups*. He was director of the London Clinic of Psycho-Analysis (1956–1962) and president of the British Psycho-Analytical Society (1962–1965). From 1968 he worked in Los Angeles, returning to England two months before his death.

Major Contributions

Bion was a prolific writer; however, his writings do not make easy reading. During the 1960s and 1970s Bion focused on developing the work of Melanie Klein (see entry). At Northfield Military Hospital, Birmingham, England, he introduced a psychoanalytic approach to working with the rehabilitation of officers suffering from a variety of war-related mental illnesses. Later, at the Tavistock Clinic, London, Bion focused on how a group will try to push the observer into the role of leader to satisfy group needs. By the observer refusing to accept any other role, the group is forced to do its own work. Two sets of forces operate: one is directed toward the accomplishment of the task and the other seems to oppose it. The latter relates to the regressive id-function.

Although Bion is better known for his work on groups, his contributions to psychoanalysis and the study of psychosis are profound, developing Klein's ideas about psychotic anxieties and defenses. He also worked to see how far psychoanalysis could be used with psychotic patients. For Bion, the mother's failure to contain her infant's fear of dying results in psychosis. He postulated that a psychotic or depressed mother herself would be unable to contain and modify her child's fears. So instead of being contained and modified by the mother, all the infant's anxiety is projected into the mother, where it grows and develops. The mother then returns these feelings to the child, and the child cannot cope with such feelings, and resorts into psychosis.

Bion's interest in the analysis of schizophrenics led him to formulate new ideas about the thinking process — how it develops in healthy individuals and also how it can go wrong. Bion's theory of thinking and creativity marks a big step forward in psychoanalytic theory.

Major Literature

Bion, Wilfred Ruprecht. *Experiences in Groups.* London, England: Tavistock, 1961.
___. "A Theory of Thinking." *International Journal of Psycho-Analysis* 43 (1962). Reprinted in *Second Thoughts.* London, England: Karnac Books, 1967.
___. *Elements of Psychoanalysis.* London, England: William Heinemann, 1963. London, England: Karnac Books, 1984.
___(Ed.). *War Memoirs 1917–1919.* London, England: Karnac Books, 1997.

Bleuler, Eugen (1857–1939)
STUDIES OF SCHIZOPHRENICS

Born in Zollikon, near Zürich, Switzerland, Eugen Bleuler studied medicine in Zürich and later in Paris, London and Munich, after which he returned to Zürich to take a post as an intern at the Burghölzli, a university hospital. In 1886 Bleuler became the director of a psychiatric clinic at Rheinau, a hospital located in an old monastery on an island in the Rhine where he set about improving conditions for the patients. He was appointed professor of psychiatry at the University of Zürich and director of the Burghölzli Asylum in Zürich, where he served from 1898 to 1927; Carl Jung (see entry) was one of his interns. Bleuler was a member of the Vienna Psycho-Analytical Society and was one of the first psychiatrists to accept psychoanalysis and to apply psychoanalytical methods in his research. His *Textbook of Psychiatry* (1916) was a standard text and went through many editions.

Major Contributions

One of the most influential psychiatrists of his time, Bleuler is best known today for his introduction of the term schizophrenia to describe the disorder previously known as *dementia praecox* (premature dementia) and for his studies of schizophrenics. The term "dementia praecox" was first introduced by Bénédict-Augustin Morel and popularized by Emil Kraepelin (see entries). In two papers written in 1908 and 1911, Bleuler argued that dementia was not a feature of dementia praecox, so he called it "schizophrenia," a splitting of the mind. Bleuler identified four major symptoms, called the four A's:

- Abnormal association;
- Autistic thinking and behavior, denoting the loss of contact with reality, frequently through indulgence in bizarre fantasy;
- Abnormal affect; and
- Ambivalence, denoting mutually exclusive contradictions within the psyche existing at the same time.

In his work for the group of schizophrenias he set out to understand and interpret the patients' way of expressing themselves. He attempted to show how the various mechanisms Freud had found in neurotic patients could also be recognized in psychotic patients, and that schizophrenia was not incurable. Bleuler challenged the prevailing belief that psychosis was the result of organic brain damage, insisting instead that it could have psychological causes. His son, Manfred Bleuler, continued his work.

Schizophrenia is a broad term that encompasses several mental disorders, usually of psychotic proportions, with disturbances in thoughts, feelings and behavior, with far-reaching personal, familial and social implications. The main characteristics are:

- Difficulty handling abstract concepts.
- Not in touch with reality.

• Often associated with hallucinations (a sensory perception for which there is no external stimulus) or delusions (a persistent false belief which is both untrue and that cannot be shaken by reason or contradictory evidence, and which is inconsistent with the person's knowledge or culture).

Major Literature

Bleuler, Eugen. *Dementia Praecox*. 1911. Translated, Madison, Connecticut: International Universities Press, 1950.
Bleuler, Manfred. *The Schizophrenic Disorders: Long-term Patient and Family Studies*. New Haven, Connecticut: Yale University Press, 1978.

Bonaparte, Princess Marie (1882–1962)
FRENCH INSTITUTE OF PSYCHOANALYSIS

Princess Marie Bonaparte was born at Saint-Cloud, a town in Hauts-de-Seine, Île-de-France. She was the only daughter of Prince Roland Bonaparte (great-nephew of Napoléon Bonaparte) and Marie-Félix Blanc (who died soon after Marie's birth). In 1907 Bonaparte married Prince Georges of Greece and Denmark, and was thereafter officially also known as Princess Georges of Greece; she had two children, Eugénie and Pierre.

In 1925 she entered psychoanalysis with Sigmund Freud (see entry) for treatment of her frigidity. Perhaps it was her release from frigidity that provoked Freud to say to her (so the story goes): "The great question that has never been answered and which I have not yet been able to answer, despite my thirty years of research into the feminine soul is 'What does a woman want?'" It may have been this that promoted Bonaparte to explore the feminine soul and to publish *Female Sexuality*. In the book she advanced a biological theory of bisexuality to explain why a masculinity complex is more common in women than a femininity complex in men and why women must grieve for and accept the loss of her penis. Although later writers have challenged her ideas, she is, nonetheless, a pioneer in the study of female development.

Bonaparte became a lay analyst and writer of many papers and books. Her most ambitious task was a 700-page psychoanalytic study of Edgar Allan Poe, first published in French in 1933. It is thought that some of the similarities between Poe's experience and Bonaparte's own life enabled her to bring insights into her analysis of her subject. She was sensitive and empathetic to Poe's inner world because her own inner world was similar. The result of this psychological fit between Poe and Bonaparte was also her own psychobiography. Her work on Edgar Allan Poe marked a milestone in psychobiographical literature, and raised Bonaparte's status as an independent psychoanalyst and not a mere clone of Freud.

The second major contribution was her generosity toward Sigmund Freud, for it was she who provided the money for him to flee Austria in 1938. She also supported the anthropological explorations in Australia of the Hungarian anthropologist Professor Geza Róheim (see entry). She founded the French Institute of Psychoanalysis (*Société Psychanalytique de Paris*) in 1915 and was a practicing psychoanalyst until she died. In the first meeting of the International Psycho-Analytical Association held after she died, it was recorded that Marie Bonaparte had not missed a single meeting since 1927.

Major Literature

Bonaparte, Marie. *Five Copy Books*: [Written by a little girl between the ages of seven-and-a-half and ten, with commentaries.] London, England: Hogarth Press, 1952.
___. *Female Sexuality*. Madison, Connecticut: International Universities Press, Inc., 1953.
___. *Life and Works of Edgar Allan Poe: A Psychoanalytic Interpretation*. New York: Harper Torchbooks, 1959. London, England: Hogarth Press, 1971.

Boring, Edwin Garrigues (1886–1968)
HISTORY OF PSYCHOLOGY

Born in Philadelphia, Pennsylvania, Edwin Garrigues Boring gained a master of engineering degree in 1908 and a Ph.D. in 1914 from Cornell University in Ithaca, New York, and from 1914 to 1917 was instructor there. From 1917 to 1919, Robert M. Yerkes (see entry) employed Boring to help test the intelligence of draftees during World War I; he also served as captain in the U.S. Army. He was associate professor, Clark University, Worcester, Massachusetts (1920–1922), and from 1922 to 1968 Boring was at Harvard University in Cambridge, Massachusetts, as director (1924) of the Psychological Laboratory and professor emeritus of psychology (1957–1968).

He was editor of the *American Journal of Psychology* (1926–1946), president of the American Psychological Association (1928), and secretary of the American International Congress of Psychology (1929). In 1934, Boring established psychology as a separate department at Harvard, which in 1936 became completely independent of philosophy. He was chair of Harvard's Department of Psychology (1936–1938) and on the editorial board for the *Journal of the History of the Behavioral Sciences* (1965–1968).

Major Contributions

Although Boring started off in engineering, he switched to psychology and was a student of Edward Bradford Titchener (see entry) and was influenced by the experimental work of Wilhelm Max Wundt (see entry). His research interests focused on psychophysical issues, such as the size-constancy problem and carrying on the work of Titchener on the "stimulus error"—an example would be looking at a full moon and describing the visual perception as a circle.

Boring's experimental work focused on sensory stimulation of the alimentary tract and the physiological consequences of dividing nerve fibers. However, his research also covered a vast number of other topics, and prepared him to write his best-known work, *A History of Experimental Psychology*, which established him as one of the first historians in the field of psychology in the U.S. This book was a huge success; however, his next, *The Physical Dimensions of Consciousness*, was not. He took this as a sign that his age was against him, and falling into depression, he undertook psychoanalysis. The reality is that his view of consciousness had gone out of fashion. What analysis might have done is to help him focus on his writing, which he continued to do until his death.

Major Literature

Boring, Edwin Garrigues. *A History of Experimental Psychology*. Chicago, Illinois: University of Chicago Press, 1929. New Jersey: Appleton-Century-Crofts, G.A. Noble, 1950.

___. *Physical Dimensions of Consciousness*. Mineola, New York: Dover Publications, Inc., 1933.

___. *Sensation and Perception in the History of Experimental Psychology*. New Jersey: Appleton-Century-Crofts, 1942. New York: Irvington Publishers, 1977.

___(Ed.). *Foundations of Psychology*. New Jersey: John Wiley and Sons, Inc., 1948.

Boring. Edwin G. *History, Psychology and Science*. New Jersey: John Wiley and Sons, Inc., 1963.

___(Ed.). *History of Psychology in Autobiography: 005*. New York: Irvington Publishers, 1967.

Herrnstein, Richard J., and Edwin Garrigues Boring (Eds.). *Source Book in the History of Psychology*. Cambridge, Massachusetts: Harvard University Press, 1965, 1973.

Boss, Medard (1903–1990)
DASEINSANALYSIS

Born in St. Gallen, Switzerland, Medard Boss received his medical degree from the University of Zürich in 1928, having spent time undergoing analysis by Sigmund Freud (see entry). From 1928 to 1932 he worked at the Burghölzli Asylum, Zürich, as an assistant to Eugen Bleuler (see entry), then studied in Berlin and London with Karen Horney (see entry). In 1938 he met Carl Jung (see entry), who introduced him to his alternative psychoanalysis, not bound up in Freudian interpretations. His meeting in 1946 and eventual friendship with the philosopher Martin Heidegger (1889–1976) turned him forever to existential psychology. His impact on existential therapy has been so great that he is often mentioned together with Ludwig Binswanger (see entry) as its co-founder.

Major Contributions

Boss set himself to the ambitious task of humanizing medicine and psychology from a new existential foundation. He spent his career developing his theory *Daseinanalysis*, strongly influenced by the philosophy of Martin Heidegger. (*Dasein* is a German word meaning "being there.") The existential view is that as human beings we flee from death and the awareness of our mortality. Boss suggests that the most dignified human relationship to death involves being aware of death without fleeing from it.

The analogy of light plays an important part in Boss's theory. Boss views Dasein as that which brings things "to light." His idea of light transforms traditional psychoanalytical concepts; defensiveness is choosing not to live in the light, and psychopathology is choosing to live in the darkness. Therapy, therefore, is helping the person to move from darkness into the light. Boss introduced the term "attunement" (another name for mood). We are constantly illuminating (focusing) one thing more than another. For example, in an angry mood, we are "attuned" to angry things, angry thoughts, angry actions; we "see red." If we are in a cheerful mood, we are "attuned" to cheerful things, and the world seems "sunny."

Boss has studied dreams more than any other existentialist and considers them important in therapy. But instead of interpreting them as Freudians or Jungians do, he allows them to reveal their own meanings. Everything is not hiding behind a symbol, hiding from the always-present censor (a Freudian concept). Instead, dreams show us how we are illuminating our lives: If we feel trapped, our feet will be bound by cement; if we feel free, we will fly; if we feel guilty, we will dream about sin; if we feel anxious, we will be chased by frightening things.

Major Literature

Boss, Medard. *The Analysis of Dreams*. New York: Random House Inc., Rider, 1957.
___, and Stephen Conway (Translator). *I Dreamt Last Night: New Approach to the Revelations of Dreaming and Its Uses in Psychotherapy*. New Jersey: John Wiley and Sons, Inc., 1978.
Boss, Medard. *Psychoanalysis and Daseinsanalysis*. Cambridge, Massachusetts: Da Capo Press, 1982.
___. *Existential Foundations of Medicine and Psychology*. Lanham, Maryland: Rowman and Littlefield Publishers, Inc., Jason Aronson, 1995.

Bowden, Blake Sperry (1967–)
STUDY OF ADOLESCENTS

Born in Columbus and raised in Wooster, Ohio, Blake Sperry Bowden received a B.A. in psychology and linguistics from Northwestern University in Illinois (1990), an M.A. in clinical psychology from DePaul University in Chicago (1993), a Ph.D. in clinical psychology (1995) from University of Dayton in Ohio, and a specialist in education (Ed.S.) in school psychology (2005).

Following a fellowship in pediatric neurodevelopment disorders, Bowden has served as a clinical psychologist with Cincinnati Children's Hospital Medical Center and regularly taught at colleges and universities in Ohio. A scientist-practitioner, he is currently working with students and teachers in public schools as a pediatric clinical school psychologist. He resides in Cincinnati and was named a member of the city's "creative class" by *Cincinnati Magazine*. He also is managing director of Clear Stage Cincinnati, a theater company that promotes new talent in the area.

Major Contributions

Bowden received national attention for his study of some 1,200 American adolescents and the social support they received from their parents and how this support affected stress levels. The results suggested that too little or too much support could increase stress levels. This research received a Dissertation Research Award from the American Psychological Association in 1995.

A segment of 527 teenagers categorized as either well-adjusted or not well-adjusted was then stud-

ied by Bowden and Jennie M. Zeisz, Ph.D., from DePaul University. They looked into the factors that make a teenager "well adjusted" and out of trouble. Their definition of "well-adjusted" adolescents were those who were less likely to do drugs, less likely to be depressed, more motivated at school, and had better peer relationships.

What they found was that the adjusted teens ate with their families an average of five days a week compared to the non-adjusted teens, who only ate with their families three days a week or less. He discovered the power of storytelling as he read J.R.R. Tolkien's *The Hobbit* to a dying teenager to help the lad face his own death. Between 2001 and 2003 Bowden adapted *The Lord of the Rings* at the Aronoff Center of the Arts, Cincinnati, Ohio.

Major Literature

Bowden, Blake Sperry. "'Supper's On!' Adolescent Adjustment and Frequency of Meals with Important Adults." Poster presented at the 105th annual national convention of the American Psychological Association, Chicago, Illinois, August 1997.
___. "Parent Ratings (CBCL) of Youngsters with Rubinstein-Taybi Syndrome (RTS): Comparison with Parents of Youngsters with Down Syndrome (DS) and Autism/PDD." Paper presented at the 123rd annual national convention of the American Association on Mental Retardation, New Orleans, Louisiana, 1999.
___. "Integrating Computers into Speech and Language Intervention: Transitioning from Tradition to Technology." *Hearsay, Journal of the Ohio Speech and Hearing Association* 13(2) (2003).

Bowlby, John (1907–1990)
ATTACHMENT THEORY

Born in London, England, John Bowlby earned a B.A. (1928), M.A. (1932), B.Ch. (1933), and M.D. (1939), all from the University of Cambridge in England. At the British Psychoanalytical Society, Bowlby was head of the Department for Children and Parents, the Tavistock Clinic, London (1945); training secretary (1944–1947); and deputy president, (1956–1957, 1958–1961). He was fellow, Center for Advanced Study in the Behavioral Sciences, Stanford, California (1957–1958); chairman, Association for Child Psychology and Psychiatry (1958–1959); president, International Association for Child Psychology and Psychiatry (1962–1966); and on the editorial board of the *Journal of Child Psychology and Psychiatry* (1963).

His awards were: honorary D.Litt., University

of Leicester, England (1971); Commander of the British Empire (1972); James Spence Medal, British Pediatric Association (1974); G. Stanley Hall Medal, American Psychological Association (1974); honorary Sc.D., University of Cambridge (1977); honorary Fellow Council, Royal College of Psychiatrists (1980); foreign honorary member, American Academy of Arts and Science (1981); Distinguished Scientific Contribution Award, Society for Research in Child Development (1981); Blanch Ittleson Award, American Orthopsychiatric Association (1981); and Salmon Medal, New York Academy of Medicine (1984).

Major Contributions

For Bowlby, child psychoanalysis focused too much on the fantasy world of the child and not enough on actual events and circumstances. He advised mothers to maintain contact with their children while in hospital; children deprived of maternal contact are likely to develop characters without affection. His collaboration with James Robertson, studying the effects of children separated in hospital, led to a film with world-wide influence. In 1951 the World Health Organization published a report by Bowlby on maternal care in post-war Europe. He studied the work of Harry Frederick Harlow (see entry) with rhesus monkeys reared in social groups, where both mother and baby suffered obvious emotional trauma when separated. His theory created an uproar in psychoanalytic circles, where social influences were discounted. Robertson and Bowlby identified three phases of separation response: protest (related to separation anxiety); despair (related to grief and mourning); and detachment or denial (related to defense).

Bowlby extended his theory so that threat of separation, rejection by parents or significant others, illness or death many also trigger anxiety, particularly where the child feels responsible. Bowlby challenged Anna Freud's (see entry) view that young children cannot grieve, but only experience brief bouts of anxiety because they have not developed an ego. He also challenged Melanie Klein (see entry), whose view that the loss of the breast is the most traumatic loss in infancy. His view was that grief and mourning appear whenever attachment behaviors are activated but the mother continues to be unavailable.

Major Literature

Bowlby, John. *Attachment and Loss*, Vol. 1, "Attachment." London, England: Penguin Books Ltd., 1969.
___. *Attachment and Loss*, Vol. 2, "Separation." London, England: Penguin Books Ltd., 1973.
___. *Attachment and Loss*, Vol. 3, "Loss." London, England: Penguin Books Ltd, 1980.

Related Reading

Robertson, J., and J. Robertson. "Young Children in Brief Separations." In R.K. Eissler, et al. *The Psychoanalytic Study of the Child* (Vol. 26). New Haven, Connecticut: Yale University Press, 1971.

Branden, Nathaniel (1930–)
SELF-ESTEEM

Born Nathan Blumenthal in Brampton, Ontario, Canada, Branden received a B.A. in psychology from the University of California at Los Angeles and his Ph.D. in psychology from the California Graduate Institute. Branden is a psychotherapist and author of psychology books and numerous articles on ethical and political philosophy. In addition to his work on the psychology of self-esteem, Branden has also played a prominent role in developing and promoting Ayn Rand's philosophic system, known as objectivism. (Rand, a Russian novelist and philosopher [1905–1982], characterizes objectivism as a philosophy "for living on earth," grounded in reality and aimed at achieving knowledge about the natural world and harmonious, mutually beneficial interactions between human beings.)

Branden met Rand when he was 19 years of age, and a deep friendship developed that eventually led to a love affair in 1954, undertaken, so it is said, with the knowledge of their respective spouses, although Branden and his wife Barbara divorced in 1965. Rand considered Branden to be her soul mate and designated him her "intellectual heir." However, the deep relationship ended in acrimony in 1968. Branden's books have been translated into 18 languages and sold over 4 million copies.

Major Contributions

Although Branden did contribute to the study of objectivism, he is better known for his work on self-esteem, which he began pioneering over thirty years ago. Self-esteem can be defined as the degree to which one feels valued, worthwhile or competent. Very low self-esteem equates to feeling worthless.

- *Lowered self-esteem* is accompanied by feelings of unhappiness, anger, sense of threat, fatigue, withdrawal, tension, disorganization, feelings of constraint, conflict and inhibition.

- *High self-esteem* is accompanied by feelings of integration, freedom, positive emotion and availability of energy.

Branden's sentence completion method (SCM) (1955) is a powerful and sophisticated psychotherapeutic tool that can be used both to make unconscious thoughts and feelings conscious, and to transform limiting beliefs and attitudes. For example, a client or a couple would be asked to complete, say, 12 times, the stem "If I weren't so...." "If I could be...." "If I trusted you [the partner] I would...." Branden continues to write and practice psychotherapy in Los Angeles, California, as well as present seminars and workshops on self-esteem. He lectures and consults with corporations all over the world, teaching how to develop self-esteem.

Major Literature

Branden, Nathaniel. *Judgment Day: My Years with Ayn Rand*. New York: Harper Collins Publishers, Inc., Avon Books, 1991.
___. *How to Raise Your Self-esteem*. New York: Random House USA, Inc., 1997.
___. *Self-esteem at Work: How Confident People Make Powerful Companies*. New Jersey: John Wiley and Sons, Inc., Jossey Bass Wiley, 1998.
___. *A Woman's Self-esteem: Struggles and Triumphs in the Search for Identity*. New Jersey: John Wiley and Sons, Inc., Jossey Bass Wiley, 1999.
___. *My Years with Ayn Rand*. New Jersey: John Wiley and Sons, Inc., Jossey Bass Wiley, 1999.
___. *Six Pillars of Self Esteem*. New York: Random House USA, Inc., 2004.

Brentano, Franz Clemens (1838–1917)
FOUNDER OF ACT PSYCHOLOGY

Franz Clemens Brentano made important contributions to many fields in philosophy, especially to ethics, ontology, logic, the history of philosophy, and philosophical theology. Born in Marienberg, Hesse-Nassau, Germany, he received his Ph.D. in 1862 from Berlin University with his thesis "On the Several Senses of Being in Aristotle." He was ordained a Roman Catholic priest (1864), appointed *privatdozent* (unsalaried lecturer) in philosophy (1866), and professor in philosophy, University of Würzburg (1872). Between 1870 and 1873 Brentano's strong opposition to the doctrine of papal infallibility, defined in the First Vatican Council of 1870, led to his resignation as professor and priest, in 1873.

In 1874 Brentano was appointed professor at the University of Vienna, but in 1880 his decision to marry was blocked by the Austrian authorities, who refused to accept his resignation from the priesthood; they considered him still a cleric. He was deprived of his Austrian citizenship, forced to resign his professorship, and moved with his wife to Leipzig. In 1881 he was allowed to return to the University of Vienna as a privatdozent, where he remained until 1895. Among his students were Sigmund Freud, Carl Stumpf (see entries), the philosopher Edmund Husserl, and Tomáš Masaryk, the founder of modern Czechoslovakia.

In *Psychology from an Empirical Standpoint* (1874), he presented a systematic psychology, a science of the soul. Act psychology, or intentionalism, in opposition to structuralism, concerns itself with the *acts* of the mind — what the mind does rather than what is contained within it — rather than with the *states* of mind or the impact of stimuli upon consciousness. In other words, psychology should focus on experience as an activity rather than on experience as a structure.

Brentano divided mental acts into three basic classes: ideating (e.g., sensing), judging (e.g., acknowledging), and loving/hating (e.g., wishing). He noted that every act always refers to (or intends) something outside of itself (intentionality); thus, acts are inseparable from the objects to which they intend. In contrast to the rigid analytical introspective methodology of Wilhelm Wundt and Edward Titchener (see entries), Brentano proposed phenomenological introspection as a means to study mental acts and intentionality. Phenomenological introspection is directed toward intact, meaningful experience.

Act psychology was a forerunner to the Würzberg school and helped provided the philosophical foundation for the founding of functionalism. After his retirement Brentano moved to Florence in Italy and at the outbreak of the First World War he transferred to Zürich, Switzerland, where he died. Brentano's theories had a profound influence on the development of Gestalt psychology.

Major Literature

Brentano, Franz Clemens. *Psychology from an Empirical Standpoint*. (1973) First English Edition. London: Routledge, 1874.
___. *The Origin of the Knowledge of Right and Wrong*. (1969) 2nd translation, Roderick Chisholm and Elizabeth Schneewind. London: Routledge, 1902.
___. *Descriptive Psychology*. Translated by Benito Müller. London: Routledge, 1995.

Breuer, Josef (1842–1925)
FORERUNNER OF PSYCHOANALYSIS

Josef Breuer was born in Vienna to a Jewish family. His father, Leopold, taught religion in Vienna's Jewish community. Breuer was a conscientious medical student who passed his medical exams in 1867 then went to work with Johann Oppolzer at the university. He gave up a university career to dedicate himself to his private patients. He was carrying out research at the Institute of Physiology when, in 1880, he met Freud, fourteen years his junior. Breuer was regarded as one of the finest physicians and scientists in Vienna. In 1894, he was elected to the Viennese Academy of Science.

Major Contributions

Although Breuer was acknowledged by Sigmund Freud and others as the forerunner of psychoanalysis, he had contributed in 1868 to medical science by describing the Hering-Breuer reflex — the rhythmic inflation and deflation of the lungs in normal breathing. In 1873 he discovered the sensory function of the semicircular canals in the inner ear and their relation to positional sense or balance. By 1880, Breuer was working with hypnosis to relieve patients' symptoms of hysteria; the most renowned was the patient called Anna O. His conclusion was that neurotic symptoms result from unconscious processes and disappear when these processes become conscious. This formed the basis of psychoanalysis.

Breuer and Freud became close friends, and Breuer referred patients to Freud. They collaborated in publishing *Studies in Hysteria* in 1895. Their conclusions were that traumatic experiences could cause diseases, because they stay in the unconscious mind. In order to release the trauma of these events, the patient would have to undergo abreaction. The relationship of Breuer to Freud was one of mentor, and at times it was paternal. At times he supported Freud financially. Later disagreement on basic theories of therapy ended their collaboration.

Anna O. was a twenty-one-year-old woman who had fallen ill while nursing her father, who eventually died of a tubercular abscess. Her illness began with a severe cough. She subsequently developed a number of other physical symptoms, including paralysis of the extremities of the right side of her body, contractures, disturbances of vision, hearing and language. She also began to experience lapses of consciousness and hallucinations. So intense was the rapport between Breuer and Anna that she divulged her strong sexual desire for him. Breuer, recognizing reciprocal feelings in him, broke off his treatment.

Freud's observation of the session led him to develop the concept of transference and countertransference. Allowing Anna to talk about her symptoms seemed to act cathartically to produce an abreaction, or discharge, of the pent-up emotional blockage at the root of the pathological behavior. By the end Anna was becoming too dependent on Breuer and told him she was pregnant with his baby. Breuer, a married man, was worried what society would think about him. He stopped treating her. Anna O. became a social worker and feminist. She never married. Although Freud did not continue using hypnosis, there is little doubt that Breuer's influence on Freud was enormous.

Briggs Myers, Isabel (1897–1979)
PERSONALITY TYPING

Isabel Briggs was the only daughter of Katherine and Lyman Briggs, the latter an American scientist. Although Briggs had no formal psychological training, around the time of World War I she became interested in the similarities and differences of human personality. When she became acquainted with the work of Carl Jung (see entry), she quickly adopted and expanded what he had done. Marrying Clarence Myers when she was young, Briggs, in addition to being a mother, published two mystery novels.

World War II gave her the impetus to continue developing what was to become the Myers-Briggs Type Indicator (MBTI), getting her subjects from school students or from any interested person, then later, medical and nursing students. Her work was not received warmly by the psychology fraternity, and her lack of any formal qualifications made the whole system suspect. However, she persisted and with perseverance gained ground. Now the indicator is accepted as a reliable personality measure for people who are not mentally ill.

The MBTI measures eight personality preferences along four dimensions:

1. Extraversion (E) or Introversion (I). Extraversion/introversion describes the way we relate to the world around us.
2. Sensing (S) or Intuition (N). Sensing/intuition describes the way we perceive the world.
3. Thinking (T) or Feeling (F). Thinking/feeling describes the way we make judgments.

4. Judgment (J) or Perception (P). Judgment/ perception describes the way we make decisions.

There are sixteen types, made up from the dominant element of each dimension. The MBTI is used in a wide variety of situations and is a useful counseling tool clients easily understand and can relate to.

A person's type is made up of the four dominant functions. Helping a client to understand his or her personality preferences is just one more way in which the client will gain insight into how to manage life with less stress.

Personality preferences might influence counseling in several ways.

- People who are too extroverted often get on people's nerves; someone who is too introverted often has difficulty making contact with people at all.
- People who are high on sensing can get so caught up in counting the trees that they miss the beauty of the wood; people who are too intuitive often seem "away with the fairies."
- People who are too high on thinking often intellectualize everything; people who are too high on feeling often swamp others by their warmth.
- People who are too high on judgment often become judge, jury and executioner; people who are too high on perception often give the impression of being grown up children.

Major Literature

Briggs Myers, Isabel. *Gifts Differing*. Palo Alto, California: Consulting Psychologists Press, 1980. Mountain View, California: Davies-Black Publishing, U.S., 1995.

___. *Introduction to Type*. Palo Alto, California: Consulting Psychologists Press, 1980, 1998.

___, and M.H. McCaulley. *Manual: A Guide to the Development and Use of the Myers-Briggs Type Indicator*. Palo Alto, California: Consulting Psychologists Press, 1985.

Broadbent, Donald Eric (1926–1993)
EXPERIMENTAL PSYCHOLOGY

Born in Birmingham, England, Donald Eric Broadbent served in the Royal Air Force until 1947, then gained a B.A. (1949), an M.A. (1951), and an Sc.D. (1965) from the University of Cambridge, England. He worked at the Applied Psychology Research Unit at the University of Cam-

bridge from 1949 to 1958, serving as director from 1958 to 1974. From 1974 to 1991 he was external staff member of the Medical Research Council, Department of Experimental Psychology, University of Oxford. He was a fellow of the British Psychological Society (1957), Acoustical Society of America (1963), Royal Society (1968), and Human Factors Society (1968), and honorary fellow on the faculty of occupational medicine, Royal College of Physicians (1981), and Royal College of Psychiatrists (1985). He was president, Psychology Section, British Association for the Advancement of Science, in 1973–1974.

His awards include Commander of the British Empire (1974), Distinguished Scientific Contribution Award of American Psychological Society (1975), and honorary D.Sc., University of Wales (1992). From 1979 to 1993 he was on the editorial panel (psychology) at Oxford University Press. Broadbent received honorary doctorates from six universities.

Major Contributions

From 1974 until he retired in 1991, Broadbent did research at Oxford University, funded by the Medical Research Council. In 1991 the British Psychological Society launched the annual Broadbent Lecture series, with the inaugural lecture being given by Donald Broadbent himself. Although much of the work of the Applied Psychology Research Unit was directed at practical issues of military or industrial significance, Broadbent rapidly became well known for theories of selective attention and short-term memory. These were developed at a time when digital computers were beginning to become available to the academic community and were among the first to use computer analogies to make a serious contribution to the analysis of human cognition.

Selective attention theories suggest that people have a tendency to focus, or process information, from only one part of the environment to the exclusion of other parts. Too much incoming information forms a bottleneck and creates confusion. Broadbent developed the Filter Model theory, which proposed that the physical characteristics (e.g., pitch, loudness) of an auditory message are used to focus attention on only a single message, so that information from only one channel at a time passes into working memory. For example, hearing your name called in a crowded place, you are more likely to respond to the person whose voice you recognize.

His various theories were brought together in

Perception and Communication (Elsevier, 1958, re-published by Oxford University Press, 1987), which remains one of the classic texts of cognitive psychology. Another area of study was implicit and explicit learning; one we are unaware of and the other is deliberate.

Major Literature

Broadbent, Donald Eric. "Noise in Industry" (*Ergonomics for Industry* series, No. 6). London: Department of Scientific and Industrial Research (Information Division), 1964.

Pribram, Karl H., and Donald Eric Broadbent (Eds.). *Biology of Memory.* London: Academic Press, Inc., 1970.

Broadbent, Donald Eric. *Decision and Stress.* London: Academic Press, 1971.

___. *In Defense of Empirical Psychology.* London, England: Methuen Publishing Ltd., 1973.

___. "Interactive Tasks and the Implicit-Explicit Distinction." *British Journal of Psychology* 79. (1988): 251–272.

Bronfenbrenner, Urie
(1917–2005)
HEAD START PROGRAM

Born in Moscow, Urie Bronfenbrenner immigrated to the United States at the age of 6. He graduated with a B.A. from Cornell University, New York (1938), completing a double major in psychology and music. He completed an M.A. in developmental psychology at Harvard University and a Ph.D. at the University of Michigan in 1942. He served as a psychologist in the American Army from 1942 to 1946, after which he worked two years as an assistant professor of psychology at the University of Michigan, then joined the Cornell faculty in 1948, where he remained for the rest of his professional life.

At the time of his death, Bronfenbrenner was Jacob Gould Schurman distinguished professor emeritus of Human Development and of Psychology at Cornell University. His research also furthered the goals of Cornell's Life Course Institute, which was renamed the Bronfenbrenner Life Course Institute in 1993. Bronfenbrenner was awarded six honorary degrees, three of them from European universities. The Bronfenbrenner Award for Lifetime Contribution to Developmental Psychology in the Service of Science and Society is awarded annually by the American Psychological Association.

Major Contributions

Bronfenbrenner's primary contribution was his ecological systems theory, in which he identified four types of inter-related systems. Each system contains roles, norms, and rules that can powerfully shape development. The four systems:

1. microsystem — family, home, work, classroom
2. mesosystem — school, religion, neighborhood
3. exosystem — a system influencing development, i.e., parental workplace, community, culture, society
4. macrosystem — the larger cultural context, global.

Bronfenbrenner's theory had widespread influence on the way psychologists and others approached the study of human beings and their environments. Child psychologists, sociologists, anthropologists and economists started looking at the child and the family outside of their own boxes, built bridges and started considering human ecology from the cradle to the grave. In addition to creating his ecological systems theory, Bronfenbrenner was a co-founder of the national Head Start program. (Head Start is a program of the United States Department of Health and Human Services, created in 1965, which provides comprehensive education, health, nutrition, and parent involvement services to low-income children and their families.) He spent many years warning Americans that children were being deprived of their birthright of virtues, such as honesty, responsibility, integrity and compassion, as evidenced the ever-growing rates of alienation, apathy, rebellion, delinquency and violence among American youth. He died from complications of diabetes.

Major Literature

Bronfenbrenner, Urie. *Two Worlds of Childhood—US and USSR.* New York: Penguin Group (USA), Inc., 1974.

___. *Influences on Human Development.* Orlando, Florida: Holt, Rinehart and Winston, 1975.

___. *The Ecology of Human Development: Experiments by Nature and Design.* Cambridge, Massachusetts: Harvard University Press, 1979.

___. "Ecology of the Family as a Context for Human Development." *Developmental Psychology* 22 (1986): 723–742.

___, et al. *The State of Americans: This Generation and the Next.* New York: The Free Press, 1996.

___. *On Making Human Beings Human.* Thousand Oaks, California; Sage Publications Ltd., 2004.

Brooks-Gunn, Jeanne (1946–)
CHILD DEVELOPMENT

Jeanne Brooks was born in Bethesda, Maryland, gained a B.A. in psychology from Connecticut College, New London, Connecticut (1969), an Ed.M. in human learning and development from Harvard University, Cambridge, Massachusetts (1970), and a Ph.D. in human learning and development from the University of Pennsylvania, Philadelphia (1975). From 1975 to 1984 she was at the Colleges of Arts and Sciences, Barnard College, Columbia University; University of Pennsylvania; from 1977 to 1982 she was associate director of the Institute for the Study of Exceptional Children, Educational Testing Service and St. Luke's-Roosevelt Hospital Center, Columbia University, New York City.

Since 1991 she has been a Virginia and Leonard Marx Professor in Child Development and Education, Teachers College, Columbia University. In 1991 she founded and co-directed the National Center for Children and Families, Teachers College, Columbia University, was a founding director of the Columbia University Institute on Child and Family Policy (1998), and since 2000 has been a professor of pediatrics, Medical School, College of Physicians and Surgeons, Columbia University. She is the recipient of more than fifteen awards, including the Distinguished Contributions to the Public Policy for Children Award from the Society for Research in Child Development (2005). She married Robert W. Gunn.

Major Contributions

In her early research Brooks-Gunn explored the attitudes of young female children toward menstruation and with Diane Ruble developed the Menstrual Attitude Questionnaire. Some major findings in this area were that female children have specific expectations about menstruation as early as the fifth grade, and that early symptom expectations are positively related to later menstrual distress. Her main research focuses on designing and evaluating interventions aimed at enhancing the development and well-being of children living in poverty and conditions associated with poverty. She is also involved with the Head Start program and other similar programs related to early childhood and family support intervention.

She is interested in the factors that contribute to positive and negative outcomes and changes in well-being, as well as the biological and psychological processes contributing to disparities in well-being. Some of her most impressive research has been on the transition to adolescence in females; she argues that many of the transitional problems usually attributed to "female hormones" are derived more from social events. Family income and poverty status are powerful influences on the cognitive development and behavior of young adolescents. With Professor Frank Furstenburg she carried out a longitudinal study of 300 African-American adolescent mothers from the Baltimore area, examining the direction their lives took, and the problems they experienced.

Major Literature

Brooks-Gunn, Jeanne, and D.N. Ruble. "The Menstrual Attitude Questionnaire." *Psychosomatic Medicine*, Vol. 42, Issue 5 (1980): 503–512.

Brooks-Gunn, Jeanne, and Wendy Schempp Matthews. *He and She: Children's Sex Role Development.* New Jersey: Prentice-Hall, 1980.

Brooks-Gunn, Jeanne, F.F. Furstenberg, and P. Morgan. *Adolescent Mothers in Later Life.* New York: Cambridge University Press, 1987.

Brooks-Gunn, Jeanne, Greg J. Duncan, and J. Lawrence Aber (Eds.). *Neighborhood Poverty: Context and Consequences for Children.* 2 Volumes. New York: Russell Sage Foundation, 1997.

Brooks-Gunn, Jeanne, Allison Sidle Fuligni, and Lisa J. Berlin (Eds.). *Early Child Development in the 21st Century.* New York: Teachers' College Press, 2003.

Brown, Laura S. (1952–)
FEMINIST THERAPY

Born into a Jewish family in Michigan, Laura S. Brown was brought up in Cleveland Heights, Ohio, from the age of three. She received a B.A. (1972) in psychology from Case Western Reserve University, Cleveland, Ohio, and an MBA (1975) and Ph.D. (1977) in clinical psychology from Southern Illinois University at Carbondale. She completed an internship in clinical psychology at the Seattle Veterans Administration Medical Center and has taught and lectured throughout the U.S., Canada, Europe and Israel. In the early 1980s Brown hosted one of the first radio call-in shows by a psychologist, and in 2000, she worked as the on-site psychologist for the reality show *Survivor: The Australian Outback*.

Brown has been honored for her scholarship, her activism, and her work as a mentor and leader on social justice issues in psychology. The most recent awards are: Raymond Fowler Award for Promotion of Student Professional Development, American Psychological Association of Graduate Students, 2003; Distinguished Contributions

Award, Society for the Psychology of Women Section on Lesbian and Bisexual Women's Issues, 2004; and Carolyn Wood Sherif Memorial Award, Society for the Psychology of Women, 2004. Brown is currently professor of psychology at the Washington School of Professional Psychology, Argosy University, Seattle.

Major Contributions

Brown's work has included the areas of feminist psychology, childhood sexual abuse, sexual abuse by therapists, homosexuality and legal issues. She was the first open lesbian psychologist and feminist psychologist in the area. Her stance served to open career doors and create opportunities rather than holding her back. She pursued the fields of childhood sexual abuse, psychotherapy malpractice, and psychological consequences in being discriminated against.

She was an expert witness in the case of *Simmons v. U.S.* (sexual misconduct by therapists and nature of transference). This case encouraged Brown to pursue the area of forensic psychology, which has served to make her valuable in testimony for many other court cases. She has been involved in cases such as the right of women in prison to not be pat-searched by male guards and the rights of homosexuals to serve in the military in the U.S. Brown places emphasis on social justice and applies it to psychology when possible. She continues to be available to attorneys to serve as an expert witness in legal matters involving questions of trauma, dissociation, abuse, victimization, discrimination, and harassment.

Major Literature

Brown, Laura S., and Maria P.P. Root (Eds.). *Diversity and Complexity in Feminist Therapy*. New York: The Haworth Press, 1990.

Brown, Laura S., and Mary Ballou (Eds.). *Personality and Psychopathology: Feminist Reappraisals*. New York: Guilford Publications, 1992.

Brown, Laura S. *Subversive Dialogues: Theory in Feminist Therapy*. New York: Basic Books, 1994.

Pope, Kenneth S. and Laura S. Brown. *Recovered Memories of Abuse: Assessment, Therapy, Forensics*. Washington, D.C.: American Psychological Association, 1996.

Ballou, Mary, and Laura S. Brown (Eds.). *Rethinking Mental Health and Disorder*. New York: Guilford Publications, 2002.

Brown, Roger William (1925–1997)
LANGUAGE DEVELOPMENT

Born in Detroit, Michigan, Roger Brown served in the U.S. Navy in the Pacific Theater during the Battle of Okinawa (1945) and was on the first ship to enter Nagasaki harbor following the explosion of the atomic bomb. He received his B.A. (1948), M.A. (1949) and Ph.D. (1952) from the University of Michigan, Ann Arbor. He was an instructor in social psychology at Harvard University, Cambridge, Massachusetts (1952), then assistant professor (1953–1957). He held various professorial appointments, including professor of psychology at Massachusetts Institute of Technology (MIT), Cambridge, in 1960. From 1962 until he retired in 1995, he was at Harvard as the John Lindsley Professor in Memory of William James (see entry).

Among his many awards were honorary degrees from three universities and the Distinguished Scientific Achievement Award of the American Psychological Association (APA) (1971). He served as chair of the Department of Psychology of Harvard, and was president of the Division of Personality and Social Psychology of APA and president of the Eastern Psychological Association. He was awarded the Phi Beta Kappa Teaching Prize, which recognizes excellence in teaching and the ability to inspire personal and intellectual development beyond the classroom.

Major Contributions

Brown is considered the father of developmental psycholinguistics. While assistant professor at Harvard (1953–1957) he wrote his acclaimed book, *Words and Things*. The ten chapters deal with the nature of meaning and the relation between language and thought. Around 1962, while professor of social psychology at Harvard, he was granted five year funding (extended to ten years) from the National Institute for Mental Health for the study of how children acquire their first language. The results were published in *A First Language* (Cambridge, Massachusetts: Harvard University Press, 1973).

He focused on three children, whom he called Adam, Eve, and Sarah. In this monumental study, and on the basis of careful examination of these children's utterances, he established practical principles for the way in which any language is acquired. He completed his textbook, *Social Psychology* (Prentice Hall), in 1965 with a second edition in 1985. The book was widely adopted in many universities and it remained in print for more than 20 years.

Major Literature

Brown, Roger William. *Words and Things: An Introduction to Language*. Glencoe, Illinois: Free Press, 1958.

___. "How Shall a Thing be Called?" *Psychology Review* (1958): 65: 14–21.

___, and J. Berko. "Psycholinguistic Research Methods." In *Handbook of Research Methods in Child Psychology*, P.H. Mussen (Ed.). New Jersey: John Wiley and Sons, Inc., 1960.

Brown, Roger William, and U. Bellugi. "The Acquisition of Language." *Monographs of the Society for Research in Child Development*, No. 92, 1964.

Brown, Roger William (Ed.). *Psycholinguistics: Selected Papers*. Glencoe, Illinois: Free Press, 1972.

___. *Against My Better Judgment: An Intimate Memoir of an Eminent Gay Psychologist*. New York and London: Harrington Park/Haworth Press, 1996.

Bruner, Jerome Seymour (1915–)

COGNITIVE LEARNING THEORY IN EDUCATION

Jerome Seymour Bruner was born in New York City of Polish immigrant parents. Congenital cataracts rendered him blind and an operation was necessary at the age of two years. Bruner gained an A.B. in psychology from Duke University, Durham, North Carolina (1937), and an M.A. (1939) and Ph.D. (1941) from Harvard University, Cambridge, Massachusetts. His doctoral thesis was "A Psychological Analysis of International Radio Broadcasts of Belligerent Nations."

During World War II, he served in United States Army's Intelligence Corps under General Eisenhower in the Psychological Warfare Division of Supreme Headquarters Allied Expeditionary Force in Europe, where his work focused upon propaganda. From 1945 to 1972 he was at Harvard and rose from lecturer to full professor. With George Miller (see entry) Bruner co-founded the Center for Cognitive Studies at Harvard.

He received the Distinguished Scientific Contribution Award of the American Psychological Association (APA) in 1962 and was president of the APA in 1964–1965. He was Watts Professor of Experimental Psychology, Oxford University, England (1972) and New York University Law School Meyer Visiting Professor (1991–1998). He has been a university professor and research professor of psychology since 1998.

Major Contributions

From the late 1950s on, Bruner became interested in schooling in the United States, particularly the cognitive development of children and the appropriate forms of education for students. Bruner has made outstanding contributions to the study of the process of education and the devel-

opment of curriculum theory. In his theory, learning is an active process in which students construct new ideas or concepts based on their current and past knowledge. The child is an active problem-solver who has his or her own ways of making sense of the world. He emphasized three ordered ways in which children convert experience into knowledge: action, imagery and, eventually, a range of symbolic systems.

Discovery learning was a continuing theme in Bruner's educational work; in his view, knowledge and understanding are more effectively gained by personal discovery. In his examination of poverty, he found that children from such a background lack goal-orientated behavior. This is not surprising when it is placed alongside Abraham Maslow's (see entry) hierarchy of needs. When energy is taken up with basic needs, that is the main goal — to survive. What his studies did show was that communication is present long before formal language develops, and that language is a problem-solving tool, and language contributes to one's awareness of self.

Major Literature

Bruner, Jerome Seymour. *The Process of Education*. Cambridge, Massachusetts: Harvard University Press, 1962.

___. *Toward a Theory of Instruction*. Cambridge, Massachusetts: Harvard University Press, 1966.

___. *The Relevance of Education*. Penguin Books, 1974.

___. *Actual Minds, Possible Worlds*. Cambridge, Massachusetts: Harvard University Press, 1986.

___. *Acts of Meaning*. Cambridge, Massachusetts: Harvard University Press, 1990.

___. *The Culture of Education*. Cambridge, Massachusetts: Harvard University Press, 1996.

___. *In Search of Mind: Essays in Autobiography*. New York: Harper Collins Publishers, Inc., 1983.

Brunswick, Ruth Mack (1897–1946)

EMOTIONAL DEVELOPMENT

Ruth Mack was born in Chicago, the only child of American parents who were of German-Jewish stock. Refused entry to Harvard medical school because of her gender, she attended Radcliffe College, Cambridge, Massachusetts, and graduated in 1918. She graduated from Tufts Medical School, Medford, Massachusetts, in 1922, then traveled to Vienna to be psychoanalyzed by Sigmund Freud and began practicing psychoanalysis herself in 1925. She was a member of the Vienna Psychoanalytic Society and an instructor at the Psychoanalytic Institute. In 1928 she married Mark Brunswick, an American composer. In 1932 she became an editor of the American journal *Psychoanalytic Quarterly.*

Brunswick became Freud's favorite collaborator, a fact that led Anna Freud to express her discontent with Dr. Brunswick's privileges in Freud's research. For years, rumors of their fierce rivalry flooded the psychoanalyst's circle. In 1938 the Brunswicks left Nazi-occupied Vienna and settled in New York City. There she joined the New York Psychoanalytic Society, taught courses in psychoanalytic technique and dream analysis, and kept up a private practice in spite of declining health. In 1944 she resumed her connection with the *Psychoanalytic Quarterly.* Health problems drove her to become dependent on drugs and she died from a fall in the bathroom.

Major Contributions

Brunswick pioneered the psychoanalytic treatment of psychoses and the study of emotional development between young children and their mothers, and the importance of this relationship in creating mental illness. In 1926–1927 she continued Sigmund Freud's treatment of the "Wolf Man," a fact that deepened the rift between her and Anna Freud, who believed she should have taken on the task.

Freud's Wolf Man was a Russian émigré, Sergei Konstantinovitch Pankejeff (1886–1979), whose analysis was started by Freud in 1910. The man's problems were his inability to have bowel movement without the assistance of an enema, and debilitating depression. It seems that his problems stemmed from a dream as a child in which he was terrified by white wolves. Freud's eventual analysis (along with Pankejeff's input) of the dream was that it was the result of Pankejeff having witnessed a "primal scene"—his parents having coïtus *a tergo* ("from behind")—at a very young age. Later Freud suggested the possibility that Pankejeff had instead witnessed copulation between animals that was displaced to his parents.

A few years after finishing psychoanalysis with Freud, Pankejeff developed a psychotic delusion. He was observed walking the streets staring at his reflection in a mirror, convinced that some sort of doctor had drilled a hole in his nose. Brunswick explained the delusion as displaced castration anxiety. She concludes her paper "A Note on the Childish Theory of Coitus a Tergo" (*International Journal of Psycho-Analysis*, Vol. 10, No. 1, 1929, pp. 93–95) by stating that coïtus a tergo is certainly not exclusively a fantasy on the part of the child.

Brunswik, Egon (1903–1955)
COGNITIVE PSYCHOLOGY

Born in Budapest, Hungary, in 1921, Egon Brunswik graduated in mathematics, science, classics, and history from the Theresianische Akademie in Vienna, Austria. He qualified in engineering but changed to psychology at the University of Vienna and was an assistant in Karl Bühler's (see entry) Psychological Institute. Two of his student colleagues were Paul F. Lazarsfeld and Konrad Lorenz. He received his Ph.D. in 1927. Brunswik established the first psychological laboratory in Turkey while he was visiting lecturer in Ankara during 1931–1932. In 1933, Edward C. Tolman (see entry), chairman of the department of psychology at the University of California, Berkeley, spent a year in Vienna. He and Brunswik found that although they had been working in different areas of psychological research, their theories of behavior were complementary, and in 1935–1936 Brunswik received a Rockefeller fellowship that enabled him to visit the University of California, Berkeley.

In 1937 Brunswik married Else Frenkel, also a former assistant in Bühler's institute. He remained at Berkeley, where he became an assistant professor of psychology in 1937 and a full professor in 1947. He became an American citizen in 1943. He committed suicide and three years later his wife ended her life with an overdose of barbiturates.

Major Contributions

All of Brunswik's work was devoted to extending and developing his fundamental premise, that psychology should give as much attention to the properties of the organism's environment as it does to the organism itself. His approach, which he called "probabilistic functionalism," was the first behavioral system founded on probabilism (the belief that certainty is impossible, and that therefore decisions must be based on probabilities). Brunswik asserted that the environment in which we live can never be certain, however much we try to make it so. The best we can do is to adapt by employing probabilistic means to achieve goals and learn to use what is probabilistic and uncertain evidence about the world.

Brunswik's theory has been used in decision-making, thinking, perception, communication and the study of curiosity. Brunswik wrote a great deal about the history of psychology, not in creating masses of data — names, dates, and places — but how psychology developed, the kinds of variables that have traditionally been employed in psychological theory and research, and a description of the changes in the emphasis of these variables over time.

His main field of empirical research was perception, but he also brought his probabilistic approach to bear on problems of interpersonal perception, thinking, learning, and clinical psychology. His research findings were published in *Perception and the Representative Design of Experiments* (Berkeley: University of California Press, 1947), which also includes Brunswik's methodological innovations and related research by others.

Major Literature

Brunswik, Egon. *The Conceptual Framework of Psychology (International Encyclopedia of Unified Science*, Vol. 1, No. 10). Chicago, Illinois: University of Chicago Press, 1952.
___. *Conceptual Framework of Psychology*. Chicago, Illinois: University of Chicago Press, 1979.
___. *The Essential Brunswick: Beginnings, Explications, Applications*. New York: Oxford University Press, Inc., 2001.

Bryan, William Lowe (1860–1955)
LEARNING AND
EXPERIMENTAL PSYCHOLOGY

Born William Julian Bryan on a farm near Bloomington, Indiana, the son of a Presbyterian minister, he graduated with a B.A. from Indiana University in 1884. Upon graduation Bryan was appointed as assistant instructor of Greek and in the latter part of 1884–1885 he taught English as well. In 1885–1886, he was appointed assistant professor of philosophy and acting instructor of English. In 1886–1887 he was associate professor of philosophy on leave of absence for study in Berlin.

In June 1887, the recommendation that Bryan be made professor of philosophy and instructor in elocution was approved. Bryan earned a master's degree in philosophy at Indiana in 1886 with a thesis on ancient Greek logic. He became interested in psychology and spent the year 1886-1887 studying psychology at the University of Berlin and was promoted full professor on his return to Indiana. In January 1888 Bryan opened the Indiana University Psychological Laboratory, the second such facility established in the United States.

Bryan married Charlotte Augusta Lowe, a Greek scholar, in 1889 and in her honor replaced his given middle name with her last name. They collaborated on writing two books on Plato. Bryan received his Ph.D. in psychology in 1892 from Clark University, Worcester, Massachusetts, for a dissertation on the development of voluntary motor abilities in children. He helped organize the American Psychological Association, founded in July 1892, and became one of its twenty-six charter members. He served as an officer in several national organizations, including as secretary of the National Association for the Study of Children (1893) and president of the Child-Study Section of the National Educational Association (1894).

Bryan was vice-president of Indiana University from 1893 to 1902, and tenth president until 1937, when he retired as president emeritus. He was elected president of the American Psychological Association in 1903.

Major Contributions

In the 1890s Bryan conducted pioneering psychological experiments investigating what process of learning is necessary to send and receive messages in Morse code on the telegraph. His identification of the "learning curve" became a classic in the study of human learning. It was through Bryan's efforts that Indiana University became an undergraduate training ground for notable future psychologists such as Lewis M. Terman (see entry). Possibly Bryan's major contribution was the transformation of Indiana University from a small, traditional liberal arts college into a modern research university. During his administration, schools of medicine, education, nursing, business, music, and dentistry were established, along with many graduate programs and several satellite campuses around Indiana.

The institution he developed commemorated his work with many memorials, including the William Lowe Bryan Hall, the main administration building at Indiana University, and Bloomington named its large municipal commons Bryan Park.

Bucke, Richard Maurice (1837–1902)
STAGES OF CONSCIOUSNESS

Richard Maurice Bucke was born in Methwold, Norfolk, England, son of the Reverend Horatio Walpole Bucke, a descendant of Robert Walpole,

Earl of Orford (1676–1745) and British prime minister. The family immigrated to Canada in 1838 and settled near London, Ontario. Between 1843 and 1858 Bucke worked as a laborer, joined a covered wagon train, prospected for gold, and lost all of one foot and part of the other through frostbite. He qualified as a doctor at McGill College (now University) at Montreal in 1862.

From 1863 to 1876 he practiced medicine in Sarnia, Ontario, then for almost the rest of his life superintended the Asylum for the Insane in London, Ontario. Bucke and the American poet Walt Whitman (1819–1892) formed a deep friendship until Whitman died, and in 1883 Bucke published the authorized biography of Walt Whitman. Bucke was one of the founders of the University of Western Ontario Medical school. He was elected a charter member of the Royal Society of Canada in 1882, and appointed first professor of nervous and mental diseases at Western University of London, Ontario. In 1897 he became president of the British Medical Association's psychological section. The following year was elected president of the American Medico-Psychological Association.

Major Contributions

Bucke introduced new ideas into how mentally ill patients were looked after. He abandoned the medicinal use of alcohol, discontinued most forms of physical restraint and initiated an open-door policy allowing the majority of patients free access to the hospital grounds. His lifelong interest in philosophy found expression in his book *Man's Moral Nature* (1879), which put forward two arguments: that human beings possess an innate moral sense located in the sympathetic nervous system, a part of the autonomic nervous system; and that this innate moral sense was increasing. Fewer than 300 copies were sold, but this was the first Canadian monograph on neuropsychiatry.

His most significant publication was *Cosmic Consciousness*. At one level it was an attempt to grapple with an emerging awareness of the unconscious mind. Bucke believed in three types of human consciousness: simple self-awareness, moral consciousness, and a third profoundly deep consciousness that he called "cosmic consciousness." The book (still in print) is composed of case studies of some 50 famous men who were said to have possessed the faculty, including Walt Whitman. A Canadian film about the lives of Bucke and Whitman, *Beautiful Dreamers,* was released in 1990, with the tag line: "The World Changes Some People. Some People Change the World."

Major Literature

Bucke, Richard Maurice. *Walt Whitman's Autograph Revision of the Analysis of "Leaves of Grass."* New York University Press, 1974.
___, and Artem Lozynsky. *Bucke, Richard Maurice, Medical Mystic: Letters of Dr. Bucke to Walt Whitman and His Friends.* Detroit, Michigan: Wayne State University Press, 1977.
___. *Cosmic Consciousness: A Study in the Evolution of the Human Mind.* Cambridge, Massachusetts: Applewood Books, 2001.
___. *From Self to Cosmic Consciousness.* Whitefish, Montana: R.A. Kessinger Publishing Co., 2005.

Bühler, Charlotte Malachowski (1893–1974)

LIFE SPAN DEVELOPMENT

Born Malachowski in Berlin, Germany, Charlotte Malachowski Bühler gained her B.S. degree from the University of Berlin in 1915 and completed her Ph.D. in 1918 at the University of Munich. In 1916 she married Karl Bühler (see entry), who was her supervisor at Munich. The couple moved to Vienna in 1923; Karl to the chair of the University of Vienna and Charlotte to the newly founded Psychological Institute, first as lecturer and then in 1929 as associate professor. In 1923 Bühler was awarded a Rockefeller Exchange fellowship to study child and youth psychology with Edward Lee Thorndike (see entry) at Columbia University, New York City. The Rockefeller Foundation awarded her a ten-year grant to continue her research in Vienna into adolescent thought processes through her innovative life biography approach — the therapeutic use of diaries.

In 1929 she returned to the United States as a guest professor of psychology for a year at Barnard College, New York. She had consulting and supervisory responsibilities at child guidance centers in England, Holland and Norway. When the Nazis invaded Austria (1938) they closed the Vienna Psychological Institute and destroyed all of Bühler's research records. Karl was imprisoned; Charlotte, who was in England, negotiated his release, and via Norway, the couple immigrated to the U.S. and settled in Los Angeles. She worked as a psychotherapist until 1972 and as chief clinical psychologist at the Los Angeles County Hospital, then as clinical professor of psychiatry at the University of Southern California School of Medicine. She died in Stuttgart, West Germany.

Major Contributions

With Abraham Maslow, Carl Rogers, and Viktor Frankl (see entries), who were concerned at the deficiencies in behaviorism and psychoanalysis, Bühler organized the Old Saybrook Conference in 1964. This led to the establishment of the Association for Humanistic Psychology, of which she was president from 1965 to 1966. She also presided over the First International Conference on Humanistic Psychology in Amsterdam in 1970. Bühler's major thesis is that people develop through their life span. She considered that developmental (maturational) age is much more significant psychologically than "mental age" or "intelligence quotient."

She included children in her theories, influenced by her earlier work with the diaries of 135 adolescents, in which many of them questioned what they are here for and what their purpose in life is. According to Bühler, fulfillment results from living constructively and thoughtfully, in ways consistent with the person's best gifts (this includes profiting from misfortune).

Major Literature

Bühler, Charlotte, and H. Hetzer. *The First Year of Life.* New York: John Day, 1930.
___. "The Social Behavior of Children." In C. Murchison (Ed.), *Handbook of Child Psychology* (2nd ed.). Worcester: Clark University Press, 1931, 374–416.
___. *From Birth to Maturity.* London: Kegan Paul, Trench, and Trubner, 1935.
___. *The Child and His Family.* Westport, Connecticut: Greenwood Press, 1972 (translated by H. Beaumont).
___, and Melanie Allen. *Introduction to Humanistic Psychology.* Pacific Grove, California: Brooks/Cole Publishing Company, 1973.

Bühler, Karl (1879–1963)
THOUGHT PROCESS

Born in Meckesheim, Heidelberg, Germany, Bühler qualified as a medical doctor from Frieburg, Germany (1903), and Ph.D. in philosophy from the University of Strasbourg (1904). He worked in the Institute for Psychology in Berlin until he moved to Würzburg, Southern Germany, in 1906 to work with Oswald Külpe on thought processes. There he developed a method of asking subjects a series of questions that required explanation, and from those he elicited their thought processes, which closely resembles the current structured interview employed by some clinicians.

Bühler was appointed professor of psychology at the University of Bonn in 1909, where his interest in Gestalt theory developed. In 1913 he moved as professor of psychology to the University of Munich, where he married Charlotte Malachowski (see entry, Charlotte Malachowski Bühler). In 1918 he published what is considered the first comprehensive dissertation on child psychology and was appointed professor of psychology at Dresden. Then in 1923 the he was appointed professor of psychology at the University of Vienna, and with Charlotte he developed the Department of Psychology into one of the leading centers for research into child psychology.

Buhler spent 1927–1928 in the U.S. as a visiting professor at Stanford, John Hopkins, Harvard and Chicago. He was offered a post at Harvard, which he declined.

Major Contributions

Karl Bühler's three main interests of research are language, developmental psychology and Gestalt theory. He taught the Austrian-British philosopher Karl Popper (1902–1994) at the University of Vienna. Bühler's work distinguished three aspects of psychological activity: instinct, training and intellect. These three develop separately and are not reducible one to another. Buhler was disappointed with the way American behaviorism was heading and was drawn to a more holistic approach to the study of personality, no doubt influenced by his increasing interest in Gestalt.

In his 1927 book, *The Crisis in Psychology*, he points to the disunity that exists in psychology methods, and at the same time seeks to reconcile the differences by acknowledging that each has a contribution to make. In the early 1930s Buhler turned to linguistics and applied Gestalt principles to linguistics. *The Theory of Language* was published in 1934. Buhler never achieved the same sort of fame in America that he enjoyed in Germany.

Major Literature

Buhler, Karl. *Theory of Language: The Representational Function of Language (Foundations of Semiotics).* Philadelphia, Pennsylvania: John Benjamins Publishing Company, 1990. (Translated by Donald Fraser Goodwin.)
___. *Mental Development of the Child: A Summary of Modern Psychological Theory.* London, England: Taylor and Francis Books Ltd., Routledge, 1999.

Related Literature

Eschbach, Achim (Ed.). *Karl Büehler's Theory of Language: Proceedings of the Conference Held at Kirchberg, August 26, 1984 and Essen, November 21–24, 1984.* (Viennese Heritage). Philadelphia, Pennsylvania: John Benjamins Publishing Company, 1987.

Burt, Sir Cyril Ludowic (1883–1971)

EDUCATIONAL PSYCHOLOGY

Born in Stratford-Upon-Avon, Warwickshire, England, Cyril Ludowic Burt earned a B.A. in 1907, teacher's diploma in 1908, an M.A. in 1909, and a D.Sc. in 1923 at Oxford University, England. He studied psychology under Oswald Külpe, University of Würzburg, Germany. He was lecturer in experimental psychology, University of Liverpool (1908–1913); chief psychologist, London County Council (1913–1932); professor of educational psychology, London Day Training Centre (1924–1932); and Charles Spearman chair of Psychology, University College, London (1932–1950).

He received an honorary LL.D. at the University of Aberdeen, Scotland (1939), and an honorary D.Litt. at the University of Reading, England (1948). Burt was the first psychologist to be knighted (1946) and the first British subject to win the American Thorndike Prize (1971). He was editor and co-editor of the *British Journal of Statistical Psychology* from 1947 to 1963 and president of British Psychological Society in 1942. He published more than 200 articles after his retirement from teaching.

Major Contributions

- Founded educational psychology in Great Britain by creating and implementing a system for identifying mentally retarded students.
- Founded child and vocational guidance services.
- Helped to establish the Eleven-Plus testing program in Great Britain.
- Helped to expand the statistical technique of factor analysis.
- Investigated differences in intelligence among social classes, gender and race.
- Traced family offenders' trees to examine the possibility of a genetic influence.
- Studied the effects of poverty and environment on development and on behavior.
- Published nine books and more than three hundred articles, lectures and book chapters.

Soon after he died, two American psychologists — Leon J. Kamin and Arthur Jensen (see entries) — found fault with Burt's research on identical twins who were reared apart. Dr. Oliver Gillie, the medical correspondent to the *London Sunday Times*, on October 24, 1976, publicly challenged Burt's findings. Gillie accused Burt of sci-entific fraud and of fabricating data to prove that intelligence was inherited; he charged that two of his collaborators were fictitious. Hans Eysenck (see entry), in defense of Burt, attributed the errors to carelessness. Others claimed to have known at least one of the "fictitious" collaborators. Leslie Hearnshaw, Burt's biographer, concluded from a close examination of Burt's papers that the accusations were true. However, the "Burt affair" debate still rumbles on, emphasizing the importance of intellectual honesty in research.

Major Literature

Burt, Cyril Ludowic. *The Young Delinquent*. London: University of London Press, 1925, 1974.
___. *The Subnormal Mind*. London, England: Oxford University Press, 1935, 1977.
___. *The Causes and Treatments of Backwardness* (4th ed.). London: University of London Press, 1957.
___. *The Gifted Child*. New Jersey: John Wiley and Sons, Inc., 1975.
___. *Mental and Scholastic Tests* (4th ed.). London, England: Staples Press, Ltd., 1962.

Related Literature

Hearnshaw, L. *Cyril Burt: Psychologist*. Ithaca, New York: Cornell University Press, 1979.
Joynson, R.B. *The Burt Affair*. New York: Taylor and Francis Books Ltd., Routledge, 1989.
Mackintosh, N.J. (Ed.). *Cyril Burt: Fraud or Framed?* Oxford University Press, 1995.

Buxbaum, Edith (1902–1982)

CHILD DEVELOPMENT

Born in Vienna, Edith Buxbaum was going to lectures on psychoanalysis and had read Sigmund Freud's (see entry) *Interpretation of Dreams* (1900) before she was 14 years old. She earned a Ph.D. at the University of Vienna and taught high school history in Vienna. From her salary she paid to undergo and study psychoanalysis with Anna Freud (see entry), and was a member of Anna Freud's first seminar on child analysis in 1927.

She fled Austria in 1937 for New York, her escape being made possible by the director of New York's Bank Street Cooperative for Teachers, who created a fake job for her and provided her with a U.S. visa. He mother and her future husband, the Viennese lawyer Fritz Schmidl (1897–1969), fled Vienna in 1938 and joined her in America. Her father had died years earlier. Bruno Bettelheim (see entry) was her cousin and lived with the family for a while.

Buxbaum worked as an analyst in Manhattan and taught for the New York Psychoanalytic

Institute and at the New School for Social Research. She ran into difficulties in New York because she was not medically qualified, and lay analysts were not welcome, so she and Fritz moved to Seattle in 1947. Buxbaum died of ovarian cancer and her ashes are interred at Evergreen-Washelli Cemetery, Seattle.

Major Contributions

Buxbaum put Seattle on the psychoanalytic map. She helped build the Seattle Psychoanalytic Institute (founded in 1946) and became the Seattle Institute's Child Analysis Division head, as well as clinical professor of psychiatry at the University of Washington. She helped found and direct a school for disturbed children at the Northwest Clinic for Neurology and Psychiatry. In 1969, she helped found Project P for the prevention of difficulties between parents and infants. Seattle became a satellite of Anna Freud's Hampstead Clinic in England. She was a leading psychoanalyst in Seattle for more than 30 years, and made her mark as a child psychoanalyst.

In 1954 Buxbaum noted that in treating the child, some parents react with apprehension, jealousy and feelings of guilt. When this happens then the amount of time spent with the parents needs to be increased. She was devoted to children and had a burning desire to improve the quality of their lives by emphasizing the child's individuality and creativity. She advocated that parents listen more, discipline less and provide a nuclear family with the mother preferably at home.

Major Literature

Buxbaum, Edith. "Review of Adult Attitudes to Children's Misdemeanors." *Psychoanalytic Quarterly* 8 (1939): 546–547.
___. "The Role of Detective Stories in a Child Analysis." *Psychoanalytic Quarterly* 10 (1941): 373–381.
___. *Your Child Makes Sense: A Guidebook for Parents.* London, England: George Allen and Unwin, 1951. New York: International Universities Press Inc., 1998.
___. "Techniques of Child Therapy: A Critical Evaluation." *Psychoanalytic Study of the Child* 9 (1954): 297.
___. *Troubled Children in a Troubled World.* New York: International Universities Press, Inc., 1970.

Cade, John Frederick Joseph (1912–1980)
BIPOLAR DISORDER

Born in Murtoa, Horsham, Victoria, Australia, the son of a doctor, John Frederick Joseph Cade graduated with M.B. and B.S. degrees in 1934 and an M.D. in 1938 from the University of Melbourne. He was resident medical officer St. Vincent's Hospital, Melbourne, in 1935 and at the Royal Children's Hospital there in 1936. In 1936 he joined the mental hygiene branch of the Department of the Chief Secretary and was appointed medical officer at Mont Park Mental Hospital, Melbourne.

He joined the Australian Army Medical Corps in 1940 (Australian Imperial Force, A.I.F.), arrived in Singapore in February 1941, and from February 1942 to September 1945 he was a prisoner of war in Changi camp on the east coast of Singapore. Demobilized in January 1946, Cade returned to the mental hygiene branch, now in the Department of Health, becoming medical superintendent and psychiatrist at the Repatriation Mental Hospital, Bundoora, a suburb of Melbourne.

In 1952 he was appointed psychiatrist superintendent and dean of the clinical school at Royal Park Psychiatric Hospital, Melbourne. He was a founding fellow of the Royal Australian and New Zealand College of Psychiatrists and a member (1970–80) of the Medical Board of Victoria. In 1970 he received the psychiatric award of the Taylor Manor Hospital in Maryland and was made a distinguished fellow of the American Psychiatric Association. In 1974 he shared the second international award of the Kittay Scientific Foundation in New York with Danish professor Mogens Schou, whose large clinical trials had validated Cade's research. Appointed to the Order of Australia in 1976, he retired from his hospital appointments in 1977.

Major Contributions

Following a visit to Britain in 1954, Cade introduced modern facilities and replaced the authoritarian approach to patient care with a more personal and informal style that included group therapy. Concerned at the number of alcohol-related cases, he supported voluntary admission to aid early detection and later proposed the use of large doses of thiamin in the treatment of alcoholism.

The work for which he is most famous is the introduction of lithium carbonate for the treatment of mania. His discovery of the efficacy of a cheap, naturally occurring and widely available element in dealing with bi-polar affective disorders (formerly manic depression) provided an alternative to the existing therapies of shock treatment or prolonged hospitalization.

The John Cade award was inaugurated in 1982

by the Victorian branch of the Royal Australian and New Zealand College of Psychiatrists. In 1983 the faculty of medicine at the University of Melbourne established the John Cade memorial prize. In 1985 the American National Institute of Mental Health estimated that Cade's discovery of the efficacy of lithium in the treatment of manic depression had saved the world at least $17.5 billion in medical costs.

Major Literature

Cade, J.F. "Lithium Salts in the Treatment of Psychotic Excitement." *Medical Journal of Australia* 2 (1949): 349–352.

Calkins, Mary Whiton (1863–1930)

SELF-PSYCHOLOGY

Mary Kalkins was born in Hartford, Connecticut, the daughter of a Presbyterian minister. In 1880 the family moved to Newton, Massachusetts, where she lived the rest of her life. She graduated with a double major in the classics and philosophy from Smith College, Northampton, Massachusetts, having had a break for a year when her sister died. After a spell in Europe, in 1887 she became a tutor in Greek at Wellesley College, Massachusetts, where she remained until 1890. Harvard University in Cambridge, Massachusetts, did not accept women in psychology courses, and although she satisfied several eminent psychologists with her thesis, "An Experimental Research on the Association of Ideas," Harvard would still not accept it as evidence of a Ph.D.

From 1895 Calkins was an associate professor of psychology and philosophy at Wellesley, and in 1898 she became a full professor, a position she held until she retired in 1927. Based on research, she wrote hundreds of papers divided between psychology and philosophy. She founded the psychology department at Wellesley College, and was the first female president of the American Psychological Association (1905) and the American Philosophical Association (1918). Columbia University, New York, bestowed a doctor of letters degree on her in 1909, and Smith College a doctor of laws degree in 1910. In spite of all her recognition, Harvard still did not award her a Ph.D. She retired in 1929 and died one year later of inoperable cancer.

Major Contributions

In her research Calkins originated a technical method for studying memory, later referred to as the method of paired associates. G.E. Müller (see entry) refined the technique, and later Edward B. Titchener (see entry) included it in his *Student's Manual*, taking full credit for himself.

Possibly as a result of constant refusal by Harvard, after 1900, Calkins developed and advocated a self-based psychology, even as behavioral psychology began to dominate the field. She considered self-psychology to be as useful as Freud's psychoanalysis. Her work in this field dealt primarily with such topics as space and time consciousness, emotion, association, color theory and dreams. Her theory held, in contrast to behaviorist views, that the conscious self is the central fact of psychology. Not surprisingly, in view of the discrimination she experienced, Calkins was a supporter of equality and the franchise for women.

Major Literature

Calkins, Mary Whiton. *An Introduction to Psychology.* New York: Macmillan, 1901.
___. *The Persistent Problems of Philosophy: An Introduction to Metaphysics.* New York: Macmillan, 1907. Whitefish, Montana: R.A. Kessinger Publishing Co., 2005.
___. *The Good Man and the Good: An Introduction to Ethics.* New York: Macmillan, 1918.
___ (Ed.). *Metaphysical System of Hobbes.* Chicago, Illinois: Open Court Publishing Co., 1977.

Campbell, Donald Thomas (1916–1996)

EVOLUTIONARY EPISTEMOLOGY

Born at Grass Lake, Michigan, Donald Thomas Campbell gained an A.B. degree at the University of California Berkeley (1939), then served in Naval Reserve during World War II. He gained a Ph.D. at the University of California Berkeley in 1947. From 1953 to 1979 he was on the faculty of Northwestern University, Evanston, Illinois, and from 1979 to 1982, the faculty of Maxwell School at Syracuse University, New York.

In 1970 he received the Distinguished Scientific Contribution Award, National Academy of Sciences. He became a member of the American Psychological Association (APA) in 1973 and served as president in 1975. Campbell received the Kurt Lewin Memorial Award, APA (1974); the Myrdal Prize in Science, Society for the Psychological Study of Social Issues (1977) and delivered the William James Lecture at Harvard University, Cambridge, Massachusetts (1977). In 1981 he received the Distinguished Contributions to Research in Education, Evaluation Research Society Award. In his lifetime was awarded honorary doctorates from six universities. He was also on the faculties at Ohio State University, Athens, and the University of Chicago, Northwestern University, Evanston, Illinois.

Major Contributions

Campbell was a pioneering social psychologist in social science methodology, evaluation research, and the application of social science to the understanding of and solutions to of a wide variety of social issues. Campbell specialized in research methodology. One of his best selling and most cited publications was *Experimental and Quasi-Experimental Designs for Research* (Houghton Mifflin, 1966), co-authored by the statistician Julian Stanley.

His major focus throughout his career was the study of false knowledge — the biases and prejudices that poison everything from race relations to academic disciplines where those with vested interests in them perpetuate erroneous theories. He was the founder of "evolutionary epistemology" (a label he created), the attempt to explain animal and human cognition, including science, in a Darwinian fashion. It aims to explain how our eyes, brains, inference structures, and the like have evolved by natural selection.

Campbell made contributions in a wide range of disciplines like psychology, sociology, anthropology, biology and philosophy, as witnessed in that he was emeritus professor of sociology, anthropology, psychology and education at the Department of Psychology and Social Relations, Lehigh University, Bethlehem, Pennsylvania, from 1983 until he died.

Major Literature

Campbell, Donald Thomas, and D.W. Fiske. "Convergent and Discriminant Validation by the Multitrait-Multimethod Matrix." *Psychological Bulletin* 56 (2) (1959): 81–105.

Levine, Robert A., and Donald Thomas Campbell. *Ethnocentrism: Theories of Conflict, Ethnic Attitudes, and Group Behavior*. New Jersey: John Wiley and Sons Inc., 1972.

Campbell, Donald Thomas. "Evolutionary Epistemology." In *The Philosophy of Karl R. Popper*, 412–463. P.A. Schilpp (Ed.). Chicago, Illinois: Open Court, 1974.

___. "Levels of Organization, Downward Causation, and the Selection-theory Approach to Evolutionary Epistemology." In G. Greenberg and E. Tobach (Eds.), *Theories of the Evolution of Knowing*, pp. 1–17. Mahwah, New Jersey: Lawrence Erlbaum Associates, Inc., 1990.

___. "How Individual and Face-to-face Group Selection Undermine Firm Selection in Organizational Evolution." In J.A.C. Baum and J.V. Singh (Eds.), *Evolutionary Dynamics of Organizations*, pp. 23–38. New York: Oxford University Press, 1994.

Carmichael, Leonard (1898–1973)
Military Psychology

Born in Philadelphia, Pennsylvania, Leonard Carmichael gained a B.S. from Tufts University, Medford, Massachusetts, in 1920, was named to Theta Delta Chi fraternity in 1921, and earned a Ph.D. in psychology at Harvard University, Cambridge, Massachusetts, in 1924. His professorships include Princeton University, New Jersey (1924–1926), Brown University, Providence, Rhode Island (1926–1936), and the University of Rochester, New York (1936–1938).

He was administrator and president, Tufts University, 1938–1952. Carmichael was president of the American Psychological Association (1940); Army Scientific Advisory Panel and Naval Research Advisory Committee (1947–1952); chairman, American Council of Education (1947–1953); chief executive of the Smithsonian Institution, Washington, D.C. (1953–1964); vice-chairman, Harvard Foundation for Advanced Study and Research, National Advisory Committee for Aeronautics (1956–1958); president of the American Philosophical Society (1970–1973); and vice president for research and exploration, National Geographic Society (1964). Carmichael received twenty-three honorary degrees and presidential citations from presidents Truman and Eisenhower.

Major Contributions

Carmichael's most significant contributions were made in the field of child psychology with a special emphasis on the importance of genetic determinants of behavior. In 1935, with Herbert Henri Jasper (1906–1999) at the Department of Neurology and Neurosurgery, McGill University, Montreal, Quebec, Carmichael reported the first electroencephalogram (EEG) carried out in America, measuring abnormalities in the electrical activity of the brain.

He also developed a machine for the electrical recording of eye movements of animals, which led to research into reading and visual fatigue. As administrator at Tufts he guided the university's activities through the World War II period, when he headed the National Roster of Scientific and Specialized Personnel, which recruited scientists and engineers for the war. Carmichael's name was linked to Project MKULTRA, the code name for a CIA mind-control research program that began in the 1950s and continued until the late 1960s. A project involved not only the use of drugs to manipulate people, but also the use of electronic signals to alter brain functioning.

During his time with the National Geographic Society, it sponsored ground-breaking research, including the British palaeoanthropologist Louis S.B. Leakey's studies in East Africa, Jane Goodall's work on primate behavior, and the underwater explorations of Jacques-Yves Cousteau. The Carmichael Auditorium at the National Museum of History and Technology at the Smithsonian Institution was dedicated in his name in 1974. The Leonard Carmichael Society at Tufts University was started in 1958 and originally consisted of a group of students who would make regular visits to a nearby mental hospital. It now consists of over 1,500 volunteers, with 36 programs to help disadvantaged people.

Major Literature

Carmichael, Leonard. "Heredity and Environment: Are They Antithetical?" *Journal of Abnormal Psychology* 20 (1925): 245–260.
___. "Electrical Potentials from the Intact Human Brain." *Science* 89 (1935): 51–52 (with H.H. Jasper).
___. *Reading and Visual Fatigue.* Westport, Connecticut: Greenwood Press, 1972.
___, and P.H. Mussen. (Eds.). *Handbook of Child Psychology.* Vol. 1, *Theoretical Models.* Vol. 2, *Infancy and Developmental Psychobiology.* Vol. 3, *Cognitive Development.* Vol. 4, *Socialization, Personality and Social Development.* New Jersey: John Wiley and Sons Inc., 1983.

Carpenter, Clarence Ray (1905–1975)

ANIMAL BEHAVIOR

Born in Lincoln County, North Carolina, Clarence Ray Carpenter gained a B.A. (1928) and an M.A. (1929) from Duke University in Durham, North Carolina. He earned his Ph.D. (1932) from Stanford University, California. In 1932 he did a field study on howler monkeys at Barro Colorado Island, Panama. He was assistant professor and lecturer at Bard College, Columbia University (1934), and a member of the Asiatic Primate Expedition (1937). He was with the College of Physicians and Surgeons and School of Tropical Medicine in Puerto Rico, planning and develop-

ing the Cayo Santiago Rhesus Colony, in 1938. From 1940 to 1970 he was at Pennsylvania State College, Lewistown, Pennsylvania.

In 1963 he was a member of a team sponsored by the Ford Foundation to study the communication systems of India. He was visiting scientist under the auspices of the U.S.-Japan Cooperative Science Program and the Japan Science Council in 1964. Carpenter retired as research professor emeritus of psychology and anthropology at the University of Georgia, Athens. He also held a visiting research post at the East-West Communication Institute in Honolulu (1970).

Major Contributions

During World War II Carpenter served as a technical advisor in the production of Army training films. After the war he conducted extensive research on learning through instructional films. His first article concerning primate behavior appeared in 1934, and he went on to write over 40 professional journal articles, books, book chapters and special publications dealing with primates. He was also active concerning employment discrimination based on race, color, religion, sex or national origin, and he worked continuously in some relationship with the U.S. Office of Education from 1958 until his death in Athens, Georgia.

Carpenter noted that human behavior is similar to animal behavior, and that the two should be studied simultaneously. Over a thirty year period almost all of the accurate information available on the behavior of monkeys and apes living in natural environments was the result of Carpenter's research in different parts of the world and his writing. He was responsible for the production of primate films and videotapes, the establishment of Pennsylvania State University as a depository for the Psychological Cinema Register, and for developing an internationally known collection of psychological, psychiatric and animal behavior films. He was involved in planning Pennsylvania State University Medical School at Hershey and drafting plans for the Florida Atlantic University.

Major Literature

Carpenter, Clarence Ray. "A Field Study in Siam of the Behavior and Social Relations of the White-handed Gibbon (Hylobates Lar)." *Comparative Psychology Monographs* 84 (1940): 1–212.
___. *Naturalistic Behavior of Non Human Primates.* University Park, Pennsylvania: Pennsylvania State University Press, 1964.
___. *Field Study in Siam of the Behavior and Social Re-*

lations of the White-handed Gibbon (Hylobates Lar). New York: Ams Press Inc., 1985.

Related Literature

Robinson, Nancy K. *Jungle Laboratory: The Story of Ray Carpenter and the Howling Monkeys.* Winter Park, Florida: Hastings House/Day Trip Publisher, 1973.

Carr, Harvey A. (1873–1954)
FUNCTIONALISM

Born in Indiana, Harvey A. Carr graduated with a B.S. in psychology (1901) and an M.S. (1902) from the University of Colorado, Boulder. He gained his Ph.D. in experimental psychology (1905) from the University of Chicago, Illinois, where he studied with John Dewey, James Rowland Angell, and John B. Watson (see entries). His doctoral dissertation was on a visual illusion of motion during eye closure. From 1905 to 1908, unable to find a university placement, he taught high school in Texas and at the State Normal School in Michigan, then at the Pratt Institute in Brooklyn, New York.

In 1908 he replaced Watson at Chicago, where he remained until his retirement in 1938. In that time he served as chairman of the Department of Psychology at Chicago from 1919 to 1938. He was elected president of American Psychological Association in 1926, and in 1937, he was president of the Midwestern Psychological Association. He was advisory editor for the *Journal of Experimental Psychology* from 1916 to 1925 and associate editor of the *Journal of General Psychology* from 1929 to 1954. He also served for many years as general editor of the *Longman's Psychology Series.*

Major Contributions

Carr's functionalism (see Angell for a short explanation of structuralism and functionalism) differed from the classic stimulus-response behaviorism of Ivan Pavlov (see entry) and of J.B. Watson because he acknowledged that mental processes exist that do influence behavior. So far as Carr was concerned, functional psychology was *the* American psychology, over and above the others, such as Gestalt and psychoanalysis, which deal only with limited aspects of psychology.

For Carr, psychology was mental activity, which dealt with memory, perception, feeling, imagination, judgment, and will. The purpose of these mental activities is to determine specific action(s), a process he calls adaptive or "adjustive" behavior. Carr took charge of the animal laboratory at Chicago and continued Watson's study of the senses used by albino rats for getting through mazes. He discovered that vision was by far the most important sense to them. He went on to develop an improved maze, which was widely used for experiments with rats.

Space perception was another of Carr's contributions. Another contribution was in the field of learning, specifically memorization, perceptual-motor learning, and the conditions affecting how we acquire adaptive behaviors. Over his thirty years as professor at Chicago he supervised 29 theses on memorization, perceptual-motor learning, and the conditions affecting acquisition of adaptive behaviors.

Major Literature

Carr, Harvey A. *Psychology: A Study of Mental Activity.* New York: Longmans, Green, 1925.
___. "Functionalism." In C. Murchison (Ed.), *Psychologies of 1930.* Worcester, Massachusetts: Clark University Press, 1930, pp. 59–78.
___. *An Introduction to Space Perception.* New York: Longmans, Green, 1966. New York: Hafner, 1935.

Carterette, Edward Calvin Hayes (1921–1999)
AUDITORY PERCEPTION

Born in Mt. Tabor, North Carolina, Edward Calvin Hayes Carterette entered the U.S. Army as a private in 1937 and retired as a lieutenant colonel in 1946. He was a graduate of the U.S. Army Command and General Staff College and served in Hawaii, Japan and the Philippines. He graduated with an A.B. in mathematics from the University of Chicago (1949); A.B. in psychology from Harvard (1952); and an M.A. in experimental and mathematical psychology (see entry) (1954) and Ph.D. from Indiana University (1957).

Carterette spent his entire academic career at University of California, Los Angeles (UCLA), rising from instructor in the psychology department in 1956 to professor in 1968. He was appointed a member of the UCLA Brain Research Institute in 1974. From 1988, he also held the rank of adjunct professor of ethnomusicology and systematic musicology. He retired from UCLA as professor emeritus of cognitive psychology in 1991. He was a fellow of the American Psychological Association, American Psychological Society, the Acoustical Society of America, the Society of Experimental Psychologists, and the Society for Music Perception and Cognition.

Major Contributions

Carterette made important research contributions in the field of perception and cognition, particularly psychoacoustics, language, and the psychology of music. He continued his research on music until his death. He was the editor or author of 17 books and over 160 scholarly papers. Carterette focused his research on theoretical and experimental problems of hearing and speech perception. Many of his students went on to research in places such as NASA and the Bell Laboratories.

In addition to his scholarly work, Carterette also had an active career as a consultant on human factors to many commercial and educational institutions. Carterette (Ed, as he was commonly called) was active in the Harvard-Radcliffe Club of Southern California, serving as president from 1984 to 1986. (The Harvard-Radcliffe Club of Southern California is a non-profit with origins dating to 1901. It sponsors social, entertainment, and educational programs for its members throughout Southern California.)

Major Literature

Carterette, Edward Calvin Hayes. "Message Repetition and Receiver Confirmation of Messages in Noise." *Journal of the Acoustic Society of America* 30 (1958): 846–885.

___ (Ed.). *Brain Function.* Berkeley, California: University of California Press, 1967.

___, and Margaret H. Jones. *Informal Speech: Alphabetic and Phonemic Texts.* Berkeley, California: University of California Press, 1974.

___, and Morton P. Friedman (Eds.). *Handbook of Perception* [series of 10 books]. New York: Academic Press, 1974–1979. Vol. 1: *Historical and Philosophical Roots of Perception.* Vol. 2: *Physiological Judgement and Measurement.* Vol. 3: *Biology of Perceptual Systems.* Vol. 4: *Hearing.* Vol. 5: *Seeing.* Vol. 6: *Tasting and Smelling.* Vol. 7: *Language and Speech.* Vol. 8: *Perceptual Coding.* Vol. 9: *Perceptual Processing.* Vol. 10: *Perceptual Ecology.*

Carterette, Edward Calvin Hayes. "Communication of Musical Expression." *Music Perception* 2 (1990): 129–163 (with R. Kentall).

Cattell, James McKeen (1860–1944)

PSYCHOLOGICAL TESTING

James McKeen Cattell was born in 1860 in Easton, Pennsylvania. He gained his bachelor's degree from Lafayette College, Easton (1880). From 1883 to 1886 he was assistant to Wilhelm Wundt (see entry) at Leipzig University and gained a Ph.D. in 1886. He was professor of psychology, University of Pennsylvania, Philadelphia (1888–1891), the first professorship in psychology ever offered there. In 1891 he was appointed professor of psychology and head of the department at Columbia University, New York City. He became a member of American Psychological Association (APA), serving as secretary in 1894 and president in 1895.

With James Mark Baldwin (see entry) he founded *Psychological Review* (1897). In 1901 he was the first psychologist to be admitted to the National Academy of Sciences. He was president of the New York Academy of Sciences in 1902. In 1903 Baldwin bought Cattell out of *Psychological Review* and in 1915 Cattell established the weekly *School and Society.* He was president, American Association for the Advancement of Sciences (1924).

Major Contributions

At Leipzig, Cattell helped Wundt to establish the formal study of intelligence, and with Wundt's guidance, Cattell became the first American to publish a dissertation in the field of psychology, *Psychometric Investigation.* He aroused controversy by his use of hashish, morphine and caffeine to explore his mind. At Pennsylvania he established a laboratory and developed a series of mental measurement tests for college students. At Columbia University he devoted much of his career to the improvement and advancement of mental testing. He was dismissed from Columbia in 1917 when he publicly expressed criticism of the draft in World War I. Cattell was one of the American Psychological Association's founding members and the fourth president (1917). The James McKeen Cattell Fund was established by a gift from him in 1942; it provides support for the science and application of psychology.

Cattell's major contribution to psychology was the realization of the importance of, and subsequent implementation of, quantifiable methods and techniques, something that ultimately changed the course of the discipline. Cattell introduced the term "mental test" to the world in 1890.

His tests did not prove reliable so he abandoned this work and began work on administration, science editing, and publishing, and the development of a method for ranking according to merit. He compiled the *Biographical Directory of American Men of Science*, published by Bowker, New York, which he edited through the first six editions, then it changed to *American Men of Science.* In 1895 he purchased *Science* from Alexander Graham Bell, which in 1900 became official publication of the

American Association for the Advancement of Science. In 1897 Cattell founded *Psychological Review* with James Mark Baldwin, who bought Cattell out in 1903. Cattell purchased *Popular Science Monthly* in 1900.

Major Literature

Cattell, James McKeen. "The Psychological Laboratory at Leipzig." *Mind* 13 (1888): 37–51.
___. "Mental Tests and Measurements." *Mind* 15 (1890): 373–381.
___. *James McKeen Cattell, 1860–1944: Man of Science.* Manchester, New Hampshire: Ayer Co. Publishers, 1947.
___. *An Education in Psychology: Journals and Letters from Germany and England, 1880–88.* Cambridge, Massachusetts: MIT Press, 1981.

Cattell, Psyche (1893–1989)

MEASUREMENT OF INTELLIGENCE IN CHILDREN

The daughter of James McKeen Cattell (see entry), Psyche Cattell was born in Garrison, Putnam County, New York, and educated at home. Psyche suffered from dyslexia (word blindness), and because her father did not support her wish for a university education, she worked as a research assistant to pay her own tuition. She gained a diploma in physical education from Sargent School for Physical Education in New York; an M.A. (1925) from Cornell University, New York; and an Ed.M. (1925) and Ed.D. (1927) from Harvard, Cambridge, Massachusetts.

From 1922 to 1936 she worked as research assistant and research fellow at Harvard University, then Stanford University. From 1936 to 1938 she was instructor in mental testing at the Nursery Training School of Boston, Massachusetts. From 1939 to 1942 she was psychologist, Lebanon County Mental Health Clinic, Lebanon, Pennsylvania, and from 1939 to 1963, chief psychologist at the Guidance Clinic of Lancaster, Pennsylvania, where she worked with children who had emotional difficulties and school problems. She maintained a private practice from 1939 to 1972.

Although single, and against much opposition, she adopted a son in 1931, and in 1940, a daughter. Dr. Cattell died following a stroke.

Major Contributions

Cattell's book *The Measurement of Intelligence of Infants and Young Children* (The Psychological Corporation, New York, 1940) was the outcome of a study involving nearly three hundred babies at the Center for Research in Child Health and Development at Harvard. (The Psychological Corporation was formed by James McKeen Cattell in 1921 to develop psychological tests; it is now Harcourt Assessment, Inc., a part of Elsevier PLC.)

On realizing that existing tests needed improvement, Psyche Cattell began working on new tests in 1932 that would find ways for babies — 3 to 30 months — to show their abilities. One important use of the test was by the New York Psychological Corporation, which used them to test pre-adoptive children. Its success is evidenced by its continuing use. The Cattell Infant Intelligence Scale (a downward extension of the Stanford-Binet Scale) is quoted on page 2192 of *Comprehensive Textbook of Psychiatry* (6th edition, eds. H.J. Kaplan and B.J. Sadock, Williams and Wilkins, Baltimore, Maryland).

In 1941 she opened an early childhood school in her own home, which she ran until it closed in 1974. Its focus was on developing the children's intelligence rather than on day-care. In 1945, the name was officially changed to The Cattell School. In 1964, she started a twice-weekly column for the *Lancaster New Era* titled "Children Under Eight." The columns gave down to earth advice on early childhood rearing, such as how to handle a toddler's jealousy of a new baby in a family.

In her last book, *Raising Children with Love and Limits* (Chicago, Nelson-Hall Co., 1972), Cattell asserted that while she couldn't prevent the minor childhood catastrophes that happen to almost all parents, she could offer workable solutions. Her view was that love and limits have to be combined; either by itself is not enough.

Cattell, Raymond Bernard (1905–1998)

PERSONALITY THEORIST

Born in Hill Top, Staffordshire, England, Raymond Bernard Cattell gained a B.Sc. with first-class honors in chemistry (1924), a Ph.D. in psychology (1929) and a D.Sc. (1939) from University of London. From 1927 to 1932 he was a lecturer in psychology, University of Exeter, England, then became advisory psychologist at the Dartington Hall progressive school (1932–1937). Cattell was also director of the Child Guidance Clinic, Leicester, England. In 1937 Cattell was research associate to Edward L. Thorndike (see entry), Columbia University, New York City, and G. Stanly

Hall Professor of Genetic Psychology, Clark University, Worcester, Massachusetts (1938–1941).

He was also lecturer, Harvard University, Cambridge, Massachusetts (1941–1943), and research professor of psychology, University of Illinois in Urbana, where he founded the Laboratory of Personality Assessment and Group Behavior (1945). Cattell was first president of the Society for Multivariate Experimental Psychology (1960 and 1961). He was professor emeritus, School of Professional Psychology, University of Illinois (1974); director, Institute for Research on Morality and Adjustment, Boulder, Colorado (1974–1978); and professor and advisor at the University of Hawaii (1978), where he taught at the Hawaii School of Professional Psychology, now the American School of Professional Psychology.

His many awards include the Lifetime Contribution Award from Division 5 of the American Psychological Association (1997) and honorary doctorates from the Hawaii School of Professional Psychology (1986) and the Forest Institute of Professional Psychology (1987).

Major Contributions

Raymond Cattell achieved distinction as a trait psychologist. Traits such as sociability, impulsiveness, meticulousness, truthfulness, and deceit are assumed to be more or less stable over time and across situations. He suggested that general ability can be subdivided into two: *fluid abilities*— reasoning and problem-solving abilities; and *crystallized abilities*—derived from fluid abilities and including vocabulary, general information, and knowledge about specific fields. From data collected over several decades he created the Sixteen Personality Factor Questionnaire (16 PF, for short). Hans Eysenck (see entry) referred to Cattell as one of the most influential and original psychologists working in the field of individual differences in intelligence and personality, in psychometrics and in behavior genetics.

Cattell was a prolific researcher and writer who contributed much to the development of a scientific psychology. He ranks among the 20th century's most influential behavioral scientists. In 1997, Cattell was nominated to receive the American Psychological Foundation Gold Medal Award for Lifetime Achievement in Psychological Science. However, following media publicity over his alleged racism in some of his writings — claims he refuted — he declined. He died in Honolulu.

Major Literature

Cattell, Raymond Bernard. *Scientific Analysis of Personality.* New York: Penguin Group (USA), Inc., 1970.
___. *Factor Analysis: An Introduction and Manual for the Psychologist and Social Scientist.* London: Greenwood Press, 1973.
___. *Personality and Learning Theory: 002.* New York; Springer Publishing Co., 1980.
___. *Structured Personality Learning Theory.* New York: Praeger, 1983.
___. *Functional Psychological Testing: Principles and Instruments.* London: Brunner-Routledge, Taylor and Francis Group, 1986.
___. *Psychotherapy by Structured Learning Theory.* New York: Springer Publishing Co., 1987.

Cerletti, Ugo (1877–1963)
ELECTRIC SHOCK THERAPY

Born in Conegliano, Italy, Ugo Cerletti studied medicine in Rome and Turin, specializing in neurology and neuropsychiatry. He was head of the Neurobiological Institute at the Mental Institute of Milan, Italy (1919–1924), and took a lecturing post in neuropsychiatry in Bari, Italy (1924). In 1928 he was appointed chair of the Department of Mental and Neurological Diseases, University of Rome, where he developed electroconvulsive shock for the treatment of several kinds of mental disorder, a discovery that made him world-famous. He also did some important research into blood and brain histology.

Major Contributions

Shock therapy has its roots in ancient history, when electric eels were used to treat headaches and mental illness. The treatment of schizophrenia by convulsions, originally induced by the injection of camphor, was reported in 1935 by the psychiatrist Ladislaus Joseph von Meduna in Budapest. Electric shock was revived in 1938 when Ugo Cerletti, in collaboration with Lucio Bini, first used electroconvulsive therapy (ECT) on a patient diagnosed as schizophrenic with delusions, hallucinations and confusion. After twelve treatments the patient was able to return to work, declaring himself to be enthusiastic about the treatment.

ECT was used as a way of producing convulsions, which it was hoped would alleviate psychosis. It was used mainly in schizophrenia and manic-depressive psychosis. Subsequently, it has proved of more use in depression than in schizophrenia. The technique is essentially that of passing alternating current through the head between two electrodes placed over the temples. The passage of the current causes an immediate cessation of consciousness and the induction of a convulsive seizure, akin to a *grand-mal* epileptic fit.

In general, electroconvulsive treatments are given three times a week for a period ranging from two to six weeks. In the early days of the treatment, "straight" ECT was used. Later this was replaced with a modified form, where the patient is sedated and given a muscle relaxant to reduce risk of damage to limbs. Following a course of treatment there is usually an impairment of memory, varying from a slight tendency to forget names to severe confusion. The memory defect diminishes gradually over several months.

Electroconvulsive therapy, as with several other shock-like therapies, declined in use after the tranquilizing drugs were introduced, although it is still used. In the late 1930s and 1940s, ECT took off. During World War II interest in the treatment increased, and it was used in military psychiatric hospitals. There has been fierce debate about the treatment, and it is banned in some states in America and in some countries.

In his long career as a psychiatrist and neurologist, Cerletti published 113 papers, including the pathology of senile plaques in Alzheimer's disease. In 1950, he received an honorary degree by the Sorbonne (University of Paris); he also has a long list of awards and degrees.

Major Literature

Cerletti, Ugo. "Old and New Information About Electroshock." *American Journal of Psychiatry* 107 (1950): pp. 87–94.

Chapanis, Alphonse (1917–2002)
FATHER OF ERGONOMICS

Born in Meriden, Connecticut, Chapanis earned a B.A. from the University of Connecticut, Storrs (1937) and a Ph.D. (1943) at Yale University, Connecticut. He worked at the Army Air Force Aero Medical Laboratory at Wright Field in Ohio and was aviation physiologist at the School of Aviation Medicine, Texas. From 1946 he was at Johns Hopkins University, Maryland, and retired as professor emeritus (1982). He received the Franklin V. Taylor Award, Society of Engineering Psychologists (1963); the Paul M. Fitts Award, Human Factors Society (now the Human Factors and Ergonomics Society) (1973); and Distinguished Contribution for Applications in Psychology Award, American Psychological Association (1978). Cha-

panis was president of the International Ergonomics Association (1976–1979) and fellow of the American Psychological Association, the American Association for the Advancement of Science and several other organizations.

As professor emeritus, Chapanis was active as a professional consultant, particularly for IBM, the U.S. Army, Bell Labs, and others in the computer industry. The Human Factors and Ergonomics Society award for the outstanding student paper at its annual conference bears his name.

Major Contributions

Ergonomics, or human factors, is the study of how a workplace and the equipment used there can best be designed for comfort, efficiency, safety, and productivity. During World War II Chapanis was concerned with helping pilots learn new techniques for attacking Japanese planes at night and improving aviation safety. A simple but effective solution was to attach a circle to one control and triangle to the other to prevent them being confused with each other. He authored, co-authored, or edited numerous books, including the first textbook in the field: *Applied Experimental Psychology: Human Factors in Engineering Design*. In his autobiography, *The Chapanis Chronicles,* he disclosed that his activities behind the Iron Curtain were sometimes for the purpose of gathering intelligence for one or another of the U.S. security departments. Some of his other contributions:

- Research that led to the design of the standard telephone touchtone keypad.
- Improving teleconferencing and videoconferencing.
- Digitized speech, a precursor to satellite-based telephony and digital wireless telephony.
- Research into the nature of color blindness and night vision.
- Championed the importance of the user in human-computer interaction.
- Worked to improve safety labels.

Major Literature

Morgan, Clifford Thomas, Alphonse Chapanis, and Wendell R. Garner. *Applied Experimental Psychology: Human Factors in Engineering Design*. New Jersey: John Wiley and Sons Inc., 1949.

Chapanis, Alphonse. "Color Blindness." *Scientific American* 184 (1951): 48–53.

___. *Research Techniques in Human Engineering*. Baltimore, Massachusetts: Johns Hopkins University Press, 1959.

___. *Human Factors in Engineering Design*. New Jersey: John Wiley and Sons Inc., 1996.

___. *Ethnic Variables in Human Factor Engineering*. Baltimore, Massachusetts: Johns Hopkins University Press, 1975.

___. *The Chapanis Chronicles: 50 Years of Human Factors Research, Education, and Design*. Walnut Creek, California: Agean Park Press, 1999.

Charcot, Jean-Martin (1825–1893)
MEDICAL TEACHER AND CLINICIAN

Known as the founder of modern neurology, Jean-Martin Charcot is one of France's greatest medical teachers and clinicians. He was born in Paris and educated at the University of Paris, from where he graduated with an M.D. (1853). He worked at the Central Bureau of Hospitals (1856) and was professor of pathological anatomy in the faculty of medicine at the University of Paris (1860). In 1862 Charcot joined the staff of the Salpêtrière Hospital and opened the most highly regarded neurological clinics of his day. After the Franco-Prussian war of 1870–1871, he occupied himself with epidemics of typhoid and smallpox.

Major Contributions

Charcot was one of a select group of physicians who made the Salpêtrière Hospital in Paris a world-renowned medical center. His powers as a teacher drew students from all parts of the world, one of whom (in 1885) was Sigmund Freud (see entry). Charcot's use of hypnosis stimulated Freud's interest in the psychological origins of neurosis. Charcot contributed greatly to the study of neurology, and he conducted pioneering research into cerebral function and discovered seed-like aneurysms that are important in cerebral hemorrhage. Seventeen different medical conditions are associated with the name Charcot, either on his own or in association, for example, Charcot's disease, or Charcot's joint. His interest extended to working with the elderly at a time when declining health was regarded as an inevitable accompaniment to old age. His work led to what we now call gerontology.

By the 1880s Charcot was using hypnosis to study the symptoms of female patients and through hypnosis was able to reproduce many of the symptoms the patient exhibited. Although he believed (erroneously) that only hysterics could be hypnotized, he fully defined and classified the many different forms that hysteria may take. He was the first to show that hysteria is of the mind and that some of its symptoms are the result of ideas that dominate the mind of the hysteric. Charcot was the first physician to describe multiple sclerosis (MS) (at that time called disseminated sclerosis). Charcot identified three classical psychological symptoms which, in the intervening years, still stand in many cases: mental depression, stupid indifference and foolish laughter.

Although Charcot contributed much to the study of MS, he attempted to make a link between that and hysteria. More recent studies show that hysteria occurs no more frequently in people with MS than in any other group of patients. Charcot's influence as a founder of neurology was recognized after his death by the erection of his bronze statue at the Salpêtrière, which was destroyed in 1942 during the Nazi occupation of Paris.

Major Literature

Charcot was a prolific writer and founded the journal *Archives de neurologie*, which he edited until his death. His works are stored in the Library of Professor J.-M. Charcot at the Salpêtrière Hospital, Paris.

Chomsky, Noam (1928–)
LINGUISTICS

Born in Philadelphia, Pennsylvania, the son of a Hebrew scholar, Noam Chomsky gained a B.A. (1949), M.A. (1951) and Ph.D. in linguistics (1955) from the University of Pennsylvania, Philadelphia. He was a junior fellow of the Harvard University Society of Fellows (1951–1955). Since 1955 he has been at the Massachusetts Institute of Technology (MIT). He became a professor, Department of Modern Languages and Linguistics (now the Department of Linguistics and Philosophy), in 1961; he was Ferrari P. Ward Professor of Modern Languages and Linguistics (1966–1976), and was named Institute Professor of Linguistics, Linguistic Theory, Syntax, Semantics and Philosophy of Language in 1976.

Chomsky has received honorary degrees from more than twenty universities worldwide. Among his awards are the Distinguished Scientific Contribution Award of the American Psychological Association, the Kyoto Prize in Basic Sciences, the Helmholtz Medal, the Dorothy Eldridge Peacemaker Award, and the Ben Franklin Medal in Computer and Cognitive Science.

Major Contributions

Chomsky's claim that linguistics is a "branch of cognitive psychology" has not met with total agreement. Whatever the argument, linguistics fits more easily as a sub-field of psychology than into any other discipline. His theory of transformational generative grammar in his book *Syntactic Structures* revolutionized theoretical linguistics. He maintained that far from being a system of syntactical and grammatical habits established by means of training and experience, humans have a built-in facility for understanding the formal principles underlying the grammatical structures of language. Children are thus able to infer the grammatical, abstract rules underlying ordinary sentences and then use those rules to generate an infinite number and variety of sentences that they had never heard before, the "generative grammars."

He identified "surface structures"— the actual words and sounds used — and "deeper structures"— which carry the sentence's underlying meaning. These abstract rules are what Chomsky calls "grammatical transformations," or "transformational rules." Further, he argues that these rules are the same in any language.

Chomsky is a renowned political activist who has not been slow to express his disapproval of American foreign policy. He was against he Vietnam War and is against U.S. involvement in the affairs of other nations. He favors free speech, something he has been criticized for when what he said seemed to support terrorism. He was accused of being anti–Semitic when he supported Robert Faurisson's right to publish his controversial book denying the Holocaust. He continues to write books on such themes as the abuse of power, global dominance, propaganda, mass media, thought control, the American Empire, and the 9/11 attacks.

Major Literature

Chomsky, Noam. *Syntactic Structures.* New York: Walter de Gruyter, 1957, 2002.
___. *Rules and Representations.* Lake Oswego, Oregon: Blackwell Publishers, 1980.
___. *Studies in Semantics in Generative Grammar.* New York: Walter de Gruyter, 1980.
___. *Language and Problems of Knowledge.* Cambridge, Massachusetts: The MIT Press, 1988.
___. *Hegemony or Survival: America's Quest for Global Dominance.* New York: Penguin Group Inc., 2004.
___. *Failed States: The Abuse of Power and the Assault on Democracy.* London, England: Penguin Books Ltd., Hamish Hamilton, 2006.

Cialdini, Robert Beno (1945–)
PERSUASION

Born in Milwaukee, Wisconsin, Robert Beno Cialdini gained his B.S. (1967) from the University of Wisconsin and an M.S. (1969) and Ph.D. (1970) in social psychology from University of North Carolina, Chapel Hill. His post-doctoral training was at Columbia University, New York City. He has held visiting scholar appointments at Ohio State University in Athens, the University of California, the Annenberg School of Communications in Los Angeles and the Graduate School of Business at Stanford University, California. He is currently Regent's Professor of Psychology at Arizona State University, Tempe, where he has also been named Distinguished Graduate Research Professor. He is on the editorial board of several influential psychology journals.

Major Contributions

At North Carolina he concentrated mainly on the psychology of persuasion, and at Arizona he has developed the whole field of personal influence. To get data for his highly popular books, he spent three years applying for jobs and training at used car dealerships, fund-raising organizations, telemarketing firms and the like, observing real-life situations of persuasion. Cialdini defines six "weapons of influence":

1. *Reciprocation.* People tend to return a favor. Thus, the widespread practice of giving free samples in marketing, even though the sample does not hold much value.
2. *Commitment and Consistency.* If people agree to make a commitment toward a goal or idea, they are more likely to honor that commitment. However, even if the incentive or motivation is removed after they have already agreed, they will continue to honor the agreement.
3. *Social Proof.* People will do things they see other people doing. One person looking up into the sky and pointing will invariably attract a crowd, also looking.
4. *Authority.* People will tend to obey authority figures, even if they are asked to perform objectionable acts. This was highlighted at the Nuremburg Trials after World War II, when many accused of war crimes pleaded that they were only obeying orders. The same thing has happened more recently in Iraq (see Milgram, Stanley).
5. *Liking.* People are easily persuaded by other

people that they like. Cialdini cites the marketing of certain commodities in what might now be called viral marketing — techniques that seek to exploit pre-existing social networks and grow much like a virus invading an organism. (The first to write about viral marketing was media critic Douglas Rushkoff in his 1994 book *Media Virus*, New York, Random House, Ballantine Books.)

6. *Scarcity.* Perceived scarcity will generate demand. For example, saying offers are available for a "limited time only" encourages sales.

Why do people say yes? Cialdini maintains people say yes mostly without thinking. Saying no would complicate things.

Major Literature

Cialdini, Robert Beno. *Influence: How and Why People Agree to Things.* Boulder, Colorado: William Morrow and Co., 1984.

___. *Influence: Science and Practice.* Upper Saddle River, New Jersey: Pearson Education, Longman Group, 1998, 2003.

___. *Influence: Psychology of Persuasion.* Colorado, Boulder: William Morrow and Co., 1999.

Claparède, Édouard
(1872–1940)
CHILD PSYCHOLOGY

Édouard Claparède was a Swiss doctor and psychologist who was born in Geneva and spent most of his life in that city. He qualified for an M.D. degree in Geneva (1897), then spent a year in research in Paris, where he met Alfred Binet (see entry). Returning to Geneva, he joined the laboratory of his psychologist cousin, Theodore Flournoy, and began lecturing at the University of Geneva. He succeeded Flournoy as professor of psychology in 1915, a post he held until his death. He was founder and joint editor of *Archives de Psychologie*, 1901–1940; general secretary, Second International Congress of Psychology, 1904; general secretary, Sixth International Congress of Psychology, 1909; professor of psychology, University of Geneva, 1915–1940; permanent secretary, International Congress of Psychology; and life president, Comité de l'Association Internationale des Conferences de Psychothechnique.

Major Contributions

Claparède's research interests included neurology, psychiatry, comparative psychology, intelli-

gence, problem-solving, and education, and in 1905 he advanced a biological theory of sleep. He considered sleep to be a defensive reaction necessary to halt activity of the organism and thereby prevent exhaustion. His research on sleep led him to the study of hysteria and the conclusion that hysterical symptoms may also be regarded as defensive reactions. From his research he developed his complex "Law of Becoming Conscious," which states that mental activity is working in the background and only emerges in to consciousness when it ceases to function adequately.

A second aspect of Claparède's "Law" is that the last process to be brought into consciousness is one that started earlier and has taken longer to develop. After the appearance of his influential book *Experimental Pedagogy and the Psychology of the Child* (1905; Eng. trans., 1911), he began to conduct a seminar in educational psychology (1906). In 1912 he established the Institut J.J. Rousseau at the University of Geneva for the advancement of child psychology and its application to education. His work was continued by Jean Piaget (see entry). Claparède's work is detailed in Robert J. Sternberg's *International Handbook of Intelligence* (New York: Cambridge University Press, 2004).

Major Literature

Claparède, Édouard. "Autobiography." In C. Murchison (ed). *History of Psychology in Autobiography* Vol. 1. Worcester, Massachusetts: Clark University Press, 1930.

___. *Inediti psicologici (Inediti claparediani).* Rome: Bulzoni, 1981.

___. *Inediti pedagogici.* Perugia, Italy: Università degli studi di Perugia, 1984.

___, and Robert H. Wozniak (Eds.). *Classics in Psychology, 1911: Experimental Pedagogy and the Psychology of the Child* Vol. 47 *(History of Psychology).* Bristol, England: Thoemmes Press (an imprint of the Continuum International Publishing Group, Ltd. London, England), 1998.

Clark, Eve Vivienne (1942–)
LINGUISTICS

Born in Camberley, Surrey, England, Eve Vivienne Clark earned an M.A. in French language and literature with minors in Spanish and phonetics (1965) from the University of Edinburgh, Scotland. She received a postgraduate diploma in general linguistics (1966) and a Ph.D. (1969) at Edinburgh. She was research assistant, Social Science Research Council Cognition Project, University of Edinburgh (1966–1967), and was assistant instructor and instructor in the Department of French, University of Pittsburgh, Pennsylvania (1967–1969). At Stanford University, California, she was research associate, Language Universals Project (1969–1970); lecturer, Committee on Linguistics (1970–1971); assistant professor of linguistics (1971–1977); associate professor of linguistics (1977–1983); professor of linguistics (1983–1994); and professor of linguistics and symbolic systems (since 1995).

Clark's awards and scholarships have been many, including one from the John Simon Guggenheim Memorial Foundation (1983–1984), and in 2003 she was elected a fellow of the American Association for the Advancement of Science. She has been or is on the editorial board of several journals, such as *Child Development, Cognition: International Journal of Cognitive Psychology, Journal of Memory and Language, Journal of Child Language,* and *Cognitive Science.*

Major Contributions

Clark has done extensive observational and experimental research into how people acquire their first language, particularly the meanings and the use of word formation. Some of her detailed comparative studies were of English and Hebrew in children and adults. She has also explored the practicalities of coining words, with particular reference to conventions and contrasts in the language used, and to how the language is acquired. She considers conventional words and contrasting words to be at the core of language acquisition, thus she starts with the words and meanings children already know and how they then develop those meanings into different structures.

In her most recent work, she has examined the kinds of information adults offer children about unfamiliar words and their meanings, and the amount of negative evidence children may receive in the course of conversation. Part of this is the concept of gaze vs. language of adults with one- and two-year-olds. An important part of all this is how children form new words and show their understanding of the words they use, and whether they assume that new words have the same meaning as old ones until they discover otherwise.

Major Literature

Clark, H. H., and Eve Vivienne Clark. *Psychology and Language: An Introduction to Psycholinguistics.* New York: Harcourt Brace Jovanovich, 1977.

Clark, Eve Vivienne. *The Ontogenesis of Meaning.* Wiesbaden: Athenaion, 1979.

___. "The Lexicon in Acquisition." In *Cambridge Studies in Linguistics,* Vol. 65. Cambridge, Massachusetts: Cambridge University Press, 1993.

___. *The Proceedings of the 30th Annual Child Language Research Forum (Annual Child Language Research Forum Proceedings).* Cambridge, Massachusetts: Cambridge University Press, 2000.

___. *First Language Acquisition.* Cambridge, Massachusetts: Cambridge University Press, 2003.

Kelly, Barbara, and Eve Vivienne Clark. (Eds.) *Acquisitions of Constructions* (lecture notes). Stanford University, California: Center for the Study of Language and Information, 2006.

Clark, Kenneth Bancroft (1914–2005)
SOCIAL PSYCHOLOGY

Born in the Panama Canal Zone, Kenneth Clark gained a B.A. (1935) from Howard University in Washington, D.C., where he studied race relations. His Ph.D. is from Columbia University, New York (1940). He taught psychology at Howard (1937–1938) and at Hampton Institute (now Hampton University) in Virginia from 1940 to 1941.

Not only was Clark the first African American to receive a Ph.D. in psychology from Columbia University, he became the first African American tenured full professor at the City College of New York in 1960. Later he was the first African American on the New York State Board of Regents and the first African American to be president of the American Psychological Association. He retired from City College in 1975, but remained an active advocate for integration. He died from cancer in Hastings-on-Hudson, New York.

Major Contributions

During Columbia's student protests in 1968, Clark, whose son Hilton was a leader of the Society of Afro-American Students, served as mediator between the black student protesters in Hamilton Hall and the administration. In 1946, Kenneth and his wife Mamie (see entry) founded the Northside Center for Child Development in Harlem, where they conducted experiments on racial biases in education. Their findings were presented at school desegregation trials in Virginia, South Carolina, and Delaware.

Their research challenged the notion of differences in the mental abilities of black and white children and so played an important role in the desegregation of American schools. The Clarks testified as expert witnesses in several school desegregation cases, including *Briggs v. Elliott*, one of the cases that was later combined into the famous *Brown v. Board of Education* case, in which the U.S. Supreme Court officially overturned racial segregation in public education.

This was a landmark case, argued by the National Association for the Advancement of Colored People (NAACP) legal team before the Supreme Court in 1954. It declared school segregation a violation of the Fourteenth Amendment of the U.S. Constitution, and Clark's 1950 report on racial discrimination was cited. The social science testimony of Kenneth Clark was a significant factor in the court's decision, and this secured his place in the historical record among social psychologists whose research has influenced significant social change in the twentieth century. It appears that this was the first time the court ever admitted social science studies as hard evidence.

Major Literature

Clark, Kenneth Bancroft. *Pathos of Power*. New York: Harper Collins College Division, 1974.
___. *A Class Divided: Then and Now*. Foreword, William Peters. New Haven, Connecticut: Yale University Press, 1987.
___. *Prejudice and Your Child*. Foreword, Stuart W. Cook. Middletown Connecticut: Wesleyan University Press, 1988.
___. *Dark Ghetto: Dilemmas of Social Power*. Foreword, Gunnar Myrdal. Middletown, Connecticut: Wesleyan University Press, 1989.

Clark, Mamie Phipps (1917–1983)

PSYCHOLOGY OF SELF-ESTEEM

Mamie Phipps was born in Hot Springs, Arkansas, the daughter of a medical doctor, but this slightly privileged status did not exempt her from the racism of the South. She enrolled in the psychology course at Howard University, Washington, D.C., where she met Kenneth Clark (see entry). She wished to marry but realized doing so might prejudice her final year, so they eloped in 1937.

Psychology offered the chance to explore her interest in children, although she was aware that there were no black women on the psychology faculty at Howard. She began working with children in an all-black nursery school and conducted psychology tests using dolls; her master's thesis was "The Development of Consciousness of Self

in Negro Pre-School Children." She and Kenneth developed these studies further in a fellowship proposal that enabled Clark to continue her work at Columbia University.

In 1943 she became the first African-American woman and the second African American (after her husband) in the university's history to receive a psychology doctorate. In 1946 the Clarks founded the Northside Center for Child Development, the first center to provide therapy for children in Harlem, at a time when many black children were being forcibly enrolled in programs for the mentally handicapped. In 1966, Columbia University recognized the couple's work by awarding each the Nicholas Murray Butler Silver Medal. Clark retired from the Northside Center in 1980 and died in New York.

Major Contributions

Using drawings and dolls of black and white children, the Clarks investigated black children's racial identification and preference by using dolls and line drawings. The Clarks found that black children often preferred the white doll and drawing, and frequently colored the line drawing of the child a shade lighter than their own skin. Samples of the children's responses illustrated that they viewed white as good and pretty, but black as bad and ugly. That young black children by the age of five years felt themselves inferior was one of the findings in the *Brown v. Board of Education* case of Topeka, Kansas (see Clark, Kenneth). The Clarks further demonstrated that feeling inferior led to scholastic underachievement. Mamie Clark served on the boards of organizations such as the American Broadcast Company, Mount Sinai Medical Center, the Museum of Modern Art, and the New York Public Library.

Major Literature

Clark, Kenneth Bancroft, and Mamie K. Clark. "The Development of Consciousness of Self and the Emergence of Racial Identification in Negro Preschool Children." *Journal of Social Psychology* 10 (1939): 591–599.
___. "Segregation as a Factor in the Racial Identification of Negro Pre-School Children: A Preliminary Report." *Journal of Experimental Education* 8 (1939): 161–163.
___. "Skin Color as a Factor in Racial Identification of Negro Preschool Children." *The Journal of Social Psychology* 11 (1940): 159–169.
___. "Emotional Factors in Racial Identification and Preference in Negro Children." *Journal of Negro Education* 19 (1950): 341–350.

Clarke, Charles Kirk (1857–1924)
CANADIAN NATIONAL COMMITTEE FOR MENTAL HYGIENE

Born in Elora, Ontario, Canada, Charles Kirk Clarke gained an M.D. at the University of Toronto, Canada (1879). He was assistant superintendent, Hamilton asylum, Ontario (1880–1881); assistant superintendent, Rockwood Asylum in Kingston, Ontario (1881–1885); superintendent, Rockwood (1885–1905); superintendent, Toronto Asylum (1905–1911); superintendent, Toronto General Hospital; professor of psychiatry and dean of the faculty of medicine at University of Toronto (1911); and co-founder and first medical director of the Canadian National Committee for Mental Hygiene, later the Canadian Mental Health Association (1918).

Major Contributions

Clarke's work in psychiatry started when he served as clinical assistant to his brother-in-law Dr. Joseph Workman at the Provincial Lunatic Asylum in Toronto. At the time Clarke entered psychiatry, inmates were treated like criminals: handcuffed, kept in tiny cells, poorly clothed and fed, and generally mistreated. When he joined Dr. William Metcalf— another brother-in-law — at Rockwood, the two like-minded men set about making humanitarian changes. The reforms ended abruptly when Metcalf was murdered by a paranoid patient. Clarke survived a vicious attack by a patient.

When Clarke succeeded Metcalf as superintendent, he carried on with their reforms — the elimination of physical restraints, the introduction of various crafts, and the encouragement of hobbies. Brush making was a success and provided the patients with pocket money, but the local brush makers complained to the government and the enterprise was stopped. Clarke said that this was typical of the obstructionism he experienced in his reforms.

Toronto Asylum was in a dilapidated and overcrowded state when he took over. A proposed new building did not receive the support of the psychiatric community and as a result many of the patients were incarcerated in Toronto jails. In 1914, he and Dr. Clarence Hincks opened a clinic for so-called feeble-minded children. With major funding from the Rockefeller Foundation, he oversaw both the creation of a fully functional Department of Psychiatry at the University of Toronto and the transformation of the medical school into a first-class institution with an international reputation. His name is commemorated in the Clarke Institute of Psychiatry in Toronto, which, in 1998, merged with several other Ontario institutions to form the Centre for Addiction and Mental Health (CAMH), which is now called the CAMH College St. Site.

An early proponent of eugenics, Clarke recommended restrictive laws to limit the immigration and marriage of the "mentally defective." He argued that such laws were necessary to stem the dramatic growth of state and provincial mental asylums where foreign-born patients made up more than 50 percent of the hospital population. By 1905, Clarke had abandoned eugenics, and many of the other leading psychiatrists would follow suit by the end of World War I, when it was clear that eugenic measures were not having the desired effects.

Coles, Michael G. H. (1944–)
PSYCHOPHYSIOLOGY

Michael Coles grew up in Watford, Hertfordshire, England, and received his B.A. degree in psychology and philosophy (1967) and his Ph.D. in psychology (1971) from the University of Exeter, England. In 1970, he went to the University of Illinois at Urbana-Champaign and was appointed full professor in 1984. He has also served as chair of the biological psychology division in the Department of Psychology. He has been president of the Society for Psychophysiological Research, editor-in-chief of *Psychophysiology*, and has served as consulting editor for *Consciousness and Cognition*, the *Journal of Experimental Psychology* and *Human Perception and Performance*.

He has held visiting positions at several universities in America and overseas, including the Max Planck Institute for Psycholinguistics, Nijmegen, Holland. He was appointed as a fellow in the Center of Advanced Study at the University of Illinois in 1976, 1985, and 2000, and received the Liberal College of Arts and Science (Illinois) Award for Distinguished Teaching at the University of Illinois Urbana-Champaign (1984). Coles retired formally from Illinois in 2001 and is emeritus professor in the Department of Psychology and an emeritus faculty member in the Beckman Institute Cognitive Neuroscience group, Urbana, Illinois. In 2002 he received the Society for Psychophysiological Research Award for distinguished contributions to psychophysiology. He is a prolific writer of several books and articles that have appeared in many distinguished journals.

Major Contributions

Michael Coles' work at the Beckman Institute, along with that of other members of the Cognitive Neuroscience Group, is concerned with specifying the functional significance of the electrical potentials of the electroencephalogram (EEG). He uses electrophysiological, computational, and imaging approaches to explore error processing in the brain. One of the significant findings — detailed in a paper written in 1985 — was that when an error occurred in the reading it suggested that the subject was aware that his or her response was incorrect. This paper made a significant contribution to experimental psychology; it opens up the field for studying how people monitor their own behavior and initiate remedial actions if necessary.

Major Literature

Coles, Michael G.H. "Physiological Activity and Detection: The Effects of Attentional Requirements and the Prediction of Performance." *Biological Psychology* 2 (1974): 113–125.

Porges, Stephen W., and Michael G.H. Coles. *Psychophysiology.* Stroudsburg, Pennsylvania: Hutchinson Ross Publishing Company, 1976.

Jennings, J. Richard, and Michael G.H. Coles. *Handbook of Cognitive Psychophysiology: Central and Autonomic Nervous System Approaches.* New Jersey: John Wiley and Sons, Inc., 1991.

Coles, Michael G.H., et al. *Psychophysiology: Systems, Processes, and Applications.* New York: Guilford Press, 1993.

Jennings, J.R., P.K. Ackles, and M.G.H. Coles (Eds.). *Advances in Psychophysiology,* Vol. 5. London, England: Jessica Kingsley Publishers, 1994.

Kramer, A., M.G.H. Coles, and G.D. Logan (Eds.) *Converging Operations in the Study of Visual Selective Attention.* Washington, D.C.: American Psychological Association, 1996.

Conolly, John (1794–1866)
Asylum Reform

Born at Market Rasen, Lincolnshire, England, of Irish descent, John Conolly spent some time as a soldier, qualified as a doctor at Edinburgh University in 1821, and subsequently practiced successively in Lewes, Chichester, Sussex, and Stratford-on-Avon, Warwickshire. From 1828 to 1830 he was professor of practical medicine at University College, London, where he concerned himself with the introduction of the teaching of clinical psychiatry. From 1830 to 1838 he lived in Warwick, where he supported his friend Sir John Forbes

(1788–1839) in the publication of the *British and Foreign Medical Review* and the *Cyclopaedia of Practical Medicine.*

With Forbes and Sir Charles Hastings (1794–1866) he laid the groundwork for a medical society that was later to become the British Medical Association. In 1839 he was appointed resident physic to Hanwell Lunatic Asylum, Middlesex, the largest institution of its kind in England, first erected in 1829–1831 for 2,520 inmates.

Major Contributions

At Hanwell, Conolly immediately began practicing the methods of Philippe Pinel and William Tuke (1732–1822, a Quaker and founder of the Retreat, an asylum in York, England). Conolly abolished the use of all kinds of mechanical restraints and later chemical restraints, such as bromide and chloral hydrate. In the early part of the 19th century there had been appalling scandals involving embezzlement, rape and murder at the York Lunatic Asylum and at Bethlehem (Bedlam) in London.

In his 1842 report, *Treatment of the Insane without Mechanical Restraints,* Conolly reported widespread use of all manner of restraints — straitjackets, hand and leg cuffs, and coarse devices of leather and iron. Although care and cure were among the aims of the more enlightened asylums, the key requirement of asylums was safe custody. In 1856, after more than twenty years at Hanwell, Conolly reported that in 24 English mental institutions, mechanical restraints had been almost completely abandoned.

Major Literature

Conolly, John. "De Statu Mentis in Insania et Melancholia." Doctoral thesis, Edinburgh, 1821.

___. *An Inquiry Concerning the Indications of Insanity, With Suggestions for the Better Protection and Care of the Insane.* London, England: J. Taylor, 1830.

___. *Construction and Government of Lunatic Asylums and Hospitals for the Insane.* London: Dawsons of Pall Mall, 1847. London: John Churchill, Psychiatric Monograph Series, Volume 6, 1969.

___. *On Some of the Forms of Insanity.* Croonian lectures delivered at the Royal College of Physicians, London, in 1849. Contributions to the *History of Psychology* Series, Vol. XIII, Westport, Connecticut: University Publications of America, 1983.

___. *Treatment of the Insane Without Mechanical Restraints.* Smith, Elder, and Co., 1856. Manchester, New Hampshire: Ayer Co. Publishers, 1973.

___. *A Study of Hamlet.* London, E. Moxon, (1863). [The first psychiatric study of Hamlet.]

Cooper, Cary Lynn (1940–)
STRESS MANAGEMENT

Born in Los Angeles, California, Cary Lynn Cooper gained a B.S. (1962) and an MBA (1964) from University of California, Los Angeles, a Ph.D. from the University of Leeds, England (1969), and an M.Sc. from the University of Manchester, England (1970). Cooper was professor of organizational psychology, University of Manchester Institute of Science and Technology (1975–2003); professor of organizational psychology and health at the Lancaster, England, University Management School (since 2003); chairman, Management and Education Development Division of the (American) Academy of Management (1979–1980); fellow, British Psychological Society (1980); advisor, World Health Organization (1981–1983); Leverhulme Trust Fellowship (1982–1983); and adviser, International Labor Organization (1983). He was founding president of the British Academy of Management (1986–1990) and fellow of the Royal Society of Arts (1990).

He received the Distinguished Service Award for his contribution to management science from the Academy of Management (1998). Cooper holds honorary doctorates from several universities and many distinctions, including the Commander of the Order of the British Empire (2001). Cooper is editor (jointly with Chris Argyris [see entry]) of the international scholarly *Blackwell Encyclopedia of Management* (12 volume set), and the editor of *Who's Who in the Management Sciences*. He published a major report, "Stress Prevention in the Workplace," for the European Union's European Foundation for the Improvement of Living and Work Conditions. He is president of the Institute of Welfare Officers, vice president of the British Association of Counseling and Psychotherapy, and an ambassador of The Samaritans and patron of the National Phobic Society.

Major Contributions

Cooper's focus is on the structural and systemic sources of stress. He explores the correlation between working hours and the quality of work and private life, and the impact that changing practices have on individuals and organizations. Cooper's original research was in the field of group psychology and experimental group techniques. In the 1970s he changed to exploring occupational stress. Since then he and his team have carried out in-depth studies in many different white- and blue-collar occupations.

The high profile of Cooper has brought the whole subject of stress and stress management into the forefront of awareness at all levels of society, as he has focused on how the workplace can affect health and the feel-good factor. Professor Cooper designed a stress policy for the staff at Aston University, Birmingham, England, making it one of the first UK universities to have one.

Major Literature

Cooper, Cary Lynn. *Executive Families Under Stress*. Englewood Cliffs, New Jersey: Prentice Hall, 1981.
___. *Managing Workplace Stress*. California: Sage Publications, 1997.
___, and Robertson, Ivan. *Well-being in Organizations: A Reader for Students and Practitioners*. New Jersey: John Wiley and Sons, Inc., 2001.
Cooper Cary Lynn, and Philip Dewe. *A Brief History of Stress*. Ames, Iowa: Blackwell Publishing, 2004.
Cooper, Cary Lynn. *Handbook of Stress Medicine and Health* (2nd ed.). Boca Raton, Florida: CRC Press Inc, 2004.
___(Ed.). *Organizational Psychology: A Reader*. London: Taylor and Francis Books Ltd., Routledge, 2006.

Cosmides, Leda (1957–)
EVOLUTIONARY PSYCHOLOGY

Born in Philadelphia, Pennsylvania, Leda Cosmides gained her A.B. in biology (1979), A.M. in psychology (1984), and Ph.D. in psychology (1985) from Harvard University in Cambridge, Massachusetts. She was a postdoctoral scholar in the Department of Psychology, Stanford University, California (1985–1989). She was on the faculty of the University of California, Santa Barbara (UCSB) Department of Psychology; visiting assistant professor (1990–1991); assistant professor (1991–1994); associate professor (1994 to 2000); and professor (2000).

Cosmides received the American Psychological Association Distinguished Scientific Award for an Early Career Contribution to Psychology in the area of Human Learning and Cognition (1993) and the American Association for the Advancement of Science Prize for Behavioral Science (1998) for her research on reason. She was the G. Stanley Hall Lecturer, American Psychological Association (1998), and received the Director's Pioneer Award, National Institutes of Health (2004 and 2005).

Major Contributions

Professor Cosmides focuses on:

- Evolutionary psychology and cognitive science;

- Using evolutionary theory to develop computational theories of adaptive information-processing problems;
- Testing for presence of evolutionarily predicted information-processing mechanisms, their neural basis, and cultural sequelae; and
- Empirical work on cooperation, threat, coalitional psychology, incest avoidance and intuitive statistics.

Together with anthropologist husband John Tooby, Cosmides pioneered evolutionary psychology, and they founded the Center for Evolutionary Psychology at UCSB. Evolutionary psychology (or EP) proposes that human and primate cognition and behavior could be better understood by examining them in light of human and primate evolutionary history. Cosmides coordinates research teams with expertise in evolutionary biology, psychology, anthropology, and neuroscience to identify:

1. Adaptive problems human hunter-gatherer ancestors faced.
2. The psychological mechanisms that evolved to solve these problems.
3. Their neurological basis.
4. How they generate culture and impose systematic patterns of social behavior both within and across cultures.

These activities are linked to the Institute of Neurology, University of London, and include field work among the Shiwiar and Achuar in the Amazonian rainforest of Ecuador.

Major Literature

Cosmides, Leda. *Deduction or Darwinian Algorithms? An Explanation of the "Elusive" Content Effect on the Wason Selection Task*. Doctoral dissertation, Department of Psychology, Harvard University: University Microfilms, #86–02206, 1985.
___. "The Logic of Social Exchange: Has Natural Selection Shaped How Humans Reason? Studies With the Wason Selection Task." *Cognition* 31 (1989): 187–276.
Barkow, J., Leda Cosmides, and J. Tooby. *The Adapted Mind: Evolutionary Psychology and the Generation of Culture*. New York: Oxford University Press, 1992.
Cosmides, Leda, and John Tooby. *What is Evolutionary Psychology? Explaining the New Science of the Mind (Darwinism Today)*. New Haven, Connecticut: Yale University Press, 2005.
Cosmides, Leda, and J. Tooby. "Neurocognitive Adaptations Designed for Social Exchange." In D.M. Buss (Ed.), *Evolutionary Psychology Handbook*. New Jersey: John Wiley and Sons, Inc., 2005.
Tooby, J., Leda Cosmides, and H.C. Barrett. "Resolving the Debate on Innate Ideas: Learnability Constraints and the Evolved Interpenetration of Motivational and Conceptual Functions." In P. Carruthers, S. Laurence, and S. Stich (Eds.), *The Innate Mind: Structure and Content*. New York: Oxford University Press, 2005.

Craik, Fergus I.M. (1935–)
ADULT DEVELOPMENT AND AGING

Born in Edinburgh, Scotland, Fergus I.M. Craik gained a B.Sc. at the University of Edinburgh, Scotland (1960), and a Ph.D. at the University of Liverpool, England (1965). He was visiting associate professor at the University of Toronto, Ontario, Canada (1968–1969); associate professor, Erindale College, University of Toronto (1971–1975); professor, University of Toronto (1975–1989); associate scientist, Rotman Research Institute, Toronto (1989); Glassman Chair in Neuropsychology, University of Toronto (1996–2000); university professor, University of Toronto (1997–2000); scientist, Rotman Research Institute (since 2000); and university professor emeritus, University of Toronto (since 2000).

He has been editor of: *Journal of Verbal Learning and Verbal Behavior*; *Journal of Experimental Psychology: Learning, Memory and Cognition*; *Canadian Journal of Psychology*; *Quarterly Journal of Experimental Psychology*; *Journal of Gerontology*; and *Canadian Journal on Aging*. Craik's honors include fellowships in the Canadian and American Psychological Associations; fellow, Center for Advanced Study in the Behavioral Sciences, Stanford University, California; and honorary president of the Canadian Psychological Association.

Major Contributions

Craik's first publications were on adult age differences and short-term retention, using information-processing models. However, Craik became dissatisfied with the mechanistic approach of such models and with his colleague, Robert S. Lockhart, in 1972 he published an influential article on levels of processing theory. This was a more flexible approach to remembering; it proposed three levels, the deeper the processing the better the memory, and memory performance is influenced by the level of initial processing. The three levels are:

- *Shallow processing*— superficial or incidental details, the shape of the letters of a word.
- *Deeper processing*— the sound of the word.
- *Deepest processing*— The significance and meaning of the word.

The levels of processing theory is not without its critics. One criticism is that it does not pay enough attention to the circumstances and conditions pertaining at the time. Craik turned his attention to the problem of aging. Since 1998 he and his colleagues have been exploring the relations between the effects of normal aging and the effects of withdrawing processing resources in young adults by means of the divided attention model, which in its simplest form is trying to do two things at once. Craik was involved in setting up a large-scale study of memory rehabilitation in patients and older people and co-edited two handbooks, one on cognitive aging and one on memory. This research is supported by the National Institutes of Aging, the Ontario Mental Health Foundation, the Medical Research Council of Canada, and the McDonnell Foundation.

Major Literature

Cermak, Laird S., and Fergus I.M. Craik, *Levels of Processing in Human Memory.* New Jersey: John Wiley and Sons, Inc., 1979.

Craik, Fergus I.M., and Timothy Salthouse (Eds.). *Handbook of Aging and Cognition.* New Jersey: Lawrence Erlbaum Associates, Inc., 1992.

Tulving, Endel, and Fergus I.M. Craik. *The Oxford Handbook of Memory.* New York: Oxford University Press, Inc., 2005.

Bialystok, Ellen, and Fergus I.M. (Eds.). *Lifespan Cognition: Mechanisms of Change.* New York: Oxford University Press, Inc., 2006.

Cronbach, Lee Joseph (1916–2001)
EDUCATIONAL PSYCHOLOGY

Born in Fresno, California, Lee Joseph Cronbach gained a B.A. at Fresno State College in Fresno, California (1934), an M.A. from the University of California, Berkeley (1937), and a Ph.D. in educational psychology, University of Chicago, Illinois (1940). He was instructor to associate professor, State College, Washington (1940–1946); assistant professor, University of Chicago, Illinois (1946–1948); associate professor, then professor of educational psychology, Chicago (1948–1964); and scientific liaison officer, Office of Naval Research, London, England (1955–1956).

He was a member of the Institute for Advanced Study at Princeton University, New Jersey (1960–1961), and fellow at the Center for Advanced Study in Behavioral Studies, Stanford, California (1963–1964). At Stanford University he was professor of education (1964–1966), Vida Jacks Professor of Education (1966–1980), and professor

emeritus (1980). He was Fulbright lecturer, University of Tokyo (1967–1968).

He received the Distinguished Scientific Contribution Award of the American Psychological Association in 1994 and honorary degrees from five universities in America, Sweden and Spain. He was a member of the National Academy of Science, the National Academy of Education, the American Philosophical Society and the American Academy of Arts and Sciences.

Major Contributions

Professor Cronbach's career was devoted to designing and developing educational tests. He devised tests that allowed for possible variations rather than a simple right or wrong. In 1944 he worked on military training projects, which included one for anti-submarine personnel, and contributed fresh understanding on the use of sonar detection. In his research into evaluation he worked on the principle that the evaluator should be an enquirer and should give feedback. For him, however laudable precision is, the context should not be ignored.

A cautious man, he refused to be drawn into the Jensen debate (see Burt, Sir Cyril). Cronbach developed the most frequently used measure of the reliability of a psychological or educational test, known as "Cronbach's alpha." This formula measures the reliability of a test when it is taken only once. Cronbach retired from teaching in 1980 but remained active in debates on educational and psychological testing. At the time of his death, he was working on a paper commemorating the 50th anniversary of the publication of the alpha paper. The initial work on the alpha led to his developing a theory of test reliability, "Generalizability Theory," a comprehensive statistical model for identifying sources of measurement error.

Major Literature

Cronbach, Lee Joseph. *Educational Psychology.* New York: Harcourt, Brace and Company, 1954.

___. *Text Materials in Modern Education.* Champaign: University of Illinois Press, 1955.

___. "Five Decades of Public Controversy Over Mental Testing." *American Psychologist* 30 (1975): 1–14.

___, and Richard E. Snow. *Aptitudes and Instructional Methods: Handbook for Research of Interactions.* New Jersey: John Wiley and Sons, Inc., 1977.

Cronbach, Lee Joseph. *Designing Evaluations of Educational and Social Programs.* New Jersey: John Wiley and Sons, Inc., Jossey-Bass, Inc., 1982.

___. *The Essentials of Psychological Testing.* Upper Saddle River, New Jersey: Pearson Education, Longman Group, 1990.

Crutchfield, Richard Stanley
(1912–1977)
PERSONALITY ASSESSMENT

Born in Pittsburgh, Pennsylvania, Richard Stanley Crutchfield gained a B.A. with honors in civil engineering from the California Institute of Technology (1934) and his Ph.D. in psychology from the University of California, Berkeley (1938). He worked at Swarthmore College, Pennsylvania, and Mount Holyoke College, South Hadley, Massachusetts. From 1940 to 1946 he held research and administrative appointments with the U.S. Department of Agriculture, the Office of War Information, and the U.S. Strategic Bombing Survey in Germany. For distinguished service in this last position, he was awarded the Medal of Freedom by the U.S. War Department.

From 1946 to 1953 he worked in the Swarthmore's department of psychology, then joined the Berkeley faculty as professor of psychology and research psychologist in the Institute of Personality Assessment and Research, and remained there until his death. He was several times elected to the Council of Representatives in the American Psychological Association. He also served on the Council for the Society for the Psychological Study of Social Issues, on the board of directors of the Eastern Psychological Association, and in 1953–1954, as president of the Division of Personality and Social Psychology.

Crutchfield's research accomplishments were recognized by his appointments as a fellow to the Institute for Advanced Study, Princeton, in 1958–1959, and in 1962–1963 as a research professor in the Miller Institute for Research in Basic Science, Berkeley. He was professor emeritus and director, Institute of Personality Assessment and Research. In 1976, in recognition of his many contributions to the Berkeley campus, he was awarded the prestigious Berkeley Citation.

Major Contributions

In the 1930s Crutchfield was a pioneer in moving psychology from a tradition of single-factor experiments to experimental designs based on a wider analysis that took more account of variables. During World War II, he made significant contributions to the then-developing methodology of opinion surveys. In 1948 his *Theory and Problems of Social Psychology*, written in collaboration with Professor David Krech of Berkeley, was recognized immediately as a landmark in the field.

In the 1950s, his papers and studies helped to establish a link between cognition, perception and significant facets of personality. He also developed precise methods for studying decision making under conditions of social interaction, and in the 1950s — at the height of the U.S. era of conformity — he conducted a series of investigations into the nature of conformity. In the late 1950s and 1960s he published a series of analyses of the process of creative thinking in both children and adults.

Major Literature

Crutchfield, Richard, and David Krech. *Elements of Psychology*. New York: Knopf, 1958. New York: Random House, Inc., 1982.
Crutchfield, Richard. *Psychology* (teachers manual). New York: Random House, Inc., 1976.
___. *Psychology* (workbook). New York: Random House, Inc., 1976.

Csikszentmihalyi, Mihaly
(1934–)
FLOW THEORY

Born in Hungary, Mihaly Csikszentmihalyi (pronounced *Me-high Chick-sent-me-high-ee*) gained his B.A. (1960) and Ph.D. (1965) from the University of Chicago, Illinois. His academic career has taken him from associate professor and chairman, Department of Sociology and Anthropology, Lake Forest College, Chicago (1965–1970), to emeritus professor of human development at the University of Chicago. He is on the advisory board, J.P. Getty Museum and the board of governors, Center for the Study of Peace and Religion. His research has been supported by the United States Public Health Service, the J. Paul Getty Trust, the Sloan Foundation, the W.T. Grant Foundation, the Hewlett Foundation, and the Spencer Foundation.

Csikszentmihalyi holds honorary doctor of science degrees from Colorado College, Colorado Springs, and from Lake Forest College and a doctor of fine arts degree from the Rhode Island School of Design. He is the C.S. and D.J. Davidson Professor of Psychology at the Peter F. Drucker Graduate School of Management at Claremont Graduate University and director of the Quality of Life Research Center at the Drucker School of Management, Claremont, California. This is a non-profit research institute (founded in 1999) that studies "positive psychology"; that is, human strengths such as optimism, creativity, intrinsic motivation, and responsibility.

The Thinker of the Year Award was given to Mihaly Csikszentmihalyi in 2000.

Major Contributions

His life's work has been to study what makes people truly happy. Drawing upon years of systematic research, he developed the concept of "flow." Csikszentmihalyi was influenced by Carl Jung's writings and, like Jung, he explored many different religions, which shaped his philosophy and the development of his "flow theory." He uses flow as a metaphor to describe the rare mental state associated with feelings (similar to peak experiences of Abraham Maslow [see entry]) of optimal satisfaction and fulfillment. Flow theory states that people are most happy when they are in a state of flow — a Zen-like state of total oneness and harmony with the activity at hand and the situation, a state where the ego takes a back seat.

Csikszentmihalyi is also a leading researcher on creativity. He explored the lives of more than 90 of the world's most creative people to find out how creativity has been a force in their lives. He discovered that some highly creative people find satisfaction by inventing a career or job for themselves, like a scientist who creates a new field of study.

Major Literature

Csikszentmihalyi, Mihaly. *Flow: The Psychology of Optimal Experience.* New York: Harper and Row, 1990.
___. *Creativity: Flow and the Psychology of Discovery and Invention.* New York: Harper Perennial, 1996.
___. *Finding Flow: The Psychology of Engagement With Everyday Life.* Tennessee, Jackson: Basic Books, 1998.
___. *Good Business: Flow, Leadership and the Making of Meaning.* New York: Viking, 2003.
Csikszentmihalyi, Mihaly, and Isabella Selega Csikszentmihalyi (Eds.). *A Life Worth Living: Contributions to Positive Psychology.* New York: Oxford University Press, Inc., 2006.

Culbertson, Frances Mitchell (1921–)

GENDER AND DEPRESSION

Born in Boston, Massachusetts, Frances Mitchell was the daughter of Russian immigrant parents. The family name was originally Uchitelle, but they changed it to Mitchell on the advice an immigration officer. Mitchell studied biochemistry at University of Michigan, East Lansing. She married John Culbertson, a discharged World War II veteran, and she supported him through university.

The couple moved to Washington, D.C., after her husband was offered a job with the Federal Reserve Board.

Culbertson finished her dissertation in 1955 and it was published in 1957. The couple moved again, when John took a position at the University of Wisconsin-Madison, and it was there where she and Dr. Maressa Orzack developed a research lab for severely developmentally disabled children and adolescents. (Orzack is the founder and coordinator of the Computer Addiction Service at McLean Hospital, Belmont, Massachusetts.)

Major Contributions

Culbertson's 1981 paper discusses an educational program for autistic children in a public school. The experimental class was composed of eight children age 4–12. The experiment focused on four areas of training; language, socialization, play, and behavior. Culbertson concluded that the schooling of autistic children does lead to learned and positive social, educational, and other behavioral responses but these need to be continuously maintained and monitored.

The major findings Culbertson discusses in her 1997 article *Depression and Gender* are:

1. For several decades, in the United States and internationally, women have experienced depression about twice as frequently as men.
2. For major depression, the ratio has been reported as four women for every man. Rates vary with ethnicity and culture.
3. For bipolar disorder (manic depression), the rates are equal between the sexes.
4. Gender is an important variable in cross-cultural assessment and treatment of depression.

A version of this article was originally presented as part of an Award for Distinguished Contributions to the International Advancement of Psychology address at the 103rd annual convention of the American Psychological Association, held in August 1995 in New York.

Culbertson retired from the University of Wisconsin-Whitewater in 1988 and moved into private practice. She then joined the Mental Health Associates; her current focus is hypnotherapy with children, adolescents, and adults, especially women. She is also doing research on resilience behaviors of aging women around the world.

Major Literature

Culbertson, Frances Mitchell. "Autistic Children and Public School Education." *School of Psychology International* 2 (1981): 27–30.

___. "Depression and Gender: An International Review." *American Psychologist* 52 (1997): 25–31.

___. "Frances Mitchell Culbertson." In Agnes N. O'Connell (Ed.), *Models of Achievement: Reflections of Eminent Women in Psychology* Vol. 3. Mahwah, New Jersey: Lawrence Erlbaum Associates, Inc., 2001.

Cummings, Nicholas Andrew (1924–)

BEHAVIORAL HEALTH

Born in Salinas, California, Nicholas Andrew Cummings received a B.A. from the University of California at Berkeley and his Ph.D. in clinical psychology from Adelphi University in New York. Cummings is president of the Foundation for Behavioral Health and chair of the boards of the Nicholas and Dorothy Cummings Foundation and the University Alliance for Behavioral Care in Scottsdale, Arizona. He was the founding chief executive officer of American Biodyne (MedCo/Merck, then Merit, now Magellan Behavioral Care). He was president of the American Psychological Association (1979). He was also the chief psychologist (retired) at Kaiser Permanente (the United States' largest integrated health maintenance organization) and the former executive director of the Mental Research Institute. Currently, Cummings is distinguished professor at the University of Nevada, Reno. He received the American Psychological Association's (APA) Distinguished Professional Contributions Award (1985).

Major Contributions

One of Cummings' contributions is the development of the Nicholas and Dorothy Cummings Foundation, headquartered in Reno, Nevada. It was incorporated in 1994 as a non-profit educational and research institute solely dedicated to excellence, innovation and the importance of behavioral health services, especially as these pertain to organized systems of care in which behavioral health is integrated into primary care. The Cummings Foundation fulfills its mission by funding a number of internally generated research, educational and demonstration projects.

Cummings has been a tireless campaigner for professionalism. He helped shape the professional school movement; he founded the four campuses of the California School of Professional Psychology, the National Academies of Practice, the American Managed Behavioral Healthcare Association, and the National Council of Professional Schools of Psychology. He helped shape the industrialization of health care and the psychologist as behavioral primary-care physician.

He also implemented the first comprehensive psychotherapy insurance and the first pre-paid comprehensive mental health plan in the U.S. As APA president he appointed the first Committee on Ethnic Minority Affairs and the first Task Force on Lesbian and Gay Issues. He co-founded the California Psychological Association, the San Francisco Bay Area Psychological Association and the San Joaquin County Psychological Association.

Major Literature

Cummings, Nicholas, and Mike Sayama. *Focused Psychotherapy: A Casebook of Brief Intermittent Psychotherapy Throughout the Life Cycle.* Philadelphia, Pennsylvania: Taylor and Francis Books, Ltd., Brunner-Mazel, 1995.

Cummings, Nicholas, et al. *The Value of Psychological Treatment: Collected Papers of Nicholas A. Cummings* Vol. 1. Phoenix, Arizona: Zeig, Tucker and Theisen, Inc., 2000.

___, and Thomas J. Lawrence (Eds.). *The Entrepreneur of Psychology: The Collected Papers of Nicholas A. Cummings.* Phoenix, Arizona: Zeig, Tucker and Theisen, Inc., 2002.

Cummings, Nicholas, and Rogers H. Wright (Eds.). *Destructive Trends in Mental Health: The Well-Intentioned Path to Harm.* Philadelphia, Pennsylvania: Taylor and Francis Books, Ltd., Routledge, 2005.

Dąbrowski, Kazimierz (1902–1980)

POSITIVE DISINTEGRATION

Psychologist, psychiatrist, physician, and poet Kazimierz Dąbrowski was born in Lublin, Poland. He gained his M.A. at the University of Poznan, Poland, then studied psychology and education in Geneva under Édouard Claparède (see entry), where Jean Piaget (see entry) was a fellow student. He received his M.D. at the University of Geneva (1929); the title of his thesis was "Le conditions psychological de suicide." In the same year he received his teaching certificate from the same university.

In Vienna, Austria, in 1930, he studied psychoanalysis with Karl and Charlotte Bühler under Wilhelm Stekel, and had additional training in clinical psychology and child psychiatry in Paris and Boston, Massachusetts. He studied child psychiatry and gained a second M.D. at Poznan and a Ph.D. in experimental psychology from Poznan in 1931. In 1934 he gained a certificate of the School of Public Health, Harvard University, Cambridge,

Massachusetts. From 1935 to 1948 (except for the German occupation) he was the director of the Polish State Mental Hygiene Institute and High School for Mental Hygiene in Warsaw, which had been organized with the aid of the Rockefeller Foundation. He died in Aleksandrow, Poland.

Major Contributions

Dąbrowski's theory of positive disintegration maintains that crises and disintegration are necessary for psychological growth and through these crises we attain wholeness of personality. He believed that inner conflict is a sign of development rather than a sign of collapse. In order to move to a higher level of development we must break down the old structures. This has echoes of Gestalt theory, where one Gestalten has to be completed before another can be built. Dąbrowski's proposal, then, makes sense when viewed from a Gestalt perspective.

An essential part of Dąbrowski's theory is what he calls "overexcitabilities." Overexcitabilities are a positive force for the gifted, as they feed, enrich, empower and amplify talent. Overexcitabilities are frequently observed in gifted children, as detailed by M.M. Piechowski and N. Colangelo ("Developmental Potential of the Gifted," *Gifted Child Quarterly* 28, 1984). Overexcitabilities appear in five forms, although not everyone demonstrates all five:

1. Psychomotor — surplus of energy
2. Sensual — sensory and aesthetic pleasure
3. Intellectual — learning, problem solving
4. Imaginational — vivid imagination
5. Emotional — intensity of feeling

In *Positive Disintegration,* Dąbrowski describes his own heightened excitability as a youth and the profound impact of wartime experiences on his development and on the development of his theory.

Major Literature

Dąbrowski, Kazimierz. *Positive Disintegration.* London: Churchill, 1964.
___. *Personality Shaping Through Positive Disintegration.* London: Churchill, 1968.
___. *Mental Growth Through Positive Disintegration.* London: Gryf Publications Ltd., 1970.
___. *Psychoneurosis Is Not an Illness: Neuroses and Psychoneuroses from the Perspective of Positive Disintegration.* London: Gryf Publications Ltd., 1972.
___. *Dynamics of Concepts.* London: Gryf Publications Ltd., 1973.

Deaux, Kay (1941–)
PSYCHOLOGY OF WOMEN

Born in Warren, Ohio, Kay Deaux gained a B.A. (1963) from University of Chicago, Northwestern University, and a Ph.D. in psychology from the University of Texas at Austin. Deaux is a distinguished professor of psychology and women's studies at the City University New York (CUNY) Graduate Center. In addition to an active research program involving both pre-doctoral and postdoctoral students, she teaches and co-teaches seminars on topics such as social identity, social psychological aspects of immigration, and gender and the law. She is past president of the Society for the Psychological Study of Social Issues (SPSSI) and she has served as president of the American Psychological Society and the Society of Personality and Social Psychology.

She has received a variety of awards and honors, including the Committee of Women in Psychology Leadership Award, the SPSSI Gordon Allport Inter-group Relations Prize (with Brenda Major), and the Carolyn Wood Sherif Award from Division 35 of the American Psychological Association. She was visiting scholar at the Russell Sage Foundation (2001-2002) and a fellow at the Center for Advanced Studies in the Behavioral Sciences. With professors Diane Ruble (New York University) and Jacquelynne Eccles (University of Michigan), Deaux directs the Social Identity in Context project, a group of investigators who are working on issues of gender, ethnicity, and social identity, funded by the Russell Sage Foundation since 2000.

Major Contributions

One of Deaux's main areas of research is immigration. This includes the complexity of ethnic identities, attitudes and stereotypes about immigrants and immigration, and how first- and second-generation immigrants from Africa and the Caribbean, Asia, Europe, and Latin America fit into American culture. She quotes the case of a Muslim woman from Bangladesh who, after 9/11, experienced an identity crisis. Where she had previously been a confident lawyer and feminist, now she regarded herself as brown woman whom people might regard as a terrorist suspect. She no longer feels a part of the New York community. One of the consequences of stereotyping is that those discriminated against tend to band together, thereby increasing their sense of identity, and to gear themselves up against attack. Another option is for immigrants to flee back to their land of origin. In her study of identity, Deaux identified four key themes:

1. A need for greater understanding of what is involved in multiple identities.
2. The functions that the several identities serve.
3. How the context influences the development and behaviour of identities.
4. The need for longitudinal studies of identity change.

Major Literature

Deaux, Kay. *Behavior of Women and Men.* Pacific Grove, California: Brooks-Cole, 1976.

Wrightsman, Lawrence, and Kay Deaux. *Social Psychology in the Seventies.* Pacific Grove, California: Brooks-Cole, 1977.

___. *Social Psychology in the Eighties.* Pacific Grove, California: Brooks-Cole, 1981.

___. *Social Psychology.* Belmont, California: Wadsworth, 1988.

Deaux, Kay. "Reconstructing Social Identity." *Personality and Social Psychology Bulletin* 19 (1993): 4–12.

Delabarre, Edmund Burke (1863–1945)

MENTAL IMAGERY

Born in Dover, Maine, Edmund Burke Delabarre graduated from Amherst College, Massachusetts, in 1883. Until 1889 he studied at Harvard University, Cambridge, Massachusetts, under William James, at Freiburg University, Germany, with Hugo Munsterberg, and at the Sorbonne, Paris, with Alfred Binet (see entries). He gained his M.A. (1889) from Harvard and his Ph.D. (1891) from Freiburg. He was a member of the Phi Beta Kappa and Alpha Delta Phi societies.

He was appointed associate professor of psychology, Brown University, Providence, Rhode Island, in 1891 and promoted to full professor in 1896. He was Brown's first professor of psychology, and established the Brown Laboratory of Experimental Psychology, the twelfth of its kind in America. In 1896–1897 he was director of Harvard's Psychological Laboratory during the absence of Professor Munsterberg.

Major Contributions

Professor Delabarre was a pioneer in the field of shape perception and on the interaction between mental processes and the involuntary movements of the body — the subject of his doctorate dissertation. For many years his principal research was

confirming that slight muscular movements, conscious or unconscious, were crucial to consciousness. He devised and put together a number of delicate instruments for the recording and measuring of, for example, eye movements. He was one of the first to use ink blots to encourage mental imagery (See Rorschach, Hermann) and published accounts of his experiments in professional journals. William James in *Principles of Psychology* (1890) refers to Delabarre's work.

Though his psychology work was important, he is possibly better known for his archæological study. His farm at Assonet Neck in Massachusetts was not far from Dighton Rock, a ten foot by four foot sandstone boulder weighing some forty tons, covered with mysterious markings. Although the rock, at the edge of the Taunton River, was submerged by tides much of the time, Delabarre deciphered the markings (partly obscured by Indian inscriptions) as referring to two Portuguese brothers, Gaspar Cortereal, who explored the coast of Newfoundland in 1501 and did not return to Portugal, and his brother Miguel Cortereal, who set out the next year to search for him and also did not return. He interpreted a shield-like marking on the rock as the insignia of Prince Henry, "The Navigator of Portugal" (1394–146).

Delabarre was decorated by the Portuguese government with the insignia of St. James of the Sword for his work. He retired in 1932 and died at Providence, Rhode Island. Dighton Rock State Park covers 85 acres in the town of Berkley, Massachusetts.

Major Literature

Delabarre, Edmund Burke. "Report of the Brown-Harvard Expedition to Nachvak, Labrador, 1900." *Bulletin of the Geographical Society of Philadelphia*, Vol. 3, No. 4., 1902.

___. *Dighton Rock: A Study of the Written Rocks of New England.* New York: Walter Neale, 1928.

Delabarre, Edmund B. "Alleged Runic Inscription in Rhode Island." *Rhode Island Historical Society Collections* 28 (1935): 49–57.

Delay, Jean (1907–1987)

PSYCHOPHARMACOLOGY

Born in Bayonne, France, the son of a surgeon, Jean Delay proved to be a gifted child and entered medical school in 1923. In 1936 he was appointed neuropsychiatrist in the famous La Salpétrière Hospital in Paris and one year later he joined the Sainte Anne Hospital in Paris as one of the few professors of psychiatry. His doctoral thesis on

"Les astéréognosies" (astereognosis, tactile agnosia — the inability to recognize objects by touch) studied the organization of tactile functions and foreshadowed a lifelong interest in the links between physiology and psychology.

In 1939, he created the first French laboratory of electroencephalography and used it to study normal and pathological aspects of cerebral waves. In 1946, Delay was appointed to the chair of mental illness and brain diseases and later held the Charcot chair until 1970, when he retired. Delay was chair of the first International Congress in Psychiatry held in Paris in 1950 and was elected member of the Académie de Médicine in 1955.

From 1959 until he died he was a member of the Académie Française, the only psychiatrist ever elected to this prestigious institution. He was a pioneer in introducing Electroconvulstive therapy (ECT) in France and examined physiological and psychological effects of shocks, following the works of Ugo Cerletti (see entry). A recognized remarkable clinician, he officiated as a psychiatric expert in the Nuremberg trial of Rudolph Hess and Julius Streicher after World War II.

Major Contributions

Jean Delay invented the word "psychopharmacology" along with a whole field of research on psychological and behavioral modifications induced by drugs such as LSD, mescaline, and psilocybin (a psychedelic drug derived from certain mushrooms). He coined the term "neuroleptic" (the effects on cognition and behavior of antipsychotic drugs) and introduced the use of reserpine (used to treat high blood pressure) into psychiatry.

In 1952, along with his co-worker Pierre Deniker (1917–1998) he was the first psychiatrist to recognize the therapeutic value of phenothiazines in the treatment of schizophrenia (Largactil being the most widely used phenothiazine). In 1956, he and Deniker established the first classification of psychotropic drugs. In his philosophy dissertation, "Les dissolutions de la mémoire: Bibliothèque de Philosophie contemporaine" (Paris, Presses Universitaires de France, 1942), Delay studied the complex relationship between neurosis and creation. During his last years he devoted himself to his masterly work *Les Avant Mémoires* (Paris, Editions Gallimard, 1979), a genealogical "psychosociobiography" of his own family through several centuries.

He made decisive contributions to the growth of the fields of psychiatry and mental health in France and in the world at large by the creation of the World Psychiatric Association (WPA), and by the recognition of the importance and the promotion of a systematic multidisciplinary approach in psychiatry. The Jean Delay Prize is the most important award of the WPA (it has been called the "Nobel Prize'" of the association).

De Mause, Lloyd (1931–)

PSYCHOHISTORY

Born in Detroit, Michigan, Lloyd De Mause graduated from Columbia College and did his post-graduate training in political science at Columbia University and in psychoanalysis at the National Psychological Association for Psychoanalysis, New York. He has taught psychohistory at the City University of New York and the New York Center for Psychoanalytic Training. He is a member of the Society for Psychoanalytic Training, and has lectured widely in Europe and America.

De Mause is director of the Institute for Psychohistory, New York City, with 17 branches in various countries. He is founder and editor of *The Journal of Psychohistory* and president of the International Psychohistorical Association (IPA). He has written several books, and his articles have appeared in many journals. He is on the editorial board of several international journals.

Major Contributions

De Mause is well-known for his work in psychohistory. Psychohistory combines the insights of psychotherapy with the research methodology of the social sciences. It studies the psychology of historical events that shape human history, particularly related to childbirth, parenting practice and child abuse, as well as the impact of incest, infanticide, and child sacrifice. In the view of De Mause, the history of childhood has been a nightmare from which we have only recently begun to awaken. Psychohistorians suggest that destructive social behavior now may be a re-enactment of past destructive parenting, abuse and neglect.

De Mause and others have argued that psychohistory is a separate field of scholarly inquiry with its own particular methods, objectives and theories that set it apart from conventional historical analysis and anthropology. Some historians, social scientists and anthropologists have, however, argued that their disciplines already describe psychological motivation and that psychohistory is not, therefore, a separate subject.

There are three inter-related areas of psychohistorical study:

1. *The History of childhood,* which looks at such questions as:

- How have children been raised throughout history?
- How has the family been constituted?
- How and why have practices changed over time?
- How has the place and value of children in society changed over time?
- How and why our views of child abuse and neglect have changed.
- Why there is still denial in modern societies of the reality of child abuse.

2. *Psychobiography,* which seeks to understand individual historical people and their motivations in history.

3. *Group psychohistory,* which seeks to understand the motivations of large groups, including nations, in history and current affairs. In doing so, psychohistory advances the use of group-fantasy analysis of political speeches, political cartoons and media headlines since the fantasy words therein offer clues to unconscious thinking and behaviors.

Major Literature

De Mause, Lloyd. *Foundations of Psychohistory.* New York: Creative Roots, Inc. 1982.
___. *History of Childhood: The Untold Story of Child Abuse.* New York: Peter Bedrick Books, Inc., 1988.
___. *The Emotional Life of Nations.* New York: The Other Press, 2002.

Denmark, Florence Harriet Levin (1931–)

PSYCHOLOGY OF WOMEN

Florence Levin was born in Philadelphia, Pennsylvania; she studied at University of Pennsylvania in the same city and gained an A.B. with double honors in history and psychology (1952), an A.M. in psychology (1954), and a Ph.D. in social psychology (1958). She married Stanley Denmark, an orthodontist, in 1953.

After earning her doctorate, she was an adjunct professor at Queens College of the City University of New York (CUNY), then full professor at Hunter College in the Bronx. She is now the Robert Scott Pace Distinguished Research Professor at Pace University, New York City. She was president, New York State Psychological Association (1972–1973); president, American Psychological Association (APA) (1980–1981); president, Eastern Psychological Association (1985–1986); national president, Psi Chi (1978–1980); and vice president, New York Academy of Sciences (1984).

Among Denmark's many awards are several doctorates; the Distinguished Leader Award of the APA; the Outstanding Woman in Science Award of the Association for Women in Science; the Association of Women Psychologists Distinguished Career Award for her contributions to mentoring, policy and scholarship; and the APA's Distinguished Contributions to Education and Training, Public Interest and the Advancement of International Psychology award. From 1971 to 1984 Denmark served as an associate editor for the *International Journal of Group Tensions,* and from 1985 to 1988, she was on the committee for Lesbian and Gay Concerns.

Major Contributions

Denmark's major work is or has been on racial prejudice in preschool, discrimination against women, the effects of college on women and the psychology of gender. She served from 1968 to 1970 as the first director of SEEK, Search for Education, Elevation, and Knowledge. SEEK was formed to help high school students of poverty to find psychology programs in colleges across America.

Her pioneering work in the psychology of women, and her carefully documented cases of discrimination and the disadvantaged status of women, has led to the psychology of women being a highly regarded field of study. Denmark was the first to integrate psychology of women in introductory psychology courses. In 1973 she was instrumental in having the American Psychological Association create its 35th division — the Psychology of Women. In 1981, Denmark established the first International Interdisciplinary Congress on Women, held at the University of Haifa, Israel.

Major Literature

Denmark, Florence L. *Women's Realities, Women's Choices: An Introduction to Women's Studies.* Hunter College Women's Studies Collective. New York: Oxford University Press, Inc., 1983.
___. "Autobiography." In A.N. O'Connell and N.F. Russo (Eds.), *Models of Achievement: Reflections of Eminent Women in Psychology,* Vol. 2, Hillsdale, New Jersey: Erlbaum, 1988.

___, and Leonore Loeb Adler (Eds.). *International Perspectives on Violence*. Westport, Connecticut: Greenwood Press, 2003.

Denmark, Florence L., et al. *Engendering Psychology: Women and Gender Revisited*. Boston, Massachusetts: Allyn and Bacon/Longman, 2004.

___, et al. *Handbook of International Psychology*. Philadelphia, Pennsylvania: Taylor and Francis, Brunner-Routledge, 2004.

Dercum, Francis Xavier (1856–1931)

PSYCHOBIOLOGY

Born in Philadelphia, Francis Xavier Dercum gained his medical degree in 1877 from the University of Pennsylvania, Philadelphia. From 1878 to 1883 he was a demonstrator of histology and physiology at Pennsylvania and later, associate professor of physiology. He lectured on practical biology and demonstrated various protozoa, algae and bacteria, laying the foundations for what was later to be called bacteriology. His particular medical interest was neuropathology (the branch of pathology concerned with the nervous system), and early in his career he worked as a pathologist at the State Hospital for the Insane in Norristown, Montgomery County, Pennsylvania.

In 1884 Dercum was made head of the neurological clinic at the University of Pennsylvania, and was one of the founders of the Philadelphia Neurological Society in 1884. He became a member of the American Neurological Society in 1885 and president in 1886. In 1885 he also became a member of the College of Physicians of Philadelphia. In 1887 he became neurologist at the Philadelphia Hospital, where many neurological patients were being treated. In 1892 he was appointed to the new chair of clinical neurology at the Jefferson Medical College, Philadelphia. A separate clinic was established in 1900 and Dercum was then appointed professor of nervous end mental diseases. He headed this department until 1925, when he was awarded emeritus status. In 1927 he was elected president of the American Philosophical Society, of which he had been a member for 35 years.

Major Contributions

Around 1884 Dercum had the photographer and scientist Eadweard Muybridge (1830–1904) (who had commenced his studies of the movements of horses) photograph patients with a pathological gait pattern and patients with convulsions elicited through hypnosis. These pictures were the first to document neurological diseases. Muybridge published an eleven volume work *Animal Locomotion* (1887) with photographs, in which volume 8 contained Dercum's patients. (Muybridge's pioneering moving photography was the forerunner of the movie industry.)

Dercum co-founded the Anthropological Society and agreed to leave his brain for study. In 1888 Dercum described what became known as Dercum's disease or syndrome, a disease accompanied by painful localized fatty swellings and by various nerve lesions. Mental depression and deterioration have been observed in an appreciable number of these patients. It is usually seen in women and may cause death from cardiac failure complications. Dercum was held in high esteem as a teacher of mental illness, and in particular dealing with patients who, in the terminology of the day, lived in the no-man's land between sanity and insanity.

Major Literature

Dercum, Francis X. *Description of the Brain of John M. Wilson, Recently Hanged at Norristown*. Philadelphia: J.B. Lippincott, 1887.

___. "A Subcutaneous Connective-Tissue Dystrophy of the Arms and Back, Associated with Symptoms Resembling Myxoedema." *University Medical Magazine of Philadelphia* 1 (1888): 140–150.

___. "Three Cases of a Hitherto Unclassified Affection Resembling in Its Grosser Aspects Obesity, But Associated with Special Nervous Symptoms — Adiposis Dolorosa." *American Journal of Medical Science* 104 (1892): 521–535.

Deutsch, Helene (1884–1982)

PSYCHOLOGY OF WOMEN

Born Helen Rosenbach, the youngest child of four of Jewish parents in Przemysl, a non–Russian part of Poland, Deutsch studied medicine and psychiatry in Vienna and Munich with Emil Kraepelin (see entry). She became a doctor before it was socially acceptable for women to have a career, and before most universities allowed women in. She then studied psychiatry and became a pupil, assistant, and colleague of Sigmund Freud (see entry) and was accepted into his elite Wednesday night meetings.

She was the first woman who was concerned with the psychology of the woman, an area that was alien to Freud. She married Felix Deutsch in 1912. In 1935 she fled Germany, immigrating to Cambridge, Massachusetts, in the United States. Her husband and son joined her a year later, and she worked there as a well-regarded psychoanalyst up until her death in 1982.

Major Contributions

Shortly after graduation Deutsch began her work in the Vienna University's Psychiatric Clinic. In the mid–1920s, she started her life-long work with the sexuality of women. Her first book, *The Psychology of Women's Sexual Functions* (1925), was the first by a psychoanalyst on the subject of women's psychology. She postulated that for a woman, menstruation meant castration, and that morning sickness and miscarriage in pregnancy are anal and oral fixations being played out.

She became an associate psychiatrist at the Massachusetts General Hospital, Cambridge (1936). Her two-volume *The Psychology of Women* (1945) for several years was the major Freudian view of the life cycle of women. She proposed that trauma during birth, infancy and childhood predisposed to adult psychosomatic illnesses. She believed that problems experienced by girls were caused by insufficient detachment from their mothers. Furthermore, she said women's sexuality depends wholly on the male and on mothering, and that the entire goal of women's sex drive is to have babies to mother. She held that infertility is caused by either the hatred of the woman's own mother's sexuality or that the woman felt she would be an incompetent mother.

Deutsch considered Beatlemania and the sexual liberation of the '60s, as a lack of fathering, which led to loneliness, thus causing people to look to their own peers for company and advice. Helene Deutsch's rebellions helped lead the way for other women to rise above their proscribed stations in life.

Major Literature

Deutsch, Helene. *Neuroses and Character Types: Clinical Psychological Studies*. Madison, Connecticut: International Universities Press, Inc., 1965.

___. *Selected Problems of Adolescence: With Special Emphasis on Group Formation*. Madison, Connecticut: International Universities Press, Inc., 1967.

___. *Deutsch: Confrontations with Myself*. New York: W.W. Norton and Co., Ltd., 1973.

___, and Paul Roazen. *The Therapeutic Process, the Self and the Female Psychology: Collected Psychoanalytical Papers*. New Jersey: Transaction Publishers, 1992.

Related Literature

Sayers, J. *Mothers of Psychoanalysis: Helene Deutsch, Karen Horney, Anna Freud, Melanie Klein*. New York: W.W. Norton, 1991.

Deutsch, Morton (1920–)
CONFLICT RESOLUTION

Born in New York, Deutsch earned a B.S. at City College, New York (1939), an M.A. at the University of Pennsylvania, Philadelphia (1940), a Ph.D. from the Massachusetts Institute of Technology, Cambridge (1948); and a certificate in psychoanalysis, Postgraduate Center for Mental Health, New York (1958).

At New York University he was assistant professor (1948–1952), associate professor (1952–1956), and adjunct professor (1961–1963). He was a member of technical staff (in charge of interpersonal process) at Bell Telephone Laboratories (1956–1963); a member of the staff, Postgraduate Center for Psychotherapy (1954–1963); professor, Teachers College, Columbia University (1963–1981); Edward Lee Thorndike Professor of Psychology and Education, Teachers College, Columbia University (1981–1990); director, International Center for Cooperation and Conflict Resolution (1986–1998); and professor emeritus (since 1990).

Deutsch is a fellow of many of the American psychology societies and has held office in most of them, including first president, Division of Peace Psychology and the American Psychological Association. He has been on the editorial board of many distinguished journals, including *Contemporary Psychoanalysis*. His distinctions have been many, including the Kurt Lewin Memorial Award, the G.W. Allport Prize, the Carl Hovland Memorial Award, the American Psychological Association's Distinguished Scientific Contribution Award, the Association for Psychological Science's James McKeen Cattell Fellow Award, and the Society of Experimental Social Psychology Distinguished Scientist Award.

Major Contributions

Deutsch's areas of specialization are conflict resolution, distributive justice, social perception, inter-group relations, developmental social psychology, small group processes, and social psychology of mental health. His Ph.D. dissertation was an investigation of the effects on groups of cooperation and competition and what determines whether the conflict will be constructive or destructive. Trust and suspicion influence people's willingness to cooperate. Developing this theme has been the major part of his life's work.

In 1986, he founded the International Center for Cooperation and Conflict Resolution (ICCCR) at Teachers College, Columbia University, New York. The aim of the center is to help individuals, schools, communities, businesses, and governments to have a better understanding of the nature of conflict and to develop the skills and settings that enable them to resolve conflict fairly and constructively. Where conflict resolution is used in schools, students report that they feel better about themselves and safer at school; they handle conflicts quickly, sometimes taking only minutes to deal with situations. Many schools report that student mediators help solve large numbers of conflicts and that the disputes remain settled in the vast majority of cases. Often the best student mediators are those who had been considered troublemakers.

Major Literature

Deutsch, Morton. "Trust And Suspicion." *Journal of Conflict Resolution* 2 (1958): 265–279.
___, and R.M. Krauss. *Theories in Social Psychology.* Jackson, Tennessee: Basic Books, 1966.
Deutsch, Morton, and Harvey A. Hornstein. *Applying Social Psychology: Implications for Research, Practice and Training.* New Jersey: John Wiley and Sons, Inc., 1975.
Deutsch, Morton. *Distributive Justice: A Social-psychological Perspective.* New Haven, Connecticut: Yale University Press, 1985.
___, et al. *The Handbook of Conflict Resolution.* New Jersey: John Wiley and Sons, Ltd., Jossey Bass Wiley, 2006.

Dewey, John (1859–1952)
PRAGMATISM

John Dewey was one of the founders of the philosophical school of pragmatism, a pioneer in functional psychology, and a leader of the progressive movement in education in the United States. Born in Burlington, Vermont, Dewey gained a B.A. at the University of Vermont, Burlington (1879), and a Ph.D. in philosophy from the Johns Hopkins University, Baltimore, Maryland (1864). From 1884 to 1894 Dewey taught at the University of Michigan, Ann Arbor, where he became professor of philosophy and psychology, with one year (1888–1889) as professor of philosophy at the University of Minnesota (psychology hadn't yet become a separate discipline).

From 1894 to 1904 he was professor of philosophy and chairman of the department of philosophy, psychology, and pedagogy at the newly created University of Chicago. A disagreement with the administration over the status of the Labora-

tory School (run by Dewey and his wife) led to Dewey's resignation from his post at Chicago in 1904. He joined the Department of Philosophy at Columbia University (now in New York), where he remained until he retired in 1930.

Major Contributions

Dewey's philosophical orientation has been labeled a form of pragmatism, though Dewey himself seemed to favor the terms "instrumentalism" or "experimentalism." Dewey's idea of democracy is a system that provides the members of a society with the opportunity for maximum experimentation and personal growth. The ideal society, for Dewey, was one that provided the conditions for enlarging the experience of all its members. His contributions to psychology are also noteworthy, and mark the beginning of functional psychology — one that focuses on the total organism in its endeavors to adjust to the environment.

Dewey disagreed with the mechanistic interpretation of the terms "stimulus" and "response." He believed that stimulus and response should be interpreted much more broadly. Dewey was in the forefront of educational reform; he believed that education should be a process where the child learns to solve problems as distinct from learning by rote. He helped found the New School for Social Research in 1919 and the University-in-Exile in 1933, established for scholars being persecuted in countries under totalitarian regimes.

In 1937 he headed a commission of inquiry that went to Mexico City to hear Leon Trotsky's rebuttal of the charges made against him in exposing Stalin's political machinations behind the Moscow show trials of 1936 and 1937. He also defended his fellow philosopher Bertrand Russell against an attempt by conservatives to remove him from his chair at the College of the City of New York in 1940.

Major Literature

Dewey, John. *Art as Experience.* (1980) New York: G.P. Putnam's Sons, 1930.
___. *How We Think.* Lexington, Massachusetts: D.C. Heath, (1910). Loughton, Essex, England: Prometheus Books, 1991.
___. *Democracy and Education.* The Macmillan Company, 2004. Montana: R.A. Kessinger Publishing Co., 1915.
Boydston, Jo Ann (ed). *The Collected Works of John Dewey.* 37 Vols. Carbondale, Illinois: Southern Illinois University Press, 1967–1991.

Dollard, John (1900–1980)
RACE RELATIONS

Born in Menasha, Wisconsin, John Dollard received his A.B. degree (1922) from the University of Wisconsin, Madison, and his Ph.D. in sociology (1931) from the University of Chicago, Illinois; then he trained in psychoanalysis in Berlin (1931–1932). He was appointed researcher at the Institute of Human Relationship, Yale University (1932), where he conducted some of his most influential work. From 1942 to 1945 Dollard served as a consultant for the United States Department of War. In 1952 he became a professor in Yale University's Department of Psychology and in 1969 he retired as professor emeritus.

Major Contributions

Possibly because of his eclectic training, Dollard was a pioneer in integrating the social and behavioral sciences. In 1959 he and Neal Miller (see entry) attempted to integrate certain psychoanalytic concepts into learning theory. For example, fear can be viewed as a drive that motivates learning, particularly responses that reduce fear. They looked at such concepts as dependency, aggression, identification and conscience formation, though such attempts had no lasting influence on psychoanalytic thought and practice.

However, what has endured is the work of Dollard and his colleagues on aggression. Dollard proposed the frustration-aggression hypothesis in which blocking of an ongoing goal-directed behavior leads to the arousal of an aggressive drive and a counter attack on the source of the frustration. Their work had a strong influence on the research into frustration and aggression by other psychologists in the 1960 and 1970s.

During the period of time with the Department of War, Dollard and fellow psychologists at Yale University's Institute of Human Relations produced a study titled "Fear and Courage under Battle Conditions." This study investigated fear and morale of soldiers in modern combat conditions. Three hundred veterans who had served as volunteers with the Abraham Lincoln Brigade during the Spanish Civil War were used as research subjects for the study. With the aid of a Rockefeller grant, Dollard and his team summarized their findings in *Fear in Battle* (a self-help handbook for World War II military personnel).

Major Literature

Dollard, John. *Criteria for the Life History with Analyses of Six Notable Documents* (Select Bibliographies Reprint Services). Manchester, New Hampshire: Ayer Co. Publishers, 1935.
___, et al. *Frustration and Aggression.* Newhaven, Connecticut: Yale University Press, 1980. Westport, Connecticut: Greenwood Press, 1939.
___, et al. *Fear in Battle.* New York: Ams Press Inc., 1944. Westport, Connecticut: Greenwood Press, 1977.
___, and Neal E. Miller. *Personality and Psychotherapy.* Columbus, Ohio: McGraw-Hill Education, 1950, 1963.
Davis, Allison, and John Dollard. *Children of Bondage: Personality Development of Negro Youth in the Urban South.* New York: Harper and Row, 1964.
Miller, Neal E., and John Dollard. *Social Learning and Imitation.* Westport, Connecticut: Greenwood Press, 1979.
Dollard, John. *Caste and Class in a Southern Town.* Madison, Wisconsin: The University of Wisconsin Press, 2006. New York: ACLS History E-Book Project, 1989.

Downey, June Etta (1875–1932)
PERSONALITY

Born in Laramie, Wyoming, Downey graduated in Greek and Latin from the University of Wyoming in 1895 and gained an M.A. in philosophy and psychology (1898) from the University of Chicago, where she published "A Musical Experiment" in the *American Journal of Psychology* (1897). She became an instructor of English and philosophy at the University of Wyoming, and in 1901 she studied psychology under Edward Bradford Titchener (see entry) at Cornell University, Ithaca, New York.

She became a full professor at Wyoming in 1905, was awarded her Ph.D. in 1908, and headed the combined Department of Psychology and Philosophy at Wyoming, the first woman to hold such a position at a state university. The title of her professorship was changed formally to philosophy and psychology in 1915. From 1923 to 1925 she served on the Council of the American Psychological Association, a rare appointment for a woman at that time. In the last decade of her life she received many recognitions, including appointment to the American Psychological Association Council, membership in the Society of Experimentalists, and election as a fellow of the American Association for the Advancement of Science.

Major Contributions

Downey was one of the original psychologists to study personality scientifically. In 1912, she published "The Imaginal Reaction to Poetry,"

University of Wyoming, Bulletin No. 2, one of her most important experiments involving the arts. This study examined the images people had in response to reading poetry. Downey believed that variation in such images revealed differences in character.

Her main contribution was the development of one of the most interesting and controversial personality tests, the Downey Individual Will-Temperament Test (see also, Roberto Assagioli, Isabel Briggs Myers and Carl Jung). This test assessed personality primarily through the use of handwriting analysis and simplified "muscle reading" of involuntary motor actions. It contained 10 subtests and the scores could be added to obtain a total score representing the general level of "will-capacity." Downey hypothesized that the subtests reflected three underlying personality types:

- the quick, by the seat of the pants, *hairtrigger* type
- the forceful, decisive, *willful* type
- the slow, careful, *accurate* type

Downey was open to the possibility that some individuals would exhibit mixed traits. It was one of the first tests to evaluate character traits separately from intellectual capacity. It was not without its critics because of its unreliability and poor correlation; however, it was one of the first tests to evaluate character traits separately from intellectual capacity.

Major Literature

Downey, June Etta. *Graphology and the Psychology of Handwriting*. Baltimore, Maryland: Warwick and York, Inc., 1919.
___, and Edward E. Slosson. *Plots and Personalities*. New York: The Century Co., 1922.
Downey, June Etta. *The Will-Temperament and Its Testing*. London: George G. Harrap and Company, 1923.
___. *Creative Imagination: Studies in the Psychology of Literature*. New York: Harcourt, Brace and Company, 1929.

Dreikurs, Rudolf (1897–1972)

FAMILY PSYCHIATRY

Bon in Vienna, Austria, Rudolf Dreikurs graduated in medicine from the University of Vienna (1923). One of his residencies was in psychiatry and neurology in Vienna. A student and colleague of Alfred Adler (see entry) he joined Adler in the United States in 1937, just before Adler died. In the same year Dreikurs founded the Society of Individual Psychology, Rio de Janeiro.

He was professor of psychiatry, Chicago Medical School (1942–1972), vice president, American Humanist Association (1944–1951), and president of the Alfred Adler Institute of Chicago (1950–1972). He was a founding member of the American Psychological Society and president (1955–1956); president, American Society of Group Psychotherapy and Psychodrama (1954); founding member, International Association of Individual Psychology and vice president (1957–1960); and vice president, American Academy of Psychotherapists in Portland, Oregon (1959).

Major Contributions

Dreikurs developed the work that Adler had started and simplified many of Adler's ideas for use by parents and teachers. He introduced psychodrama and group therapy into his private psychiatric practice in the early days of their existence, and applied Adlerian principles to business and large organizations. He constructed probably the most effective tool — and what may well be Dreikurs' finest contribution — in helping to understand children's behavior: the *Four Goals of Misbehavior* and the techniques of effectively revealing these to a misbehaving child. Although much of Dreikurs' writing is directed at educationalists, what he says applies equally to parents. Dreikurs said that discouraged children use four primary "misbehaviors" in their mistaken ideas on how to achieve belonging:

- Excessive attention seeking (many class clowns seek attention this way).
- Vying to be the boss (being right).
- Seeking revenge for the hurt they experience from the lack of acceptance.
- Giving up because they feel they cannot possibly win.

Children will always do better when they feel better. The teacher (parent) must reach the heart before she can reach the head. The remedy Dreikurs suggested is to confront the child with the four goals. The purpose of confrontation is to disclose and confirm the mistaken goal to the child. Use the four "could it be..." questions:

1. Could it be that you want special attention?
2. Could it be that you want your own way and hope to be boss?
3. Could it be that you want to hurt others as much as you feel hurt by them?
4. Could it be that you want to be left alone?

Major Literature

Dreikurs, Rudolf. *Coping with Children's Misbehavior: A Parent's Guide*. New York: Penguin Group, Inc., Dutton Books, 1972.
___. *Children That Challenge*. New York: Penguin Group, Inc., Dutton Books, 1976.
___. *Psychodynamics, Psychotherapy, and Counseling: Collected Papers*. Chicago, Illinois: Adler School of Professional Psychology, 1982.
___. *Discipline Without Tears*. New York: Penguin Group, Inc., Dutton Books, 1986.
___. *The Challenge of Parenthood*. New York: Penguin Group, Inc., Plume Books, 1992.

Dunbar, Helen Flanders (1902–1959)
PSYCHOSOMATIC MEDICINE

Born in Chicago, Illinois, Helen Flanders Dunbar graduated from Bryn Mawr College, Pennsylvania, in 1923. Over the next seven years she received four graduate degrees. At one point, she was studying in three programs at three different institutions simultaneously, including a B.A. in divinity at Union Theological Seminary in Charlotte, North Carolina. Columbia University awarded her an M.A. in philosophy (1924) and a Ph.D. in philosophy (1929). Her doctoral dissertation on Dante, *Symbolism in Medieval Thought and Its Consummation in the Divine Comedy*, was published 1929. She graduated with an M.D. (1930) at Yale University School of Medicine, New Haven, Connecticut.

During the summer of 1925, she trained at Worcester State Hospital, Massachusetts, with Anton Boisen (1876–1965), one of the co-founders of the Clinical Pastoral Education (CPE) movement. Dunbar later became the medical director the Council for Clinical Pastoral Training of Theological Students in New York City. In 1929 Dunbar worked at the General and Psychiatric-Neurological Hospital and Clinic of the University of Vienna. She underwent psychoanalysis with Helene Deutsch, worked at Carl Jung's Burgholzli Psychiatric Clinic in Zurich, and visited Lourdes as a continuation of her interest in the relationship between faith and healing.

From 1931 to 1949 she held appointments in medicine and psychiatry at the Columbia Presbyterian Hospital, New York, and the Vanderbilt Clinic, New York, while teaching at Columbia University's College of Physicians and Surgeons. Between 1942 and 1947 she taught at the New York Psychoanalytic Institute. Dunbar drowned at her home in Connecticut on the day that she had received the first copy of her *Psychiatry in the Medical Specialties*.

Major Contributions

Within psychology, Dunbar is generally known as "the mother of holistic medicine." From 1932 to 1949 she directed the psychosomatic research at the Columbia-Presbyterian Hospital that established the relationship between certain personality characteristics and psychosomatic disorder. Demonstrating that emotional factors influence the course of disease became her major intellectual contribution to the medical and psychiatric fields. Dunbar founded what is now the American Psychosomatic Society (1942) and its journal, *Psychosomatic Medicine: Experimental and Clinical Studies*.

She edited *Psychosomatic Medicine* (1939–1947), *Psychosomatic Medicine Monographs* (1939–1946), and *Psychoanalytic Quarterly* (1939–1940), and served on the editorial board of *Personality: Symposia on Topical Interests* (1950–1959). She was an instructor at the New York Psychoanalytic Institute (1941–1949). During the height of her career, she maintained concurrent positions at a variety of institutions, carried out scientific studies, and wrote prolifically.

Major Literature

Dunbar, Helen Flanders. *Psychosomatic Diagnosis*. New York: Paul B. Hoeber, Inc., 1943.
___. *Mind and Body: Psychosomatic Medicine*. New York: Random House Inc., 1947.
___. *Synopsis of Psychosomatic Diagnosis and Treatment*. St. Louis, Missouri: C.V. Mosby Co., 1948.
___. *Your Child's Mind and Body: A Practical Guide for Parents*. New York: Random House, Inc., 1949.
___. *Emotions and Bodily Changes: A Survey of Literature on Psychosomatic Interrelationships, 1910–1953*. New York: Columbia University Press, 1954. Manchester, New Hampshire: Ayer Co. Publishers, 1976.

Dunlap, Knight (1875–1949)
BEHAVIORISM

Born at Diamond Spring, California, Knight Dunlap received his Ph.D. from Harvard University, Cambridge, Massachusetts, in 1903 under Hugo Munsterberg (see entry). From 1904 to 1906 he worked at University of California, Berkeley, then was appointed instructor in psychology at the Johns Hopkins University, Baltimore, Maryland, where, by 1916, he was professor of experimental psychology. He published some influential work on imagery, consciousness, instincts and habits, something that highlighted the relationship between cognition and learning.

John B. Watson (see entry) was appointed full professor of comparative psychology and experimental psychology, and thereafter Dunlap moved in Watson's shadow and has been largely forgotten. Though Watson was younger than Dunlap, he regarded Dunlap as his "junior," though he did give credit to Dunlap's ability, and it does seem that Dunlap influenced Watson in some of his thinking. When Watson was forced to resign from Johns Hopkins on account of his affair with a colleague, Dunlap became chair of the psychology department and was instrumental in resurrecting the dying Ph.D. psychology program. He remained at Johns Hopkins until 1936, when he accepted an offer to develop a graduate psychology program at University of California, Los Angeles (UCLA).

Watson was pure behaviorist; Dunlap and Watson disagreed about the role of cognition in psychology, although they did share the same opposition to psychoanalysis. Dunlap believed that conscious experience was a type of behavior and that it could be studied scientifically. Seventy years later cognitive-behavioral psychology has a definite place in therapy. Dunlap was president of the American Psychological Association (1922) and first editor of the *Journal of Comparative Psychology* (originally *Psychobiology*). Dunlap's papers are housed at the Archives of the History of American Psychology, University of Akron, Ohio.

Major Contributions

- Dunlap conducted important research on color vision, audition, and the nystagmus reflex (an involuntary rhythmic movement of the eyes, usually from side to side, caused by some illnesses that affect the nerves and muscle behind the eyeball).
- He was among the first to demonstrate practice effects in intelligence testing.
- He wrote books on physiological psychology, the psychology of religion, social psychology, general psychology, psychoanalysis, and personal adjustment.
- He was an important leader of national and regional organizations, including the Western Psychological Association, the National Institute for Psychology, the National Research Council, and the Southern Society for Philosophy and Psychology.

Major Literature

Dunlap, Knight. *Mysticism, Freudianism, and Scientific Psychology.* St. Louis, Missouri: C.V. Mosby, 1920. Montana: R.A. Kessinger Publishing Co., 2003.

___. *Old and New Viewpoints in Psychology.* St. Louis, Missouri: C.V. Mosby Co., 1925.

___. *Social Psychology.* Philadelphia, Pennsylvania: Lippincott, Williams and Willkins, 1927.

___. *Religion: Its Functions in Human Life; A Study of Religion from the Point of View of Psychology.* Columbus, Ohio: McGraw-Hill, 1946.

___. *Habits: Their Making and Unmaking.* New York: W.W. Norton and Co., Ltd., Liverlight Books, 1949.

Dunnette, Marvin D. (1926–)
COUNSELING PSYCHOLOGY

Born in Austin, Minnesota, Marvin D. Dunnette graduated with a bachelor's degree from the Institute of Technology at the University of Minnesota, Minneapolis, with high distinction in chemical engineering (1948). He worked for a year in the Department of Mines and Metallurgy as a research chemist, and gained an M.A. in industrial psychology (1951) and Ph.D. (1954) from the University of Minnesota. For his doctoral dissertation he validated the Minnesota Engineering Analogies Test.

From 1954 to 1960 he was manager of employee relations research for the 3M Company, St. Paul, Minnesota, where he developed new procedures for selecting and appraising research scientists, sales personnel, and clerical employees. From 1960 to 1967 he was associate professor of psychology at the University of Minnesota; then he formed his own management consulting company, Personnel Decisions, Inc. In 1974 he co-founded Personnel Decisions Research Institute. The institute does behavioral science research in areas related to improved and more productive utilization of human resources.

He is a fellow of the American Psychological Association and holds the Diplomat in Industrial Psychology designation granted by the American Board of Professional Psychology. He served as president of the American Psychological Association's Division of Industrial and Organizational Psychology, 1966-67, and was the 1985 recipient of the Division's Award for Outstanding Scientific Contributions.

Major Contributions

Dunnette either singly or through his research organizations has developed improved selection procedures for police officers, lawyers, managers, firefighters, Navy recruiters, salesmen, prison guards, and power plant operators. Another area of research has involved motivation, morale, and job satisfaction, improved methods of job analysis and job performance appraisal. He has served as academic advisor to Ph.D. students in fields of industrial psychology, counseling psychology, and psychometrics. He is a professor emeritus of psychology at the University of Minnesota, and chairman emeritus of Personnel Decisions Research Institutes, Inc. and Personnel Decisions, Inc.

Major Literature

Dunnette, Marvin D. "The MN Engineering Analogies Test." *Journal of Applied Psychology* 37 (1953): 170–175.

___. *Personnel Selection and Placement*. London: Taylor and Francis Books Ltd., Tavistock Publications, 1967.

Dunnette, Marvin D., and Leaetta M. Hough. *Handbook of Industrial and Organizational Psychology* Vol. 1. Mountain View, California: Davies-Black Publishing, 1990.

___. *Handbook of Industrial and Organizational Psychology* Vol. 2. Mountain View, California: Davies-Black Publishing, 1991.

___. *Handbook of Industrial and Organizational Psychology* Vol. 3. Mountain View, California: Davies-Black Publishing, 1992.

Dunnette Marvin D. "Emerging Trends and Vexing Issues in Industrial and Organizational Psychology." *Applied Psychology*, Volume 47 2 (1998): pp. 129–153.

Ebbinghaus, Hermann (1850–1909)
STUDY OF MEMORY

Born at Barmen (now Wuppertal), near Bonn, Germany, Hermann Ebbinghaus studied languages and philosophy at the University of Bonn (1867–1870). Following service in the army during the Franco-Prussian War (1870–1871), he returned to Bonn and gained his Ph.D. in 1873. His dissertation was based on the views on the unconscious of the German philosopher Eduard von Hartmann (1842–1906).

Ebbinghaus spent several years studying at various universities and tutoring students as a means of support. He spent the year 1878-1879 at the University of Berlin researching rote learning and memory and setting up experiments. From 1880 to 1894 he was assistant professor at the University of Berlin, where he continued his studies of memory, repeated many of the original experiments and added new ones. He was professor at the University of Breslau from 1894 until 1905 and was professor at the University of Halle from 1905 until his death.

Major Contributions

Ebbinghaus studied his own memory processes and those of subjects by devising a list of 2,300 three-letter "nonsense syllables" deliberately composed to avoid meaning and determining how well these examples of nonsense syllables would be remembered or forgotten. This learning invention, together with the stringent control factors he developed and his meticulous treatment of data, brought him to the conclusion that memory is orderly.

His findings included the well-known "forgetting curve" that relates forgetting to the passage of time. Ebbinghaus discovered that people forget 90 percent of what they learn in a class within thirty days, something that has been confirmed by those who followed him. In assessing the retention of lists containing nonsense syllables, he also found that there occurs a very rapid forgetting in the first hour. This forgetting, he discovered, flattened out at about 30 percent for delays of up to two days.

After completing his work on memory, Ebbinghaus turned to research on color vision, and in 1890, with the physicist Arthur König (1856–1901), founded *Zeitschrift für Psychologie und Physiologie der Sinnesorgane* (*Journal of the Psychology and Physiology of the Sense Organs*). In conjunction with a study of the mental capacities of Breslau schoolchildren (1897), he created a word-completion test. Both nonsense syllables and word-completion tests in various forms are still used in mental assessment. Ebbinghaus also developed early versions of intelligence tests.

Major Literature

Ebbinghaus, Hermann. *Psychology: An Elementary Text Book*. Manchester, New Hampshire: Ayer Co. Publishers, 1908.

___. *Memory: A Contribution to Experimental Psychology*. New York Teachers College, Columbia University, 1913. (Originally published in 1885 and translated by Henry A. Ruger and Clara E. Bussenius. Mineola, New York: Dover Publications, Inc., 1988.

Related Literature

Shamow, D. "Hermann Ebbinghaus." *American Journal of Psychology* 43 (1930): 505–518.

Postman, L. "Hermann Ebbinghaus." *American Psychologist* 23 (1968): 149–157.

Egan, Gerard
THE SKILLED HELPER

The Rev. Gerard Egan, Ph.D., is professor emeritus of organizational development and psychology in the Center for Organization Development of Loyola University, Chicago. He is a world-renowned psychology and organization development consultant and psychotherapist and a registered psychologist. He serves as professor of psychology and chair of the Department of Psychology at North Park Theological College, Chicago. He has been a highly successful writer over many years, both in the field of counseling and in management and has lectured in all continents.

Major Contributions

Egan's contribution to counseling theory and practice is enormous, and few people have not heard of, or used, *The Skilled Helper*. The main thrust of Egan's work is to help the client focus on goals. One important part of problem-solving that can sometimes be difficult is goal-setting — working out a satisfactory solution. Goal-setting is a highly cognitive approach that many people have difficulty working with. Egan takes into account the affective and behavioral factors as well as the creative potential of the client. Problem-solving counseling is successful only if it results in problem-handling action. Listening, as part of problem-solving, is effective only if it helps clients to set realistic goals.

- The advantages of goal-setting are that it focuses attention and action, mobilizes energy and effort, increases persistence and is strategy oriented.

EGAN'S MODEL

- Stage 1. Where the client is. The task: explore. Identify themes and demonstrate primary empathy. The counselor helps clients to tell their story, focus, and develop insight and new perspectives.
- Stage 2. Where the client wants to be. The task: understand. Develop the themes identified in Stage 1 and demonstrate advanced empathy. The counselor helps clients to create new scenarios, evaluate possible scenarios, and develop choice and commitment to change.
- Stage 3. How to get from 1 to 2. The task: to help the client to take action. Without action, little will have been achieved. The counselor helps clients to identify and assess action strategies, formulate plans and implement plans.

In *The Skilled Helper*, Egan lays out a clear structure of what helping involves. The subtitle develops the theme: *A Problem-Management and Opportunity-Development Approach to Helping*.

Thus the focus is promoting a structured approach to helping. While Egan concentrates on developing the skills of helping, he does not overlook the qualities of empathy, genuineness, and respect, enshrined in the person-centered approach. This blending of skills and qualities makes the book more than a skills approach. However, the fundamental premise of *The Skilled Helper* is a blend of cognitive and behavioral, with an emphasis on goals.

Major Literature

Egan, Gerard. *Essentials of Skilled Helping: Managing Problems, Developing Opportunities.* Belmont, California: Wadsworth Publishing Company, 2005.
___. *The Skilled Helper: A Problem-Management and Opportunity-Development Approach to Helping* (8th ed.). Pacific Grove, California: Brooks/Cole Publishing Company, 2006.
Egan, Gerard, and Rich McGourty. *Exercises in Helping Skills for the Skilled Helper.* Pacific Grove, California: Brooks/Cole Publishing Company, 2006.

Ekman, Paul (1934–)
FACIAL EXPRESSIONS

Born in Washington, D.C., Paul Ekman gained a B.A. (1954) from New York University, and an M.A. (1955) and Ph.D. (1958) from Adelphi University, New York. Drafted into the army in 1958, he became chief psychologist at Fort Dix, New Jersey. He received the National Institute of Mental Health Award in 1972, 1976 and 1981. He was Fulbright Senior Professor, Leningrad State University (1983) and faculty research lecturer, University of California, San Francisco (1983). He is currently professor of psychology in the Department of Psychiatry at the University of California Medical School (UCSF) San Francisco.

Major Contributions

In 1969 Ekman developed a classification of non-verbal behaviors with particular reference to facial expressions, drawing particularly on studies carried out in New Guinea. Ekman found that some facial expressions and their corresponding emotions are not culturally determined, but appear to be universal to human culture and thus presumably biological in origin, as Charles Darwin had once theorized. Expressions he found to be universal included anger, disgust, fear, joy, sadness and surprise. He focused on how non-verbal behavior can betray deceit, and coined the term "leakage."

He developed the Facial Action Coding System

(FACS) — the first and only comprehensive technique for measuring facial movement — now widely used for deciphering which of the 43 muscles in the face are working at any given moment, even when an emotion is so fleeting that the person experiencing it may not be conscious of it.

The Dalai Lama gave Ekman $50,000 in seed money to learn how to improve emotional balance in schoolteachers and other people in high pressure jobs. The American Psychological Association designated Paul Ekman one of the 100 most important psychologists of the twentieth century. The Federal Bureau of Investigation, the Central Intelligence Agency and state and local police forces have turned to Ekman for help learning to read subtle emotional cues from the faces, voices and body language of potential assassins, terrorists and questionable visa applicants. His detailed knowledge of facial expression earned Ekman a supporting role in the movie industry, where he has consulted with animators from Pixar and Industrial Light and Magic to give lifelike expressions to cartoon characters. In 2001, Ekman collaborated with John Cleese for the BBC documentary series *The Human Face*.

Major Literature

Ekman, Paul, and Erika Rosenberg (Eds.). *What the Face Reveals: Basic and Applied Studies of Spontaneous Expression Using the Facial Action Coding System (FACS)*. New York: Oxford University Press Inc., 1989.

Ekman, Paul. *Telling Lies: Clues to Deceit in the Marketplace, Politics and Marriage*. New York: W.W. Norton and Co. Ltd., 1992.

Ekman, Paul, and Wallace V. Friesen. *Unmasking the Face: A Guide to Recognizing Emotions from Facial Expressions*. Cambridge, Massachusetts: Malor Books, 2003.

Ekman, Paul. *Emotions Revealed: Understanding Faces and Feelings*. Troy, Michigan: Phoenix Press, 2004.

Elkind, David (1931–)
CHILD DEVELOPMENT

Born in Detroit, Michigan, Elkind gained a B.A. (1952) and Ph.D. (1955) from the University of California at Los Angeles. He was a National Science Foundation senior postdoctoral fellow at Piaget's Centre d'Epistémologie Génétique in Geneva, Switzerland. He is professor of child study, senior resident scholar at Tufts University, Medford, Massachusetts; president of the National Association for the Education of Young Children; and G. Stanley Hall Lecturer and Scandinavian Lecturer.

He is editorial board member for several prestigious journals, including *Journal of Youth and Adolescence* and *Montessori Life*. He is with the National Parenting Association and Institute for Family Values, and the National Forum on Leadership in Early Childhood Education. He is consultant to schools, mental health associations and private foundations.

Elkind is the author of more than 400 articles and book chapters, as well as several children's stories published in *Jack and Jill* magazine for 7–10 year olds. His work has also been published in more popular publications such as *Good Housekeeping* and *The Boston Globe Magazine*, and he is a contributing editor to *Parents Magazine*. He has appeared on several television shows. He was awarded with an honorary D.Sc. in 1987.

Major Contributions

Building on the theories of Jean Piaget (see entry), Elkind has done extensive research in the areas of perceptual, cognitive, social and religious development in children and adolescents and the causes and effects of stress on children, youth and families. One of his findings is that variety is an important element in healthy learning and development. He stresses the danger of hurrying children to grow up too quickly, for in so doing they miss out on some important ingredients of learning. A linked theme is stress caused by parents who push their children into becoming geniuses.

His studies of adolescent egocentrism (referred to as adolescent vulnerability) shows that young people often fall into the error of being unable to differentiate between their own thought processes and what other people are thinking. This results in inability to distinguish transient thoughts from abiding thoughts, the objective from the subjective, and the unique from the universal.

In five films produced by Davidson Films Inc., San Luis Obispo, California (http://www.davidsonfilms.com), Elkind illustrates Jean Piaget's theory of how children think and discover, and discusses their knowledge of the world.

Major Literature

Elkind, David. *Children and Adolescents: Interpretive Essays on Jean Piaget*. New York: Oxford University Press, Inc., 1974.

___. *The Hurried Child*. Reading, Massachusetts: Addison-Wesley, 1981, 1988, 2001.

___. *Ties That Stress: The New Family Imbalance*. Cambridge, Massachusetts: Harvard University Press, 1994.

___. *All Grown Up and No Place to Go* (2nd edition). Reading, Massachusetts: Addison-Wesley, 1988.

___. *Miseducation*. New York: Knopf, 1987.
___. *Reinventing Childhood*. Rosemont, New Jersey: Modern Learning Press, 1988.
Coles, R., and David Elkind. *The Ongoing Journey: Awakening the Spiritual Life in At-Risk Youth*. Boys Town, Nebraska: Boys Town Press, 2000.

Ellis, Albert (1913–)
RATIONAL EMOTIVE BEHAVIOR THERAPY

Born in Pittsburgh and raised in New York, Albert Ellis graduated in business administration from New York City University in 1934. From 1934 to 1942 he had various work, started studying clinical-psychology at Columbia University, New York, and had a part-time private practice in family and sex counseling. He gained an M.A. in clinical psychology at Teachers College, Columbia (1943), and Ph.D. at Columbia (1947).

He is executive director, Institute for Rational-Emotive Therapy, and Humanist of the Year, American Humanist Association. He received the Distinguished Psychologist Award, American Psychological Association (APA) Division 29; Distinguished Psychologist Award, Academy of Psychologists in Marital and Family Therapy; Distinguished Sexologist Award, Society for the Scientific Study of Sex; Distinguished Sex Educator and Therapist Award, American Society of Sex Educators, Counselors and Therapists; and APA Distinguished Award for Professional Contributions to Knowledge. He is member of the National Academy for Practice in Psychology and on the editorial board of many distinguished journals.

Major Contributions

Ellis started off with the idea of becoming a fiction writer, but discovered that he had a flair for non-fiction and turned his attention to writing about the field of human sexuality, a field in which he had developed a noted expertise. Following his Ph.D. degree he turned his attention to clinical psychology and then to psychoanalysis. In 1947 Ellis began a personal analysis and program of supervision with Richard Hulbeck (1892–1974), who was a leading Jungian training analyst at the Karen Horney Institute.

While conducting his part-time practice in New York, Ellis worked full-time as a psychologist for the state of New Jersey and became chief psychologist of the state in 1950. In 1951, Ellis became the American editor of the *International Journal of Sexology* and began publishing a number of articles advocating sexual liberation. Disillusioned

with psychoanalysis, Ellis concluded that clients whom he saw weekly or even less frequently made as much progress as when he saw them daily.

He became more active and concentrated on changing people's behavior by confronting them with their irrational beliefs and persuading them to adopt rational ones. The fundamental premise of Rational Emotive Behavior Therapy (REBT) is that our emotions and behaviors are controlled by what we believe. Highly charged emotional consequences are invariably created by our belief systems. Undesirable emotional consequences can usually be traced to irrational beliefs. When irrational beliefs are disputed, disturbed consequences disappear.

Major Literature

Ellis, Albert. *Hold Your Head Up High (Overcoming Common Problems)*. London, England: Sheldon Press, 1991.
___. *How to Make Yourself Happy and Remarkably Less Disturbed*. Ascadero, California: Impact Publishers, 1999.
___. *Anger: How to Live With and Without It*. New York: Citadel Press, 2003.
___. *Rational Emotive Behavior Therapy: It Works for Me, It Can Work for You*. Loughton, Essex, England: Prometheus Books, 2004.
___. *How to Stubbornly Refuse to Make Yourself Miserable About Anything—Yes, Anything!* New York: Citadel Press Inc., 2005.

Ellis, Henry Havelock (1859–1939)
HUMAN SEXUAL BEHAVIOR

Born in Croydon, Surrey, England, Havelock Ellis graduated as a medical doctor and was awarded a physician's license from St. Thomas's Hospital, London, in 1889. He practiced only for a short time before turning to writing. He married the English writer Edith Lees (1861–1916) in 1881, a marriage that was highly unconventional and stormy. During his time as a medical student, Ellis began writing for magazines and become a staff member of the *Westminster Review*. In 1887 he became editor of the Mermaid Series of unexpurgated reprints of Elizabethan and Jacobean drama.

His first work of non-fiction, *The Criminal* (1890), appeared in the Contemporary Science Series, which he edited until 1914. *Man and Woman* (1894) was translated into many languages. In his 1922 novel *Kanga Creek: An Australian Idyll*, and in his autobiography, *My Life* (1939), he recounts his time as teacher in New South Wales, where he underwent some inner transformation (his first orgasm) at a place called Sparke's Creek. He was elected to a fellowship of the Royal College of Physicians in 1936. Havelock Ellis's library was purchased by Yale University in 1941. The FBI also has files on Ellis.

Major Contributions

Ellis is remembered for his work on sexuality at a time when most of his readers in England were raised in the Victorian climate of asexuality, ignorance, and prejudice. *Studies in the Psychology of Sex* appeared in six volumes from 1897 to 1910; a seventh volume was published in 1928. The *Studies* explored sexual relations largely from a biological and multicultural perspective. What he did then paved the way for the surveys of Alfred Kinsey and other modern writers on sexual topics.

He agreed with Sigmund Freud that childhood sexuality did exist but objected to Freud's application of adult sexual terms to infants. He tried to demystify human sexuality, and assured his readers that masturbation did not inevitably lead to serious illness and that homosexuality was not a crime. This was only a few years after Oscar Wilde was imprisoned for homosexuality (1895).

A British judge declared *Studies in the Psychology of Sex* obscene. *Sexual Inversion* was published in Germany in 1896 and when it was published in England a year later, George Bedborough, the bookseller who had stocked it, was prosecuted. Ellis was a prolific writer, not only on sexual matters. He wrote *The Nationalization of Health* (1892), *A Study of British Genius* (1904), *The Soul of Spain* (1908), *The Philosophy of Conflict* (1919), *Sonnets, with Folk Songs from the Spanish* (1925), and *From Rousseau to Proust* (1935).

Major Literature

Ellis, Havelock. *The Dance of Life*. London: Constable, 1973. London: Greenwood Press, 1923.
___. *Studies in the Psychology of Sex: The Evolution of Modesty, the Phenomena of Sexual Periodicity, Auto-Erotism*. Honolulu, Hawaii: University Press of the Pacific, 2001.
___. *Studies in The Psychology Of Sex: Sexual Inversion*. Honolulu, Hawaii: University Press of the Pacific, 2001.

Entwistle, Noel J. (1936–)
EDUCATIONAL PSYCHOLOGY

Born in Bolton, Lancashire, England, Noel J. Entwistle gained a B.Sc. (1960) from the University of Sheffield, England, and a Ph.D. (1967) from the University of Aberdeen, Scotland. He was professor of educational research at the University of Lancaster, England, until 1978, then Bell Professor of Education at Edinburgh until 2003. He is currently professor emeritus of education at the University of Edinburgh.

He is a fellow of the British Psychological Society, the Scottish Council for Educational Research, and the Society for Research into Higher Education. He has been editor of the *British Journal of Educational Psychology* and the *International Journal, Higher Education*.

Major Contributions

Entwistle's interest in learning dates from his time as schoolmaster and researching the transfer from primary to secondary education. Since 1968 his main research interest has been on student learning in higher education. He has directed major studies that have contributed greatly to the understanding of how teaching and assessment affect the quality of learning. Entwistle concludes that *what* students learn depends on *how* they learn, and *why* they have to learn it. How well students learn depends on their intelligence, effort, and motivation. Academic learning is influenced by the individual characteristics of learners, their experiences in education, current experiences with courses they are taking, quality of the teaching, and the nature of assessment procedures

According to Entwistle, two orientations influence the way a student learns — academic and vocational — as well as their expectations. Two contrasting approaches can be identified. Using the *deep approach*, students focus more deeply on the underlying meaning, examine the logic of the argument, and seek to integrate the ideas. In the *surface approach*, students focus on memorizing facts on the surface level of the text and fail to recognize the principles.

A deep approach is consistent with academic interest in the subject for its own sake and with self-confidence, and has been found to be more common in classes that have good teaching and freedom in learning. A surface approach is associated with anxiety and fear of failure, and to some extent with vocational motives. Classes that students rated as having a heavy workload, or as having assessment procedures emphasizing the accurate reproduction of detailed information, are likely to induce a surface approach to learning and studying.

Major Literature

Entwistle, Noel J. "Improving Teaching Through Research on Student Learning." In J.J.F. Forest (Ed.),

University Teaching: International Perspectives (pp. 73–112). New York: Garland, 1998.

___. *Styles of Learning and Teaching: An Integrated Outline of Educational Psychology for Students, Teachers and Lecturers.* London: David Fulton Publishers Ltd., 1988.

___(Ed.). *Influences of Instructional Settings on Learning and Cognitive Development: Findings from European Research Programs.* Hillsdale, New Jersey: Erlbaum Associates Inc., 1995.

___, and A.C. Entwistle. "Revision and the Experience of Understanding." In F. Marton, D.J. Hounsell, and N.J. Entwistle (Eds.), *The Experience of Learning* (2nd ed.) (pp. 145–158). Edinburgh: Scottish Academic Press, 1997.

Erickson, Milton (1902–1980)

Pardoxical and Strategic Therapy

Overcoming severe dyslexia, profound tone deafness, color blindness and polio in his teens, which left him paralyzed for a year, Milton Erickson went on to qualify as a doctor and psychiatrist, and later became one of the world's most renowned and influential hypnotherapists. He has been long considered the father of modern clinical hypnosis and is best appreciated today as a psychotherapy innovator. His therapy was molded by his early career research into the nature of suggestion, hypnotic states, the mental mechanisms underlying psychodynamic processes, and the psychophysiological aspects of trance.

Erickson realized he could be most effective when not using formal or directive hypnosis. The nondirective, naturalistic style he invented is called Ericksonian hypnosis, and his revolutionary psychotherapeutic approach is called Ericksonian psychotherapy. Erickson believed that treatment should be specifically constructed for each patient because each patient is unique. He advocated a "utilization" approach whereby a clinician utilizes whatever behavior, ideas, or attitudes patients exhibit. Among the many therapeutic approaches he developed were one-session therapy, brief therapy, strategic family therapy, systems-oriented therapy, solution-focused therapy, ordeal therapy, neurolinguistic programming, and dental hypnoanalgesia.

As a psychiatrist he worked in a number of institutions and later was a professor of psychiatry. He was a fellow of many international professional bodies and was founding president of the American Society for Clinical Hypnosis.

Paradoxical Intention

In addition to his legacy of hypnotherapy, Milton Erickson is known for the technique of *paradoxical intention.* The technique was developed by Viktor Frankl, but Erickson brought it to a new level of use. Paradoxical intention is where the therapist encourages clients — with appropriate humor (something both Frankl and Erickson strongly emphasize) — to do exactly and deliberately what they believe they do involuntarily, and over which they believe they have no control. Interest in paradoxical therapy reached its height in the late 1970s and early 1980s.

Paradoxical therapy is less about seeking a cause and more about working for amelioration of some condition that causes distress to the sufferer. In this respect it embraces behaviorism. Paradoxical therapy also recommends defining the problem clearly, establishing clear goals for the treatment, offering a plan, and enlisting the collaboration of the patient or the family in the suggested strategy. Paradoxical therapy is clearly not a psychotherapy itself but a set of techniques usable in therapy.

Major Literature

Erickson, Milton H., and Lawrence Rossi. *The February Man: Evolving Consciousness and Identity in Hypnotherapy.* London, England: Taylor and Francis Books Ltd., Routledge, 1989.

Erickson, Milton H., and Sidney Rosen. *My Voice Will Go with You: Teaching Tales of Milton H. Erickson.* New York: W.W. Norton and Co. Ltd., 1991.

Cooper, Linn F., and Milton Erickson. *Time Distortion in Hypnosis: An Experimental and Clinical Investigation.* New York: Irvington Publishers, 1981. Wales, Carmarthen: Crown House Publishing, 2002.

Erikson, Erik Homburger (1902–1994)

Lifespan Model of Development

Born in Frankfurt, Germany, of German-Danish parents, Erik Erikson was a psychiatrist whose theories influenced professional approaches to psychosocial problems and attracted much popular interest. Invited by Anna Freud, he taught art, history, and geography at a small private school in Vienna, and underwent a training analysis with Anna Freud. In 1933 Erikson was elected to the Vienna Psychoanalytic Institute.

He immigrated to the United States in 1933, practiced child psychoanalysis in Boston, Massachusetts, joined the faculty of the Harvard Medical School, Cambridge, Massachusetts, and in 1936 joined the Institute of Human Relations at Yale University, New Haven, Connecticut, where he was appointed professor at the medical school.

In 1938 Erikson began his first studies of cultural influences on psychological development working with Sioux Indian children at the Pine Ridge Reservation in South Dakota. He was appointed professor of psychology at the University of California, Berkeley (1942). During Senator Joseph McCarthy's "reign of terror" in the 1950s Erikson left Berkeley when professors there were asked to sign "loyalty oaths" on the grounds that it infringed on the First Amendment. He spent ten years working and teaching at a clinic in Massachusetts, ten more years back at Harvard, and retired in 1970.

Major Contributions

During the war years, Erikson studied scores of children on the West Coast in an effort to explore psychodynamics through experimental play. Out of that came his initial attempt to relate the Freudian stage theory of infantile sexuality to the needs of developing children within particular surroundings. His findings were reinforced by his treatment of emotionally disturbed war veteran patients whom, he concluded, were bewildered and anxious but not mentally ill, mostly normal men undergoing the normal crises of readjustment to post-war society.

In his classic study *Childhood and Society,* Erikson introduced his theories on identity, identity crisis (a term he popularized) and psychosexual development. Erikson proposed that people grow through experiencing a series of crises. They must achieve trust, autonomy, initiative, competence, their own identity, generativity (or productivity), integrity and acceptance. Lifespan psychology is the study of people throughout life. Erikson, building on the work of earlier theorists, is the name most associated with lifespan psychology. Erikson's view of personality development has widely influenced the views of educators. Erikson's enduring legacy is his psychosocial development model.

Major Literature

Erikson, Erik Homburger. *Childhood and Society.* New York: W.W. Norton and Co. Ltd., 1950. 2nd ed., 1963. New York: Vintage and Anchor Books, 1995.
___. *Insight and Responsibility.* New York: W.W. Norton and Co. Ltd., 1964, 1995.
___. *Identity: Youth and Crisis.* New York: W.W. Norton and Co. Ltd., 1968, 1995.
___. *The Life Cycle Completed: A Review.* New York: W.W. Norton and Co. Ltd., 1982, 1998.
___. *The Erik Erikson Reader.* New York: W.W. Norton and Co. Ltd., 2001.

Esquirol, Jean Etienne Dominique (1772–1850)
ASYLUM REFORM

Born in Toulouse, France, the son of wealthy wholesale cloth merchant, Jean Etienne Dominique Esquirol studied at Toulouse and completed his education at Montpellier. He went to Paris in 1799, where he worked at the Salpêtrière Hospital and became a student of Philippe Pinel (see entry). With financial help from Pinel, Esquirol set up a private asylum in 1801 or 1802 in Paris, which was quite successful, being ranked in 1810 as one of the three best such institutions in Paris. In 1805 he published his thesis, titled *Des Passions considérées comme causes, symptômes et moyens curatifs de l'aliénation mentale* ["The passions considered as causes, symptoms and means of cure in cases of insanity"]. *Des Passions* was an influential work for understanding the origin of modern psychiatric theory.

Major Contributions

Esquirol succeeded Pinel as physician in chief at the Salpêtrière Hospital in Paris in 1811, further developing Pinel's diagnostic techniques and continuing his efforts to achieve more humane treatment of the mentally ill. Esquirol was the most influential psychiatrist of his time. He developed the theory and practice of moral therapy, seeing the asylum as the most powerful weapon against mental illness, and was one of the authors of an 1838 law providing an asylum in every department of France, with detailed provisions for patient care.

Esquirol anticipated modern views in his suggestion that some mental illnesses may be caused by emotional disturbances rather than by organic brain damage. He provided the first accurate description of mental retardation as an entity separate from insanity. He differentiated between hallucination (a term he coined) and illusion. He classified insanities into monomania, a partial insanity, such as paranoia, and a general delirium-like mania.

He inaugurated what was probably the first course in psychiatry and trained physicians to be asylum directors. Two of his pupils, Jean-Pierre Falret (1794–1870) and Jules Baillarger (see entry). independently described and named circular insanity (now called bipolar disorder). Esquirol was the first psychiatrist to delineate the symptoms of a drug-induced psychosis. Esquirol, like Pinel, believed that the origin of mental illness lies in the passions of the soul and was convinced that although madness does affect a patient's reason, it is not necessarily permanent.

In 1822 he was appointed inspector general of medical faculties, and in 1823, when Pinel and other liberals were forced from the Faculty of Medicine by the government, Esquirol was promoted to the position of inspector general of the Faculty of Medicine. J.B. Baillière, Paris, published Esquirol's (1838) *Des maladies mentales, considérées sous les rapports médical, hygiénique, et médico-légal,* which has been called the first modern treatise on clinical psychiatry, and it remained a basic text for 50 years.

Estes, William Kaye (1919–)
EXPERIMENTAL PSYCHOLOGY

Born in Minneapolis, Minnesota, William Kaye Estes studied at the University of Minnesota in Minneapolis and earned a B.A (1940) and a Ph.D. under the guidance of B.F. Skinner (1943). From 1943 to 1945 he was a psychologist in the Army Air Force. He rose to research professor of psychology at Indiana University, Bloomington (1945–1962), and was professor of psychology, Stanford University, California (1962–1968), Rockefeller University, New York (1968–1979), and Harvard University, Cambridge, Massachusetts (1970–1999). Estes has been professor of psychology and Distinguished Scholar of Psychology and Cognitive Science at Indiana University since 1999.

His awards are include honorary D.Sc., Indiana University (1976) and University of Minnesota (1998). Positions held by Estes include founder and chair of the Psychonomic Society and chair of the organizing group of the Society for Mathematical Psychology. His posts include president of the Midwestern Psychological Association; president of the Division of Experimental Psychology of the American Psychological Association; chair of the Mathematical Social Science Board; vice president of the Federation of Behavioral, Psychological, and Cognitive Sciences; and chair of the Psychology Section of the American Association for the Advancement of Science.

His awards have been many, and include the U.S. National Medal of Science and the Gold Medal Award for Life Achievement in Psychological Science from the American Psychological Foundation.

Major Contributions

In his work with Skinner (see entry) on animals, Estes developed a method (that is now standard) for tracing the emotional reactions related to fear. Estes is one of the founders of the field of mathematical psychology, broadly defined to include work of a theoretical character that uses mathematical methods, formal logic. Mathematical psychology mathematically explores principles in the mental world, and should begin with the attempt to make a theory on phenomena occurring in human brains when we think. Mathematical psychology is closely connected with linguistics because we usually think in our mother tongue.

Estes developed a statistical theory of elementary learning, and in over 60 years of research, he has produced various models that address human learning, memory, perception, choice, and categorization and decision-making. Estes demonstrated how experimental observations of behavior can be compared to the predictions of a mathematical or computer simulation model. His theory includes how humans profit or fail to profit from experiences that involve reward and punishment.

Major Literature

Estes, William K. "Toward a Statistical Theory of Learning." *Psychological Review* 57 (1950): 94–107.

Estes, William Kaye. "Some Targets for Mathematical Psychology." *Journal of Mathematical Psychology* 12 (1975): 263–282.

___. *Handbook of Learning and Cognitive Processes: Attention and Memory* Vol. 4. New Jersey: John Wiley and Sons, Inc., 1976. Hillsdale, New Jersey: Lawrence Erlbaum Associates, Inc., 2006.

___. *Models of Learning, Memory and Choice: Selected Papers.* Westport, Connecticut: Greenwood Press, 1982.

___. *Statistical Models in Behavioral Research.* Hillsdale, New Jersey: Lawrence Erlbaum Associates, Inc., 1991.

___. *Classification and Cognition.* New York Oxford University Press, Inc., 1994.

Eysenck, Hans Jurgen (1916–1997)
BEHAVIOR THERAPY

Born in Berlin, Hans Jurgen Eysenck left Nazi Germany in 1934. At the University of London he earned a B.A. (1938) and a Ph.D. (1940). From 1942 to 1945 he was at Mill Hill Emergency Hospital, London. He was also a psychologist, University of London, Maudsley Hospital (1946–1950); reader and director of the Psychology Unit at the Institute of Psychiatry, London (1950–1955); professor of psychology (1955–1984); and professor emeritus at the University of London (1984–1997).

Major Contributions

Behavioral psychologist Eysenck is renowned for his detailed research into the human personality. The Eysenck Personality Inventory (EPI) places people's personalities into a hierarchy of divisions rooted in Jungian theory, ranging from habitual reactions and traits at the lower end of the scale, through personality and neuroticism, to, at the top, psychoticism. What the EPI showed was that very introverted people (high on the neurotic scale) are easily conditioned and have many inhibitions. They are predisposed to such disorders as depression, anxiety, and obsessive compulsion. High levels of both extraversion (outgoing tendencies) and neuroticism (emotionality or heightened emotional behavior) are associated with criminal behavior.

Eysenck aroused fierce controversy by linking people's racial origins with their IQs. This led to the claims by certain groups that they were genetically superior to other races. His contributions to behavior therapy is immense, particularly in the field of conditioning, and aversion therapy. While behavior therapy proved successful for certain types of behavior problems, such as phobias, it failed when it was used to attempt to change a person's sexual orientation. Eysenck and other British psychologists focused on diagnosis and research, and on scientific observation and statistical analysis, as a sound basis for treatment, whereas the American tradition focused on therapy and treatment.

For Eysenck there is no experimental evidence to substantiate psychoanalysis as a scientific discipline. And in a paper written in 1952 he found no evidence for the effectiveness of psychotherapy. He maintained that recovery with psychotherapy was no more than one would expect from spontaneous recovery. Thus Eysenck laid the foundations for the scientific study of psychotherapy with well-controlled studies. In the two decades until the mid 1970s, the emphasis on training for British clinical psychologists was dominated by behaviorism. This was due mainly to the fact that many Maudsley-trained psychologists went on to run other training courses in universities throughout the country. Eysenck was possibly one of the most prolific writers on psychology ever.

Major Literature

Eysenck, Hans Jurgen. "The Effects of Psychotherapy: An Evaluation." *Journal of Consulting Psychology* 16 (1952): 319–324.

___. *Personality at Work: Role of Individual Differences in the Workplace.* London, England: Taylor and Francis Books Ltd., Routledge, 1994.

___. *Test Your IQ.* New York: HarperCollins, Publishers Inc., 1994.

___. *Rebel with a Cause: The Autobiography of Hans Eysenck.* New Jersey: Transaction Publishers, 1997.

___. *The Biological Basis of Personality.* Springfield, Illinois: Charles C. Thomas, 1967. New Jersey: Transaction Publishers, 2006.

Fairbairn, William Ronald Dodds (1889–1964)
OBJECT RELATIONS SCHOOL

Born in Edinburgh, Scotland, William Ronald Dodds Fairbairn graduated from Edinburgh University, then spent three years in divinity and Hellenic Greek studies. After the war, in which he served with General Allenby in the Palestinian campaign (1917), he trained as a doctor, and shortly after qualifying he began thirty years of working with war neuroses. Despite being without the requisite formal training, he began psychoanalytic work in 1925 and obtained his M.D. in 1927, and started his clinical writing soon after. From 1927 to 1935 he was a lecturer in psychology at Edinburgh University and was elected a member of the British Psychoanalytical Society.

Major Contributions

Fairbairn exerted tremendous influence on British object relations and the relational schools of psychoanalysis. Fairbairn was one of the theory-builders for the Middle Group (now called the Independent Group) of psychoanalysts. The Independent Group contained analysts who identified with neither the Kleinians nor the Anna Freudians. They were more concerned with the relationships between people than the "drives" within them. Although acknowledging the place of the drives and the pleasure principle, he maintained that these were not dominant.

The object relations theory is that people's struggles and goals in life focus on maintaining relations with others, while at the same time ensuring that they are different from others. The concept of self and others is acquired in childhood and is later played out in adult relations. Fairbairn also established the dissociative nature of the schizoid personality in particular and the schizoid aspects of all psychopathology in general. For Fairbairn, the primary aim of human behavior is contact with another, even if it is unpleasant. For him, psychopathology is failure to establish good object relationships in infancy. Maternal absence or withdrawal during the paranoid-schizoid position leads the infant to regard love as noxious or bad. The resultant schizoid conflict — to love or not to love — sets off a withdrawal from relatedness, with the development of compensatory defensive internal object relations that provide a sense of security and continuity that is absent in real relationships, especially the earliest ones with the parents.

Another theme Fairbairn dealt with is that of "working through." He stresses that the relationship formed between the psychoanalyst and the patient forms another object-relation. Thus the patient attaches to the analyst, who becomes the center of the patient's psyche, in much the same way as did the mother. Fairbairn's work has had widespread influence on the study of the self, trauma, multiple personality, infant development, religion, and pastoral care.

Major Literature

Fairbairn, William Ronald Dodds. *Psychoanalytic Studies of the Personality.* London: Taylor and Francis Books Ltd., Tavistock Publications, 1952, 1994.
___. *An Object Relations Theory of the Personality.* New York: Basic Books, 1954.
___. "Review of the Six Schizophrenias: Reaction Patterns in Children and Adults." *International Journal of Psychoanalysis* 36 (1955): 414–415.
___. "On the Nature and Aims of Psychoanalytical Treatment." *International Journal of Psychoanalysis* 39 (1958): 374–385.

Farrington, David Philip (1944–)

CRIMINOLOGY

Born in Ormskirk, Lancashire, England, David Philip Farrington gained a B.A. (1966), an M.A. (1970) and a Ph.D. (1970) in psychology from the University of Cambridge, England. He is professor of psychological Criminology at the Institute of Criminology, Cambridge University, and adjunct professor of psychiatry at Western Psychiatric Institute and Clinic, University of Pittsburgh, Pennsylvania. His fellowships are at the British Academy, Academy of Medical Sciences, European Association of Psychology and Law, and Academy of Experimental Criminology, British Society of Criminology. He is past chairman of

the British Psychological Society Division of Forensic Psychology and past president of the American Society of Criminology. He was awarded the Order of the British Empire in 2004.

In addition to nearly 400 published papers and chapters on criminological and psychological topics, he has published nearly 50 books, monographs and government publications, one of which — *Understanding and Controlling Crime* (1986) — won the prize for distinguished scholarship of the American Sociological Association Criminology Section. He received the Sellin-Glueck Award of the American Society of Criminology in 1984 for international contributions to criminology, and the Sutherland Award of the American Society of Criminology in 2002 for outstanding contributions to criminology. He received the Beccaria Gold Medal of the Criminological Society of German Speaking Countries in 2005, and the Joan McCord Award of the Academy of Experimental Criminology in 2005.

Major Contributions

Farrington's major research interest is in developmental criminology, and he is director of the Cambridge Study in Delinquent Development, which is a prospective longitudinal survey of over 400 London males from age 8 to age 48. He is co-principal investigator of the Pittsburgh Youth Study, a longitudinal survey of 1500 Pittsburgh males from age 7 to age 25. He has carried out studies of stealing, shoplifting, sentencing, prison overcrowding, police cautioning and crime rates. His main focus remains why people commit crimes, crime prevention, and reaction to crimes of the police, courts and prisons.

He is co-chair of the Campbell Collaboration Crime and Justice Group, an international network of researchers that prepares, updates, and rapidly disseminates systematic reviews of high-quality research conducted worldwide on effective methods to reduce crime and delinquency and improve the quality of justice. He has a long-term commitment to developing criminological and legal psychology as a recognized academic and professional activity.

Major Literature

Farrington, David Philip. "Criminal Career Research: Lesson for Crime Prevention." *Studies on Crime and Crime Prevention* 1 (1992): 7–29.
___. *Psychological Explanation of Crime.* Sudbury, Massachusetts: Darmouth Publishing Inc., 1994.
Tonry, Michael, and David Philip Farrington (Eds.). *Building a Safer Society: Strategic Approaches to Crime*

Prevention. Chicago, Illinois: University of Chicago Press, 1995.

Farrington, David Philip, et al. *Causes of Conduct Disorder and Juvenile Delinquency*. New York: Guilford Press, 2003.

___, and Jeremy W. Coid (Eds.). *Early Prevention of Adult Antisocial Behavior* (Cambridge Studies in Criminology). New York: Cambridge University Press, 2003.

Welsh, Brandon C., and David Philip Farrington (Eds.). *Preventing Crime: What Works for Children, Offenders, Victims and Places*. Notre Dame, Indiana: Kluwer Academic Publishers, 2006.

Fechner, Gustav Theodor (1801–1887)

PSYCHOPHYSICS

Born in Gross-Sächen, Prussia, Gustav Theodor Fechner became a key figure in the founding of psychophysics — the science concerned with measurable relations between sensations and the stimuli producing them. In 1817, he enrolled in medicine at the University of Leipzig, Germany, where he studied anatomy, mathematics and physics. He was appointed lecturer in physics 1824. In 1834, with over 40 publications to his credit, including an important paper on the measurement of direct current, he was appointed professor of physics at Leipzig.

In 1844, following a major breakdown in health, prostration, and partial blindness and sensitivity to light, (thought to have been brought on by his gazing at the sun during the study of visual afterimages), he was pensioned by the university. Thereafter he began delving more deeply into philosophy and conceived of a highly animistic universe with God as its soul. In 1848 he was appointed professor of philosophy, University of Leipzig.

Major Contributions

Hours spent in meditation and reflection deepened Fechner's religious awareness and his concern over the problem of the soul. He postulated that mind and body, though appearing to be separate entities, are actually different sides of one reality. The experimental procedures he developed are still useful in experimental psychology for measuring sensations in relation to the physical magnitude of stimuli. Most important, he formulated Fechner's Law, an equation to express the theory of the just-noticeable difference, advanced earlier by Ernst Weber. This theory concerns the sensory ability to discriminate when two stimuli (e.g., two weights) are just noticeably different

from each other. The combined work of Weber and Fechner has been useful, especially in hearing and vision research, and has had an impact on attitude scaling and other testing and theoretical developments.

From about 1865 Fechner delved into experimental aesthetics and sought to determine by actual measurements which shapes and dimensions are most aesthetically pleasing. Fechner defended the thesis of panpsychism — the theory that all nature has a psychic side; that even trees are living and conscious. In the United States, Josiah Royce (1855–1916), an absolute idealist philosopher, not only followed Fechner in affirming that heavenly bodies have souls but also adopted a unique theory that each species of animal is a single conscious individual incorporating into itself the individual souls of each of its members.

In 1838 Fechner reported the phenomenon that spinning a disc with a certain black and white pattern can give the impression that colors are present, when in fact they are not, known as the Fechner color illusion.

Fechner's greatest achievement was in the investigation of exact relationships in psychology and aesthetics. The formal beginnings of experimental psychology can, therefore, be traced to Gustav Fechner, and he ranks among the great psychologists. In his *Elements of Psychophysics* (1880) (republished, Holt, Rinehart and Winston, 1966), he discusses the functional relations of mind and body and reports investigations of his own and others on the various senses — sight, sound, and the cutaneous and muscular senses.

Feigenbaum, Edward Albert (1936–)

ARTIFICIAL INTELLIGENCE

Born at Weehawken, New Jersey, Edward Albert Feigenbaum gained a B.S. in engineering (1956) and a Ph.D. in artificial intelligence (1960) at the Carnegie Institute of Technology, Carnegie Mellon University, Pittsburgh, Pennsylvania. He won a Fulbright Research Scholarship (1959–1960); was assistant professor at the University of California, Berkeley (1960–1965); computer and biomathematical sciences, member of study section, National Institutes of Health (1968–1972); on the Committee on Mathematics in the Social Sciences, Social Science Research Council (1977–1978); and a member of the Computer Science Advisory Committee, National Science Foundation (1977–1980).

His awards are: National Computer Conference Award, Best Technical Paper (1978); elected to Productivity Hall of Fame, Republic of Singapore (1986); Career Achievement Medal, World Congress on Expert Systems (1991) (the "Feigenbaum Medal" named in his honor); and U.S. Air Force Exceptional Civilian Service Award (1997). He was on the Cognitive Science Society governing board (1979–1982) and was president, American Association for Artificial Intelligence Council (1980–1981).

His fellowships are American Association for the Advancement of Science (1983), American College of Medical Informatics (1984), and American Institute of Medical and Biological Engineering (1994). He is a member of the American Academy of Arts and Sciences (1991), was founding editor of the McGraw-Hill Computer Science Series, and is currently professor emeritus of computer science, Stanford University, California.

Major Contributions

In 1959 Feigenbaum developed the computer program EPAM, a theoretical model of human perception and memory; the most up-to-date version IV (1994) has been adapted to deal with various short-term and long-term memory tasks. Feigenbaum moved to Stanford in 1965, where he founded the Knowledge Systems Laboratory (KSL) to begin the development of expert systems — computer programs that demonstrate the knowledge of a human expert in a specialized domain. His first major success at Stanford was DENDRAL, an expert system capable of determining the structure of chemical compounds. The next expert system was MYCIN, designed to diagnose infectious blood diseases and recommend antibiotics, with the dosage adjusted for patient's body weight.

In 1994 he received the Turing Award from the Association for Computing Machinery for pioneering the design and construction of large scale artificial intelligence systems, demonstrating the practical importance and potential commercial impact of artificial intelligence technology. Expert systems have played a role in many manufacturing industries as well as the military, as evidenced by Feigenbaum's appointment as chief scientist of the United States Air Force from 1994 to 1997.

Major Literature

Feigenbaum, Edward Albert, and Julian Feldman (Eds.). *Computers and Thought*. Columbus, Ohio: McGraw-Hill Education, 1963.

Feigenbaum, Edward Albert, B.G. Buchanan, and J. Lederberg. *Application of Artificial Intelligence of Organic Chemistry: The DENDRAL Project*. Columbus, Ohio: McGraw-Hill Education, 1980.

Feigenbaum, Edward Albert, and Pamela McCorduck. *The Fifth Generation: Artificial Intelligence and Japan's Computer Challenge to The World*. New York: Macmillan, 1984.

Feigenbaum, Edward Albert. "Computer Assisted Decision Making in Medicine." *Journal of Philosophy and Medicine* 9 (1984): 135–160 (with J. Kunz, E.H. Shortliffe and B.G. Buchanan).

___. et al. *The Rise of the Expert Company: How Visionary Companies are Using Artificial Intelligence to Achieve Higher Productivity and Profits*. New York: Vintage and Anchor Books, 1990.

Ferenczi, Sandor (1873–1933)
ACTIVE ANALYTIC TECHNIQUES

Born in Miskolc, Hungary, the son of Jewish parents, Sandor Ferenczi qualified as a doctor in Vienna (1894). He served as an army doctor specializing in neurology and neuropathology and acquiring skills in hypnosis. He was appointed chief neurologist for the Elizabeth Poorhouse in Budapest, and subsequently was appointed as a psychiatric expert to the Royal Court of Justice.

He met Sigmund Freud (1908) and became a member of the Vienna Psychoanalytic Society. Ferenczi was noted for his contributions to psychoanalytic theory and his experimentation with techniques of therapy. He founded the Hungarian Psychoanalytic Society (1913) and was Professor of psychoanalysis, University of Budapest (1919).

Major Contributions

Ferenczi is one of the most innovative of all early psychoanalysts. He believed in being more active than was usual in traditional psychoanalysis. A more controversial approach was where he advocated abstention from sex and other pleasurable biological acts, the rationale being that this would store up libido (emotional energy) that could then be used to hasten the therapeutic process. However, this evoked strong opposition in patients and proved counterproductive.

Ferenczi recommended a loving, permissive therapeutic relationship to counterbalance the rejection and emotional deprivation so many patients had experienced with their parents. He went further and asserted that the therapist could openly express his affection for the patient, an approach that was severely criticized by other psychoanalysts.

His exploration of ways to improve therapeutic technique caused a split between him and Freud (see entry). His book *The Development of Psychoanalysis* (1924), written in collaboration with Otto Rank (see entry), included the view — denounced by many psychoanalysts of the day — that the full recollection of certain traumatic memories is not essential for modifying neurotic patterns. He later suggested another revolutionary idea, that the wish to return to the comfort of the womb symbolizes a wish to return to the origin of life, the sea.

Ferenczi's work can be summed up as active, nurturing, and with an emphasis on setting time limits. He argued that analytic neutrality is a fiction, and that the training analysis should be a personal analysis, not a merely an educational one. He originated such psychoanalytic constructs as "identification with the aggressor," "splitting," "projective identification," and the "corrective emotional experience." Possibly one of the most controversial ideas was that analyst and patient should analyze each other, thus expanding the emotional awareness of both. This turned on its head the premise that the analyst was in some way superior. In many ways the working premise of Carl Rogers is similar, that the analyst should be humanly authentic. Ferenczi established Budapest as a psychoanalytic center.

Major Literature

Ferenczi, Sandor. *Final Contributions to the Problems and Methods of Psychoanalysis Ú Selected Papers of Sandor Ferenczi* Vol. III (Michael Balint, ed.). New York: Basic Books, Inc., 1955.
___. *Bausteine zur Psychoanalyse* (*The Fundamentals of Psychoanalysis*) Second Edition. Berne: Hans Huber Verlag, 1964.
___, et al. *The Clinical Diary of Sandor Ferenczi.* Cambridge, Massachusetts: Harvard University Press, 1995.

Festinger, Leon (1919–1989)
COGNITIVE DISSONANCE THEORY

Born in New York to Russian immigrant parents, Leon Festinger earned a B.S. at York City College (1939), an M.A. at State University, Iowa (1940), working on field theory under Kurt Lewin (see entry), and a Ph.D. in psychology from State University, Iowa, Ames (1942). From 1943 to 1945 he was statistician for the Committee on Selection and Training of Aircraft Pilots, University of Rochester, New York. He was assistant professor of social psychology with Lewin at the Research Center for Group Dynamics at the Massachusetts Institute of Technology (1945); at the University of Minnesota, Minneapolis (1951); and Else and Hans Staudinger Professor of Psychology, the New School for Social Research at Stanford, California (1955–1989).

He received the Distinguished Scientist Award, American Psychological Association (APA) (1959); an honorary doctorate, University of Mannheim, Germany (1978), was Einstein Visiting Fellow, Israel Academy of Sciences and Humanities (1980–1981), and a member of the National Academy of Science.

Major Contributions

Festinger formulated theories dealing with social influence, communication in small groups, and social comparison processes, although he is probably most widely known for his theory of cognitive dissonance. Cognitive dissonance theory proposes that when a person's actions are inconsistent with his or her attitudes, the discomfort produced by this dissonance leads the person to bring the attitudes in line with the actions, and to maintain a cognitive balance. Mental conflict occurs when beliefs or assumption are contradicted by new information, when the new information is perceived to be incompatible or inconsistent with what is already established. Groups also strive to maintain the balance of their interpersonal relationships.

People cope with dissonance by:

* Rejecting the new information.
* Explaining away the new information.
* Avoiding the new information.
* Persuading themselves that there is no conflict.
* Reconciling the difference.

The original idea stemmed from Festinger's observation that people generally like consistency in their daily lives. Cognitive dissonance occurs whenever we make decisions and, if the theory is correct, then we will (unconsciously) take steps to reduce the unpleasant feelings of dissonance.

To summarize the theory:

* Two thoughts, attitudes or beliefs are not in harmony.
* Disharmony creates psychological discomfort.
* Something must be done to reduce the discomfort.
* Avoidance action is taken.

An example of cognitive dissonance is that many people know that cigarettes cause cancer and other diseases, but nonetheless continue to smoke. People going through cognitive dissonance will find some rationale for whatever is causing the conflict, or they may choose to ignore the event in question altogether. Festinger believed that people want balance in their lives and that cognitive dissonance is a way to bring back a lost sense of balance. Dissonance is present in both conflict resolution and decision-making.

Major Literature

Festinger, Leon. *A Theory of Cognitive Dissonance*. Palo Alto, California: Stanford University Press, 1957.
___ (Ed.). *Retrospections on Social Psychology*. New York: Oxford University Press Inc., 1981.
___. *The Human Legacy*. New York: Columbia University Press, 1987.

Forel, Auguste-Henri (1848–1931)

NEUROANATOMY

Born in LaGracieuse, near Morges, Switzerland, on the shore of Lake Geneva, Auguste-Henri Forel studied medicine at the University of Zürich from 1866 to 1871, then worked under Theodor Meynert at the University of Vienna, where he did a comparative study of the thalamus. He received his medical degree from Vienna in 1872. He went to the Ludwig-Maximilians-Universität in Munich in 1873, becoming assistant physician under Bernhard Aloys von Gudden (see entry).

In 1875, Forel made the first complete section of the whole brain, and in 1877 he carried out his groundbreaking study of the part of the brain called the tegmentum, in the region of the thalamus and sub-thalamus, three zones called Haubenfeld (H fields) — the "tegmental fields of Forel."

He was appointed director of the Burghölzli Asylum in Zürich and professor of psychiatry at the University of Zürich Medical School in 1879 and was succeeded by Eugen Bleuler (see entry). During his tenure at Zurich he formulated the concept of cellular and functional units (later termed the neuron theory). In 1885 he discovered the origin of the acoustic nerve, *Nervus acusticus*, in the brain.

His neuroanatomical studies with Gudden's method led him to formulate the neuron theory in 1887, four years before Wilhelm von Waldeyer, who received most of the credit for it. Forel then turned his back on neuroscience. In 1889 he founded an institute at Zürich for the medical treatment of alcoholism, and throughout his career he worked for social reforms to prevent such causes of mental illness as syphilis and alcoholism. He himself practiced complete abstinence, as an example, and fought in every way possible the effects of alcoholism on the working classes.

Forel retired in 1893 and devoted the remainder of his life to social reform and the study of the psychology of ants (myrmecology), which had been a lifelong passion, and publishing papers on insanity, prison reform, and social morality. Forel became interested in the therapeutic value of hypnotism, while continuing his work on brain anatomy and ants. After his retirement from the Burghölzli asylum in 1898, he had a stroke in 1911 that paralyzed his right side. He taught himself to write with his left hand and was able to continue his studies.

He introduced the IOGT (International Order of Good Templars, now International Organization of Good Templars) to Switzerland. He also concerned himself with public education, and he was engaged in the peace cause. His interest in psychology led him to effect innumerable reforms that not only influenced psychiatry in Switzerland but brought about important changes in the penal code. In 1920 he became a member of the Bahá'í Faith, out of respect for its social work and because it lacked "dogmas or priests." Before his death Forel published *Le Monde Social des Forimis* on the social world of the ants, in which he made insightful observations on the neural control of sensory and instinctive behavior common to both humans and insects.

Foulkes, Sigmund Heinrich (1898–1976)

GROUP ANALYTIC THERAPY

Michael Foulkes, as he later liked to be called, was born of a Jewish family in Karlsruhe, Rhineland. He served in World War I as a wireless operator, after which he completed his medical studies. He was drawn to neurology and psychiatry and was profoundly influenced by two years of work under the direction of Kurt Goldstein, who had organized and directed a hospital for the treatment of brain-injured soldiers from the German army.

Major Contributions

Foulkes absorbed from Goldstein the Gestalt holistic dictum — the whole is more than the sum of its parts. Group analytic therapy (GAT) differed from other group psychotherapies in that Foulkes believed that it was essential to recognize and not underestimate the importance of the social nature and the need for and to understand communication.

In GAT everyone and no one is a therapist. The analysis is carried out by the group. Only in a group situation can one do full justice to each individual. Disturbance of communication can only be understood by a careful analysis of the conflict within the group. Analyzing communication is the function of every member of the group, not just the facilitator. Each member brings his or her part of the outside world into the group, and the group is then influenced in some way by what each person contributes.

Foulkes resisted the term "leader," which had connotations of being led, and that went against the concept of the group authority. Foulkes saw a group as being made up of equals. However, the refusal of the facilitator to accept the role of omnipotent leader can, and often does, generate fierce emotional reactions, which may be reminiscent of rejection by some significant figure or figures.

Foulkes also believed that one of the individual's main tasks in life is to attain maturity. This maturity, so maintained Foulkes, is to find courage to probe into the deeper layers of one's self in order to illuminate those aspects of himself from which one has long been separated; to increase self-awareness that is the gateway to freedom. By entering into self-knowledge people learn to love not only themselves in a healthy way, but also others who, as they discover, share their experience of being human.

Foulkes was a prolific writer of articles in many psychological and psychoanalytical journals. Foulkes was involved during World War II in the Northfield Experiments.

Major Literature

Foulkes, Sigmund Heinrich. *Introduction to Group-Analytic Psychotherapy.* London: William Heinemann, 1949. London, England: Karnac Books, 1983.

___. *Group Analytic Psychotherapy: Method and Principles.* London, England: Penguin Books Ltd., 1957. London, England: Karnac Books, 1986.

___. *Therapeutic Group Analysis.* New York: International University Press, 1964. London, England: Karnac Books, 1984.

___. *Psychiatry in a Changing Society.* London, England: Taylor and Francis Books Ltd., Routledge, 1969, 2001.

Related Literature

Harrison, Tom. *Bion, Rickman, Foulkes and the North-*

field Experiments: Advancing on a Different Front. London, England: Jessica Kingsley Publishers, 2000.

Fowler, James W. (1940–)
STAGES OF GROWTH IN FAITH

Son of a North Carolina Methodist minister, James W. Fowler earned a B.A. at Duke University, North Carolina; a master of divinity degree at Drew University, New Jersey, and a Ph.D. at Harvard University, Cambridge, Massachusetts. He taught at the Harvard Divinity School's department of applied theology, was C.H. Candler Professor of Theology and Human Development, and was director of the Center for Faith Development, Emory University in Atlanta, Georgia, until he retired in 2005.

Major Contributions

Drawing inspiration from other theologians and from Erik Erikson's (see entry) stages of adult growth, Jean Piaget's (see entry) stages of early childhood learning capacities, and Laurence Kohlberg's (see entry) moral development, the main thrust of Fowler's work has been to research and clarify the stages through which adult faith passes on its way to greater maturity.

THE STAGES OF FAITH

Stage 1 Intuitive-Projective faith. Two to six or seven years of age. The age of fantasy and imitation, where the examples, moods, actions and stories of the visible faith of significant adults powerfully influence the infant.

Stage 2 Mythic-Literal faith. The stage of the school child in which the child begins to take on for himself or herself the stories, beliefs and rituals of his or her community. Beliefs, symbols and stories, moral rules and attitudes are interpreted literally, though they may touch or move the child at a deeper level.

Stage 3 Synthetic-Conventional faith. Associated with early adolescence, and links with what Piaget calls formal operational thinking. Many adults never progress beyond this stage. This is the stage of the emerging self-identity, and increasing awareness of relationships and feedback from other significant people and their values. The relationship with God takes on a new and personal meaning.

Stage 4 Individuative-Reflective faith. From roughly mid-adolescence to early 20s, where the process of self-identity is continued. In this critical stage of transition the individual must begin to take responsibility for his or her own commitments, lifestyle, beliefs and attitudes. It is in this stage that the individual firms up the boundaries between self and others.

Stage 5 Conjunctive faith. Around 35 or 40 or beyond, some people undergo a change of being in faith. The boundaries between self and others become more fluid, as the individual recognizes the relationship with others, including God. Some of the idealism, the images and prejudices of the past need to be reworked. This is often associated with deep and painful soul-searching and letting go of outdated values.

Stage 6 Universalizing faith. Not many people move into this stage. For those who do, God becomes the center of their lives. God becomes a reality, and not just a concept. They learn to participate with God in moving out toward other people in service.

Major Literature

Fowler, James W. *Stages of Faith: The Psychology of Human Development and the Quest for Meaning.* New York: HarperCollins Publishers, Inc., 1989.
___. *Faithful Change.* Nashville, Tennessee: Abingdon Press, 2001.

Frank, Jerome David (1909–2005)
CLASSIFICATION OF PSYCHOTHERAPIES

Born in New York, City, Jerome David Frank gained an A.B. (1930), a Ph.D. in psychology (1934) and a medical doctorate (1939) from Harvard University, Cambridge, Massachusetts. From 1940 to 1943 he was on the faculty of the Johns Hopkins University School of Medicine. He trained at the Henry Phipps Psychiatric Clinic there and spent most his working life at Johns Hopkins. In 1974 he became professor emeritus of psychiatry, Johns Hopkins Medical School.

He was a member Maryland Psychiatric Society (1949) and president (1955–1956). Frank received the Award for Distinguished Contributions to Psychology in the Public Interest (1985) and was made a life fellow, American Psychiatric Association (1997).

Major Contributions

Frank's research ranged from classification of psychotherapies to faith healing, the psychology of leadership, and nuclear war. Frank believed that mental health is more than devising programs of prevention. If society is to take prevention seriously it must also consider social reform.

When a society focuses on trying to repair damaged adults in one-to-one relationships, as in therapy, the time and energy expended would be more profitably occupied in trying to fix up a society in ways that will increase the strength and stability of the family. When we get healthy families, the mental health of future generations will be put onto a more sure footing. What society needs for prevention to be effective are teachers, researchers and social activists who are focused on social change.

Jerome Frank's book *Persuasion and Healing* focuses on "psychological healing," a belief system and its effects on the healing process. The book examines such topics as religious revivalism, magical healing, contemporary psychotherapies, the role of the shaman in non-industrial societies, and the traditional mental hospital. It offers perspectives of contemporary American psychotherapy and psychotherapists.

The Jerome Frank Collection of papers, held at the Johns Hopkins Medical Institutions, spans his career at Johns Hopkins. It contains professional and patient correspondence, case notes, patient records, student records, teaching notes, a dissertation, manuscripts, reprints, committee records, reports, guidebooks, appointment books, publications, slides, and audiocassettes. These documents represent Frank's contributions to the Johns Hopkins University as a clinician, teacher, and researcher. His involvement with the Physicians for Social Responsibility and their efforts to control the proliferation of nuclear weapons is also documented.

Major Literature

Frank, Jerome David. *Persuasion and Healing: A Comparative Study of Psychotherapy.* Baltimore: Johns Hopkins Press, 1961. New York: Random House Inc., Schocken Books, 1974.
Powdermaker, Florence B., and Jerome David Frank. *Group Psychotherapy: Studies in Methodology of Research and Theory.* Westport, Connecticut: Greenwood Press, 1973.
Frank, Jerome David. *Sanity and Survival in the Nuclear Age: Psychological Aspects of War and Peace.* Lanham, Maryland: University Press of America, 1987.
___, and Park Elliott Dietz (Ed.). *Psychotherapy and the Human Predicament: A Psychosocial Approach.* Lanham, Maryland: Rowman and Littlefield Publishers, Inc., Jason Aronson, 1994.

Frankl, Viktor (1905–1997)
LOGOTHERAPY

Born in Vienna, Austria, Viktor Frankl graduated with an M.D. from the University of Vienna

Medical School (1930). He was director of the Neurological Department of the Rothschild Hospital in Vienna from 1940 to 1942. He was interred in Nazi concentration camps from 1942 to 1945; his family, all but one sister, died in Auschwitz.

He gained his Ph.D. in 1949 and was made associate professor of neurology and psychiatry at the University of Vienna. He founded and became president of the Austrian Medical Society for Psychotherapy (1950). In 1985, he was the recipient of the Oksar Pfister Award presented by the American Psychiatric Association. He was also the recipient of 29 honorary doctorates and the Great Cross of Merit with Star of the Republic of Austria (1995).

Major Contributions

Logotherapy is officially recognized by the American Medical Society, the American Psychiatric Association, and the American Psychological Association as a scientifically based school of psychotherapy. During his career Frankl lectured at universities on all five continents, and was visiting professor at several major universities in America. He founded the Viktor Frankl Institute for Logotherapy and Existential Analysis, now at Abilene, Texas.

Man's Search for Meaning portrays the courageous confrontation and transformation of suffering that is a hallmark of existential psychology. In it Frankl did not consider himself a hero; rather he describes the heroes or "saints" to be among the minority in the concentration camps; those who gave up their portions of bread to others, or gave their lives in order to save someone else from the gas chambers. The "existential" aspect of logotherapy maintains that man always has the ability to choose, no matter what biological or environmental forces stand against him. He talks of the "tragic triad" — pain, guilt, and death — and how it is possible to maintain optimism in the face of tragedy, and that the human potential is able to:

- turn suffering into a human achievement and accomplishment;
- derive from guilt the opportunity to change oneself for the better; and
- derive an incentive to take responsible action from the transitory nature of life.

Logotherapy means "therapy through meaning." It is an active-directive therapy aimed at helping people specifically to find meaning in crises, which manifest themselves either in a feeling of aimlessness or indirectly through addiction, alcoholism or depression. Frankl says we have a will to meaning, so in spite of physical and psychological restraints, we are free to stand against whatever circumstances confront us. We all have the potential to rise above even the most adverse conditions. Each of us has to find our own unique meaning of life.

Major Literature

Frankl, Viktor. *The Doctor and the Soul: From Psychotherapy to Logotherapy*. Netherlands: Springer, 1955. London: Souvenir Press Ltd., 2004.
___. *Man's Search for Meaning*. London Hodder and Stoughton, 1959. New York: Random House Inc., Rider, 2004.
___. *The Will to Meaning*. Austin, Texas: World Publishing, 1969. New York: Penguin Group, New American Library, 1988.
___. *Recollections: An Autobiography*. Jackson, Tennessee: Perseus Books, 2000.

Franz, Shepherd Ivory (1874–1933)
BRAIN FUNCTIONING

Born in New Jersey of German ancestry, Shepherd Ivory Franz gained a B.A. (1894) and a Ph.D. in psychology (1899) from Columbia University in New York. From 1899 to 1901 he was assistant in physiology, Harvard Medical School, Boston, Massachusetts. He was then instructor in physiology, Dartmouth Medical School, New Hampshire (1901–1904). In 1904 he established a psychological laboratory at McLean Psychiatric Hospital in Belmont, Massachusetts, to develop psychological testing methods to be used with psychiatric patients.

He was psychologist, Government Hospital for the Insane in Washington, D.C. (founded in 1852 and later renamed St. Elizabeth's Hospital) (1907–1924); established a psychological laboratory; scientific director (1909–1919); and was director of the laboratories (1919–1924). At George Washington University in Washington, D.C., he was professor of physiology (1906–1921) and professor of experimental psychology (1906–1924). From 1920 to 1924 he was instructor of neurology at the Naval Medical School in Washington. He was also lecturer in psychology at Johns Hopkins University, Baltimore, Maryland (1922–1923).

In 1924, serious lapses in his administrative duties resulted in Franz being demoted to psychologist, causing his resignation from the Government Hospital. He joined the University of California,

Los Angeles (UCLA) (1924), and from 1925 to 1933, he was professor and head of the psychology department and chief of the psychological clinic at the Children's Hospital in Hollywood.

Major Contributions

Franz worked hard to repair the rift between psychiatrists and psychologists; he maintained that psychologists were every bit experts as were psychiatrists. In 1922 he developed a six-month course in neuro-psychiatry for qualified physicians working within the Veterans Bureau (founded in 1921), one of the earliest and most comprehensive courses of its kind.

His inaugural lecture to the Southern Society for Philosophy and Psychology (founded 1904) was "The Functions of the Anterior and Posterior Areas of the Cerebrum." He concluded that the frontal lobes had motor associational functions while the posterior areas had sensory-associational functions. Franz claimed that phrenology was not a science and that there was no evidence to suggest that mental processes could be linked to anatomical regions of the brain.

He received an honorary M.D. degree from George Washington University (1915) and an honorary LL.D. degree from Waynesburg College, Pennsylvania (1915). He edited the *Psychological Bulletin* (1912–1924), *Psychological Monographs* (1924–1927), and *Journal of General Psychology* (1927–1929). In 1940, Franz Hall was newly opened to house the psychology department at UCLA.

Major Literature

Franz, Shepherd Ivory. *Handbook of Mental Examination Methods*. New York: The Journal of Nervous and Mental Disease Publishing Company, 1912.
___. "New Phrenology." *Science* 35 (1912): 321–328.
___. "Psychology and Psychiatry." *Psychological Review* 29 (1922): 241–249.
___. *Nervous and Mental Re-Education*. New York: Macmillan Co., 1923.
___. "Shepherd Ivory Franz." In C. Murchison (Ed.), *A History of Psychology in Autobiography* Vol. II (pp. 89–113). Worcester, Massachusetts: Clark University Press, 1932.
___. *Persons One and Three: A Study in Multiple Personalities*. New York: McGraw Hill Book Company, Inc., 1933.
___, and K. Gordon. *Psychology*. New York: McGraw-Hill Book Company, Inc., 1933.

Freud, Anna (1895–1982)
CHILD PSYCHOANALYSIS

Born in Vienna, the youngest daughter of Sigmund Freud, Anna Freud was educated at the Cottage Lyceum, Vienna. She traveled to England to improve her English (1914) after which she was a teacher at her old school. In 1918, she started analysis with her father; she attended the International Psychoanalytical Congress at The Hague in 1920, and in 1922, she presented her paper *Beating Fantasies and Daydreams* to the Vienna Psychoanalytical Society and became a member.

She began her own psychoanalytical practice with children in 1923. In 1925, she ran a teaching seminar at the Vienna Psychoanalytic Training Institute on the technique of child analysis. From 1925 to 1928 she was chairman of the Vienna Psychoanalytic Society, and in 1927, published a paper outlining her approach to child psychoanalysis. She was general secretary of the International Psychoanalytical Association (1927–1934) and director of the Vienna Psychoanalytical Training Institute (1935).

From the 1950s until the end of her life Anna Freud lectured in the United States. During the 1970s she was concerned with the problems of working with emotionally deprived and socially disadvantaged children, and she studied deviations and delays in development and taught seminars on crime and the family at Yale Law School, New Haven, Connecticut.

Major Contributions

• Originated the concept of identification with the aggressor in ego psychology.
• Formulated the basic concepts in the theory and practice of child psychoanalysis.
• Began systematic charting of theoretical normal growth from dependency to emotional self-reliance, a psychoanalytic concept of psychological development, which was a new approach to assessing the indications for treatment in a child.

In 1938 Anna Freud and her father escaped from Nazi-dominated Austria and settled in London, where she worked at a Hampstead nursery (which provided foster care for over 80 children of single-parent families) until 1945. Sigmund Freud (see entry) died from cancer within weeks of the outbreak of World War II.

Anna Freud identified repression as the principal human defense mechanism; it is an unconscious process that develops as the young child learns that some impulses, if acted upon, could prove dangerous to himself. The other defense mechanisms she identified include projection, or directing aggressive impulses against the self (suicide being the extreme example); identification with an overpowering aggressor; and the divorce of ideas from feelings.

Freud founded the Hampstead Child Therapy Course and Clinic in London in 1947 and served as its director from 1952 to 1982. She was one of the pioneers of play therapy. She worked closely with parents and believed that analysis should have an educational influence on the child.

Major Literature

Freud, Anna. *The Ego and the Mechanisms of Defense.* London: Hogarth Press and Institute of Psycho-Analysis, 1936.
___. *The Psychoanalytic Treatment of Children.* London: Imago Publishing Co., Ltd., 1946.
___. *Normality and Pathology in Childhood: Assessments of Development.* New York: International Universities Press, Inc., 1965.
Burlingham, Dorothy, and Anna Freud. *Young Children in Wartime.* London: George Allen and Unwin, 1942.
Bergmann, Thesi, and Anna Freud. *Children in the Hospital.* New York: International Universities Press, Inc., 1965.

Freud, Sigmund (1856–1939)

FOUNDER OF PSYCHOANALYSIS

Born of Jewish parents, in Moravia, now in the Czech Republic, Sigmund Freud worked with Josef Breuer (see entry) in 1877, earned an M.D. at the University of Vienna (1881), and studied in Paris under Jean-Martin Charcot (see entry), who was using hypnosis to treat hysteria (1885). He married in 1886, remained married for 50 years and had six children.

Between 1892 and 1895, he developed his psychoanalytic method and the technique of free association. In 1896 he coined the term "psychoanalyse" (psyche=soul) and started his self-analysis. He formed the Psychological Wednesday Society in 1902 and the International Psychoanalytical Association in 1908. He presented his structural model of id, ego, and superego in 1923. The Nazis burned Freud's books in Berlin in 1933 and he left Vienna for London in 1938 (see Bonaparte, Princess Marie).

Major Contributions

While working with patients under hypnosis with Joseph Breuer, Freud observed that often there was improvement in the condition when the sources of the patients' ideas and impulses were brought into the conscious. Also, observing that patients talked freely while under hypnosis, he evolved his technique of free association. Noting that sometimes patients had difficulty in making free associations, he concluded that painful experiences were being repressed and held back from conscious awareness.

Freud deduced that what was being repressed were disturbing sexual experiences, real or in fantasy, and that repressed sexual energy and its consequent anxiety finds an outlet in various symptoms that serve as ego defenses. His basic theory was that neuroses are rooted in suppressed sexual desires and sexual experiences in childhood. He maintained that many of the impulses forbidden or punished by parents are derived from innate instincts. Forbidding expression to these instincts merely drives them out of awareness into the unconscious. There they reside to affect dreams, slips of speech or mannerisms and may also manifest themselves in symptoms of mental illness.

Freud's view that the conscious and the unconscious are sharply divided and that access to the unconscious is denied except by psychoanalysis does not meet with universal acceptance. Rather, many believe that there are various layers of awareness.

In summary, Freud's view was that humans are driven by sex and aggression, the same basic instincts as animals. Society is in constant struggle against any expression of these. Psychoanalysis includes investigating mental processes not easily accessed by other means. It is a method of investigating and treating neurotic disorders and the scientific collection of psychological information. The main purpose of psychoanalysis is to make unconscious material conscious. Freud died of cancer in London.

Major Literature

Freud was a prolific writer. Many of his more than 300 articles and books have been republished many times. The most comprehensive is still available.
Freud, S. (Ed. James Strachey). *Standard Edition of the Complete Psychological Works of Sigmund Freud, 1953–1974.* London: Hogarth Press, 1953–1974. New York: W.W. Norton and Co. Ltd., 2000.

Fromm, Erich Pinchas (1900–1980)

INTERACTIVE PSYCHOLOGY

Born in Frankfurt, Germany, of Orthodox Jewish parents, Erich Pinchas Fromm gained a Ph.D. at the University of Heidelberg, Germany (1922), and took psychoanalytic training at the University of Munich and at the Psychoanalytic Institute of Berlin. He moved to America (1934) and was at Columbia University, New York from 1934 to 1941. From 1941 to 1950, he was a member of the faculty at Bennington College, Bennington, Vermont, then professor of psychoanalysis at the National Autonomous University of Mexico, Mexico City (1951–1976). He was a professor at Michigan State University, East Lansing, Michigan (1957–1961) and professor of psychiatry, New York University, while still working in Mexico (1962).

Major Contributions

A social philosopher, Fromm explored the interaction between psychology and society. He believed that by applying psychoanalytic principles to the remedy of cultural ills, mankind could develop a psychologically balanced "sane society." He soon took issue with Freud's preoccupation with unconscious drives and consequent neglect of the role of society in human psychology.

For Fromm, an individual's personality was the product of his culture as well as his biology. As early as 1930 he was promoting the view that an understanding of basic human needs is essential to the understanding of society and mankind itself. When these basic needs are not met at an individual and wider social level, conflicts are created that influence the formation of mental disorders.

In *Escape from Freedom*, he charted the growth of human freedom and self-awareness from the Middle Ages to modern times. Using psychoanalytic techniques, he shows how modern man is alienated from place and community. Alienation produces insecurities and fears and this helps to explain how people seek the security and rewards of authoritarian social orders such Nazism.

The theme of alienation is continued in *The Sane Society*, where modern man is estranged from himself within consumer-oriented industrial society. Fromm called for a rebirth of enlightenment in a new and perfect society that would allow each person to fulfill his individual needs while maintaining his sense of belonging through bonds of social brotherhood. He brought to his work a strong religious understanding, a humanistic ethic and a vision of possibility, yet wrote in such a way that he appealed to a wide and popular audience.

His criticism of Freud led to him being suspended from supervising students by the New York Psychoanalytic Institute in 1944. His last major work, in 1976, points to the competing cultures of having or being. The having society, based on aggression and greed, is materialistic. The being mode is rooted in love and is concerned with shared experience and productive activity.

Major Literature

Fromm, Erich Pinchas. *Escape from Freedom*. New York: Farrar and Rinehart, Inc., 1941. New York: Henry Holt, 1994.

___. *The Art of Loving*. London, England: Thorsons, 1957. New York: HarperCollins Publishers, Inc., 1994.

___. *The Anatomy of Human Destructiveness*. New York: Henry Holt, 1973. New York: Random House Inc., Pimlico, 1997.

___. *To Have or To Be*. London, England: Abacus, 1976. New York: Continuum Publishing Group, 2005.

Fromm-Reichmann, Frieda (1889–1957)
PSYCHODYNAMIC PSYCHOTHERAPY

Frieda Reichmann was born in Karlsruhe, Germany, of a middle-class German Jewish family, the oldest of three daughters. She graduated from medical school in 1914, then studied neurology, war-related brain injuries, and dementia praecox (schizophrenia) before pursuing psychoanalytic training and practice in Berlin and Heidelberg. She married Erich Fromm, and together they founded the Psychoanalytic Training Institute of South-western Germany. Although they later divorced, they continued as colleagues. In 1935 she immigrated to America and joined the staff of Chestnut Lodge Hospital, Rockville, Maryland, where she remained until her death.

Major Contributions

Although primarily a psychoanalyst, she introduced modifications to the classical model that were considered heretical at the time, such as:

- not using a couch
- insisting that patients with schizophrenia can form transferences
- focusing on the here-and-now as well as working on the past
- stressing the impact of counter-transferences and the therapist's values on the therapeutic work
- seeking the origins of psychotic conflict before and beyond the oedipal period of development
- focusing less on classical libido and structural theory in favor of interpersonal, object relations theory
- attempting to help psychotic patients integrate rather than reject their disorder.

From her experiences of working with severely mentally ill patients at Chestnut Lodge, Fromm formulated her theories of intensive psychodynamic psychotherapy. She was renowned for her work with the most severely ill patients, focusing on the quality of the therapeutic relationship.

I Never Promised You a Rose Garden is a fictionalized depiction of Joanne Greenberg's psychoanalytic treatment with Frieda Fromm-Reichmann at Chestnut Lodge. The story takes place in the late 1940s and early 1950s, at a time when Fromm, Harry Stack Sullivan, and Clara Thompson (see entries) were establishing the basis for the interpersonal school of psychiatry and psychoanalysis, focusing specifically, though by no means exclusively, on the treatment of schizophrenia.

In summary, Frieda Fromm developed a comprehensive theory of therapy and technique in working with patients suffering from severe mental illness, including schizophrenia. Her writing and her practice laid the foundations of what later became known as psychodynamic psychotherapy. Although derived from psychoanalysis, it tends to differ in two obvious ways. First, it is usually shorter, and second, there tends to be a more specific aim, for example, sorting out a phobia. Psychoanalysis will tend to look to affect a lot more of a person's personality. The mission of Chestnut Lodge Hospital is to provide expert and compassionate care for patients with psychiatric disorders, particularly those with severe and persistent mental illness. Chestnut Lodge Hospital is now owned by a non-profit community mental health agency.

Major Literature

Fromm-Reichmann, Frieda. *Principles of Intensive Psychotherapy*. Chicago, Illinois: The University of Chicago Press, 1950.

___. *Psychoanalysis and Psychotherapy; Selected papers of Frieda Fromm-Reichmann*. Chicago, Illinois: University of Chicago Press, 1959, 1974.

Related Literature

Greenberg, Joanne. *I Never Promised You a Rose Garden*. New York: Macmillan, 1972. (Now available on DVD.)

Gagné, Robert Mills (1916–2002)
CONDITIONS OF LEARNING

Born in North Andover, Massachusetts, Robert Mills Gagné graduated with an A.B. (1937) at Yale University, New Haven, Connecticut, and a Ph.D.

in psychology (1940) from Brown University, Providence, Rhode Island. From 1940 to 1949 he was a professor of psychology and educational psychology, Connecticut College for Women, New London, Connecticut. He was at Pennsylvania State University and Princeton University, New Jersey (1958–1962) and the University of California at Berkeley (1966–1969).

He served throughout World War II as an aviation psychologist, producing tests of motor and perceptual skills for use in selecting air crews. He was research director of the perceptual and motor skills laboratory of the U.S. Air Force from 1949 to 1958, then was consultant to the U.S. Department of Defense from 1958 to 1961 at Lackland, Texas, and Lowry, Colorado, and to the United States Office of Education (1964–1966). He also served as a director of research at the American Institute of Research in Pittsburgh (1962–1965).

From 1969 Gagné was a professor in the Department of Educational Research at Florida State University in Tallahassee. He received the American Psychological Association's Distinguished Scientific Award for the Applications of Psychology in 1982.

Major Contributions

Gagné developed a comprehensive learning theory called the "conditions of learning." From his research he identified five unique categories of learning that represent different capacities and performances: verbal information, intellectual skills, attitudes, motor skills, and cognitive strategies.

A major contribution to the theory of instruction was the model "Nine Events of Instruction":

1. Gain attention
2. Inform learner of objectives
3. Stimulate recall of prior learning
4. Present stimulus material
5. Provide learner guidance
6. Elicit performance
7. Provide feedback
8. Assess performance
9. Enhance retention transfer.

Gagné identified eight kinds of learning from the simplest to the most complex:

1. signal learning (Pavlovian conditioning)
2. stimulus-response learning (operant conditioning)
3. chaining (complex operant conditioning)
4. verbal association
5. discrimination learning

6. concept learning
7. rule learning
8. problem solving.

Gagné's eight steps or phases of learning:

1. *Motivation.* Self-motivation is preferred.
2. *Apprehending.* Getting and keeping the learner's attention.
3. *Acquisition.* The learner translates the information into his own language and stores it in short-term memory.
4. *Retention.* Information stored in long-term memory.
5. *Recall.* As and when needed.
6. *Generalization.* Transfer of learning.
7. *Performance.* Information is put to use.
8. *Feedback.* The process of encouragement and consolidation.

Major Literature

Gagné, Robert Mills. "Military Training and Principles of Learning." *American Psychologist* 17 (1962): 263–276.
___. *The Conditions of Learning.* Orlando, Florida: Holt, Rinehart and Winston, 4th ed., 1985.
___. *Instructional Technology Foundations.* Hillsdale, New Jersey: Lawrence Erlbaum Associates, Inc., 1987.
___, and M. Driscoll. *Essentials of Learning for Instruction.* Englewood Cliffs, New Jersey: Prentice-Hall, 1988 (2nd Ed.).
Gagné, Robert Mills. *Studies of Learning: 50 Years of Research.* Tallahassee: Florida State University, 1989.
___, L. Briggs, and W. Wager. *Principles of Instructional Design.* Fort Worth, Texas: HBJ College Publishers, 1992. (4th Ed.).

Galton, Sir Francis (1822–1911)

INTELLIGENCE

Born in Duddeston, Warwickshire, England, Galton was Charles Darwin's half-cousin. The Galtons were famous, rich and highly successful Quaker gun manufacturers and bankers, while the Darwins were distinguished in medicine and science. Galton gained a B.A. (1844) and M.A. (1847) from the University of Cambridge, England. Originally intent on a medical career, he suffered some sort of mental breakdown and when his father died in 1844, leaving Galton well provided for, he abandoned medicine.

In 1853 he was awarded the Royal Geographical Society Gold Medal for his expedition to Lake Ngami, in Botswana, north of the Kalahari Desert, Africa, some 550 miles east of Walvis Bay. His awards and achievements were: Fellow of the Royal Society (1856); president, British Association Geography Section (1872); president, British Association Anthropology Section (1885); Gold Medal, Royal Society (1886); honorary degree, University of Oxford (1894); honorary Sc.D., University of Cambridge (1895); Darwin Medal, Royal Society (1902); Huxley Medal, Anthropological Institute (1902); Darwin-Wallace Medal, Linnean Society (1908); knighted (1909); and Copley Medal, Royal Society (1910). Galton produced over 340 papers and books throughout his lifetime.

Major Contributions

Galton created the statistical concepts of regression and correlation, discovered regression toward the mean, was the first to apply statistical methods to the study of human differences and inheritance of intelligence, and introduced the use of questionnaires and surveys for collecting data on human communities, which he needed for genealogical and biographical works and for his anthropometric studies. He was a pioneer in eugenics, coining the term "eugenics" and the phrase "nature versus nurture." He founded psychometrics and investigated visual memory as to illumination, definition, coloring, and the like. He also experimented with taste, smell, the muscular sense of weight, the judgment of experts in guessing the weight of cattle, and many similar points.

To psychology Galton also made contributions that were important and original. He showed that different minds work in different ways, and, for example, that visual images play a large part with some but not with others. In 1879 Galton devised a word-probe task used to assess patients' past memory, useful in psychiatry. He initiated scientific meteorology: invented the weather map, proposed a theory of anticyclones and was the first to establish a complete record of short-term climatic phenomena on a European scale. He also invented the silent dog whistle and devised a method for classifying fingerprints useful in forensics. Under the terms of his will, a eugenics chair was established at the University of London.

Major Literature

Galton, Francis. *Hereditary Genius.* New York: Macmillan, 1869. Boston: Adamant Media Corporation, 2000.
___. *Inquiries Into Human Faculty and its Development.* New York: Macmillan, 1883. Honolulu, Hawaii: University Press of the Pacific, 2003.
___. *Natural Inheritance.* New York: Macmillan, 1889. Placitas, New Mexico: Genetics Heritage Press, 1996.
___. *Fingerprints.* New York: Macmillan, 1892. New York: William S. Hein and Co., 2002.

Gardner, Howard Earl (1943–)
MULTIPLE INTELLIGENCES

Born in Scranton, Pennsylvania, the son of refugees from Nazi Germany, Gardner gained a B.A. (1965) and Ph.D. (1971) from Harvard University, Cambridge, Massachusetts. He is John H. and Elisabeth A. Hobbs Professor in Cognition and Education at the Harvard Graduate School of Education and adjunct professor of neurology at the Boston University School of Medicine. He is chair of the steering committee of Project Zero, working on the design of performance-based assessments.

Gardner was the first American to receive the University of Louisville's Grawemeyer Award in education (1990). In 2004 he was named an honorary professor at East China Normal University in Shanghai. In 2005, *Foreign Policy* and *Prospect* magazines named him one of 100 most influential public intellectuals in the world. Gardner has received honorary degrees from twenty colleges and universities, including institutions in Ireland, Italy and Israel.

Major Contributions

Gardner is best known for his theory of multiple intelligences, rather than a single intelligence that can be assessed by standard psychometric tests. Gardner identifies nine distinct types of intelligence:

1. *Linguistic.* The ability to use language to express what's on your mind and to understand other people; to enjoy writing, reading, telling stories or doing crossword puzzles.
2. *Logical-Mathematical.* The ability to understand patterns, categories and relationships, arithmetic problems, strategy games and experiments.
3. *Bodily-kinesthetic.* The ability to use the whole body or parts of the body to solve a problem. Such people are often athletes, dancers, actors, or good at crafts such as sewing or woodworking.
4. *Spatial.* The ability to think in images and pictures, to form cognitive maps. These people are often fascinated with mazes or jigsaw puzzles, or spend free time drawing or playing chess.
5. *Musical.* The ability to think in music, to be able to hear patterns, recognize them, and perhaps manipulate them. Musical children are always singing or drumming to themselves.
6. *Interpersonal.* The ability to understand other people, be leaders among their peers, be good at communicating, seem to understand others' feelings and motives, possess interpersonal intelligence.
7. *Intrapersonal.* Knowing who you are, what you can do, what you want to do, how you react to things, which things to avoid, and which things to gravitate toward.
8. *Naturalist.* The ability to discriminate among living things (plants, animals) and sensitivity to other features of the natural world (clouds, rock configurations).
9. *Existential.* The ability and inclination to pose (and ponder) questions about life, death, and ultimate realities.

Major Literature

Gardner, Howard Earl. *Art, Mind, and Brain: A Cognitive Approach to Creativity.* Jackson, Tennessee: Basic Books, 1982.

___. *Frames of Mind: The Theory of Multiple Intelligence.* Jackson, Tennessee: Basic Books, 1993.

___. *The Unschooled Mind: How Children Think and How Schools Should Teach.* Jackson, Tennessee: Basic Books, 1993.

___. *Multiple Intelligences: The Theory in Practice.* Jackson, Tennessee: Basic Books, 1993.

___. *Changing the World: A Framework for the Study of Creativity.* Westport, Connecticut: Greenwood Press, 1994.

Gazzaniga, Michael S. (1939–)
NEUROPSYCHOLOGY

Born in Los Angeles, Gazzaniga gained an A.B. (1961) from Dartmouth College, Hanover, North Hampshire, and a Ph.D. in psychobiology (1964) from the California Institute of Technology, Pasadena. From 1964 to 1966 he was post-graduate fellow, California Institute of Technology.

Since 1967 he has had a distinguished academic career at several major American universities, including director, Center for Neuroscience; professor of Neurology and of Psychology, University of California (1992–1996); David T. McLaughlin Distinguished Professor, Dartmouth College; director, Center for Cognitive Neuroscience (1996), and from 2002, dean of the faculty, Dartmouth College. He is now full professor at the University of California, Santa Barbara, heading the new SAGE Center for the Study of the Mind, opened 10 November 2005.

Major Contributions

Gazzaniga worked for his Ph.D. under the guidance of Roger Sperry (see entry) whose primary responsibility was split-brain research. Gazzaniga subsequently made remarkable advances in our understanding of how the two cerebral hemispheres communicate, whether they function independently, and whether they have separate and unique abilities.

He observed that some people who underwent surgery to sever the connecting corpus collosum ended up with "split brain." Cutting apart the two hemispheres of the human brain is a drastic step, and it is one of the most controversial operations ever performed. Yet it can succeed, when all else fails, in relieving violent, drug-resistant epileptic seizures. Gazzaniga developed a special apparatus which demonstrated that the left side of the brain is the language center — speaking, writing, mathematics and reading; the right half of the brain is better for recognizing faces, for visualization and the use of imagery.

The idea of left and right brain has become part of modern culture and it has left the inference that somehow people with predominantly right brain functioning are in some way superior to people who use their left brain more. However, no one functions entirely on either one side or the other. Indeed, most activities make use of both sides. The following table illustrates the differences between left-brain and right-brain thinking:

LEFT BRAIN	RIGHT BRAIN
Logical	Random
Sequential	Intuitive
Rational	Holistic
Objective	Subjective
Looks at parts	Looks at wholes
Analytical	Synthesizing

Gazzaniga's books and his television appearances have brought brain functioning to a wide audience. *The Cognitive Neurosciences* is recognized as the sourcebook for the field. Gazzaniga founded the Cognitive Neuroscience Society in 1993 and the *Journal of Cognitive Neuroscience* in 1989.

Major Literature

Gazzaniga, Michael S., and Joseph E. Ledoux. *The Integrated Mind*. Notre Dame, Indiana: Kluwer Academic Publishers/Plenum, 1978.
Gazzaniga, Michael S. *Social Brain: Discovering the Networks of the Mind*. Jackson, Tennessee: Basic Books, 1987.
___ (Ed.). *The Cognitive Neurosciences*. Cambridge, Massachusetts: MIT Press, 1995, 2004.
___ (Ed.). *Cognitive Neuroscience: A Reader*. Iowa, Ames: Blackwell Publishing, 2000. New York: W.W. Norton and Co. Ltd., 2006.
___. *The Ethical Brain: The Science of Our Moral Dilemma*. New York: HarperCollins Publishers, Inc., Harper Perennial, 2006.

Gerard, Harold Benjamin (1923–2003)

EXPERIMENTAL SOCIAL PSYCHOLOGY

Born in Brooklyn, New York, Gerard began his studies as a physics major at Brooklyn College. After serving in the signal corps during World War II and taking part in the invasion of Europe (1944), he graduated with a B.A. from Brooklyn College in 1947. He then enrolled in the graduate program in sociology at Columbia University, New York, working under the anthropologist Margaret Mead.

Mead offered Gerard a scholarship to accompany her on field work to New Guinea, but he chose instead to study social psychology at the University of Michigan and at the Research Center for Group Dynamics. He received his Ph.D. under Leon Festinger (see entry) in 1952. Thereafter, he held professorial and research appointments at the Research Center for Human Relations of New York University, at the University of Buffalo, New York. He was a Fulbright scholar at the University of Nijmegen in the Netherlands and worked at the Social Science Communications Center of Bell Telephone Laboratories and the University of California, Riverside.

Gerard joined the faculty of the Department of Psychology at University College Los Angeles in 1962, where he continued to teach and conduct research in social psychology until his retirement in 1992. Among many distinctions, Gerard was awarded a Guggenheim Fellowship and was twice a fellow at the Center for Advanced Study in the Behavioral Sciences, Stanford, California.

Major Contributions

One of the pioneers of experimental social psychology, at Riverside, Gerard collaborated with Norman Miller and others there in a huge field experiment made possible by a court-ordered desegregation of a school system. In 1969, Gerard married Desy Safán, a psychoanalytic clinical psychologist, and in 1982, with his wife's encouragement, Gerard entered psychoanalytic training and became a psychoanalyst, maintaining for years a limited private practice.

He carried out a series of studies on unconscious psychodynamics and emotions, and compared the developmental theories of Sigmund Freud and Melanie Klein (see entries) and relating psychoanalytic theory to social phenomena. He came to believe that cooperation and competition, close relationships, altruism and aggression, prejudice, and so on, could all be illuminated through understanding unconscious and psychodynamic factors. He also researched group influences on attitudes and behavior and cognitive dissonance theory.

Major Literature

Gerard, Harold Benjamin, and Norman Miller. *Foundations of Social Psychology*. New York: Plenum Publishing Corporation, 1967.
___. *School Desegregation: A Long-Term Study*. New York: Plenum Publishing Corporation, 1975.

Gerbner, George (1919–2005)
CULTIVATION THEORY

Born in Budapest, Hungary, George Gerbner immigrated to America in late 1939 and earned his B.A. in journalism (1942) at the University of California, Berkeley. He enlisted into the U.S. Army in 1943, served with the 541st Parachute Infantry (101st Airborne) and the Office of Strategic Services (OSS) — the U.S. intelligence agency — and received the Bronze Star for service behind enemy lines. He gained his master's degree (1951) and his Ph.D. (1955) from the University of Southern California, Los Angeles.

He was dean emeritus of the Annenberg School for Communication at the University of Pennsylvania (1964–1989). He then became an independent researcher and teacher, with appointments as visiting lecturer at home and abroad, including the Bell Atlantic Professor of Telecommunication at Temple University, Philadelphia, from 1997. He was former director, the Cultural Indicators Project, and founder and former president, the Cultural Environment Movement.

He was executive editor of the quarterly *Journal of Communication* and chair of the editorial board of the *International Encyclopedia of Communication*. He also served on the staff of the *San Francisco Chronicle* and other newspapers, and was series co-editor, Oxford Communication Books and Longman Communication Books.

Major Contributions

Gerbner's cultivation theory grew out of his master's thesis, "Television and Education," and his Ph.D. thesis, "Toward a General Theory of Communication." Gerbner and his colleagues analyzed television content and the influence on the attitudes and perceptions of reality on people. According to the theory, television creates a false image of reality. The values perpetuated may involve gender roles, ethnicity, political attitudes, violence, science, religion, aging and how various minority groups are represented. What is on the "box" must be correct, and the more a person watches, the more likely they are to be influenced by what they see and hear. Light viewers may have more outlets and sources to influence their version of reality than heavy viewers.

Gerbner's theory asserts that most often heavy viewers tend to be men and those of lower income brackets. The "mean world" syndrome is one of the main effects of the cultivation theory — heavy viewers see the world as a much nastier place than do light viewers, and "the double dose effect" is where heavy viewers believe that violence is more prevalent than it actually is. Cultivation theory is often criticized because it ignores other variables, including sex, education, race, and geographic location in the gathering of information, and any beneficial effects of television.

Major Literature

Gerbner, George (Ed.). *Child Abuse: An Agenda for Action*. New York: Oxford University Press, Inc., 1980.
___, and Marsha Siefert (Eds.). *World Communications: A Handbook*. Upper Saddle River, New Jersey: Pearson Education, Longman Group, 1984.
Gerbner, George (Ed.). *The Global Media Debate: Its Rise, Fall and Renewal*. Norwood, New Jersey: Ablex Publishing Corporation, 1993.
___, and Michael Morgan (Eds.). *Against the Mainstream: Selected Works of George Gerbner*. New York: Peter Lang Publishing, Inc., 2002.

Gesell, Arnold Lucius (1880–1961)
CHILD DEVELOPMENT

Born in Alma, Wisconsin, Arnold Lucius Gesell gained his B.Ph. (1903) at the University of Wisconsin Madison, became a high school teacher and principal, gained his Ph.D. (1906) in child psychology at Clark University, Worcester, Massachusetts, where he was influenced by G. Stanley Hall (see entry), one of the earliest psychologists to study child development. In 1911 he went to New Haven, Connecticut, to head the Yale Psycho-Clinic (later the Clinic of Child Development). He gained his M.D. in 1915 from Yale University, and from 1915 to 1948 he was professor of child hygiene at Yale. The Yale Clinic was the primary United States center for the study of child behavior in its time.

Clark University awarded Gesell an honorary D.Sc. in 1930, as did the University of Wisconsin in 1953. After his retirement, his friends set up the Gesell Institute of Child Development and Gesell worked as a consultant there until his death. The Gesell Institute of Child Development still carries on its research to this day, and publishes books on child development that are popular with parents and teachers. He was a member of the White House Conference on Childhood in a Democracy (1939–1940) and was made a member of Kappa Delta Phi in 1958.

Major Contributions

Gesell was one of the first to attempt a quantitative study of child development. From 1926 the movie camera became his principal tool of investigation. About 12,000 children of various ages and levels of development were filmed candidly through the Gesell dome, a one-way mirror shaped as a dome, under which children could be observed without being disturbed. Measurements contributed to a set of milestones — motor, perceptual, cognitive, and behavioral — which are still being used by child health professionals.

His initial work focused on developmentally disabled children, but he believed that it was necessary to understand normal infant and child development in order to understand those with disabilities. In addition to his studies of normal development, Gesell also studied the psychological factors in child adoption and the effect of premature birth on mental development, Down syndrome, cretinism, and cerebral palsy.

Major Literature

Gesell, Arnold Lucius. *Infancy and Human Growth*. New York: Macmillan, 1928.
___. *An Atlas of Infant Behavior*. New Haven, Connecticut: Yale University Press, 1934.
___, and Francis L. Ilg. *Infant and Child in the Culture of Today*. London, England: Penguin Books Ltd., Hamish Hamilton, 1940.
Gesell, Arnold Lucius, et al. *The Child from Five to Ten*. London, England: Penguin Books Ltd., Hamish Hamilton, 1946.
___, and Francis L. Ilg. *Child Development: An Introduction to the Study of Human Growth*. Saddle River, New Jersey: Pearson Education, Longman Group, 1949.
___. *Youth: The Years from Ten to Sixteen*. London, England: Penguin Books Ltd., Hamish Hamilton, 1956.

Gibson, Eleanor Jack
(1910–2002)
DEVELOPMENTAL PSYCHOLOGY

Eleanor Jack was born in Peoria, Illinois. She gained a B.A. (1931) and an M.A. (1933) at Smith College, Northampton, Massachusetts, and a Ph.D. (1938) from Yale University, New Haven, Connecticut. She married James Jerome Gibson (see entry) and raised a family. In 1949 she moved with her husband, as unpaid research associate, to Cornell University, Ithaca, New York. She became a professor at Cornell in 1966 and the Susan Linn Sage Professor of Psychology in 1971, the first woman at Cornell to occupy an endowed chair.

During her lifetime she accrued many honors and awards: the Wilbur Cross Medal, the American Psychology Association Distinguished Contribution Award, and the 1969 Century Prize for her book *Principles of Perceptual Learning and Development*. She was a fellow of the American Academy of Arts and Sciences, a fellow of the National Academy of Sciences, and recipient of the National Medal of Science in 1992. She received eleven honorary doctorates and was an elected member of the National Academy of Sciences and the American Academy of Arts and Sciences. She was the author of five books on perception, infant development, and reading.

Major Contributions

Gibson was a pioneer in the study of perceptual learning and development. Her contribution to psychology has been her research on the way children learn to perceive their environment, although her work did include animal studies and learning. Gibson, along with her husband, argued that perceptual learning was done through a process called *differentiation*. Before perceptual learning, children over-generalize and see things similarly to each other. As children develop perceptual learning they can make distinctions between objects and events they were not able to make initially. Young children easily confuse stimuli with one another, but with repetition, the stimuli eventually become differentiated.

In 1960 Gibson and Richard Walk devised a novel piece of apparatus called the "visual cliff" to study depth perception and the fear of falling. The behavior of most infants suggested that they could perceive depth and that depth perception is not learned. She set up her own infant laboratory in 1975.

Major Literature

Gibson, Eleanor Jack. *Principles of Perceptual Learning and Development*. New Jersey: Prentice-Hall, 1969.
___, and H.T. Levin. *The Psychology of Reading*. Cambridge, Massachusetts: MIT Press, 1978.
Gibson, Eleanor Jack. *An Odyssey of Learning and Perception*. Cambridge, Massachusetts: MIT Press, 1991, 1994.
___, and A.D. Pick. *An Ecological Approach to Perceptual Learning and Development*. New York: Oxford University Press Inc., 2000, 2003.
Gibson, Eleanor Jack. *Perceiving the Affordances: A Portrait of two Psychologists*. Hillsdale, New Jersey: Erlbaum Associates, Inc., 2002.

Gibson, James Jerome
(1904–1979)
VISUAL PERCEPTION

Born in McConnelsville, Ohio, James Jerome Gibson studied at Princeton and Edinburgh universities and gained a B.A. (1925) and Ph.D. (1928) from Princeton University, New Jersey, where his dissertation was on memory and focused on the role of learning. From 1928 to 1949 he taught psychology at Smith College, Northampton, Massachusetts, and at Cornell University in Ithaca, New York (1949–1972). During World War II he served as director of the Research Unit in Aviation Psychology for the U.S. Air Force.

Major Contributions

Gibson and his wife, Eleanor Jack Gibson (see entry), formed a remarkable partnership. Although they worked together, they also worked separately, yet influenced each other's work. She formulated a theory of development that complemented his theory of perception. While at Smith College, he met Kurt Koffka (see entry) whose work on Gestalt psychology profoundly influenced his thinking and work. While working with the Air Force he implemented a new approach for pilot selection by using motion pictures to present the test material. This experience led him to propose that moving pictures present more information than static pictures.

Gibson is primarily known for his research in, and theories of, perception. He became a leader of a new movement in that field by considering that perceptions come to us direct and complete, without any steps, variables, or associations. He formulated the concept of "stimulus ecology," referring to the stimuli that surround a person. These include the light from slanting and reflecting surfaces, and the gravitational forces we all experience in walking, sitting, and lying down.

Gibson emphasized the need to study vision in terms of people behaving in the real world performing meaningful tasks rather than subjects responding under the artificial and information-poor conditions of the laboratory. He also invented the word "affordance"—the property of an object, or a feature of the immediate environment, that indicates how to interface with that object or feature. The empty space within an open doorway, for instance, affords movement across that threshold. A couch affords the possibility of sitting down on it. This concept is used by workers in the fields of cognitive psychology, environmental psychology, industrial design, human-computer interaction, design, ergonomics and artificial intelligence.

Gibson's work is referred to as "ecological psychology," which is also known as "environmental psychology." Gibson coined the term "ecological psychology" to emphasize his belief that more traditional psychologies of the "mind" or of "behavior" were too narrowly conceived. Ecological psychology, on the other hand, recognizes the place and contribution of animals and their environments, and the need to take into account the animal environment and the reciprocity between it and ours.

Major Literature

Gibson, James Jerome. *The Perception of the Visual World*. Westport, Connecticut: Greenwood Press, 1950.
___. *The Senses Considered as Perceptual Systems*. Westport, Connecticut: Greenwood Press, 1966, 1983.
___. *The Ecological Approach to Visual Perception*. Houghton Mifflin, 1986. Hillsdale, New Jersey: Erlbaum, Associates, Inc., 1970.

Gilbreth, Lillian Moller
(1878–1972)
INDUSTRIAL PSYCHOLOGY

Lillian Evelyn Moller was born in Oakland, California, and gained a B.A. (1900) and an M.A. in literature (1902) from the University of California at Berkeley. She married Frank Bunker Gilbreth (1864–1924) in 1904 and had twelve children. Four of them accompanied their mother when she was awarded her Ph.D. (1915) at Brown University, Providence, Rhode Island. In 1926, she became the first woman member of the American Society of Mechanical Engineers.

From 1935 to 1948 she was professor of management at Purdue University, West Lafayette, Indiana, the first female professor in their engineering school. In 1966, she won the Hoover Medal of the American Society of Civil Engineers. Three of her 22 honorary degrees were from Princeton University, Brown University and the University of Michigan. She was an advisor to Presidents Hoover, Roosevelt, Eisenhower, Kennedy and Johnson on matters of civil defense, war production and rehabilitation of the physically handicapped. She and her husband have a permanent exhibit in the Smithsonian National Museum of American History. Her portrait hangs in the National Portrait Gallery, Washington, D.C. In 1984, the United States Postal Service issued a stamp in her honor.

Major Contributions

Lillian Gilbreth and her husband were pioneers in the field of industrial engineering; some of their industrial management techniques are still in use today. When they married, Frank was a contracting engineer in New York City with a keen interest in workplace efficiency; together they began their study of scientific management principles. They launched a time and motion studies consulting firm in Providence, Rhode Island, which later moved to Montclair, New Jersey. Frank was concerned with the technical aspects of worker efficiency, Lillian, with the human aspects of time management.

She recognized that workers are motivated by indirect incentives (among which she included money) and direct incentives, such as job satisfaction. Her work with Frank helped create job standardization, incentive wage plans, and job simplification. She was among the first to recognize the effects of fatigue and stress on time management. After Frank's death she assumed the presidency of the firm and remained active in research, lecturing, and writing. She was a pioneer in making the environment easier for the physically handicapped. She also sought to apply business methods to home economics and the management of the home. The book *Cheaper by the Dozen* (1949; filmed 1950, DVD, 2004) is a hilarious account of their family life.

Major Literature

Gilbreth, Lillian. *Psychology of Management*. Easton, Pennsylvania: Hive Publishing Co., 1914.
___. *Fatigue Study*. New York: Sturgis and Walton Co., 1916. New York: The Macmillan Co., 1920. Easton, Pennsylvania: Hive Publishing Co., 1973.
Gilbreth, Frank, and Lillian Gilbreth. *Applied Motion Study*. New York: Sturgis and Walton Co., 1917. London: George Routledge and Sons, 1919. New York: The Macmillan Co., 1920. Easton, Pennsylvania: Hive Publishing Co., 1973.
Gilbreth, Lillian. *Motion Study for the Handicapped*. New York: The Macmillan Co., 1920. Easton, Pennsylvania: Hive Publishing Co., 1973.

Gilligan, Carol (1936–)
PSYCHOLOGY OF WOMEN

Born in New York City, Gilligan received an A.B. in English literature from Swarthmore College, Pennsylvania (1958); an M.A. in clinical psychology at Radcliffe College, Cambridge Massachusetts (1961); and a Ph.D. in social psychology from Harvard University, Cambridge, Massachusetts (1964). In 1997 she became Harvard's first professor of gender studies. From 1992 to 1993 she was Pitt Professor of American History and Institutions, and 1993 to 1994 was visiting professorial fellow, University of Cambridge, England. From 1998 to 1999 she was Visiting Meyer Professor; 1999 to 2001, visiting professor, then from 2002, university professor at New York University.

She is a visiting professor, University of Cambridge, England (affiliated with the Centre for Gender Studies and with Jesus College). She received a senior research scholarship award from the Spencer Foundation, a Grawemeyer Award for her contributions to education, a Heinz Award for her contributions to understanding the human condition and was named by *Time* magazine as one of the 25 most influential Americans.

Major Contributions

In 1970 Gilligan became a research assistant to Lawrence Kohlberg (see entry). Her rise to fame came with the publication of *In a Different Voice: Psychological Theory and Women's Development* in which she criticized Laurence Kohlberg's research on the moral development of children. Gilligan's criticisms were that Kohlberg only studied privileged, white men and boys and this caused a biased opinion against women. Secondly, in his stage theory of moral development, the male view of individual rights and rules was considered a higher stage than women's point of view of development in terms of its caring effect on human relationships. Kohlberg saw reason to revise his scoring methods as a result of Gilligan's critique, after which boys and girls scored evenly.

Gilligan helped to form a new psychology for women by listening to them and rethinking the meaning of self and selfishness. Her work formed the basis for what has become known as the "ethics of care," a theory of ethics that contrasts so-called ethics of justice to ethics of care. The justice view of morality focuses on doing the right thing no matter who or what suffers. The care view says that we should cultivate our natural capacity to care for others and ourselves and put the interests of those who are close to us above the interests of complete strangers.

Major Literature

Gilligan, Carol. *In a Different Voice: Psychological Theory and Women's Development.* Cambridge, Massachusetts: Harvard University Press, 1982.

___ (Ed.). *Women, Girls and Psychotherapy: Reframing Resistance.* San Francisco, California: Harrington Park Press, 1992.

Brown, Lyn Mikel, and Carol Gilligan. *Meeting at the Crossroads: Women's Psychology and Girls' Development.* Cambridge, Massachusetts: Harvard University Press, 1992.

Gilligan, Carol. *Between Voice and Silence: Women and Girls, Race and Relationship.* Cambridge, Massachusetts: Harvard University Press, 1995.

___. *The Birth of Pleasure: A New Map of Love.* New York: Random House Inc., Chatto and Windus, 2002.

Glasser, William (1925–)
REALITY THERAPY

Born and raised in Cleveland, Ohio, William Glasser gained B.S. and M.A. degrees in clinical psychology from Case Western Reserve University in Cleveland and his M.D. from the University of California, Los Angeles. Between 1954 and 1957 he trained in psychiatry at the Veterans Administration Hospital in West Los Angeles and at the University of California, Los Angeles. In 1965 he created reality therapy, which is now taught worldwide. He founded the Institute for Reality Therapy (1967); it was renamed the William Glasser Institute in 1996.

Major Contributions

Although trained in Freudian psychoanalysis, Glasser rejected it in favor of his own idea of reality therapy. Glasser does not believe in the concept of mental illness unless there is something organically wrong with the brain. Reality therapy is based on the idea that individuals are responsible for what they do. Responsible behavior is defined as that which satisfies one's needs while, at the same time, not keeping others from satisfying theirs. Reality therapy focuses on the present and upon getting people to understand that all choices are made in order to meet needs. When needs are not met, people suffer, and often they cause others to suffer also.

Glasser emphasizes reality as the basis for responsible behavior. He posits that people have failed to learn the behaviors necessary for them to meet their psychological needs. The reality therapist educates people to become more responsible and realistic and hence more successful at attaining their goals.

Glasser has more recently developed "choice theory," the principles of which are:

- The only person whose behavior we can control is our own.
- All we can give another person is information.
- All long-lasting psychological problems are relationship problems.
- The problem relationship is always part of our present life.
- What happened in the past has everything to do with what we are today, but we can only satisfy our basic needs right now and plan to continue satisfying them in the future.
- We can only satisfy our needs by satisfying the pictures in our "quality world."
- All we do is behave; all behaviors are "total behaviors" and are made up of four components — acting, thinking, feeling and physiology.
- All total behaviors are chosen, but we only have direct control over the acting and thinking components.
- We can only control our feeling and physiology indirectly through how we choose to act and think.
- All total behavior is designated by verbs and named by the part that is the most recognizable.

Major Literature

Glasser, William. *The Identity Society.* New York: Harper Collins Publishers, Inc., 1972.

___. *Control Theory: A New Explanation of How We Control Our Lives.* New York: HarperCollins Publishers, Inc., 1986.

___. *Choice Theory: A New Psychology of Personal Freedom.* New York: HarperCollins Publishers, Inc., 1998.

___. *Reality Therapy in Action.* New York: HarperCollins Publishers, Inc., 2001.

___. *Warning: Psychiatry can be Hazardous to Your Mental Health.* New York: HarperCollins Publishers, Inc., 2003.

Goddard, Henry Herbert
(1866–1957)

EUGENICS

Henry Herbert Goddard gained a B.A. (1887) and M.A. in mathematics from Haverford College (1889) in Pennsylvania and a Ph.D. in psychology from Clark University, Worcester, Massachusetts (1899). From 1887 to 1888 he was football coach and instructor of Latin, history, and botany at the University of Southern California, Los Angeles, then teacher, Damascus Academy, Damascus, Ohio (1889–1891); teacher and principal, Oak Grove Seminary, Vassalboro, Maine (1891–1896); professor of psychology and pedagogy, State Normal School, West Chester, Pennsylvania (1899–1906); and director of research, Training School for Feeble-minded Girls and Boys, Vineland, New Jersey (1906–1918).

In 1910 and 1912 he was invited to Ellis Island to assist in identifying mental defectives. He was a member of the Army Alpha and Beta Testing Team under Robert Yerkes (see entry) (1917–1919). He served at the Ohio State Bureau of Juvenile Research (1918–1938) and was professor of abnormal and clinical psychology, Ohio State University (1922–1938).

Major Contributions

- 1908, translated the Binet-Simon intelligence scale into English.
- 1908–1915, distributed 22,000 copies of the translated Binet scale and 88,000 answer blanks across the United States.
- 1910, established the first laboratory for the psychological study of mentally retarded persons.
- 1911, helped to draft the first American law mandating special education, and stressed the need for public school reform, suggesting that normal children could benefit from the instructional techniques originally developed for use with retarded students.

An advocate of eugenics, Goddard believed that "feeble-mindedness" resulted from a single recessive gene. In addition to their learning difficulties, Goddard characterized "morons" (as he called feeble-minded people) as lacking self-control, thus making them susceptible to sexual immorality and vulnerable to other individuals who might exploit them for use in criminal activity. He hesitated to promote compulsory sterilization; instead he suggested that colonies should be set up where the feeble-minded could be segregated.

His book *The Kallikak Family: A Study in the Heredity of Feeblemindedness* was one of the many best-selling books (which has been challenged as mainly fiction) that led to the enactment of sterilization laws, in which he attempted to demonstrate that mental retardation and anti-social behavior were genetically determined. The eugenicist movement won substantial recognition in early 20th century America; by 1941, 33 U.S. states had endorsed sterilization policies and some 60,000 individuals were involuntarily sterilized. The movement swept much of the globe, including Nazi Germany. Later in his career, Henry Goddard withdrew his previous beliefs on the hereditary nature of feeblemindedness and questioned the need for eugenic solutions to the problem of mental deficiency.

Major Literature

Goddard, Henry Herbert. *The Kallikak Family: A Study in the Heredity of Feeble-Mindedness.* New York: Macmillan, 1912.
___. *Feeble-Mindedness: Its Causes and Consequences.* New York: Macmillan, 1914.
___. "Mental Tests and the Immigrant." *Journal of Delinquency* 2 (1917): 243–277.
___. "Who is a Moron?" *Scientific Monthly* 24 (1927): 41–46.
___. "In Defense of the Kallikak Study." *Science,* 95 (1942): 574–576.

Golden, Charles Joshua (1949–)

NEUROPSYCHOLOGY

Born in Los Angeles, California, Charles Joshua Golden gained a B.A. in psychology from Pomona College, Claremont, California (1971), and an M.A. (1973) and Ph.D. in clinical psychology (1975) from the University of Hawaii, Honolulu. He was assistant professor of psychology, University of South Dakota, Vermillion (1975); assistant professor and full professor of medical psychology at the University of Nebraska, Lincoln (1978–1987); professor of neuropsychology, Drexel University, Philadelphia (1987–1994); and professor of psychology, Nova Southeastern University, Fort Lauderdale, Florida (since 1994).

Since 1995 he has been on the board of directors, American Board of Assessment Psychology (vice-president). In 2002 was president, Section 9 (Assessment Psychology), Division 12, American Psychological Association (APA) and in 2003 he received the APA's Distinguished Neuropsychologist Lifetime Award. He was editor, *International Journal of Clinical Neuropsychology* (1980–1993), and has been consulting editor of *Psychological Assessment* since 1991.

Major Contributions

Golden's involvement in psychological assessment and neuropsychology created a desire to develop a test that would be both statistically accurate and useful in assessing the neurological damage in patients. The result was the Luria-Nebraska Neuropsychological Battery (LNNB), which incorporated Alexander R. Luria's (see entry) techniques into American clinical neuropsychology.

The LNNB generates fourteen scores: motor, rhythm, tactile, visual, receptive speech, expressive speech, writing, reading, arithmetic, memory, intellectual processes, indicators of specific diseases, left hemisphere, and right hemisphere. Unlike other tests, the LNNB was designed to test variations of a skill, not just a specific skill. The battery is used by clinicians as a screening tool to determine whether a significant brain injury is present or to learn more about known brain injuries. The LNNB may be used to determine which intellectual or cognitive tasks a patient may or may not be able to complete.

The battery can also be used to arrive at underlying causes of a patient's behavior; specifically, information regarding the location and nature of the brain injury or dysfunction causing a patient's problems is collected. The LNNB is also used to help distinguish between brain damage and functional mental disorders such as schizophrenia. In addition to its clinical use, the battery is sometimes used for legal purposes; the presence or severity of a brain injury may be given as evidence in court.

Major Literature

Golden, Charles Joshua. *Clinical Interpretation of Objective Psychological Tests*. New York: Grune and Stratton, 1979.
___, and S. Anderson. *Learning Disabilities and Brain Dysfunction*. Springfield, Illinois: Charles C. Thomas, 1979.
Golden, Charles Joshua. *Diagnosis and Rehabilitation in Clinical Neuropsychology*. 2nd ed. Springfield, Illinois: Charles C. Thomas, 1981.
___. *The Luria-Nebraska Children's Battery*. Los Angeles: Western Psychological Services, 1987.
___. *Screening Battery for the Luria-Nebraska Adult and Children's Battery*. Los Angeles: Western Psychological Services, 1987.
___. *Clinical Interpretation of Objective Psychological Tests*. Boston: Taylor and Francis, 1991 (2nd revised ed.).
___, W.L. Warren, and P. Espe-Pfeiffer. *LNNB Handbook: 20th Anniversary*. Los Angeles: Western Psychological Services, 2000.
Golden, C.J., and S. Freshwater. "Luria-Nebraska Neuropsychological Battery." In W. Dorfman and M. Hersen (Eds.), *Understanding Psychological Assessment*. New York: Kluwer, 2001.

Goodenough, Florence Laura (1886–1959)
INTELLIGENCE TESTING

Born in Honesdale, Pennsylvania, Florence Laura Goodenough gained a bachelor of pedagogy (B.Pd.) from Millersville, Pennsylvania Normal School (1908), and was then a teacher until 1920, when she gained a B.S (1920) and an M.A. (1921) from Columbia University, New York, under Leta Hollingworth (see entry). From 1920 to 1921 she was director of research for the Rutherford and Perth Amboy, New Jersey, public schools, the equivalent of today's school psychologist.

She gained a Ph.D. under Lewis Terman (see entry) from Stanford University, California (1924), and from 1924 to 1925, she worked at the Minneapolis Child Guidance Clinic, St. Paul University of Minnesota, Minneapolis. She was professor, Institute of Child Welfare, University of Minnesota, Minneapolis (1925–1947), professor emeritus (1947–1959), and president of the Society for Research in Child Development (1946–1947).

Major Contributions

Goodenough spent the main portion of her intellectual life developing tools for assessing intelligence in young children. Goodenough was one of the first individuals to question the use of the intelligence quotient (IQ). She contended that mental age may not have the same meaning for all children and that a better way of reporting results was in the form of percentages. She claimed that percentages, in addition to being more easily understood by lay people, were more useful because they would allow comparison among children who were the same chronological age. She worked on developing the Stanford-Binet IQ test for children, under Terman's direction, with particular interest in gifted children.

In 1926, she introduced her "draw-a-man test" of intelligence, intended for children aged two to thirteen. It took about ten minutes to administer (significantly less time than other nonverbal tests of the time), it was highly reliable and it correlated well with standard IQ tests of the time. It was listed as the third most frequently used test by clinical psychologists, and remained popular with them.

Revised in the late 1940s with the assistance of Dale Harris, it is now known as the "Goodenough-Harris drawing test." The revised test featured a new standardization, a drawing quality score, and the draw-a-woman test. Another revised edition was published in 1964 by the Psychological Corporation, Washington, D.C., aimed at children from 5 to 17 years of age. Goodenough also revised the Stanford-Binet test to include smaller children. The result was the Minnesota Preschool Scale. A degenerative illness caused her premature retirement in 1947 and eventually made her blind.

Major Literature

Goodenough, Florence Laura. *Anger in Young Children.* Westport, Connecticut: Greenwood Press, 1931.
___. *Measurement of Intelligence by Drawings.* 1975. Manchester, New Hampshire: Ayer Co. Publishers, 1926.
___, and Katherine M. Maurer. *Mental Growth of Children from Two to Fourteen Years: A Study of Predictive Value of The Minnesota Preschool Scales.* University of Minnesota, the Institute of Child Welfare Monograph Series No. XX. Minneapolis: The University of Minnesota Press, 1942.
Goodenough, Florence Laura. *Mental Testing: Its History, Principles and Applications.* New York: Rinehart, 1950.
___, and Leona Elizabeth Tyler. *Developmental Psychology: An Introduction to the Study of Human Behavior.* New York: Irvington Publishers, 1959.

Goodnow, Jacqueline Jarrett (1924–)

INFLUENCE OF CULTURE ON THINKING

Born in Toowoomba, Queensland, Australia, Jacqueline Jarrett Goodnow gained a B.A. with honors in psychology (1944) from the University of Sydney, Australia, where she was demonstrator in teaching, fellow and lecturer (1944–1948). She gained a Ph.D. from Radcliffe College (Harvard), Cambridge, Massachusetts (1951); was research psychologist for the United States Army in Munich, Germany (1951–1953); was lecturer and research associate, Harvard (1953–1955); research psychologist, Walter Reed Army Institute, Silver Springs, Maryland (1956–1959); and consultant at the Department of Education, University of Hong Kong (1960–1961).

She was also assistant professor, associate professor and professor, George Washington University, Washington, D.C. (1962–1972). At Macquarie University in New South Wales, Australia, she was senior lecturer and associate professor in the School of Education (1973–1975); professor of psychology, School of Behavioral Sciences (1975–1990); and emeritus professor and professional research fellow since 1990.

Goodnow's awards include an honorary D.Sc. from Macquarie University (1976); fellow, Center for Advanced Studies in Behavioral Sciences, Stanford University, California (1984–1985); G. Stanley Hall Award for Distinguished Contributions to Developmental Psychology, American Psychological Association (1989); Companion of the Order of Australia (1992); Award for Distinguished Scientific Contributions to Child Development, Society for Research in Child Development (1997); Inaugural Distinguished Scientific Contribution Award, Australian Psychological Society (1998); and Award for Distinguished Scientific Contributions to Developmental Psychology, Society Research in Child Development (1999).

Major Contributions

Goodnow's interests lie in the meeting place of developmental, social cognition (perceptions of the social rather than the physical world) and social psychology. She has concentrated her work on family, community, culture, development over the whole span of life, family norms and the practices related to the distribution of work and wealth. Her work has extended into the outcomes of beliefs about parenting and how social values are transmitted between generations.

During the 1970s she included research into the nature of children's drawings, then moved into studying how children and adults deal with everyday life. This included analyzing child development and the issue of discipline. One of her studies was to examine how children are assigned and how they perform their allocated household chores. This focus on everyday events helped to reveal how goals relate to problem solving, and how children are introduced to the rules and norms of society such as fairness and justice. She extended her work into lifelong learning and some of the issues facing women.

Major Literature

Goodnow, Jacqueline. *Children's Drawing* (Developing Child Series). London: Fontana Press, 1983.
___. *Home and School: Child's Eye View.* Allen and Unwin with A. Burns. London: George Allen and Unwin, 1985.

___, and Jennifer M. Bowes. *Men, Women and Household Work.* Melbourne, Victoria: Oxford University Press, Australia and New Zealand, 1993.

Goodnow, Jacqueline, et al. *Cultural Practices as Contexts for Development: New Directions for Child and Adolescent Development.* New Jersey: John Wiley and Sons Inc., Jossey Bass Wiley, 1996.

Goodwin, Frederick K. (1936–)
MANIC DEPRESSIVE ILLNESS

Born in Cincinnati, Ohio, Frederick K. Goodwin gained a B.S. from Georgetown University in Washington, D.C. (1958). At St. Louis University, St. Louis, Missouri, he held a graduate fellowship (1959–1959) and earned an M.D. (1963). His psychiatric residency was at the University of North Carolina, Chapel Hill. From 1969 to 1971 he was a fellow, Washington School of Psychiatry in Washington, D.C.

He was then adjunct professor, George Washington University School of Medicine, Department of Psychiatry (1972–1982); director, Intramural Research Program at the National Institute of Mental Health (1982–1988); scientific director, National Depression Awareness, Recognition, and Treatment Program (1985); and administrator, Alcohol, Drug Abuse, and Mental Health Administration (1988–1992). Since 1994 he has been research professor of psychiatry at George Washington University Medical Center. He is a member of the Institute of Medicine's National Academy of Sciences and the American College of Neuropsychopharmacology in Nashville, Tennessee.

He serves on the editorial boards of *Archives of General Psychiatry* and *The Journal of Clinical Psychopharmacology*, and is a founder of *Psychiatry Research.* Since 1998, Goodwin has been the host of the award-winning *The Infinite Mind* weekly radio program.

Major Contributions

Goodwin is a recipient of many major awards in his field, and many honors both scientific and civic. The author of over 400 publications, Goodwin collaborated with Kay Jamison, Ph.D., in writing *Manic-Depressive Illness*, the first psychiatric text to win the Best Medical Book Award from the Association of American Publishers. The book (which was ten years in the writing) comprehensively surveys the massive body of evidence and assesses its meaning for both clinician and scientist. It also vividly portrays the experience of manic-depressive illness (bi-polar disorders) from the perspective of patients, their doctors, and researchers, and recounts the torments of some of the great poets and composers whose art was almost certainly enriched, energized, and deepened by the extremes of manic-depressive illness. Special emphasis is given to fostering compliance with medication regimens and treating bi-polar patients who abuse drugs and alcohol or who pose a risk of suicide. Although aimed at doctors, it is a book for all professionals who work in the field of depression.

Major Literature

Goodwin, Frederick K., and Kay Redfield Jamison. *Manic-Depressive Illness.* New York: Oxford University Press Inc., 1990.

Gottfredson, Linda Susanne (1947–)
EDUCATIONAL PSYCHOLOGY

Linda Susanne Howarth was born in San Francisco; she married Gary Don Gottfredson in 1967, divorced in 1979, and married Robert Arthur Gordon (1980). She was research assistant, Alameda County Human Relations Commission in Oakland, California (1968–1969). She gained a B.A. in psychology from the University of California at Berkeley, where she was a member of Phi Beta Kappa (1969). From 1969 to 1972 she was a Peace Corps volunteer in family planning and health statistics, Penang State Health Office, Georgetown, Malaysia. She gained a Ph.D. in sociology from Johns Hopkins University, Baltimore, Maryland (1977) and served in various academic and research capacities there from 1972 to 1985.

From 1985 to 1986 she was with the Research Department of Counseling and Personnel Services, College of Education, University of Maryland, College Park. At the College of Education, University of Delaware, Newark, she was associate professor, Department of Educational Studies (1987–1990), and is currently professor, Department of Educational Studies; affiliated faculty, honors program, University of Delaware, and co-director of the Delaware–Johns Hopkins Project for the Study of Intelligence and Society from 2000.

In 1994 she was fellow, Society for Industrial and Organizational Psychology; fellow, American Psychological Association; 1995, Johns Hopkins University Society of Scholars; 1998, fellow, Association for Psychological Science; 1999–2000,

Mensa Research Foundation Award for Excellence in Research; 2005, Faculty Senate Commendation for Extraordinary Leadership and Service, University of Delaware; 2005, Mensa Award for Excellence in Research.

Gottfredson currently sits on the boards of Intelligence, Learning and Individual Differences, and Society, the International Society for the Study of Individual Differences (ISSID), and the International Society for Intelligence Research (ISIR).

Major Contributions

Gottfredson's work has been influential in shaping U.S. public and private policies regarding affirmative action (positive discrimination), hiring quotas, and "race-norming" (the practice of giving every applicant for employment the same aptitude skills test, but then grading the test differently depending on the applicant's race). At the Johns Hopkins Center for Social Organization of Schools (1986) she investigated issues of occupational segregation and personality types based on skill sets and intellectual capacity.

Her research and views have stirred considerable controversy, especially her testimony on public affirmative action policy and her defense of the bell curve, and especially "Mainstream Science on Intelligence," an editorial written by her, signed by 52 colleagues, and published in the *Wall Street Journal* (1997). Since that time she has written a number of articles on race and intelligence, especially as it applies to occupational qualification.

Major Literature

Gottfredson, Linda Susanne. "The Egalitarian Fiction." In Nathaniel J. Pallone and James J. Hennessy (Eds.), *Fraud and Fallible Judgment: Varieties of Deception in the Social and Behavioral Sciences*, 95–106. New Jersey: Transaction Publishers, 1995.

___. "Gottfredson's Theory of Circumscription and Compromise." *Career Choice and Development*. Duane Brown and Linda Brooks (Eds.) (3rd ed.). New Jersey: John Wiley and Sons, Inc., Jossey Bass Wiley, 1996.

___. "Confronting the New Particularism in Academe." *Journal of Management Inquiry* 2 (1996): 319–325.

___. "Why g Matters: The Complexity of Everyday Life." *Intelligence* 24 (1997): 79–132.

Green, André (1927–)
PSYCHOANALYTIC CRITICISM

Born in Cairo, Green studied medicine at the Paris Medical School and psychiatry at the Sainte-Anne Hospital, Paris (1953). In 1965, having worked in several different hospitals and after having finished his training as a psychoanalyst, he became a member of Paris Psychoanalytic Society, of which he was the president from 1986 to 1989. From 1975 to 1977 he was a vice president of the International Psychoanalytical Association and from 1979 to 1980 a professor at University College, London.

Major Contributions

Green is one of the most influential psychoanalysts in France, but also in America and internationally. A major contributor to psychoanalysis as a theorist and a clinician, he has always linked his theory with practice. Green acknowledges the influence of Jacques Lacan, Wilfred Bion, Donald Winnicott, and most importantly, Sigmund Freud (see entries), but has developed his own original ideas.

His independence of thought was demonstrated early on when he criticized Lacan for the damage done to psychoanalytic theory by his view of the unconscious. Green was of the opinion that psychoanalysis was being too much influenced by American ego psychology, with its emphasis on adaptation. Green favored a return to Freud's theory of drives, negation, sexuality, and object relationships.

For Green, psychoanalysis is based on the negative and is about restoring that which was lost and latent. His paper *The Dead Mother* provides the most suggestive metaphor of where the mother is physically present but psychically dead. Green's idea puts an entirely different emphasis on Winnicott's "absent mother;" the non-presence (emotionally) of the mother becomes an object which tenaciously occupies a central position in the child's psyche. (Although "child" is referred to, the analyst will work with the child part of the adult to attempt to recover that which was lost.)

Major Literature

Green, André. *On Private Madness*. Classics of Psychoanalysis. Eltham, Victoria, Australia: Rebus Press Limited, 1996.

___. *The Fabric of Affect in the Psychoanalytic Discourse*. (Alan Sheridan, translator.) London, England: Taylor and Francis Books Ltd., Brunner-Routledge, 1999.

___. *The Work of the Negative*. London, England: Free Association Books Ltd., 1999.

___. *André Green at the Squiggle Foundation*. Winnicott Studies Monographs. London, England: Karnac Books, 2000.

___. *Time in Psychoanalysis: Some Contradictory Aspects.* (Andrew Weller, translator.) London, England: Free Association Books Ltd., 2002.

___. *Key Ideas for a Contemporary Psychoanalysis: Misrecognition and Recognition of the Unconscious.* New Library of Psychoanalysis. (Andrew Weller, translator.) London, England: Taylor and Francis Books Ltd., Brunner-Routledge, 2005.

___, and Gregorio Kohon. *Love and its Vicissitudes.* London, England: Taylor and Francis Books Ltd., 2005.

Green, André. *Play and Reflection in Donald Winnicott's Writing.* Winnicott Clinic Lecture Monograph Series. London, England: Karnac Books, 2005.

___. *Psychoanalysis: A Paradigm for Clinical Thinking.* London, England: Free Association Books Ltd., 2005.

Related Literature

Kohon, Gregorio (Ed.). *The Dead Mother: The Work of André Green.* New Library of Psychoanalysis. London, England: Taylor and Francis Books Ltd., Brunner-Routledge, 1999.

Gregory, Richard Langton (1923–)

PERCEPTION

Born in London, England, Richard Langton Gregory served in the Royal Air Force (1941–1947), read philosophy and experimental psychology at Downing College, Cambridge University (1947–1950), and earned an M.A. from Canterbury University (1950). From 1950 to 1953, he was at the Medical Research Council Applied Psychology Unit, Cambridge. He spent one year at the Royal Navy Physiological Laboratory, Whale Island, Portsmouth, designing and running experiments on escaping from submarines following the 1951 disaster when the British submarine *Affray* sunk with 75 officers and men aboard.

From 1953 to 1967 he was university demonstrator and then lecturer in the Department of Experimental Psychology, Cambridge University, where he lectured on perception, scientific method and cybernetics. He was visiting professor at the University of California, Los Angeles (UCLA) (1963), the Massachusetts Institute of Technology, Cambridge (MIT) (1964) and University of New York graduate school (1966).

He co-founded the Department of Machine Intelligence and Perception, University of Edinburgh (1967–1970); was professor of bionics and department chairman (1968–1970); professor of neuropsychology and director of the Brain and Perception Laboratory at the Medical School, University of Bristol (1970–1988). He is currently emeritus professor of neuropsychology at the University of Bristol. Gregory has received nine honorary degrees; Bristol University in England awarded him a D.Sc. (1983). In 1989, he was made a Commander of the British Empire.

Major Contributions

At Cambridge, Gregory designed and directed the Special Senses Laboratory. This was used to investigate perceptual problems to be anticipated for astronauts, such as judgment of speed and distance for moon landing and docking for the U.S. Air Force. He devised the "Inappropriate Constancy Scaling" theory of distortion illusions, which stressed the brain's "software" rather than its physiology for explaining many perceptual phenomena. This led to interest in artificial intelligence for investigating brain strategies: the "software" might be transferred to intelligent machines.

At Edinburgh he built one of the first intelligent robots, "Freddie." At Bristol he founded and is the scientific director of the Bristol Exploratory Science and Technology Centre, a hands-on center, the first of its kind in the U.K. In 1989 he was appointed Osher Visiting Fellow of the Exploratorium, a similar scientific education center in San Francisco, California.

Gregory's view of perception is a development of Hermann von Helmholtz's view, that perception is influenced by unconscious processes. Gregory's interests lie in the anomalies of perception such as illusions, which he explains as being caused by a three-dimensional shape being projected in two dimensions. Another area is that of motion perception, which involves both the eyes and the eye-head movement systems.

Major Literature

Gregory, Richard Langton. *Odd Perceptions.* London, England: Taylor and Francis Books Ltd., Routledge, 1988.

___. *Mind in Science: History of Explanations in Psychology and Physics.* London, England: Penguin Books Ltd., 1993.

___. *Even Odder Perceptions.* London, England: Taylor and Francis Books Ltd., Routledge, 1994.

___. *Eye and Brain: The Psychology of Seeing.* Oxford, England: Oxford University Press, 1997.

___ (Ed.). *The Oxford Companion to the Mind.* Oxford, England: Oxford University Press, 2004.

Grinder, John (1940–)

NEURO LINGUISTIC PROGRAMMING

John Grinder graduated from the University of San Francisco with a degree in psychology in the early 1960s and saw military service as a Green Beret in Europe during the Cold War. Returning to college in the late 1960s, he studied linguistics and received his Ph.D. from the University of California at San Diego. He studied cognitive science with George Miller at Rockefeller University, and was appointed professor of linguistics at Santa Cruz, where he met Richard Bandler (see entry), a student of psychology. Both were students of Gregory Bateson (see entry)

Major Contributions

At Santa Cruz, Grinder started working alongside Bandler, who was running therapy groups. There Grinder became fascinated by the language used by effective therapists. Together, Bandler and Grinder drew up a theory of transformational grammar, of the language patterns used by Gestalt therapy founder Fritz Perls, family therapist Virginia Satir and hypnotherapist Milton Erickson (see entries). Grinder drew on Noam Chomsky's (see entry) theories of transformational grammar, and of general semantics by Count Alfred Korzybski (1879–1950). General semantics is a system of linguistics that attempts to increase people's capacity to transmit ideas from generation to generation through the study and refinement of ways of using and reacting to language.

Neuro-linguistic programming (NLP) describes the fundamental dynamics between mind (neuro) and language (linguistic) and how their interplay affects our body and behavior (programming). NLP is also about self-discovery — exploring identity and purpose. It also takes into consideration the "spiritual" part of human experience that reaches to family, community and beyond. NLP is not only about competence and excellence, it is about wisdom and vision. NLP argues that we should never confuse our perception of reality with reality itself. Our perception is limited by our internal "neuro-linguistic" maps. Thus we are limited in what we do by our perception of reality.

The way we interact is influenced by our desire and need for balance, or homeostasis, and how we interact is influenced by others around us. We create a map of the world, but that map is never static nor is it wholly objective or perfect. The goal is to create the richest map possible that represents ourselves and the world we live in. The people who are most effective are the ones who have a map of the world that allows them to perceive the greatest number of available choices and perspectives. NLP is a way of enriching the choices that

you have and perceive as available in the world around you. Excellence comes from having many choices. Wisdom comes from having multiple perspectives.

Major Literature

Grinder, John. *Guide to Transformational Grammar.* Orlando, Florida: Holt, Rinehart and Winston, 1973.
___. *Framework for Excellence.* Scots Valley, California: Grinder DeLozier Associates, 1990.
___, and Michael McMaster. *Precision.* Scots Valley, California: Grinder and Associates, 1993.
Grinder, John, and Judith DeLozier. *Turtles All the Way Down.* Portland, Oregon: Metamorphous Press, 1995.

Grof, Stanislav (1931–)
TRANSPERSONAL PSYCHOLOGY

Born in Prague, Czechoslovakia, Stanislav Grof received his M.D. from Charles University, Prague (1957), and his Ph.D. in medicine at the Czechoslovakian Academy of Sciences (1965), having also trained as a Freudian psychoanalyst. From 1967 to 1969 he was research scientist and professor of psychiatry at Johns Hopkins University School of Medicine, Baltimore, Maryland. He was then chief of psychiatric research at the Maryland Psychiatric Research Center and assistant professor of psychiatry at the Henry Phipps Clinic of Johns Hopkins University.

From 1973 to 1987 he was scholar-in-residence at the Esalen Institute in Big Sur, California. He was president of the International Transpersonal Association (ITA), founded in 1977 in Santa Rosa, California. He is currently professor of psychology at the Department of Philosophy, Cosmology, and Consciousness at the California Institute of Integral Studies, San Francisco (CIIS) and at the Pacifica Graduate School in Santa Barbara.

Major Contributions

For the past 35 years Grof has conducted research on the use of psychedelic drugs in psychotherapy, the therapeutic aspects of non-ordinary states of consciousness for purposes of healing, growth, and insight, alternative approaches to psychoses, spiritual crises and transpersonal crises, and the implications for psychiatric theory and the emerging scientific models of recent developments in quantum physics, information and systems theory, biology, brain research, and consciousness studies.

Grof went on to discover that many of the altered states of mind could be explored without drugs by using certain breathing techniques in a supportive environment. He continues this work today under the title "holotropic breathwork." He is one of the founders of the field of transpersonal psychology. Sometimes referred to as the "fourth force," transpersonal psychology is the successor to humanistic psychology.

The term "transpersonal" means "beyond the personal." A common assumption in transpersonal psychology is that transpersonal experiences involve a higher mode of consciousness in which the ego self is transcended. What matters is the experience of being at one with humanity. Transpersonal experiences are distinguished from "religious" or "spiritual" experiences in that they are not required to fit into some prearranged pattern of dogma. Transpersonal work is not about learning something new but unlearning distorted knowledge already acquired. Over time, his theory developed into an in-depth cartography of the deep human psyche.

Major Literature

Grof, Christina, and Stanislav Grof. *Stormy Search for the Self: A Guide to Personal Growth Through Transformational Crisis.* Los Angeles, California: J.P. Tarcher, 1992.

Grof, Stanislav, and Hal Zina Bennett. *The Holotropic Mind: Three Levels of Human Consciousness and How They Shape Our Lives.* New York: HarperCollins Publishers, Inc., 1993.

Grof, Stanislav. *The Cosmic Game: Explorations of the Frontiers of Human Consciousness.* Albany, New York: State University of New York Press, 1998.

___. *Psychology of the Future: Lessons from Modern Consciousness Research.* Albany, New York: State University of New York Press, 2000.

___. *When the Impossible Happens.* Louisville, Colorado: Sounds True Publishing, 2006.

Gudden, Johann Bernhard Aloys Von (1824–1886)

NEUROPSYCHIATRY

Born in Kleve, in Lower Rhineland near the Dutch frontier, Johann Bernhard Aloys Von Gudden received his doctorate in 1848 at Halle for the study of eye movement. He passed the state medical examination with distinction in Berlin, and also commenced his one-year of military service. In 1848 Gudden worked at the Siegburg Asylum, and from 1851 to 1855, at the asylum at Illenau in Baden, a hospital known even outside Germany for its outstanding organization.

In 1855 Gudden was appointed director of the newly founded Unterfränkische Landes-Irrenanstalt in Werneck, Bavaria. He transformed the former Episcopal palace into Germany's most modern asylum, an achievement that demonstrated his administrative skills. In 1869 Gudden became director of the recently constructed mental hospital Burghölzli, near Zürich, and in 1872 became professor of psychiatry at the University at Munich. He enlarged and reorganized the Oberbayerische Kreis-Irrenanstalt Haar hospital in Munich and a second hospital in Gabersee, Oberbayern. From 1870 Gudden was a co-editor of the *Archiv für Psychiatry und Nervenkrankheiten.*

He was knighted in 1875 and appointed physician to the mad king Ludwig II of Bavaria. In 1886 the king was diagnosed with what was probably paranoid schizophrenia, relieved of all official duties and taken by Gudden to Schlossberg, on Lake Starnberg, Bavaria, which was to serve as the king's residence. At 6:45 P.M. on June 13, 1886, the king and Gudden took a walk, and at 11 P.M. both the king and Gudden were found dead; the cause of death was never made public. A new musical on the life of Ludwig II was premiered in the Festspielhaus Neuschwanstein theatre in Füssen in March 2005.

Major Contributions

Gudden rejected physical force and the belief that "moral influence" and "educational strictness" were beneficial in treating mental patients. He advocated no restraint, and a liberal and humane approach to the treatment of the mentally ill. Going beyond even John Conolly (see entry) he granted his patients an unprecedented measure of personal freedom. He insisted that proper treatment required communal social life for the patients, constant contact between physicians and patients, and a well-trained staff with a strong sense of duty.

Gudden's research did not deal with clinical psychopathology, an area that was investigated by his student, Emil Kraepelin (see entry). Two other students were Franz Nissl and Auguste-Henri Forel (see entry). In 1876 von Gudden devised a microtome for sectioning the whole human brain and described important neuroanatomical centers; Forel relates that this enabled him (Forel) to make the first complete serial sections.

Through his research Gudden was the first to set forth many of the neuroanatomical facts generally accepted today concerning the paths, origins and termini of the nerves, as well as many concerning the nuclei of the cranial nerves. The accomplishments of Gudden's pupils paved the way for contemporary psychiatry, and his laboratory of neuroanatomy and brain physiology became the germ-cell of the Research Institute for Psychiatry in Munich, which was founded by his master pupil Kraepelin. Gudden conclusively verified through skillful clinical observations that scabies is a parasitic disease caused by mites.

Guilford, Joy Paul
(1897–1987)
PSYCHOPHYSICS

Born in Marquette, Nebraska, Joy Paul Guilford gained a B.A. from the University of Nebraska, Lincoln (1922) and a Ph.D. from Cornell University in Ithaca, New York (1926). From 1927 to 1928, he taught at University of Kansas, Lawrence, and from 1928 to 1940 at University Southern California. He was emeritus professor of psychology, University of Southern California, Los Angeles. Guilford was president, Psychometric Society (1939), and in 1941, director of Psychological Research, working in selection and ranking of aircrew trainees at the Army Air Base in Santa Ana, California. He gained an LL.D. at the University of Nebraska (1952) studying under Edward Titchener (see entry).

He was a member of the National Academy of Sciences (1954) and gained an Sc.D. at the University of Southern California, Los Angeles (1962). His awards include the Distinguished Scientific Award from the American Psychological Association (1964); Richardson Creativity Award (1966); Founder's Medal, Creative Educational Foundation (1970); Thorndike Award, American Psychological Association (1975); and Gold Medal Award, American Psychological Foundation (1982).

Major Contributions

Among Guilford's major contributions is his theory on "convergent and divergent production," which is one of the most basic principles of creative thinking. In a nutshell, convergent thinking is working toward a single solution to a problem; divergent thinking is coming up with numerous diverse solutions to a problem. The left hemisphere of the brain is related to convergent thinking, while the right hemisphere relates more to divergent thinking (see Gazzaniga, Michael).

Guilford specialized in psychometrics of human intelligence, and went on to develop the Guilford's Structure of Intellect (SI) theory, where intelligence is viewed as comprising:

1. *Operation*: cognition, memory, divergent production, convergent production, evaluation;
2. *Products*: units, classes, relations, systems, transformations, implications; and
3. *Contents*: visual, auditory, symbolic, semantic, behavioral.

Each of these dimensions is independent, so theoretically there are 150 different components of intelligence. Guilford was the first to use factor analysis to determine which tests appeared to measure the same or different abilities. Further,

1. Reasoning and problem-solving skills (convergent and divergent operations) can be subdivided into 30 distinct abilities (6 products × 5 contents).
2. Memory operations can be subdivided into 30 different skills (6 products × 5 contents).
3. Decision-making skills (evaluation operations) can be subdivided into 30 distinct abilities (6 products × 5 contents).
4. Language-related skills (cognitive operations) can be subdivided into 30 distinct abilities (6 products × 5 contents).

With Wayne S. Zimmerman, Guilford developed the Guilford-Zimmerman Temperament Survey, which provides a non-clinical description of an individual's personality characteristics for use in career planning, counseling, and research. It has the following symptom scales: G — general activity; R — restraint; A — ascendance; S — sociability; E — emotional stability; O — objectivity; F — friendliness; T — thoughtfulness; P — personal relations; and M — masculinity.

Major Literature

Guilford, Joy Paul. *Personality.* Psychology Series. Columbus, Ohio: McGraw-Hill Education, 1959.
___. *Nature of Human Intelligence.* Columbus, Ohio: McGraw-Hill Education, 1967.
___. *Analysis of Intelligence.* Columbus, Ohio: McGraw-Hill Education, 1971.
___, and Benjamin Fruchter (Eds.). *Fundamental Statistics in Psychology and Education.* Psychology Series. Columbus, Ohio: McGraw-Hill Education, 1978.

Gulliksen, Harold Oliver
(1903–1996)
EDUCATIONAL PSYCHOLOGY

Born in Washington, D.C., Harold Oliver Gulliksen earned his bachelor's degree in 1926 and his master's degree in 1927 at the University of Washington, Seattle, and after subsequent study at the University of Ohio, he completed his Ph.D. in psychology at the University of Chicago in 1931. He worked for two years at the Mooseheart Laboratory for Child Research before returning to the University of Chicago, where he served successively as a research assistant in psychology to L.L. Thurstone, examiner on the Board of Examinations, then assistant and associate professor of psychology.

During World War II, Gulliksen directed a research and development project for the Navy by the College Board at its offices in Princeton, New Jersey, where he was involved in the development of assessment procedures ranging from officer screening tests to performance tests for gun crews. President Harry Truman awarded him the Certificate of Merit in 1948. In 1945, Gulliksen was appointed research secretary of the College Board and professor of psychology at Princeton University.

When the Educational Testing Service (ETS) was founded in 1948, Gulliksen was named research advisor and director of the ETS Pyschometric Fellowship Program at Princeton. Gulliksen retired from Princeton University in 1972 and from ETS in 1974. He was a founding member of the Psychometric Society in 1935 and served on the initial editorial board of the society's journal *Pyschometrika*. He was managing editor of the journal from 1942 to 1949 and president of the Psychometric Society in 1944. He was also a fellow of the American Statistical Association and the American Psychological Association, and a member of the Institute of Mathematical Statistics.

Major Contributions

For over 60 years Gulliksen was an expert in psychometrics, particularly in the areas of test theory, psychological scaling, and mathematical models of learning, and was dedicated to the development of psychology as a quantitative rational science. The fields of Gulliksen's interests were in various aspects of mathematical psychology, broadly defined to include work of a theoretical character that uses mathematical methods, formal logic, or computer simulation. The Psychometric Society's journal is the *Journal of Mathematical Psychology*.

Gulliksen collaborated with two colleagues in developing a test to predict college grades. While working at Ohio he became more interested in mathematical learning theory and developed a tachistoscope (apparatus for perception and memory tests: an instrument for displaying visual images very briefly, used to test perception and memory).

Major Literature

Gulliksen, Harold Oliver. *Theory of Mental Tests*. New Jersey: John Wiley and Sons Ltd., 1950.

___. "Mathematical Solutions for Psychological Problems." *American Scientist* 47 (1959) 178–201.

___. *Psychological Scaling: Theory and Application*. New Jersey: John Wiley and Sons Ltd., 1960.

Frederiksen, Norman, Harold Gulliksen, and L.L. Thurstone. *Contributions to Mathematical Psychology*. New York: Holt, Rinehart and Winston, 1964.

Guthrie, Edwin Ray
(1886–1959)
THEORY OF LEARNING

Born in Lincoln, Nebraska, Edwin Ray Guthrie gained a B.A. with Phi Beta Kappa honors in mathematics (1907) and an M.A. in philosophy with a minor in mathematics and psychology (1910) from the University of Nebraska, Lincoln. At the University of Pennsylvania, Philadelphia, he was a Harrison Fellow in philosophy (1910) and gained a Ph.D. in symbolic logic (1912). He taught high school mathematics at Boys Central High School in Philadelphia (1912–1914). At University of Washington, Seattle he was: instructor, Department of Philosophy (1914); assistant professor in philosophy (1918); in the Department of Psychology (1919); assistant professor in psychology (1920); associate professor in psychology (1926); professor in psychology (1928); and dean of graduate studies (1943–1951); emeritus professor (1951). He retired from the University of Washington in 1956.

He served as a high-ranking civilian consultant to the War Department in Military Intelligence in Washington, D.C. (1941–1942) and served in the Office of War Information (1942–1943). Guthrie was president of the American Psychological Association and received an honorary LL.D. from the University of Nebraska (1945) and a Gold Medal for outstanding lifetime contributions from the American Psychological Foundation (1958).

Major Contributions

The Psychology Department at the University of Washington, Seattle, is in a building named Guthrie Hall. Guthrie made contributions in the philosophy of science, abnormal psychology, social psychology and educational psychology, and he played a significant part in the development of the contiguity theory of learning, a classical account of how learning takes place. Guthrie's law of contiguity states that a combination of stimuli that has accompanied a movement will on its recurrence tend to be followed by that movement; contiguity — closeness or contact — in time is the basis of associative learning.

Guthrie believed in one-trial learning, which states that a stimulus pattern gains its full associative strength on the occasion of its first pairing with a response. He did not believe that learning is dependent on reinforcement, which he defined as anything that alters the stimulus situation for the learner. Guthrie stated that forgetting is due to interference because the stimuli become associated with new responses. In his theory, Guthrie avoids any mention of drives, successive repetitions, rewards, or punishment. He refers to stimuli and movement in combination. Between 1936 and 1939, he collaborated on stereotyped behavior of cats in a puzzle box to illustrate the associative theory of learning.

Major Literature

Guthrie, Edwin Ray. "Conditions as a Principle of Learning." *Psychological Review* 37 (1930): 412–428.
___. *The Psychology of Human Conflict: The Clash of Motives*. New York: Harper and Brothers Publishers, 1973. Westport, Connecticut: Greenwood Press, 1938.
___. *Cats in a Puzzle Box*. New York: Rinehart and Co. Inc., 1946.
___, and F. Powers. *Educational Psychology*. New York: Ronald Press Co., 1950.
Guthrie, Edwin Ray. *The Psychology of Learning*. York: Harper and Brothers Publishers, 1952.

Haber, Ralph Norman (1932–)
EXPERIMENTAL PSYCHOLOGY

Born in Lansing, Michigan, Ralph Norman Haber earned a B.A. in philosophy with honors from the University of Michigan, Ann Arbor (1953) and an M.A. in psychology from Wesleyan University, Connecticut (1954). At Stanford University, California, he gained a Ph.D. in psychology (1957) and was a research associate at the Institute for Communication Research (1957–1958). From 1957 to 1958 he was instructor in psychology at San Francisco State College in California. He was also assistant professor at Yale University, New Haven, Connecticut, from 1958 to 1964.

At the University of Rochester, New York, he was associate professor of psychology, professor

of psychology, and chairman of the Department of Psychology (1964–1979). From 1970 to 1971 he was post-doctoral fellow in human factors, Applied Psychology Unit, Medical Research Council, Cambridge, England. Since 1979 he has been professor of psychology, research professor of psychology, and professor emeritus of psychology at the University of Chicago, Illinois.

Haber's honors and awards include the Society of the Sigma Xi, associate member (1954) and full member (1957); fellow, American Psychological Association, Division 3 (1970); Division 2 (1983); fellow, American Association for the Advance of Science (1971); Outstanding Achievement Award, Ann Arbor (1977); fellow, Institute of the Humanities, University of Chicago, Illinois (1984–1985); and fellow, American Psychological Society (1989).

Major Contributions

In 1987, with his wife, Lyn, Haber formed the company Human Factors Consultants in Swall Meadows, California. They provide government and business clients with human factors expertise in areas of product and equipment design and operation, development and evaluation of training programs, performance assessment, risk and accident analysis, and cost-benefit analysis of proposed changes in operations.

The company specializes in providing legal expertise, consultation and testimony on eyewitness identification, including issues of perception, memory, line-up procedures, and recovered memory. They also include the factors that affect the accuracy of fingerprint comparisons; language, including comprehension, verbal and nonverbal harassment, children's understanding, memory and testimony; and safety failures, including human factors analyses of product design, warning, and training, and of accidents. Haber is consulting editor for 15 scientific journals and three publishers, scientific reviewer for six governmental and three military agencies, and research consultant to two universities and four agencies of the government.

The main thrust of his work has been on visual perception, creativity in motivation and personality. His early studies with Naomi Weisstein showed that subjects who were repeatedly exposed to short durations of an image reported that they actually found the image becoming clearer. This led to many years' study of eidetic imagery. He and his wife have designed training programs for low-altitude flying for the Air Force and teaching train drivers how to drive. They have also designed programs for visually handicapped people, train dispatching and air traffic control.

Major Literature

Haber, Ralph Norman (Ed.). *Current Research in Motivation.* New York: Henry Holt and Company, Inc., 1966.

___. "Eidetic Images." *Scientific American* 220 (1969): 36–55.

___. *Information Processing Approaches to Visual Perception.* New York: Henry Holt and Company, Inc., 1970.

___. "Twenty Years of Haunting Eidetic Imagery: Where's the Ghost?" *Behavioral and Brain Science* 24 (1979): 583–629.

___, and Maurice Hershenson. *Psychology of Visual Perception.* New York: Henry Holt and Company, Inc., 1980.

Hackman, J. Richard (1940–)
INDUSTRIAL PSYCHOLOGY

Born in Joliet, Illinois, Richard J. Hackman earned an A.B. degree, with honors, in mathematics and minors in psychology and physics at MacMurray College, Jacksonville, Illinois (1962). At the University of Illinois, Urbana, Champaign, he gained an M.A. (1964) and a Ph.D. in social psychology with minors in sociology and psychological measurement (1966). From 1966 to 1999 he had professorships in psychology at Yale University, New Haven, Connecticut, the University of Michigan, Ann Arbor, and Harvard University in Cambridge, Massachusetts. Since 2005 he has been Edgar Pierce Professor of Social and Organizational Psychology at Harvard.

His honors and awards are: Distinguished Scientific Contribution Award, Division 14 of the American Psychological Association (1992); Distinguished Educator Award, Academy of Management (1996); Distinguished Scholar Award, Academy of Management (1997); and American Psychological Association Distinguished Scientist Lecturer (2005). Hackman is on the editorial board of several professional journals, and has consulted to a variety of organizations on issues having to do work design, leadership, and team effectiveness.

Major Contributions

Richard Hackman is an industrial and organizational psychologist with a focus on group effectiveness. His research has included studies of social influences on behavior in organizations, task and work design, the dynamics and performance of work teams, and the design and leadership of self-managing organizational units, motivation, job satisfaction and performance. He and G.R. Oldham developed the job characteristics model and the Hackman-Oldham Job Diagnostic Survey (JDS), which assesses the five core dimensions and has become a widely used instrument in industrial psychology.

Three critical psychological states influence motivation, satisfaction and performance of employees: experienced meaningfulness of work; experienced responsibility for the outcome of the work; and knowledge of the actual results. The three states are affected by five core dimensions: skill variety, task identity, task significance, autonomy and feedback.

His more recent research includes looking at how professional symphony and chamber orchestras are organized and how the players relate to one another. He researches how the U.S. intelligence community measures performance of its teams. He is developing educational materials to enhance leadership skills for various creative groups, either as performers or those that develop creative products.

Major Literature

Hackman, J. Richard, and G.R. Oldham. "Development of the Job Diagnostic Survey." *Journal of Applied Psychology* 60 (1975): 159–170.

Hackman, J. Richard. *Perspectives on Behavior in Organizations.* Columbus, Ohio: McGraw Hill Higher Education, 1977.

Hackman, J. Richard, and G.R. Oldham. *Work Redesign.* Upper Saddle River, New Jersey: Addison Wesley, 1980.

Hackman, J. Richard. *Groups That Work and Those That Don't: Creating Conditions for Effective Teamwork.* New Jersey: John Wiley and Sons, Inc., Jossey Bass Wiley, 1990.

___. "Group Influences on Individuals in Organizations." In Marvin D. Dunnette and Leaetta M. Hough (Eds.). *Handbook of Industrial and Organizational Psychology* Vol. 8, 2nd ed. San Francisco, California: Consulting Psychologists Press, 1992.

___. *Leading Teams: Setting the Stage for Great Performances.* Boston, Massachusetts: Harvard Business School Press, 2002.

Hall, Granville Stanley (1844–1924)
CHILD AND EDUCATIONAL PSYCHOLOGY

Born in Ashfield, Massachusetts, Granville Stanley Hall studied with Wilhelm Wundt (see entry) and Hermann von Helmholtz in Germany. He gained a B.A. (1867) and M.A. (1870) from Williams College, Williamstown, Massachusetts. From 1867 to 1868 he studied at the Union Theological Seminary, New York, and earned a Ph.D. in Psychology from Harvard University, Cambridge, Massachusetts (1878), one of the first doctorates granted in America. At Johns Hopkins University in Baltimore, Maryland, he was lecturer in philosophy (1883) and professor of psychology and pedagogics (1884).

Hall founded the *American Journal of Psychology* (1887), the first such American journal and the second of any significance outside Germany. He founded the Child Study Association of America (1888), was the first president of the American Psychological Association, and was professor of psychology at Clark University, Worcester, Massachusetts (1889–1919). He also founded what is now the *Journal of Genetic Psychology*, the chief outlet for research in child study and educational psychology (1891).

Major Contributions

Hall is frequently regarded as the founder of child psychology and educational psychology. Two of his early significant papers dealt with children's lies (1882) and the other with the contents of children's minds (1883). At Harvard, he developed one of the first psychological laboratories in the United States. The philosopher-psychologist-educator John Dewey (see entry) was one of the first to use it. In 1888 Hall helped to establish Clark University, Worcester, and was the university's president and professor of psychology.

He became a major force in shaping experimental psychology into a science. By 1893 he had supervised 11 of the 14 doctorates in psychology granted in the United States. He was a leading figure in the founding of the American Psychological Association, and in 1892 was its first president. Hall pioneered the use of surveys; later he and his students would devise more than 190 questionnaires, which were largely instrumental in stimulating the upsurge of interest in the study of child development.

Hall's influence was not as a theorist but as a great teacher; he inspired research that reached into all areas of psychology. Among his students were the notable psychologists Arnold Gesell, Lewis Terman, James McKeen Cattell, John Dewey, Joseph Jastrow (see entries), and Edmund C. Sanford. Hall researched the psychology of religion, and he offered a course in the psychology of Christianity. Hall published 489 works covering most of the major areas of psychology.

Major Literature

Hall, Granville Stanley. *The Content of Children's Minds.* New York: D. Appleton, 1883.
___. *The Study of Children, Adolescence, Its Psychology and Its Relation to Physiology, Anthropology, Sociology, Sex, Crime.* New York: D. Appleton, 1883.
___. *Religion and Education.* New York: D. Appleton, 1904.
___. *Youth: Its Education, Regimen and Hygiene.* New York: D. Appleton, 1906.
___. *Educational Problems* 2 vols. New York: D. Appleton, 1911.
___. *Founders of Modern Psychology.* New York: D. Appleton, 1912.
___. *Jesus, the Christ, In the Light of Psychology.* New York: D. Appleton, 1917.

Hamilton, Gilbert Van Tassel (1877–1943)
OBJECTIVE PSYCHOPATHOLOGY

Born in Frazeysburg, Ohio, Gilbert Van Tassel Hamilton gained an A.B. (1898) from Ohio Wesleyan University in Delaware, Ohio, and an M.D. (1901) from Medical College, Philadelphia, working on nervous diseases under Francis X. Dercum (see entry). He started clinical practice as resident physician at the Jewish Hospital, Philadelphia, then spent three years as a clinical neuropsychiatrist at the State Hospital in Warren, Pennsylvania.

In 1905 Hamilton resigned his position to study psychology at Harvard University, Boston, Massachusetts. His choice of Boston might have been influenced by the arrival in 1896 of Adolf Meyer (see entry) to head the hospital's scientific staff; Meyer's influence drew psychiatry and psychology closer. Hamilton was appointed to the McLean Psychiatric Hospital, Boston, whose director at that time was Shepherd Ivory Franz (see entry). Franz had been appointed in 1904 with the task of investigating the abnormal physiological and psychological conditions of the insane.

In 1906 Hamilton, then serving as a resident physician, was assigned to the financier and philanthropist Stanley McCormick. When McCormick was discharged in 1907, Hamilton resigned from McLean and moved with McCormick to a nearby private residence as his personal physician. After about one year, McCormick returned to his estate near Santa Barbara, California, accompanied by Hamilton and his family. Before long, Hamilton had established a private comparative psychology laboratory, including a small primate colony, funded through a Stanley McCormick grant.

In 1916 McCormick's mental health deteriorated and a psychoanalytically oriented doctor criticized Hamilton's handling of his patient, so he resigned. From 1917 to 1919 he was commissioned as a captain in the army air service, stationed in Pittsburgh. Between 1922 and 1924 he was psychopathologist to the Santa Barbara clinic, and in 1935, director of psychobiological research at the Bureau of Social Hygiene, New York.

Major Contributions

From Freud, Hamilton adopted a strong tendency to seek psychopathology in childhood sexual trauma or adult sexual dysfunction, sometimes directly expressed, but often manifest in what Hamilton referred to as an "indirect reaction." Indeed, for the remainder of his professional career, Hamilton was to involve himself in the scientific study of sexual behavior—first in animals, especially sub-human primates, and eventually in humans. Between 1908 and 1917, Hamilton carried out a series of comparative psychological studies, some of which were experimental, some of which involved naturalistic observation.

The focus of the research was on sexual behavior, habit formation, and the identification of general behavioral and emotional reaction tendencies in situations presenting insoluble problems. In 1921 he studied the mental state of some 30,000 inhabitants of a small city in the Mississippi Valley. So far as psychology is concerned, Hamilton's behavioral approach was in keeping with the times, but as a psychiatrist, he rejected psychoanalysis outright. Smith Ely Jelliffe, a renowned psychoanalyst, criticized Hamilton for his handling of the McCormick case and also rejected Hamilton's objective psychopathology. Hamilton wrote one book: *An Introduction to Objective Psychopathology* (St. Louis, Missouri: C.V. Mosby Co., 1925).

Hamilton, Max (1912–1988)

PSYCHOPHARMACOLOGY

Born in Offenbach, Germany, at the beginning of World War I, Max Hamilton went with his parents to England and received his medical training at University College Hospital Medical School, London. He gained his M.A. from the University of London and his M.D. while senior registrar at King's College Hospital, London, his thesis being on the personalities of patients with dyspepsia. He was a Royal Air Force medical officer during World War II, where he became interested in psychiatry. He subsequently worked as senior hospital medical officer at Tooting Bec Hospital Psychiatric Hospital, London.

He devoted much of his life to the study of psychometrics, statistics, and experimental design. In 1956 he was appointed senior lecturer in the department of psychiatry in the University of Leeds. He spent two years as visiting scientist at the National Institute of Mental Health in Bethesda, Maryland, before returning to Leeds as a member of the external staff of the Medical Research Council. From 1964 to 1977 he was Nuffield Professor of Psychiatry, then emeritus professor of psychiatry, 1987–1988, University of Leeds. He won the South West Regional Hospital Research Prize, 1953; was president of the British Association of Pharmacology; honorary professor of psychiatry, University of Missouri, Columbia, 1970; and fellow, Royal College of Psychiatrists, 1971.

Major Contributions

Hamilton was one of the first to carry out controlled double-blind studies for clinical trials and psychotropic drugs. It is the Hamilton Anxiety Scale (HAS) (1959) and the Hamilton Rating Scale for Depression, (HAM-D) (1960) for which he is best known. Both are still widely used in psychiatry. The HAM-D scale contains 21 items that evaluate the severity of depressive symptoms. Some of the items are scored on a scale of 0 to 4 and others on a scale of 0 to 2. The items are depressed, guilt feelings, suicide, insomnia (early), insomnia (middle), insomnia (late), work and activities, retardation (psychomotor), agitation, anxiety (psychological), anxiety (somatic), somatic symptoms (gastro-intestinal), somatic symptoms (general), sexual dysfunction (menstrual disturbance), hypochondrias, weight loss, insight, diurnal variation, depersonalization and derealization, paranoid symptoms, and obsessional and compulsive symptoms.

Hamilton developed the HAS to be appropriate for adults and children; although it is most often used for younger adults there has been support for the test's use with older adults as well. It has 14 items: anxious mood, tension, fears, insomnia, intellectual, depressed mood, somatic complaints (muscular), somatic complaints (sensory), cardiovascular symptoms, respiratory symptoms, gastrointestinal symptoms, genitourinary symptoms, autonomic symptoms, and behavior.

Major Literature

Hamilton, Max. *Psychomantics*. London, England: Chapman and Hall, 1955.

___. "The Assessment of Anxiety States by Rating." *British Journal of Medical Psychology* 33 (1959): 50–55.

___. "A Rating Scale for Depression." *Journal of Neurology, Neurosurgery and Psychiatry* 2 (1960): 3, 56–62.

Harding, Mary Esther
(1888–1971)
FIRST AMERICAN JUNGIAN ANALYST

Born in Shropshire, England, Harding graduated as a doctor from the London School of Medicine for Women in 1914, then served as an intern at the Royal Infirmary in London, the first hospital in London to accept women interns. Here she wrote her book on diphtheria and later contracted the disease. After reading *Psychology of the Unconscious* by Carl Jung (see entry) and translated by Beatrice Hinkle (see entry), she entered psychoanalysis in Jung's Küsnacht home near Zurich, Switzerland.

In 1919 Harding met the Americans Eleanor Bertine and Kristine Mann at an international conference of medical women in Zurich. Bertine and Harding developed a lasting relationship and in 1924 Harding relocated to New York, and each traveled to Zurich for two months of analysis. The two friends spent every summer at Bailey Island, Maine, the home of Kristine Mann, and continued their analysis with therapists from the United States and Canada in settings conducive to profound experiences of the unconscious.

Major Contributions

Harding was an influential figure in the New York Jungian analytical psychology community and a prodigious writer who lectured frequently in America and Canada. Her main contributions are in her writing. Her first Jungian book, *The Way of All Women*, was acclaimed as one the best books on feminine psychology and was an instant best seller. It has been translated into many languages and has introduced many people to Jung's psychology.

In it she discusses topics such as work, marriage, motherhood, old age, and women's relationships with family, friends, and lovers. Harding, who was best known for her work with women and families, stresses the need for a woman to work toward her own wholeness and develop the many sides of her nature, and emphasizes the importance of unconscious processes.

Harding also helped to found many Jungian organizations, such as the Analytical Psychology Club of New York (1936); the Medical Society for Analytical Psychology, Eastern Division (1946) and the C.G. Jung Foundation for Analytical Psychology (1962). The foundation is dedicated to helping men and women grow in conscious awareness of the psychological realities in themselves and society, find healing and meaning in their lives, reach greater depth in their relationships, and live in response to their discovered sense of purpose. The foundation is in New York.

Major Literature

Harding, M. Esther. *The Circulatory Failure of Diphtheria: A Thesis for the Degree of Doctor of Medicine in the University of London.* London: University of London Press, 1920.

___. *The Way of All Women.* New York: Harper and Row, 1933. New York: Putnam Publishing, 1970.

___. *Psychic Energy, Its Source and Goal.* New York: Pantheon Books, 1948.

___. *Woman's Mysteries Ancient and Modern: A Psychological Interpretation of the Feminine Principle as Portrayed in Myth, Story, and Dreams.* New York: Pantheon Books, 1955.

Harlow, Harry Frederick
(1905–1981)
STUDY OF AFFECTION IN PRIMATES

Born Harry Frederick Israel in Fairfield, Iowa, Harlow gained an A.B. (1927) and a Ph.D. (1930) in psychology from Stanford University, California. While at Stanford, he studied under Lewis Terman (see entry) and on advice changed his name from Israel to Harlow. Although he was Protestant, it was thought that his Jewish name might hinder his search for work.

He was appointed assistant professor (1930) at the University of Wisconsin, Madison, where he stayed for the rest of his career, becoming full professor in 1944, and becoming chair of his department in 1949. Harlow was a member of several science and psychological associations, including the American Psychological Association, National Academy of Arts and Sciences, and Sigma Xi. He lectured nationally and was consultant to the Army's Scientific Advisory Panel. During his career, he was awarded with several distinctions, including the Howard Crosby Warren Medal (1956), National Medal of Science (1967), and the Gold Medal from the American Psychological Foundation (1973).

Major Contributions

Harlow studied the behavior of former U.S. prisoners of war servicemen from Korea, but it is his research with rhesus monkeys for which he will be remembered. Harlow focused on the learning of problem-solving, curiosity and manipulation, and the development of affectional systems.

Harlow found that rhesus monkeys are more mature at birth than humans, and like human babies, show a range of emotions and need to be nursed and loved. He separated infant monkeys from their real mothers, giving them instead two surrogate mothers, one model made of wire and the other made of cloth. The wire model was outfitted with a bottle to feed the baby monkey. But the babies rarely stayed with the wire model no longer than it took to get the necessary food. They clearly preferred cuddling with the softer cloth model, especially if they were scared. (When the cloth model had the bottle, they didn't go to the wire model at all.)

What Harlow and others did then would not be ethically or morally acceptable in the 21st century. However, his research has shed light on brain development and functioning, intelligence, learning, psychological abnormalities, social behavior, and affectional relationships, and the research he began continues even today. His work on attachments influenced other psychologists such as John Bowlby (see entry) in his attachment theory and the zoologist Robert Hinde, who works with mother-infant relationships in rhesus monkeys.

Major Literature

Harlow, Harry Frederick. *Biological and Biochemical Bases of Behavior*. Madison, Wisconsin: University of Wisconsin Press, 1958.
___. *Learning to Love*. Sudbury, Massachusetts: Jones and Bartlett Publishers International, 1971.
___, and Clara Mears. *The Human Model: Primate Perspectives*. New Jersey: John Wiley and Sons Inc., 1979.
___. *Learning to Love: The Selected Papers of H.F. Harlow*. Centennial Psychology Series. Westport, Connecticut: Greenwood Press, 1986.

Hartmann, Heinz (1894–1970)
EGO PSYCHOLOGY

Born in Vienna, Austria, Heinz Hartmann qualified in medicine from the University of Vienna. He underwent analysis with Sandor Rado and in 1927 he published *Les fondements de la psychanalyse*, which he followed with studies on psychoses, neuroses, and twins. He also participated in the creation of a manual of medical psychology.

At the same time that Sigmund Freud (see entry) offered him a free analysis if he stayed in Vienna, Hartmann was offered a position at Johns Hopkins University, New York. He chose the analysis with Freud and was noted as a shining star among analysts of his generation.

In 1938 he fled Austria with his family to escape the Nazis. He arrived in New York in 1941 and quickly became one of the foremost thinkers of the New York Psychoanalytic Society. Hartmann, with Anna Freud (see entry) and Ernst Kris, founded the publication *The Psychoanalytic Study of the Child* at Yale University Press, which is now in its 60th volume.

From 1951 to 1957 he was president of the International Psychological Association, and after several years of his presidency, he received the honorary title of lifetime president. The American Psychoanalytical Association honored him with its Charles Frederick Menninger Award in 1958. He drew on his horrifying experiences in Buchenwald when interviewed by Steven Spielberg's Shoah Foundation in its research for *Schindler's List* (1993).

Major Contributions

In Freud's view, the ego itself takes shape as a result of the conflict between the id and the external world. The ego, therefore, is inherently a conflicting formation in the mind. Freud viewed the functions of the ego as reality-testing, impulse-control, judgment, affect tolerance, and defense; Hartmann argued that the healthy ego includes a sphere of autonomous ego functions that are independent of mental conflict, that do not have their origins in the id. These functions, which include perception, motility, memory and intelligence, are present from birth and to some extent are genetically determined.

According to Hartmann, psychoanalytic treatment aims to expand the conflict-free sphere of ego functioning. By doing so, Hartmann believed, psychoanalysis facilitates *adaptation*, that is, more effective mutual regulation of ego and environment. Many authors have criticized Hartmann's conception of a conflict-free sphere of ego functioning as both incoherent and inconsistent with Freud's vision of psychoanalysis as a science of mental conflict. As part of his theory of adaptation, Hartmann put forward the view that some defense mechanisms, for example intellectualization and sublimation, can be coping devices and autonomous from the id. Further, one of the functions of the ego is to promote homeostasis — a harmonious balance between the drives of sex and aggression.

Major Literature

Hartmann, Heinz. *Essays on Ego Psychology: Selected Problems in Psychoanalytic Theory.* New York: International Universities Press, 1965.

___. *Once a Doctor, Always a Doctor: The Memoirs of a German-Jewish Immigrant Physician.* Loughton, Essex, England: Prometheus Books, 1986.

___. *In Search of Self, In the Service of Others.* Loughton, Essex, England: Prometheus Books, 1998.

Havighurst, Robert James (1900–1991)
ADULT DEVELOPMENT AND AGING

Born in Depere, Wisconsin, Robert James Havighurst earned a B.A. at Ohio Wesleyan University in Delaware, Ohio (1921), and an M.A. (1922) and Ph.D. in chemistry (1924) from Ohio State University, Columbus. He was National Research Council Fellow in Physics at Harvard University, Cambridge, Massachusetts (1924–1926). Between 1927 and 1934 he had academic appointments in both chemistry and physics. From 1934 to 1944 he worked for the Rockefeller Foundation, General Education Board, and from 1941 to 1991 he was professor of education and human development at the University of Chicago, and emeritus professor.

He was Fulbright scholar at the University of Canterbury, New Zealand (1953–1954), co-director of the Government Center for Educational Research in Brazil (1956–1958), a Fulbright scholar at the University of Buenos Aires (1961), visiting professor at the University of Missouri in Kansas City and Fordham University in New York (1965–1968), and director of a national study on American Indians (1968–1970). He was awarded an honorary D.Sc. at Adelphi University, New York (1962), an honorary LL.D. at Ohio Wesleyan University (1963), and a Thorndike Award for Research, Division of Educational Psychology, American Educational Association (1967).

Major Contributions

At Rockefeller, Havighurst became the central figure in developing educational programs at major universities and research centers throughout America. He was also instrumental in raising funds for European refugee scholars to settle in America; two well-known are Bruno Bettelheim and Erik Erikson (see entries). In his appointment to Chicago in 1941 he began a series of collaborative studies with sociologists, anthropologists and educationalists on personality and moral development of children and adolescents. In his book *Developmental Tasks and Education*, Havighurst posited eight developmental tasks of adolescence that young people needed to complete if they were to successfully make the passage from adolescence to adulthood:

1. Achieve new and more mature relations with age-mates of both sexes
2. Achieve a masculine or feminine social role
3. Accept one's physique and use the body effectively
4. Achieve emotional independence of parents and other adults
5. Prepare for marriage and family life
6. Prepare for an economic career
7. Acquire a set of values and an ethical system as a guide to behavior
8. Desire and achieve socially responsible behavior.

Havighurst was active in civil rights and much of his work focused on the education of minority youth and the relationship between social class and educational development. His survey of Chicago public schools, published in 1964, recommended desegregation of schools and communities. He also directed the Kansas City Studies of Adult life, focusing on the sociology and psychology of aging.

Major Literature

Havighurst, Robert James. *Human Development and Education.* New York: Longmans, Green, 1953.

___. *Growing Up in River City.* New Jersey: John Wiley and Sons, Inc., 1962.

___, and J.R. Moreira. *Society and Education in Brazil.* Pittsburgh, Pennsylvania: University of Pittsburgh Press, 1965.

Havighurst, Robert James, B.L. Neugarten, and J.M. Falk. *Society and Education: A Book of Readings.* 3rd Ed. Boston, Massachusetts: Allyn and Bacon, 1967.

___. *Developmental Tasks and Education.* New York: David McKay Company, 1972.

Hebb, Donald Olding (1904–1985)
NEUROPSYCHOLOGY

Born in Chester, Nova Scotia, Canada, Donald Olding Hebb gained a B.A. from Dalhousie University in Halifax, Nova Scotia (1925), where he later became professor emeritus of psychology

(1976). In 1931, Hebb became bedridden due to tuberculosis in his hip but gained his M.A. with honors later that year. Hebb earned his Ph.D. at Harvard University, Cambridge, Massachusetts, under Karl Lashley (see entry) (1936); his thesis was on the effects of early visual deprivation upon size and brightness perception in rats.

From 1937 to 1939 he was research fellow, Montreal Neurological Institute, researching the effect of brain surgery and injury on human brain function. From 1939 to 1942 he was lecturer, then assistant professor, at Queen's University in Ontario, Canada, and research associate at Yerkes Laboratories of Primate Biology in Orange Park, Florida (1942–1947). At McGill University in Montreal, Quebec, Canada, Hebb was professor of psychology (1947–1974) and professor emeritus (1974).

He was president of the Canadian Psychological Association (1952); fellow, Royal Society of Canada (1959); and president of the American Psychological Association (1960). He received the Distinguished Scientific Contribution Award from the APA (1961) and seventeen honorary degrees from universities in Canada, England and America.

Major Contributions

Under Lashley, Hebb worked on the question, is perception innate or acquired? To test this he set up an experiment with rats reared normally and those reared in the dark. His conclusion was that perception does not require previous experience, though he later realized that the dark-reared rats took longer to learn a task. Before Hebb turned to psychology, he was a teacher, and in 1928 he was headmaster of a troubled school in Montreal.

Hebb was critical of the Stanford-Binet and Wechsler intelligence tests for use with brain surgery patients, because they were designed to measure overall intelligence. Hebb believed tests should be designed to measure more specific effects that surgery could have had on the patient, so he created the Adult Comprehension Test and the Picture Anomaly Test. Using the Picture Anomaly Test, he provided the first indication that the right temporal lobe was involved in visual recognition. He also showed that removal of large parts of the frontal lobe had little effect on intelligence.

In 1939, he was appointed to a teaching position at Queen's University, Ontario, Canada, where he developed human and animal intelligence tests, including the "Hebb-Williams" maze, which has subsequently been used to investigate the intelligence of many different species in hundreds of

studies, making it the "Stanford-Binet" of comparative intelligence. At the Yerkes Laboratory of Primate Biology, Hebb explored fear, anger, and other emotional processes in the chimpanzee. The Donald O. Hebb Award, named in his honor, is awarded to distinguished Canadian scientists.

Major Literature

Hebb, Donald Olding. *The Organization of Behavior.* New Jersey: John Wiley and Sons, Inc., 1949. New Jersey: Erlbaum Associates, Inc., 2002.
Hebb, Donald Olding, and Charles C. Torrey. *Textbook of Psychology.* St Louis, Missouri: W.B. Saunders Company, 1958, 1972.
Hebb, Donald Olding. *Essay on Mind.* Hillsdale, 1981.
___. *Conceptual Nervous System: Selected Papers.* London, England: Reed Elsevier Group, 1982.

Heider, Fritz (1896–1988)
BALANCE THEORY

Born in Vienna, Fritz Heider received his Ph.D (1920) from Karl Franzens University in Graz, Austria, then studied at the Psychological Institute, Berlin. At the invitation of Wolfgang Köhler (see entry) Heider immigrated to the United States in 1930 to conduct research at the Clarke School for the Deaf in Northampton, Massachusetts, and to be an assistant professor at nearby Smith College. He was professor of psychology at the University of Kansas, Lawrence, from 1947 until her retired in 1966. He received the Distinguished Scientific Contribution Award from the American Psychological Association (1965) and was named a University Distinguished Professor in 1965.

Major Contributions

How we interpret our own behavior, as well as that of others, formed the basis for Heider's work on relationships and for his two theories — attribution and balance. Attribution theory explains how we attribute the behavior of others. We may attribute behavior to disposition; for example, we might decide that altruism is what makes a particular person donate money to a charity. Or we may attribute behavior to situations; the donor gives money to charity because of social pressure. Heider believed that we generally tended to give more attribution than we should to personality, and, conversely, less than we should to situations. In other words, personality is not as consistent an indicator of behavior as people tend to believe.

The Psychology of Interpersonal Relations is regarded as having established attribution theory as separate area of study within social psychology. Heider proposed that behavior is the product of the personal forces of ability, intention and effort, and the environmental forces of opportunity, task difficulty and luck. An everyday example of attribution theory is: A student passes one of her tests with flying colors, so she attributes that success to her high IQ. She fails another test and attributes that failure to a headache she suffered that day. In reality, she didn't study for that test, as she didn't like the lecturer.

Balance theory, which was influenced by Gestalt theory, asserts that we will favorably evaluate people we like and that we will also like the people our friends like and vice versa. Heider argued that the way we perceive the social world is influenced by our need to belong, and that we prefer relationships that fit well with each other and make us feel balanced. If consistency or balance is not achieved, we feel under strain and we try to restore balance.

Major Literature

Heider, Fritz, and G.M. Heider. "Studies in the Psychology of the Deaf." *Psychological Monographs* 52, 53, 1940.

Heider, Fritz. *The Psychology of Interpersonal Relations.* Hillsdale, New Jersey: Erlbaum Associates, Inc., 1958, 1982.

___. "On Balance and Attribution." In P.W. Holland and S. Leinhardt, Eds., *Perspectives on Social Network Research.* London: Reed Elsevier Group, Academic Press Inc., 1979.

___. *The Life of a Psychologist.* Lawrence, Kansas: University Press of Kansas, 1986.

Hilgard, Ernest Ropiequet (1904–2001)

HYPNOSIS

Born in Belleville, Illinois, Ernest Ropiequet Hilgard gained a B.A. in chemical engineering from the University of Chicago, Illinois (1924). At Yale University in New Haven, Connecticut, he earned a Ph.D. (1930) and was instructor in psychology (1920–1933). At Stanford University, California, he was assistant professor, associate professor, professor of psychology, chairman of the Department of Psychology, dean of the graduate division, director of the Laboratory of Hypnosis Research, and emeritus professor (1933–1979).

Following the attack on Pearl Harbor in 1941, Hilgard served on a program of national opinion surveys at Washington. Hilgard's awards and honors include an honorary D.Sc. from Kenyon College, Gambier, Ohio (1964); the American Psychological Foundation's Gold Medal (1978); the National Academy of Science Award for Excellence in Scientific Reviewing (1984); an honorary D.Sc. from Colgate University, Hamilton, New York (1987); an honorary D.Sc. Northwestern University, Evanston, Illinois (1987); and an honorary Ph.D. from the University of Oslo (1994).

After World War II, Hilgard helped establish a nursery school at Stanford University, California, to assist married students returning from the war. He was part of a delegation of educators invited by General MacArthur to advise his staff and the Japanese ministry of education on demilitarizing the Japanese school system.

Major Contributions

In 1940, Hilgard co-authored *Conditioning and Learning*, which quickly became the standard text in the field; it is still in print. Another major contribution is his study of hypnosis. In the 1950s, Hilgard and his wife, Josephine (1906–1989), made headlines as pioneers when they established the Laboratory of Hypnosis Research at Stanford University. To learn the basics, he brought in the former stage hypnotist Andre Weitzenhoffer.

The Hilgards and other colleagues began experimenting and collecting data on hypnosis as a means of, among other things, helping people to overcome harmful habits such as smoking and to treat pain. It does not mean that the pain is not there, the patient feels no conscious pain. Hilgard discovered that the more susceptible a person is to hypnosis, the more effective the technique as an analgesic.

In 1959, the Hilgards developed what became known as the Stanford Hypnotic Susceptibility Scale, a system of measurement still used by medical practitioners to determine a person's likelihood of being hypnotized and to what degree. Their research on the use of hypnosis in bone marrow aspirations in the treatment of childhood cancer earned them grants from the National Cancer Institute. Other hypnosis projects brought funding from the Ford Foundation and the National Institute of Mental Health. Hilgard served as president of the International Society of Hypnosis in the 1970s.

Major Literature

Hilgard, Ernest Ropiequet. *Conditioning and Learning.* New Jersey: Prentice-Hall, 1961.

___(Ed.). *Theories of Learning and Instruction.* Chicago, Illinois: University of Chicago Press, 1965.

___. *Hypnotic Suggestibility*. New York: Harcourt, Brace and Company, 1965.
___, and Josephine R Hilgard. *Hypnosis in the Relief of Pain*. London: Taylor and Francis Books Ltd., Brunner/Mazel Publisher, 1994.

Related Literature

Hilgard's *Introduction to Psychology*, first published in 1953, is now: Edward Smith, Susan Nolen-Hoeksema, Barbara Fredrickson, and Geoffrey R. Loftus, 14th ed, *Atkinson and Hilgard's Introduction to Psychology*. Belmont, California: Wadsworth, 2003.

Himmelweit, Hilde Therese (1918–1989)

COGNITIVE PSYCHOLOGY

Born in Berlin, Germany, Hilde Therese Himmelweit gained a B.A. (1940) and an M.A. (1942) from the University of Cambridge, England, and a Ph.D. from the University of London (1945). Himmelweit was a fellow, British Psychological Society; chairman, Social Psychology Section (1953); founder and member, European Association of Experimental Social Psychology (1953); chairman, Academic Advisory Committee, Open University (1969–1974); trustee, International Institute of Communications (1973–1979); member, Committee on Television and Social Behavior, United States Social Science Research Council (1973–1979); Annan Committee on the Future of Broadcasting in Britain (1974–1977); vice-president, International Society of Political Psychology (1978–1981); and Center for Contemporary Studies (1980–1989).

She was awarded an honorary doctorate at Open University (1976), received the Nevitt Sanford Award from the International Society of Political Psychology (1981) and was professor emeritus of social psychology at the University of London. Himmelweit was on the editorial boards of the *Journal of Social and Clinical Psychology*, *Journal of Communication*, *International Journal of Communication Research*, *Interdisciplinary Science Review*, and *Media, Culture and Society*.

Major Contributions

Himmelweit worked with Sir Frederic Charles Bartlett (see entry) at Cambridge University, then as a clinical research psychologist with children and in the Army Neurosis Centre, Northfield Military Hospital in England (see Wilfred Bion and Sigmund Foulkes). She taught at London School of Economics (LSE) from 1948 to 1983 and from 1964 she was the first professor of social psychol-ogy in Britain, founding LSE's social psychology department and establishing the discipline on the university curriculum.

One of her research projects, for which she received great publicity in the media, was concerned with the effect of horror television on young audiences. As director of the Nuffield television inquiry from 1954 to 1958, she contributed to the understanding of television's impact in society, the subsequent book *Television and the Child* establishing her reputation in Europe and in the U.S. Three different models have been developed that have stood the test of time, and in every case, a longitudinal element was introduced into the study to trace change over time:

1. the displacement and stimulation effects of television
2. the relative impact of home and school on the young
3. a cognitive model of individuals' voting decisions, which greatly strengthened the understanding of human decision-making by voters.

The Hilde Himmelweit scholarship is awarded to M.Sc. applicants to the Department of Social Psychology and the Hilde Himmelweit Prize is given for the best overall performance in the program.

Major Literature

Himmelweit, Hilde Therese. "The Measurement of Personality in Children." *British Journal of Educational Psychology* 21 (1951): 9.
___. *Television and the Child: An Empirical Study of the Effect of Television on the Young*. Published for the Nuffield Foundation by Oxford University Press, 1958.
___ (with P. Humphreys, M. Jaeger and M. Katz). *How Voters Decide in 1981*. London, England: Reed Elsevier Group, Academic Press Inc., 1981.
Himmelweit, Hilde Therese. *Societal Psychology*. Sage Focus Editions. New York: Sage Publications, 1990.

Hinde, Robert Aubrey (1923–)

COMPARATIVE AND PHYSIOLOGICAL PSYCHOLOGY

Born in Norwich, England, Robert Aubrey Hinde was a flight lieutenant in the Royal Air Force Coastal Command, flying between Scotland and the Maldive Islands (1941–1945). He gained a B.Sc. at the University of London (1948). At University of Oxford he was research assistant, Edward Grey Institute of Field Ornithology (1948–1950); he earned a Ph.D. there in 1950.

At University of Cambridge he was curator, Ornithological Field Station (now a sub-department of Animal Behaviour), Madingley (1950–1989). He earned an Sc.D. (1958) and was professor (1963–1989). From 1970 to 1979 he was honorary director of the Medical Research Council Unit on Development and Integration of Behavior. He was Hitchcock Professor, University of California (1979), and Green Visiting Scholar, University of Texas (1983).

Hinde has received honorary doctorates from seven universities in Britain, Europe and Canada, and many other awards in zoology, psychiatry and medicine. They include the Distinguished Scientists Award from the Society for Research in Child Development in 1991 and Commander of the British Empire in 1988. Formerly master of St. John's College, Cambridge, he is the emeritus Royal Society Research professor of zoology at the University of Cambridge.

Major Contributions

Trained as a biologist, Hinde is best known for his studies of the effects on infants of short-term separation from their mothers. During the late 1950s, Hinde established a colony of rhesus monkeys to serve as his laboratory. There he conducted extensive research that led to new information on human interpersonal relationships. He observed that rhesus mothers encouraged independence in their infants before the infants themselves appeared to seek it. Later he concentrated on children ages three to six and their relationships with their mothers and their peers.

Influenced by John Bowlby (see entry), Hinde demonstrated that an infant's presence affected the mother's relationship to other adults. He argued that an attachment relationship more likely reflected the contributions of both the mother and infant, rather than that of the infant alone. The relationship itself reflects what goes on between the traits of the individuals involved and the nature of the relationship.

In the last few years he has tried to show how far a biological-psychological approach can help us to understand the ubiquity of religious systems, and the similarities and differences between the moral codes of different cultures. In that way he hopes to strengthen the links between biology and the social sciences. For over two decades Hinde has also been seeking ways to reduce the incidence of war. He is chair of the British Pugwash Conference, an international organization that seeks to reduce armed conflicts.

Major Literature

Hinde, Robert Aubrey. "A Biologist Looks at Anthropology." *Man Now Journal of the Royal Anthropological Institute* 26 (1991): 583–608.
___. "War: Some Psychological Causes and Consequences." *Interdisciplinary Science Reviews* 22 (1997): 229–245.
___. *Relationships: A Dialectical Perspective*. Hove, England: Psychology Press, 1997.
___. *Why Gods Persist: A Scientific Approach to Religion*. London, England: Taylor and Francis Books Ltd., Routledge, 1999.
___. *Why Good is Good*. London, England: Taylor and Francis Books Ltd., Routledge, 2002.
___, and J. Rotblat. *War No More: Eliminating Conflict in the Nuclear Age*. London, England: Pluto Press, 2003.

Hinkle, Beatrice Moses (1874–1953)
JUNGIAN ANALYST

Beatrice Moses was born in San Francisco. In 1892 she married Walter S. Hinkle and entered the Cooper Medical School in San Francisco (now part of Stanford University). Her husband died seven years later and when Hinkle graduated from the medical school she was appointed as San Francisco's city physician, the first time a female doctor was given such a responsibility.

She became interested in psychoanalysis for the treatment of mental illness, and to find out more, she moved to New York to attend the New School of Psychoanalytic Society, founded in 1911 (now the New York Psychoanalytic Society and Institute). In 1908 she co-founded America's first psychotherapeutic clinic at Cornell Medical School, New York, and in 1909 she went to Vienna to study under Sigmund Freud (see entry).

However, she disagreed with Freud's views on women's psychology — he believed that the psyche of the woman is derived from the psyche of man — so she quickly became aligned with the less biased theories of Carl Jung (see entry). Another fundamental difference was that in Freud's view the father was the dominant figure in the life of a child, whereas for Jung, it was the mother. This significant switch allowed Hinkle to come to grips with the emphasis that Jung placed on the masculine and feminine parts of the personality.

She returned to New York in 1915 determined to spread Jung's theories in America, although she remained keenly interested in Freud's work, particularly in the neuroses and hysteria. In 1916 she published a translation of Jung's theories of the unconscious titled *The Psychology of the Unconscious*, the first publication in America of Carl Jung's work, and she added several theories of her own that were arrived at through her personal experience with both Freud and Jung.

In 1916, Hinkle was included in the faculties of Cornell Medical College and the New York Post-Graduate Medical School. She became one of the most famous female psychoanalysts within the psychological society of New York, and probably the earliest practitioner of Jung's theories in the United States. Relating the feminine principle to artists, she said that the male artist is closer to the psychology of women than to the psychology of men. On her retirement, she moved to Washington, Connecticut, and opened a sanatorium to continue her practice in psychoanalysis.

Major Literature

Hinkle, B. *Psychology of the Unconscious: A Study of The Transformations and Symbolisms of the Libido.* New York: Vail-Ballou Press, 1916. (Translation from Carl Jung). New Jersey: Princeton University Press, Bollingen Foundation, 1922.

Hinkle, B. *The Recreating of the Individual.* New York: Dodd, Mead and Company, 1923.

Hoffer, Abram (1917–)

ORTHOMOLECULAR PSYCHIATRY

Born in Saskatchewan, Canada, Hoffer gained a bachelor of science and arts (1938) and a master of science and arts (1940) from the University of Saskatchewan. His Ph.D. was from the University of Minnesota, Minneapolis (1944). From 1940 to 1944, Hoffer was research cereal chemist, Purity Flour Mills. He gained an M.D. at the University of Toronto (1949) and was intern at City Hospital, Saskatoon, Saskatchewan (1949–1950).

He was director of psychiatric research, Department of Public Health, Regina, Saskatchewan (1950–1957) and in 1954 was certificant, psychiatry, Royal College of Physicians, Canada. From 1955 to 1958 he was assistant professor (research) of psychiatry at the College of Medicine, University of Saskatchewan, and was associate professor (research) in psychiatry from 1958 to 1967. He has been in private practice since 1967. He became a fellow, Royal College of Physicians and Surgeons, in Canada in 1972.

Major Contributions

Hoffer became interested in psychiatry during his internship at Saskatoon, especially psychosomatic medicine, and wanted to combine his interest in medicine, chemistry and psychiatry in a research position. He joined Dr. D.G. McKerracher at Regina, Saskatchewan, where his aim was to initiate a program of research into psychiatry. From Dr. Franz Alexander (see entry) at the Chicago Psychoanalytic Institute, he learned that psychosomatic medicine had no basis in fact. Heinrich Kluver (see entry) introduced him to the possibilities of the hallucinogens, especially mescaline.

Hoffer was joined by Dr. Humphrey Osmond in 1952 and together they directed the research program until Osmond left in 1960, and Hoffer went into private practice in 1967. They decided to tackle the most important single problem—schizophrenia. Half of the mental hospital beds at that time, and one quarter of all hospital beds in Canada, were occupied by patients suffering from schizophrenia. However, they were conscious that a biological approach would meet opposition from the disciples of the flourishing psychoanalysis.

Osmond discovered that the mescaline experience resembled the schizophrenic experience, and from that Hoffer and Osmond developed the adrenochrome (a product of adrenalin) hypothesis of schizophrenia. The outcome was the discovery that massive doses of vitamin B-3 and ascorbic acid were therapeutic for schizophrenia and that niacin lowers cholesterol levels. The Hoffer-Osmond Diagnostic tests were developed for assisting in the diagnosis of schizophrenia.

Hoffer's work has met with apathy from the psychiatric fraternity and no encouragement from the drug companies. He is editor of the *Journal of Orthomolecular Medicine*.

Major Literature

Altschul, R., Abram Hoffer, and J.D. Stephen. "Influence of Nicotinic Acid on Serum Cholesterol in Man." *Archives of Biochemical and Biophysics* 54 (1955): 558–559.

Hoffer, Abram. *Chemical Basis of Clinical Psychiatry.* Springfield, Illinois: Thomas, 1960.

___. *Niacin Therapy in Psychiatry.* American Lecture Series. Springfield, Illinois: Charles C. Thomas Ltd., 1962.

___, H. Osmond, and H. Kelm. *Hoffer-Osmond Diagnostic Test.* Tuscaloosa, Alabama: Behavior Science Press, 1975.

Hoffer, Abram, and L. Pauling. *Healing Cancer: Complementary Vitamin and Drug Treatments.* Toronto: Canadian College of Naturopathic Medicine Press, 2004.

___. *Healing Schizophrenia: Complementary Vitamin and Drug Treatments.* Toronto: Canadian College of Naturopathic Medicine Press, 2004.

Hollingworth, Leta Stetter (1886–1939)
DEVELOPMENTAL PSYCHOLOGY

Born in Dawes County near the town of Chadron, Nebraska, Leta Stetter Hollingworth gained a B.A. from University of Nebraska, Lincoln (1906). At Teachers College, Columbia University, New York, she earned an M.A. in education (1913) and a Ph.D. in educational psychology under Edward L. Thorndike (see entry) (1916); she was later professor of educational psychology.

She was appointed the first Civil Service psychologist, in New York in 1913, worked as a clinical psychologist at Bellevue Hospital in New York (1915), and was a consulting psychologist with the New York Police Department (1915). In 1917 Hollingworth helped establish the American Association of Clinical Psychologists. In 1921 she was cited in *American Men* [now *and Women*] *of Science* for her contributions to the psychology of women, and was nominated as a "Builder of a Nation" by the Nebraska International Women's Year Coalition (1974).

Major Contributions

Leta Stetter married Henry Hollingworth (1880–1956) in 1908 and moved to New York when her husband was appointed an assistant professor at Barnard College. As a married woman Hollingworth found it impossible to secure a teaching post. In 1911, Henry was hired as assistant director by the Coca-Cola Company to investigate the effects of caffeine on mental and motor tasks performed by humans, therefore, the couple was able to save up enough money for Hollingworth to continue her schooling.

Her job for the Civil Service was to administer Binet intelligence tests, which, having no experience, she quickly taught herself to do. During her graduate work, Hollingworth examined the role of women in society and questioned the assumption that the biology of women made them inferior. She hypothesized that women were disadvantaged because of the male-dominated society.

She challenged another prevalent assumption that women should be incapacitated by menstruation. She extended her work into challenging the idea that women had an inborn instinct for motherhood and that they should gain their satisfaction in life by bearing children. She also dismissed the idea that a woman's desire to achieve satisfaction outside of marriage and family was abnormal or unhealthy. She attributed these falsehoods to sociocultural attitudes.

At Bellevue she administered testing, supervised the psychology laboratory, helped to establish the Classification Clinic for Adolescents, and focused much of her attention on gifted children. In addition to her teaching duties at Columbia, she was the principal of a school for exceptional children.

Major Literature

Hollingworth, Leta Stetter. *The Psychology of Subnormal Children*. New York: Macmillan, 1920.
___. *Special Talents and Defects: Their Significance for Education*. New York: Macmillan, 1923.
___. *Gifted Children: Their Nature and Nurture*. New York: Macmillan, 1926.
___. "The New Woman in the Making." *Current History* 27 (1927): 15–20.
___. *The Psychology of the Adolescent*. New York: D. Appleton and Company, 1928.
___. *Children Above 180 IQ Stanford-Binet: Origin and Development*. Yonkers-on-Hudson, New York: World Book Company. 1975 Manchester, New Hampshire: Ayer Co. Publishers, 1942.

Hooker, Evelyn (1907–1996)
MALE SEXUALITY

Born in North Platte, Nebraska, Evelyn Hooker gained her bachelor's and master's degrees in psychology at the University of Colorado, Boulder, and her Ph.D. (1932) from Johns Hopkins University in Baltimore, Maryland. She then taught in a small women's college near Baltimore. From 1934 to 1936 she was a patient in tuberculosis sanitarium in California, followed by one year part-time teaching at Whittier College, St. Whittier, California.

A fellowship took her to Germany in 1937-1938 to study at the Institute for Psychotherapy, Berlin. She then spent a year traveling in England and Russia, and her experience of the repression in two totalitarian states strengthened her ambition to correct social injustice. From 1940 to 1970, when she resigned to set up a private practice, she was psychology professor at the University of California, Los Angeles (UCLA). In 1951 she married for the second time to Edward Niles Hooker, a distinguished professor of English at UCLA, who died in 1957.

Hooker received the 1991 Award for Distinguished Contribution to Psychology in the Public Interest, presented by the American Psychological Association. She died at her home in Santa Monica.

Major Contributions

Evelyn Hooker has been among the most influential figures in the highly successful movement to convince the American people that homosexuality is a normal variant of human sexual behavior. In 1953, Hooker received a grant from the National Institute of Mental Health to study the adjustment of non-clinical homosexual men and a comparable group of heterosexual men. At that time homosexuality was considered not only a mental illness but illegal.

The grant continued until 1961, when she received the Research Career Award. Her study is the most frequently cited scientific source for the argument that homosexuality is not a pathology, that homosexuals are as free from mental disorder as heterosexuals. Not until 1973 did the American Psychological Association (APA) change its diagnosis "from a disease to a condition that can be considered a disease only if it is subjectively disturbing to the person" (H.J. Kaplan and B.J. Sadock, Eds. *Comprehensive Textbook of Psychiatry*, 6th ed., Williams and Wilkins, Baltimore, Md., 1995, p. 2795).

In the Diagnostic and Statistical Manual of Mental Disorders III, the classification was removed entirely. Hooker was honored with the 1991 APA Award for Distinguished Contributions to Psychology in the Public Interest. She was appointed chair of the National Institute of Mental Health's Task Force on Homosexuality, a group that recommended the repeal of sodomy laws and encouraged better public education on homosexuality.

Major Literature

Hooker, Evelyn. "A Preliminary Analysis of Group Behavior of Homosexuals." *Journal of Psychology 42* (1956): 217–225.
___. "The Adjustment of the Male Overt Homosexual." *Journal of Projective Techniques* 21 (1957): 18–31.
___. "Male Homosexuality in the Rorschach." *Journal of Projective Techniques* 23 (1958): 278–281.
___. "Homosexuality." In *The International Encyclopedia of the Social Sciences*. David L. Sills and Robert K. Merton, Eds. New York: MacMillan and Free Press, 1968.
Berzon, Betty, and Evelyn Hooker. *Positively Gay*. Madison, Wisconsin: Celestial Arts, 1992.

Horney, Karen Clementine Danielsen (1885–1952)

PERSONALITY DISORDERS

Karen Danielsen was born in Hamburg in 1906 and entered medical school against parental wishes. She married Oscar Horney (pronounced horn-eye) in 1909 and started psychoanalysis with Karl Abraham (see entry) in 1911. She gained her medical degree from Berlin University (1913) and moved to the U.S. to become associate director of the Institute for Psychoanalysis in Chicago (1932).

Horney returned to private practice in New York City in 1934 and to teaching at the New School for Social Research. She settled in Brooklyn, where she developed her theories on neurosis based on her experiences as a psychotherapist. She was professor, New York Medical College (1942). She founded the *American Journal of Psychoanalysis* and served as its editor until her death.

Major Contributions

Horney founded a neo–Freudian school of psychoanalysis based on the conclusion that neuroses result from emotional conflicts arising from childhood experiences and later disturbances in interpersonal relationships. She observed that the majority of her patients complained of unhappiness and lack of fulfillment in their lives, and the difficulty of establishing and maintaining relationships of quality. According to Horney, feelings of helplessness and despair drive us into making decisions that are not fulfilling and leave us feeling dissatisfied. Such feelings (formed early in childhood into defensive patterns) are self-perpetuating strategies against anxiety.

Her views on the concept of repression brought her into conflict with the New York Psychoanalytic Institute, and forced her expulsion as an instructor. By 1941, Horney established and became dean of the American Institute for Psychoanalysis, a training institute for those interested in her own Association for the Advancement of Psychoanalysis, a program that resulted from her dissatisfaction with the orthodox approach to psychoanalysis.

Horney believed that passivity was not restricted to women, but is determined by culture. She rejected the notion of penis envy and other manifestations of male bias in psychoanalytic theory. She also rejected the libido, the death instinct, and the Oedipus complex, which she believed could be more adequately explained by cultural and social conditions.

She outlined three strategies that are available to the child in its search for safety:

1. *Compliant, self-effacing*: Moving toward others, seeking affection approval — this "moving toward" only emphasizes helplessness.

2. *Aggressive, expansive*: Moving against others and in so doing accepting a hostile environment.

3. *Detached, resigned*: Moving away from others and in so doing accepting the difficulty of relating to people at an intimate level.

Behavior is influenced by the strategy that is found to bring the greatest rewards.

Major Literature

Horney, Karen. *The Neurotic Personality of Our Time*. New York: W.W. Norton and Co. Ltd., 1937, 1994.

___. *New Ways in Psychoanalysis*. New York: W.W. Norton and Co. Ltd., 1939, 2000.

___. *Self-Analysis*. New York: W.W. Norton and Co. Ltd., 1942, 1994.

___. *Our Inner Conflicts*. New York: W.W. Norton and Co. Ltd., 1945, 1993.

___. *Neurosis and Human Growth*. New York: W.W. Norton and Co. Ltd., 1950, 1991

___. *Feminine Psychology*. New York: W.W. Norton and Co. Ltd., 1967, 1994.

Hovland, Carl Iver (1912–1961)
PERSUASION

Born in Chicago, Illinois, to Lutheran parents of Scandinavian descent, Carl Iver Hovland gained his B.A. (with highest distinction) (1932) and M.A. (1933) from Northwestern University, Evanston, Illinois. His Ph.D. (1936) was from Yale University, New Haven, Connecticut. He then joined the faculty of psychology at Yale, where he worked on experimental psychology on problems of conditioned responses. From 1942 to 1945 he worked for the War Department.

Returning to Yale after World War II, Hovland served as chairman of the department of psychology (1945–51) and was appointed Sterling professor of psychology (1947). He directed further studies in attitude and communication, particularly on the prestige of the communicator and the order of presentation of arguments as they influence the effectiveness of persuasive communication.

He received the Distinguished Scientific Contribution Award of the American Psychological Association (1957) and the Howard Crosby Warren Medal by the Society of Experimental Psychologists (1961). Awarded close to the time of his death, the medal was received for his father by his nineteen-year-old son, David.

Major Contributions

During the war, Hovland was director of experimental studies and chief psychologist for the U.S. War Department at Washington, D.C. The primary mission of Hovland's section of some fifteen researchers was to study military morale and to evaluate the training programs and films being prepared by the Information and Education Division for American troops in the United States and Europe. The particular emphasis was audience resistance to persuasive communications and methods of overcoming such resistance.

He first reported the "sleeper effect" after studying the effects of the Frank Capra's propaganda film series *Why We Fight* on soldiers while in the Army. In later studies on this subject, Hovland collaborated with Irving Janis (see entry), who would later become famous for his theory of groupthink. The sleeper effect refers to the "hidden" effect of a propaganda message even when it comes from a low-credibility source. The greater the personal involvement with the source of information, the higher the credibility rating.

Hovland also worked as scientific consultant to a number of industrial organizations and government departments. He further developed the social judgment theory of attitude change. The judgment theory attempts to explain how attitude change is influenced by judgmental processes. In the late 1950s he was one of the psychologists anxious to bring information technology into psychology. He died of cancer less than one year after the death of his wife.

Major Literature

Sherif, Muzafer, and Carl I. Hovland. *Social Judgment: Assimilation and Contrast Effects in Communications and Attitude Change*. New Haven, Connecticut: Yale University Press, 1961. Westport, Connecticut: Greenwood Press, 1981.

Hovland, Carl Iver, and Irving L. Janis. *Personality and Persuasibility*. New Haven, Connecticut: Yale University Press, 1966.

Hovland, Carl Iver. *Communication and Persuasion: Psychological Studies of Opinion Change*. New Haven, Connecticut: Yale University Press, 1953. Westport, Connecticut: Greenwood Press, 1982.

___ (Ed.). *Order of Presentation in Persuasion*. New Haven, Connecticut: Yale University Press, 1957, 1966.

Howard, Ruth Winifred (1900–1997)
DEVELOPMENTAL PSYCHOLOGY

Born in Washington, D.C., the daughter of a Baptist minister, Ruth Winifred Howard was the first African American woman to complete a doctorate in psychology. She graduated in social work in 1921 from Simmons College, Boston, then earned her master's degree in 1927 and her Ph.D. in 1934 from the University of Minnesota, Minneapolis, where her mentor was Dr. Florence Goodenough (see entry).

She began social work practice through the Cleveland Urban League, then with the Cleveland Child Welfare Agency, where she worked with children living in dysfunctional family situations or foster homes. The lack of understanding of the needs of the black community among people in schools and medical and child clinics spurred her on to pursue a career in psychology. Her doctoral research was a study of the developmental history of 229 sets of triplets ranging in age from early infancy up to 79 years, the most comprehensive study of triplets of its time.

At Minnesota she registered at the Institute of Child Development. Sometime after 1934 she married psychologist Albert Sidney Beckham (who died in 1964) and the couple moved to Chicago. She was a psychologist for Chicago's Provident Hospital School of Nursing while consulting schools in Kansas City and Jacksonville. In Chicago, she completed an internship at the Illinois Institute of Juvenile Research, which prepared her for subsequent clinical work with children and young people. She also worked at a community hospital and state school for delinquent girls.

Following her internship, she became a supervisor at the National Youth Administration and, with her husband, began a private practice. Howard pursued postdoctoral studies at the University of Chicago, where she studied projective techniques with Dr. Robert Havighurst (see entry); client-centered therapy with Dr. Carl Rogers (see entry); reading therapy with Dr. Helen Robinson; and play therapy with Virginia Axline. In 1944, Howard published her own study of play interviews with kindergartners and fourth-graders, focusing on how these play interviews could be used to detect war attitudes.

She helped organize the National Association of College Women and joined the American Psychological Association, the International Psychological Association, the International Council of Women Psychologists, the Women's International League for Peace and Freedom, and the Friends of the Mentally Ill. In addition, she was a long time volunteer for the Young Women's Christian Association and Bartelme Homes for juvenile girls. She consulted for children's programs at the Abraham Lincoln Center for Character Development,

Wheaton, Illinois, and served as psychologist for the McKinley Center for Retarded Children (1964–66) and the Chicago Board of Health, Mental Health Division (1968–1972).

Major Literature

Howard, Ruth Winifred. "Fantasy and Play Interview." *Character and Personality* 13 (1944): 151–165.
___. "Intellectual and Personality Traits of a Group of Triplets." *Journal of Psychology* 21 (1946): 25–36.
___. "The Developmental History of a Group of Triplets." *Journal of Genetic Psychology* 70 (1947): 191–204.

Howes, Ethel Dench Puffer
(1872–1950)
SEXUAL EQUALITY

Ethel Puffer was born in Framingham, Massachusetts, and graduated from Smith College, Northampton, Massachusetts (1891). She took a teaching job at Keene High School, Keene, New Hampshire, then taught mathematics for three years at Smith College. In 1895 she went to the University of Berlin, where she experienced sex discrimination against women in psychology. While there she met Hugo Munsterberg (see entry) and in 1896 attended Freiberg University working with Munsterberg in his laboratory. She followed him to Harvard, Boston, Massachusetts to work for her Ph.D. But again, being a women she experienced the same sex discrimination and was officially considered a Radcliffe College student.

She received her Ph.D. from Radcliffe College, Massachusetts, in 1902 and stayed in the Boston area and taught at Radcliffe, Wellesley College, Massachusetts, and Simmons College, Boston. In 1908 she married Benjamin Howes. She saw society as the cause of discrimination, and in 1925, working out of Smith College, she founded and was the director of the Institute for the Coordination of Women's Interests, funded for three years by the Laura Spelman Rockefeller Fund.

The institute's interests dealt with domestic responsibilities, mostly with researching families through demonstration programs. The aims of the institute were to bring about change in society's attitudes toward men and women and to accept the twofold need of women — marriage and career. Her message was that every woman should have the right to marry and go on with her job; "the right" meaning a fair field and no disfavor from administrators, employers of whatever type, or from her social fellows. Not only is it the right, but it is the need, of every human being to live a normal, emotional life and to fully develop latent powers, and that whether in personal relationships or in profession, women and men should be treated equally.

In her article "Continuity for Women," Howes stated that women should strive to replace the notion "career woman" with the idea of "contributing professional." Howes gained credence for her ideas in that she was a mother as well as a professional woman.

Major Literature

Howes, Ethel Puffer. *The Psychology of Beauty*. Boston, Massachusetts: Houghton Mifflin, 1905.
___. "Accepting the Universe." *Atlantic Monthly* 129 (1922): 444–453.
___. "Continuity for Women." *Atlantic Monthly* 130 (1922): 731–739.
___. "True and Substantial Happiness." *Women's Home Companion,* December 1923.
___, and Dorthea Beach. "The Cooperative Nursery School: What it Can Do for the Parents." *Institute for the Coordination of Women's Interests* No. 3: (1928).
Howes, Ethel Puffer. "The Meaning of Progress in the Women's Movement." *Annals of the American Academy of Political and Social Science* 143 (1929): 14–20.
___. "The Golden Age." *Radcliffe Quarterly* 21 (1937): 14–16.

Hull, Clark Leonard (1884–1952)

DRIVE REDUCTION THEORY

Born in Akron, New York, Clark Leonard Hull gained a B.A. at the University of Michigan, Ann Arbor (1913) and a Ph.D. in psychology from the University of Wisconsin, Madison (1918). At Yale University, New Haven, Connecticut (1920–1952), he rose from assistant professor to Sterling Professor of psychology. In 1936 Hull was president of the American Psychological Association.

Major Contributions

Although one of Hull's first experiments was an analytical study of the effects of tobacco on behavioral efficiency, his life long emphasis was on the development of objective methods for psychological studies designed to determine the underlying principles of behavior. Hull was a primary representative of the neo-behaviorist school. (The neo-behaviorists bridged the gap between behaviorism and cognitive theories of learning.)

His experimental studies on learning attempted to put psychology on a par with such an exact science as geometry. He was also the first known psychologist to apply quantitative experimental methods to the phenomena of hypnosis. The basic concept of his theory of learning was "habit strength," which was said to develop as a function of practice. According to Hull, responses (rather than perceptions or expectancies) participate in habit formation; the process is gradual, and reward is an essential condition.

A major influence in learning is practice. But practice alone does not make perfect; psychological feedback is also necessary. The consensus among theoreticians is that feedback must be relevant and reinforcing to effect permanent increments of habit strength. Once developed, habit never dies; it does not even fade away. Hull took certain ideas on conditioning from Ivan Pavlov (see entry) and also borrowed from American psychologists, including John B. Watson (see entry), who emphasized the objective study of behavior, and Edward L. Thorndike (see entry), who asserted the importance of reinforcement in learning — the tendency for an association to be made is strengthened when reinforcement is given, that is, when the response reduces a physiological or psychological need.

On the other hand, Hull hypothesized that animals would learn more quickly the stronger the physiological need or drive and the more immediate the reward or reinforcement; this he later confirmed by experiment. Complex behavior could be explained by a series of such simple response mechanisms. Hull believed that psychology had its own quantitative laws that could be stated in mathematical equations. His lasting legacy to psychology is his approach to the study of behavior rather than the specifics of his theories.

Major Literature

Hull, Clark Leonard. "Quantitative Aspects of the Evolution of Concepts: An Experimental Study." *Psychological Monographs* 28, 123, 1920.
___. "A Functional Interpretation of the Conditioned Reflex." *Psychological Review* 26 (1929): 498–511.
___. *Hypnosis and Suggestibility: An Experimental Approach.* New Jersey: Appleton-Century-Crofts, 1933. Bancyfelin Carmarthen, South Wales: Crown House Publishing, 2002.
___. "Mind, Mechanism, and Adaptive Behavior." *Psychological Review* 44 (1937): 1–32.
___. *Essentials of Behavior.* New Haven, Connecticut: Yale University Press, 1951.
___. *A Behavior System.* New Haven, Connecticut: Yale University Press, 1952.

Humphrey, Jeanne Block
(1923–1981)
EGO DEVELOPMENT

Jeanne Block Humphrey, born in Tulsa, Oklahoma, was commissioned an ensign in SPARS, the women's unit of the Coast Guard, in 1944. In 1945 she nearly died from serious scalds but returned to active service after many painful skin grafts. She graduated with honors in psychology (1947) from Reed College, Portland, Oregon. While studying clinical psychology for her Ph.D. at Stanford University, California, under Earnest Hilgard (see entry) she met Jack Block, a fellow psychology student; they presented joint doctoral theses, married in 1950, and Humphrey completed her thesis in 1951, pregnant with her first baby.

Part of her work was in the Department of Psychiatry at the University of California Medical School on the study of the comparison of parents with schizophrenic children and the parents of neurotic children. She also studied the psychopathology of allergic predisposition in childhood asthma at the Children's Hospital of the East Bay, Oakland, California.

In 1963, she received the Special Research Fellowship from the National Institute of Mental Health, and for one year she and her family lived in Norway while she worked at the Norwegian Institute for Social Research, Oslo. She completed several studies comparing the socialization practices of Norway, Sweden, Denmark and Finland with America and England. In the process, she evolved her widely used assessment instrument, the Child-rearing Practices Report (CRPR), a set of items for the *Description of Parental Socialization Attitudes and Values*, published by the Institute of Human Development, University of California, Berkeley (1965).

In 1968, Humphrey received the National Institute of Mental Health Research Scientist Development Award. With her husband she started an ambitious longitudinal study of 130 children at ages three, four, five, seven, eleven, fourteen, and later including eighteen and twenty-three-year-olds. The purpose was to study the developmental of ego-control and ego resiliency; sex role development and gender differences; self-esteem; and parenting styles and their consequences.

She was a member of the National Institute of Mental Health Personality and Cognition Research Review Committee (1972–1975) and a member of the National Institute of Child Health and Development's Maternal and Child Health Research Review Committee (1977–1981). She received the Hofheimer Prize in 1974 (the American Psychiatric Association's most prestigious award for research on asthma). She was appointed adjunct professor of psychology at Berkeley in 1979 and elected fellow of the American Association of the Advancement of Science in 1980.

Major Literature

Haan, N., M.B. Smith, and Jean H. Block. "Moral Reasoning of Young Adults: Political-Social Behavior, Family Background, and Personality Correlates." *Journal of Personality and Social Psychology* 10 (1968): 183–201.

Block, Jean. H. "Parents of Schizophrenic, Neurotic, Asthmatic, and Congenitally Ill Children." *Archives of General Psychiatry* 20 (1969): 659–674.

Lippe, von der, A., and Jean H. Block. "Sex Role and Socialization Patterns: Some Personality Concomitants and Environmental Antecedents." *Journal of Consulting and Clinical Psychology* 41 (1973): 321–341.

Block, Jean H. *Sex Role Identity and Ego Development.* New Jersey: John Wiley and Sons, Inc., Jossey Bass Wiley, 1983.

Hunt, Joseph Mcvicker
(1906–1991)
DEVELOPMENTAL PSYCHOLOGY

Born Scottsbluff, Nebraska, Joseph Mcvicker Hunt gained a B.A. (1929) and an M.A. (1930) from University of Nebraska, Lincoln and a Ph.D. from Cornell University in Ithaca, New York (1933). From 1936 to 1946 he was instructor to associate professor at Brown University, Providence, Rhode Island, and research consultant, Institute of Welfare Research of the Community Service Society of New York (1944–1946) and director (1946–1951). He was professor of psychology (1951–1974) and professor emeritus (1974–1991) at the University of Illinois, Urbana, Champaign.

At the American Psychological Association (APA) he was on the board of directors (1949–1954), president (1951–1952), and member of the Council of Representatives (1967–1970).

Hunt's awards and honors include Research Career Award, National Institute of Mental Health (1962–1974); Gold Medal Award, American Psychological Foundation (1970); Distinguished Scholar Award, Hofstra College, Hempstead, New York (1973); Distinguished Contribution Award, Clinical Division, APA (1973); and G. Stanley Hall Award, Developmental Division, APA (1976).

Major Contributions

Inspired by Sigmund Freud (see entry) on the importance of early experience, Hunt carried out a series of feeding-frustration studies, which demonstrated that rats who had been deprived in infancy hoarded food as adults. As director of the Institute of Welfare Research, Hunt focused on the effects of social case work, and concluded that "talking therapy" was not of itself enough to cope with the problems seen in patients. He believed that children who are reared in early-impoverished environments suffer from intellectual deficit.

Intelligence and Experience, a landmark book that argued against the traditional concept of fixed intelligence, was an important factor in persuading the Kennedy and Johnson administrations to make the Head Start program a part of the war on poverty in the U.S. The idea that intelligence can be developed provided programs like Head Start with the rationale they needed to develop interventions designed to maximize children's potential. Hunt chaired a White House task force on the government's role in early childhood education, resulting in extensions of Project Head Start to older children.

His study of orphaned children in Tehran, Iran, found that appropriate attention from caregivers can enable such children to attain normal development growth; they may even be slightly ahead of home-reared offspring of middle-class parents in the West.

Major Literature

Hunt, Joseph Mcvicker. "The Effects of Infant Feeding Frustration Upon Adult Hoarding in the Albino Rat." *Journal of Abnormal and Social Psychology* 36 (1941): 338–360.

___, and N.S. Endler. *Personality and the Behavior Disorders.* New York: Ronald Press, 1944. New Jersey: John Wiley and Sons, Inc., Rev. ed., 1984.

Hunt, Joseph Mcvicker. *Intelligence and Experience.* New York: Ronald Press, 1961.

___. *The Challenge of Incompetence and Poverty.* University of Illinois Press, 1969.

___. *Human Intelligence.* New Jersey: Transaction Books, 1972.

___, K. Mohandessi, M. Ghodssi, and M. Akiyama. "The Psychological Development of Orphanage-Reared Infants: Interventions with Outcomes." *Genetic Psychology Monographs* 94 (1976): 177–226.

Inhelder, Bärbel (1913–1997)

HUMAN INTELLIGENCE

Born in St. Gallen, Switzerland, Inhelder graduated with a B.A. from Rorschach Teacher's College, Switzerland (1932). Inhelder studied under Édouard Claparède and Jean Piaget (see entries) at the Institut Jean-Jacques Rousseau, Geneva, and was Piaget's volunteer assistant (1932–1938). She returned to St. Gallen in 1938 and set up the first Educational Testing Service of the Canton. She gained her Ph.D. (1943), then was appointed director of studies at Geneva, was full professor of child and adolescent psychology (1948 to 1971), and continued her collaboration with Piaget.

In 1961 she spent four months at the newly created Center of Cognitive Sciences at Harvard University, Cambridge, Massachusetts, run by Jerome Bruner (see entry). After Piaget's retirement in 1971, she was professor of genetic and experimental psychology until 1983, when she retired from teaching but not from scientific work.

In 1974 Inhelder created the Jean Piaget Archives Foundation, aimed at gathering all of Piaget's publications as well as all researches inspired by him. She was the first director and then chair of the scientific committee. Inhelder was awarded several scientific distinctions and prizes, as well as a dozen honorary degrees from various universities all over the world.

Major Contributions

When working with children with learning difficulties, Inhelder rejected the traditional intelligence test. Through her analysis of these children she found that they follow the same developmental pattern as fully functioning children, just at a slower rate. In the late 1960s she started working on learning and cognitive structures, and during the seventies, she directed an intercultural research project in West Africa using Piagetian tasks to study the development of Baoulé (Ivory Coast) children.

In her retirement she undertook experimental work on children's strategies in problem solving. While studying the development of the experimental method in children and adolescents, with a team of young and talented researchers, she discovered the stage of formal operations. She investigated the transition of thought that occurs between childhood and adolescence, which involves the emergence of experimental or inductive thinking. She and her colleagues found that when children were in a transition between stages, training the children on concepts related to the next stage of development was successful in facilitating the promotion to the next stage.

Major Literature

Inhelder, Bärbel. *Diagnosis and Reasoning in the Mentally Retarded.* New York: John Day, 1943.

___, and Jean Piaget. *The Psychology of the Child.* London: Routledge and Kegan Paul, 1966.

Inhelder, Bärbel. *Early Growth of Logic in the Child.* New York: W.W. Norton and Co. Ltd., 1969.

___, H. Sinclair and M. Bovet. *Learning and the Development of Cognition.* Cambridge, Massachusetts: Harvard University Press, 1974.

Inhelder, Bärbel, and Jean Piaget. *The Growth of Logical Thinking from Childhood to Adolescence: An Essay on the Construction of Formal Operational Structures.* International Library of Psychology. London, England: Taylor and Francis Books Ltd., Brunner/Mazel, 1999.

Irigaray, Luce (1930–)
FEMINISM

Luce Irigaray is a Belgian-born French feminist, psychoanalyst and philosopher who has examined the uses and misuses of language in relation to women. She received her master's degree (1955) from the University of Louvain, Belgium, taught high school in Brussels (1956–1959), and gained her master's degree in psychology (1961) and her diploma in psychopathology from the University of Paris (1962). From 1962 to 1964 she worked for the Fondation Nationale de la Recherche Scientifique in Belgium. After this she began work as a research assistant at the Centre National de la Recherche Scientifique in Paris.

She trained as a psychoanalyst and received her doctorate in linguistics in 1968. Irigaray was a member of the Freudian School of Paris, founded by Jacques Lacan (see entry) and taught at the University of Vincennes, Paris, from 1968 until she was dismissed in 1974. Her second doctoral thesis, *Speculum de l'autre femme* (*Speculum of the Other Woman*), argues that history and culture are written in patriarchal language, that they exclude women's needs and desires, and that the thinking of Sigmund Freud was based on hatred of women. Irigary made the point that the male-centered society cannot accept sexual difference and the existence of a different female perspective.

Major Contributions

Although obviously a feminist, Iragary has resisted all attempts to get her to align herself with any one group. She has been involved in demonstrations for contraception and abortion rights, has given seminars and has been a speaker at conferences throughout Europe. In the second semester of 1982, Irigaray held the chair in philosophy at the Erasmus University in Rotterdam. Research here resulted in the publication of *An Ethics of Sexual Difference*, establishing Irigaray as a major Continental philosopher.

She is an interdisciplinary thinker who works between philosophy, psychoanalysis, and linguistics. She is currently director of research at the Centre National de Recherche Scientifique, where her more recent work is on the difference between the language of women and the language of men. Her work has generated productive discussions about how to define femininity and sexual difference, what strategies should be employed, and assessing the risks involved. Irigaray offers suggestions for changing contemporary attitudes toward women in Western culture: through art and nature (mimesis), how women present themselves (strategic essentialism), idealism and perfection (utopian ideals), and using examples of oppression from history.

Major Literature

Irigaray, Luce, et al. *This Sex Which is Not One.* New York: Cornell University Press, 1985.

___. *Speculum of the Other Woman.* New York: Cornell University Press, 1985.

___, and Alison Martin. *Je, Tu, Nous: Towards a Culture of Difference Thinking Gender.* London, England: Taylor and Francis Books Ltd., Routledge, 1993.

Irigaray, Luce. *To Speak is Never Neutral.* Athlone Contemporary European Thinkers Series. London: Continuum International Publishing Group, Mansell, 2002.

___. *An Ethics of Sexual Difference.* New York: Cornell University Press, 1993. Continuum Impacts Series. London, England: Continuum International Publishing Group-Academic, 2004.

Jackson, Donald De Avila (1920–1968)
CON-JOINT FAMILY THERAPY

Donald De Avila Jackson graduated from Stanford Medical School (1944) and was chief of neurology for the U.S. Army, Letterman Hospital, San Francisco, California. In 1947, he entered training at Washington School of Psychiatry and Chestnut Lodge under the tutelage of Harry Stack Sullivan, Freda Fromm-Reichmann (see entries), and other leaders in interpersonal psychiatry.

In 1951 he started private practice in Palo Alto and was training interns at the Menlo Park Veterans Hospital, California; he began to experiment with seeing a schizophrenic patient conjointly, first with the young adult and her mother, then later with the mother, father, and young adult. Jackson was invited by Gregory Bateson (see entry) in 1954 to join his research group as a consultant. He was co-founder with Virginia Satir (see entry) of the Mental Research Institute in Menlo Park, California (1958).

In 1962, Jackson received the Freda Fromm-Reichmann Award for his contribution toward understanding schizophrenia; he was named Salmon Lecturer by the American Psychiatric Association and the New York Academy of Medicine (1967), and named one of the top ten most influential psychiatrists of his era by his peers in the field of psychiatry and the behavioral sciences (1970).

Major Contributions

"Conjoint family therapy" is a term coined by Jackson to characterize therapy in which two or more people who are vitally important to one another are seen simultaneously in therapy. Jackson will be remembered for the contributions he made to family theory — family homeostasis, family rules, and the concept of the double bind, with Gregory Bateson (see entry). Family therapy is a talking treatment given to the family of a person with schizophrenia; it aims to reduce the hostility within that family, may include education, and is usually given as an adjunct to drug treatment. Family therapy may work by reducing such expressed emotions as hostility and criticism in the relatives of people with schizophrenia, or may act by improving concordance with medication.

Although influenced by Harry Stack Sullivan, Jackson differed in approach. Sullivan developed his interpersonal theory while working with mentally ill individuals in isolation from their families. In contrast, Jackson extended Sullivan's theory by focusing on the actual relationship between one individual and other individuals, particularly family relationships.

Major Literature

Jackson, Donald D. *The Etiology of Schizophrenia*. Jackson, Tennessee: Basic Books, 1960.
___. *Myths of Madness: New Facts for old Fallacies*. New York: Macmillan, 1964.
Haas, Albert, and Donald D. Jackson. *Bulls, Bears and Dr. Freud*. Cleveland and New York: World Publishing, 1967.
Watzlawick, Paul, Janet Helmick Beavin, and Donald D. Jackson. *Pragmatics of Human Communication: A Study of Interactional Patterns, Pathologies and Paradoxes*. New York: W.W. Norton and Co. Ltd., 1967.

Jackson, Donald D. *Communication, Family and Marriage*, 2 volumes. Palo Alto, California: Science and Behavior Books, 1968.
Lederer, William J., and Donald D. Jackson. *Mirages Of Marriage*. New York: W.W. Norton and Co. Ltd., 1968.

Jackson, John Hughlings (1835–1911)
CLINICAL NEUROLOGY

Born in Green Hammerton, Yorkshire, England, John Hughlings Jackson was physician to the London Hospital (1859–1894) and gained an M.D. at St. Andrews University, Scotland (1860). He was a member of the Royal College of Physicians London (1861) and from 1862 to 1906, he worked at the National Hospital for Paralysis and Epilepsy, now the National Hospital for Neurology and Neurosurgery, London. Jackson was fellow of the Royal College of Physicians in London (1868); fellow, Royal Society (1878); president, Pathology and Bacteriology Section, British Medical Association (1882); first president, Neurological Society (1885); and president, Opthalmological Society (1890).

His awards include the Moxon Gold Medal, Royal College of Physicians (1903); LL.D., Universities of Glasgow and Edinburgh; D.Sc., University of Leeds; D.M., University of Bologna; honorary FRCP, Ireland; and corresponding member, Royal Academy of Medicine, Belgium.

Major Contributions

Hughlings Jackson, the "father of English neurology," was one of the founders of *Brain: Journal of Neurology* (1878), now in its 129th volume. He is best remembered for his influential contributions to the diagnosis and understanding of all forms of epilepsy. Jackson's wife suffered from epilepsy; observation of her seizures showed him that they followed a certain pattern and affected the same parts of the body. He described this form of epilepsy associated with localized convulsive seizures, now known as Jacksonian epilepsy or Jacksonian seizures.

Jackson believed that seizures were electrical discharges within the brain, with the discharges starting at one point and radiating out from that point. This suggested to him that the brain was divided into different sections, and that each section controlled the motor function (or movement) of a different part of the body. He also investigated temporal lobe epilepsy. This activity does not cause *grand mal* seizures; rather, it causes unusual behaviors and patterns of cognition, and may cause sudden outbursts of unexpected aggression or agitation, or it may be characterized by aura-like phenomena.

In 1864 Jackson confirmed the discovery by Paul Broca, a French surgeon, that the speech center of right-handed persons is located in the left cerebral hemisphere, and vice versa, by finding that, in most cases, he was able to associate aphasia (a speech disorder) in right-handed persons with disease of the left cerebral hemisphere. From 1870 to 1900 Jackson developed the thesis that psychiatric symptoms are a repression from higher functions that are the products of evolution. He also contributed to the discussion of whether sleep disturbance causes mental disorders or vice versa; he suggested (before the influential work on dreams by Sigmund Freud) that if the psychiatrist found out about the patient's dreams he would find out about psychosis.

Jackson wrote no books but contributed over 300 articles on such disparate subjects as syphilis, vertigo, chorea, tobacco smoking and the psychology of joking.

Related Literature

York, George K. and David A. Steinberg. *An Introduction to the Life and Work of John Hughlings Jackson with a descriptive Catalogue of His Writings.* London, England: Wellcome Institute for the History of Medicine, 2006.

James, William (1842–1910)
PRAGMATISM AND FUNCTIONALISM

Born in New York City, William James was educated by tutors and at private schools in New York. The family moved between America and Europe, where young James studied science and painting. He studied at Lawrence Scientific School at Harvard University, Cambridge, Massachusetts (1861), and at Harvard School of Medicine, Boston, Massachusetts (1864). He joined the 1865 Amazon expedition and contracted a mild form of smallpox. He returned to medical school, but suffered eye strain, back problems, and suicidal depression.

He studied physiology, philosophy and psychology in Germany (1866). He qualified for an M.D. (1869) but never practiced; he taught an undergraduate course in comparative physiology at Harvard (1872). Between 1874 and 1875, James established the first American psychology laboratory, at Harvard. From 1880 until he resigned in 1907, he was assistant professor of philosophy at Harvard.

Major Contributions

James was one of the principle figures in developing the philosophy of pragmatism, a term first used by the American logician C.S. Peirce. Pragmatism holds that the function of thought is to guide action, and that truth is pre-eminently to be tested by the practical consequences of belief. James was one of the most influential thinkers of his time and advanced the principle of functionalism in psychology.

He was influential in removing psychology as a branch of philosophy and establishing it among the laboratory sciences based on experimental method. Functionalism emphasized such techniques as human intelligence tests and controlled experiments designed to test the ability of animals to learn and solve problems. This type of investigation represented a clear break with the introspective methods favored by other 19th-century psychologists. Functionalism is no longer regarded as a separate psychological doctrine, but its viewpoint has had a lasting influence on such fields of modern applied psychology as intelligence and aptitude testing (see entry for James Rowland Angell for definitions of functionalism and structuralism).

James applied his empirical methods of investigation to philosophical and religious issues. He explored the questions of the existence of God, the immortality of the soul, free will, and ethical values by referring to human religious and moral experience. For James, the meaning of ideas is found only in terms of their possible consequences. If consequences are lacking, ideas are meaningless. Meaningful theories, James argued, are instruments for dealing with problems that arise in experience.

By the end of his life, James had become world-famous as a philosopher and psychologist. He was more an originator of new thought than a founder of dogmatic schools. His pragmatic philosophy was further developed by the American philosopher John Dewey (see entry) and others.

Major Literature

James, William. *Principles of Psychology.* New York: Henry Holt and Company, Inc., 1890.
___. *Pragmatism.* New York: Longmans Green, 1907, 1979.
___. *The Meaning of Truth.* New York: Longmans Green, 1909, 1979.

___. *Some Problems of Philosophy.* New York: Longmans Green, 1911, 1979. Boston, Massachusetts: Adamant Media Corporation, 2005.
___. *The Works of William James*, 17 volumes. Cambridge, Massachusetts: Harvard University Press, 1975.

Jamison, Kay Redfield (1946–)
BIPOLAR DISORDER

The daughter of an Air Force officer, Jamison was brought up in the Washington, D.C., area and in Los Angeles. She gained a B.A., M.A. (1971) and a candidate in philosophy (C.Phil.) (1973) from the University California Los Angeles (UCLA). She joined the faculty of UCLA in 1974; her clinical psychology internship (1973–1974) was at UCLA-Neuro Psychiatric Institute and she gained her Ph.D. in 1975. She later founded the UCLA Affective Disorders Clinic, which became a large teaching and research facility. She also studied zoology and neurophysiology at the University of St. Andrews in Scotland.

She has received numerous awards and in 2002 she was one of 23 people to receive a $500,000, "no-strings-attached" fellowship from the John D. and Catherine T. MacArthur Foundation. She was selected as UCLA Woman of Science, has been named one of the "Best Doctors in the United States," and was chosen by *Time* magazine as a "Hero of Medicine." She was also chosen as one of the five individuals for the public television series "Great Minds of Medicine." She is professor of psychiatry at the Johns Hopkins University School of Medicine, Baltimore, Maryland, and is an honorary professor of English at the University of St. Andrews, Scotland.

Major Contributions

With Frederick K. Goodwin (see entry) Jamison co-authored *Manic-Depressive Illness*, the standard medical text on the illness. It was chosen in 1990 as the "Most Outstanding Book in Biomedical Sciences" by the American Association of Publishers. "This book ... offers the most comprehensive review to date of all information on the disease and all aspects of treatment, including medical—acute and prophylactic—and the role of psychotherapy." (H.J. Kaplan and B.J. Sadock [Eds.]. *Comprehensive Textbook of Psychiatry,* 6th ed. Baltimore, Maryland: Williams and Wilkins, 1995, p. 2797.)

Her memoir about her own experiences with manic-depressive illness, *An Unquiet Mind*, was on the *New York Times* Bestseller List for more than five months and was translated into fifteen languages. Her most recent book, *Night Falls Fast: Understanding Suicide*, was a national bestseller, translated into twelve languages, and selected by *The New York Times* as a "Notable Book of 1999." She is involved in suicide prevention, and her work now focuses on genetic research and psychological aspects of mania.

Major Literature

Goodwin, F.K., and Kay Redfield Jamison. *Manic-Depressive Illness.* New York: Oxford University Press, 1990.
Jamison, Kay Redfield. *Touched With Fire: Manic Depressive Illness and the Artistic Temperament.* New York: Simon and Schuster, 1993.
___. *An Unquiet Mind: A Memoir of Moods and Madness.* New York: Alfred A. Knopf, 1995.
___, and Thomas C. Caramagno. *The Flight of the Mind: Virginia Woolf's Art and Manic-Depressive Illness.* Berkeley, California: University of California Press, 1996.
Jamison, Kay Redfield. *Night Falls Fast: Understanding Suicide.* New York: Alfred A. Knopf, 1999.
___. *Exuberance: The Passion for Life.* New York: Alfred A. Knopf, 2004.

Janet, Pierre (1859–1947)
PATHOLOGICAL PSYCHOLOGY

A French psychologist and neurologist, from childhood Pierre Janet was interested in the natural sciences. Being of a religious disposition and the nephew of a distinguished philosopher, Janet studied philosophy. It was his uncle Paul who encouraged him to study medicine. He was appointed professor of philosophy at the Lycée at Havre (1881) and worked as teacher in the lycées of Châteauroux and Havre (1882–1889). He became Dr. ès lettres in 1889 and director of the psychological laboratory at the Salpêtrière, the largest Paris mental institution. There he completed his work for his M.D., which he received for the thesis *L'état mental des hystériques* in 1892.

In 1898 Janet was appointed lecturer in psychology at the Sorbonne, and in 1902 he succeeded Theodule Ribot (see entry) in the chair of experimental and comparative psychology at the Collège de France, a position he held until 1936. He was a member of the Institut de France from 1913. In 1904, with his friend Georges Dumas (1866–1946), he founded the *Journal de psychologie normal et pathologique*, to which he contributed numerous articles.

Major Contributions

Janet was influential in bringing about in France and the United States a connection between academic psychology and the clinical treatment of mental illnesses. He introduced the words "dissociation" and "subconscious" into psychological terminology and attributed hysteria and hypnotic susceptibility to inherited dispositions toward imbalances in psychic energy and psychic tension.

It was to hypnosis that Janet was drawn, following on the work of Jean-Martin Charcot (see entry), and to the study of neuroses. He contributed to the modern concept of mental and emotional disorders involving anxiety, phobias, and other abnormal behavior. Janet originated the concept of *dissociation,* where under certain conditions some thoughts, feelings and actions become split off, or dissociated, from the rest of consciousness and function outside of awareness or voluntary control, or both.

This concept has become the cornerstone of what was known as multiple personality disorder (MPD), now known as dissociative identity disorder (DID). In his numerous case histories, Janet demonstrated the role of memories in the origins of the mind and in the treatment of hysterical disorders. (In the *Diagnostic and Statistical Manual of Mental Disorders* [DSM-IV] and the *ICD-10 Classification of Mental and Behavioral Disorders* [ICD-10], the term hysteria has been replaced with somatoform disorder.)

His writings had a profound influence in France, Britain, and the United States. Josef Breuer and Sigmund Freud (see entries) credit Janet and other Parisian dissociationists with some of the fundamental discoveries that made their *Studies on Hysteria* possible. Janet saw "somnambulism" as the essential condition of which hysteria, hypnosis, multiple personality, and spiritualism were variations.

Major Literature

Janet, Pierre. *Psychological Healing: A Historical and Clinical Study.* 2 vols. London, England: Hodder and Stoughton, 1919. (Classics in Psychiatry.) Manchester, New Hampshire: Ayer Co. Publishers, 1976.
Janet, Pierre: *The Mental State of Hystericals.* New York: G.P. Putnam's Sons (French, 1892–1894; English, 1901.) Westport, Connecticut: University Publications of America, 1977.

Janis, Irving Lester (1918–1990)
GROUPTHINK

Born in Buffalo, New York, Janis gained a B.S. at the University of Chicago, Illinois (1939) and a Ph.D. from the University of Columbia, New York (1948). He was adjunct professor, University of Berkeley, California, and professor emeritus, Yale University, New Haven, Connecticut. His awards and honors include Fulbright Award, University of Oslo (1957–1958); Hofheimer Prize, American Psychiatric Association (1959); Socio-Psychological Prize, American Association for the Advancement of Science (1967); Kurt Lewin Memorial Award for Research in Social Psychology, American Psychological Association (APA) Division 9 (1985); and Distinguished Scientific Contributions Award, APA.

His fellowships include the Center for Advanced Study in the Behavioral Sciences (1973–1974); Guggenheim (1974–1974); and senior fellowship, Netherlands Institute for Advanced Study in the Social Services and Humanities (1981–1982). He was on the editorial boards of the *Journal of Experimental Social Psychology; American Scientist; Journal of Conflict Resolution* (chairman); and *British Journal of Social Psychology* (overseas editorial board). He was associate editor, *Journal of Behavioral Medicine.*

Major Contributions

Janis and Carl Iver Hovland (see entry) worked together on communication and attitude change. Janis's research included pioneering work on the effects of fear. *Psychological Stress* presents systematic data and case study observations on reactions of patients awaiting major surgery. Three patterns emerged:

1. *Excessive worry before surgery.* Wanted to postpone the operation. More likely than the other two groups to be anxiety-ridden postoperatively.
2. *Moderate worry before surgery.* Asked for realistic information, focused on realistic threats rather than on imaginary fears. Less likely than group one to display emotional disturbance postoperatively.
3. *Little fear before surgery.* Cheerful, optimistic, denied feeling worried. Gave the impression of being totally invulnerable. Their vulnerability showed after the operation. More likely than the other two groups to display anger and resentment toward the staff. They complained and were uncooperative.

Late in the 1950s Janis focused on real-life personal health decisions. *Counseling on Personal Decisions* presents the theory and reports twenty-three controlled field experiments that help to explain when, how and why people succeed in adhering to difficult decisions, such as going on a diet, as a consequence of verbal interchanges with a counselor. Janis also developed the theory of groupthink, the phenomenon whereby individuals intentionally conform to what they perceive as the consensus of the group. Groupthink may cause the group (typically a committee or large organization) to make bad or irrational decisions that each member might individually consider to be unwise.

Major Literature

Janis, Irving Lester. *Psychological Stress.* New Jersey: John Wiley and Sons, Inc., 1958.
___. "Effectiveness of Emotional Role Playing in Modifying Smoking Habits and Attitudes." *Journal of Experimental Research in Personality* 1 (1965): 84–90.
___. *Stress and Frustration.* New York: Harcourt, Brace and Company, 1971.
___, et al *Counseling on Personal Decisions: Theory and Research on Short-Term Helping Relationships.* New Haven, Connecticut: Yale University Press, 1982.
Janis, Irving Lester. *Groupthink: Psychological Studies of Policy Decisions and Fiascos.* Boston, Massachusetts: Houghton Mifflin, 1982.
___. "International Crisis Management in the Nuclear Age." In S. Oskamp, ed. *Applied Psychology Annual,* Vol. 6. New York: Russell Sage Foundation, 1986.

Janov, Arthur (1924–)

PRIMAL THERAPY

Born in Los Angeles, Arthur Janov gained his B.A. and master's degree in psychiatric social work from the University of California, Los Angeles, and his Ph.D. in psychology from Claremont Graduate School, California. He worked for the Veterans Administration at Brentwood Neuropsychiatric Hospital and was in private practice from 1952 till 1967. He was also on the staff of the Psychiatric Department at Los Angeles Children's Hospital, where he was involved in developing their psychosomatic unit.

In the mid–1960s, he discovered primal therapy (PT) when a male client, lying on the floor, uttered a piercing scream that seemed to come the depths of his unconscious. Janov has treated thousands of clients and conducted extensive research to support his thesis — that both physical and psychic ailments can be linked to early trauma.

He concludes that PT can dramatically reduce such debilitating medical problems as depression, anxiety, insomnia, alcoholism, drug addiction, heart disease and many other serious diseases. *The Primal Scream* (1970) has since sold more than a million copies worldwide. Primal therapy was never "screaming" therapy; it encourages clients to tap into the pain of trauma. Sometimes the person will sob; not everybody screams. Janov is the founder and director of the Primal Center in Venice, California.

Major Contributions

Several universities in America, Denmark, and England have examined his results and supported his theory that PT can produce measurable positive effects on the function of the human brain and body. PT deals with "primal pain" arising from the "major primal scene"— the infantile experience, or fantasy about, parental intercourse — and helps clients to recognize and then express their deepest feelings about their parents and their primal traumas.

"Primal trauma" refers to some painful experience: the experience of birth, an especially severe punishment, the death of a parent, the primal scene, or the knowledge of not being loved. The theory is that the pain of the trauma experienced before, during and in the early months after birth, is kept from conscious awareness, but at the cost of neurotic symptoms and psychological disorders in later life.

In summary, PT deals with the traumas of conception, implantation (the struggle of the fertilized ovum to implant itself on the wall of the womb), birth and infancy. It consists of helping the client through catharsis to unblock repressed, painful feelings and relive primal scenes until the "primal pool" has been systematically emptied; dismantling the defenses to leave only a "real self."

Major Literature

Janov, Arthur. *The Anatomy of Mental Illness.* New York: G.P. Putnam's Sons, 1971.
___, and E.M. Holden (Eds.). *Primal Man: The New Consciousness.* London, England: Time Warner Books, Abacus, 1975.
Janov, Arthur. *The New Primal Scream.* London, England: Time Warner Books, Abacus, 1991.
___. *The Biology of Love.* Loughton, Essex, England: Prometheus Books, 2000.
___. *Primal Healing: Access the Incredible Power of Feelings to Improve Your Health.* Franklin Lakes, New Jersey: New Page Books, 2006.

Jaspers, Karl Theodor (1883–1969)

EXISTENTIALIST PSYCHOTHERAPY

Born in Oldenburg, Germany, Karl Theodor Jaspers studied law at the universities of Heidelberg and Munich, then medicine at the universities of Berlin, Göttingen, and Heidelberg, and registered as a doctor in 1909. From 1909 to 1915 Jaspers was a research assistant at the University of Heidelberg psychiatric clinic under Franz Nissl.

Unorthodox in his approach, he studied psychiatry in his own time and in his own way, choosing the patients to work with; this was allowed only because he agreed to work without a salary. Diagnosis was of paramount importance; therapy was largely neglected. Jaspers brought the methods of phenomenology — the direct investigation and description of phenomena as consciously experienced, without theories about their causal explanation — into the field of clinical psychiatry.

Between 1913 and 1922 he was assistant professor in psychology, assistant professor in philosophy, then professor in philosophy at University of Heidelberg. Because his wife was Jewish, Jaspers qualified as an enemy of the Nazi state, and from 1933 he was gradually excluded from university life. After the war Jaspers devoted himself to rebuilding Heidelberg University and helping to bring about a moral and political rebirth of the people. From 1948 he was professor in philosophy in Basel, Switzerland, and in 1967 he took out Swiss citizenship.

Major Contributions

Although Japers is possibly better known for his existential philosophy, this section will consider only his contribution to existential psychotherapy; Jaspers rejected any attempt to label him an existentialist. Other significant figures in existential psychotherapy are Ludwig Binswanger, Medard Boss, Victor Frankl, R.D. Laing, Rollo May (see entries), and Irvin Yalom.

Enshrined in this approach is a belief in the individual's capacity to become healthy and fully functional, to rise above self through self-consciousness and self-reflection. This is achieved as the client concentrates on what is happening in the present; accepting that what happens in life is partly his or her personal responsibility and influenced by decisions. Existentially oriented psychotherapists concern themselves with how the client experiences life rather than with diagnosis and cause.

Existentialism is similar to humanistic therapies, although it may be more confronting. It is the opposite of the more technical, behavioral and strategy-dominated therapies. Psychoanalysis, conversely, concentrates on cause and effect and on trying to reduce complicated patterns to individual parts. Existential psychotherapy is an attempt to grapple with the meaninglessness and extinction that threaten present-day societies.

Major Literature

Jaspers, Karl. *General Psychopathology* Volumes 1 and 2 (translated to English by J. Hoenig McHugh and Marian W. Hamilton). Baltimore, Maryland: Johns Hopkins University Press, 1913, 1997.
___. *Philosophy of Existence*. Philadelphia: University of Pennsylvania Press, 1971.
___. *The Question of German Guilt*. New York: Fordham University Press, 2000.
___. *Myth and Christianity: An Inquiry into the Possibility of Religion Without Myth*. Loughton, Essex, England: Prometheus Books, 2005.

Jastrow, Joseph (1833–1944)

OPTICAL ILLUSIONS

Born in Warsaw, Poland, son of Jewish scholar, Joseph Jastrow gained an A.B. (1882) and A.M. (1885) from the University of Pennsylvania, Philadelphia, and was a fellow in psychology (1885–1886) and gained a Ph.D. (1886) from Johns Hopkins University in Baltimore, Maryland. Jastrow founded the psychology department at the University of Wisconsin, Madison (1888), and was professor of psychology until 1927. From 1927 to 1933 he was lecturer at the New School for Social Research, New York City.

He was in charge of the psychological section of the Chicago World Exposition (1893); was president of the American Psychological Association (APA) (1900); wrote a daily newspaper column titled "Keeping Mentally Fit" (1928–1932) and lectured weekly over NBC radio from 1935 to 1938.

Major Contributions

In 1869, Jastrow accompanied William James (see entry) to the first International Congress of Psychology, held in Paris. They were the only two American academics in attendance, and this was the beginning of lasting friendship between the two men. Both Jastrow and James spent summers vacationing near each other on the coast of Maine. On those occasions both were under the care of the same physician for recurring depression, an illness that eventually caused Jastrow to leave teaching for a year (1894–1895).

In the 1890s, Jastrow introduced hypnosis research at Wisconsin and for years thereafter taught a medical hypnosis course in the university's medical school, and eventually turned that course over to Clark Hull (see entry).

Jastrow invented the "automatograph," a scientific-instrument version of the Ouija board. The automatograph was designed to study distinctions between voluntary and involuntary behavior. For instance, the automatic writing sometimes produced with hypnosis might be assessed for its essential characteristics with this instrument. With piles of squiggly records of unconscious hand movements, Jastrow claimed to have found important and revealing patterns.

He also worked on the phenomena of optical illusions. A number of well-known optical illusions were either discovered or popularized in his work. Jastrow taught his last course at Wisconsin in 1925. On September 28, 1988, psychologists trained at the University of Wisconsin returned to their alma mater in Madison to launch a three-day celebration of the Wisconsin psychology department's first century and to remember the two pioneers — Joseph Jastrow and Clark Hull.

Major Literature

Jastrow, Joseph. "Perception of Space by Disparate Senses." PhD. dissertation, Johns Hopkins University. *Mind* Vol. 2, 1886.

____. *Time Relations of Mental Phenomena*. New York: Hodges, 1890.

____. *Fact and Fable in Psychology*. New York: Houghton Mifflin, 1901.

____. *The Subconscious*. New York: Houghton Mifflin, 1906. Whitefish, Montana: R.A. Kessinger Publishing Co., 2005.

____. *Keeping Mentally Fit: A Guide to Everyday Psychology*. Garden City, New York: Garden City Publishing Co., 1928. Whitefish, Montana: R.A. Kessinger Publishing Co., 2003.

____. *The House That Freud Built*. Waukesha, Wisconsin: Greenberg Publishing, 1932.

____. *Freud: His Dream and Sex Theories*. England: Pocket Books; Thorpe and Porter, 1954.

Jaynes, Julian (1920–1997)

THE ORIGIN OF CONSCIOUSNESS

Born in West Newton, Massachusetts, Julian Jaynes received his bachelor's degree from McGill University in Montreal, Quebec, Canada, and master's and doctorate degrees from Yale Univer-

sity in New Haven, Connecticut. He lectured in the Psychology Department at Princeton University, New Jersey, from 1966 to 1990, as well as lecturing at other universities in North America and abroad. Jaynes was an associate editor of the internationally renowned journal *Behavioral and Brain Sciences* and on the editorial board of the *Journal of Mind and Behavior*.

Major Contributions

Jaynes published widely, his earlier work focusing on the study of animal behavior and ethology, which eventually led him to the study of human consciousness. The arguments created by his politically unacceptable, provocative and controversial book, *The Origin of Consciousness in the Breakdown of the Bicameral Mind* (a nominee for the National Book Award in 1978) tended to overshadow his other significant contributions to the study of animal learning.

The unusual scope of his book spanned psychology, anthropology, history, philosophy, religion, and literary studies. He argues that ancient peoples were not conscious as we consider the term today, and that the change of human thinking occurred over a period of centuries about three thousand years ago. Controversial though his theory was, he influenced, among others, the work of Steven Pinker (see entry). One reviewer wrote, "It's quite heavy going, and to review it properly I think you'd need a degree in psychology, another in ancient history and languages."

Jaynes's central idea is the minds of "preconscious" humans were split in two (the "bicameral mind"), probably as a result of a dissociation between the left and right hemispheres of the brain. In earlier times human mentality was characterized by auditory and sometimes visual hallucinations, in which people heard the voices of the gods speaking to them and ordering them what to do.

Jaynes finds evidence of this in Homer's *Iliad*, in which the characters continually receive orders and advice from various deities. The *Iliad*, Jaynes believes, stands at a watershed between two different types of human mentality and affords us an insight into an older mode of being. Only later, in the *Odyssey* do individuals begin to take responsibility for their own decisions and actions. With the breakdown of the bicameral mind came the "unicameral mind," and only when this process became internalized and recognized as coming from within the person's own minds did truly modern consciousness begin.

Leftovers of the bicameral mind today, according to Jaynes, include possession states, religious prophecy, hypnosis schizophrenia and the general sense of need for external authority in decision-making. Jaynes noted that many schizophrenics have "command hallucinations" wherein the "voices" command the schizophrenic to commit certain acts. In Jaynes' argument, these command hallucinations are little different from the commands from gods which feature so prominently in ancient stories. Continuing research has failed to either further confirm or refute the thesis.

Major Literature

Jaynes, Julian. *The Origin of Consciousness in the Breakdown of the Bicameral Mind.* Boston, Massachusetts: Houghton Mifflin, 1976. Houghton Mifflin, Mariner Books, 2000.
___. "The Evolution of Language in the Late Pleistocene." In S.R. Harnad, H.D. Steklis, and J. Lancaster, editors, *Origins and Evolution of Language and Speech.* Annals of the New York Academy of Sciences, Volume 280, 1977.

Jensen, Arthur Robert (1923–)
DEVELOPMENTAL PSYCHOLOGY

Born in San Diego to a Polish Jewish mother and a Danish father, Arthur Robert Jensen gained a B.A. at the University of California, Berkley (1945), an M.A. at San Diego State College, California (1952), and a Ph.D. from Columbia University, New York (1956).

Jenson was assistant in medical psychology at the University of Maryland Psychiatric Institute in Baltimore (1955–1956); research fellow, Institute of Psychiatry at the University of London (1956–1958); professor, University of California, Berkeley (1958–1992); and professor emeritus of educational psychology at Berkeley (since 1992). He was honored as one of the most eminent psychologists of the 20th century (2002) and awarded the Kistler Prize, Foundation for the Future (2003).

Major Contributions

Jensen did his post-doctoral research under Hans Eysenck (see entry) at the Institute of Psychiatry, University of London, and was influenced by Eysenck's quantitative and experimental approach to personality research. He has concentrated much of his work on the learning difficulties of culturally disadvantaged students, black, Mexican-American, and other minority-group school children. He worked on developing a series of "culturally-free" intelligence tests that could be administered in any language. He distinguished two separate types of learning ability (or intelligence). Level I, or associative learning, is simple retention of input (rote memorization of simple facts and skills). Level II, or conceptual learning, is roughly equivalent to the attribute measured by IQ tests, which is the ability to solve problems.

Statistical analysis of his findings led Jensen to conclude that Level I abilities were distributed equally among members of all races, but that Level II occurred with significantly greater frequency among whites than among blacks (and among Asians somewhat more than among whites). His findings convinced Jensen that Sir Cyril Burt (see entry) was correct — 80 percent of intelligence is based on heredity, and 20 percent on environment. (Although Jensen agreed with Burt on that issue, he criticized Burt's findings on twins.) Further, the genes for superior intelligence tend to be dominant.

His findings created a storm of protest, many people labeling him racist, particularly those who had invested heavily in Head Start programs. The violent reaction to his 1969 article led to students and faculty protests outside Jensen's office. He received death threats and the abusive term "Jensenian" was coined. Jensen said that he did not claim that blacks were deficient in intelligence, but that that at that time, no scientifically satisfactory explanation existed for the differences between the IQ distributions in the black and white populations.

Major Literature

Jensen, Arthur Robert. "How Much Can We Boost I.Q. and Scholastic Achievement?" *Harvard Educational Review* 39 (1969): 1–123.
___. *Genetics and Education.* New York: Harper Collins Publishers, Inc., 1973.
___. "The Relationship Between Learning and Intelligence." *Learning and Individual Differences* 1 (1989): 37–62.
___. "Psychological Research on Race Differences." *American Psychologist* 50 (1995): 41–42.
___. *The g Factor: The Science of Mental Ability.* Westport, Connecticut: Greenwood Press, 1998.
___. *Clocking the Mind: Mental Chronometry and Individual Differences.* London, England: Reed Elsevier Group, 2006.

Jones, Ernest (1879–1958)
APPLIED PSYCHOANALYSIS

Born in Rhosfelyn, Glamorgan, Wales, Ernest Jones graduated in medicine (1903), became a member of the Royal College of Physicians in London (1904), and held several successive hospital and clinical posts in that city. His career path to psychoanalysis was by way of clinical medicine, neurology and psychiatry. He met Carl Jung (see entry) in 1907 and in 1908 he traveled with Jung to the first historic congress of what became known as the International Psychoanalytic Association held in Salzburg. There he met Sigmund Freud (see entry) and soon became a member of Freud's inner circle.

From 1908 to 1913 he taught psychoanalysis at the Toronto General Hospital and was director of the Ontario Clinic for Nervous Diseases. From 1911 to 1913 he served as the first secretary of the American Psychoanalytic Association. In 1909, Jones accompanied Freud to Clark University, Worcester, Massachusetts, where Freud and Jung received honorary degrees. Jones left Canada following an obscure matter of morals involving one of his patients, and on his return to London in 1913 he founded the London Clinic for Psychoanalysis and became president of the British Psychoanalytical Society in 1920, the year he founded the *International Journal of Psychoanalysis,* which he edited until 1939.

It was largely through his efforts that the British Medical Association recognized psychoanalysis in 1929. During the 1930s, Jones helped many displaced German analysts to resettle in England and other countries, including, in 1938, bringing the ailing Freud and his family. His 1,500-page authoritative biography, *The Life and Works of Sigmund Freud* (1953–1957) is still a primary source for the history of psychoanalysis and is a monument to Ernest Jones as well as to Sigmund Freud.

Major Contributions

Jones's principal contributions to psychoanalytic theory developed from his application of psychoanalytic principles to anthropology, folklore, art, and literature. He wrote monographs on the study of suggestion, symbolism, character formation, and obsessional neuroses, and coined the term *rationalization* as one of the defense mechanisms. With the exception of Freud, no other analyst had a greater influence on psychoanalysis in the English-language community. In addition to his involvement with the British Society of Psychoanalysis, he also led the International Psychoanalytic Association and was involved in the *International Journal of Psycho-Analysis.*

Major Literature

Jones, Ernest. *Papers on Psycho-Analysis.* London: Ballière, Tindall and Cox, 1913.

___. *On the Nightmare.* New York: Liveright, 1915.
___. *What is Psychoanalysis?* London: George Allen and Unwin, 1949.
___. *The Life and Work of Sigmund Freud.* London: Hogarth Press and Institute of Psycho-Analysis, 1953–1957. Jackson, Tennessee: Basic Books, 1981.
___. *Free Associations.* London: Hogarth Press, 1959.
___. *Essays in Applied Psychoanalysis.* New York: International Universities Press Inc., 1964.
___. *Hamlet and Oedipus.* The Norton Library, N799. New York: W.W. Norton and Co. Ltd., 1976.
Ferenczi, Sandor, and Ernest Jones. *First Contributions to Psychoanalysis.* Maresfield Library. London: Karnac Books, 1994.

Jones, Mary Cover
(1896–1987)
BEHAVIOR THERAPY

Mary Cover was born in Johnstown, Pennsylvania, and graduated in psychology from Vassar College, New York, in 1919. Her desire to pursue graduate work in psychology was sparked by attending a lecture given by J.B. Watson in New York City, in which he described the Little Albert study. She began graduate work at Columbia University in 1919, completed her master's degree in 1920, and in that same summer married fellow graduate student Harold Jones. In 1923, she was appointed associate in psychological research at the Institute of Educational Research, Columbia University Teachers' College, New York. She received her Ph.D. from Columbia in 1926.

Around 1927 Jones was appointed research associate at the Institute for Child Welfare at the University of California, Berkeley, and in 1932 she became involved in the longitudinal Oakland Growth Study. In 1952, she was appointed assistant professor of education at Berkeley; protocol denied her full professor status until 1959 because her husband was director of research.

In 1968, she received the prestigious G. Stanley Hall Award from the American Psychological Association. Her friend and colleague Joseph Wolpe (see entry) dubbed Jones "the mother of behavior therapy." In 1960 (the year her husband died) she served as president of the Division of Developmental Psychology of the APA.

Major Contributions

Following on Watson's study of Little Albert, Jones's study of unconditioning a fear of rabbits, which she conducted at the Institute of Educational

Research, Columbia University Teachers' College on a three-year-old named Peter, is her most often cited work. Jones treated Peter's fear of a white rabbit; as the rabbit was gradually brought closer to him in the presence of his favorite food, Peter grew more tolerant, and was able to touch it without fear.

The Oakland Growth Study, begun in 1932, was designed to follow a group of approximately 200 fifth- and sixth-grade students from puberty through adolescence. Several follow-up studies were undertaken as members of this group moved well into middle and older adulthood. Jones published over 100 studies using data from the study. Among these was a series of studies on the long-term psychological and behavioral effects of early- and late-physical maturing in adolescence. Another series of papers examined the developmental antecedents of problem drinking.

Despite her behaviorist beginnings, her work reflected an eclectic theoretical outlook and an emphasis on the whole person in his or her developmental, environmental, and social context.

Major Literature

Jones, Mary Cover. "A Laboratory Study of Fear: The Case of Peter." *Pedagogical Seminary* 31 (1924): 308–315.

___. "The Development of Early Behavior Patterns in Young Children." *Pedagogical Seminary* 33 (1926): 537–585.

___. "The Later Careers of Boys Who Were Early- or Late- Maturing." *Child Development* 28 (1957): 113–128.

___. "Personality Correlates and Antecedents of Drinking Patterns in Adult Males." *Journal of Consulting and Clinical Psychology* 31 (1968): 2–12.

___. "Albert, Peter, and John B. Watson." *American Psychologist* 29 (1974): 581–583.

Jung, Carl Gustav (1875–1961)
ANALYTICAL PSYCHOLOGY

Born in Kesswil, Switzerland, Carl Jung gained an M.D. at the University of Basel (1900) and Burgholzli Psychiatric Hospital, Zurich, under Professor Eugen Bleuler (see entry) (1900–1909) and a Ph.D. with the dissertation "On the Psychology and Pathology of So-Called Occult Phenomena" (1902). He visited the U.S. with Sigmund Freud (see Jones, Ernest) (1909), and from 1909 to 1961, had a private psychoanalysis practice in Küssnacht, Switzerland.

Jung was elected president of International Psychoanalytic Society and lectured at Fordham University, New York (1910). In 1912, he declared himself scientifically independent of Freud, and in 1914, resigned as president of the society — his final break with Freud.

He was professor of psychology, Federal Polytechnical University in Zurich (1932–1940), and professor of medical psychology, University of Basel (1944–1945). He founded the C.G. Jung Institute in Zurich (1948). Jung received seven honorary degrees from universities in America, India, and England, and was made a member of the Royal Society, London (1939). He was founding editor (1913) of the *International Journal of Psychoanalysis*.

Major Contributions

Jung and Sigmund Freud became close working colleagues and Freud eventually came to regard Jung as the crown prince of psychoanalysis and his heir apparent. Partly for temperamental reasons and partly because of differences of viewpoint, the collaboration ended. Jung developed his own school, which he called analytical psychology.

Principal differences between Jung and Freud:

- Jung attached less importance to the role of sexuality in the neuroses.
- He believed that the analysis of patient's immediate conflicts were more important than the uncovering of the conflicts of childhood.
- He defined the unconscious as including both the individual's own unconscious and that which he inherited — the "collective unconscious."
- He emphasized the use of the phenomenon of transference.

Jung developed a typology of personality involving the categories extraversion or introversion, thinking or feeling, and sensing or intuition (See also Briggs Myers, Isabel).

Other terms associated with analytical psychology:

- *Archetypes*, common symbols, that enshrine universal, even mystical, perceptions and images.
- *Anima*, the feeling function, and *Animus*, the thinking function.
- *The shadow*, the thing a person has no wish to be, the negative, dark, primitive side of the self, or what is inferior, worthless, uncontrollable and unacceptable.
- *Persona*, the mask or public face we put on to meet the world, which develops from the pressures of society

- *Dreams,* forward-looking, creative, instructive and, to some extent, prophetic. Jung believed that dreams draw on the collective unconscious.
- *Complexes,* emotionally charged clusters of associations withheld from consciousness because of their disagreeable, immoral (to them), and frequently sexual content.

The goals of Jungian therapy are to help the individual gain insight and journey toward individuation, and to facilitate greater integration of both conscious and unconscious components.

Major Literature

Jung was a voluminous writer and his works are available as *C.G. Jung Collected Works,* published by the Brunner-Routledge division of Taylor and Francis Books Ltd., London, England.

Kagan, Jerome (1929–)

PHYSIOLOGY IN
PSYCHOLOGICAL DEVELOPMENT

Born in Newark, New Jersey, Jerome Kagan gained a B.S. from Rutgers University in New Jersey (1950). At Harvard University in Cambridge, Massachusetts, he earned an M.A. (1954) and Ph.D. (1954), and since 1964, he has been the Daniel and Amy Starch Professor of Psychology. From 1955 to 1958 he was instructor in psychology, Ohio State University, and psychologist, U.S. Army Hospital at West Point, New York. Between 1958 and 1964 he was at Fels Research Institute in Yellow Springs, Ohio, and was chairman of the Department of Psychology there in 1959.

Kagan was awarded the Hofheimer Prize of the American Psychiatric Association (1963); the Wilbur Lucius Cross Medal from Yale University, New Haven, Connecticut (1982), and the G. Stanley Hall Award of the American Psychological Association (APA) (1994). Kagan has served on numerous committees of the National Academy of Sciences, as well as the President's Science Advisory Committee and the Social Science Research Council and is on the editorial board of *Child Development* and *Developmental Psychology.*

Major Contributions

Kagan pioneered in re-introducing physiology as a determinate of psychological characteristics. At Fels, Kagan carried on the long tradition of the study of children from infancy through adolescence in order to better understand human development. On re-examining some of the Fels subjects

as adults, Kagan discovered that certain behavioral characteristics, such as aggression, dominance, competitiveness, and dependence, present in childhood did not persist into adulthood. However he did find that for a small group who had been very fearful as toddlers, fear still influenced their behavior as adults.

In his 1986 study of 500 infants, roughly 20 percent of the babies who screamed at toys and other unfamiliar stimuli grew into 11-year-olds who were shy with interviewers and who showed biological signs of alarm in stressful situations. By contrast, 33 percent of the calm, cool babies grew into composed, sociable preteens. He also discovered that the development of memory skills, the understanding of symbolism, a sense of morality, and self-awareness arise in a particular order during the first two years of life.

In *Nature of the Child,* Kagan argues that biology and environment are both important factors in development, and he questions the widespread belief that adult personality was determined by childhood experience alone. In 2002 Kagan ranked 22nd on one psychology journal's list of the top psychologists of the 20th century, one notch above Carl Jung. Kagan is a firm believer in temperament and his research has re-opened the whole debate about temperament and the part played by heredity.

Major Literature

Kagan, Jerome. *Birth to Maturity.* New Jersey: John Wiley and Sons, Inc., 1962. New Haven, Connecticut: Yale University Press, 1983.
___. *Galen's Prophecy: Temperament in Human Nature.* London, England: Free Association Books Ltd., 1994.
___. *Nature of the Child.* Jackson, Tennessee: Basic Books, 1994.
___. Herschkowitz, Norbert. *A Young Mind in a Growing Brain.* Hillsdale, New Jersey: Erlbaum Associates Inc., 2005.
___. *An Argument for Mind.* New Haven, Connecticut: Yale University Press, 2006.

Kahneman, Daniel (1934–)

BEHAVIORAL FINANCE

Born in Tel Aviv, Israel, Daniel Kahneman was brought up in Paris. At the Hebrew University, Jerusalem, he gained a B.A. in mathematics and psychology (1954); was lecturer (1961–1970), and was professor of psychology (1970–1978). He has held a fellowship at the Center for Rationality since 2000. His Ph.D. is from the University of California, Berkeley (1961). He was Eugene Higgins Professor of Psychology, Princeton University, New Jersey, and professor of public affairs at Princeton's Woodrow Wilson School of Public and International Affairs (1993).

He received the Distinguished Scientific Contributions Award, American Psychological Association (1982), and in 2002 was co-recipient of the Nobel prize (with American economist Vernon L. Smith) for his pioneering work that examined human judgment and decision making under uncertainty.

Major Contributions

Kahneman is most noted for his pioneering work on behavioral finance (how we think about finance and the emotions involved in making financial decisions) and hedonic psychology (or psychological egoism, which is the view that we are always motivated by self-interest, even in seeming acts of altruism). With Amos Tversky (see entry) and others, Kahneman established a cognitive basis for common human errors using heuristics (a particular technique of directing one's attention in learning, discovery, or problem-solving) and in developing prospect theory — how individuals evaluate losses and gains.

In 1955 he joined Israeli Defense Forces, serving his time as a psychologist responsible for the classification and selection of recruits. He constructed and validated a semi-structured interview schedule for personality assessment. When training interviewers he noted that they were often poor judges of the quality of their work. Only when they were forced to think in concrete terms of the candidate's past did they make accurate predictions. His collaboration with Amos Tversky started in 1969, when Kahneman invited Tversky to lecture on probability assessment. They concentrated mainly on:

- *anchoring and adjustment* — the way people assess probabilities intuitively
- *availability* — a rule of thumb, or cognitive bias, where people base their prediction of an outcome on the vividness and emotional impact rather than on actual probability
- *representativeness* — where we assume commonality between objects of similar appearance. While often very useful in everyday life, it can also result in neglect of relevant base rates and other errors
- *loss aversion* — the tendency for people to strongly prefer avoiding losses than acquiring gains

The insights derived from Kahneman and Tversky's studies of the psychological processes in the way people make decisions have helped to develop new ways of improving how we think.

Major Literature

Kahneman, Daniel, Paul Slovic, and Amos Tversky. *Judgment Under Uncertainty: Heuristics and Biases.* New York: Cambridge University Press, 1982.

Kahneman, Daniel, and Amos Tversky. *Choices, Values, and Frames.* New York: Cambridge University Press, 2000.

Gilovich, Thomas, Dale Griffin, and Daniel Kahneman. *Heuristics and Biases: The Psychology of Intuitive Judgment.* New York: Cambridge University Press, 2002.

Kahneman, Daniel, Ed Diener, and Norbert Schwarz (Eds.) *Well-Being: Foundations of Hedonic Psychology.* New York: Russell Sage Foundation, 2003.

Kamin, Leon J. (1927–)
INTELLIGENCE

Born in Taunton, Massachusetts, son of a Polish rabbi, at Harvard University in Cambridge, Massachusetts, Leon J. Kamin gained a B.A. in psychology (1949) and a Ph.D. in psychology and social relations under Gordon Allport (see entry) in 1954. He was associate professor of Queens University, Kingston University, Ontario, and McGill University, Ontario, Canada (1955–1957); professor and chairman (1964–1968), McMaster University, Hamilton, Ontario (1957–1968); professor, Princeton University, New Jersey (1968–1987), and since 1987, professor at Northeastern University in Boston, Massachusetts, and honorary professor of psychology, University of Cape Town, South Africa.

Major Contributions

Although Kamin began his career as an animal researcher, it is not for these studies that he is best remembered, even though they are important, but for his attack on the findings of Sir Cyril Burt (see entry) that IQ is 80 percent hereditary and only 20 percent culturally determined. Kamin, an expert statistician and methodologist, was shocked to find that other respected psychologists such as Robert Yerkes (see entry) had put forth racial theories about IQ in the 1920s. He found a bias in the retention time and mental processing research. He also found a bias regarding "non white adults."

Kamin concluded that the unsupported assumption that IQ was inherited led to unjust social policy at that time. He also saw dangerous parallels between the 1920s and the 1970s. Feeble data and unjustified claims were again being used politically as a rationale for denying programs and assistance to minorities. Richard Herrnstein (one of the authors of the best-selling and controversial *The Bell Curve* (1994) supported Burt, as did Arthur Jensen (see entry) and Hans Eysenck (see entry). Herrnstein and Charles Alan Murray's book has renewed the nature versus nurture debate.

Kamin, in "Lies, Damned Lies," severely criticizes *The Bell Curve* for being divisive and perpetuating flawed arguments. Kamin's studies have emphasized the weakness in the genetic argument and provided continued support for the environmental argument. Not surprisingly, his work has caused a good deal of controversy in the nature vs. nurture debate surrounding intelligence.

Major Literature

Kamin, Leon J. "Predictability, Surprise, Attention, and Conditioning." In B. Campbell and R. Church, *Punishment: Symposium.* New York: Appleton-Century, pp. 279–296, 1968.

___. *The Science and Politics of I.Q.* Hillsdale, New Jersey: Erlbaum Associates, Inc. Potomac, 1974.

Eysenck, H.J., and Leon J. Kamin. *The Intelligence Controversy.* New Jersey: John Wiley and Sons, Inc., 1981.

Lewontin, Richard C., Steve Rose, and Leon Kamin. *Not in Our Genes: Biology, Ideology, and Human Nature.* New York: Pantheon Books, 1984.

Kamin, Leon J., and Grant Henry Sharon. "Reaction Time, Race, and Racism." *Intelligence,* 11 (1987): 299–304.

Kamin, L.J. "Lies, Damned Lies, and Statistics." In R. Jacoby and N. Glaoberman, Eds. *The Bell Curve Debate.* New York: Times, Random House, 1995.

Kanner, Leo (1894–1981)
INFANT AUTISM

Born in Klekotow, Austria, Leo Kanner graduated in 1913 from the Sophiengymnasium (secondary school) in Berlin, but service with the Austrian Army in World War I interrupted his medical studies at the University of Berlin. He gained his M.D. in 1921 and worked in the Berlin Charité hospital for clinical physiology until 1924, when he immigrated to the United States to take a position as an assistant physician at the State Hospital in Yankton County, South Dakota.

With no more training in pediatrics or child psychiatry than he had received as a medical student, Kanner taught himself pediatric psychiatry. In 1930, shortly after coming to Johns Hopkins University School of Medicine, he was selected by professors Adolf Meyer (see entry), director of psychiatry, and Edward A. Park, director of pediatrics, to develop the United States' first child psychiatry service in a pediatric hospital. Kanner became an associate professor of psychiatry at Johns Hopkins in 1933 and professor of child psychiatry from 1957 until he retired in 1959, although he remained active until his death.

Major Contributions

Kanner was the first physician in the United States to be identified as a child psychiatrist. His textbook, *Child Psychiatry,* was the first English language textbook to focus on the psychiatric problems of children. His influential 1943 paper "Autistic Disturbances of Affective Contact," together with the work of the pediatrician Hans Asperger (1906–1980), forms the basis of the modern study of autism. (Asperger, in a paper published in 1944, came to almost the same conclusions as Kanner; he described children who had difficulty integrating socially into groups and labeled the condition "autistic psychopathology." He believed that such children were not as seriously disturbed as autistic children.)

Kanner described 11 children whose fundamental feature was inability to relate themselves in the ordinary way to people and situations from the beginning of life, and this included failure to use language to communicate, an inability to accommodate change, a fascination with objects and pictures, and good cognitive potential. Before Kanner noticed and recorded a pattern of symptoms, such children would be classified as emotionally disturbed, schizophrenic, or mentally retarded. Kanner observed that these children often demonstrated capabilities that showed that although they might be slow learners, they didn't fit the patterns of emotionally disturbed children. Thus he invented a new category, which he called early infantile autism, which has since sometimes been called Kanner's Syndrome.

Major Literature

Kanner, Leo. *Child Psychiatry.* Springfield, Illinois: Charles C. Thomas Publisher Ltd., 1935, 1979.

___. "Autistic Disturbances of Affective Contact." *Nervous Child* 2 (1943): 217–250.

___. "Irrelevant and Metaphorical Language in Early Infantile Autism." *American Journal of Psychiatry* 1516 Supplement (1946): 161–164.

___, and L. Eisenberg. "Early Infantile Autism 1943–1955." *American Journal of Orthopsychiatry* 26 (1956): 55–65.

Kanner, Leo. "Follow-up Study of Eleven Autistic Children Originally Reported in 1943." *Psychiatr Enfant* 38, 2 (1971): 421–461.

___. *Childhood Psychosis: Initial Studies and New Insights.* New Jersey: John Wiley and Sons, Inc., 1973.

Kaufman, Alan S. (1944–)
INTELLIGENCE TESTING

Born in Brooklyn, New York, Kaufman gained a B.A. at the University of Pennsylvania in Philadelphia (1965). At Columbia University, New York, he gained an M.A. in educational psychology (1967) and a Ph.D. under Robert L. Thorndike, specializing in measurement, research, and evaluation (1970). He was assistant director of test research and director of statistics at The Psychological Corporation in San Antonio, Texas (1968–1974); project manager for the Wechsler Intelligence Scale for Children-Revised (WISC-R), working directly with David Wechsler (see entry) (1970–1974); associate professor at the University of Georgia, Athens (1974–1979); professor and adjunct professor, California School of Professional Psychology at San Diego (1982–1986 and 1995–1997); research professor, University of Alabama, Tuscaloosa (1984–1995); and since 1997, clinical professor of psychology, School of Medicine, Child Study Center, Yale University, New Haven, Connecticut.

Major Contributions

When Kaufman joined The Psychological Corporation, San Antonio, the debate about left-right brain functions was topical but Kaufman and his wife, having explored several theories, concluded that the two processes (regardless of their localization in the brain) corresponded to two fundamental types of mental processing or problem solving. If you can measure how well (or poorly) children solve problems either by sequential (left-brain) or simultaneous (right-brain) methods, then you are one step closer to making meaningful school-based recommendations for children who have learning difficulties.

While assistant director at The Psychological Corporation he worked closely with David Wechsler on the revision of the Wechsler Intelligence Scale for Children (WISC) and supervised the standardization of the revised version (WISC-R). Other scales developed by Kaufman or by him and his wife, Nadeen Kaufman (see entry), include:

- Kaufman Assessment Battery for Children (K-ABC)
- Kaufman Test of Educational Achievement (K-TEA/NU)
- Kaufman Brief Intelligence Test (K-BIT),

- KTEA-II and KBIT-2
- Kaufman Survey of Early Academic and Language Skills (K-SEALS)
- Cognitive/Language Profile of the Early Screening Profiles (which address the preschool level)
- Kaufman Adolescent and Adult Intelligence Test (KAIT)
- Kaufman Short Neuropsychological Assessment Procedure (K-SNAP)
- Kaufman Functional Academic Skills Test (K-FAST) (which extend through the adult life span)

In 1994 Kaufman was one of 52 signatories on "Mainstream Science on Intelligence," an editorial written by Linda Gottfredson (see entry) and published in the *Wall Street Journal*, defending the findings on race and intelligence in *The Bell Curve* (see Kamin, Leo).

Major Literature

Kaufman, Alan S., and Nadeen L. Kaufman. *Clinical Evaluation of Young Children with the Mccarthy Scales.* New York: Grune and Stratton, 1977.

Kaufman, Alan S., and Nadeen L. Kaufman. *K-ABC Interpretive Manual.* Circle Pines, Minnesota: American Guidance Service, 1983. 2nd ed., 2004, KABC-II.

Kaufman, Alan S. *Assessing Adolescent and Adult Intelligence.* Boston: Allyn and Bacon, 1990. revised 2002 with Elizabeth Lichtenberger; 2006 edition with Elizabeth Lichtenberger New Jersey: John Wiley and Sons Inc.

Kaufman, Alan S. *Intelligent Testing With The WISC-III.* Wiley Series on Personality Processes New Jersey: John Wiley and Sons Inc., 1994.

___, and Elizabeth Lichtenberger. *Essentials of WAIS-III Assessment.* New Jersey: John Wiley and Sons, Inc., 1999.

Kaufman, Alan S., and Nadeen L. Kaufman. *Specific Learning Disabilities and Difficulties in Children and Adolescents: Psychological Assessment and Evaluation.* Cambridge Child and Adolescent Psychiatry Series. New York: Cambridge University Press, 2001.

Kaufman, Alan S. "WAIS-III IQs, Horn's Theory, and Generational Changes from Young Adulthood to Old Age." *Intelligence* 29: (2001) 131–167.

Kaufman, Alan S., et al. *Essentials of KABC II Assessment.* New Jersey: John Wiley and Sons, Inc., 2005.

Kaufman, L. Nadeen (1945–)
INTELLIGENCE TESTING

Nadeen L. Kaufman was born in Brooklyn, New York, and married to Alan S. Kaufman in 1964. She gained a B.S. in education at Hofstra University, Long Island, New York (1965). At Columbia

University, New York, she gained an M.A. in educational psychology, Teachers College (1972); an Ed.M. in learning and reading disabilities (1975); and an Ed.D. in special education-neurosciences (1978). Since 1997 she has been lecturer at the Yale University School of Medicine, Child Study Center, New Haven, Connecticut.

Major Contributions

The career of Nadeen Kaufman is closely tied into her husband's; they have been successful in the development of the various scales for measuring intelligence. However, Nadeen Kaufman has made her own contributions. Immediately prior to 1997 she was professor at California School of Professional Psychology. She has worked as a school psychologist, taught learning-disabled children and is a learning disabilities specialist. She was founder-director of several psycho-educational clinics for the assessment of children and adults (including clinics at Mesa Vista Hospital and the California School of Professional Psychology, both in San Diego), as well as psychologist at the Rutland Psychoeducational Center in Athens, Georgia.

Kaufman traces her approach to assessment of intelligence to the training she received at Teachers College, where each child referred for learning disabilities assessment was treated with respect. She learned to apply a humanistic approach to solving each individual's particular set of learning problems, to identify individual differences and pinpoint strengths and weaknesses within the child's ability spectrum, and to interpret these profiles within the broad framework of developmental psychology.

In her eyes, the clinician is a cross between a psychological detective and psychological midwife; the one to discover the problems and the other to help bring out a hidden parts of the child. The blend of neurology, psychology, and education helped focus Kaufman's approach to assessment and, ultimately, to the development of new intelligence tests. With her husband she trained school psychologists and clinical psychologists, and supervised graduate student research at the University of Georgia, the National College of Education in Evanston, Illinois, the California School of Professional Psychology in San Diego, and the University of Alabama, Tuscaloosa, and worked with him on the development of new scales. She was one of 52 signatories on "Mainstream Science on Intelligence" (see Kaufman, Frank).

Major Literature

Kaufman, Alan S., and Nadeen L. Kaufman. *Clinical Evaluation of Young Children with the Mccarthy Scales.* New York: Grune and Stratton, 1977.

Kaufman, Alan S., and Nadeen L. Kaufman. *K-ABC Interpretative Manual.* Circle Pines, Minnesota: American Guidance Service, 1983. 2nd ed., 2004, KABC-II.

Kaufman, Alan S., and Nadeen L. Kaufman. *Specific Learning Disabilities and Difficulties in Children and Adolescents: Psychological Assessment and Evaluation.* Cambridge Child and Adolescent Psychiatry Series. New York: Cambridge University Press, 2001.

Kaufman, Alan S., et al. *Essentials of KABC II Assessment.* New Jersey: John Wiley and Sons Inc., 2005.

Keller, Fred Simmons (1899–1996)
EXPERIMENTAL PSYCHOLOGY

Born on a farm near Rural Grove, New York, Fred Simmons Keller left school at an early age to become a Western Union telegrapher. He enlisted in the U.S. Army during World War I and served with the American Expeditionary Force on an ammunition train, rising to the rank of sergeant. He earned a B.S. (1926) from Tufts University, Medford, Massachusetts, and an M.A. (1928) and Ph.D. (1931) in psychology from Harvard University, Cambridge, Massachusetts, where he was a classmate of B.F. Skinner (see entry). (Skinner dedicated *Science and Human Behavior* [1953] and *The Shaping of a Behaviorist* [1979] to Keller.)

Keller taught at Colgate University at Hamilton, New York, from 1931 to 1938, when he joined the Columbia University, New York, faculty as an instructor of psychology. He became assistant professor (1942), associate professor (1946), and professor of psychology (1950). He served as chairman of the department from 1959 to 1962 and became professor emeritus of psychology in 1964. He was a fellow of the American Psychological Association and a past president of the Eastern Psychological Association. He received the Distinguished Teaching Award from the American Psychological Foundation in 1970.

Major Contributions

In the early 1940s, based on his research in behavior, Keller developed the "code-voice method" for teaching Morse code to radio operators and military personnel, which gave students instant feedback, allowing them to correct mistakes immediately. The U.S. Army Signal Corps adopted it officially in 1943, and in 1948 Keller received the Certificate of Merit from President Truman.

In 1947 Keller, with his colleague William Schoenfeld, instituted at Columbia College, Chicago, the first undergraduate psychology course to use Skinner's experimental methods. Keller gave his name to "the Keller Plan," or the Personalized System of Instruction (PSI), an individually paced, mastery-oriented teaching method that has had a significant impact on college-level science education. The five essential components are:

- an emphasis on the written word
- unit mastery
- self-pacing
- student proctors (invigilators)
- the use of lectures and demonstrations.

With the publication of his paper "Good-bye, Teacher!" the Keller Plan received national recognition and college instructors began to experiment with it. Students have responded positively to the plan, and, in published studies, their final examination performance equals and often exceeds performance in lecture sessions. In 1964 Keller went to the University of Brasilia, Brazil, where he helped found the psychology department and offered the first course using his personalized instruction method.

Major Literature

Keller, Fred Simmons. *The Definition of Psychology*. New Jersey: Appleton-Century-Crofts, 1937.
___. *Learning Reinforcement Theory*. New York: Random House Inc., 1954, 1969.
___. "Good-Bye, Teacher!" *Journal of Applied Behavior Analysis* 1 (1968) 79–89.
___, and J.G. Sherman *The Keller Plan Handbook*. Menlo Park, California: W.A. Benjamin Co., 1974.
___. *The PSI Handbook: Essays on Personalized Instruction*. Lawrence, Kansas: TRI Publications, 1982.

Kelley, Harold Harding (1921–2003)

RELATIONSHIPS

Born in Boise, Idaho, and brought up in Delano, California, Harold Harding Kelley earned a B.A. in psychology (1942) and M.A. in psychology (1943) from the University of California, Berkeley. He served on the U.S. Air Force Aviation Psychology Program, assisting in the construction and validation of selection tests and analyzing air crew behavior. He gained a Ph.D. in group psychology from the Massachusetts Institute of Technology (MIT) in Cambridge (1948), and worked on the new Research Center for Group Dynamics at MIT, headed by Kurt Lewin (see entry).

Kelley's posts include assistant professor, Yale University, New Haven, Connecticut; joined the Communications and Attitude Change program (1950); professor, University of Minnesota, Minneapolis; professor, Psychology Department, University of California, Los Angeles, from 1961, professor emeritus from 1981 and Walker-Ames professor, University of Washington.

He was president of the American Psychological Association (APA) Division 8 (1965–1966) and president of the Western Psychological Association (1969–1970). He received the Distinguished Scientist Award from the APA in 1971 and the Distinguished Scientific Award (with John W. Thibaut) from the Society of Experimental Social Psychology in 1981.

Major Contributions

Kelley's principal contributions are on attribution theory: we form attributions by gathering information in order to make judgments. Kelley draws attention to three different types of information:

- *consensus information* refers to the extent to which other people behave in the same way toward the stimulus as the actor (the person being watched)
- *distinctiveness information* refers to the extent to which one actor behaves in the same way toward different stimuli
- *consistency information* refers concerns the extent to which the behavior between one actor and one stimulus is the same across time and circumstances.

Two patterns can be detected:

- *Internal attribution* (deciding that the behavior is something to do with the actor) when the consensus and distinctiveness of the act are low;
- *External attribution* (deciding that the behavior has something to do with the other person, not the actor) if consensus, distinctiveness and consistency are all high.

Kelley's other focus was on *interdependence theory*. Interdependence theory suggests that social behavior is best understood by examining the manner in which partners influence each other's actions and outcomes. It focuses on interaction as the core of all social psychological phenomena. That is, individuals communicate with other persons, they create products for one another, or they emit behaviors that will affect the behavior or experiences of one or more interacting partners.

Major Literature

Kelley, Harold Harding, and J.W. Thibaut,. *The Social Psychology of Groups.* New Jersey: John Wiley and Sons, Inc., 1959.

___. *Interpersonal Relations: A Theory of Interdependence.* New Jersey: John Wiley and Sons, Inc., 1978.

Kelley, Harold Harding. *In Search of Your Family Tree.* New York: St. Martins Press, 1978.

___. *Personal Relationships.* Hillsdale, New Jersey: Erlbaum Associates, Inc., 1979.

___. *Close Relationships.* New York: W.H. Freeman and Co. Ltd., 1983.

___, et al. *An Atlas of Interpersonal Situations.* New York: Cambridge University Press, 2003.

Kelly, George Alexander (1905–1967)

PERSONAL CONSTRUCT THEORY

Born near Perth, Sumner County, Kansas, George Alexander Kelly graduated with a B.A. (1926) in physics and mathematics from Park College, Kansas; an M.A. (1928) in sociology from the University of Kansas, Lawrence; a B.Ed. (1930) from the University of Edinburgh, Scotland; and a Ph.D. in psychology (1931) on speech and reading disabilities at the State University of Iowa. He was professor and director of clinical psychology at Ohio State University (OSU) from 1945 to 1965 and president, American Psychological Association Divisions 12 and 13. He held a distinguished professorship, the Riklis Chair of Behavioral Science, at Brandeis University in Waltham, Massachusetts, 1965–1967. He was also president of the American Board of Examiners in Professional Psychology.

Major Contributions

For some years, based at Fort Hays Kansas State College before World War II, Kelly worked in school psychology, developing a unique program of traveling clinics, serving the entire state, for teachers, students, parents and children. During the war he worked as an aviation psychologist; among other things, he was responsible for a training program for local civilian pilots. Later he went to the Bureau of Medicine and Surgery of the Navy in Washington and remained in the Aviation Psychology Branch until 1945.

When *The Psychology of Personal Constructs* was published in 1955 — a unique and major development in the psychology of personality — it achieved immediate international recognition, gaining him visiting appointments at various universities in the U.S, Europe, the Soviet Union, South Amer-ica, the Caribbean, and Asia. Personal construct theory is based on the belief that our understanding of others and interactions with them are dependent upon getting inside their psychological world. Our thoughts, feelings and behaviors are bound up with our system of constructs.

A construct is a cluster of characteristics shared by one event that distinguishes and makes it different from another event. Each construct is bipolar in nature, happy and sad being the two poles of one construct. Core constructs are so central to the person's identity that, if shaken, the individual is likely to experience great anxiety. In Kelly's view, people are "scientists," constantly developing theories about events, creating hypotheses, then experimenting with their behavior to test the theories. People whose predictions or anticipations are proved correct have a fair amount of control over their personal world. If we don't like what we experience from our behavioral experiments, we may change constructs and subsequent behavior. Personal construct theory is a highly systematized, rational, intellectual, precise and "scientific" method of psychotherapy and counseling, which might not appeal to some people who prefer to work more with feelings.

Major Literature

Kelly, G. A. *The Psychology of Personal Constructs* Vol. I, II. New York: W.W. Norton and Co. Ltd., 1955. London, England: Taylor and Francis Books Ltd., Routledge, 1991.

Kelly, G. A. *A Theory of Personality: The Psychology of Personal Constructs.* New York: W.W. Norton and Co. Ltd., 1963, 1980.

Related Literature

Maher, B. (Ed.). *Clinical Psychology and Personality: The Selected Papers of George Kelly.* New Jersey: John Wiley and Sons, Inc., 1969.

Kent, Grace (1875–1973)

CLINICAL PSYCHOLOGY

Grace Kent was born in Michigan City, Indiana. At the University of Iowa, Ames, she gained a B.A. (1902) and an M.A. (1904) under Carl Seashore (see entry). From 1905 to 1906 she did graduate work with Hugo Munsterberg (see entry) at Harvard University, Cambridge, Massachusetts, and from 1906 to 1907 she was researcher, Philadelphia Hospital for the Insane in Pennsylvania. Kent earned a Ph.D. in psychology from George Washington University in Washington, D.C. (1911).

Between 1922 and 1926, she inaugurated the first psychology department in state hospitals and worked as psychologist at Worcester State Hospital, Massachusetts. She has held the posts of psychologist, Danvers State Hospital, Massachusetts (1928–1946); part-time clinical psychology professor, University of Miami, Florida (1946–1948); and psychologist, Waterbury State Hospital, Vermont 1948–1952). She retired in Arlington, Vermont, in 1952.

Major Contributions

From 1907 to 1910, while at Kings Park State Hospital, Long Island, New York, Kent researched associationism (the theory that man's understanding of the world occurs through ideas associated with sensory experience rather than through innate ideas, which then become associated through principles such as similarity and contrast). This led to the development of the Kent-Rosanoff Association Test (1910), a psychiatric screening instrument that was one of the first to have objective scoring and objective norms. The Association Adjustment Inventory (AAI) is a modified form of the Kent-Rosanoff test, and is designed for use as a screening instrument for maladjustment and immaturity.

She later worked at the Government Hospital for the Insane under Dr. Shepherd Ivory Franz (see entry) while attending George Washington University. Between 1911 and 1926, she worked at various hospitals and state mental institutions as well as with mentally retarded patients. At Danvers State Hospital (asylum) she established a successful psychology department that took care of all the psychometric work, such as the preparation of case studies, writing of clinical papers and the training of different teaching groups consisting mostly of nurses.

She "retired" several times but it seems that she was unable to give up work. Eventually she did retire in 1969 to Friends House in Sandy Springs Retirement Home, Maryland, where she remained until her death.

Major Literature

Kent, Grace, and A.J. Rosanoff. "A Study of Association in Insanity." *American Journal of Insanity* 67 (1910): 37–96, 317–390. Also published in *State Hospital Bulletin of New York* 4 (1911): 165–302.

Kent, Grace. "Experiments on Habit Formation in Dementia Praecox." *Psychological Review* 18 (1911): 375–410. Also published in *Bulletin of the Government Hospital for the Insane* No. 5 (1913): 21–50.

___. "An Experiment on the Instruction of Insane Subjects." *Journal of Nervous and Mental Disease* 48 (1918): 313–324.

___. "Modification of the Kohs Block Test Design." *Journal of Applied Psychology* 18 (1934): 578–598.

___. "Use and Abuse of Mental Tests in Clinical Diagnosis." *Psychological Record* 2 (1938): 391–400.

___. "Emergency Battery of One-Minute Tests." *Journal of Psychology* 13 (1942): 141–164.

___. *Mental Tests in Clinics for Children.* New York: D. Van Nostrand Company, Inc., 1950.

Kernberg, Otto F. (1928–)

BORDERLINE PERSONALITY DISORDER

Otto F. Kernberg was born in Vienna; the family fled from Nazi Germany to Chile in 1939. Kernberg studied biology and medicine at Santiago, Chile, and afterward psychiatry and psychoanalysis with the Chilean Psychoanalytic Society. He gained a Rockefeller Foundation fellowship to research psychotherapy with Jerome Frank (see entry) at the Johns Hopkins Hospital, Baltimore, Maryland (1959). In 1961, Kernberg immigrated to the U.S.; he joined and later became director of the C.F. Menninger Memorial Hospital in Topeka, Kansas, where he was supervising and training analyst of the Topeka Institute for Psychoanalysis, and director of the Psychotherapy Research Project of the Menninger Foundation.

He was director of the General Clinical Service of the New York State Psychiatric Institute (1973); professor of Clinical Psychiatry at the College of Physicians and Surgeons of Columbia University, New York (1974); professor of psychiatry, Cornell University; director of the Personality Disorders Institute of the New York Hospital-Cornell Medical Center (1976–1995); president of the International Psychoanalytic Association (1995); clinical director of the Borderline Personality Disorder Resource Center, New York-Presbyterian Hospital, Westchester Division; professor of psychiatry, Weill Medical College, Cornell University; and training and supervising analyst of the Columbia University Center for Psychoanalytic Training.

Kernberg's awards and honors include the Heinz Hartmann Award of the New York Psychoanalytic Institute and Society (1972); Edward A. Strecker Award from the Institute of Pennsylvania Hospital (1975); George E. Daniels Merit Award of the Association for Psychoanalytic Medicine (1981); honorary doctorate from the University of Buenos Aires, Argentina (1998); and the Austrian Cross of Honor for Science and Art (1999).

Major Contributions

One of the world's leading teachers of object relations, Kernberg is widely regarded as the world's leading expert on borderline personality disorder and narcissistic personality disorder. Influenced by Melanie Klein (see entry), Kernberg has cited "splitting" as the key defensive operation in borderline patients.

Psychiatrists and some other mental health professionals describe borderline personality disorder as a serious mental illness characterized by pervasive instability in mood, interpersonal relationships, self-image, identity, and behavior. This instability often disrupts family and work life, long-term planning, and the individual's sense of self. Pathological narcissism is characterized by a pervasive pattern of grandiosity in fantasy or behavior, an excessive need for admiration, and may include having an exaggerated sense of self-importance, having a feeling of being special.

Major Literature

Kernberg, Otto F. *Severe Personality Disorders: Psychotherapeutic.* New Haven, Connecticut: Yale University Press, 1993.
___. *Borderline Conditions and Pathological Narcissism.* Lanham, Maryland: Rowman and Littlefield Publishers, Inc., Jason Aronson, 1995.
Clarkin, John F., Frank E. Yeomans, and Otto F. Kernberg. *Psychotherapy for Borderline Personality: Focusing on Object Relations.* Washington, D.C.: American Psychiatric Publishing, Inc., 2006.

Related Literature

Diagnostic and Statistical Manual of Mental Disorders (DSM IV). American Psychiatric Association, Washington, D.C. (1994): 650.
Classification of Mental and Behavioral Disorders (ICD-10). World Health Organization, Geneva, (1992): 205.

Kety, Seymour Solomon
(1915–2000)
PSYCHIATRIC GENETICS

Born in Philadelphia, Pennsylvania, Seymour Solomon Kety graduated (1940) in medicine from the University of Pennsylvania, Philadelphia, with an internship at the Philadelphia General Hospital. His first noted research was into lead poisoning in children, due to their chewing on the lead-containing paint on their cribs or toys. He treated the poisoning with citrate, which forms a soluble chelate of lead that is relatively rapidly excreted in the urine. This was the first proof of principle that chelating agents can be used in the treatment of heavy metal intoxication.

In 1942, he became involved in a wartime project of traumatic and hemorrhagic shock, and in 1943 he returned to the University of Pennsylvania to work with Carl Schmidt (1888–1985), then a leading figure in the field of the cerebral circulation. Together they worked out a system for measuring blood flow using nitrous oxide, which led to much knowledge of the human brain in health and disease. In 1951 Kety left Pennsylvania to undertake the organization of the research programs of the National Institute of Mental Health and the National Institute of Neurological Diseases and Blindness, now National Institute of Neurological Disorders and Stroke.

Kety will be best remembered for his research into schizophrenia, which he suspected might be a biochemical disorder that is at least partly inherited. He established in the Laboratory of Clinical Science a program of research on the biology of schizophrenia, and although no definitive evidence of a biochemical defect linked to schizophrenia was derived from these studies, they laid the foundation for modern biological psychiatry.

Although previous studies of siblings and identical and fraternal twins had suggested a genetic influence, Kety had the idea of studying the adoptive and biological family lines of schizophrenics who had been adopted at birth. Using Danish national birth registries, he tracked the transmission of mental illness in people who were separated at birth from their biological parents. He discovered that heredity played a significant role in the development of schizophrenia and laid to rest the theory that the disorder was the result of bad parenting. The results demonstrated far greater incidence of the disease in the biological than in the adoptive family lines and thus provided unequivocal evidence of a major genetic component in the etiology of schizophrenia. Kety acknowledged that schizophrenia was not a purely genetic disease, only that there was an inherited susceptibility in a group of patients that fell within what he called a "schizophrenia spectrum."

In 1967 he moved to Harvard University, Cambridge, Massachusetts, first as director of psychiatric research at the Massachusetts General Hospital, then as director of the Laboratories for Psychiatric Research, Mailman Research Center, McLean Hospital, and finally professor of neuroscience in the Department of Psychiatry. In 1983 he retired from Harvard and returned to the National Institute of Mental Health, from which he retired once again in 1996.

Major Literature

Kety, Seymour Solomon. *The History of Neuroscience Videos*. London, England: Reed Elsevier Group, Academic Press Inc., 2000.

Kimura, Doreen (1933–)
CLINICAL NEUROPSYCHOLOGY

Doreen Kimura was born in Winnipeg, Manitoba, Canada. At McGill University in Montreal, Quebec, she gained a B.A. in psychology (1956), an M.A. in experimental psychology (1957), and a Ph.D. in physiological psychology (1961). From 1967 to 1998 she was professor in psychology at the University of Western Ontario, London. She served in the Department of Psychology at Simon Fraser University, Burnaby, British Columbia, in 1998, and has been distinguished researcher, Canadian Society for Brain, Behavior, and Cognitive Science, since 2005.

Her awards and honors include the Canadian Psychology Association Award for Distinguished Contributions to Canadian Psychology as a Science (1985); Canadian Association for Women in Science Award for Outstanding Scientific Achievement (1986); John Dewan Award, Ontario Mental Health Foundation (1992); honorary doctorate from Simon Fraser University, Burnaby, British Columbia, Canada (1993); Sterling Prize in support of controversy, Simon Fraser University (2000); and the Furedy Academic Freedom Award, Society for Academic Freedom and Scholarship (2002). Kimura has been visiting professor, Department of Psychology, Simon Fraser University, and is a fellow of the American Psychological Society and the Royal Society of Canada.

Major Contributions

Several tests Kimura devised helped improve the diagnosis of disorders after brain damage and became widely used in clinical neuropsychology. In January 2005, Lawrence Summers, the American economist and president of Harvard University, continuing the discussion on *The Bell Curve*, suggested at an economic conference that one reason there are fewer women than men in science and engineering professorships might be innate sex differences in the distribution of intelligence. Summers unleashed a storm of protest from many quarters; Kimura (a believer in "nature" rather than "nurture") threw her weight behind Sum-

mers by pointing to some significant differences between the sexes, mainly in mathematical reasoning, and spatial tasks (men) and verbal memory (women).

Women are more likely to thrive in biological sciences than physical sciences. Kimura believes it's natural for men and women to choose different careers, preferring jobs that best fit their innate talents. According to Kimura, the larger number of men in fields of mathematics, computing, engineering, and physics is a fact of life. She criticizes recent initiatives to increase the representation of women in these disciplines (affirmative action or positive discrimination), as it is demeaning to women.

Concerned about political correctness — certain research being frowned upon, as it might offend certain groups (like obese people or women, or people of different ethnic groups)— in 1992 she founded, and was first president of, the Society for Academic Freedom and Scholarship (SAFS). The goals of this society, which is primarily concerned with institutions of higher learning in Canada, are maintaining freedom in teaching, research, and scholarship, and maintaining standards of excellence in academic decisions about students and faculty. She also has a small consulting business that sells neuropsychological tests she developed.

Major Literature

Kimura, Doreen. *Speech and Language*. Readings from the *Encyclopedia of Neuroscience*. New York: Springer-Verlag, Birkhauser, 1989.
___. *Neuromotor Mechanisms in Human Communication*. Oxford Psychology Series. New York: Oxford University Press Inc., 1993.
___. *Sex and Cognition*. Bradford Book Series. Cambridge, Massachusetts: MIT Press, 2000.

Klein, Melanie (1882–1960)
ANALYTICAL PLAY THERAPY

Born in Vienna, Melanie Reisez chose to marry Arthur Stephen Klein, an engineer, when she was twenty-one, rather than study medicine; the marriage failed after some years. In 1914, she started analysis with Sandor Ferenczi (see entry) and continued with Karl Abraham (see entry) in Berlin in 1924; both encouraged her to develop her own system of child analysis; it is her contribution to child psychiatry for which she is mostly remembered.

Klein demonstrated that how children play with toys reveals earlier infantile fantasies and anxieties. She was a member (1921–1926) of the Berlin

Psychoanalytic Institute, using psychoanalytic techniques with emotionally disturbed children. At the invitation of Ernest Jones (see entry), Klein moved to London in 1926 and became linked with the British object relations school. In her later work, Klein's theories came into conflict with those of other psychoanalysts, particularly Anna Freud. Kleinian theory is still influential as a distinctive strain of psychoanalytic theory.

Major Contributions

One of Klein's major departures from Freud was in her interpretation of the Oedipus complex which she maintains dates from the first year of life. The desire in both sexes for the good breast (feeding) becomes a desire for the father's penis. Likewise, the bad breast (withdrawal of feeding) is displaced on to the bad penis. The "good breast" is responsible for all positive, gratifying feelings associated with the life instinct, feelings that reinforce trust and balance the life and death instincts.

Some other Kleinian concepts:

- *Splitting.* Splitting characterizes the very young. It is the active separation into good or bad experiences, perceptions and emotions linked to objects. Splitting interferes with the accurate perception of reality and nurtures denial. The opposite of splitting is synthesis. This takes place when the infant is able to distinguish part from whole objects.
- *Paranoid-schizoid position.* The paranoid-schizoid position occurs during the first 6 months of life and relates the to the love-hate relationship with the "good breast" and the "bad breast." Fixation at the paranoid-schizoid position may result in either a paranoid or a schizoid personality.
- *Depressive position.* The depressive position, adopted during the second 6 months of life, is characterized by idealization of the good object to avoid destroying the object. Depressive idealization creates an over-dependence on others in later stages of development. Fixation at the depressive position may result in pathological mourning or the development of manic defenses.
- *Kleinian therapy.* Klein believed that analysis of children could protect them from serious guilt-producing impulses. In interpreting play as the symbolic expression of conflicts and anxieties, the analyst does not offer the child reassurance but works exclusively with the

transference, in language the child can understand.

Major Literature

Klein, Melanie. *The Psychoanalysis of Children.* London, England: Hogarth, 1998. London, England: Karnac Books, 1932.
___. *Contributions to Psychoanalysis, 1921–1945.* London: Hogarth, 1948.
___. *Envy and Gratitude: A Study of Unconscious Sources.* New York: Basic Books, 1957.
___. *Narrative of a Child Analysis.* New York: Basic Books, 1961. New York: Vintage and Anchor Books, 1998.

Kleinman, Arthur (1941–)
PSYCHIATRIC ANTHROPOLOGY

Born in New York, Arthur Kleinman gained an A.B. (1962) and an M.D. (1967) from Stanford University, California. From 1969 to 1970 he was surgeon, United States Public Health Service, and gained an M.A from Harvard University, Cambridge, Massachusetts (1974).

He founded the journal *Culture, Medicine and Psychiatry* in 1976. Since 1978 he has been co-director of a National Institute of Mental Health-funded postdoctoral training program in clinically applied anthropology. In 1996 he directed the *World Mental Health Report.* He is Esther and Sidney Rabb Professor and Chair, Department of Anthropology, Harvard University, and professor of medical anthropology in social medicine and professor of psychiatry, Harvard Medical School. He received an honorary D.Sc. from York University, Toronto, Canada (1996), and the Doubleday Award at the University of Manchester, United Kingdom (2004).

Major Contributions

Kleinman's current research interests include the experience of chronic illness, social suffering, depression, emerging infectious diseases, substance abuse, suicide, political violence, trauma, aging, ethnicity, and disabilities. Between 1969 and 1970 he was seconded to the Nave Medical Research Unit 2 at the National Taiwan University Hospital, where he conducted research on leprosy, tuberculosis and stigma in Taiwan and on the Taiwanese health care system.

From 1980 to 1983, he conducted a study of patients with neurasthenia, pain and depression in the People's Republic of China, the first systematic study of survivors of China's cultural revolution. He also conducted studies of epilepsy among poor peasants in the Chinese provinces of Ningxia and Shanxi, the elderly in hospice care in Shanghai, depression in Guangzhou, and suicide among rural and urban women. He was awarded a key to the city of Shanghai by the office of the mayor of Shanghai. Kleinman's work with Chinese or East Asian patients demonstrated that mental distress is much more likely to be expressed as a bodily ailment than as psychological distress.

He co-chaired the American Psychiatric Association's Taskforce on Culture and DSM-IV and co-chaired the 2002 Institute of Medicine report on reducing suicide, and the 2002 National Institute of Health conference on stigma. In a talk Kleinman gave on March 12, 2004, titled "Stigma, SARS, and AIDS in China" (SARS stands for severe acute respiratory syndrome), he said that stigma encompasses the individual, the family, and society as a whole. It causes tensions within families, widens fault lines in society, and induces a climate of fear and prejudice within which the individual is increasingly isolated.

His other honors include the Franz Boaz Award from the American Anthropological Association and the Welcome Prize in Medical Anthropology.

Major Literature

Kleinman, Arthur. *Patients and Healers in the Context of Culture.* Berkeley: University of California Press, 1979.

___. *Social Origins of Distress and Disease: Neurasthenia, Depression and Pain in Modern China.* New Haven, Connecticut: Yale University Press, 1986.

___.*The Illness Narratives: Suffering, Healing and the Human Condition.* Jackson, Tennessee: Basic Books, 1989.

Kleinman, Arthur, and James L. Watson. *SARS in China: Prelude to Pandemic?* Palo Alto, California: Stanford University Press, 2005.

Klineberg, Otto (1899–1992)

PERSONALITY AND
SOCIAL PSYCHOLOGY

Born in Quebec, Canada, Otto Klineberg gained a B.A. (1919) and an M.D. (1925) from McGill University, Montreal, Quebec, Canada, and an M.A. in philosophy from Harvard University, Cambridge, Massachusetts (1920). At Columbia University, New York City, he gained a Ph.D., studying performance test speed from children of difference races under Robert Woodworth (see entry) (1927). He was research associate in the Anthropology Department (1928) and Department of Psychology (1929). From 1961 to 1982 he was

director, the International Center for Inter-group Relations, University of Paris; then he taught part-time at City University, New York (1982–1989).

His awards and honors include Distinguished Contributions in the Public Interest, American Psychological Association (APA) (1979); Contribution to Development of Psychology in Brazil (1979); honorary life member, New York Academy of Science (1983); and Distinguished Contributions to the International Advancement of Psychology from the American Psychological Association (1991).

Major Contributions

During World War II, Klineberg served with the U.S. Strategic Bombing Survey and conducted research on the effects of the air war on Germany. In 1966–1967 he was president of the World Federation for Mental Health (which he helped establish in 1948). He organized research for UNESCO on social tensions, stereotypes and their connection with international understanding, and conducted ground-breaking studies on intelligence scores of black students.

In his study of cross-cultural differences, he found that pupils migrating from the less affluent southern states of America to integrated schools in the north improved their IQ scores to a level matching their northern-born black peers. His pioneering findings helped influence the United States Supreme Court's landmark 1954 school desegregation case, *Brown v. Board of Education.* (See Clark, Kenneth B., and Clark, Mamie.) He highlighted cross-cultural comparisons in human behavior and was known for his work on the relativity of experience and emotional expression.

Kleinberg was president of the Society for the Psychological Study of Social Issues. The Otto Klineberg Intercultural and International Relations Award of $1000 is given annually to "the best paper or article of the year on intercultural or international relations."

Major Literature

Klineberg, Otto. *Negro Intelligence and Selective Migration.* New York: Columbia University Press, 1935.

___. *Social Psychology.* Orlando, Florida: Holt, Rinehart and Winston, 1940, 1954.

___. "Race Differences: The Present Position on the Problem." *International Social Science Bulletin* 2 (1950): 460–467.

___. *Tensions Affecting International Understanding: A Survey of Research Bulletin.* New York: Social Science Research Council, 1950.

___. *The Human Dimension in International Relations,* Holt, 1964.

___. *Perspectives in Social Psychology.* Orlando, Florida: Holt, Rinehart and Winston, 1965.

___. *International Educational Exchange: An Assessment of Its Nature and Its Prospects.* New York: Mouton De Gruyter, 1976.

Kluver, Heinrich (1897–1979)
GESTALT PSYCHOLOGY

Born in Schleswig-Holstein, Germany, Heinrich Kluver served as an infantry soldier in the German army during World War I, then studied at the Universities of Hamburg and Berlin (1920–1923). In 1923 Kluver immigrated to the United States to attend Stanford University, California, where he is credited with having introduced German Gestalt psychology to North America. He gained a Ph.D. in physiological psychology from Stanford (1924) and was instructor in psychology (1924–1926) at the University of Minnesota, Minneapolis, where he met psychologist Karl Spencer Lashley (see entry). He was fellow of the Social Science Research Council, Columbia University, New York (1926–1928). From 1928 to 1933, he worked with Lashley at the Institute for Juvenile Research and was a member of the Sprague Memorial Institute, University of Chicago. Kluver took U.S. citizenship in 1934.

He was associate professor of psychology (1936) and full professor of experimental psychology (1938) at University of Chicago, Illinois. He retired from teaching at Chicago as Sewell Avery distinguished professor of biological psychology (1963). Kluwer was awarded three honorary doctorates from German universities, and as professor emeritus he continued to pursue laboratory research on the University of Chicago campus until a year before his death. Kluver was a member of innumerable professional and honorary societies, including the National Academy of Sciences, the National Academy of Arts and Sciences, the American Physiological Society, the Society for Experimental Biology and Medicine, and the Society of Biological Psychiatry.

Major Contributions

Kluver is a key contributor to the discovery of how brain physiology and neurochemistry influence both normal behavior and the treatment of abnormal behavior. He began experimenting with monkeys in an attempt to discover precisely what area of the brain is affected by the psychotropic drug mescaline (he also studied its effects upon himself) and why mescaline produces particular hallucinatory perceptions. He noticed that when he gave mescaline to monkeys they exhibited unusually frequent mouth manipulation. Kluver's efforts to learn which part of the brain was responding to the drug by producing this behavior led to the surgical removal of the temporal lobes of the brain. This procedure produced a further regular pattern of characteristics and behaviors, which is known as the Kluver-Bucy Syndrome, when present in humans.

Major Literature

Kluver, Heinrich. *Mescal: The Divine Plant and Its Psychological Effects.* London, England: Kegan Paul, 1928.

___. *Behavior Mechanisms in Monkeys.* Chicago: University of Chicago Press, 1935, 1957.

___. *Mescal and Mechanisms of Hallucinations.* University of Chicago Press, 1966.

___. *Experimental Study of the Eidetic Type.* Manchester, New Hampshire: Ayer Co. Publishers, 1975.

Koch, Sigmund (1917–1996)
HUMAN MENTALITY
AND FUNCTIONING

Born and brought up in New York City, Koch received a bachelor's degree in philosophy and psychology from New York University, a master's degree (1939) from University of Iowa, Ames, and a Ph.D. in psychology (1942) from Duke University, Durham, North Carolina. He stayed on at Duke to become a full time faculty member and remained there for 22 years, initially as an assistant professor and later as a full professor. From 1964 to 1967 Koch was director of the Ford Foundation's Program in the Humanities and Arts, New York City. From 1967 to 1971 he was full professor at the University of Texas at Austin, and from 1971 to his death, university professor of psychology and philosophy professor at Boston University, Massachusetts.

In 1978 he was elected president of the American Psychological Association (APA) in both general psychology and philosophical psychology. Koch was elected president of several APA divisions during his tenures at Boston and Texas. He was also awarded fellowships from the American Association for the Advancement of Science and the Psychonomic Society. He was a member of the Jewish War Veterans, Washington, D.C., and an educational consultant at the New York Institute of Technology.

Major Contributions

During his tenure at Duke, Koch developed his own critique of psychology, culminating in perhaps his best-known work, *Psychology: A Study of a Science*, a six-volume status report on the discipline. At the Ford Foundation he directed funding to support orchestras, conventions, and public and private lectures generally directed at an interdisciplinary approach to the arts and sciences.

In his opinion, over several decades psychology had become impersonal and sterile, enmeshed in behaviorism. Koch was instrumental in redirecting the discipline's inquiries into the areas of human mentality and functioning. Later in his life Koch compiled hours of videotape interviews of artists from many disciplines, researching their creative drive. He found that the common thread between artists of every genre was the loss of self to the creation urge, which he believed was a heightened mental state. An APA conference was being held in Toronto when his death was announced and a spontaneous memorial service was held. The International Society for Theoretical Psychology offers an award in honor of Sigmund Koch.

Major Literature

Koch, Sigmund. *Psychology: A Study of a Science*. Columbus, Ohio: McGraw-Hill Education, 1959–1963.
___, and David E. Leary (Eds.). *A Century of Psychology as Science*. Columbus, Ohio: McGraw-Hill Education, 1985.
Koch, Sigmund, David Finkelman, and Frank Kessel. *Psychology in Human Context: Essays in Dissidence and Reconstruction*. Chicago, Illinois: University of Chicago Press, 1999.

Koffka, Kurt (1886–1941)
GESTALT PSYCHOLOGY

Born in Berlin, Germany, Kurt Koffka studied philosophy at the University of Berlin and spent 1904 to 1905 studying at the University of Edinburgh, Scotland, improving his English. Upon returning to Berlin, he changed from philosophy to psychology and gained his Ph.D. (1909) from the University of Berlin. In 1909, he became assistant to the physiologist Johannes von Kries, a professor on the medical faculty at the University of Freiburg, Germany. He was then assistant to Oswald Külpe at the University of Würzburg, a major center of experimental psychology, where he was particularly interested in visual perception, suffering as he did from color blindness.

In 1910 Koffka and Wolfgang Köhler (see entry) went to work as assistants to Friedrich Schumann at the Psychological Institute, Frankfurt, sharing a laboratory with Max Wertheimer (see entry), who was studying the perception of motion. Their findings led Koffka, Wertheimer, and Köhler to stress the holistic approach, which led to establishing the theoretical and experimental basis of Gestalt psychology.

From 1911 to 1927 Koffka taught at the University of Giessen, Germany. From 1924 Koffka began a series of visits to several American universities, and in 1927 he was appointed professor of psychology at Smith College in Northampton, Massachusetts, where he remained for the rest of his life.

Major Contributions

In his book *The Growth of the Mind* (translated into many languages, including Russian, Chinese and Japanese), Koffka applied the Gestalt viewpoint to child psychology and argued that infants initially experience organized wholes before they learn to differentiate the world about them. Koffka promoted Gestalt in Europe and introduced it to the United States, and his fluency in English made him a popular writer.

He was responsible for systematizing Gestalt psychology into a coherent body of theories. He extended Gestalt theories to developmental psychology, and his ideas about perception, interpretation, and learning influenced American educational theories and policies. Gestalt, when translated loosely, means "pattern" or "form." When the pattern or *Gestalten* is incomplete, we talk of "unfinished business."

The chief tenet of Gestalt psychology is that analysis of parts, however thorough, cannot provide an understanding of the whole — the whole is more than the sum of the parts. An analogy is the human body, each part of which has its distinct function yet all are integrated to make up the body. Parts are not understood when analyzed in isolation. Mental processes and behaviors come complete. An example is that we hear a melody as a whole and not merely as a collection of individual notes.

Major Literature

Koffka, Kurt. "Perception: An Introduction to the *Gestalt* Theory." *British Journal of Psychology* 33 (1922): 69–76.
___. *The Growth of the Mind*. London, England: Taylor and Francis Books Ltd., Routledge, 1924. New Jersey: Transaction Publishers, 1980.
___. *Growth of The Mind: An Introduction to Child Psychology*. London, England: Taylor and Francis Books Ltd., Routledge, 1928.

___. *Principles of Gestalt Psychology*. New York: Harcourt, Brace and Company, 1935.

Kohlberg, Lawrence (1927–1987)
THEORY OF MORAL DEVELOPMENT

Born in Bronxville, New York, during World War II he served as an engineer in the merchant Marines on a carrier ship that was involved in smuggling Jews escaping from Europe to Palestine. At University of Chicago, Illinois, he gained a B.A (1949), was veterans administrator trainee (1953–1954), was research associate (1955–1957), and gained a Ph.D. on moral judgment (1958). From 1958 to 1959 Kohlberg worked at the Child Medical Center, Boston, Massachusetts; from 1959 to 1961 he was assistant professor at Yale University, New Haven, Connecticut. He was also a fellow, Center of Advanced Study of Behavioral Science, Chicago, Illinois, and on the Committee on Human Development (1962). From 1963 to 1967 Kohlberg was on the faculty of University of Chicago and then professor of education and social psychology at Harvard University in Cambridge, Massachusetts (1968–1987).

Because of a tropical disease contracted in 1971 while doing cross-cultural work in Belize, Central America, Kohlberg struggled with depression and physical pain for the remainder of his life. In 1987, he requested a day of leave from the Massachusetts hospital where he was being treated and committed suicide by drowning himself in the Atlantic Ocean.

Major Contributions

In his work rescuing Jews, Kohlberg and his comrades had to run a British blockade, but he was determined to do this and managed to cope with the moral dilemma of breaking the law. During a visit to an Israeli kibbutz in 1969, Kohlberg observed how much more the youths' moral development had progressed compared to those who were not part of kibbutzim. He started a new school called the Cluster School within Cambridge Rindge and Latin High School, Cambridge, Massachusetts. The school ran as a "just community" where students had a basic and trustworthy relationship with one another, using democracy to make all the school's decisions. Armed with this model he started similar "just communities" in other schools and even one in a prison.

Seeking to expand on Jean Piaget's work in cognitive development, and to determine whether there are universal stages in moral development, Kohlberg developed his own work on moral reasoning in children and adolescents. His studies led to his theory of moral reasoning with three levels and six stages, moving from obeying rules in order to avoid punishment to being guided by ethical standards and the ability to formulate abstract moral principles, though not all adolescents negotiate the passage to final state, postconventional morality. Kohlberg believed, as did Piaget, that most moral development occurs through social interaction. The discussion approach is based on the insight that individuals develop as a result of cognitive conflicts at their current stage.

Major Literature

Kohlberg, Lawrence. *The Philosophy of Moral Development: Moral Stages and the Idea of Justice*. New York: HarperCollins Publishers, Inc., 1981.
___. *Child Psychology and Childhood Education: A Cognitive Developmental View*. Upper Saddle River, New Jersey: Addison Wesley, 1987.

Köhler, Wolfgang (1887–1967)
EXPERIMENTAL PSYCHOLOGY

Wolfgang Köhler was born in Revel (now Tallinn), Estonia. He gained a Ph.D. at the University of Berlin (1909) and was assistant and lecturer at the University of Frankfurt (1911). From 1913 to 1920 Köhler was director of the Anthropoid Research Station at the Prussian Academy of Sciences, Tenerife, Canary Islands (founded by Max Rothmann in 1912), then worked at the Psychological Laboratory, University of Berlin (1920). Köhler was professor, University of Gottingen, Germany, (1921); head of the Department of Psychology at the University of Berlin (1922–1935); William James Lecturer, Harvard University, Cambridge, Massachusetts (1934); and a visiting professor at the University of Chicago (1935).

He fled to the United States in 1935. He was professor at Swarthmore College in Swarthmore, Pennsylvania, and Dartmouth College, New Hampshire (1935–1958). His awards and honors include the Distinguished Scientific Contribution Award, American Psychological Association (APA) (1957); president, APA and Gifford Lecturer, University of Edinburgh (1958); honorary citizen, City of Berlin (1965); and honorary president, Deutsche Gesellschaft fur Psychologie (1967). He received honorary doctorates from six universities in America, Sweden and Germany. He was a member of the American Academy of Arts and Sciences, the American Philosophical Society and the National Academy of Science.

Major Contributions

Köhler is a key figure in the development of Gestalt psychology. His doctoral thesis under Carl Stumpf (see entry) and physicist Max Planck at the University of Berlin was on psycho-acoustics, research he continued at Frankfurt. In 1912 he and Kurt Koffka (see entry) were subjects for experiments on perception conducted by Max Wertheimer (see entry), whose report on the experiments launched the Gestalt movement. Thereafter Köhler was associated with Wertheimer and Koffka as the three endeavored to gain acceptance for the new theory.

On Tenerife, Köhler conducted experiments on problem-solving by chimpanzees, demonstrating their ability to devise and use simple tools and build simple structures. His two chief goals for this work on chimpanzees was to find out in what ways humans and apes were similar and to find out how humans differed. Contrary to what Edward L. Thorndike and Ivan Pavlov (see entries) believed — that learning by association (e.g., trial-and-error) was the only way animals could solve problems — Köhler believed that chimpanzees could work out solutions. His findings emphasized insight and led to a radical revision of learning theory.

Between 1922 and 1935 he directed a series of investigations that explored many aspects of Gestalt theory. Köhler's experiments in perception and learning in apes and chimpanzees inspired science fiction writers: *Planet of the Apes* (Pierre Boulle, 1912–1994); *2001: A Space Odyssey* (Arthur C. Clarke, 1917–); and the 1933 film *King Kong*. The ape cognition research facility in Leipzig, Germany, was named after Köhler in honor of his contributions.

Major Literature
(Dates relate to English translations)

Köhler, Wolfgang. *The Mentality of Apes.* New York: Harcourt, Brace and Company, 1925.
___. *Gestalt Psychology.* New York: Liveright, 1929, 1992.
___. *The Place of Value in a World of Facts.* New York: Liveright, 1938.
___. *Dynamics in Psychology.* New York: Liveright, 1940, 1973.
___. *The Task of Gestalt Psychology.* New Jersey: Princeton University Press, 1969, 1972.

Kohut, Heniz (1913–1981)
SELF-PSYCHOLOGY

Born and raised in an upper middle-class Jewish family in Vienna, Heniz Kohut graduated in medicine from the University of Vienna in 1938. In 1937 he entered psychoanalysis with August Aichhorn (see entry) which, among much else, that was terminated when the Nazis took over Austria in 1938. Kohut fled to England for a year and arrived in the United States in March 1940, where he trained in neurology and psychiatry at the University of Chicago. He re-entered psychoanalysis and began course work at the Chicago Institute for Psychoanalysis in 1946. He graduated from the institute in 1950 and immediately joined the faculty, and although he left the university, he continued as a lecturer in psychiatry, and worked full-time for the rest of his life as a clinical psychoanalyst.

Kohut served one term as president of the American Psychoanalytic Association (1964–1965); from the mid–1960s until his death, Kohut devoted himself to writing and academic work. Although for the last decade of his life, Kohut was living with cancer — a fact that he kept secret from all but his family — he carried on working and almost completed his last book, *How Does Analysis Cure?*, which was completed and published posthumously.

Major Contributions

Kohut was a leading post–Freudian psychoanalyst and the creator of the first authentically American psychoanalytic movement that he called "psychoanalytic self-psychology." It has emerged as one of the major schools of theoretical psychoanalysis; it emphasizes the development of a stable sense of self through mutually empathic contacts with other humans. At its core, self-psychology is psychoanalytic, but in self-psychology, deficits or defects are emphasized, not conflicts; faulty structures are held to be responsible for faulty functioning; the emphasis is on infantile needs, rather than on repressed wishes and drives. The therapeutic goals in self-psychology are to understand those needs, rather than — as in psychoanalysis' — frustrating infantile wishes that must ultimately be renounced.

There are crucial differences in how the patient-therapist relationship is viewed. In psychoanalytic theory, the psychoanalyst keeps an emotional distance from the patient in order to objectively analyze the information received from the patient. Empathy is the centerpiece of self-psychology; without empathy, there will be no trust. Once the patient trusts the therapist, he or she will talk more, thus enabling the therapist to gather more and better information and thus make more accurate interpretations.

Major Literature

Kohut, Heinz. *Analysis of the Self: Systematic Approach to Treatment of Narcissistic Personality Disorders.* New York: International Universities Press, Inc., 1971, 2000.
___. *Restoration of the Self.* New York: International Universities Press, Inc., 1977.
___, and Arnold Goldberg (Eds.). *How Does Analysis Cure?* University of Chicago Press, 1984.
___, and Charles B. Stozier (Ed.). *Self Psychology and the Humanities: Reflections on a New Psychoanalytic Approach.* New York: W.W. Norton and Co. Ltd., 1986.
Kohut, Heinz, and Miriam Elson (Eds.). *The Kohut Seminars on Self-Psychology and Psychotherapy With Adolescents and Young Adults.* W.W. Norton and Co. Ltd., 1988.

Korsakoff, Sergei (1853–1900)
Amnestic Disorders

Russian-born Sergei Korsakoff studied medicine at the University of Moscow, graduated in 1875 and subsequently became a physician in a mental hospital. From 1876 to 1879 he gained postgraduate experience in a clinic for nervous diseases. His thesis, "Alcoholic Paralysis," won him the medical doctorate in 1887. He was prepared for the position of professor in 1888 and in 1892 appointed superintendent of a new university psychiatric clinic and professor extraordinarius (professor without a chair). He was professor ordinarius (with a chair) of neurology and psychiatry from 1899 until his death the next year.

Korsakoff was one of the great psychiatrists of the 19th century and published numerous works in neuropathology, psychiatry, and forensic medicine (none is available in English). He was instrumental in founding the Moscow Society of Neuropathologists and Psychiatrists and also organized the 12th International Medical Congress in Moscow in 1897. *The Zhurnal nevropatologii i psikhiatrii imenia Korsacov (S.S. Korsakoff Journal of Neuropathology and Psychiatry)* was named after him.

Major Contributions

Korsakov — the first great Russian psychiatrist — is universally known for the disorder which bears his name. Although he studied alcoholic polyneuritis with mental symptoms, his "Korsakov's psy-

chosis" was the term used only when the mental disorder was accompanied by neuritis symptoms. It is a disease associated with chronic alcoholism, resulting from a deficiency of vitamin B_1. Patients sustain damage to part of the thalamus and cerebellum. Symptoms include inflammation of nerves, muttering delirium, insomnia, illusions, and hallucinations. It is now generally referred to as Wernicke-Korsakoff syndrome.

Korsakoff was the first to give a clear account of paranoia, and he classified psychiatric illnesses. Known as a humanitarian, he improved conditions in mental institutions, although his reforms did not meet with general approval: the less constraints and restraint, the more the medical staff would have to give alert attention and devotion to the patients.

As chairman of the Society for Aid to Needy Students, he did much to alleviate their financial difficulties, but he stressed that being educated meant students must be ready to sacrifice, even to pay with their lives if necessary, for the good of the country and for the ideals of mankind. His heart was set on establishing a Russian Association of Psychiatrists and Neurologists (now the Russian Society of Psychiatrists). He worked out the constitution in all details, but died just before the association came into being.

Kraepelin, Emil (1856–1926)
Classification of Mental Illness

Born in Neustrelitz, Germany, Emil Kraepelin studied medicine in Würzburg, Bavaria and Leipzig Saxony, Germany, where he made the personal acquaintance of Wilhelm Max Wundt (see entry). While still a student he decided to become a psychiatrist and was awarded a prize for a work on psychiatry from the University of Würzburg, where he became assistant to the zoologist Professor Franz von Rinecker (1811–1183) in 1977. The thesis for his medical doctorate (from the department of medicine, Leipzig University) was on the influence of acute illnesses on the origin of mental illnesses.

He worked in various asylums and from 1886 to 1891; he was fellow professor of psychiatry at Dorpat University, Estonia; fellow professor of psychiatry at Heidelberg University (1891–1903); and fellow professor of psychiatry at Munich University (1903–1917). The German Psychiatric Research Institution, Munich — substantially designed and prepared by Kraepelin — was opened in 1917. He remained in charge until 1922, when he was given emeritus status, but remained one of the major personalities on the board until he died.

Major Contributions

Kraepelin traveled as far as India, Java, the United States and Mexico to work in comparative psychiatry and was one of the most influential psychiatrists of his time. His classification system for mental illness influenced subsequent classifications, and his distinctions between schizophrenia and manic-depressive psychosis remain valid today. Kraepelin divided mental illnesses into exogenous disorders, those caused by external conditions and were treatable, and endogenous disorders resulting from biological causes such as organic brain damage, metabolic dysfunctions, or hereditary factors, and were thus regarded as incurable.

He collaborated with Alois Alzheimer (see entry) and in 1911 he attached the eponym "Alzheimer's disease" to pre-senile dementia. He first made the distinction between manic-depressive psychosis and dementia praecox, now called schizophrenia. He was the "father" of the modern and humane psychiatric clinic.

His three clinical varieties of dementia praecox were: *catatonia*, in which motor activities are disrupted, either excessively active or inhibited; *hebephrenia*, characterized by inappropriate emotional reactions and behavior; and *paranoia*, characterized by delusions of grandeur and persecution. Although he did not identify these conditions, he was the first to systematize them into a workable model that could be used to diagnose and treat mental patients, and he pioneered the use of drugs to treat mental illness.

Kraepelin was a fierce campaigner against smoking and alcohol and investigated the psychiatric effects of alcohol. He published many works on the topic, and in the Munich psychiatric clinic alcohol was banned; instead the patients were offered lemonade.

Major Literature

Kraepelin, Emil. *Manic-Depressive Insanity and Paranoia*. Edinburgh: Livingstone, 1921.
___. *Memoirs*. New York: Springer-Verlag, 1987.
___. *Lifetime Editions of Kraepelin in English*. England, Bristol: Thoemmes Press, 2002.
___. *Kraepelin's Psychiatrie: Ein Lehrbuch*. Foundations of Modern Psychiatry Series. England, Bristol: Thoemmes Press, 2002.
___. *Dementia Praecox and Paraphrenia*. Foundations of Modern Psychiatry Series. England, Bristol: Thoemmes Press, 2002.

Krafft-Ebing, Richard Von (1840–1902)

SEXUAL PERVERSION

Born in Mannheim, Baden, Germany, Richard von Krafft-Ebing graduated in medicine and then psychiatry from the University of Heidelberg, then worked in a number of asylums. He was professor at several universities, including Strasbourg (1872) and was also a forensic expert at Vienna. His interests ranged from genetic functions in insanity and sexual deviation to epilepsy, paralysis agitans (obsolete term for Parkinson's Disease, and hemicrania (pain on one side of the head). He also established the relationship between syphilis and general paresis (called general paralysis of the insane; third stage syphilis) and performed experiments in hypnosis.

He published his first major book, *A Textbook of Insanity* in 1879, in which he provided extensive systems for categorizing and classifying mental disorders. In 1891 he described the symptoms of delusional jealousy in alcoholics and believed that extreme jealousy was specifically distinctive for alcoholism.

Most of his other contributions have been overshadowed by his famous study of sexual perversion, *Psychopathia Sexualis* (1886), in which he included every variant in sexual activity. He coined the terms sadism and masochism. *Psychopathia Sexualis* (*Psychopathy of Sex*) was intended as a forensic reference for doctors and judges and was deliberately written in high academic tone and in scientific language to discourage lay readers. Case reports were so lurid and detailed that early editions were published in Latin. Despite this, the book was highly popular with lay readers and it went through many printings and translations (and is still in print).

In the 1886 edition Krafft-Ebing divided sexual deviance into the following categories:

1. *paradoxia*, sexual desire at the wrong time of life, i.e. childhood or old age
2. *anesthesia*, insufficient desire
3. *hyperesthesia*, excessive desire
4. *paraesthesia*, sexual desire for the wrong goal or object. This included homosexuality (or "contrary sexual desire"), sexual fetishism, sadism, masochism, and so on. (See *Diagnostic and Statistical Manual of Mental Disorders [DSM IV]*. Washington, D.C.: American Psychiatric Association, 1994, Paraphalias, pp. 522–532.)

In his later editions — contrary to common belief — Krafft-Ebing reached the conclusion that both male and female homosexuals were not suffering from mental illness. However, it was to be many years before homosexuality was removed from the list of mental illnesses.

Before the towering figures of Sigmund Freud and Carl Jung (see entries) dominated psychiatry in the early twentieth century, Richard von Krafft-Ebing monopolized the nineteenth century spotlight, yet his contributions, other than his *Psychopathia Sexualis,* have been largely ignored.

Major Literature

Krafft-Ebing, Richard von. *Aberrations of Sexual Life, After the "Psychopathia Sexualis" of Dr. R. v. Krafft-Ebing: A Medico-legal Study for Doctors and Lawyers.* Richmond, Virginia: The Staples Group LLC, 1951.

___. *Experimental Study in the Domain of Hypnosis.* Hypnosis and Altered States of Consciousness Series. Cambridge, Massachusetts: Da Capo Press, 1982.

___. *Psychopathia Sexualis.* Burbank, California: Bloat Books, 1999.

Kretschmer, Ernest (1888–1964)
BODY TYPES AND MENTAL ILLNESS

One of the most important psychiatrists during the first half of the 20th century, Ernest Kretschmer was born near Stuttgart (Württemberg), Germany. He studied philosophy and medicine at Tübingen University in Stuttgart, and gained his M.D. in 1913 from München University. He started his psychiatric career in Tübingen, where he stayed until 1926, with time out for World War I. In 1914 he published his dissertation on manic-depressive delusions, the forerunner of his life's work in mental illness. As a military physician during the war, he studied hysteria and developed a treatment in which victims of battle hysteria were quieted in dark chambers and treated with electrical impulses.

After the war, he returned to Tübingen as a lecturer, and from 1926 to 1933 he was director of the psychiatric university clinic in Marburg. In 1933 he resigned as president of the German Society of Psychotherapy in protest against the Nazi takeover of the government but remained in Germany during the war, returning to the University of Tübingen as director of the psychiatry department, where he remained until his retirement in 1959. In 1956, Kretschmer was awarded the Golden Kraepelin Medal, together with Ludwig Binswanger (see entry).

Major Contributions

His best-known work, *Physique and Character,* advanced the theory that certain mental disorders were more common among people of specific physical types. He identified three fundamental types of physique:

1. the asthenic: tall, fragile, narrowly built
2. the athletic: muscular
3. the pyknic: short and rotund.

Kretschmer's data supported the idea that types 1 and 2 would be more prone to develop schizophrenia (the schizoid personality), type 1 being more prone than type 2. The pyknic type is more likely to be diagnosed as manic depressive (bipolar disorder). His work was criticized because his thinner, schizophrenic patients were younger than his pyknic, manic-depressive subjects, so the differences in body type could be explained by differences in age. Nevertheless, Kretschmer's ideas entered into popular culture and generated further psychological research (see entry for Sheldon, William). Kretschmer identified two subtypes — the hyperaesthetic or overly sensitive type (the forerunner of avoidant personality disorder) and the anesthetic or insensitive type (the forerunner of the current schizoid personality disorder).

After 1946 Kretschmer continued studying physical constitution as well as mental illness in children and adolescents. He developed new methods of psychotherapy and hypnosis, and studied compulsive criminality, recommending adequate provisions be made for the psychiatric treatment of prisoners. In his work on the theory of paranoia, Kretschmer identified that certain sensitive personalities who developed paranoid features acutely at certain critical times in their lives where less likely to develop schizophrenia.

Major Literature

Kretschmer, Ernest. *Hysteria, Reflex, and Instinct.* Westport, Connecticut: Greenwood Press, 1923.

___. *Physique and Character: An Investigation of the Nature of Constitution and of the Theory of Temperament.* Translator, W.J.H. Sprott. New York: Harcourt, Brace and Company, 1925.

___. *The Psychology of Men of Genius.* International Library of Psychology. London: Routledge, 1929.

Kübler-Ross, Elisabeth (1926–2004)
DEATH, DYING AND BEREAVEMENT

Born in Zurich, Switzerland, in the aftermath of World War II, Elisabeth Kübler-Ross was a volunteer in International Voluntary Service for Peace (IVSP). She spent time in Poland and Germany aiding survivors of the concentration camps, as well as the defeated Germans, to rebuild their lives. She returned to Switzerland and went to medical school, eventually marrying an American student studying there. She graduated from medical school at the University of Zurich in 1957. She immigrated to the United States in 1958 and until 1962 worked in various New York hospitals.

From 1962 to 1969 Kübler-Ross taught psychiatry at the universities of Colorado and Chicago, and was staff member at LaRabida Children's Hospital and Research Center in Chicago (1969–1970). She was medical director at Family Service and Mental Health Center in South Cook County, Illinois, Chicago Heights (1970–1973). She was also president, Ross Medical Association, Southern County, Flossmoor, Illinois (1973–1976); chairman, Shanti Nilaya Growth and Healing Center, Escondido, California (1977–1995); clinical professor of Behavioral Medicine and Psychiatry, University of Virginia, Charlottesville, Virginia (1985); and president, Elisabeth Kübler-Ross Center, Head Waters, Virginia (1997–1995). She received more than 50 awards and 20 honorary doctorates, and served on the board of 38 different institutes.

Major Contributions

Kübler-Ross's experience of the way dying patients were ignored led her to focus on helping them express their feelings about death. She found that many dying patients are comforted if someone sits and listens to their openly expressed fears and thoughts. She began giving seminars for students and their teachers on helping people to die with dignity. This experience led to the publication of her book *On Death and Dying*. Kübler-Ross conceptualized five stages in facing one's terminal illness: denial, anger, bargaining, depression, and acceptance.

These stages occur neither with predictable regularly nor in any set order. Further, the stages are simply general reactions to many situations involving loss, not necessarily dying. Seldom does a dying person follow a regular, clearly identifiable series of responses. Patients may be assisted in reaching acceptance by the hospital staff's and family's openly talking about death when the patient so desires. Other people have developed different models; one is J.W. Worden's *Grief Counseling and Grief Therapy: A Handbook for the Mental Health Practitioner* (London: Routledge,

1983). Yet they, and the whole world, all owe a great debt to Elisabeth Kübler-Ross. The Elisabeth Kübler-Ross Foundation (EKR Foundation) was formed in Scottsdale, Arizona, to keep alive the spirit of this pioneering woman.

Major Literature

Kübler-Ross, Elisabeth. *On Death and Dying*. New York: Collier Books, 1969. New York: Simon and Schuster Inc., 1993.
___. *Life Lessons: How Our Mortality Can Teach Us About Life and Living*. New York: Simon and Schuster Ltd., 2001.
___. *The Wheel of Life: A Memoir of Living and Dying*. London, England: Random House Group, Bantam, 2004.
___. *On Grief and Grieving: Finding the Meaning of Grief Through the Five Stages of Loss*. New York: Simon and Schuster Ltd., 2005.

Lacan, Jacques (1901–1981)
LANGUAGE OF THE UNCONSCIOUS

Born in Paris, France, Jacques Lacan began studying medicine in 1920 and specialized in psychiatry from 1926. He earned a medical degree in 1932 and was a practicing psychiatrist and psychoanalyst in Paris for much of his career, having completed his own psychoanalysis in 1938. Lacan presented his first analytic paper titled "Mirror Stage" at the 1936 Congress of the International Psychoanalytical Association in Zurich. The mirror stage is the period when the child begins to draw rudimentary distinctions between self and other, the period when the child's sense of self and the first steps in the acquisition of language emerge, where the child sees itself mirrored in other people and objects.

Lacan served as a doctor during World War II, and from 1951 until his death, he held weekly seminars on psychoanalysis at the St. Anne Hospital Paris. His controversial innovation of variable-length sessions and the critical stance he took toward much of the accepted orthodoxy of psychoanalytic theory and practice led, in 1963, to his being expelled from the Société Parisienne de Psychanalyse and the International Psychoanalytical Association. He founded and headed the Freudian School of Paris from 1964 until he disbanded it in 1980 for what he claimed was its failure to adhere with sufficient strictness to Freudian principles.

Lacan stressed the unconscious more than many other modern psychoanalysts. He likened the unconscious to an ancient language, with its own structures, rules and meanings and nuances, so in order to interpret the unconscious, one first has to learn to the language and what is peculiar and specific to the individual.

The unconscious, he argued, was not a more primitive or archetypal part of the mind separate from the conscious, the ego, rather it is a formation every bit as complex and structurally sophisticated as consciousness itself. If the unconscious is structured like a language (a language different from the language of the ego), then the self is denied any communication with it. In this way, Lacan's thesis of the structurally dynamic unconscious is also a challenge to the ego psychology that Freud himself opposed; that is possibly one reason that Lacan was out of step with the majority of his fellow psychoanalysts; while they were concentrating on strengthening the ego, Lacan was reapplying the old concepts.

Major Literature

Lacan, Jacques. "Some Reflections on the Ego." *International Journal of Psychoanalysis* 34 (1953): 11–17.
___. *Ecrits: A Selection.* New York: W.W. Norton and Co. Ltd., 1977, 2004.
___. *The Four Fundamental Concepts of Psychoanalysis.* New York: W.W. Norton, 1978. London, England: Karnac Books, 2004.
___. "The Neurotic's Individual Myth." *Psychoanalytic Quarterly* 48 (1979): 405–425.
___. *Returning to Freud: Clinical Psychoanalysis in the School of Lacan.* New Haven: Yale University Press, edited and translated, S. Schneiderman, 1980.
___. *The Language of the Self: The Function of Language in Psychoanalysis.* Anthony Wilden, translator. Baltimore: Johns Hopkins University Press, 1997.

Ladd, George Trumbull (1842–1921)

EXPERIMENTAL PSYCHOLOGY

Born in Painesville, Lake County, Ohio, George Trumbull Ladd was a philosopher, theologian, preacher and psychologist. He graduated from Western Reserve College, Connecticut (1864), and from Andover Theological Seminary, Massachusetts (1869). From 1869 to 1871 he preached in Edinburg, Ohio, and in the Spring Street Congregational Church of Milwaukee from 1871 to 1879. He was professor of theology at Bowdoin College, Brunswick, Maine, from 1879 to 1881; Clark Professor of metaphysics and moral philosophy at Yale University, New Haven, Connecticut, from 1881 to 1901, and university professor, department of philosophy and psychology at Yale (1901–1905).

Between 1892 and 1907 he lectured at universities in Japan, India and Korea, and became professor emeritus in 1905. He was co-founder of the American Psychological Association (1892) and was its second president (1893). He received the Japanese Order of the Rising Sun, 3rd Class (1899) and 2nd Class (1907), and was awarded the Gold Medal of the Imperial Educational Society of Japan. The degree of D.D. was conferred on him by Western Reserve College in 1881.

Major Contributions

During his years at Bowdoin College, Ladd investigated the relationship between the nervous system and mental phenomena and introduced the first study of experimental psychology in the United States. At Yale he established one of the first American laboratories in experimental psychology. (Most scholars credit G. Stanley Hall [see entry] with establishing the first American psychological laboratory at Johns Hopkins University in 1883.) His textbooks influenced the establishment of experimental psychology in the United States.

Although he called for a scientific psychology, he viewed psychology as ancillary to philosophy. Ladd's main interest was in writing *Elements of Physiological Psychology*, the first handbook of its kind in English; because of its emphasis on neurophysiology, it long remained a standard work. His large-scale *Psychology, Descriptive and Explanatory*— a theoretical system of functional psychology — was another textbook that established him as one of the pioneers of scientific psychology.

He occupied his retirement by writing magazine articles on contemporary social and political issues, generally from a Republican standpoint — he opposed the formation of the League of Nations in 1919. He was particularly influential in establishing psychology as a discipline in Japan, and one of his former students, Matataro Matsemoto, became a leading figure there. Several of Ladd's textbooks were translated into Japanese.

Major Literature

Ladd, George Trumbull. *Elements of Physiological Psychology.* New York: Charles Scribner's Sons, 1887.
___. *Psychology, Descriptive and Explanatory.* New York: Charles Scribner's Sons, 1894.
___. *Primer of Psychology.* New York: Charles Scribner's Sons, 1894.
___. *Philosophy of Knowledge: An Enquiry Into the Nature, Limits and Validity of Human Cognitive Faculty.* New York: Charles Scribner's Sons, 1897.

___. *Knowledge, Life and Reality.* New York, Longmans Green, 1909.

___. "The Conference of Pragmatism." *Hibbert Journal* 7, 4 (1909), 784–801.

___. *The Secret of Personality.* New York, Longmans Green, 1918.

Ladd-Franklin, Christine (1847–1930)

COLOR VISION

Christine Ladd (known as Kitty) was born at Windsor, Connecticut; she studied Greek at Wesleyan Academy in Massachusetts (1863–1865) and was the only female in that department. She gained an A.B. at Vassar College, Poughkeepsie, New York (1869); taught in Washington, Pennsylvania (1871); studied mathematics at Harvard University, Cambridge, Massachusetts (1872); and studied mathematics at Johns Hopkins University in Baltimore, Maryland (1878–1882) (the "men only" rule denied her a Ph.D. until 1926).

She married Fabian Franklin of Hopkins' mathematics department (1882); was awarded an honorary LL.D. degree from Vassar College (1887); studied in Germany (1891–1892); lectured on logic and philosophy at Johns Hopkins (1904–1909); and lectured on logic and philosophy at Columbia University in New York City (1910–1930). She was associate editor for *Logic and Psychology* and helped publish the *Dictionary of Philosophy and Psychology* (1902).

Major Contributions

Although her work with color vision and logic are her main contributions, Ladd's struggle for academic equality for women should not be ignored, something that many of the early women psychologists fought for. For seventeen years she helped to administer the Sarah Berliner fellowship to support recent Ph.D. women in their research. At Johns Hopkins, Ladd developed her interest in symbolic logic and wrote a dissertation titled "The Algebra of Logic," published several articles in *The Analyst*, and contributed to Mathematical Questions section of the London based *Educational Times*.

She continued working on symbolic logic as well as the field of physiological optics, and this latter area carried her into research in the optics of color vision, an area in which she worked for thirty-seven years. While studying in Germany she developed the Ladd-Franklin theory — that gray is the earliest form of vision, from which is derived two paired substances that detect yellow and blue, and that the yellow gives rise to paired substances for detection of red and green. This theory criticized the views of Ewald Hering (1834–1918), whose hypothesis was that red-green was the more primitive, giving rise to blue-yellow.

In 1887 she published "A Method for the Experimental Determination of the Horopter," a mathematical investigation of binocular vision. (Horopter is the sum of all the points seen in binocular vision with the eyes fixed.) Her model on binocular vision was the entry that she needed to be accepted into the world of psychologists. From then on her theories developed and prospered until she had an evolutionary-based model on her theory of color vision that she presented to the International Congress of Psychology in London in 1892. Her theory of color vision has never been proved or disproved.

Major Literature

Marquand, Allan, Christine Ladd, Oscar Howard Mitchell, and Benjamin Ives Gilman. *Studies in Logic.* London, England: Little, Brown, and Company, 1883. Boston, Massachusetts: Adamant Media Corporation, 2005.

Ladd, Christine. *Color and Color Theories.* London, England: Taylor and Francis Books Ltd., Routledge, 1928, 1999.

___. "The Experimental Determination of the Horopter." *American Journal of Psychology* 1 (1997): 99–111.

Laing, Robert David (1927–1989)

ANTI-PSYCHIATRY

Born in Govanhill, Glasgow, Scotland, Robert David Laing gained an M.B. and Ch.B. (medicine) at Glasgow University in 1951. From 1951 to 1953 Laing was medical officer in the Royal Army Medical Corps, British Army Psychiatric Unit, Royal Victoria Hospital, Netley, Southampton, and Military Hospital, Catterick, Yorkshire. He worked at Gartnavel Royal (psychiatric) Hospital, Glasgow (1953), and gained his diploma in psychological medicine (qualification as psychiatrist) at the University of London (1956).

He was senior registrar at the Tavistock Clinic in London, qualified as a psychoanalyst at the Institute of Psychoanalysis (1960), and set up a private practice at Wimpole Street, London. Laing died of a heart attack while playing tennis in St. Tropez, France. The Society for Laingian Studies was founded in 2002.

Major Contributions

At Netley, confronted with the traditional approach to treating psychiatric patients — electroconvulsive therapy, insulin coma therapy, restraint, psychotropic drugs — Laing began to formulate his alternative approach. At Gartnavel, Laing set up the "Rumpus Room" where schizophrenic patients spent time in a comfortable room; staff and patients wore normal clothes. Patients were allowed to spend time doing activities such as cooking and art, the idea being to provide a setting where patients could respond to staff and each other in a social, rather than institutional setting. The patients all showed a noticeable improvement in behavior. Laing knew that time spent listening to and talking with patients (what he referred to as "real therapy") was productive.

In 1965 he and a number of colleagues founded a charity, the Philadelphia Association (then at Kingsley Hall, East London, now at Hampstead, North London), whose central aim was the relief of mental illness of all descriptions, in particular schizophrenia, and to question the way in which the "facts" of "mental health" and "mental illness" are seen. Laing said that the strange behavior and seemingly confused speech of people undergoing a psychotic episode were ultimately understandable as an attempt to communicate worries and concerns, often in situations where this was not possible or not permitted.

Although Laing, denounced the label of antipsychiatry, he argued that individuals can often be put in impossible situations where they are unable to conform to the conflicting expectations of others, leading to a "lose-lose situation" and immense mental distress for the individuals concerned.

Major Literature

Laing, Robert David. *The Divided Self: An Existential Study in Sanity and Madness.* London, England: Penguin Books Ltd., 1960, 1990.

___, and A. Esterson. *Sanity, Madness and the Family.* London, England: Penguin Books Ltd., 1964. London, England: Taylor and Francis Books Ltd., Routledge, 1998.

Laing, Robert David. *Self and Others.* London, England: Penguin Books Ltd., 1969. London, England: Taylor and Francis Books Ltd., Routledge, 1998.

___. *The Politics of the Family and Other Essays.* London, England: Taylor and Francis Books Ltd., Tavistock Publications, 1971.

___. *The Voice of Experience: Experience, Science and Psychiatry.* London, England: Penguin Books Ltd., 1982.

___. *Wisdom, Madness and Folly: The Making of a Psychiatrist 1927–1957.* London, England: Macmillan, 1985. Edinburgh, Scotland: Canongate Books, 2001.

Lambert, Nadine M. (1926–2006)
DEVELOPMENTAL PSYCHOLOGY

Born in Ephraim, Utah, Lambert gained a B.A. in psychology (1948) from the University of California Los Angeles, an M.A. in education (1955) from Los Angeles State University, and a Ph.D. in psychology with a specialty in psychometrics (1965) at the University of Southern California, Los Angeles. She received numerous awards, including the Senior Scientist Award from the National Association of School Psychologists (2005); the Distinguished Service Award, Division of School Psychology, American Psychological Association; and the Sandra Goff Award for Outstanding Contribution to School Psychology in California.

She was professor emeritus of education and an advisor and mentor at the school's joint doctoral program in education leadership, Graduate School of Education, University of California, Berkeley. A fellow of the American Psychological Association, she also served on its board of directors (1984–1987) and chaired its board of educational affairs from 1992 to 1994. Lambert died in a car accident near campus.

Major Contributions

Lambert founded the school psychology program at the education school, Berkeley, in 1964, her first year. The National Institute of Mental Health supported the program for 18 years as a model for preparing school psychologists. More than 160 graduates have completed the program and gone on to become school psychologists, researchers, consultants and university educators.

Early in her career, Lambert was part of a team of investigators for the California State Department of Education assigned to establish and evaluate programs for children with educational handicaps, including those with what is commonly known today as attention deficit hyperactivity disorder (ADHD). The team's work led the first state legislation supporting educational programs for children with learning and behavioral disorders.

At Berkeley she carried out a 30-year longitudinal study of 492 children, about half of them with ADHD, documenting life histories of the participants from kindergarten into early adulthood, including the prevalence of hyperactivity and the various treatments for it. In a report to the

National Institutes of Health in 1999 she stated that the children in the study who were treated with stimulant drugs such as Ritalin to control ADHD started smoking cigarettes earlier, smoked more heavily and were more likely as adults to abuse cocaine and other stimulants than those not taking such medications. The report was not well received, as the implication was that Ritalin was a gateway to drug abuse. The debate rumbles on.

In 1995, she was a signer of a collective statement, "Mainstream Science on Intelligence," written by Linda Gottfredson (see entry) in support of *The Bell Curve*.

Major Literature

Lambert, Nadine M. *The Educationally Retarded Child.* New York: Grune and Stratton, 1974.
___. "The Prevalence of Learning Disabilities in a Sample of Children Considered Hyperactive." *Journal of Abnormal Child Psychology* 8 (1980): 32–50.
___. *Moral Development and Socialization.* Upper Saddle River, New Jersey: Pearson Education, Allyn and Bacon, 1980.
___, and Barbara L. McCombs. *How Students Learn: Reforming Schools Through Learner-centered Education.* Washington, D.C.: American Psychological Association, 1998.

Langer, Ellen J. (1947–)
ADULT DEVELOPMENT AND AGING

Born in New York City, Ellen J. Langer gained a B.A. (1970) from New York University and a Ph.D. (1974) in social and clinical psychology from Yale University, New Haven, Connecticut. In 1980 she was the recipient of a Guggenheim Fellowship. Other honors include the Award for Distinguished Contributions to Psychology in the Public Interest, the American Psychological Association; the Distinguished Contributions of Basic Science to Applied Psychology Award, the American Association of Applied and Preventive Psychology; the James McKeen Cattel Award; and the Gordon Allport Intergroup Relations Prize. Langer is a fellow of The Sloan Foundation, the American Psychological Association, the American Psychological Society, the American Association for the Advancement of Science, Computers and Society, the Society for the Psychological Study of Social Issues, and the Society of Experimental Social Psychologists. In addition to other honors, she has been a guest lecturer in Japan, Malaysia, Germany, and Argentina.

Major Contributions

Langer is a professor in psychology and chair of the Social Psychology Department at Harvard University, Cambridge, Massachusetts. Her projects have been in the general areas of decision-making, behavioral medicine, deviance, the social psychology of aging, control, and socially induced performance debilitations. Her main interest is trying to extend human potential, not limited by age.

According to Langer many of the limitations placed upon us are of our own making. She shoots down the belief that aging always brings deterioration in mental capacity. The way something is presented influences the way we learn. For example, presenting something to an elderly person as "This is difficult, I will help you," might be self-defeating and increase dependency. She examines intelligence, the importance of basic skills, and learning to delay gratification. She presents simple but not simplistic approaches that can allow people to learn in more effective ways.

More recently Langer has concentrated on mindfulness/mindlessness and has developed the Langer Mindfulness Scale. This is a 21-item questionnaire intended for use as a training, self-discovery, and research instrument. It assesses four domains associated with mindful thinking: novelty-seeking, engagement, novelty producing, and flexibility. An individual who seeks novelty perceives each situation as an opportunity to learn something new. An individual who scores high in engagement is likely to notice more details about his or her specific relationship with the environment. A novelty producing person generates new information in order to learn more about the current situation. Flexible people welcome a changing environment rather than resist it. Well-ingrained habits can work against mindfulness and lead to what we call absent-mindedness, because the novelty factor is missing.

Major Literature

Langer, Ellen J. "The Illusion of Control." *Journal of Personality and Social Psychology* 32 (1975): 311–328.
___. *The Psychology of Control.* New York: Russell Sage Foundation, 1983.
___. *Mindfulness.* Reading, Massachusetts: Addison Wesley, 1989.
___. *The Power of Mindful Learning.* Reading, Massachusetts: Addison-Wesley, 1997.

Laplanche, Jean (1924–)

PSYCHOSEXUAL DEVELOPMENT

Born in Paris into a family of wine-producers who owned the prestigious Chateau de Pommard in Burgundy, Jean Laplanche grew up in the Côte d'Or region of Eastern France. He planned to study philosophy at the École Normale Supérieure, Paris, but the war intervened. In 1943–1944, during the Vichy regime, Laplanche joined the French Resistance and was active in Paris and Bourgogne. He entered university in the 1944–1945 academic year.

In 1946–1947, he visited Harvard University, Cambridge, Massachusetts, on a scholarship and studied in the Department of Social Relations. He became interested in psychoanalytic theory, and on his return to France he underwent psychoanalysis with Jacques Lacan (see entry) until 1963. Acting on Lacan's advice, Laplanche qualified as a medical doctor (1959), then became France's most renowned psychoanalyst, philosopher, and professor of psychoanalysis at the University of Paris.

From 1969 to 1971 Laplanche was president of the Association Psychoanalytique de France, and in 1986 he was granted the honorary professorship at the University of Lausanne, given the Mary S. Sigourney Award (1995), and made a Knight of Arts and Letters in 1990.

Major Contributions

Over more than four decades Laplanche has developed a systematic re-reading of Freud's work, seeking to bring more radical insights of psychoanalysis. He retrieved and reworked Freud's "seduction hypothesis," which was that many of the neuroses were caused by incest, real or fantasized, at the Oedipal stage of psychosexual development. Psychiatrists in modern times have become aware that incest (as well as other forms of sexual and physical abuse) is frequently a forerunner of subsequent borderline disorders, especially in women hospitalized with borderline personality disorder (BPD).

All the clinical manifestations of BPD can be related to the prior incest experiences. Incest is an autoerotic act and, therefore, narcissistic. When a father makes love to his daughter, he is making love to himself because she is 50 percent himself. It is a form of masturbation and reassertion of control over oneself.

What Laplanche has done is to encourage a new debate on an old topic. One key distinction between Laplanche's approach to psychoanalysis and most of those in the English-speaking world — object relations theory, Ego psychology and Kleinian thought — is Laplanche's insistence on a distinction between drive and instinct, which is in contrast to the English-speaking schools, even though drive and instinct (derived as they are from biology) present some difficulties.

Major Literature

Laplanche, Jean, and Jean-Baptiste Pontalis. *The Language of Psychoanalysis.* London, England: The Hogarth Press, 1973.

Laplanche, Jean, and Jeffrey Mehlman. *Life and Death in Psychoanalysis.* Baltimore, Maryland: The Johns Hopkins University Press, 1976.

Laplanche, Jean. *New Foundations for Psychoanalysis.* England, Oxford, Blackwell Publishing, 1989.

___. *Seduction, Translation, Drives.* London, England: Institute of Contemporary Arts, 1992.

___, John Fletcher and Luke Thurston. *Essays on Otherness.* London, England: Taylor and Francis Books Ltd., Routledge, 1998.

Laplanche, Jean. *The Unconscious and the Id: A Volume From Laplanche's Problématiques.* London, England: Karnac Books, 1999.

Lashley, Karl Spencer (1890–1958)

BEHAVIORISM

Born in Davis, West Virginia, Karl Spencer Lashley gained a B.A. at the University of West Virginia, Morgantown, West Virginia (1910), an M.S. in bacteriology, University of Pittsburgh, Pennsylvania (1911), and a Ph.D. at Johns Hopkins University, Baltimore, Maryland (1914). Lashley was at St. Elizabeth's Hospital in Washington, D.C. (1915–1917), working under Shepherd Ivory Franz (see entry) and at the University of Minnesota, Minneapolis (1917–1918), working under Robert M. Yerkes (see entry).

From 1918 to 1920 he worked for the U.S. Interdepartmental Social Hygiene Board and was assistant professor (1920–1924) and professor (1924–1926) at Minneapolis. From 1926 to 1929 he worked for the Behavior Research Fund. He was professor at the University of Chicago, Illinois (1929–1935); professor at Harvard University in Cambridge, Massachusetts (1935–1955), worked at the Yerkes Laboratory of Primate Biology in Orange Park, Florida (1942–1955), and was emeritus professor from 1955. Lashley was president, American Psychological Association (1929) and president of the Eastern Psychological Association (1938). Lashley died in Poitiers, west-central France.

Major Contributions

At St. Elizabeth's Hospital, Lashley studied spinal injuries in patients, so developing his interest in neurology. He studied many animals, including primates, but his major work was done on the measurement of behavior before and after specific, carefully quantified, induced brain damage in rats. He trained rats to perform specific tasks, then created lesions in specific areas of the rat cortex, either before or after the animals received the training. The cortical lesions had specific effects on acquisition and retention of knowledge. He tried but did not find any one focal point where learning occurred, the engrams; this suggested to him that memories were widely distributed throughout the cortex. From these findings, he evolved two principles:

- The principle of mass action (size critical), which states that the cerebral cortex acts as one — as a whole — in many types of learning.
- The principle of equipotentiality (locus not important) states that if certain parts of the brain are damaged, other parts of the brain may take on the role of the damaged portion.

Lashley, more than any other scientist, shaped and developed the field of physiological psychology. The Karl Spencer Lashley Award of the American Philosophical Society was established in 1957 by Lashley and is made in recognition of work on the integrative neuroscience of behavior.

Major Literature

Lashley, Karl Spencer. "Studies of Cerebral Function in Learning, III: The Motor Areas." *Brain* 44 (1921): 255–86.

___. *Brain Mechanisms and Intelligence: A Quantitative Study of Injuries to the Brain.* Chicago, Illinois: University of Chicago Press, 1929.

___. *The Mechanism of Vision, Part 12: Nervous Structures Concerned in the Acquisition and Retention of Habits Based on Reactions to Light.* Comparative Psychology: Monographs 11 (1935): 43–79.

___. *In Search of the Engram.* Society of Experimental Biology, Symposium 4 (1950): 454–482.

___. "Cerebral Organization and Behavior." In *The Brain and Human Behavior: Proceedings of the Association for Research in Nervous and Mental Disease.* New York: Lippincott, Williams and Wilkin, 1958.

Latané, Bibb (1937)

SOCIAL IMPACT THEORY

Born in New York City, Bibb Latané gained a B.A. in culture and behavior at Yale University in New Haven, Connecticut (1958) and a Ph.D. in psychology with journalism from the University of Minnesota, Minneapolis (1963). He was assistant then associate professor of social psychology at Columbia University, New York (1963–1968); associate then full professor of psychology at Ohio State University in Athens (1968–1981); professor of psychology at the University of North Carolina, Chapel Hill (1982–1989); director, Institute for Research in Social Science, Chapel Hill (1982–1988); professor of psychology at Florida Atlantic University in Boca Raton, Florida (since 1989); chair of psychology, Boca Raton (1989), and *professeur invite* at the Universite Blaise Pascal, France (1997).

Latané was president of the American Psychological Association Executive Committee (1970–1980). His awards and honors include the Behavioral Science Award, American Association for the Advancement of Science (AAAS) (1968); Richard M. Elliot Memorial Award (1968); AAAS Behavioral Science Award (1980); Cattell Fellowship (1981); Donald T. Campbell Award, Society for Personality and Social Psychology (1986); and Distinguished Scientific Contribution Award, Society of Experimental Social Psychology (1997). Latané was editor, associate editor or on the editorial board of several distinguished psychology journals.

Major Contributions

Latané and John Darley developed the theory of social impact, partly to explain the diffusion of responsibility. Diffusion of responsibility is the concept that each person is only responsible for an equal proportion of effort based on the number of people in a group. One explanation is that in a group an individual is anonymous and is not readily pointed out as an individual who can or should help. Another possibility is that of not wanting to push one's self forward as an expert. The three principles in Latané and Darley's theory of social impact are:

- the number of people present and the influence the people have on an individual both contribute to the social effect
- the impact of others increases as the number of people increases, but the rate of impact does not increase with the number of others added
- each person influences others, but as the audience size increases the influence decreases.

On group influence, Latané hypothesizes that the evangelist Billy Graham would be more effective speaking to small audiences than to larger audiences. The number of people who responded to Graham's call for converts in different sized audiences was examined. Consistent with the theory, those in smaller audiences were more willing to let local ministers contact them.

Major Literature

Latané, Bibb, and J.M. Darley. "Bystander Apathy." *American Scientist* 57 (1969): 244–268.
___. *The Unresponsive Bystander: Why Doesn't He Help?* New Jersey: Appleton-Century-Crofts, 1970.
Latané, Bibb and James M. Dabbs, Jr. "Sex, Group Size and Helping in Three Cities." *Sociometry* 38, No. 2 (1975): 180–194.
Latané, Bibb. "The Psychology of Social Impact." *American Psychologist* 36 (1981): 373.
___, and S. Nida. "Ten Years of Research on Group Size and Helping." *Psychological Bulletin* 89 (1981): 308–324.

Lazarus, Arnold Allan (1932–)

MULTIMODAL THERAPY

Born in Johannesburg, Transvaal, South Africa, Arnold Allan Lazarus earned a B.A. with honors (1956) and an M.A. (1957) and Ph.D. in clinical psychology (1960) at the University of Witwatersrand, Johannesburg. He was visiting assistant professor of psychology at Stanford University, California (1963); lecturer in psychiatry, University of Witwatersrand (1964); director, Behavior Therapy Institute, Sausalito, California (1966); professor of behavioral science, Temple University Medical School, Philadelphia (1967); visiting professor of psychology and director of clinical training, Yale University, New Haven, Connecticut (1970); distinguished professor of psychology, Rutgers University, New Jersey (1972), and is professor emeritus in the Graduate School of Applied and Professional Psychology at Rutgers University.

His awards and honors include election to the National Academy of Practice in Psychology (1982); Lifetime Achievement Awards from the California Psychological Association and the Association for Advancement of Behavior Therapy (1999); the Distinguished Career Award from the American Board of Medical Psychotherapists; fellow of the Academy of Clinical Psychology; and diplomate of the International Academy of Behavioral Medicine, Counseling, and Psychotherapy. In addition to his many books and articles, Lazarus has made videos and sound recordings of his methods.

Major Contributions

Lazarus was the first psychologist to apply desensitization techniques (see entry for Wolpe, Joseph) for treating phobias in group therapy sessions. He founded the Multimodal Therapy Institute in Kingston, New Jersey, in 1976, which he continues to direct. He established additional multimodal therapy institutes in New York, Virginia, Pennsylvania, Illinois, Texas, and Ohio. Lazarus developed multimodal therapy (MMT) in part by questioning clients about the factors that had helped them in their therapy.

Multimodal therapy involves examining and treating seven different but interrelated modalities, or psychological parameters that have the acronym BASIC ID:

1. Behavior
2. Affect
3. Sensation
4. Imagery
5. Cognition
6. Interpersonal relationships
7. Drugs/biology

Multimodal therapists seek the answer to the question: What works, for whom, and under what conditions? The therapy is tailor-made to the individual's needs. MMT overlaps cognitive behavior therapy and rational emotive therapy. The major points all three have in common are:

1. Most problems arise from deficient or faulty social learning.
2. The client is related more to as a trainee than as a sick person.
3. Transfer of learning to the client's everyday life is deliberately fostered through homework and other assignments.
4. Labels, diagnoses, traits and generalized descriptions are avoided.

Major Literature

Lazarus, Arnold Allan. "Multi Modal Behavior Therapy: Treating the BASIC I.D." *Journal of Nervous and Mental Disease* 156 (1973): 404–411.
___ (Ed.). *Multi Modal Behavior Therapy.* New York: Springer-Verlag, 1976.
___. *The Practice of Multi Modal Therapy.* New York: McGraw-Hill, 1981. Baltimore: Johns Hopkins University Press, 1989.
___. *Dual Relationships and Psychotherapy.* New York: Springer-Verlag, 2002.
___. *Brief but Comprehensive Psychotherapy: The Multimodal Way.* New York: Springer-Verlag, 2006.

Lazarus, Richard S. (1920–2002)
STRESS APPRAISAL

Born in New York City, Richard S. Lazarus graduated (1942) from City College, New York, then served for three and a half years in the U.S. Army during World War II. He gained his Ph.D. (1947) from the University of Pittsburgh, Pennsylvania, and subsequently served on the faculties of Johns Hopkins University, Baltimore, Maryland, and Clark University, Worcester, Massachusetts, before becoming professor of psychology at the University of California, Berkeley.

Lazarus received many awards, including a Guggenheim Fellowship, honorary doctorates from the University of Haifa and the Johannes Gutenberg University in Mainz, Germany, and in 1989, the Distinguished Scientific Contribution to Psychology Award from the American Psychological Association. Although he retired from Berkeley in 1991, his writing and research did not stop; of his 13 books, five were written after his retirement. He was named by *American Psychologist* as one of the most influential psychologists in the history of the psychology of stress.

Major Contributions

Lazarus's work influenced psychology in many ways. At a time when psychology was focused on behavior learned by associations, rewards or punishments, Lazarus stressed the study of cognition. His experiments on the role of unconscious processes in perception were well ahead of their time. He also made significant contributions to the study of emotions, and helped keep alive the concept of emotion during a time when it was virtually ignored by other psychologists.

His theory of emotion centered on the concept of appraisal — how an individual evaluates the impact of an event on his or her self or well-being — a concept which he elaborated upon extensively in his classic work *Emotion and Adaptation*. He showed how appraisal explains the meaning of a person's emotional behavior, how a single response, like a smile, can be in the service of many different emotions; and how totally different responses, like retaliation or passive aggressiveness, can be in the service of the same emotion.

He moved into the study of stress and coping and established the Berkeley Stress and Coping Project, in which he extended his ideas on the importance of appraisal to explain exactly what stress is and what coping involves. This led to the development of the Daily Hassles and Uplift Scale and Ways of Coping Checklist. Lazarus proposed that the way we respond to a stressful event depends on how we appraise it, and if we believe we have the ability to cope with it. The reality of the stress is less important than our perception of the threat in determining how we react emotionally and physiologically.

Major Literature

Lazarus, Richard S. and Susan Folkman. *Stress, Appraisal, and Coping.* New York: Springer-Verlag, 1984.

Lazarus, Richard S., and Bernice N. Lazarus. *Passion and Reason: Making Sense of Our Emotions.* New York: Oxford University Press Inc., 1995.

Lazarus, Richard S., *Stress and Emotion: A New Synthesis.* London: Free Association Books Ltd., 1999, 2006.

Lazarus, Richard S., and Carolyn M. Aldwin. *Stress, Coping, and Development: An Integrative Perspective.* New York: Guilford Press, 2000.

Lewin, Kurt (1890–1947)
GESTALT PSYCHOLOGY

Born in Moglino, Germany (now Poland), Kurt Lewin joined the German army (1914). He was injured in combat and awarded the Iron Cross. He received a Ph.D. from the University of Berlin (1916). He was lecturer (1921–1926) and professor (1927) at the Psychological Institute, University of Berlin, and visiting professor at Stanford University in California (1932). Lewin fled Germany to United States via England (1933) and was on the faculty of Cornell University, Ithaca, New York. He was granted American citizenship in 1940. He was professor, State University of Iowa's Child Welfare Research Station (1935), and president of the Society for the Psychological Study of Social Issues (1942).

Lewin established and directed the Kurt Lewin Research Center for Group Dynamics, Massachusetts Institute of Technology (MIT) at Cambridge (1944–1947); established the Commission on Community Interrelations (1944); and created National Laboratories Training (1947). The Society for the Psychological Study of Social Issues founded the Lewin Memorial Award (1950); Gordon Allport (see entry) was first recipient (1950).

Major Contributions

Lewin is universally recognized as the founder of modern social psychology. He believed that prejudice causes discrimination, rather than being a result of it, altering that behavior could change attitudes. He was one of the first researchers to study group dynamics, sensitivity training and organizational development. He looked to the nature of group task in an attempt to understand the uniformity of some groups' behavior.

Influenced by Gestalt psychology, Lewin developed a theory that emphasized the importance of individual personalities, interpersonal conflict, and situational variables. His "field theory" had a major impact on social psychology, supporting the notion that our individual traits and the environment interact to cause behavior. The whole psychological field, or "lifespace," within which people act has to be viewed in order to understand behavior. Individuals participate in a series of life spaces (such as the family, work, school and church) and have to be viewed in the context of the particular lifespace in order to understand the person.

Out of his field theory Lewin developed force field analysis (FFA), a decision-making technique widely used in counseling. It is designed to help people understand the various internal and external forces that influence the way they make decisions. Mostly, these forces are in relative balance, but when something disturbs the balance, decisions are more difficult to make. When the forces are identified, counselor and client work on strategies to help the client reach the desired goal. The underlying principle is that by strengthening the facilitating forces and diminishing the restraining forces, a decision will be easier to make because energy, trapped by the restraining forces, has been released. This is an example of how Lewin turned theory into practice.

Major Literature

Lewin, Kurt. *A Dynamic Theory of Personality*. Columbus, Ohio: McGraw-Hill Education, 1935.

___. *Field Theory in Social Science: Selected Theoretical Papers*. New York: Harper Collins Publishers, Inc., 1951.

___. *Resolving Social Conflicts*. Washington, D.C.: American Psychological Association, 1997.

___. *The Complete Social Scientist: A Kurt Lewin Reader*. Washington, D.C.: American Psychological Association, 1999.

Lewis, Michael (1937–)

DEVELOPMENTAL PSYCHOLOGY

Born in Brooklyn, New York, Michael Lewis gained a B.A. (1958) and Ph.D. (1962) from the University of Pennsylvania, Philadelphia. He is university distinguished professor of pediatrics and psychiatry and director of the Institute for the Study of Child Development at Robert Wood Johnson Medical School, University of Medicine and Dentistry of New Jersey. He also is professor of psychology, education, cognitive science, and biomedical engineering at Rutgers University, New Jersey.

He is fellow of the American Psychological Association; fellow of the American Association for the Advancement of Sciences; consulting editor for *Journal of Sex Roles*, *Psychological Enquiry*, and *Infant Behavior and Development*. Lewis is a fellow of the New York Academy of Sciences, American Psychological Association, and American Association of the Advancement of Science, as well as the Japan Society for the Promotion of Science. In 1995, he was ranked by a University of Notre Dame study number 1 in terms of the impact of scientists who are most referenced and productive in the field of developmental sciences. He serves or has served on many national committees concerned with mental health and development.

Major Contributions

Lewis has focused his research on normal and deviant emotional and intellectual development, particularly on how the central nervous system is organized and functions. He has developed a computer-based technique for enhancing intellectual ability in children suffering from a variety of disorders associated with learning difficulties, such as Down syndrome and cerebral palsy. He has also done work on mirror recognition, a simple test used since 1970 to determine whether an animal is self-aware. Few animal species pass this test, and children one year old and below typically fail the test as well.

Lewis argues that children's environments, at whatever age, determine how children behave, and he suggests that altering environments should be the major task in effecting social adjustment and mental health. More recently still Lewis has been working on gifted children, particularly those from low socioeconomic status. The Gifted Child Clinic, New Brunswick, New Jersey, a research and parental resource center, serves as a referral agency for children who are thought to be gifted or talented. *Children's Emotions and Moods* was the first book devoted to emotional development. He has had published over 350 articles and chapters in professional journals and scholarly texts.

Major Literature

Lewis, Michael, and J. Brooks-Gunn. *Social Cognition and the Acquisition of Self*. New York: Plenum Publishing Corporation, 1979.

Lewis, Michael. *Children's Emotions and Moods: Developmental Theory and Measurement.* New York: Plenum Publishing Corporation, 1983.

___. *Shame: The Exposed Self.* New York: Simon and Schuster Inc., The Free Press, 1992.

___. *Altering Fate: Why the Past Does Not Predict the Future.* New York: Guilford Press, 1997.

___, and Jeanette M. Haviland-Jones. *Handbook of Emotions.* New York: Guilford Press, 2000.

Slater, Alan, and Michael Lewis. *Introduction to Infant Development.* New York: Oxford University Press Inc., 2002.

Lifton, Robert Jay (1926–)

PSYCHOHISTORY

Born in Brooklyn, New York, Robert Jay Lifton graduated in medicine from New York Medical College (1948). His internship was at the Jewish Hospital, Brooklyn (1948–1949) and his psychiatric residence training at Downstate Medical Center, Brooklyn (1949–1951). He was an Air Force psychiatrist (1951–1952) in the United States, Japan, and Korea and on the teaching staff at Washington School of Psychiatry. At Harvard University, Cambridge, Massachusetts (1956–1961), he was research associate in psychiatry and affiliated with the Center for East Asian Studies.

He was visiting professor of psychiatry, Harvard Medical School and Cambridge Hospital, Massachusetts; former distinguished professor of psychiatry and psychology, Graduate School University Center; and director of the Center on Violence and Human Survival at John Jay College of Criminal Justice, the City University of New York.

Major Contributions

During the 1960s, Lifton, together with Erik Erikson (see entry) and the historian Bruce Mazlish, formed the Wellfleet Psychohistory Group, which focused mainly on psychological motivations for war, terrorism and genocide in recent history. In 1965, the group received sponsorship from the American Academy of Arts and Sciences to establish psychohistory as a separate field of study. Lifton studied thought reform or "brainwashing" (mind control) and was a defense witness in the 1976 trial of the American heiress Patty Hearst. He stated that the Symbionese Liberation Army had used similar techniques to produce a temporary behavioral change in Hearst. Lifton describes eight methods that are used to change people's minds without their agreement:

1. *milieu control*, controlled relations with the outer world
2. *mystic manipulation*, events are orchestrated to appear miraculous or spontaneous
3. *confession*, strong pressure to make a person confess past and present "sins"
4. *self-sanctification through purity*, pushing the individual toward perfection
5. *aura of sacred science*, beliefs of the group are sacrosanct and perfect
6. *loaded language*, new meanings to words, encouraging black and white thinking
7. *doctrine over person*, ideology and the group are more important than the individual
8. *dispensed existence*, insiders are saved, outsiders are doomed

Lifton spoke vigorously against the Vietnam War, the U.S. nuclear strategy, and the Iraq War, believing that they arose from irrational and aggressive aspects of American politics motivated by fear. He has also criticized the current "war on terrorism" as misguided and dangerous. On the lighter side, Lifton refers to cartooning as his real vocation; he has published two books of humorous cartoons about birds.

Major Literature

Lifton, Robert Jay. *Death in Life: Survivors of Hiroshima.* New York: Random House, 1968.

___. *Birds, Words, and Birds* (cartoons). New York: Random House, 1969.

___. *Home From the War: Vietnam Veterans — Neither Victims Nor Executioners.* New York: Simon and Schuster, 1973.

Olson, Eric, and Robert Jay Lifton. *Explorations in Psychohistory: The Wellfleet Papers.* New York: Simon and Schuster, 1975.

Lifton, Robert Jay. *The Nazi Doctors: Medical Killing and the Psychology of Genocide.* Jackson, Tennessee: Basic Books, 1986.

___. *Destroying the World to Save It.* New York: Henry Holt and Company, Inc., Owl Books, 1999.

Loevinger, Jane (1918–)

DEVELOPMENTAL PSYCHOLOGY

Born into a Jewish family from St. Paul, Minnesota, Jane Loevinger earned a B.A. with honors (1937) and an M.S. in psychometrics (1938) from the University of Minnesota, Minneapolis, and a Ph.D. (1944) at the University of California, Berkeley. Women Jewish graduates did not find employment easy in 1937 but in 1938 she took a teaching assistantship at Berkeley, where she became a research assistant to Erik Erikson (see entry).

During World War II she moved between Berkeley and Stanford University, California, then spent one year working on her dissertation — construction and evaluation of tests of ability — in which she carried out a critique of psychometric theory and test reliability, proving that all definitions of test reliability were circular (a circular definition is one that assumes a prior understanding of the term being defined). Nobody would publish such a heretical paper, so she paid for it to be published.

In July 1943, she married Sam Weissman a scientist stationed at Los Alamos National Security Laboratory, New Mexico. The family (now with two children) stayed at Los Alamos until shortly after the second atomic bomb was dropped, on Nagasaki. In the immediate post-war period, Loevinger felt unfulfilled; jobs were more likely to be given to men and she felt that employers were prejudiced against women. This situation led her to develop an interest in the experience of women and motherhood; she was one of the first people in psychological research to focus on women as a slice of the population.

Her research — funded by the National Institute for Mental Health — began with an objective test of mothers' attitudes, working in an informal weekly group, at first discussing whatever problems mothers, and women in general, faced throughout the day and throughout the life cycle. She, and others working with her, developed the sentence completion test (SCT), which measures ego development (not to be confused with any psychoanalytic connotations of the word "ego"), which included moral development, interpersonal relations and grasp of concepts. The SCT correlates the answers of thirty-four open-ended sentences such as "most men think that women..." or "sometimes she wished that...." Loevinger identifies nine sequential ego stages of development, each of which represents a progressively more complex way of perceiving oneself in relation to the world:

1. *Infancy*— not differentiated from the world
2. *Impulsive*— curbed by restraints, rewards and punishments
3. *Self-Protective*—"don't get caught"
4. *Conformist*— security equals belonging
5. *Self-Aware*— self distinct from norms and expectations
6. *Conscientious*— sense of responsibility
7. *Individualistic*— inner reality versus outward appearance
8. *Autonomous*— integrates different identities
9. *Integrated*— self-actualizing

Major Literature

Loevinger, Jane. *Measuring Ego Development Construction and Use of a Sentence Completion Test: 001.* San Francisco: Jossey-Bass, 1970.
___. *Ego Development.* San Francisco: Jossey-Bass, 1976.
___. *Paradigms of Personality.* New York: Freeman, 1987.
___. *Technical Foundations for Measuring Ego Development: Washington University Sentence Completion Test.* Personality and Clinical Psychology Series. Hillsdale, New Jersey: Erlbaum Associates Inc. 1998.

Loftus, Elizabeth F. (1944–)
STUDY OF MEMORY

Born in Los Angeles, California, Elizabeth F. Loftus gained a B.A. from the University California, Los Angeles (1966), and an M.A. (1967) and Ph.D. (1970) from Stanford University, California. She was assistant professor, New School for Social Research, New York (1970–1973); assistant, associate, and full professor at the University of Washington, Seattle (1973–2002); fellow of the American Council on Education (1975–1976); member of the National Science Foundation (1977); fellow of the Center for Advanced Study in Behavioral Science (1978–1979); distinguished professor, University of California, Irvine (since 2002); and affiliate professor, University of Washington, Psychology Department and School of Law (since 2002).

Her honorary doctorates include science, Miami University, Ohio (1982); Leiden University, the Netherlands (1990); doctor of laws, John Jay College of Criminal Justice, City University of New York (1994); science, University of Portsmouth, England (1998); and philosophy, University of Haifa, Israel (2005). Loftus received the Distinguished Contribution Award from the American Academy of Forensic Psychology (1995).

Major Contributions

Loftus studies human memory and over the last 20 years has been an expert witness where eyewitness testimony is called into question. Her experiments reveal how facts, ideas, suggestions and things that we are told can modify our memories. She has written extensively on false memory related to childhood trauma (usually sexual), memories implanted by therapists, usually under hypnosis. She is an important spokesperson for the False Memory Syndrome Foundation.

Her work in this area centers around an attempt to prevent innocent people from being prosecuted and families from being torn apart by accusations of sexual molestation based on the false memory phenomenon. She has studied over 20,000 subjects showing that eyewitness testimonies are often unreliable and that false memories can be triggered in up to 25 percent of people merely by suggestion or giving of incorrect post-event information. While not denying child sexual abuse, or that repression of a trauma is possible, she questions the accuracy of those memories and the techniques used to resurface such memories. The whole arena of refuting false memory is fraught with difficulty and danger. Loftus is currently (2006) being sued — *Taus v. Loftus*—for publishing confidential material. Loftus refutes the claim that Taus was sexually abused by her father as a child.

Major Literature

Loftus, G.R. and Elizabeth F. Loftus. Human Memory: Processing of Information. Hillsdale, New Jersey: Erlbaum Associates, Inc., 1976.

Wortman, Camille B., and Elizabeth F. Loftus. Psychology. New York: Random House, Inc., 1988.

Loftus, Elizabeth F. "The Reality of Repressed Memories." American Psychologist 48 (1993): 518–537.

___. "Desperately Seeking Memories of the First Few Years of Childhood: The Reality of Early Memories." Journal of Experimental Psychology 122 (1993): 247–277.

Loftus, Elizabeth F., and K. Ketcham. *The Myth of Repressed Memory*. New York: St. Martin's Press, 1994.

Lombroso, Cesare (1835–1909)

CRIMINAL ANTHROPOLOGY

Born into a wealthy Jewish family in Verona, Italy, Cesare Lombroso studied at the universities of Padua, Italy, Vienna, Austria, and Paris, France, and in 1859 was an army surgeon. From 1862 to 1876 he was professor of diseases of the mind (psychiatry) at the University of Pavia, Italy. In 1871 he became director of the mental asylum at Pesaro, northwest of Rome, and in 1876 he became professor of forensic medicine and hygiene at the University of Turin, where he subsequently held appointments as professor of psychiatry (1896) and then of criminal anthropology (1906).

He was a historical figure in modern criminology, and the founder of the Italian school of positivist criminology, which rejected the established classical school's stance that crime was a characteristic trait of human nature. Lombroso's theory was that criminality was inherited, and that the born criminal could be identified by physical defects, which confirmed a criminal as savage, or atavistic, biological throwbacks to a more primi-

tive stage of human evolution. He contended that such criminals exhibit a higher percentage of physical and mental anomalies than do non-criminals. If criminality were inherited, then the born criminal could be distinguished by physical atavistic stigmata, such as:

- Large jaws, forward projection of jaw, low sloping forehead
- High cheekbones, flattened or upturned nose
- Handle-shaped ears
- Hawk-like noses or fleshy lips
- Hard, shifty eyes, scanty beard or baldness
- Insensitivity to pain, long arms.

Lombroso also studied female criminals and concluded that female criminals were rare because they lacked the intelligence and initiative to become criminal. With successive research, and with more thorough statistical analysis, Lombroso modified his theories. He continued to define additional atavistic stigmata, as well as the lack of effectiveness in the treatment of born criminals.

In attempting to predict criminality by the shapes of the skulls and other physical features of criminals, Lombroso had in effect created a new pseudoscience of forensic phrenology. Lombroso's scientific study of criminals were widely influential in Europe for a time, although his emphasis on hereditary causes of crime was later strongly rejected in favor of environmental factors. His work influenced the development of the eugenics movement in the early twentieth century. Lombroso tried to reform the Italian penal system by encouraging more humane and constructive treatment of convicts through rehabilitation and the abolition of capital punishment.

Major Literature

Lombroso, Cesare. *The Criminal Man*. Durham, North Carolina: Duke University Press, 1876, 2006.

___. *The Man of Genius*. London, England: Taylor and Francis Books Ltd., 1889, 1985.

___. *Crime, Its Causes and Remedies*. Glen Ridge, New Jersey: Patterson Smith, 1899, 1968.

___. *Criminal Woman, the Prostitute, and the Normal Woman*. Durham, North Carolina: Duke University Press, 2004.

Luria, Alexander Romanovich (1902–1977)

NEUROPSYCHOLOGY

Born in Kazan, a small town east of Moscow, Russia, Alexander Romanovich Luria graduated at the age of nineteen from Kazan State University.

While a student, he established the Kazan Psychoanalytic Association and exchanged letters with Sigmund Freud. In 1923, his work with reaction times related to thought processes earned him a position at the Institute of Psychology in Moscow, where he developed the "combined motor method," which helped diagnose individuals' thought processes, creating the first lie detector device. This research was published in the U.S. in 1932 and in Russian for the first time in 2002.

In the 1930s, Luria explored Central Asia, investigating various psychological changes (including perception, problem solving, and memory). He also studied identical and fraternal twins in large residential schools to determine various cognitive factors. In the late 1930s, Luria went to medical school (partly to escape the Great Purges being carried out by Josef Stalin), and gained his doctor of padagogical sciences (psychology) in 1936.

He specialized in the study of aphasia, focusing on the relation between language, thought, and cortical function, focusing considerable attention on the development of compensatory functions for aphasia. In 1939 he moved to the Neurological Clinic of the Institute of Experimental Medicine, Moscow, where he became head of the Laboratory of Experimental Psychology.

During World War II, Luria was a medical officer at an army hospital responsible for a research team looking for ways to compensate for psychological dysfunctions after brain injuries. He was moved to the Institute of Neurosurgery in Moscow and in 1950, on account of his Jewish descent, he was removed from his position, but later restored and continued there until his death.

Luria helped to start the psychology department of Moscow State University and was one of its key professors. The Luria-Nebraska Neuropsychological Test (still used in psychiatry) is a standardized test based on his theories of neuropsychological functioning. There are 11 scales: motor functions, rhythm, tactile functions, visual functions, receptive speech, expressive speech, writing, reading, arithmetic, memory, and intellectual processes. It is used with people who are 15 years or older; however, it may be used with adolescents down to 12 years old.

Major Literature

Luria, Alexander Romanovich. *Traumatic Aphasia: Its Syndromes, Psychology, and Treatment*. New York: Mouton De Gruyter, 1970.

___. *The Working Brain*. Jackson, Tennessee: Basic Books, 1973.

___. *The Making of Mind: Personal Account of Soviet Psychology*. Cambridge, Massachusetts: Harvard University Press, 1986.

___, and Jerome Bruner. *The Mind of a Mnemonist: A Little Book About a Vast Memory*. Cambridge, Massachusetts: Harvard University Press, 1987.

Luria, Alexander Romanovich, and Lynn Solotaroff. *The Man With a Shattered World: The History of a Brain Wound*. Cambridge, Massachusetts: Harvard University Press, 1987.

Luria, Alexander Romanovich, Mike Cole, and Karl Levitin. *The Autobiography of Alexander Luria: A Dialogue With the Making of Mind*. Hillsdale, New Jersey: Erlbaum Associates Inc., 2005.

Lynn, Richard (1930–)

INTELLIGENCE

British-born, educated at Cambridge University, and a Richard Lynn is emeritus professor of psychology at the University of Ulster, Ireland. He is known for his research, controversial books, book chapters and journal articles on race and sex differences in intelligence. In the late 1970s he published that East Asians demonstrate a higher average IQ than whites, and in 1982 he published an article in *Nature* announcing that IQ scores in Japan were increasing. James R. Flynn, emeritus professor of political studies at the University of Otago in Dunedin, New Zealand, also commented on the continued year-on-year rise of IQ test scores in all parts of the world, which led to the "Flynn effect" or the "Lynn-Flynn effect."

Lynn hypothesized that the change was due to improved nutrition. Lynn's psychometric studies were cited in *The Bell Curve* and came under criticism as part of the controversy surrounding that book. Another controversial subject is skin color and IQ; he concludes that lightness of skin color in African-Americans is positively correlated with a higher IQ, derived from the higher proportion of Caucasian mix, which would suggest that he is also referring to white genes.

Lynn and others also argue that the wealthier the nation, the higher the IQ is likely to be, and that the national wealth can be attributed to the higher IQ. Lynn is not without his critics; he has been accused of disregarding scientific objectivity, misrepresenting data, and racism, and that some studies quoted by Lynn show cultural bias. On speaking at a conference in Britain in 2000, Lynn pointed to the problems of unemployment, crime, illegitimacy, and low IQ, considering African and

African-Caribbean immigrants to perform worse in these measures than Indian and Chinese immigrants.

Another controversial subject is brain size; correlating brain size and reaction time with measured intelligence led him to the conclusion that women have smaller brains than men, and that men have a higher IQ than women. Lynn proposes that history has not treated the study of eugenics kindly, probably due to the bad press it received under the Nazis. He argues that eugenics can play a positive role in the eradication of genetic diseases, increasing intelligence, and reducing personality disorders. While there is no doubt that Lynn's work has been controversial and will remain so, he has to be admired for publishing on topics that will keep alive the whole question of IQ for many years to come.

Major Literature

Lynn, Richard. "IQ in Japan and the United States Shows a Growing Disparity." *Nature* 297 (1982): 222–3.
___. "The Role of Nutrition in Secular Increases of Intelligence." *Personality and Individual Differences* 11 (1990): 273–285.
___. *Dysgenics: Genetic Deterioration in Modern Populations.* Westport, Connecticut: Praeger, 1996.
___. *Eugenics: A Reassessment.* Westport, Connecticut: Praeger, 2001.
___, and T. Vanhanen. *IQ and the Wealth of Nations.* Westport, Connecticut: Praeger, 2002.

Maccoby, Eleanor Emmons (1917–)
PSYCHOLOGY OF SEX-DIFFERENCES

Born in Tacoma, Washington, Eleanor Emmons married Nathan Maccoby in 1938. She gained a B.S. at the University of Washington, Seattle (1939), and spent the war years in Washington, D.C., examining the impact of wartime programs. She gained an M.A. (1949) and a Ph.D. in experimental psychology (1950) at the University of Michigan Ann Arbor. Maccoby was lecturer and research associate in social relations at Harvard University, Cambridge, Massachusetts (1950–1958); associate professor (1958); and the first woman chair of the Psychology Department (1973–1976) at Stanford University, California.

She was president of the Western Psychological Association (1974–1975); vice chair of the Committee on Child Development and Public Policy for the National Research Council (1977–1983); president of the Society for Research in Child Development (1981–1983); and chairwoman of the Institute for Research on Women, Gender, and Social Science (1984–1985). Her awards and honors include the Gores Award for Excellence in Teaching (1981); Gordon Stanley Hall Award (1982); Distinguishing Science Contribution to Child Development (1987); Lifetime Achievement Award from the American Psychology Foundation (1996); and president of the Consortium of Social Science (since 1997).

Major Contributions

Maccoby worked through three different research perspectives: behavioral theory, learning theory, and cognitive-developmental theory. Her study at Harvard, supervising fieldwork for interviews of mothers as part of a study on child rearing practices, focused on the socialization of children, developmental change in personality and behavior, relationships of couples after divorce, and parent-child interactions. Maccoby conducted some of the first studies on the impact of television on the lives of families, and more specifically, children, and in 1957, identification with fictional movie characters. Maccoby believed that identification and parent-child socialization were important moderating variables in the development of personality.

In their influential book *Psychology of Sex Differences*—a review of some 1600 studies of gender differences—Maccoby and Jacklin identified four major differences between the sexes: verbal ability is superior in females; visuo-spatial ability is superior in males; males have more mathematical ability; and females are less aggressive than males. In 1981, Maccoby launched a longitudinal investigation of gender differences in children during the first six years of development, and in 1990, she performed a longitudinal investigation of families going through divorce. Her more recent work has focused on children's socialization and the development of sex differences.

Major Literature

Sears, R.R., H. Levin, and Eleanor Emmons Maccoby. *Patterns of Child Rearing.* Palo Alto, California: Stanford University Press, 1957.
Maccoby, Eleanor Emmons. *Experiments in Primary Education.* New York: Harcourt, Brace and Company, 1970.
___, and C.N. Jacklin. *Psychology of Sex Differences.* Palo Alto, California: Stanford University Press, 1974.
Maccoby, Eleanor Emmons. *Social Development: Psychological Growth and the Parent-Child Relationship.* New York: Harcourt, Brace and Company, 1980.
___. *The Two Sexes: Growing Up Apart, Coming Together.*

Family and Public Policy Series. Cambridge, Massachusetts: Harvard University Press, 1999.

Mahler, Margaret Schonberger (1897–1985)

SEPARATION OF INFANT FROM MOTHER

Margaret Schoenberger was born in Sopron, Hungary, the daughter of a Jewish physician. She graduated with honors as a doctor from the University of Jena, Germany, in 1922. Her license to practice in Germany was refused on account of her being Jewish, but in 1923 she was granted a license in Vienna, where she was appointed as school doctor, but she soon moved from pediatrics to psychoanalysis, and she was accepted as an analyst in 1933.

She married Paul Mahler in 1936 and they fled from the Nazis to England, where they spent their time trying to help others escape and immigrate to America. In 1938 the British Psychoanalytic Society loaned them the money to move to America, where she received a New York medical license and started her private practice. In 1940, having given a child analysis seminar, and becoming the senior teacher of child analysis, she joined the Institute of Human Development and the Educational Institute along with the New York Psychoanalytic Society.

She received the American Psychological Association Agnes Purceil McGavin Award in 1969 and in 1981 the Distinguished Service Award. The Margaret S. Mahler Psychiatric Research Foundation (Wynnewood, Pennsylvania) was established in 1970.

Major Contributions

Her passion was, and remained, working with children. In 1950 she joined the staff of the Albert Einstein School of Medicine in New York and was the chairman of the child analysis training program, which she continued into the 1960s. During 1950 she co-founded the therapeutic nursery for psychotic children at Einstein. This was used to study if child psychosis occurs at one and a half and through the age of two. Mahler believed that the "psychological birth is not simultaneous to the biological birth."

Mahler placed great emphasis on the importance of physical and psychological holding of a child. The latter keeps tension and frustration from becoming too great. Wrong holding can include not holding a child physically or psychologically when it needs to be held, or holding it too tightly in a way that is felt as smothering, so that individuality does not have a chance to develop. If the mother isn't there for the child when it tries to move away, the child is forced to move away too soon. Until her death Mahler continued to write, teach, and supervise analysts in training in New York and Philadelphia.

Major Literature

Mahler, Margaret Schonberger. *On Human Symbosis and the Vicissitudes of Individuation: Infantile Psychoses.* New York: International Universities Press Inc., 1968.
___, Fred Pine, and Anni Bergman. *The Psychological Birth of the Human Infant: Symbiosis and Individuation.* Jackson, Tennessee: Basic Books, 1975, 2000.
Mahler, Margaret Schonberger. *Separation-Individuation: Selected Papers of Margaret S. Mahler.* Lanham, Maryland: Rowman and Littlefield Publishers, Inc., Jason Aronson, 1977.
___. *Infantile Psychosis and Early Contributions: Selected Papers of Margaret S. Mahler.* Lanham, Maryland: Rowman and Littlefield Publishers, Inc., Jason Aronson, 1994.

Martin, Lillien Jane (1851–1943)

GERONTOLOGICAL PSYCHOLOGY

Born in Olean, New York, Lillien Jane Martin graduated from Vassar College in Poughkeepsie, New York, in 1880, then taught high school physics and chemistry in Indianapolis. She studied general psychology, aesthetics, the subconscious, and humor in relation to psychology at the University of Göttingen, Germany, which awarded her a Ph.D. in 1898. She continued her studies during summers in Germany until 1914. By 1911 she was full professor at Stanford University, California, and in 1915 she became the first woman to head a department at the university.

In 1913 Martin was presented with an honorary Ph.D. from the University of Bonn for her experimental psychology and aesthetics in reducing the subject of imageless thought to exact measurement, an honor that had never been granted to an American psychologist before. In 1910, in American Men of Science's official directory of qualified scientists in the United States, Martin was one of a few women mentioned for her contributions to the field of psychology.

From 1914 to 1915, she was the vice-president of Section H of Anthropology and Psychology of the American Association for the Advancement of Science, and the first female vice president in the history of the American Association for the Advancement of Science. She was a member of the American Psychological Association, and of Sigma Xi, the honorary scientific society, and held the office of president of California Society of Mental Hygiene. After retirement Martin became the president of the College Equal Suffrage League.

Major Contributions

On retirement as emeritus professor, she moved to San Francisco to set up a private consulting psychology practice and establish mental health clinics in the Polyclinic and Mount Zion hospitals for normal children of the pre-school years. It was her dream to have mental hygiene clinics in every hospital and for this information to be used for preventive purposes. Her *Mental Training for the Preschool Age* was written to help non-professionals to learn how to apply child psychology.

In 1929 she established the Old Age Center, a psychological clinic for aging men and women. Thereafter she devoted herself to gerontological research, clinical counseling and rehabilitation. She was a firm believer (and practiced it herself) of regular exercise for people of all ages.

Major Literature

Martin, Lillien Jane. "Psychology of Aesthetics: Experimental Prospecting in the Field of the Comic." *American Journal of Psychology* 16, 1 (1905): 35–118.
___. "Introspection Versus the Subconscious." *Psychology Review* 24, 3 (1917): 242–243.
___. "Mental Hygiene and the Importance of Investigating It." *Journal of Applied Psychology* 1 (1917): 67–70.
___, and Clare DeCruchy. *Mental Training for the Pre-School Age Child.* California: Harr Wagner Publishing Co., 1923.
Martin, Lillien Jane, and Clare DeCruchy. *Salvaging Old Age.* New York: The Macmillan Company, 1930.
Martin, Lillien Jane. *A Handbook for Old Age Counselors: The Method of Salvaging, Rehabilitating and Reconditioning Old People Used in the Old Age Counseling Center in San Francisco, California.* San Francisco: Geertz Printing Company, 1944.

Maslow, Abraham H.
(1908–1970)
Needs Hierarchy

Born in Brooklyn, New York, the son of Russian Jewish immigrants, Abraham Maslow gained a B.A. (1930), an M.A. (1931) and a Ph.D. (1934) in psychology at the University of Wisconsin, Madison. From 1935 to 1937 he was assistant to professor Edward L. Thorndike (see entry) at Columbia Teachers College, New York. From 1935 to 1937, he was on a Carnegie teaching fellowship and from 1937 to 1951 he taught at Brooklyn College, New York.

He was chairman of the psychology department at Brandeis University in Waltham, Massachusetts (1951–1969); president, Massachusetts Psychological Association (1960–1962); president, New England Psychological Association (1962–1963); and president of the American Psychological Association (1967). Maslow's awards and honors include the Humanist of the Year Award, American Humanist Association (1967); Laughlin Foundation Fellowship (1960–1970); and honorary doctorate, Xavier University, Cincinnati, Ohio.

Major Contributions

Maslow was an influential figure in humanistic psychology for his work on self-actualization and peak experiences, and in the development of the human potential movement; he founded the Esalen Institute, California. He proposed that the primary goal of psychotherapy should be the integration of the self and that integration is achieved as needs are experienced and met. The term "self-actualization" is used to describe the dominating, motivating life force that drives the individual toward ever-developing.

From his theory of personality is derived Maslow's hierarchy of human needs with five levels of needs related to motivation and problem-solving. A person must have experienced secure footing on the first rung in order to proceed to the next. Inability to fulfill a lower-order needs may create locked-in, immature behavior patterns; only as each need is satisfied are people motivated to reach for the next higher level. Thus, people who lack food or shelter, or who do not feel themselves to be in a safe environment, are unable to concentrate on the highest needs of self-actualization. Our drive for self-actualization may conflict with our rights and duties and responsibilities to other people.

Maslow did not say that all needs of a certain level must be fulfilled before progress upward was possible. It is a question of how much energy is being used up at a lower level. While people might be high on self-actualization today, tomorrow something could happen that would change that and thrust them back into satisfying their basic needs, for example an earthquake or some other disaster. The hierarchy:

Level 5: Self-actualization; growth and development

Level 4: Ego-status; ambition, status, approval

Level 3: Belongingness; relationships

Level 2: Safety; security, orderliness, protective rules and risk avoidance

Level 1: Basic; physiological and survival needs.

Major Literature

Maslow, Abraham H. *Motivation and Personality*. New York: Harper Collins Publishers, Inc., 1954.

___. *Toward a Psychology of Being*. New York: Van Nostrand Reinhold, 1962. New Jersey: John Wiley and Sons Inc., 1999.

___. *The Farther Reaches of Human Nature*. London, England: Penguin Books Ltd., Viking, 1971. New York: Arkana, 1993.

___. *The Maslow Business Reader*. New Jersey: John Wiley and Sons Inc., 2000.

May, Rollo Reese (1901–1994)
EXISTENTIAL PSYCHOTHERAPY

Born, in Ada, Ohio, Rollo Reese May graduated with a B.A. from Oberlin College, Ohio, then taught English for three years at Anatolia College, Greece, and briefly studied with Alfred Adler (see entry). May received his B.D. (1938) from Union Theological Seminary, New York, where one of his teachers was the existentialist theologian Paul Tillich, who had a profound effect on May's thinking. May practiced for two years as a Congregationalist minister before starting his psychology studies at Columbia University, New York.

During a three-year isolation with tuberculosis, facing the possibility of death, May filled his hours with reading Soren Kierkegaard, the Danish religious writer who inspired much of the existential movement; this provided the inspiration for May's theory. He went on to study psychoanalysis at William Alanson White Institute of Psychiatry in New York, where he met Harry Stack Sullivan and Erich Fromm (see entries) and gained his Ph.D. in clinical psychology from Columbia University in 1949. He lectured at the New School for Social Research, New York, and was a visiting professor at Harvard University, Cambridge, Massachusetts, Yale University, New Haven, Connecticut, and Princeton University, New Jersey. From 1958 he is most associated with the White Institute.

Major Contributions

He became a pioneer of humanistic psychology, although his theoretical approach has the added dimension of existentialism, not evident in, for example, the work of Abraham Maslow and Carl Rogers (see entries). And in contrast to cognitive psychology, he emphasized individual values and uniqueness in the practice of psychotherapy. Strongly influenced by American humanism, he sought to reconcile existential psychology with other approaches, especially psychoanalysis. May bridged the gap between European and American existentialism; he has been referred to as the "father of existential psychotherapy."

May can be credited with co-editing the first American book on existential psychology; *Existence* highly influenced the emergence of American humanistic psychology. May urges that a psychologist, in order to do justice to the human being who is his patient, must participate in the world of the client. With this basic motivation, May persuasively argues that an existential psychology is best equipped to help the clinician to do so without doing violence to the client. May spent the closing years of his life in Tiburon on the San Francisco Bay, where he died.

Major Literature

May, Rollo Reese. *The Meaning of Anxiety*. New York: W.W. Norton and Co. Ltd., 1950, 1996.

___. *Man's Search for Himself*. Surrey, England: Delta Publishing, 1953. London: Souvenir Press Ltd., 1982.

May, Rollo Reese, Ernest Angel, and Henri F. Ellenberger (Eds.). *Existence: A New Dimension in Psychiatry and Psychology*. New York: Basic Books, 1958.

May, Rollo Reese. *Love and Will*. New York: W.W. Norton and Co. Ltd., 1969. Bantam Doubleday Dell Publishing Group, 1996.

___. *The Discovery of Being*. New York: W.W. Norton and Co. Ltd., 1983, 1994.

___. *The Art of Counseling*. London: Taylor and Francis Books Ltd., Psychology Press, 1990.

___. *The Cry for Myth*. Surrey, England: Delta Publishing, 1991.

Mayo, Clara Alexandria Weiss (1931–1981)
SOCIAL PSYCHOLOGY

Clara Weiss, born in Linz, Austria, fled from the Nazis with her family to Paris in 1938 and settled in New York in 1939. She graduated in philosophy from Cornell University in Ithaca, New York (1953), and moved to New Hampshire when she married. She gained a master's degree from Wellesley College, Massachusetts (1955) in a program that focused on human relations service and a community mental health program. Her Ph.D. was from Clark University in Worchester, Massachusetts (1959); her dissertation explored the degree to which first impressions could be altered in the face of subsequent discrepant information.

She was a social psychology trainee at Veterans Administration Hospital in Brockton, Massachusetts (1959–1960); research social psychologist in Boston, studying people's perceptions of and attitudes about mental illness; lecturer in the psychology department, Boston University (1960–1964); and full professor, Boston University (1974). She directed the graduate Afro-American studies program. Mayo was president of the New England Psychological Association (1976–1977); member of the Society for Experimental Social Psychology; fellow of the American Psychological Association, Division 9; and was elected president of the Society for the Psychological Study of Social Issues (1981). She died a few months into her term of office.

Major Contributions

At Cornell, Mayo majored in philosophy and studied psychology under Urie Bronfenbrenner (see entry), assisting him in a research project, working mainly on detecting small behavior cues that demonstrated women as being excellent at reading other people's nonverbal cues. Her social psychology focused on four major themes: improving the quality of life, a commitment to knowledge building, a greater understanding of mental illness, and conquering racism and sexism in society.

Mayo was appointed to work on "Operation Exodus"— people affected by racial integration — which involved black families paying to bus their children to all-white schools in Boston. The research investigated why black families chose to do this and what the outcomes of their decisions were. Mayo researched nonverbal differences in how blacks and whites talked with one another. She also researched the treatment of African-American people in American courts. She stressed the importance of racial consideration in jury selection and offered expert testimony concerning the unfair treatment of black defendants in court proceedings and her belief in the necessity of asking potential jurors about their racial attitudes.

The Society for the Psychological Study of Social Issues set up the Clara Mayo grant program to support masters' theses or pre-dissertation research on aspects of sexism, racism, or prejudice, with preference given to students enrolled in a terminal master's program; up to four grants are awarded annually.

Major Literature

Lafrance, Marianne, and Clara Weiss Mayo. *Evaluating Research in Social Psychology: A Guide for the Consumer.* Pacific Grove, California: Brooks/Cole Publishing Company, 1977.

Lafrance, Marianne, and Clara Weiss Mayo. *Moving Bodies.* Pacific Grove, California: Brooks/Cole Publishing Company, 1978.

Mayo, Clara Weiss, and Nancy Henley. *Gender and Nonverbal Behavior.* Springer Series in Social Psychology. New York: Springer-Verlag, 1981.

McClelland, David Clarence (1917–1998)
ACHIEVEMENT MOTIVATION

Born at Mount Vernon, New York, David Clarence McClelland gained a B.A. at Wesleyan University, Middletown, Connecticut (1938), an M.A. at the University of Missouri-Columbia (1939) and a Ph.D. in experimental psychology at Yale University, New Haven, Connecticut (1941). He was lecturer at Connecticut College in New London, Connecticut, and Wesleyan University (1941–1956); professor of psychology, Department of Psychology and Social Relations at Harvard University, Cambridge, Massachusetts (1956–1987); and distinguished research professor of psychology, Boston University, Massachusetts (1987–1998).

He was a fellow, American Psychological Association (APA) (1948); on the APA Education and Training Board (1951–1952); Board of Directors of the Psychological Committee, Connecticut State Hospital, Middletown (1952–1956); Fulbright Advisory Panel on Psychology (1953–1956); National Institute of Mental Health Training Grants Committee for Clinical Psychology (1956–1961); founder, McBer consultancy, helping industry assess and train staff (1963); APA Committee on Psychology in National and International Affairs (1965–1967); APA Committee on Scientific Awards (1968–1969); and past president, Connecticut Valley Association of Psychologists, Connecticut State Psychological Society. His awards and honors include an honorary Sc.D. at Wesleyan University (1957), and honorary doctorates from Mainz University in Germany, McMurray University in Abilene, Texas, and Albion College, Michigan.

Major Contributions

McClelland is chiefly known for his work, extending over four decades, on achievement motivation, personality and consciousness. He describes three types of motivational need:

1. *The need for achievement (n-ach).* The n-ach person is "achievement motivated" and therefore seeks achievement, attainment of realistic but challenging goals, and advancement in the job. There is a strong need for feedback as to achievement and progress, and a need for a sense of accomplishment. While they may be effective leaders, they may demand too much of other people. Many people who are what is called "approval hungry" also have a high achievement drive.

2. *The need for authority and power (n-pow).* The n-pow person is "authority motivated." This drive produces a need to be influential, effective and to make an impact. There is a strong need to lead and for their ideas to prevail. There is also motivation and need towards increasing personal status and prestige. While they may be attracted to leadership, they may not be flexible enough to hold a team together.

3. *The n-affil person is "affiliation motivated,"* and has a need for friendly relationships and is motivated toward interaction with other people. The affiliation driver produces motivation with a need to be liked and held in popular regard. These people are team players. A need to be liked could undermine a manager's objectivity and influence decisions adversely.

Most people are a mix of all three types.

Major Literature

McClelland, David Clarence. *Personality*. New York: William Sloane, 1951.
___. *Studies in Motivation*. New Jersey: Appleton-Century-Crofts, 1955.
___. *The Achieving Society*. New York: Van Nostrand Reinhold, 1961. New York: Simon and Schuster Inc., The Free Press, 1985.
___. *Roots of Consciousness*. New York: Van Nostrand Reinhold, 1963.
___. *Power: The Inner Experience*. New York: Irvington Publishers, 1975. New York: Halstead-Wiley, 1995.
___. *Motives, Personality and Society: Selected Papers*. Westport, Connecticut: Greenwood Press, Praeger, 1984.

McDougall, William (1871–1938)
Experimental Psychology

Born in Chatterton, Lancashire, England, William McDougall gained a B.A. in sciences at Manchester University (1890) and a B.A. in natural sciences at St. John's College, Cambridge (1894), and graduated in medicine with specialties in physiology and neurology at St. Thomas's Hospital, London, and Cambridge University (1898). He was awarded the Grainger Testimonial Prize for his research on muscle contractions. He was elected into a fellowship at St. John's College to make a systematic study of contemporary psychology (1898). He spent time with G.E. Müller (see entry) at Göttingen University, Germany, continuing laboratory work on color vision and on attention.

In 1898 McDougall was attending physician on the Cambridge anthropological expedition to the Torres Straits, Australasia. From 1902 to 1904 he lectured and demonstrated on psychology under James Sully (1843–1823) at University College, London. He helped found the British Psychological Society (1901); was elected Wilde reader in mental philosophy at Oxford University (1904–1920) and opened an experimental research laboratory, the first experimental psychologist at Oxford.

He was a fellow of the Royal Society and of Corpus Christi College, Oxford (1912), and a major with the Royal Army Medical Corps (1914–1919), working with victims of shell shock (post-traumatic stress disorder). He was also William Clark Chair of Psychology, Harvard University, Cambridge, Massachusetts (1920–1927); and chair of psychology at Duke University, Durham, North Carolina (1927–1938), where he supported the establishment of the Parapsychology Laboratory. He co-founded the Boston Society for Psychical Research (1925). He received an honorary D.Sc. from Manchester University (1919) and was honorary fellow St. John's College, Cambridge. McDougall died in Durham, North Carolina.

Major Contributions

McDougall contributed significantly to more branches and departments of psychology than anyone else writing in English at that time, and he influenced the development of the new field of social psychology. McDougall argued that all human behavior, including social relationships, could be explained by the many instincts that were related to primary emotions. For example, fleeing is an instinct related to the emotion of fear. He opposed behaviorism and argued that behavior is generally goal-oriented and purposive, an approach he called "hormic psychology" (derived from the Greek for animal impulse, or drive).

(McDougall explains goal-seeking *vis-à-vis* behaviorism in Chapter 7 of *Introduction to Social Psychology*.)

His anti-behaviorism alienated him from many behavioral psychologists in the United States. Inspired by Jean-Baptiste Lamarck (1744–1829), around 1926, McDougall began a long and detailed Lamarckian study of rats in an attempt to prove that white rats could inherit acquired traits. In 1957, the Parapsychology Laboratory at Duke established the McDougall Award for Distinguished Work in Parapsychology.

Major Literature

McDougall, William. *Physiological Psychology*. London, England: J.M. Dent, 1905.
___. *An Introduction to Social Psychology*. London, England: Methuen, 1908.
___. *Body and Mind*. London, England: Methuen, 1911.
___. *The Group Mind*. England: Cambridge University Press, 1920.
___. *An Outline of Psychology*. London, England: Methuen, 1923.
___. *An Outline of Abnormal Psychology*. New York: Charles Scribner, 1926.
___. *The Battle of Behaviorism*. New York: W.W. Norton and Co. Ltd., 1928.

McGraw, Myrtle Byram
(1899–1988)
CHILD DEVELOPMENT

Born in Birmingham, Alabama, Myrtle Byram McGraw left public school at age twelve to be a typist. She attended a small seminary, now Snead Junior College in Boaz, Alabama, and paid for her tuition, room and board by being secretary to the headmistress. Around 1914 McGraw began a correspondence with John Dewey (see entry), called a "Teacher of Teachers." She came to call him her "intellectual godfather" and he began signing his letters to her "GF."

After she gained her A.B. degree (1923) from Ohio Wesleyan University, Dewey hired her to type a book manuscript for him, thus providing her with funds to study religious education at Teachers College, Columbia University, from which she gained her M.A. in 1925. With the aid of a Laura Spelman Rockefeller fellowship, she gained her a Ph.D. (1931) in psychology under the supervision of Helen Thompson Woolley (see entry) from Teachers College.

From 1930 to 1942 she was associate director of the Normal Child Development Study at Babies Hospital, Columbia Presbyterian Medical Center.

After raising a family, from 1953 until her retirement in 1972, McGraw was professor of psychology at Briarcliff College, New York, where she trained undergraduate women to work with infants and young children. She died at her home in Hastings-on-Hudson, New York. During her eulogy her daughter Mitzi described her mother as a woman on the forefront. She stated, "My mother was born in the 19th Century, lived in the 20th Century and thought in the 21st Century."

Major Contributions

For her doctoral dissertation, McGraw compared the performance of African-American and Caucasian infants on a battery of standardized tests; the development of children remained her life's work. In the early 1930s the debate raged between the behaviorist approach of John Watson (see entry) and the developmental approach of Arnold Gesell (see entry). At the Babies Hospital she worked with project director and neurologist Frederick Tilney and neuroembryologist George Coghill.

She was the first to demonstrate the swimming reflex in 2 and 4 month old infants (if an infant is placed in water on his tummy, his legs and arms will move in a swimming motion). In her research with the Woods twins — *Growth: A Study of Johnny and Jimmy* (a study of the development of equilibrium and stepping movements) — she put 13 month old Johnny on roller skates. To the surprise of the research team and the delight of the media, Johnny became a very skillful skater. Due in part to the approaching war, the Normal Child Development Study ended in early 1940.

Major Literature

McGraw, Myrtle Byram. *Growth: A Study of Johnny and Jimmy*. New York: Institute of Child Development, 1935.
___. *The Neuromuscular Maturation of the Human Infant*. New York: Institute of Child Development, 1939.
___. "Memories, Deliberate Recall, and Speculations." *American Psychologist* 45 (1990): 934–937.

Mendel, Gregor Johann
(1822–1884)
GENETICS

Johann Mendel was born into a German-speaking family from Heinzendorf, Austria (now Hyncice in the Czech Republic). He was a botanist and plant experimenter, the first to lay the mathematical foundation of the science of genetics, in what came to be called Mendelism. He is often called the "father of genetics" for his study of the inheritance of traits in pea plants. When he entered the Augustinian Abbey of St. Thomas in Brno, Austria (now the second largest city in the Czech Republic) in 1843 he added the name Gregor.

In 1847 he was ordained as a priest, and from 1851 to 1853 was a student at the University of Vienna; he then spent his life teaching, mainly physics. On one of his frequent walks around the monastery, he found an atypical variety of an ornamental plant. He took it and planted it next to the typical variety. He grew their progeny side by side to see if there would be any approximation of the traits passed on to the next generation. He found that the plants' respective offspring retained the essential traits of the parents, and therefore were not influenced by the environment. This simple test gave birth to the idea of heredity. Between 1856 and 1863 Mendel cultivated and tested some 28,000 pea plants. His three principles were:

- that separate characteristics are inherited independently of each other via hypothesized elements called genes;
- that each reproductive cell possesses only one gene from each gene pair;
- that some factors are dominant over others.

Mendel read his paper "Experiments on Plant Hybridization" at two meetings of the Natural History Society of Brno in 1865. When Mendel's paper was published in 1866 in *Proceedings of the Natural History Society of Brno*, it had little impact and was cited about three times over the next thirty-five years.

Elevated to abbot in 1868, Mendel's scientific work largely ended, as he focused on his increased administrative responsibilities, especially a dispute with the civil government over their attempt to impose special taxes on religious institutions. Mendel died at the monastery in which he spent forty-one productive years.

The significance of Mendel's work was not recognized until the turn of the 20th century. Its rediscovery prompted the foundation of genetics. In 1900, his work was rediscovered by the Dutch biologist Hugo de Vries (1842–1935) and the German botanist and geneticist Carl Correns (1864–1933), but it was the British geneticist William Bateson (1861–1926)—the first person to use the term genetics to describe the study of heredity and biological inheritance — who popularized Mendel's work in the English-speaking world. Mendel's theory has been confirmed and extended by biol-

ogists in many countries and is the basis of a rapidly developing science of genetics. Mendel's Law influenced the understanding of evolution, physiology, biochemistry, medicine, agriculture, and social science.

Related Literature

Edelson, Edward. *Gregor Mendel and the Roots of Genetics*. Minneapolis, Minnesota: Sagebrush Library Automation, 2001.

Menninger, Karl Augustus (1893–1990)
THE MENNINGER CLINIC

Born in Topeka, Kansas, Karl Augustus Menninger graduated with honors from Harvard Medical School in Boston, Massachusetts, in 1917. Before returning to Topeka in 1919, he held an internship in Kansas City, worked at the Boston Psychopathic Hospital, and taught at Harvard Medical School. In 1925, he and his doctor father, Charles Frederick Menninger (1862–1953), and his psychiatrist brother William (1899–1966) opened the Menninger Clinic at Topeka. The doctors Menninger believed that every patient was treatable, and instilling hope, as much as diagnosing disease, became an integral part of treatment. The clinic started Southard School, Topeka, in 1926 to foster treatment programs for children and adolescents, as well as conducting research. The Menninger vision was of a better kind of medicine and a better kind of world.

Later, the Menningers turned the Kansas psychiatric hospital system into one of the nation's finest, with many governors turning to Menninger for its reform model. The Menninger Foundation — established in 1941 for research, training, and public education in psychiatry — quickly became a U.S. psychiatric and psychoanalytic center.

After World War II, Menninger was instrumental in founding the Winter Veterans Administration Hospital in Topeka, which became the largest psychiatric training center in the world, and with Southard School represented the center of a psychiatric education revolution, integrating the foundations of medical, psychodynamic, developmental, and family systems to focus on the overall health of patients. In 2003 the clinic, much smaller than in its heyday, moved to the Houston area, where it continues in association with the Baylor College of Medicine and the Methodist Hospital.

In *The Human Mind*, Menninger argued that psychiatry was a science and that mentally ill people were only slightly different from healthy individuals. In *The Crime of Punishment*, Menninger argued that crime was preventable through psychiatric treatment; punishment was a brutal and inefficient relic of the past. He advocated treating offenders like those with mental illness.

As of 2005, the Menninger Clinic has an adolescent treatment program, an eating disorders program that takes in adults and adolescents, an obsessive-compulsive disorder program, a professionals in crisis program, a young adult program for people 18–30 with mental disorders or substance abuse issues, and a Hope Adult program for people 18–60 with mental illness. Menninger was awarded the Presidential Medal of Freedom by Jimmy Carter in 1981.

Major Literature

Menninger, Karl Augustus. *Man Against Himself.* New York: Harcourt, Brace and Company, 1938, 1989.
___. *The Human Mind.* London: Random House Group, Knopf, 1945. Kila, Montana: Kessinger Publishing Co., 2005.
___. *The Vital Balance.* New York: Viking Press, 1963. Magnolia, Massachusetts: Peter Smith Pub. Inc., 1983.
___. *Theory of Psychoanalytic Technique.* New York: Harper Collins Publishers, Inc., 1966. Jackson, Tennessee: Basic Books, 1974.
___. *The Crime of Punishment.* New York: Viking Press, 1968.
___. *Whatever Became of Sin?* London, England: Random House Group, Bantam, 1973, 1988.

Mesmer, Franz Anton (1734–1815)
FORERUNNER OF MODERN HYPNOTISM

Born and raised in Iznang, the Swabia region of Germany, Franz Anton Mesmer's academic career was fragmented. From 1752 to 1753 he studied philosophy at the Jesuit university of Dillingen, Bavaria, changed to theology, then from 1753 continued theology at the University of Ingolstadt, but soon abandoned theology. In 1759 Mesmer went to Vienna, first studying law and then medicine. He received his medical doctorate in 1766 with a dissertation on how the planets affect health by moving an invisible fluid found in the human body and throughout nature. His dissertation borrowed heavily from the work of the British physician Richard Mead (1673–1754).

In 1775 Mesmer revised his theory of "animal gravitation" to one of "animal magnetism," wherein the invisible fluid in the body acted according to the laws of magnetism. According to Mesmer, "animal magnetism" could be activated by any magnetized object and manipulated by any trained person. Disease was the result of "obstacles" in the fluid's flow through the body, and these obstacles could be broken by "crises" (trance states often ending in delirium or convulsions) in order to restore the harmony of personal fluid flow. Mesmer devised various therapeutic treatments to achieve harmonious fluid flow, and in many of these treatments he was a forceful and rather dramatic personal participant.

After the medical fraternity of Vienna accused Mesmer of fraud, he settled in Paris in 1778, and in 1784 King Louis XVI appointed a commission of scientists and physicians to investigate Mesmer's methods. They reported that Mesmer was unable to support his scientific claims, and the mesmerist movement thereafter declined. Further investigation of the trance state by his followers eventually led to the development of legitimate applications of hypnotism, although Mesmer did not "invent" hypnotism, which has achieved a high status as a therapeutic treatment.

Mesmer's friend, Maximilian Hell (1720–1792), a court astronomer and Jesuit priest who used magnets in the treatment of disease, influenced Mesmer to conduct his first attempts at healing with a steel magnet. Magnet therapy is widely used in the 21st century as one of the alternative therapies.

In his time, Mesmer achieved great fame and traveled through Hungary, Switzerland, and Bavaria giving lectures, and was made a member of the Bavarian Academy of Sciences at Munich in 1775. During the Revolution he lost his entire fortune and fled to England, returned to France in 1798 and then moved finally to Frauenfeld in Thurgau, Switzerland in 1807, where he practiced medicine. In the early nineteenth century animal magnetism was in high fashion in Germany, where his system of therapeutics, mesmerism, had numerous adherents in all walks of society and influenced both natural philosophy and Romanticism.

Related Literature

Mesmer, Franz Anton, and George J. Block. *Mesmerism: A Translation of The Original Medical and Scientific Writings of F.A. Mesmer.* San Francisco, California: W. Kaufmann, 1981.

Meyer, Adolf (1866–1950)
PSYCHOBIOLOGY

Born in Niederwenigen, near Zurich, Switzerland, Meyer gained an M.D. at the University of

Zurich in 1892, having studied psychiatry and neuropathology and having worked as a neuropathologist. He immigrated to the U.S. in 1892, practiced neurology and taught at the University of Chicago, Illinois.

He was pathologist, Eastern Hospital for the Insane in Kankakee, Illinois (1893–1895); chief pathologist, state mental hospital, Worcester, Massachusetts (1895–1902); director of the Pathological Institute of the New York State Hospital, Ward's Island (now the Psychiatric Institute) (1902–1910); professor of psychiatry, Cornell University Medical College, Ithaca, New York (1904–1909); and from 1910 to his retirement in 1941, he was professor of psychiatry at Johns Hopkins University in Baltimore, Maryland. He was director of the Henry Phipps Psychiatric Clinic at Johns Hopkins Hospital from its inception in 1913.

Major Contributions

Meyer impressed generations of students with the idea that, in the diagnosis and treatment of mental illness, account must be taken of the patient as a whole person. He believed that a biographical study of personality provides both a guide for extracting essential data and for analyzing the relationship between that data and the client's symptoms. Meyer called this study of the interrelationship of all the factors in a person's life "distributive analysis." Helping the person understand and, therefore, to cope better, he called "distributive synthesis."

Therapy is based on the view that a person's personality is developed from biological, social and psychological influences, and starts with distributive analysis, and ends with distributive synthesis. Meyer believed that it was important to use words and ideas familiar to the client. Focus is on the present, conscious reactions to life, only relating to the past where there is a direct influence on the present and on attaining long-term goals. Therapy is an active process, where the therapist feels comfortable advising, suggesting, and re-educating. All of this may be called "habit training" of current life situations. Early concentration is on sleep, nutrition and regulation of daily routine.

The Life Chart is important in evaluating strengths, weaknesses and resources, with concentration on the healthy parts of the personality. The Life Chart is a chronological record of the condition and performance of eight "vulnerable systems." A psychobiogram is a record of the role each of the systems plays in shaping the biography or life of the client. It is also a record of, and the interplay between, the various experiences, memories and feelings associated with the chronological data. The eight "vulnerable systems" are the cerebrum, digestive, heart and circulation, kidneys, respiratory organs, sexual, thymus, and thyroid. The psychobiogram is useful to show the complex lateral and vertical relationships between significant life events.

Major Literature

Meyer, Adolf. "The Life Chart and the Obligation of Specifying Positive Data in Psychopathological Diagnosis." In *Contributions to Medical and Biological Research*. New York: Paul B. Hoeber, 1919.

___. *Collected Papers of Adolf Meyer*, 4 vols. John Hopkins University Press, Baltimore, 1948–1952.

___. *Psychobiology: A Science of Man*. Springfield, Illinois: Charles C. Thomas, 1957.

Michie, Donald (1923–)
ARTIFICIAL INTELLIGENCE

Born in Rangoon, Burma, Donald Michie gained an M.A. in human anatomy and physiology (1949), a D.Phil. in mammalian genetics (1953), and a D.Sc. in biological sciences (1971) from Oxford University, England. At University of Edinburgh, Scotland, he was senior lecturer in surgical science (1958); reader in surgical science (1962); founder and director, Experimental Programming Unit (1965); personal chair of Machine Intelligence (1967); founder and first chairman, Department of Machine Intelligence and Perception; director, Machine Intelligence Research Unit (1974–1984); and professor emeritus of Machine Intelligence. Michie was founder of the British Computer Society Specialist Group in Expert Systems (1980); founder and director of research, the Turing Institute in Glasgow, Scotland (1984); and was elected a founding fellow of the American Association for Artificial Intelligence, for contributions to artificial intelligence (1990).

Michie's awards and honors include the Lifetime Achievement Award, British Computer Society Specialist Group on Artificial Intelligence (2004); honorary degrees from several U.K. universities; the 1995 Achievement Medal of the Institution of Electrical Engineers (U.K.) for contributions to computing and control; and the 1996 Feigenbaum Medal of the World Congress on Expert Systems. Michie has been visiting lecturer at universities in the USSR and U.S., and is foreign honorary member of the Slovenian Academy of Sciences of the American Academy of Arts and Sciences.

Major Contributions

From 1942 to 1945, Michie's war service was working for the Foreign Office at Bletchley Park, Buckinghamshire, the code breaking center. His changes to Colossus, the world's first high-speed electronic computer, improved discovery of the daily German code patterns from several person-weeks at best to a few person-hours, an achievement beyond the original goal of Colossus. This sparked a "crash program" that yielded nine successively enhanced Colossus machines working round the clock by the war's end.

While at Bletchley, he formed a friendship with Alan Turing (1912–1954), often considered to be the father of modern computer science. Michie began his first experiments in 1960. His tic-tac-toe machine MENACE demonstrated the basic principle of a self-reinforcing learning mechanism, which was soon employed industrially to evolve strategies for automatic control, such as controlling a steel mill. A program Michie developed improved yield efficiency from less than 85 percent to about 95 percent at a uranium refining plant for Westinghouse Research, Pennsylvania. The resulting annual savings were in excess of $10 million.

From 1975 to 1984, Michie was chairman of the Board of Trustees, A.M. Turing Trust, an educational charity to further the advancement and spread of education in the fields of computation.

Major Literature

Michie, Donald. *On Machine Intelligence*. New Jersey: John Wiley and Sons, Inc., 1974.

Hayes, Jean E., and Donald Michie. *Intelligent Systems: The Unprecedented Opportunity*. New York: Longman Higher Education, 1984.

Michie, Donald, and Rory Johnson. *The Knowledge Machine: Artificial Intelligence and the Future of Man*. New York: Harper Collins Publishers, Inc., William Morrow, 1985.

___, and Rory Johnson. *The Creative Computer: Machine Intelligence and Human Knowledge*. New York: Penguin Group, 1985.

Milgram, Stanley (1933–1984)

OBEDIENCE AND AUTHORITY

Born in New York, Stanley Milgram gained a B.A. in political science from Queens College, the City University of New York (1954), and a Ph.D. in behavioral sciences from Harvard University, Cambridge, Massachusetts (1960), and worked with Gordon Allport (see entry).

Milgram was assistant professor of psychology at Yale University in New Haven, Connecticut (1960–1963); executive director, Comparative International Program, Department of Social Relations, Harvard (1966–1967); professor, City University, New York (1967); and distinguished professor of psychology, Graduate Center, City University (1980–1984). His awards and honors include the annual Socio-psychological Prize, American Academy of Arts and Science (1965); fellow, American Psychological Association (1970–1984); gellow, American Academy of Arts and Science (1971–1984); Guggenheim Fellow (1972–1973); and nomination for a National Book Award for *Obedience to Authority* (1975).

Major Contributions

In 1963 he published one of 6 popular papers on his shock experiments on authority. In 1976, Columbia Broadcasting System (CBS) presented a movie about obedience experiments — *The Tenth Level* — with William Shatner as Stephen Hunter, a Milgram-like scientist. Milgram himself was a consultant for the film. Some of his social psychology experiments are well known; one person looking into the sky will invariably attract others; people with a positive experience to life will invariably mail a stamped envelope dropped near a mailbox. His most noteworthy experiments are on authority and obedience, reported in his book *Obedience to Authority*.

Following the horror accounts of the Holocaust, Milgram was fascinated by the reports that the perpetrators were simply "carrying out orders." In his experiments (commenced in 1961, three months after the start of the trial of Adolf Eichmann in Jerusalem) he found that "ordinary" people were prepared to make subjects suffer pain because they were told to do so. (The subjects were actors, and no pain was involved.) What Milgram also found was that obedience dropped when the experimenter was not present, when the "victim" was moved closer to the participant, and when a fellow "teacher" or a second experimenter stopped cooperating. Obedience increases when the "victim" is never heard.

Examples are the My Lai massacre in the Vietnam War, and more recently, in the atrocities reported during the Iraq War, of where the moral judgment of the average person is overridden by obedience to authority. The feelings of duty and personal emotion are clearly separated. Responsibility shifts in the mind of the subordinate from himself or herself to the authority figure.

Major Literature

Milgram, Stanley. "The Small World Problem." *Psychology Today* 1 (1967): 60–67.

___. *Obedience to Authority: An Experimental View*. New York: Harper Collins Publishers, Inc., 1974. London: Pinter and Martin Ltd., 2005.

___, and Robert Lance Shotland. *Television and Anti-Social Behavior: Field Experiments*. Burlington Massachusetts: Academic Press Inc., 1974.

Milgram, Stanley. *The Individual in a Social World: Essays and Experiments, Stanley Milgram*. Upper Saddle River, New Jersey: Addison Wesley, 1977. Columbus, Ohio: McGraw-Hill, Education, 1992.

Miller, Jean Baker (1927–2006)
PSYCHOLOGY OF WOMEN

Born in the Bronx, New York, Jean Baker Miller contracted polio at l0 months of age and until the age of 10 underwent several operations; she was left with an atrophied leg and limp. Miller gained an M.D. at Columbia University in New York (1952), and a psychoanalysis certification at New York Medical College (1959). She was visiting lecturer at London School of Economics and at the Tavistock Institute and Clinic in London (1972–1973), and clinical professor of psychiatry, Boston University School of Medicine (1981–2006).

Her awards and honors include Woman of the Year in Health and Medicine from the National Organization of Women Massachusetts Chapter; Massachusetts Psychological Association Allied Professional Award for Outstanding Contributions of the Advances of Psychology (1982); honorary doctor of human letters, Brandeis University in Waltham, Massachusetts (1987); and honorary doctorate at Regis College, Weston, Massachusetts (1995). Miller died in Brookline, Massachusetts, after a 13-year struggle with emphysema and post-polio effects.

Major Contributions

Miller's interest in the psychology of women dates to the early 1960s, and she was vocal in her support for the identity of women. Her goal was to make the world aware that women were not men gone wrong, but that they had issues of their own and psychologies separate from those of men. In her view, women are the ones who know how to make relationships work, hold their families together, and help them to survive and thrive. These are the strengths she wanted to develop.

In 1981 Miller was appointed the first director of the Stone Center for Developmental Studies at Wellesley College, Massachusetts, where she spear-headed collaborative work among scholars, researchers, and clinicians on the treatment and prevention of mental health problems in women. Work at the Stone Center led to the subsequent establishment of the Jean Baker Miller Training Institute at the Wellesley Centers for Women in 1995. Miller served as director of the institute until late 2005, where relational-cultural theory — a new model of psychological development — was further elaborated on and taught to practitioners, lay persons, and most recently, business professionals.

The thrust of her approach is on developing relationships that help people to grow; she saw growth relationships as the central human necessity and disconnections as the source of psychological problems. Instead of emphasizing separateness, accruing power over others, and social stratification, nations and individuals need to emphasize mutual respect and the building of community. Human development is about movement toward increasing mutuality and better connection, rather than growth toward separateness and independence.

Major Literature

Miller, Jean Baker. *Psychoanalysis and Women: Contributions to New Theory and Therapy*. London, England: Taylor and Francis Books Ltd., Brunner-Routledge, 1973.

___. *Toward a New Psychology of Women*. Boston, Massachusetts: Beacon Press, 1976, 1987.

___, Irene Striver, and Trisha Hooks. *The Healing Connection: How Women Form Relationships in Therapy and in Life*. Boston, Massachusetts: Beacon Press, 1997.

Miller, Jean Baker. *How Connections Heal: Stories from Relational-Cultural Therapy*. New York: Guilford Press, 2004.

Miller, Neal Elgar (1909–2002)
THEORY OF MOTIVATION

Born in Milwaukee, Wisconsin, Neal Elgar Miller gained a B.S. at the University of Washington, Seattle (1931), an M.S. at Stanford University, California (1932), and a Ph.D. in psychology (1935) from Yale University, New Haven, Connecticut. At Yale he was James Rowland Angell Professor of Psychology (1952–1966) and research affiliate (1985). He was also Social Science Research Council fellow at the Vienna Psychoanalytic Institute (1935–1936); professor, Rockefeller University, New York (1966–1981); and professor emeritus and head of the Laboratory of Physiological Psychology at Rockefeller University (1981–1985).

Miller's awards and honors include being elected to the National Academy of Science (1958); receiving the Distinguished Scientific Contribution Award, American Psychological Association (APA) (1959); National Medal of Science (1964); Gold Medal Award, APA (1971); McAlpin Medal, Mental Health Association (1978); Distinguished Contributions to Knowledge Award, APA (1982); Lifetime Achievement Award, APA (1991); and honorary degrees from five American universities. He was president, APA (1960–1961); American Association for the Advancement of Science (1961); president, Society for Neuroscience (1971–1972); President, APA Division 38 (1980–1981); and president, Biofeedback Society of America (1984–1985).

Major Contributions

Miller began his scientific career with an investigation of Freudian theory and clinical phenomena using experimental analysis of behavior techniques. He asked how the Freudian phenomena could be understood in terms of the basic laws of learning and behavior as they were known in the 1940s. His work led to new perspectives on personality and social learning and to two influential books with John Dollard (see entry).

Miller's investigations revealed that fear can be learned, and if fear, why not other drives such as hunger and thirst? Combining elements of a number of earlier reinforcement theories of behavior and learning, Miller and Dollard developed a theory of motivation on how people satisfy psychosocial drives. Miller's pioneering work, using electrical and chemical brain stimulation and recording to analyze learning and behavior, formed the basis of what today is known as behavioral neuroscience.

His work led to the development of the field of behavioral medicine and health psychology. In the 1930s Miller was one of the first researchers to demonstrate experimentally the power of mind over matter by subjects being able to control their heart rate and bowel contractions, just as they learned to walk or play tennis, through a system called biofeedback. Biofeedback is now routinely used to alleviate problems such as headaches, chronically taut muscles resulting from accidents or sports injuries, asthma, and many other conditions.

During World War II Miller was asked by the U.S. government to develop better tests for selecting aircrew, and to improve pilots' and air gunners' operational success rates.

Major Literature

Miller, Neal Elgar, and J. Dollard. *Social Learning and Imitation*. New Haven, Connecticut: Yale University Press, 1941.

___. *Personality and Psychotherapy*. Columbus, Ohio: McGraw-Hill, 1950.

Miller, Neal Elgar. *Biofeedback and Self Control*. Los Angeles: Aldine Books, 1974.

Richter-Heinrich, Elisabeth, and Neal Elgar Miller. *Biofeedback: Basic Problems and Clinical Applications: Selected International Congress Papers*. London, England: Reed Elsevier Group, 1983.

Milner, Brenda (1918–)

CLINICAL NEUROPSYCHOLOGY

Brenda Milner was born in Manchester, England, during World War II. At Cambridge University, she was involved in the development of radar. She gained her bachelor's degree in experimental psychology, then she and her husband immigrated to Canada in 1944, he to help launch atomic energy research and she to teach psychology at the University of Montreal. During her time at Montreal she also completed a master's degree in experimental psychology at Cambridge University and a Ph.D. in physiological psychology at McGill University, Montreal, Quebec, Canada. Her supervisor was Donald Olding Hebb (see entry), and Wilder Penfield (1891–1976), distinguished brain surgeon, allowed her access to recovering patients as she studied the effects of temporal-lobe lesions at the Montreal Neurological Institute.

Milner rose to become one of the first world-class exponents of the new discipline of neuropsychology. In well over a hundred learned papers, she has helped to chart the pathways of memory, speech, and learning. She has received 14 honorary doctorates, including one from Cambridge University; she has been included in the Canadian Medical Hall of Fame, and is a member of the Royal Societies of Canada and of London, England. She is an officer of the Order of Canada, and also *Officier de l'Ordre national du Quebec*, and in 2004 she was honored with the Companion of the Order of Canada. She has also been given the Distinguished Scientific Contribution Award of the American Psychological Association.

Major Contributions

While working for her Ph.D. she decided to build her scientific career studying brain-function relationships, first through behavioral studies in patients who undergo focal removal of cerebral tissue for the treatment of intractable epilepsy, and more recently, through brain imaging studies using positron emission tomography (PET) and functional magnetic resonance imaging (fMRI). Her observations of one patient were the first clear demonstration of the existence of multiple memory systems in the brain.

Her work has brought new insights into the effects of lesions to the temporal and frontal regions of the brain, allowing specialists to understand better the role of these cerebral structures in different forms of memory processes, as well as in other cognitive functions. This knowledge has helped specialists to carry out neuropsychological evaluations of a variety of patients with neurological disorders.

In collaboration with Dr. Theodore Rasmussen (1910–2002), she developed the sodium amytal test (also called the Wada test) for cerebral dominance of language function, which has made a major difference in the pre–surgical care of patients and the decision making processes of neurosurgeons facing the difficult task of having to remove brain tissue that might be critical for language or memory functions. As Killam Professor at the Montreal Neurological Institute, McGill University, using state-of-the-art technology, she currently explores hemispheric specialization.

Major Literature

Milner, Brenda. "Laterality Effects in Audition." In *Interhemispheric Relations and Cerebral Dominance*, ed. V.B. Mountcastle, 177–195. Baltimore: Johns Hopkins Press, 1962.

Milner, Brenda. *Brain Function and Cognition*. Westport, Connecticut: Greenwood Publishing Group, Inc., Praeger, 1987.

Minsky, Marvin Lee (1927–)

Artificial Intelligence

Born in New York City, Marvin Lee Minsky served in the U.S. Navy (1944–1945) and gained a B.A. in mathematics at Harvard University, Cambridge, Massachusetts (1950), and a Ph.D. in mathematics at Princeton University, New Jersey (1954). At the Massachusetts Institute of Technology (MIT), Cambridge, he was with the Lincoln Laboratory (1957–1958); assistant professor of Mathematics (1958–1961); associate professor of electrical engineering (1961–1964); MIT's Artificial Intelligence Laboratory (1961); director, MIT Artificial Intelligence Laboratory (1964–1974); Donner Professor of Science (1974–1989); and Toshiba Professor of Media Arts and Sciences (since

1990). He was Doubleday Lecturer at the Smithsonian Institute in Washington D.C. (1970), and Messenger Lecturer, Cornell University, Ithaca, New York (1979).

Minsky's awards and honors include the Turing Award, Association for Computing Machinery (1978); president, American Association for Artificial Intelligence (1989); Killian Award, MIT (1981–1982); Japan Prize Laureate, Government of Japan (1990); International Joint Conference on Artificial Intelligence Award for Research Excellence (1991); Rank Prize from the Royal Society of Medicine (1995); Benjamin Franklin Medal, Franklin Institute, Philadelphia, Pennsylvania (2001); and R.W. Wood Prize, Optical Society of America (2001).

Major Contributions

After receiving his Ph.D., Minsky revisited Harvard as part of the group of scholars known as the Society of Fellows and it was there that he made his primary contribution to the field of optics. In 1955 he invented the confocal scanning microscope to examine images of neural networks in unstained samples of live brains. The result was a predecessor to today's widely used confocal laser scanning microscope. In 1951 he built the SNARC, the first neural network simulator. His other inventions include mechanical hands and other robotic devices.

At MIT he soon became one of the world leaders in the emerging field of artificial intelligence (AI). Minsky wrote with Seymour A. Papert the book *Perceptrons*, which became the foundational work in the analysis of artificial neural networks.

Minsky was an adviser on the 1968 movie *2001: A Space Odyssey* (see entry, Köhler, Wolfgang) and is referred to in the movie and book. In the early 1970s at the MIT Artificial Intelligence Laboratory, Minsky and Seymour Papert started developing what came to be called "the society of mind theory," which attempts to explain how what we call intelligence could be a product of the interaction of non-intelligent parts called agents. Minsky has made many contributions to AI, cognitive psychology, mathematics, computational linguistics, robotics, and optics. In recent years he has worked chiefly on imparting to machines the human capacity for common sense reasoning.

Major Literature

Minsky, Marvin Lee. *Semantic Information Processing*. Cambridge, Massachusetts: MIT Press, 1969.

___, and Seymour Papert. *Perceptrons: An Introduction*

to Computational Geometry. Cambridge, Massachusetts: MIT Press, 1969.

Minsky, Marvin Lee. *The Society of Mind*. New York: Simon and Schuster Inc., 1987. See also *The Society of Mind CD-ROM version*, Voyager, 1996.

___, Vernor Vinge, and James Frenkel. *True Names and the Opening of the Cyberspace Frontier*. New York: Tom Doherty Associates, Tor Books, 2002.

Minsky, Marvin Lee. *The Emotion Machine: Commonsense Thinking, Artificial Intelligence, and the Future of the Human Mind*. New York: Simon and Schuster Inc., 2006.

Mischel, Walter (1930–)
PERSONALITY STRUCTURE

Born in Vienna, Austria, Walter Mischel and his family settled in Brooklyn, New York, in 1938. Mischel gained a B.A. in psychology from New York University (1951), an M.A. in psychology at the City College of New York (1953), and a Ph.D. in psychology from Ohio State University, Athens (1956). Mischel was assistant professor, University of Colorado, Boulder (1956–1958), and assistant professor and lecturer, Harvard University, Cambridge, Massachusetts, Department of Social Relations (1958–1962). At Stanford University, California, he was associate professor of psychology (1962–1966); professor of psychology (1966–1983); and chairman, Department of Psychology (1977–1978 and 1982–1983). At Columbia University in New York, he was chairman, Department of Psychology (1988–1991); professor of Psychology (1983-Present); and Niven Professor of Humane Letters (since 1994).

Mischel's awards and honors include the Distinguished Scientist Award, American Psychological Association, Division of Clinical Psychology (1978); Social Sciences Commission, Humanities Section, Max-Planck-Gesellschaft, Germany (1981–1900); Distinguished Scientific Contribution Award of the American Psychological Association (1982); honorary doctor of science degree, Ohio State University (1997); and Distinguished Scientist Award, Society of Experimental Social Psychologists (2000).

Major Contributions

Mischel ranks among today's most influential psychologists, with all major textbooks having some reference to his work on personality. His research interests focus on self-regulation (willpower) and personality structure, process, and development. Mischel's famous longitudinal research study, "The Marshmallow Test," showed the importance of impulse control and delayed gratification for academic, emotional and social success. Mischel followed the group of four year olds and found that, 14 years later, the "grabbers" suffered low self-esteem and were viewed by others as stubborn, prone to envy and easily frustrated. The "waiters" were better copers, more socially competent and self-assertive, trustworthy, dependable and more academically successful. This group even scored about 210 points higher on their Scholastic Aptitude Test and Scholastic Assessment Test (SATs).

Mischel maintains that personality has too many variables to be consistent and is probably influenced more by situational factors than has traditionally been appreciated. Mischel opposes the idea of global traits, arguing for the uniqueness of the individual. In his social cognitive learning theory, Mischel argues that our behavior in a given situation depends on the consequences of our actions (rewards or punishments). He introduces five cognitive variables that interact and determine behavior:

1. Encoding strategies: how we see something;
2. Expectancies and beliefs: what will happen;
3. Affects: feelings, emotions and affective responses;
4. Values and goals: the worth of something; compatibility of goals with values;
5. Competencies: what you can do; alternatives for action.

All of these personal variables (sometimes referred to as cognitive social-learning variables) interact with the conditions of a particular situation to determine what an individual will do in that situation.

Major Literature

Mischel, Walter. *Personality and Assessment*. New Jersey: John Wiley and Sons, Inc., 1968. Hillsdale, New Jersey: Erlbaum Associates, Inc., 1996.

Cervone, Daniel and Walter Mischel. *Advances in Personality Science*. New York: Guilford Press, 2002.

Mischel, Walter. *Introduction to Personality: Toward an Integration*. New Jersey: John Wiley and Sons, Inc., 2003.

Moniz, António Caetano De Abreu Freire Egas (1874–1955)
FOUNDER OF MODERN PSYCHOSURGERY

Egas Moniz was born in Avanca, Portugal, and studied medicine in the University of Coimbra, Portugal, and neurology in Bordeaux and Paris,

France. He returned to the University of Coimbra as professor and chairman of the Department of Neurology (1902) and was chair of neurology at the University of Lisbon from 1911 until his retirement in 1945. He also worked for a time as a physician in the Hospital of Santa Maria, Lisbon.

From 1903 to 1917 he was minister of foreign affairs in the Portuguese parliament, and president of the Portuguese delegation at the Paris Peace Conference in 1918. He was ambassador to Spain under the First Republic from 1918 to 1919, when he returned to the University of Lisbon. His former country house in Avanca, in the north of Portugal, became a museum for his art collection.

Moniz shared the 1949 Nobel Prize for Physiology or Medicine with the Swiss neurophysiologist Walter Hess (1881–1973). Moniz was awarded the prize for the development of prefrontal leucotomy (later renamed lobotomy) as a radical therapy for certain psychoses, or mental disorders.

Major Contributions

In 1927, Moniz developed the technique of angiography, a method of using X-ray that allowed for the visualization of the brain arteries to diagnose several kinds of neurological disorders, such as tumors and malformations of blood vessels. He received the Oslo Prize for this discovery. The method is still used for the diagnosis of brain tumors and vascular diseases in the brain and other organs, and has saved thousands of lives.

Moniz recognized that the frontal lobes were important in personality structure and behavior, and concluded that interfering with frontal lobe function might alter the course of mental diseases such as schizophrenia and other chronic psychiatric disorders. With the help of Almeida Lima, a neurosurgical colleague, he introduced a simple surgical procedure for indiscriminately destroying most of the connections between the frontal lobe and the rest of the brain. During the period from 1935 through the 1940s, vast numbers of these procedures were performed throughout the world as a way of controlling mentally ill people and those considered society's worst misfits, including communists and homosexuals mostly, often done without consent.

With the advent of increasingly effective psychotropic drugs in the late 1940s and the early 1950s, frontal lobotomy as a psychotherapeutic strategy rapidly disappeared, although certain hospitals in Britain still perform a modified procedure for persistent severe depression and anxiety and obsessive-compulsive disorder (OCD).

Patients must consent to the surgery and ethical and clinical standards committees subject each case to rigid scrutiny before it goes ahead. The backlash against lobotomy has been fierce. In 1996 the Norwegian Parliament passed a temporary act of compensation that intended to offer the victims some restitution, and there have been calls for the withdrawal of the Nobel Prize from Moniz.

Montessori, Maria (1870–1952)
DEVELOPMENTAL PSYCHOLOGY

Born in Chiaravalle, near Ancona, Italy, Maria Montessori graduated in medicine from the University of Rome (1896); she was the first woman in Italy to do so. She was appointed assistant doctor at the psychiatric clinic of the University of Rome, where she became interested in the educational problems of mentally retarded children. Between 1899 and 1901 she served as director of the State Orthophrenic School of Rome. From 1896 to 1906 she was professor in hygiene at a women's college in Rome, and from 1900 to 1907 she lectured in pedagogy at the University of Rome, also holding a chair in anthropology from 1904 to 1908.

In 1907 Montessori opened the first Casa dei Bambini ("Children's House") in Rome, applying her methods now to children of normal intelligence. Montessori made her first visit to the United States in 1913, the same year that Alexander Graham Bell and his wife Mabel founded the Montessori Educational Association at their Washington, D.C., home. Among her other strong American supporters were Thomas Edison and Helen Keller.

In 1922 she was appointed government inspector of schools in Italy, but left the country in 1934 because of the fascist rule. She lived and worked in India, where she continued her work, Education for Peace, and developed many of the ideas taught in her training courses today. She was three times nominated for the Nobel Peace Prize, 1949, 1950, and 1951. She settled in the Netherlands, where she died.

Major Contributions

Montessori believed that each child is born with a unique potential to be revealed, not a "blank slate" waiting to be written upon. Montessori teachers:

- Prepare the most natural and life supporting environment for the child

- Observe the child living freely in this environment
- Continually adapt the environment in order that the child may fulfill his or her greatest potential, physically, mentally, emotionally, and spiritually.

The Montessori method, which has since spread throughout the world, stresses the development of initiative and self-reliance by permitting children to do by themselves the things that interest them, but within strictly disciplined limits. A wide variety of special equipment of increasing complexity is used to help direct the interests of the child and hasten development. When a child is ready to learn new and more difficult tasks, the teacher guides the child's first endeavors in order to avoid wasted effort and the learning of wrong habits; otherwise the child learns alone. It has been reported that the Montessori method has enabled children to learn to read and write much more quickly.

Major Literature

Montessori, Maria. *The Absorbent Mind*. Oxford, England: ABC-Clio Ltd., 1988.
___. *The Secret of Childhood*. London, England: Sangam Books, 1998.
___. *Dr. Montessori's Own Handbook: A Short Guide to Her Ideas and Materials*. New York: Random House, Inc., 1992.
___. *The Montessori Method*. London, England: Kuperard, 1992.
___. *To Educate the Human Potential*. Oxford, England: ABC-Clio Ltd., 1998.

Morel, Bénédict Augustin (1809–1873)

DEMENTIA PRAECOX (SCHIZOPHRENIA)

Born in Vienna of French parents, Bénédict Augustin Morel gained his medical doctorate in 1839 and in 1841 became assistant to the psychiatrist Jean Pierre Falret at the Salpêtrière Hospital, Paris. Between 1843 and 1845 Morel traveled in the Netherlands, Switzerland, Germany, and Italy studying their asylums. In 1848 he was appointed director of the lunatic asylum Asile d'Aliénés de Maréville at Nancy, Maréville, where he introduced important reforms for the improvement of the situation of the mentally ill, particularly regarding the use of restraining methods.

At Maréville asylum he studied the mentally retarded, searching their family histories and ex-amining such influences as poverty and early physical illnesses. In 1856 he made a scientific journey to England in order to study no-restraint methods. On his return he became a member of a Paris commission set up to investigate the causes of struma (goiter) and cretinism, and to find a cure for these conditions.

The science of Morel's day was so primitive that he had no way of knowing that cretinism is caused by iodine deficiency and he concluded that like most mental illnesses, cretins suffer from an incurable hereditary disorder. Cretins, he reasoned, contribute little to society and they present a genetic risk. He feared that if they were allowed to reproduce, they would beget more cretins and damage France's genetic heritage. He created a new medical diagnosis to account for Cretin's symptoms that he called "degeneration."

According to Morel, the over-consumption of alcohol, tobacco, and opium were the leading causes of damage to the human organism that leads to degeneration. Morel taught that a man damaged by overindulgence in these and other appetites develops illnesses and weakens his heredity. He described a progressive degeneration starting with neurosis in the first generation, mental alienation in the next, and imbecility in the third, culminating in sterility in the fourth and final generation. What was being passed on was not a specific pathology but a susceptibility of the nervous system to disturbances originating from "overindulgence" of toxic substances.

Morel's ideas quickly became popular in Continental Europe, though his new theories were less successful in England and the United States. Psychologists such as Sigmund Freud and Havelock Ellis (see entries) rejected the idea of degeneracy. Morel and his followers inadvertently provided fodder for the ethnic cleansing of the Nazi era, and the extermination of Jews, homosexuals, and other "degenerate" minorities during the Holocaust.

In *Traité des maladies mentales* (1860) Morel introduced the term *dementia praecox* to refer to a mental and emotional deterioration beginning at the time of puberty. The disorder was renamed *schizophrenia* in 1908 by the Swiss psychologist Eugen Bleuler (see entry).

Major Literature

Morel, Bénédict Augustin. *Traite Des Degenerescences Physiques, Intellectuelles Et Morales De L'Espece Humaine*. Classics in Psychiatry Series. Manchester, New Hampshire: Ayer Co. Publishers, 1976.

Moreno, Jacob Levy
(1889–1974)
PSYCHODRAMA

Born in Bucharest, Romania, of Jewish parents, Jacob Levy Moreno grew up in Vienna, studied medicine, mathematics, and philosophy at the University of Vienna, and graduated in medicine and psychiatry in 1917. He then became a health officer and set up a general practice in a suburb of Vienna. For some years in Vienna, Moreno had experience with storytelling in children's groups, followed by having the children act out the stories. He later used this method with adults, founding a theater named Das Stregreif in 1921, in which actors and audiences acted out real and imagined stories.

He immigrated to the United States in 1925 and was awarded his New York medical license in 1927. He held positions at Columbia University, New York, and the New School for Social Research, New York. In 1968 he received an honorary doctorate from the Medical Faculty, University of Barcelona, and in 1969 the Golden Doctor Diploma from University of Vienna. Before he died in Beacon, New York, near the Moreno Institute he had established in 1935, he saw psychodrama operating in many countries around the world.

Major Contributions

Moreno is the founder of psychodrama and sociometry and is one of the pioneers of group psychotherapy. Moreno entered psychodrama through the practice of sociometry — an observational charting of how people interact in groups. He carried out his first long-range sociometric study from 1932 to 1938 at the New York State Training School for Girls in Hudson, New York.

Moreno expanded his theory of psychodrama into psychotherapy; it was accepted by Adolf Meyer (see entry) and others. In 1941 he founded Beacon House to publish sociometric books and monographs, and in 1942 he founded the Theatre of Psychodrama, and Psychodramatic and Sociometric Institute, New York City. Psychodrama extended to many different settings — churches, prisons and psychiatric hospitals.

Psychodrama employs guided dramatic action to examine problems or issues raised by an individual (psychodrama) or a group (sociodrama), in which people dramatize their personal problems within a group setting. Although the situations in psychodrama are simulated, they can and do generate insight and release emotions through catharsis. It is a powerful method of working, which, in the hands of an experienced therapist, can be liberating. A stage setting is generally used, the therapist acting as the "director," with group members playing various roles. Using experiential methods, role theory, and group dynamics, psychodrama facilitates insight, personal growth, and integration on cognitive, affective, and behavioral levels. It clarifies issues, increases physical and emotional well-being, enhances learning and develops new skills.

Major Literature

Moreno, Jacob Levy. *Group Psychotherapy: A Symposium.* New York: Beacon House, 1966.
___. *Psychodrama: Action Therapy and Principles of Practice.* New York: Beacon House, 1969.
___. *Who Shall Survive? Foundations of Sociometry, Group Psychotherapy, and Sociodrama.* New York: Beacon House, 1977.
___. *Psychodrama.* New York: Beacon House, 1985.
___. *The Essential Moreno: Writings on Psychodrama, Group Method, and Spontaneity.* New York: Springer-Verlag, 1988.

Morgan, Conwy Lloyd
(1852–1936)
COMPARATIVE PSYCHOLOGY

Born in London, England, Conwy Lloyd Morgan graduated as associate in mining and metallurgy from the Royal School of Mines (comprising the departments of Earth Science and Engineering, and Materials) at Imperial College, London, in 1871. He was a tutor for a few years in North and South America then entered the Royal College of Science to continue his scientific studies under T.H. Huxley (1825–1895).

From 1878 to 1884 he taught physical sciences, English literature and, for a time, constitutional history at the Diocesan College at Rondebosch, South Africa. From 1884 to 1919, Morgan was professor of geology and zoology at University College, Bristol, and principal of the college in 1887 and vice chancellor of the university in 1910. He returned to teaching in 1911 as professor of psychology and ethics and retired in 1919 to Clifton, Bristol, and then to Hastings, Sussex, where he died.

He was elected fellow of the Royal Society in 1899, being the first fellow to be elected for psychological work, and he received the honorary degree of D.Sc. from Bristol University in 1910.

Major Contributions

Although his main focus at Bristol was zoology, the study of animal and comparative psychology, he was one of the chief founders of the scientific study of animal psychology. In addition Morgan is noted for establishing sound general principles of explanation and interpretation. The results of his investigations appeared in a long series of publications. His most important works in the field of investigation are his two courses of Gifford Lectures delivered at St. Andrews University, Scotland, in 1922 and 1923 and published as *Emergent Evolution*.

In his studies of animal psychology over the years, Morgan attempted to describe animal behavior in objective terms and without attributing human characteristics to them. He studied animal behavior for its own sake, without regard to how man's mentality evolved. "Morgan's canon" applies to what has become known as "the principle of parsimony" or "the principle of simplicity"—one should always choose the simplest explanation of a phenomenon, the one that requires the fewest leaps of logic. When applied to animals, we should not attribute human motives (or thinking) to what animals do. In his studies of animal behavior he arrived at what Robert Thorndike later labeled "the law of effect."

Major Literature

Morgan, Conwy Lloyd. *Animal Life and Intelligence*. London, England: Edward Arnold, 1890–1891.
___. *Habit and Instinct*. London: Edward Arnold, 1896. Manchester, New Hampshire: Ayer Co. Publishers, 1977.
___. *Animal Behavior*. London, England: Edward Arnold, 1900.
___. *Instinct and Experience*. New York: Macmillan, 1912.
___. *Emergent Evolution*. London: Williams and Norgate, 1923. New York: Ams Press, Inc., 1977.
___. *Life, Mind and Spirit: Gifford Lectures*. New York: Ams Press, Inc., 1926.

Morris, Robert Lyle
(1942–2004)
Parapsychology

Born in Canonsburg, Pennsylvania, Robert Lyle Morris graduated with a B.Sc. (1963) in psychology from the University of Pittsburgh, Pennsylvania, then specialized in comparative psychology and animal social behavior at Duke University, Durham, North Carolina, gaining his a Ph.D. in 1969 with a dissertation on bird behavior. While at Duke he also did research at the Center for the Study of Aging and Human Development and started to develop his interest in parapsychology, spending evenings, weekends, and summers at the Foundation for Research on the Nature of Man, the center in Durham, North Carolina, founded by J. B. Rhine. (Parapsychology is defined as the scientific study of those anomalous interactions between minds, or between minds and the physical world, which cannot be explained in conventional terms.)

After Morris finished his doctoral research, his interests in parapsychology came to the fore; he became research coordinator and then research associate at the Psychical Research Foundation in Durham until 1974. From 1974 to 1980 he was a faculty member at the University of California, first at Santa Barbara and then at Irvine, where his teaching schedule was a mix of courses in parapsychology, animal social behavior, abnormal and comparative psychology and learning theory. He also taught individual courses in parapsychology at John F. Kennedy University, Pleasant Hill, California, and the University of Southern California, Los Angeles.

In 1978 he moved to the Communications Studies Laboratory at Syracuse University, New York, and was a senior research scientist in the School of Computer Science and Information Science there from 1980 until 1985, teaching courses on computer science, frontiers of human communication, and human-machine interaction. There he became interested in how people can mislead themselves and be misled by others into thinking and believing that something "psychic" has happened.

In 1985 he moved to Scotland to become the first Koestler Professor of Parapsychology located within the School of Philosophy, Psychology and Language Sciences at the University of Edinburgh. The chair (the only chair of its kind in the U.K.) had been established out of a bequest from the writer Arthur Koestler and his wife. As Koestler Professor, he was often called upon to act as spokesman for the field of parapsychology. He was on the Council of the American Association for the Advancement of Science and for two years he was president of the Psychology Section of the British Association for the Advancement of Science. He also received the Charles Myers Award of the British Psychological Society in 1999. There are currently 10 departments in the U.K. where parapsychology is pursued; two of his former students are now professors. Morris died of a heart attack.

Major Literature

Edge, Hoyt L., Robert Lyle Morris, Joseph H. Rush, and John Palmer. *Foundations of Parapsychology*. London, England: Taylor and Francis Books Ltd., Routledge and Kegan Paul, 1986.

Wiseman, R., and Robert Lyle Morris. *Guidelines for Testing Psychic Claimants*. University of Hertfordshire Press, Hatfield, 1995.

Morris, Robert Lyle. "Parapsychology in the 21st Century." *Journal of Parapsychology* 64 (2000): 123–137.

Moscovici, Serge (1925–)

GROUP PSYCHOLOGY

Born in Bra~ila, Romania, of Jewish parents, in 1938 Serge Moscovici was excluded from the high school in Bucharest because of anti–Semitic laws, and, after the Iron Guard-instigated Bucharest Pogrom in January 1941, he was interned in a forced labor camp, until being set free by the Red Army in 1944. After the war, he became a welder in a large Bucharest factory, but in 1947, disillusioned with the communist regime, he left Romania. He studied and traveled in Palestine, Germany, Austria, and at the first signs of the Cold War he fled to Paris in 1948. Helped by a refugee fund, he studied psychology at the Sorbonne.

In the 1960s he finished his studies at Stanford University, California, and at Princeton University, New Jersey. His doctoral dissertation (1961) explored the social representations of psychoanalysis in France. Moscovici identified a series of processes in which psychoanalysis was reconstructed, and in the end, in the French mind, it was no longer what Freud had formulated. He then worked on a series of psychosocial research projects that explored the relations between nature and human society in which he elaborated his theory of social representations.

Major Contributions

Moscovici believed that social groups always carry out transformation in order to make something familiar out of something new and which is outside of common sense. Social representations are thus a vital necessity for societies in which change and the diffusion of information prevail. The theory of social representation, the theory of social influence of the minorities and the theory of collective choice and social consensus are the three most important contributions that Serge Moscovici has made to European social psychology.

1. The theory of "social representations" refers to the manner in which values, ideas, and practices are structured in and by ordinary communication, allowing people to both communicate and to order their world. They provide reference points; a position or perspective from which an individual or a group can observe and interpret situations; they provide reference points for people to communicate with one another.

2. In the theory of "social influence of the minorities," Moscovici demonstrates that individuals change when they are in groups, but he also shows that minorities are capable of changing the opinions, ways of doing things and ways of thinking of society as a whole.

3. The theory of collective choice and social consensus is important in relationships whether individual or at a national or international level.

Major Literature

Moscovici, Serge, and Gerard Duveen. *Social Representations: Studies in Social Psychology*. Cambridge, England: Polity Press, 2000.

Moscovici, Serge, Fabrizio Butera, and Gabriel Mugny. *Social Influence in Social Reality*. Cambridge, Massachusetts: Hogrefe and Huber Publishers, 2001.

Moscovici, Serge, and Ivana Markova. *The Making of Modern Social Psychology: The Hidden Story of How an International Social Science Was Created*. Cambridge, England: Polity Press, 2006.

Moscovici, Serge. *Psychoanalysis: Its Image and Its Public*. Oxford, England: Blackwell Publishing, 2006.

Müller, Georg Elias (1850–1934)

EXPERIMENTAL PSYCHOLOGY

Born in Grimma, Saxony, Georg Elias Müller completed one year of philosophy studies each at the Leipzig and Berlin universities and spent one year as a volunteer soldier in an elite Prussian regiment. His studies were influenced by the philosopher Johannes Herbart (1776–1841), who proposed that psychology is a science, grounded in experience, metaphysics, and mathematics. He received a Ph.D. from the University of Göttingen, Germany, in 1873, for his basic analysis of sensory attention, which later formed one of major sources of the work on attention by Edward Bradford Titchener (see entry).

From 1876 to 1879 he was *Privatdozent*, or lecturer, at the University of Göttingen, and in 1880 an instructor at the recently founded University of Bukovina (former province of Romania). When Professor Rudolph Hermann Lotze (1817–1881) died, Müller succeeded him at Göttingen (one of the major centers of psychological research).

Major Contributions

Müller was acknowledged, by his contemporaries, as the master experimenter and methodologist in three areas of experimental psychology: the study of memory, visual perception (including color vision), and psychophysics. In 1879 Müller began experimenting with sensory discrimination of weights, the work originated by Gustav Theodor Fechner (see entry). Müller's work on the effect of anticipation on discrimination is also viewed as one of the early experimental studies of attitude.

Müller extended the pioneer efforts of Hermann Ebbinghaus (see entry) on memory and learning. In 1887 he received his first official grant to pay for the first memory drum (to determine retention)—an apparatus where lists of 12 syllables were mounted on rotating drums and read aloud as pairs by emphasizing every other syllable. He found that learning and recall involve active processes such as grouping, rhythms, and generally conscious organizational strategies for the verbal tasks, and that judgment involves such components as anticipated sensations and feelings, as well as doubt, hesitation, and readiness. Müller devised the interference theory of forgetting, particularly the concept that new learning can interfere with the old; this is called retroactive inhibition.

In 1904, he became the chair of the German Society of Experimental Psychology, a title he held until 1927. In 1922 he was legally forced to retire and took up color theory in earnest, and in 1930, he published 1300 pages on color theory. He considered the three-process color theory was chemical, not metabolic, as Ewald Hering (1834–1918) had proposed.

Major Literature

Müller, Georg Elias. *Zur Grundlegung der Psychophysik. Kritische Beiträge (On the Founding of Psychophysics: Critical Contributions).* Berlin: T. Grieben. Bibliothek fur Wissenschaft und Literatur, 23. Band. Philosophische Abtheilung. 4. bd. (Habilitation, S. 424; 2. Aufl. Berlin: Hoffmann), 1878.

___, and A. Pilzecker. *Experimentelle Beiträge zur Lehre vom Gedächtniss (Experimental Contributions on the Theory of Memory).* Leipzig: J.A. Barth (*Zeitschrift für Psychologie.* Erganzungsband 1), 1900.

Müller, G.E. *Uber die Farbenempfindungen. Psychophysische Untersuchungen (On the Sensations of Color:* *Psychophysical Inquiries).* Leipzig: J.A. Barth (*Zeitschrift für Psychologie.* Erganzungsband 17), 1930.

Munsterberg, Hugo (1863–1916)
PSYCHOLOGY OF BUSINESS

Born in Danzig, Germany, Hugo Munsterberg gained a Ph.D. in psychology from the University of Leipzig, Germany (1885), and an M.D. at the University of Heidelberg, Germany (1887). He was assistant professor, University of Freiburg, Germany (1891), and chair of the psychology laboratory, Harvard University, Cambridge, Massachusetts. Between 1892 and 1887 he shifted between Freiburg and Harvard.

His awards and honors include president of American Psychology Association (1898); honorary LL.D., Washington University, St. Louis (1901); honorary Litt.D., Lafayette College, Easton, Pennsylvania (1907); president, American Philosophical Association (1908); and exchange professor from Harvard to the University of Berlin (1910). He was founder of the American Institute in Berlin.

Major Contributions

Hugo Munsterberg was a pioneer in the fields of industrial, experimental, and clinical psychology. He championed behaviorism, investigated the value of prayer, and challenged the effectiveness of eyewitness testimonies. He was a famous Harvard professor who reached great academic heights. He helped redefine the psychology of Wilhelm Wundt (see entry) into its modern form.

Inspired by the belief that harmony among nations could be brought about only by fostering the cultural ties between them, he devoted much of his time to the creation of the American Institute in Berlin in 1910. However, the last years of his life were spent in stress and sorrow; he was spurned by the America he loved; from the first days of World War I he continued to write in defense of Germany's motives and ideals. This resulted in violent criticism and attack, and the loss of numerous friendships, and overshadowed his remarkable contributions.

Munsterberg's chief contribution to theoretical psychology was his action theory, this making him a forerunner in the field of behaviorism. His industrial-organizational psychology—experimentally based—looked at problems with monotony, attention and fatigue, physical and social influences on the working power, the effects of advertising, and the future development of economic psychology.

Munsterberg also looked at the reliability of eyewitness testimonies. Within this area are studies that essentially deal with the mind of the witness, illusions, the memory of the witness, and the prevention of crime. Upon viewing pictures made of dots, subjects would look at the pictures for a period of time and would then be asked to write down what they saw. His findings show that each picture was interpreted differently by each subject, bringing into question the reliability of witness statements.

Major Literature

Munsterberg, Hugo. *Psychology and Life*. Edinburgh, Scotland: Archibald Constable and Co., 1899. Montana: R.A. Kessinger Publishing Co., 2004.

___. *The Americans*. Newark, Delaware: McClure Philips, 1904. Whitefish, Montana: R.A. Kessinger Publishing Co., 2005.

___. *On the Witness Stand*. New York: Doubleday, Page and Company, 1907. Littleton, Colorado: Fred B. Rothman and Co., 1981.

___. *Psychology and Industrial Efficiency*. Boston and New York: Houghton Mifflin Company, 1913. Boston, Massachusetts: Adamant Media Corporation, 2005.

___. *The War and America,* Leipzig, Germany: Bernhard Tauchnitz, 1915. Appleton and Co. New York: Cosimo Inc., 2006.

___. *Psychology, General and Applied*. New Jersey: Appleton-Century-Crofts, 1915.

Murphy, Lois Barclay
(1902–2003)

CHILD/SOCIAL PSYCHOLOGY

Lois Barclay was born in Lisbon, Iowa, and earned a B.A. in economics with a minor in religion and psychology from Vassar College, New York. In 1926 she married Gardner Murphy, who at the time was a professor of psychology at Columbia University; they formed an effective working partnership until he died in 1979. Murphy gained her B.D. from Union Theological Seminary in 1938. She taught comparative religion at Sarah Lawrence College, Bronxville, New York, and conducted a study of sympathy exhibited by preschoolers at Macy's Foundation in New York.

She gained a Ph.D. in psychology in 1973 at Columbia University, New York, on her research at Macy's. Her study showed that children as young as 2 years were capable of showing care of and defense for each other, as well as warning each other of some kind of danger. At Sarah Lawrence College she started the first child development center, using the nursery school as a site for much of her research on children and personality development.

In 1952, Lois and Gardner Murphy moved to Topeka, Kansas, to work for the Menninger Foundation (see entry, Menninger, Karl). Gardner became the director, and it was there where Lois carried out the bulk of her work. The couple moved again in 1968 to Washington, D.C., where Gardner worked for George Washington University, while Lois worked as a research consultant at the Children's Hospital. After her husband died, Murphy remained in Washington. She received the G. Stanley Hall Award for the American Psychological Association in 1981.

Major Contributions

One her most noted studies is on personality in young children. She concluded that two children interacting with each other will cause each other to "call forth" traits of an inherent capacity for growth and development that was not previously known to each child. In other words each child's new potentiality trait is specific to it and to the environment in which the two children are interacting, and that if that situation were to disappear or no longer exist, that potentiality would also disappear. For example, a particular situation may call forth the trait of heroism that would otherwise remain dormant. Murphy cautions about assessing personality in one culture into another culture. In this respect, cultural influences supersede genetic dispositions.

Major Literature

Murphy, G., Lois Barclay Murphy, and T. Newcomb. *Experimental Social Psychology: An Interpretation of Research Upon the Socialization of the Individual*. New York and London: Harper and Brothers Publishers, 1937.

Murphy, Lois Barclay. *Methods for the Study of Personality in Young Children*. Oxford, England: Basic Books, 1941.

___. *Personality in Young Children, Vol. 1: Methods for the Study of Personality in Young Children*. Oxford, England: Basic Books, 1956.

Murphy, G., and Lois Barclay Murphy. *Western Psychology: From the Greeks to William James*. Oxford, England: Basic Books, 1970.

Murphy, Lois Barclay. *Gardner Murphy: Integrating, Expanding and Humanizing Psychology*. Jefferson, North Carolina: McFarland and Co. Inc., 1991.

Murray, Henry Alexander (1893–1988)
PSYCHOLOGICAL TESTING

Born in New York City, Henry Alexander Murray gained a B.A. in history at Harvard University, Cambridge, Massachusetts (1915), and an M.A. in biology and an M.D. at Columbia University's College of Physicians, New York (1919). At Harvard he earned a Ph.D. in biochemistry (1927); taught psychology (1927–1937); was assistant director and then director of the Harvard Psychological Clinic (1937–1962); was chief researcher (1947); helped establish the Psychological Clinic Annex (1949); and became emeritus professor (1962). From 1943 to 1947, in the Army Medical Corps, he established and directed the Office of Strategic Services (OSS), an agency charged in part with selecting men for James Bond–like tasks during the war and forerunner of the CIA.

Murray's awards and honors include member, American Academy of Arts and Sciences (1935); Legion of Merit (1946); Distinguished Scientific Contribution Award from the American Psychological Association (1961); five honorary degrees, including the University of Oslo, between 1964 and 1973; and the Gold Medal Award for Lifetime Achievement from the American Psychological Foundation (1969). The Henry A. Murray Research Center is part of Harvard University.

Major Contributions

Murray helped the Allied forces understand Adolf Hitler's psychological makeup in order to predict his behavior as they pushed forward to defeat the Nazis. Murray wrote that Hitler had a personality type stimulated by real or imagined insult or injury, that held grudges, had a low tolerance for criticism, made excessive demands for attention, and had a tendency to belittle, bully or blame others and seek revenge. He predicted that Hitler would commit suicide.

Murray is also noted for his theory of personality (which he labeled "personology"), based on an individual's inborn needs and his relationship with the physical and social environment. Murray insisted that no isolated piece of behavior could ever be understood without taking into account the fully functioning person from physiological, emotional, and social viewpoints.

Influenced by both Sigmund Freud and Carl Jung (see entries), Murray and Christiana D. Morgan developed the Thematic Apperception Test (TAT), which was hailed as an important contribution to understanding a person's patterns of thought, attitudes, observational capacity, and emotions. The TAT now consists of 31 pictures that depict a variety of social and interpersonal situations. The subject is asked to tell a story about each picture to the examiner. Of the 31 pictures, 10 are gender-specific while 21 others can be used with adults of either sex and with children. The TAT is criticized as unscientific because it cannot be proved to be valid (that it actually measures what it claims to measure), or reliable (that it gives consistent results over time, due to the challenge of standardizing interpretations of the stories produced by subjects).

Major Literature

Murray, Henry Alexander, et al. *Explorations in Personality.* New Jersey: John Wiley and Sons, Inc., 1938.
___, et al. Thematic Apperception Test. Cambridge, Massachusetts: Harvard University Press, 1943.
Murray, Henry Alexander. A Psychological Profile of Hitler (1943). Accessible on CU Law Library site, *http://www.news.cornell.edu/Chronicle/05/3.17.05/Hitler_papers.html.*
___. Thematic Apperception Test: Student Manual with Cards. Cambridge, Massachusetts: Harvard University Press, 1974.

Neugarten, Bernice Levin (1916–2001)
ADULT DEVELOPMENT AND AGING

Bernice Levin was born in Norfolk, Nebraska; she married Fritz Neugarten in 1940. At the University of Chicago, Illinois, she gained a B.A. (1936), an M.A. in educational psychology (1937); and a Ph.D. (1943). At the university she was on the Human Development Committee (1951); director, Graduate Training Program in Adult Development and Aging (1958–1980); associate professor of human development (1960–1964); full professor (1964–1969); and chair of Human Development (1969–1980). She was professor of human development and social policy at Northwestern University (1980–1988); emeritus professor and Rothschild Distinguished Scholar at the Center on Aging, Health, and Society, University of Chicago (1988–2001); and president, Gerontological Society of America (1969).

Her awards and honors include first chair of the Committee on University Women (1969–1970); Kleemeier Award for Research on Aging (1971); the National Teaching Award from the American Psychological Foundation (1975); Illinois

Psychological Association Distinguished Psychologist Award (1979); American Psychological Association, Distinguished Scientific Contribution Award from the Division on Adult Development and Aging (1980); honorary D.Sc., University of Southern California, Los Angeles (1980); deputy chair, White House Conference on Aging (1981); Brookdale Award from the Gerontological Society of America for outstanding contributions to gerontology (1982); Sandoz International Prize for Research in Gerontology (1987); honorary doctorate from the University of Nijmegen, the Netherlands (1988); and Gold Medal Award for Life Contributions by a Psychologist in the Public Interest from the American Psychological Association (1994).

Major Contributions

Neugarten, regarded by many as the "grandmother of gerontology," is best known for her groundbreaking contributions to the study of adult development and aging over a period of forty years. While much of her work focused on the second half of life, she viewed older lives in terms of both earlier life experiences and social context, which led to her interest in social policy.

Neugarten and her colleagues in Chicago studied many adults in non-clinical settings. They emphasized the psychological importance of an increased awareness of aging and the personalization of death, as expressed in body monitoring and a tendency to view time in terms of time left to live rather than time since birth. Middle-aged adults develop a sense of competence that was unrealized earlier in life and have a unique perspective on the younger and older generations. As middle age progresses, people become more introspective and develop an increased sense of interiority. Late adulthood culminates in the life review, a detailed appraisal of life as it nears an end.

Major Literature

Neugarten, Bernice Levin. *Middle Age and Aging: Reader in Social Psychology*. Chicago, Illinois: University of Chicago Press, 1969.

Havighurst, Robert J., and Bernice Levin Neugarten. *American Indian and White Children: A Sociopsychological Investigation*. Chicago, Illinois: University of Chicago Press, 1969.

Neugarten, Bernice Levin. *Age or Need? Public Policies for Older People*. London, England: SAGE Publications Ltd., 1983.

Neugarten, Bernice Levin, and Dail A Neugarten. *The Meanings of Age: Selected Papers of Bernice L. Neugarten*. Chicago, Illinois: University of Chicago Press, 1996.

Neumann, Erich (1905–1960)
DEVELOPMENTAL PSYCHOLOGY

Born in Berlin, Neumann received his Ph.D. from the University of Berlin in 1927. Increasingly intrigued by psychoanalysis, Neumann began medical studies at Friedrich Wilhelm University in Berlin. He passed his examinations in 1933 but was unable to obtain an internship because of the race laws affecting Jews. Decades later, when he was already internationally famous, the university granted him a belated medical degree.

Though Freud made a deep impact on him, the pivotal figure in Neumann's career was Carl Jung (see entry), whom he studied with in Zurich. The relationship between these two prolific writers was close yet ambivalent because of Jung's anti–Semitism. Neumann and his wife Julia, who had joined Zionist organizations in their teenaged years, immigrated to Palestine in 1934. For many years, he regularly returned to Zürich, Switzerland, to lecture at the C.G. Jung Institute. He also lectured frequently in England, France and the Netherlands, and was a member of the International Association for Analytical Psychology and president of the Israel Association of Analytical Psychologists. He practiced analytical psychology in Tel Aviv from 1934 until his death.

Major Contributions

In *The Origins and History of Consciousness*, with a foreword by Jung, Neumann develops the theory that mythology reveals how the development of consciousness of the individual parallels the development in society as a whole. He charts what he calls "the mythological stages in the evolution of consciousness": the creation myth, the hero myth, and the transformation myth, identified with the Egyptian god Osiris.

He also presents his theory of centroversion in ego formation — a blend of extraversion and introversion, his contribution to Jung's theory of individuation, in which he describes three types of heroes. The first is the extroverted hero of action who changes the physical world; an example would be the warrior figure of Alexander the Great. The second is the introverted hero who brings culture and inner values, for example Sir Isaac Newton. The third type of hero does not seek to change the world, but to transform the personality.

Neumann wrote extensively on his theory of feminine development in the massive volume *The Great Mother*, in which he traces the genealogy and symbolism of goddess figures in world culture. Neumann has contributed greatly to the study of feminine psychology.

Major Literature

Neumann, Erich. *The Great Mother: An Analysis of the Archetype*. London, Routledge, 1982. London, England: Taylor and Francis Books Ltd., Routledge, 1955.

___, and R. Manheim. *Amor and Psyche: The Psychic Development of the Feminine—A Commentary on the Tale by Apuleius*. New Jersey: Princeton University Press, 1971.

Neumann, Erich. *Depth Psychology and a New Ethic*. New York: Harper Collins Publishers, Inc., 1973.

___. *The Origins and History of Consciousness*. New Jersey: Princeton University Press, 1973. London, England: Taylor and Francis Books Ltd., Routledge, 1999.

___. *The Child*. New York: Harper Collins Publishers, Inc., 1976.

Niederland, William Guglielmo (1904–1993)

SURVIVOR SYNDROME

Born into a Jewish family from Schippenbeil, East Prussia, William Guglielmo Niederland qualified as a medical doctor at the University of Würzburg in 1929, then subsequently worked as a physician in Berlin, Düsseldorf and Geilingen. In 1934 he immigrated to Italy, where he took the medical exam for a second time and established a psychiatric practice in Milan. He was forced to flee in 1939 by way of England and arrived in the United States in 1940; he become an American citizen in 1954.

After taking his medical exam for the third time in 1941 and establishing a private practice in New York, he traveled throughout the United States giving lectures on the subject of fascism in Germany and other European countries. From 1945 to 1947, he taught at the University of Tampa in Florida and he taught at the Downstate Medical Center in Brooklyn from 1952 to 1977, when he was named professor emeritus. He was president of the Psychoanalytic Association of New York from 1971 to 1973.

Major Contributions

One of Niederland's major research interests for decades was the case of Daniel Paul Schreiber, whose diaries had been analyzed by Freud in 1911. (Schreiber [1842–1911], a German judge who suffered from paranoid schizophrenia, described his condition in his book *Memoirs of My Nervous Illness*.) From 1953 onward, Niederland was a consultant to German courts ruling on indemnification claims by Holocaust survivors.

The prevailing theory was that the survivor's psychiatric diseases and mental suffering were results of the patient's disposition rather than the result of Nazi persecution. Together with a handful of other psychiatrists, Niederland submitted very detailed and empathetic psychiatric reports that not only illustrated the impact of Nazi persecution on people's mental constitution, but were a testament to the life-enduring suffering of numerous Holocaust survivors.

Niederland established an international research network with several colleagues, including Robert J. Lifton (see entry) and coined the phrase "the survivor syndrome." (Survivor syndrome is also a factor in post–traumatic stress disorder). This syndrome includes depression, apathy, chronic anxiety and fear of renewed persecution, which could, under stress, become paranoia. Survivors were found to have many somatic complaints, nightmares with Holocaust content, and insomnia. The psychiatrists also described "survivor guilt," feeling guilty for surviving when so many had died. Very few of the survivors received any treatment for these difficulties.

Major Literature

Niederland, William Guglielmo. *Man Made Plague: A Primer on Neurosis*. New York: Renbayle House, 1948.

___. "Three Notes on the Schreber Case." *Psychoanalytic Quarterly* 20 (1951): 579–591.

___. "The Problem of the Survivor: The Psychiatric Evaluation of Emotional Disorders in the Survivors of Nazi Persecution." *Journal of the Hillside Hospital* 10 (1961): 233–247.

___. "Psychiatric Disorders Among Persecution Victims: A Contribution to the Understanding of Concentration Camp Pathology and its After-effects." *Journal of Nervous and Mental Diseases* 139 (1964): 458–474.

___. *The Schreber Case: Psychoanalytic Profile of a Paranoid Personality*. Quadrangle/New York Times Book Co., 1974.

Orne, Martin Theodore (1927–2000)

HYPNOSIS

Born in Vienna, Martin Theodore Orne immigrated with his family to the United States in 1938. At Harvard University, Cambridge, Massachusetts, Orne gained an A.B. with honors (1948), an A.M. (1951) and a Ph.D. (1958). His M.D. is from Tufts University, Medford, Massachusetts (1955). His residency in psychiatry was at Massachusetts Mental Health Center (1957–1960). Orne was professor of psychiatry and director, University of Pennsylvania Medical School, Philadelphia (1967–2000).

His awards and honors include the Benjamin Franklin Gold Medal, International Society of Hypnosis (1982); Distinguished Scientific Award for the Applications of Psychology, American Psychological Association (APA) (1982); Seymour Pollack Award, American Academy of Psychiatry and the Law (1991); and James McKeen Cattell Fellow Award in Applied Psychology, APA (1992). He was a member of APA Divisions 1, 6, 8 and 30, with fellow status in 6, 8 and 30. He was the recipient of two honorary doctorate degrees, editor of the *International Journal of Clinical and Experimental Hypnosis* for 30 years; executive director of the Institute for Experimental Psychiatry Research Foundation, Inc., and past president of the International Society of Hypnosis and the Society for Clinical and Experimental Hypnosis.

Major Contributions

At Philadelphia, Orne established and directed the Unit for Experimental Psychiatry, a research laboratory in the School of Medicine. Orne was widely recognized for his work in hypnosis, memory, biofeedback, pain management, dissociative identity disorder (formerly multiple personality disorder), what is popularly known as brainwashing, lie detection, sleep and the factors that influence psychotherapy and behavioral medicine.

His interest in hypnosis started as an undergraduate at Harvard, when he wrote a paper challenging many of the myths associated with using hypnosis for age regression. He found that recall, having been filtered through adult perceptions, was not accurate. The last paper before he died examined how hypnosis could encourage witnesses to confabulate or "remember" things they could not have seen or experienced, in what has become known as "false memory syndrome."

His work led to the adoption of guidelines restricting the use of hypnosis in forensic cases. He chaired an influential panel that helped establish the American Medical Association's standards for the forensic use of hypnosis. An expert witness in legal cases involving coercion and memory distortion, Orne was involved in several high profile criminal cases, including the kidnapped heiress Patty Hearst (1974) and the case of Kenneth Bianchi (1978), who was convicted for the torture and murder of young women in the hillside strangler serial murders.

Major Literature

Orne, Martin Theodore, D.F. Dinges, and E.C. Orne. "On the Differential Diagnosis of Multiple Personality in the Forensic Context." *International Journal of Clinical and Experimental Hypnosis* 32 (1984): 118–169.

Orne, Martin Theodore. *Hypnotically Refreshed Testimony HRT: Enhanced Memory or Tampering With Evidence.* Collingdale, Pennsylvania: Diane Publishing Company, 1985.

___. "Comments on the Draft Home Office Guidelines." *British Journal of Experimental and Clinical Hypnosis* 5 (1988): 37–44.

___. *On the Social Psychology of the Psychological Experiment: With Particular Reference to Demand Characteristics and their Implications.* New York: Irvington Publishers, 1991.

Osgood, Charles Egerton (1916–1991)

SEMANTIC DIFFERENTIAL

Born in Somerville, Massachusetts, Charles Egerton Osgood gained a B.A. (1939) and a D.Sc. (1962) from Dartmouth College, Hanover, North Hampshire. At Yale University, New Haven, Connecticut, he gained a Ph.D. (1945) and was research associate (1945–1946). From 1946 to 1949 he was assistant professor of psychology, University of Connecticut, Storrs. At the University of Illinois, Urbana-Champaign, he was associate professor of psychology (1949–1952); professor of communications and psychology (1952–1984); and director of the Communications Research Center (1957–1984). From 1958 to 1959 he was at the Center for Advanced Study in the Behavioral Sciences, Stanford, California.

He was president of the American Psychological Association American Academy of Arts and Sciences (1962–1963); a Guggenheim fellow; fellow, Center for Advanced Study in Behavioral Sciences, Palo Alto, California; American Association of University Professors; Linguistic Society of America; Phi Beta Kappa and Society of Sigma Xi.

Major Contributions

Osgood's main contributions are:

1. *Behaviorism versus cognitivism.* Osgood regarded himself as a behaviorist who argued that simple stimulus-response theories were incapable of explaining most of human behavior such as language and thinking. Nevertheless, Osgood continued to regard his work as essentially behaviorist because the

core semantic features were always derived from actual behavior towards stimuli in the environment.

2. *Psycholinguistics research and theory.* Following Noam Chomsky's (see entry) criticism of the limitations of the behaviorist approach, Osgood's work on the importance of semantics over syntax was largely ignored.

3. *Theory of meaning.* Osgood suggested that words represent things because they produce an abbreviated replica of actual behavior towards those things. Osgood and others developed the *semantic differential* as an objective measure of meaning. Respondents were asked to rate a given concept on a series of seven-point, bi-polar rating scales. Evaluation (good-bad), potency (strong-weak) and activity (active-passive). The semantic differential is still widely used, although it is now regarded as measuring emotional responses to words (i.e. the affective meaning) rather than the dictionary meaning.

4. *Cross-cultural research on affective meaning and attribution of feelings.* At Stanford he conducted a cross-cultural study involving 30 language-culture groups and 620 concepts. He found fairly strong support for the universality of his theory of meaning.

5. *Peace studies.* Osgood considered that psychologists could and should become actively involved in averting war, especially nuclear war. His major contribution was his GRIT strategy (graduated and reciprocated initiatives in tension-reduction). The purpose of GRIT is to induce trust and cooperative responses among protagonists and reduce the escalation of hostility.

Major Literature

Osgood, Charles Egerton. *Method and Theory in Experimental Psychology.* New York: Oxford University Press, Inc., 1952.

Osgood, Charles Egerton, and Thomas A. Sebeok. *Psycholinguistics: A Survey of Theory and Research Problems.* Bloomington: Indiana University Press, 1954. Westport, Connecticut: Greenwood Press, 1977.

Osgood, Charles Egerton. *Alternative to War or Surrender.* Champaign, Illinois: University of Illinois Press, 1962.

___. *Measurement of Meaning.* Champaign, Illinois: University of Illinois Press, 1967.

___. *Language, Meaning and Culture: Selected Papers of C.E. Osgood.* Westport, Connecticut: Greenwood Press, 1990.

Paivio, Allan Urho (1925–)
IMAGERY, LANGUAGE AND MEMORY

Born in Thunder Bay, Ontario, Canada, Allan Urho Paivio gained a B.Sc. (1949), an M.Sc. (1957), and a Ph.D. (1959) at McGill University, Montreal, Quebec. At the University of Western Ontario, London, he was assistant professor (1962–1963); associate professor (1963–1967); professor of psychology (1967–1992); professor emeritus of kinesiology (from 1992). He was president of the Canadian Psychological Association (1974–1975).

His awards and honors include the Queen's Silver Jubilee Medal (1977); fellow of the Royal Society of Canada (1978); Distinguished Contributions to Psychology as a Science, Canadian Psychological Association (1982); Killam Research Fellowship (1990, 1991–1992); and honorary LL.D., University of Western Ontario (1993).

Major Contributions

During his undergraduate years, Paivio won the title of Mr. Canada in 1948, and was on the cover of *Muscle Power and Your Physique.* He has spent over forty years researching imagery, memory, language and cognition, and has published approximately two hundred articles and book chapters and five books. His principal work is a general theory of cognition, called dual coding theory (DCT), which assumes that all human cognition entails the cooperative activity of multimodal verbal and nonverbal (especially imagery) processing systems. DCT is related to the cognitive memory models that emerged as part of the cognitive information processing studies that attempted to describe how the mind processes information.

Paivio's DCT mainly deals with how visual information is processed and stored in memory and gives equal weight to verbal and non-verbal processing. According to the theory, human cognition consists of two subsystems that process knowledge simultaneously, one processing the nonverbal objects (imagery) and one dealing with language (verbal). The two systems have different functions; the verbal subsystem processes and stores linguistic information, (words, sentences, etc.), whereas the visual subsystem processes and stores images and pictorial information. Verbal system units are called logogens; these units contain information that underlie our use of the word. Non-verbal system units are called imagens. While the two subsystems can be activated independently, the interrelations and connections of the two systems allow the dual coding of information.

DCT has applications in many cognitive domains: concept learning, language, improving graphics for communication, decision making, memory, and problem solving. Imagery also has useful application in psychotherapy and counseling, where it is used to get at deeper feelings that words alone cannot reach.

Major Literature

Paivio, Allan Urho. *Mental Representations: A Dual Coding Approach.* New York: Oxford University Press, Inc., 1986.

___, and Mark Sadoski. *Imagery and Text: A Dual Coding Theory of Reading and Writing.* Hillsdale, New Jersey: Erlbaum, Associates, Inc., 2001.

Paivio, Allan Urho. *Imagery and Verbal Processes.* Hillsdale, New Jersey: Erlbaum Associates, Inc., 2002.

Craig, R., Diane E. Hall, and Allan Urho Paivio. *Sport Imagery Questionnaire: Test Manual.* Morgantown, West Virginia: Fitness Information Technology, Inc., 2005.

Paivio, Allan Urho. *Mind and Its Evolution: A Dual Coding Theoretical Approach.* Hillsdale, New Jersey: Erlbaum Associates, Inc., 2006.

Parke, Ross D. (1938–)

CHILD DEVELOPMENT

Born in Huntsville, Ontario, Canada, Ross D. Parke gained a B.A. (1962) and an M.A. in psychology (1963) from the University of Toronto, Ontario, Canada, and a Ph.D. in psychology at the University of Waterloo, Ontario (1965). Parke was professor in the Department of Psychology, University of Wisconsin, Madison (1970–1971); clinical professor, School of Clinical Medicine, University of Illinois at Urbana-Champaign (1970–1990); Fels Clinical Professor of Research Pediatrics, University of Cincinnati College of Medicine (1971–1975); professor of psychology, University of Illinois at Urbana-Champaign (1975–1990); presidential chair in psychology, University of California, Riverside (1990–1992); professor of psychology, University of California, Riverside (since 1990); and director, Center for Family Studies, University of California, Riverside (since 1992).

Parke's awards and honors include Belding Scholar of the Foundation for Child Development, New York (1980); University of Illinois Department of Psychology Graduate Student Organization Award for Excellence in Advising and Teaching at the Graduate Level (1989); chair, Council of Editors, American Psychological Association (1989–1990); Fellow, American Psychological Society (1990); and Sabbatical Award, James McKeen Cattell Foundation (1994). Parke was associate editor of *Child Development* (1973–1977) and editor of *Developmental Psychology* (1987–1992).

Major Contributions

Parke's research focuses on the development of social behavior in young children. As part of a long-standing exploration of mother-father differences in styles of interaction, he is examining the linkages between family and peer social systems. The lessons that are learned in the family, in turn, influence children's adaptation to peers. Three areas are of particular interest:

1. The role of parent-child interaction patterns in learning modes, of socially interacting with peers, how emotions and thinking influence social relationships.

2. How parents serve as direct instructors, tutors and models to help teach children how to interact with others of the same age.

3. How parents act as managers of their children's peer relationships by providing opportunities for peer contact.

Parke's most significant work has been in the area of parent-infant interaction, with a particular emphasis on the role fathers play in infancy and early childhood. Before Parke, the study of the attachment behavior of the newborn was almost exclusively limited to the mother-infant dyad, and the significance of the father in the theories of parenthood had been ignored. Society seems to have decided that the mother is *the* competent primary career. Yet as Harry Harlow's (see entry) work with monkeys showed, "contact comfort," as opposed to food, has primary reinforcing qualities for infant monkeys. Parke and his colleagues are now exploring the impact of economic stress on adaptations in families of different ethnic backgrounds.

Major Literature

Parke, Ross D. "Nurturance, Nurturance Withdrawal, and Resistance to Deviation." *Child Development* 38 (1967): 1101–1010.

___. *Fatherhood.* Cambridge, Massachusetts: Harvard University Press, 1996.

___, and R. O'Neil. "The Influence of Significant Others on Learning about Relationships." In S. Duck (Ed.), *The Handbook of Personal Relationships*, 2nd ed. New York: Wiley, 1997.

Parke, Ross D., and A. Brott. *Throwaway Dads: The*

Myths and Barriers That Keep Men From Being the Fathers They Want to Be. Boston, Massachusetts: Houghton-Mifflin, 1999.

Patterson, Gerald R. (1926–)
ANTISOCIAL BEHAVIOR

Born in Lisbon, North Dakota, Gerald R. Patterson served in the combat infantry in Okinawa, Japan, during World War II. He earned a B.S. (1949) and an M.A. (1951) from the University of Oregon, Eugene, and a Ph.D. from the University of Minnesota, Minneapolis (1956). He was fellow in psychology, Wilder Child Guidance Clinic, St. Paul, Minnesota (1953–1955) and instructor in medical psychology, Psychiatric Institute, University of Nebraska Medical School, Omaha (1955–1957). At the University of Oregon, Patterson was professor, Department of Psychology (1957–1966); research professor, School of Education (1967–1968); research scientist (1967–1977); and co-founder and research scientist, Oregon Social Learning Center (since 1977).

Patterson's awards and honors include the National Institute of Mental Health Career Development Award (1967–1972); Distinguished Scientist Award, Division of Clinical Psychology, American Psychological Association (APA) (1982); Distinguished Scientific Award for the Applications of Psychology, APA (1984); Distinguished Professional Contribution Award, Section on Clinical Child Psychology, APA (1986); and Founders Award for Distinguished Contributions to the Profession of Psychology, Pacific University Department of Psychology, Forest Grove, Oregon (1993).

Major Contributions

At the Wilder Clinic, Patterson concluded that psychoanalytic theory made little impact on antisocial and hyperactive children, which made up the bulk of the case load of child guidance clinics. At Omaha, he learned the therapeutic skills appropriate for working with extremely disturbed children and developed a non-verbal technique for assessment of aggression in children (1960). As a professor at Eugene, he used an eclectic approach of psychoanalysis and the approaches of Harry Stack Sullivan and Carl Rogers (see entries).

When Patterson joined the Oregon Research Institute he began to focus his attention on measurement methodology, personality and cognitive processes, and developing behavioral approaches to treating conflict in families. At the Oregon Social Learning Center the attention moved from problems of parent training for families of antisocial, abused and delinquent children to researching long-term prediction of delinquency, treatment of child abuse and analysis of resistance to treatment. His work appears in virtually all reviews of deviant family interaction, childhood aggression, and their treatment. Patterson (with others) published a series titled *A Social Learning Approach to Family Intervention* (Pacific Grove, California: Brooks/Cole Publishing Company). The five volumes, in order, are *Families with Aggressive Children* (1975); *Observations in Home Setting* (1978); *Coercive Family Processes* (1982); *Antisocial Boys* (1992); and Family Connections: *A Treatment Foster Care Model for Delinquent Youth* (1994).

Major Literature

Patterson, Gerald R. "A Nonverbal Technique for the Assessment of Aggression in Children." *Child Development* 31 (1960): 643–53.

Capaldi, Deborah M., and Gerald R. Patterson. *Psychometric Properties of Fourteen Latent Constructs From the Oregon Youth Study.* New York: Springer-Verlag, 1989.

Patterson, Gerald R. *Depression and Aggression in Family Interactions.* Hillsdale, New Jersey: Erlbaum Associates Inc., 1990.

Reid, John B., Gerald R. Patterson, and James J. Snyder. *Antisocial Behavior in Children and Adolescents: A Developmental Analysis and Model for Intervention.* Washington, D.C.: American Psychological Association, 2002.

Patterson Gerald R., and Marion Forgatch. *Parents and Adolescents Living Together: Family Problem Solving.* Champaign, Illinois: Research Press Publishers, 2005.

Pavlov, Ivan Petrovich (1894–1936)
CLASSICAL CONDITIONING

Ivan Pavlov, the son of a priest, spent his youth in Ryazan in central Russia. He left his theological studies in 1870 to study chemistry and physiology at the University of St. Petersburg, from where he graduated in 1875. After graduating with an M.D. at the Imperial Medical Academy, St. Petersburg, in 1879 (he completed his dissertation, "The Centrifugal Nerves of the Heart," in 1883), he studied physiology in Breslau and Leipzig, Germany, from 1884 to 1886.

In 1890 Pavlov organized the new Department of Physiology at the Institute of Experimental Medicine, St. Petersburg, and directed it for 45 years. This institute became one of the most important centers of physiological research; he initiated precise surgical procedures for animals, with strict attention to their postoperative care and facilities for the maintenance of their health. In 1890 he became professor of physiology in the Imperial Medical Academy, St. Petersburg, where he remained until his resignation in 1924.

He was awarded the Nobel Prize in Physiology or Medicine in 1904 for research pertaining to the digestive system. In 1922 Pavlov requested Vladimir Lenin to transfer his laboratory abroad. Lenin refused, saying that Russia needed scientists such as Pavlov. Pavlov visited the United States in 1923 and after another visit in 1929 he publicly denounced Communism, stating that the basis for international Marxism was false. In 1924, when the sons of priests were expelled from the Military Medical Academy in Leningrad (the former Imperial Medical Academy), he resigned his chair of physiology. In 1927 he wrote to Joseph Stalin saying that he was ashamed to be called a Russian.

Major Contributions

Pavlov is chiefly known for his development of the concept of the conditioned reflex. In a now-classic experiment, he trained a hungry dog to salivate at the sound of a bell, which was previously associated with the sight of food. He developed a similar conceptual approach, emphasizing the importance of conditioning, in his pioneering studies relating human behavior to the nervous system.

Beginning about 1930, Pavlov tried to apply his laws to the explanation of human psychoses. He assumed that the excessive inhibition characteristic of a psychotic person was a protective mechanism — shutting out the external world — in that it excluded injurious stimuli that had previously caused extreme excitation.

Pavlov is also known for conditioning in the areas of extreme pain and stress. He began the study of transmarginal inhibition (TMI), the body's natural response of shutting down when exposed to overwhelming stress or pain. Carl Jung studied Pavlov's work on TMI and considered that introverted people were more sensitive to stimuli and reached a TMI state earlier than their extroverted counterparts. Pavlov died in Leningrad (St. Petersburg).

Major Literature

Pavlov, Ivan Petrovich, and George Windholz. *Psychopathology and Psychiatry*. New Jersey: Transaction Publishers, 1993.

Pavlov, Ivan, and I.P. Petrovich. *Selected Works*. Honolulu, Hawaii: University Press of the Pacific, 2001.

Payton, Carolyn Robertson (1925–2001)
PSYCHOTHERAPY

Carolyn Robertson was born in Norfolk, Virginia. Although she grew up during the Depression, it was not financial hardship she most remembered but the racial segregation, where even toilets were segregated. As an American citizen she knew she was guaranteed certain rights, and all her life she was a powerful advocate for women's and minority rights, a pioneer in cross-cultural and ethnic minority psychology. She supported the movement for specialized training for psychotherapists for treating clients of an ethnic minority. She was the first woman and the first African-American psychologist to hold the position of director of the U.S. Peace Corps, in which she was responsible for the work of over 6,000 volunteers in 63 countries.

She graduated from Bennett College, Greensboro, North Carolina, a distinguished college for black women, in 1945. She gained her M.S. in clinical psychology from University of Wisconsin in 1948 and married Raymond Rudolph Payton. From 1948 to 1953 she was an instructor at Livingstone College, Salisbury, North Carolina, and was the only psychologist on the faculty. From 1953 to 1958 she was dean of women and psychology instructor at Elizabeth City State Teachers College in North Carolina, then associate professor of psychology at Virginia State College, Petersburg. This was a post that entailed half-time work as an undergraduate professor and half-time as clinical counselor, her first clinical position, where she conducted psychological testing and provided psychotherapy to students.

In 1959, Payton became an assistant professor at Howard University in Washington, D.C. Here she worked in a primate laboratory, which led to her award of a three year grant from the National Institute of Mental Health. Her work focused mostly on perception, with the ultimate goal of building on the research and studying racial perception in young children. She took a leave of absence and received her Ed.D. in 1962 from Columbia University's Teachers College.

Major Contributions

In 1970, Payton was appointed to direct the Howard University Counseling Service (HUCS), used by students, staff and the wider black community. She incorporated group therapy methods and established training and supervision components into the program. Eventually HUCS became a training institute itself, with an emphasis on training clinicians for work with ethnic and minority clients. She was also instrumental in making counseling services available to lower-income clients. She publicly advocated short-term group therapies as a way of minimizing costs and increasing availability.

In addition, she is largely responsible for making HUCS an American Psychological Association (APA) accredited counseling psychology internship site, which is still one of the few in existence at primarily black institutions. Payton won several awards and gained much recognition for her work, including the Distinguished Professional Contributions to Public Service Award from APA in 1982; the Committee on Women in Psychology Leadership Citation from APA in 1985; and the Peace Corps Leader for Peace Award in 1988.

Major Literature

Payton, Carolyn Robertson. "Who Must do the Hard Things?" *American Psychologist* 39 (1984): 391–397.

Peck, M. Scott (1936–2005)
PSYCHIATRY AND RELIGION

Born in New York City, M. Scott Peck earned a B.A. with honors (1958) at Harvard College, Cambridge, Massachusetts, and an M.D. (1963) at the Case Western Reserve University School of Medicine, Cleveland, Ohio. From 1963 until 1972, he served in the United States Army, resigning from the position of assistant chief of psychiatry and neurology consultant to become the surgeon general of the Army with the rank of lieutenant colonel and the Meritorious Service Medal with oak leaf cluster. He was the medical director of the New Milford Hospital Mental Health Clinic and a psychiatrist in private practice in New Milford, Connecticut.

In 1992 Peck was selected by the American Psychiatric Association (APA) as a distinguished psychiatrist lecturer "for his outstanding achievement in the field of psychiatry as an educator, researcher and clinician." As a result of his pioneering community building work, Peck was the recipient of the 1984 Kaleidoscope Award for Peacemaking and the 1994 Temple International Peace Prize. In 1996 he was also recipient of the Learning, Faith and Freedom Medal from Georgetown University.

Peck suffered from Parkinson's disease as well as pancreatic and liver duct cancer and died at his home on Bliss Road in Warren, Connecticut.

Major Contributions

Peck came to Christianity by way of Buddhist and Islamic mysticism and made a public commitment by a non-denominational baptism in 1980. One of his religious insights was that people who are evil attack others rather than face their own failures. In 1984, Peck, his wife and nine others established the Foundation for Community Encouragement, a non-profit, public educational foundation whose mission was to promote and teach the principles of community. It ceased operations in 2002.

Peck's works combined his experiences from his private psychiatric practice with a distinctly religious point of view. *The Road Less Traveled* (Simon and Schuster) was first published in 1978. It spent 13 years on the New York Times bestseller list to create a paperback record, sold 10 million copies worldwide and was translated into more than 20 languages.

Peck believes that it is only through suffering and agonizing that people can resolve the many puzzles and conflicts they face. This is what he calls *genuine suffering*, the Christian way. By trying to avoid genuine suffering, people ultimately end up creating more causes for suffering. Unnecessary suffering is what Scott Peck terms *neurotic suffering*. People's aim must be to eliminate neurotic suffering and work through genuine suffering to achieve their individual goals.

Major Literature

Peck, M. Scott. *People of the Lie: The Hope for Healing Human Evil.* New York: Simon and Schuster Inc., 1983.
___. *What Return Can I Make? Dimensions of the Christian Experience.* New York: Simon and Schuster Inc., 1985.
___. *The Different Drum: Community Making and Peace.* New York: Simon and Schuster Inc., 1987.
___. *Meditations from the Road.* New York: Simon and Schuster Inc., 1993.

Penrose, Lionel Sharples (1898–1972)
GENETICS OF LEARNING DISABILITY

Born in London, England of Quaker stock, Lionel Sharples Penrose served in the Friends' Ambulance Train of the British Red Cross in France until the end of World War I. He graduated in moral sciences from St. John's College, Cambridge, in 1921, then spent a postgraduate year in psychology at Cambridge. From 1923 to 1925 he studied psychiatry in Vienna, Austria, then graduated in medicine in London MRCS, LRCP in 1928, winning the Bristowe Medal (1929) for his clinical experience at St. Thomas's Hospital, London. He gained his M.D. (1930) at City Mental Hospital, Cardiff, with a study of schizophrenia.

In 1931 he moved to the Royal Eastern Counties Institution at Colchester, Essex, a hospital with a large number of mentally retarded patients. He at once became interested in this hitherto neglected branch of medicine, partly because of the human aspects, but also because (at that time) the 300,000 patients in the general population posed a serious social problem, and little thought had been given to the possibilities of prevention of mental retardation.

Over seven years he made a detailed study of 1,280 mentally defective patients and their 6,629 siblings, plus their parents and other relatives. The research showed that there were many different types and causes of mental defect, and that normality and subnormality were on a continuum. The findings were published in a Medical Research Council special report and later expanded in two books. From 1939 to 1945 he was director of psychiatric research in Ontario, Canada, where he made an important study on the efficacy of shock therapy. In 1945 he was appointed to the Galton chair of eugenics at University College, London; in 1963 he had the name of the chair changed to the "Galton chair of human genetics."

When he began his study of Down syndrome, the condition was called Mongolism (on account of the Mongoloid features of these people); he later changed the term to "Down's anomaly." Penrose wrote a notable monograph on the subject in 1966, the centenary of Dr. John Langdon Down's first description of the condition. Penrose was the first to demonstrate the significance of a mother's age in her child's healthy birth and early years. In the 1950s he was a leading figure in the Medical Association for the Prevention of War.

Major Literature

Penrose, Lionel Sharples. *Mental Defect*. London, England: Sidgwick and Jackson, 1933.
___. *Influence of Heredity on Disease*. London, England: H.K. Lewis, 1934.
___. *The Biology of Mental Defect*. London, England: Sidgwick and Jackson, 1949, 4th edition revised in 1972 by J.M. Berg and H. Lang-Brown.

___. *Outline of Human Genetics*. London, England: William Heinemann, 1963.
___, and G.F. Smith. *Down's Anomaly*. London, England: Churchill, 1966.
___. *Clinical and Genetic Study of 1280 Cases of Mental Defect: Colchester Survey*. London, England: Institute for Research into Mental and Multiple Handicap, 1975.

Perls, Fritz (1893–1970)
Gestalt Therapy

Friedrich Salomon Perls was born in Berlin, Germany, of Jewish descent. He earned his M.D. degree in 1921, and then worked at the Institute for Brain Damaged Soldiers in Frankfurt. He was influenced by Gestalt psychologists, existential philosophers, and by Karen Horney, and eventually became a psychoanalyst. In 1933, he, his wife, Laura, and their first child fled to the Netherlands. One year later they immigrated to South Africa where he taught psychoanalysis. He was an army psychiatrist from 1942 and in 1946 he moved to the United States.

He became increasingly disenchanted with psychoanalysis and existentialism, and in 1951, the Perls organized the New York Institute of Gestalt therapy. In 1964 he joined the Esalen Institute, California, where he continued to offer Gestalt therapy workshops until 1969, when he moved to start a Gestalt community at Lake Cowichan on Vancouver Island, Canada. He died almost a year later in Chicago.

Major Contributions

Fritz Perls, the "father of Gestalt therapy," brought on a revolution in psychiatry. He provided a foundation from which humanistic and transpersonal psychology was built. His approach is related to, but not identical with, Gestalt psychology and the Gestalt theoretical psychotherapy of Hans-Juergen Walter. The core of Gestalt therapy is the belief that people split off from the experiences, thoughts, sensations, and emotions that are uncomfortable. This splitting off creates a fragmentation of the personality. Perls' focus was to assist people in owning their experiences and developing a healthy gestalt or wholeness. According to Perls, there are six factors causing psychological discomfort:

1. The lack of contact: no social support.
2. Confluence: the environment takes control.
3. Unfinished business: inability to gain closure.
4. Fragmentation: denied or fragmented self.

5. Winner/loser: conflict of values and expectations.
6. Polarities: never seeing gray, always black or white.

"The Gestalt Prayer" is generally taken as a classic expression of the kind of individualism associated with the American culture of the 1960s. The key idea of the statement is the focus on living in response to one's own needs. It also expresses the idea that, by fulfilling their own needs, people can help others do the same, i.e., when they "find each other, it's beautiful." The principles of Gestalt therapy are found in most current schools of psychotherapy and provide the springboard for eclectic psychotherapy.

Major Literature

Perls, Fritz. *Ego Hunger and Aggression: A Revision of Freud's Theory and Method.* London: G. Allen and Unwin Ltd., 1947. New York: Gestalt Journal Press, 1992.
___, Paul Goodman, and Ralph Hefferline. *Gestalt Therapy: Excitement and Growth in Human Personality.* New York: Julian Press, 1951. London, England: Souvenir Press Ltd., 1994.
Perls, Fritz. *Gestalt Therapy Verbatim.* Lafayette, California: Real People Press, 1992. New York: Gestalt Journal Press, U.S., 1969.
___. *In and Out of the Garbage Pail.* Lafayette, California: Real People Press, 1981. London: Random House Group, Bantam, 1969.

Piaget, Jean (1896–1980)
COGNITIVE DEVELOPMENT THEORY

Born in Neuchâtel, Switzerland, Jean Piaget gained a doctorate in biology (1918) and was research director, Institute Jean-Jacques Rousseau, Geneva, Switzerland (1921–1925); professor of psychology, sociology and the philosophy of science, University of Neuchâtel, Switzerland (1925–1929); professor of the history of scientific thought, University of Geneva (1929–1939); director, International Bureau of Education, Geneva (1929–1967); director, Institute of Educational Sciences, University of Geneva (1932–1971); professor of experimental psychology and sociology, University of Lausanne (1938–1951); professor of sociology, University of Geneva (1939–1951); professor of experimental psychology, University of Geneva (1940–1971); professor of genetic psychology, Sorbonne, Paris (1952–1964); director, International Center for Genetic Epistemology, Geneva (1955–1980); and emeritus professor, University of Geneva (1971–1980). Piaget received honorary doctorates from 32 universities and received 12 international prizes.

Major Contributions

Piaget was the first to make a systematic study of the acquisition of understanding in children. He traced four stages in the development of children:

Stage 1—*Sensorimotor stage*: The first two years of life is when children experience the world through movement and senses; they first become aware of themselves as a separate physical entity.

Stage 2—*Preoperational stage*: Roughly from age two to age six or seven. Through the acquisition of motor skills, children learn to represent objects by words and to manipulate the words mentally.

Stage 3—*Concrete operational stage*: From age of about 7 to age 11 or 12. The beginnings of logic; the classification of objects by their similarities and differences; early grasp of concepts of time and number.

Stage 4—*The period of formal operations*: This begins at age around age 12 and extends into adulthood. Orderliness of thinking and a mastery of logical thought; more flexible kind of mental experimentation; manipulates abstract ideas, makes hypotheses, and sees the implications of his own thinking and that of others.

Piaget's concept of these developmental stages caused a reevaluation of older ideas of the child, of learning, and of education. If the development of certain thought processes was on a genetically determined timetable, simple reinforcement was not sufficient to teach concepts; the child's mental development would have to be at the proper stage to assimilate those concepts. Thus, the teacher became not a transmitter of knowledge but a guide to the child's own discovery of the world.

Major Literature

Piaget, Jean. *The Child's Conception of the World.* London, England: Routledge and Kegan Paul, 1928.
___. *The Moral Judgment of the Child.* London, England: Kegan Paul, Trench, Trubner and Co., 1932.
___. *The Child's Conception of Number.* London, England: Routledge and Kegan Paul, 1952.
___. *The Origins Of Intelligence In Children.* London, England: Routledge and Kegan Paul, 1953.
___. *The Child's Construction of Reality.* London, England: Routledge and Kegan Paul, 1955.
Inhelder, B., and Jean Piaget. *The Growth of Logical Thinking from Childhood to Adolescence.* New York: Basic Books, 1958.
Piaget, Jean. *Studies in Reflecting Abstraction.* Hove, England: Psychology Press, 2001.

Pinel, Philippe (1745–1826)
REFORMER OF ASYLUMS

Born in Saint-André, Tarn, France, Pinel gained his M.D. (1773) from the University of Toulouse, then studied four years at the Faculty of Medicine of Montpellier. When he moved to Paris in 1778, his degree was not recognized by the Paris faculty, so he earned his living for fifteen years as a writer, translator, and editor. He worked for five years in a mental institution where he gathered information and started to formulate his ideas.

In 1793 he was appointed "physician of the infirmeries" at Bicêtre Hospital, in the southern suburbs of Paris, which at the time housed about four thousand imprisoned men — criminals, petty offenders, syphilitics, pensioners and about two hundred mental patients. His previous experience at the private sanatoria made him a good candidate for the job, and Pinel's patrons hoped that his appointment would lead to therapeutic initiatives.

Pinel was elected to the Académie des Sciences in 1804 and was a member of the Académie de Médecine from its founding in 1820. He died in Paris and a statue in his honor stands outside the Salpêtrière.

Major Contributions

What he aimed for at Bicêtre was a strict, non-violent, non-medical management of mental patients, which came to be called moral treatment ("psychological" is probably a more accurate translation of the French "moral"). Pinel did away with bleeding, purging, and blistering in favor of a therapy that involved close contact with, and careful observation of, patients. He visited each patient, often several times a day, and took careful notes over two years. He engaged them in lengthy conversations. His objective was to assemble a detailed case history and a natural history of the patient's illness.

From 1795 until he died, Pinel was chief physician to the Hospice de la Salpêtrière, Paris; his right-hand man at Bicêtre, Jean-Baptiste Pussin, followed Pinel to Salpêtrière in 1802. The Salpêtrière at that time was like a large village, with seven thousand elderly, destitute and ailing women, an entrenched bureaucracy, a teeming market and huge infirmaries. Pinel created an inoculation clinic in 1799 and the first vaccination in Paris was given there in April 1800.

In 1795 Pinel was also appointed as a professor of medical pathology, a chair that he held for twenty years. In his book Traité médico-philosophique sur l'aleniation mentale; ou la manie, published in 1801, Pinel discusses his psychologically oriented approach. This book was translated into English by the English physician D.D. Davis (1777–1841) as Treatise on Insanity (1806). It had an enormous influence on both French and Anglo-American psychiatrists during the nineteenth century.

In 1802 Pinel published La Médecine Clinique, which was based on his experiences at Bicêtre and the Salpêtrière and in which he made a new classification of mental illnesses — mania, melancholia, idiocy and dementia — and stated that they were caused mainly by heredity and environmental influences. He also described how — through an asylum regimen of education, reasoning, and persuasion — many of the symptoms of insanity could be alleviated.

Pinker, Steven Arthur (1954–)
LANGUAGE DEVELOPMENT

Born, Montreal, Quebec, Canada, Steven Arthur Pinker gained a B.A. with first class honors in psychology at McGill University, Montreal (1976), and a Ph.D. in experimental psychology, Harvard University, Cambridge, Massachusetts (1979). Pinker was postdoctoral fellow, Center for Cognitive Science, Massachusetts Institute of Technology (MIT) (1979–1980); assistant professor, Department of Psychology, Harvard (1980–1981); and assistant professor, Department of Psychology, Stanford University, California (1981–1982).

At MIT he was assistant professor, Department of Psychology (1982–1985); associate professor, Department of Brain and Cognitive Sciences (1985–1989); co-director, Center for Cognitive Science (1985–1994); professor, Department of Brain and Cognitive Sciences (1989–2000); director, McDonnell-Pew Center for Cognitive Neuroscience (1994–1999); and Peter de Florez Professor (2000–2003). Since 2003 he has been Johnstone Family professor of psychology, Harvard.

Pinker's awards and honors include the Distinguished Scientific Award for an Early Career Contribution to Psychology, American Psychological Association (1984); Esquire Register of Outstanding Men and Women Under Forty (1986); Newsweek One Hundred Americans for the Next Century (1995); Golden Plate Award, American Academy of Achievement (1999); humanist laureate, International Academy of Humanism (2001); one of the 100 most influential people in the world named by Time Magazine (2004); and one of Prospect and

Foreign Policy's 100 top public intellectuals (2005). He received honorary doctorates from the four universities in England, Israel and Canada.

Major Contributions

Pinker is a prominent experimental psychologist, cognitive scientist, and popular science writer known for his lively and wide-ranging support of evolutionary psychology and the computational theory of mind. He has appeared in TV documentaries and on radio in America, Canada, England, Scotland, New Zealand, and his books have won him numerous awards. Pinker's academic specializations are visual cognition and language development in children, and he is most famous for popularizing the idea that language is an "instinct," an innate faculty of mind shaped by natural selection rather than a by-product of general intelligence.

He views the mind as a multi-faceted organism equipped by evolution with a set of specialized tools (or modules) developed by one's ancestors to deal with problems they faced. Pinker and other evolutionary psychologists believe the human mind evolved by natural selection, just like other body parts. Evolutionary psychology, pioneered by Leda Cosmides (see entry), the biologist E.O. Wilson, and the anthropologist John Tooby, is rapidly gaining interest, especially among cognitive psychologists.

Major Literature

Pinker, Steven. *The Language Instinct: The New Science of Language and Mind*. London, England: Penguin Books Ltd., 1995.
___. *How the Mind Works*. London, England: Penguin Books Ltd., 1999.
___. *Language and Mind*. Jackson, Tennessee: Basic Books, 1999.
___. *Words and Rules: The Ingredients of Language*. Troy, Michigan: Phoenix Press, 2000.
___. *The Blank Slate: The Modern Denial of Human Nature*. London: Penguin Books Ltd., 2003.
___. *Hotheads*. London, England: Penguin Books Ltd., 2005.

Plomin, Robert (1948–)

BEHAVIORAL GENETICS

Born, Chicago, Illinois, Robert Plomin was assistant to the research director, Association of School Business Officials, Research Corporation, Illinois (1968–1970), and gained a B.A. in psychology at DePaul University, Chicago, Illinois (1970), and a Ph.D. in psychology at the University of Texas, Austin (1974). At University of Colorado, Boulder, Plomin was assistant professor of psychology and behavioral genetics (1974–1986); associate professor (1978–1982); professor (1982–1986); and member, Cognition, Emotion, and Personality Research Review Committee, Bethesda, Maryland (1985–1989).

At Pennsylvania State University, University Park in Philadelphia, Plomin was professor of human development, Department of Human Development and Family Studies (1986–1994); associate director, Center for Developmental and Health Genetics (1988–1990); and faculty member, Inter-college Graduate Program in Genetics 1988–1994. Since 1994 Plomin has been Medical Research Council research professor of behavioral genetics at the Institute of Psychiatry in London, England, and deputy director of the Social, Genetic and Developmental Psychiatry Research Centre (SGDP). Plomin has received awards from the Behavior Genetics Association (2002), American Psychological Society (2005), and Society for Research in Child Development (2005).

Major Contributions

The goal of the SGDP Research Centre is to bring together genetic and environmental research strategies — nature and nurture — to study behavioral development. Behavioral genetics focuses on questions such as why individuals within a species differ in behavior (e.g., why children differ in rates of language acquisition), whereas much research in psychology investigates species-typical behavior (e.g. average age of children when they use two-word sentences).

Plomin's special interest is in harnessing the power of molecular genetics to identify genes that affect complex behavioral dimensions and disorders in order to advance understanding of the developmental interplay between genes and environment. From 1986 until 1994 he worked at Pennsylvania State University studying elderly twins reared apart and twins reared together to study aging, and developed models to identify genes in complex behavioral systems.

His current research (TEDS) includes a study of 7500 pairs of twins born in England during 1994–1996. They have been assessed at 2, 3, 4 and 7 years on measures of cognition, language and behavior problems. The team will assess each child's school and classroom environments at 10 years of age as perceived by the children themselves, as well as by their parents and teachers, in order to test the hypothesis that school environments and their relationship to educational outcomes are in part mediated by genetics and vice versa. He coined the term "non-shared environment" to refer to the environmental reasons why children growing up in the same family are so different.

Major Literature

Plomin, Robert. *Development, Genetics and Psychology.* Hillsdale, New Jersey: Erlbaum Associates Inc., 1986.

___. McClean, Gerald E. *Nature, Nurture, and Psychology.* Washington, D.C.: American Psychological Association, 1993.

Plomin, Robert, et al. *Behavioral Genetics: A Primer.* New York: H. Freeman and Co. Ltd., 2000.

___. *Behavioral Genetics in the Postgenomic Era.* Washington, D.C.: American Psychological Association, 2003.

___, and F.M. Spinath. "Intelligence: Genetics, Genes, and Genomics." *Journal of Personality and Social Psychology* 86 (2004): 112–129.

Porteus, Stanley David (1883–1972)

RACE PSYCHOLOGY

Considered to be Australia's first professional psychologist, Stanley David Porteus was born in the Melbourne suburb of Box Hill, Victoria. He qualified as a schoolteacher from Melbourne Education Institute in 1899 and taught until 1912 at country schools, mainly in Gippsland, Victoria. From 1912 to 1917 he was superintendent of special schools. In 1916 Porteus was awarded a research scholarship to work in the department of anatomy in the University of Melbourne on brain size and intelligence, and next year was appointed on a sessional basis to lecture on experimental education. In 1918 he replaced H.H. Goddard (see entry) as director of research at the Vineland Training School in New Jersey, USA, a school for mentally retarded children, established in 1845.

In 1922 he moved to Hawaii, where he founded the Psychological and Psychopathic Clinic at the University of Hawaii, Manoa, becoming professor of clinical psychology and its director, and dean of the psychology department in 1925.

Porteus was an early contributor to *Mankind Quarterly*; helped British-born American physicist and inventor of the transistor William Shockley (1910–1989) to organize the Foundation for Education on Eugenics and Dysgenics, and served on the executive committee of the International Association for the Advancement of Ethnology and Eugenics. He received an honorary doctorate of science from the University of Hawaii (1932) and

a Distinguished Contribution award from the American Psychological Association. He was made a foundation fellow of the Australian Psychological Society in 1966.

Major Contributions

Porteus experimented with notions of head size and the pencil and paper tests of intelligence that emerged in the early years of the twentieth century, and in 1914 he invented the Porteus Maze Test. At Vineland he began research on various topics, including cephalometrey (the study of head measurement and its relation to feeblemindedness), the Binet tests (see entry, Binet, Alfred), and X rays. In Hawaii he studied the intelligence of Australian aborigines in the Kimberley region and Northern Territory (1929) and Kalahari tribesmen of southern Africa (1934).

He became an American citizen in 1932 and died at Honolulu, where the university social sciences building, Porteus Hall, was named after him in 1974. His theories about the superiority of intelligence of white races led to controversy, including a full-scale student protests at the University of Hawaii, at Porteus' perceived "blatantly racist theories." In 1998, the authorities had his name removed from the building.

Major Literature

Porteus, Stanley David, and M. E. Babcock. *Temperament and Race.* Boston, Massachusetts: Richard G. Badger, Publisher, The Gorham Press, 1926.

Porteus, Stanley David. *The Psychology of a Primitive People.* London, England: Longman, Green, 1931.

___, and R.D. Kepner. *Mental Changes after Bilateral Prefrontal Lobotomy.* King George, Virginia: The Journal Press, 1944.

Porteus, Stanley David. *Porteus Maze Test: Fifty Years Application.* Gold Coast Queensland, Australia: Pacific Book House, 1965.

___. *A Psychologist of Sorts.* Gold Coast, Queensland, Australia: Pacific Book House, 1968.

Prince, Morton Henry (1854–1929)

MULTIPLE PERSONALITY

Born into a wealthy family from Boston, Massachusetts, Morton Henry Prince graduated from Harvard Medical School in Boston in 1879. While on his "grand tour" of Europe, he visited Jean-Martin Charcot (see entry) at the Salpêtrière in Paris. Although impressed by Charcot, he returned to Boston, where he established an ear, nose and throat practice, but switched to neurology. Prince taught neurology at the Harvard Medical School (1895–1898) and at Tufts College Medical School, Medford, Massachusetts (1902–1912).

Major Contributions

Prince recognized how emotional conflict motivates behavior and was among the first to use hypnosis for exploring psychopathology and for psychotherapy. A leading investigator of the pathology of mental disorders, in 1906 he founded the *Journal of Abnormal Psychology*, which he edited until 1929. The Harvard Psychological Clinic that he founded in 1927 became a major American mecca for wide-ranging psychological research into personality. The clinic included the eminent personality psychologists Gordon Allport and Henry Murray (see entries), who extended the ideas that Prince first taught them. Murray, who took over as director, developed a more systematic and approachable clinic. Prince stressed the importance of the subconscious to hysterical symptoms at the same time as Sigmund Freud (see entry) but he was critical of psychoanalysis.

Prince maintained an active professional life, not only with his psychopathologic studies, but as a practicing physician as well. He was a prolific writer, publishing some 14 books and numerous essays. He wrote mostly on dissociation and abnormal psychology but also applied his understanding of the unconscious. Prince produced one of the earliest accounts of multiple personality, now dissociative identity disorders (DID). (See *Diagnostic and Statistical Manual of Mental Disorders* [*DSM IV*], American Psychiatric Association, Washington, D.C., 1994, pp. 477–487.)

His most famous case of Sally Beauchamp, detailed in *The Dissociation of a Personality*, caused consternation due to the sensational nature of the case and his difficult and tangled prose. In the case of Sally Beauchamp, Prince discovered three distinct personalities. One was cultivated, quiet and deeply religious; another was the reverse and full of mischief; the third was proud, selfish and dignified. Two of these personalities had no knowledge of each other or of the third, except by inference. The personalities came and went in colorful succession, many changes often being made in the course of twenty-four hours. Miss Beauchamp was in therapy for seven years before some integration took place. Although rare, DID is still a disturbing psychiatric problem and requires long-term therapy.

Major Literature

Prince, Morton Henry. *The Dissociation of a Personality.* New York: Longmans, Green and Co., 1906. Westport, Connecticut: Greenwood Press, 1969.
___. *The Unconscious: The Fundamentals of Human Personality: Normal and Abnormal.* New York: Macmillan, 1921. Manchester, New Hampshire: Ayer Co. Publishers, 1980.
___. *Clinical and Experimental Studies in Personality.* Cambridge, Massachusetts: Sci-Art Publisher, 1929.
___. *Psychotherapy and Multiple Personality: Selected Essays.* N.G. Hale, Jr., Ed. Cambridge, Massachusetts: Harvard University Press, 1975.

Progoff, Ira (1921–1998)
INTENSIVE JOURNAL METHOD

Born in New York City, Ira Progoff served in the United States Army during World War II. In 1951 he received his a Ph.D. in psychology from New School for Social Research in New York. His doctoral thesis on the psychology of C.G. Jung (see entry) was published as *Jung's Psychology and Its Social Meaning.* After reading Progoff's dissertation, Jung invited him to study with him in Switzerland as a Bollingen fellow in 1952, 1953 and 1955. In addition, Progoff gave several lectures in Switzerland during the 1960s, where he presented his theories of holistic depth psychology.

He died of progressive supranuclear palsy (a rare degenerative neurological disorder involving the gradual deterioration and death of selected neurons in the brain).

Major Contributions

Progoff devoted his life to the exploration of new ways to encourage creativity and to enhance individual and spiritual growth. From 1959 to 1971 he practiced analytical (Jungian) psychology and became director of the Institute for Research in Depth Psychology at Drew University Madison, New Jersey. He was a leading authority on C.G. Jung, depth psychology and transpersonal psychology as well as journal writing.

At Drew University, Progoff conducted research on the dynamic process by which individuals develop more fulfilling lives. As a psychotherapist, he found that the clients who wrote in some form of a journal were able to work through issues more rapidly. Through this research, he then developed and refined the Intensive Journal Method, and in 1975 he published the award-winning book *At a Journal Workshop* (New York: Dialogue House), which articulates both his theory of personal and spiritual growth and how to use the Intensive Journal Method.

As interest continued to grow, Progoff formed the Progoff (National) Intensive Journal Program to make workshops available to the public through its trained and certified leaders. To further his goal of providing a tool for self-development, he made workshops available at prisons, social service agencies and health care facilities. In 1980, he completed *The Practice of Process Meditation* (New York: Dialogue House), which set forth the principles and exercises for the meaning (process meditation) dimension of the intensive journal workbook. In 1992, he issued a revised edition of *At a Journal Workshop*, which combines in one volume the original edition and *The Practice of Process Meditation*.

Major Literature

Progoff, Ira. *Depth Psychology and Modern Man*. Columbus, Ohio: McGraw-Hill, 1974.
___. *Symbolic and the Real*. Boston, Massachusetts: Coventure, 1977.
___. *Well and the Cathedral: An Entrance Meditation*. New York: Dialogue House, 1982.
___. *Life Study*. New York: Dialogue House, 1984.
___. *Jung's Psychology and its Social Meaning*. New York: Dialogue House, 1986.
___. *Dynamics of Hope: Perspectives of Process in Anxiety and Creativity, Imagery and Dreams*. New York: Dialogue House, 1986.
___, and Ronald Gestwicki. *A Life-Study of Franz Kafka 1883–1924: Using The Intensive Journal Method of Ira Progoff*. Lampeter, Dyfed, Wales: Edwin Mellen Press Ltd., 1992.

Rank, Otto (1884–1939)

WILL THERAPY

Otto Rosenfeld, born in Vienna, became one of Sigmund Freud's closest aides, colleagues and finally critic, and one of his first lay analysts. At the University of Vienna, from where he gained his doctorate in philosophy in 1912, he legally adopted the name of Otto Rank. Rank soon became a member of the Freud's inner circle, served as secretary to the Vienna Psychoanalytic Society, and from 1912 to 1924, edited the *Internationale Zeitschrift für Psychoanalyse* (*International Journal of Psychoanalysis*). In 1919 he founded a publishing house devoted to the publication of psychoanalytic works and directed it until 1924. He published *Das Trauma der Geburt und seine Bedeutung für die Psychoanalyse* (*The Trauma of Birth*) (1924, English edition 1929).

Rank maintained that birth trauma — the transition from the womb to the outside world — causes tremendous anxiety in the infant that may persist as anxiety neurosis into adulthood. He proposed that the male sex drive was a desire to return to the womb. His trauma theory was rejected by the Vienna Psychoanalytic Society, who expelled him in 1926. To remain in the society, those who had undergone analysis with Rank were forced to undergo analysis again with a Freudian practitioner.

Following the break, Rank taught and practiced in the United States and Europe (chiefly Paris) for about 10 years, settling in New York City in 1936.

Major Contributions

Rank was the first psychoanalyst to examine mother-child relationships, including separation anxiety; the earliest separation is birth, followed by weaning and discipline and school and work and heartbreaks. So we must face our fears, recognizing that, to be fully developed, we must embrace both life and death, become individuals and nurture our relationships with others. Rank's briefer form of psychotherapy — "active therapy" — stressed a more equal relationship between the patient and therapist. Many of Rank's ideas, including the importance of the ego, consciousness, and the present, have become mainstays of psychoanalytic theory.

Rank also introduced the contest between life and death. The "life instinct" pushes us to become individuals, competent and independent, and the "death instinct" pushes us to be part of a family, community, or humanity. The "fear of life" is the fear of separation, loneliness, and alienation; the "fear of death" is the fear of getting lost in the whole, stagnating, being no one.

Rank extended psychoanalytic theory to the study of legend, myth, art, and creativity. During the 1930s he developed a concept of the will as the guiding force in personality development. His work was ignored for years, until the 1970s, when it was resurrected by the psychologists Rollo May and Carl Rogers (see entries).

Major Literature (Recent editions)

Rank, Otto. *Will Therapy*. New York: W.W. Norton and Co. Ltd., 1978.
___. *The Double: A Psychoanalytic Study*. New York: Penguin Group, New American Library, 1980.
___. *The Trauma of Birth*. London, England: Taylor and Francis Books Ltd., Routledge, 1999.
___. *Psychology and the Soul*. Baltimore: Johns Hopkins University Press, 2003.

Ratliff, Floyd (1919–1999)
NEUROPSYCHOLOGY

Born in La Junta, Colorado, Ratliff served with the Army in World War II, earning the Bronze Star for combat in Europe. He gained a B.A. at Colorado College, Colorado Springs (1947), a Ph.D. at Brown University, Providence, Rhode Island (1950), and a National Research Council postdoctoral fellowship to work with H. Keffer Hartline, Johns Hopkins University (1950).

Ratliff was chair of the laboratory of biophysics, Johns Hopkins, and assistant professor, Harvard College, Cambridge, Massachusetts (1951–1954). From 1954 he took charge of the newly founded laboratory of biophysics at the Rockefeller Institute for Medical Research (now Rockefeller University, New York). He was president of the Harry Frank Guggenheim Foundation, which funds research on violence and aggressive behavior (1983–1989). Ratliff was a member of the Society of Experimental Psychologists (1957), National Academy of Sciences (1966), American Academy of Arts and Sciences (1968), and American Philosophical Society (1972).

His awards and honors include the Warren Medal of the Society of Experimental Psychologists (1966); honorary D.Sc., Colorado College (1975); Edgar D. Tillyer Award of the Optical Society of America (1976); Medal for Distinguished Service of Brown University (1980); the Pisart Vision Award of the Lighthouse, New York Association of the Blind (1983); and the Distinguished Scientific Contribution Award, American Psychological Association (1984).

Major Contributions

At Brown University, Ratliff's initial research focused on the relation between tiny, rapid oscillations in eye movements — physiological nystagmus — and visual function. In collaboration with others, he developed an optical technique that effectively stopped the movement of images on the retina that results from movement of the eyes, thereby stabilizing the image on the retina. They also showed that stabilized images quickly fade from view.

He later worked on the concept of lateral inhibition in the cutaneous (skin) senses and on lateral inhibition in the nervous system. His work led to the formulation of the Hartline-Ratliff equations, which describe inhibitory interactions in the retina. Ratliff and Professor H. Keffer Hartline were the first neurophysiologists to use digital computers in their investigations.

Ratliff is credited with combining psychology with physiology, physics and mathematics in a unique way. In medicine, Ratliff pointed out that the presence of Mach bands (an illusion of dark/light gradients) in some X-ray photographs led to misdiagnoses and unnecessary surgical procedures. In his retirement he was professor emeritus of biophysics and physiological psychology at the Rockefeller University. Late into retirement, while residing in Santa Fe, New Mexico, Ratliff continued his exploration of color vision. He died from complications arising from a tumor on the thymus.

Major Literature

Ratliff, Floyd. *Mach Bands: Quantitative Studies of Neural Networks in the Retina.* San Francisco: Holden-Day Publisher, 1965.
___. "The Logic of the Retina." *Journal of Philosophy* 68 (1971): 591–597.
___. *Studies on Excitation and Inhibition in the Retina.* Norwell, Massachusetts: Kluwer Academic Publishers, Chapman and Hall, 1974.
___, and Robert Shapley. *Visual Arts and Sciences Transactions of the American Philosophical Society.* Philadelphia, Pennsylvania: American Philosophical Society, 1985.

Reich, Wilhelm (1897–1957)
CHARACTER ANALYSIS, ORGONE THERAPY

Born of Jewish parents at Dobrzcynica, Galicia, Austria-Hungary [now in Ukraine], Wilhelm Reich fled from the Russian army in 1914 and served in the Austrian Army from 1915 to 1918, for the last two years as a lieutenant. He graduated with an M.D. (1922) from the University of Vienna. Having become interested in the work of Sigmund Freud (see entry), he was accepted for membership in the Vienna Psychoanalytic Association in October 1920. He worked in Internal Medicine at University Hospital, Vienna, and studied neuropsychiatry (1922–1924) at the Neurological and Psychiatric Clinic under Professor Julius von Wagner-Jauregg (see entry).

In 1922, Reich set up a private practice as a psychoanalyst and became first clinical assistant, and later vice-director, at Freud's Psychoanalytic Polyclinic. He joined the faculty of the Psychoanalytic Institute in Vienna in 1924 and conducted research into the social causes of neurosis.

In 1930, he moved his practice to Berlin and joined the Communist Party of Germany, becoming its spokesman, but was expelled from the party in 1933 on account of his being too outspoken. In

1933 his book — *The Mass Psychology of Fascism*, which categorized fascism as a symptom of sexual repression — was banned when the Nazis came to power. Reich was expelled from the International Psychological Association in 1934 for political militancy. German newspapers started attacking him as a womanizer, a communist, and a Jew who advocated free love. He fled to Scandinavia and then to the United States in 1939.

Major Contributions

Reich developed a system of psychoanalysis that concentrated on overall character structure rather than on individual neurotic symptoms. His early work on psychoanalytic technique and personality was overshadowed by his pseudoscientific system "orgonomy." He claimed that that the ability to achieve orgasm — called "orgastic potency" — was an essential attribute of the healthy individual; failure to dissipate pent-up sexual energy by orgasm could produce neurosis in adults. Reich built "orgone boxes" to harness "orgone," which he believed was responsible for emotions and sexuality. He conceived of mental illness as an orgone deficiency, which he attempted to treat by using the orgone box. He leased orgone boxes as a therapy for many illnesses, including cancer.

Reich's experiments and the commercialization of the orgone box brought him into conflict with American authorities. In August 1956, several tons of his publications were burned by the Food and Drug Administration (FDA); he was convicted for contempt of court and died of heart failure in prison. While the medical fraternity rejected his orgone theory, his contributions to the history of psychotherapy and personality theory continue to exert influence, particularly in the area of ego-psychology.

Major Literature (Recent editions)

Reich, Wilhelm. *Selected Writings: An Introduction to Orgonomy.* London, England: Vision Press, 1961.
___. *Character Analysis.* Third, enlarged edition. New York: Farrar Straus Giroux, 1980.
___. *Function of the Orgasm.* London, England: Souvenir Press Ltd., 1989.
___. *On Wilhelm Reich and Orgonomy.* Lancaster, Pennsylvania: Veritas Press, 1994.
___. *The Mass Psychology of Fascism.* London, England: Souvenir Press Ltd., 1997.

Rhine, Joseph Banks (1895–1980)
PSYCHICAL RESEARCH

Born in Pennsylvania, Joseph Banks Rhine gained a B.A. (1922) and an M.S. (1923), both in botany, and a Ph.D. (1925) from the University of Chicago, Illinois. In 1927 he moved to Duke University, Durham, North Carolina, to work under Professor William McDougall (see entry). At that time the field of investigation into the unexplained powers of the mind was called "psychical research" and was largely devoted to the study of mediums and questions of survival of death. Rhine began experiments to study "extrasensory perception" (ESP, a term he coined) to describe the apparent ability of some people to acquire information without the use of the known (five) senses. Later he added, "psychokinesis" (PK), the movement of objects through the will of the mind.

Rhine — widely considered to be the "father of modern parapsychology" — adopted the term "parapsychology" (psi) to distinguish his interests from mainstream psychology. By 1935, Rhine's experiments had shown sufficient promise to justify the creation of a special unit devoted to them, and the Parapsychology Laboratory came into being at Duke University. Under his guidance, a new science was built.

His studies helped develop parapsychology into a branch of science; the field is today recognized by the American Association for the Advancement of Science. He developed methodology and concepts for parapsychology as a form of experimental psychology and founded the institutions necessary for its continuance as a profession — including the establishment of the *Journal of Parapsychology*, and the formation of the Parapsychological Association. In 1962, with the help of benefactors, such as Chester Carlson (founder of Xerox), Rhine started the Foundation for Research on the Nature of Man (FRNM) to sponsor and thus ensure the continuation of his work, which in 1995 was renamed the Rhine Research Center, based at Durham.

The Duke experiments on telepathy, clairvoyance and precognition used specially designed cards called Zener cards which centered around students attempting to guess symbols on the cards that they could not directly see. The percentage of correct guesses was occasionally significantly above chance, leading Rhine to hypothesize that some students were capable of mind reading. In one set of experiments, 2400 total guesses were made and an excess of 489 hits (correct guesses) were noted. The statistical probability of this outcome is equivalent to odds of 1,000,000 to 1 (against chance) and thus show significant evidence that "something occurred." Skeptics argued and will continue to argue about the validity of the tests.

Major Literature

Rhine, Joseph Banks, and William McDougall. *Extra Sensory Perception*. Boston: Boston Society for Psychic Research, 1934. Montana: R.A. Kessinger Publishing Co., 2003.

Rhine, Joseph Banks. *Parapsychology: Frontier Science of the Mind; A Survey of the Field, the Methods and the Facts of Esp and Pk Research*. Springfield, Illinois: Charles Thomas, 1957.

Rhine, Joseph Banks, and associates. *Parapsychology from Duke to FRNM*. Durham, North Carolina: Parapsychology Press, 1965.

Rhine, Joseph Banks. *New Frontiers of the Mind: Story of the Duke Experiments*. Westport, Connecticut: Greenwood Press, 1973.

Ribot, Theodule-Armand (1839–1916)

PIONEERING WORK ON MEMORY LOSS

Theodule-Armand Ribot, the founder of scientific psychology in France, was born at Guingamp, and was a teacher from 1856 until 1862, when he was admitted to the École Normale Supérieure in Paris, from where he gained his doctorate. He taught at the Sorbonne from 1885 to 1888, and from 1889 to 1896 he held a chair of experimental and comparative psychology at the Collège de France, Paris. Ribot's main aim was to separate psychology from ethics and philosophy and bring it closer to the biological sciences. He was founder and first editor of *Revue Philosophique* (1876) and was on the editorial board of *L'Année Philosophique* (1894).

His *Les Maladies de la mémoire* (*Diseases of Memory*) was an endeavor to account for memory loss as a symptom of progressive brain disease by using principles describing the evolution of memory function in the individual, as offered by an English neurologist, John Hughlings Jackson (see entry). The progressive destruction of memory follows a logical order that became known as Ribot's "law" of regression (or progressive destruction). Memory loss advances progressively from the unstable to the stable. It begins with the most recent recollections, which, being lightly impressed upon the nervous elements, rarely repeated and consequently having no permanent associations, represent organization in its feeblest form. It ends with the sensorial, instinctive memory, which, having become a permanent and integral part of the organism, represents organization in its most highly developed stage. The notion has been applied with some success to phenomena as diverse as the breakdown of memory for language in a disorder called aphasia and the gradual return of memory after brain concussion, although here the sequence of return of memory doesn't always follow a pattern.

After studying the works of English and German psychologists, Ribot began his analysis of abnormal psychology. His published works on the subject, in addition to *Diseases of Memory*, included studies of diseases of will, personality, and attention. He was a supporter of the evolutionary theories of Charles Darwin and Herbert Spencer, and he used Spencer's theory of dissolution (the opposite of evolution) to explain certain disorders of personality, of will and of memory.

Major Literature

Ribot, Theodule-Armand. *Diseases of Memory: An Essay in the Positive Psychology*. New York: D. Appleton and Company, 1882.

___. *Heredity: A Psychological Study of its Phenomena, Laws, Causes, and Consequences*. New York: D. Appleton and Company, 1883. New York: Ams Press Inc., 1977.

___. *Diseases of the Will*. New York: D. Appleton and Company, 1884.

___. *The Psychology of Attention*. Chicago: Open Court Publishing Company, 1890.

___. *Diseases of Personality*. Chicago: Open Court Publishing Company, 1895.

___. *The Psychology of the Emotions*. New York: Charles Scribner, 1897.

___. *The Evolution of General Ideas*. Translated, F.A. Welby. Chicago: Open Court Publishing Company, 1899.

___. *Essay on the Creative Imagination*. Chicago: Open Court Publishing Company, 1906. Translated, A.H.N. Baron, 2006.

Rivers, William Halse (1864–1922)

MENTAL FUNCTIONING

Born in Luton, near Chatham, Kent, England, William Halse Rivers gained a bachelor of medicine at the University of London (1886); was ship's surgeon (1887); gained an M.D. at London University (1888) and was a fellow of the Royal College of Physicians. Rivers was physician at St. Bartholomew's Hospital, London (1889); worked at the National Hospital for the Paralyzed and Epileptic (1891–1892); worked with Emil Kraepelin (see entry) at Heidelberg University, Germany, measuring the effects of fatigue (1893); was a lecturer in experimental psychology, Cambridge University; and established an experimental laboratory dealing specifically with the physiology of the sense organs (1893).

In 1898 Rivers was part of Alfred Haddon's anthropological Torres Straits Expedition (1898). From 1907 to 1908, he worked in Melanesia, Solomon Islands, and in 1914, Australia, Melanesia, the New Hebrides, and New Zealand. From 1916 to 1918 he was a military psychiatrist and from 1918 to 1922 he was at Cambridge University concentrating on psychology, psychiatry, sociology and ethnology. He co-founded the *British Journal of Psychology* (1904).

Major Contributions

Rivers' achievements spanned physiology, neurology, psychology, psychiatry and anthropology. The published reports of the Torres Straits Expedition were used to support successful land rights claims against the Australian government. (The Torres Straits is a body of water between Australia and the Melanesian island of New Guinea.) He conducted comparative research on sensory perceptions, especially of color recognition and perspective, among English schoolchildren, Egyptians, Eskimos and the Todas, a pastoral hill people in southwest India. Rivers firmly rejected social evolution as an explanation for human diversity, arguing that circumstances and history make people what they are.

As a military psychiatrist, he worked at Mughill Military Hospital in Lancashire, a college of psychotherapy (unique in Britain), then at Craiglockhart War Hospital near Edinburgh. He dealt mainly with war trauma (erroneously called "shell shock"), and among the more famous casualties he treated there was the poet Siegfried Sassoon. (It has been estimated that shell shock affected 7–10 percent of officers and 3–4 percent of other ranks, leading to 200,000 hospital admissions.) Rivers renamed shell shock "anxiety neurosis" and rather than treating these soldiers with electroshock therapy, he preferred psychotherapy. His insights form the basis for a wider understanding of what we now call post-traumatic stress disorders.

Well-versed in Freudian theory, Rivers maintained that anxiety neuroses did not result from the war experiences themselves but from attempting to banish distressing memories from the mind. He attributed his own clinical successes mainly to encouraging patients to remember, but he also described more subtle aspects of therapy, which he termed "re-education" and "faith and suggestion," by which he meant getting the patient to talk, re-

framing painful memories and emphasizing the therapeutic relationship.

Major Literature

Rivers, William Halse. *The History of Melanesian Society.* Cambridge, England: Cambridge University Press, 1914. Boston: Adamant Media Corporation, 2001.
___. *Kinship and Social Organization.* London, England: Constable and Robinson Ltd., 1914.
___. *Instinct and the Unconscious.* Cambridge, England: Cambridge University Press, 1920.
___. *Conflict and Dream.* London, England: Kegan Paul, Trench, Tubner and Co., 1923.

Rogers, Carl Ransom (1902–1987)
PERSON-CENTERED THERAPY

Born in Oak Park, Illinois, Carl Ransom Rogers gained a B.A. at the University of Wisconsin (1924), and an M.A. (1928) and Ph.D. (1931) at Teachers College, Columbia University. He was at the Rochester Guidance Center for the Prevention of Cruelty to Children in New York (1928–1940); at Ohio State University (1940–1945); was professor, University of Chicago, Illinois; director, Counseling Center (1945); held positions in departments of psychology and psychiatry at the University of Wisconsin, Madison, (1957); and at the University of California, La Jolla, Western Behavioral Sciences Institute, he helped found the Center for Studies of the Person (1964).

He was vice-president, American Orthopsychiatric Association (1941–1942); president, American Association for Applied Psychology (1944–1945); president, American Psychological Association (APA) (1946–1947); and president, American Academy of Psychotherapists (1956). His awards and honors include the Nicholas Murray Butler Silver Medal, Columbia University (1955); Distinguished Scientific Contribution Award, APA (1956); fellow, American Academy of Arts and Sciences (1961); Humanist of the Year, American Humanist Association (1964); Distinguished Contribution Award, American Pastoral Counselors Association (1967); Award of Professional Achievement, American Board of Professional Psychology (1968); Distinguished Professional Psychologist Award, APA Division 29 (1972); First Distinguished Professional Contribution Award, APA (1972); and honorary doctorates from seven universities.

Major Contributions

Originally intending to study for the ministry, Rogers changed to clinical psychology at Teachers

College. In 1942, he wrote *Counseling and Psychotherapy*. In *Client-Centered Therapy* (1951, Houghton Mifflin, 2003, Constable and Robinson), he outlines his basic approach. Rogers regards people as basically good or healthy. He considers mental health as the normal progression of life, and sees mental illness, criminality, and other human problems as distortions of what is normal. Rogers' entire approach is built on the actualizing tendency — the built-in motivation present in every life-form to develop its potentials to the fullest extent possible.

Non-directive therapy, his initial term, was later changed to "client centered" then to "person centered," although many people simply refer to Rogerian therapy. The underlying principle is the therapist strives to understand what something means to the client (Rogers chose "client" rather than "patient" to get away from the authoritarian relationship of psychoanalysis) from the client's frame of reference. This was a fundamental shift from psychoanalysis, where what the client says is filtered and interpreted through the psychoanalytic model. The person centered approach is built upon the four core conditions of empathy, genuineness/congruence, unconditional positive regard and non-possessive warmth. At first glance, person centered therapy is simple, but practitioners and clients testify to how demanding it is, yet so rewarding.

Major Literature

Rogers, Carl Ransom, and Rosalind F. Dymond. *Psychotherapy and Personality Change*. Chicago, Illinois: University of Chicago Press, 1954, 1978.

Rogers, Carl Ransom. *On Becoming a Person*. London: Constable and Robinson Ltd., 1961. Boston, Massachusetts: Houghton Mifflin, 2004.

___. *Client Centered Therapy: Its Current Practice, Implications and Theory*. London: Constable and Robinson Ltd., 1976, 2003.

Rogers, Carl Ransom. *A Way of Being*. Boston, Massachusetts: Houghton Mifflin, 1980.

___. *Freedom to Learn for the '80s*. Columbus, Ohio: Charles Merrill Co., 1983.

Róheim, Geza (1891–1953)

PSYCHOANALYTIC ANTHROPOLOGY

Born in Budapest, Hungary, Geza Róheim gained his Ph.D. (1914) from Budapest University. Influenced by the works of Sigmund Freud (see entry), he later became one of the first psychoanalysts to successfully apply the Freudian psychoanalytical theories to the analysis of primitive cultures. Róheim joined the department of ethnology at the Magyar Nemzeti Museum, Budapest, and entered psychoanalysis in 1915 with one of Freud's closest disciples, Sandor Ferenczi (see entry). In 1919, Róheim became the first professor of anthropology at the University of Budapest and held the chair until 1938. He taught psychoanalysis and anthropology at Budapest Institute of Psychoanalysis from 1932 to 1938. In 1921, Sigmund Freud presented Róheim with an award for a paper he wrote on applied psychoanalysis related to the Oedipus complex.

From 1928 to 1931 Róheim did fieldwork in central Australia. In this study, financed by Marie Bonaparte (Princess George of Greece) (see entry), Róheim applied psychoanalytical theory to the aborigines of central Australia, and later expanded his work to the southwest United States, Duau (Normanby Island), Papua, New Guinea, and Somalia. His work focused on the individual rather than the entire culture. Some of the techniques he used were dream analysis and analysis of children's play activities. This study helped him develop his "ontogenetic theory of culture," which was a major contribution to anthropology and psychoanalysis.

In this theory, Róheim contended that cultural differences were largely the result of an individual's childhood traumas. The childhood experiences of the individual, he thought, were ultimately reflected in adult personality and in institutions. He theorized that the protracted dependence of the infant and child on the mother, resulting in emotional and social bonds, is the foundation of culture.

He fled to the United States in 1938 and joined the Worcester State Hospital, Massachusetts, as an analyst, and in 1939 he entered private psychoanalytic practice in New York City. He lived the rest of his life in New York City, lecturing to the New York Psychoanalytic Institute, and occasionally taking short trips to the southwest to study the Navaho Indians. He died in New York City.

Major Literature

Róheim, Geza. *Animism, Magic, and the Divine King*. Montana: R.A. Kessinger Publishing Co., 1930.

___. *The Riddle of the Sphinx*. London, England: Hogarth and Institute of Psychoanalysis, 1934.

___. *The Origin and Function of Culture*. Chicago, Illinois: University of Chicago Press, 1943.

___. *The Eternal Ones of the Dream*. New York: International Universities Press Inc., 1945.

___. *Psychoanalysis and Anthropology*. New York: International Universities Press Inc., 1950.

___. *The Gates of the Dream*. New York: International Universities Press Inc., 1952.

___. *Magic and Schizophrenia*. New York: International Universities Press Inc., 1955.

Rokeach, Milton (1918–1988)
OPEN-MINDEDNESS

Milton Rokeach was born into a Jewish family from Hrubieszow, Poland, who moved to New York in the mid–1920s. After graduating from Brooklyn, Rokeach's studies at University of California, Berkeley, were interrupted by World War II, and he served in the Air Force Psychology Testing Program. He gained a Ph.D. at Berkeley (1947) and from 1961 to 1962 was a fellow at the Center for Advanced Study in the Behavioral Sciences, Stanford, California. From 1976 to 1988 he directed the Unit on Human Values, Social Research Center, Washington State University, and was professor of social psychology at Michigan State University and later at Washington State University, where he held a joint appointment in the departments of sociology and psychology.

Rokeach was president, American Psychological Association (APA) Division 9 (1967), and vice-president, International Society for Political Psychology (1981–1982), His awards and honors include the Research Excellence Award, Washington State University (1983); Distinguished Psychologist Award, Washington State Psychological Association (1983); Kurt Lewin Memorial Award (1984); and an honorary doctorate from the University of Paris (1984). Rokeach was a fellow of the American Association for the Advancement of Science.

Major Contributions

Upon his return to Berkeley after the war, Rokeach and Donald T. Campbell (see entry) were employed as research staff on a study of prejudice in children. His Ph.D. was on individual differences in ethnocentrism and problem-solving rigidity among college students. At that time Dr. Else Frenkel-Brunswik was working on the concept of intolerance of ambiguity — people who are intolerant of ambiguity are relatively "closed" to new information.

Rokeach suggested that closed-mindedness is a general personality trait. In order to measure this variable he developed the Dogmatism Scale, which was an attempt to improve on Theodor Adorno's authoritarianism. Dogmatism is usually considered a measure of general authoritarianism and the Dogmatism Scale purports to be an ideologically and content-free measure of closed-mindedness. It has been used widely in studies of religion and prejudice, and contrasts authoritarianism to open-mindedness.

Open-mindedness refers to how flexible and responsive one is to examining new evidence about one's belief systems. It is partially related to one's ability to receive, evaluate and act on information from the outside on its own merits. It also relates to how one is able to free oneself from internal pressures that would obscure or interfere with incoming information. Rokeach believed that dogmatism, like authoritarianism, is linked with early family socialization experiences. His theory of dogmatism, like that of authoritarianism, was criticized for failing to pay sufficient attention to the role of socio-cultural and situational determinants of intolerance.

Major Literature

Rokeach, Milton. *The Open and Closed Mind*. New York: Basic Books, 1960.

___. *The Three Christs of Ypsilanti: A Psychological Study* [Ypsilanti is a city in Michigan]. New York: Columbia University Press, Knopf, 1964.

___. *Beliefs, Attitudes and Values: A Theory of Organization and Change*. San Francisco: Jossey-Bass, 1968.

___. *Understanding Human Values: Individual and Societal*. New York: Simon and Schuster, Inc. The Free Press, 1979, 2000.

Romanes, George J. (1848–1894)
COMPARATIVE PSYCHOLOGY

George J. Romanes was born in Kingston, Ontario, but the family moved to London, England, when Romanes was young. He graduated with a B.A. (1870) from Gonville and Caius College, Cambridge, where he studied medicine and physiology, and in 1879 he was elected fellow of the Royal Society. The University of Aberdeen awarded him honorary doctor of laws (1882); he was professor at the University of Edinburgh in 1886–1890 and Fullerian Professor of Physiology at the Royal Institution from 1888 to 1891. In 1891, the University of Oxford awarded him an M.A. degree.

Major Contributions

Romanes laid the foundation of what he called comparative psychology, postulating a similarity of cognitive processes and mechanisms between humans and animals. It was at Cambridge where he first came to the attention of Charles Darwin (1809–1882); the two remained friends for life. Despite early strong religious beliefs, Romanes was converted to Darwinism and wrote *A Candid Examination of Theism* under the pseudonym *Physicus*. At the end of his life, he wrote a second religious treatise, this time orthodox in belief, under the pseudonym of *Metaphysicus*.

Romanes compiled a systematic collection of stories and anecdotes about the behavior of animals, upon which he built an elaborate theory of the evolution of intelligence. It was largely in reaction to this anecdotal tradition, with its uncritical acceptance of tales of astounding feats by pet cats and dogs, that Robert Thorndike undertook his studies of learning under relatively well-controlled laboratory conditions.

Romanes attempted to relate psychological development and evolutionary advancement. First, he demonstrated that animals could show intelligence. Then he tried to show that the animals that act more advanced and humanlike were higher on an evolutionary scale. Finally, he argued that language could have appeared by natural selection.

Romanes' studies covered three related fields: physiology, psychology and evolution. He conducted a number of experiments on the jellyfish (medusa) in order to determine whether it has a nervous system. From this work, the synapse (the gap between nerve ends across which signals are transmitted) was later revealed. One of his controversial conclusions was that mutual infertility is the cause, rather than the effect, of separate evolution of species. Romanes believed that there were two types of barriers between species — external and internal. The external barriers are hygienic measures and the internal barriers are each organism's immune response. One of the most apparent barriers between closely related species would be the sterility barrier. Romanes had suffered ill health from childhood and he died young at Oxford.

Major Literature

Romanes, George. *Mental Evolution in Animals*. London, England: Kegan Paul, Trench, Trubner and Co., 1893. Montana: R.A. Kessinger Publishing Co., 2004.

___. *Darwin and After Darwin*. Chicago: The Open Court Publishing Co., 1897.

___. *Animal Intelligence*. London, England: Kegan Paul, Trench, Trubner and Co., 1904. Boston, Massachusetts: Adamant Media Corporation, 1904.

___. *A Candid Examination of Theism*. Boston, Massachusetts: Adamant Media Corporation, 2005.

Rorschach, Hermann
(1884–1922)
Projective Diagnostic Test

Born in Zurich, Hermann Rorschach entered medical school in Zurich in 1904 and graduated in 1909, then worked as a resident in the Thurgovian psychiatric hospital in Münsterlingen, Switzerland. He attended clinical and theoretical psychiatry lectures at the Burghölzli university clinic, Zurich, where among his teachers were Auguste-Henri Forel, Eugen Bleuler, and Carl Jung (see entries). At this stage the work of Sigmund Freud (see entry) was just beginning to gain in popularity. His doctoral dissertation, supervised by Eugen Bleuler, was published in 1912. He then spent seven months at the fashionable Krjukovo asylum near Moscow accompanied by his Russian wife Olga.

In 1914 he was appointed resident at the Waldau Psychiatric University Hospital, Berne. A year later he was appointed associate director of the asylum at Herisau, in the eastern part of Switzerland. When the Swiss psychoanalytic society was founded in 1919, Rorschach was elected vice president. His book *Psychodiagnostik*, published by Bircher in 1921, was a total disaster. The entire edition remained unsold and the publisher went bankrupt. The method presented in it became world-famous as the Rorschach Test.

Rorschach died of peritonitis, possibly from a ruptured appendix. His work won international respect and an institute was founded in his name in New York in 1939, and renamed in 1971 the Society for Personality Assessment, with its base in Washington, D.C. It is now based at Falls Church, Virginia.

Major Contributions

In 1911, Rorschach began experimenting with inkblots and Jung's word association test on school children and patients. Rorschach was impressed by symbolic associations, and in a paper, *Clock and Time*, he proposed that some neurotics' love of watches was related to a subconscious longing for the mother's breast with the ticking representing heart beats.

In Herisau, Rorschach faced a heavy workload. The hospital housed some 300 patients, with only two psychiatrists, the director and the associate director of the clinic. There were no social workers or secretaries, and at the beginning, no subordinate physicians. Here he introduced a course of lectures for the nursing staff, the first of its kind in Switzerland. His investigations of the strange religious sects in Switzerland revealed that some of them preached the holiness of incest.

The Rorschach inkblot test was widely used clinically for diagnosing psychopathology. The test is based on the tendency to project interpretations and feelings onto ambiguous stimuli — in this case, inkblots. From these cues, trained observers are supposed to be able to pinpoint deeper personality traits and impulses in the person taking the test. A similar method, the Holtzman Inkblot Test, has been developed in an effort to eliminate some of the statistical problems that beset the Rorschach test. It involves the administration of a series of 45 inkblots, the subject being permitted to make only one response per card.

Major Literature

Rorschach, Hermann. *Psychodiagnostics*. New York: Springer-Verlag, 1975.

Rosenthal, Robert (1933–)
SELF-FULFILLING PROPHECY

Born in Giessen, Germany, Robert Rosenthal gained a B.A. (1953) and Ph.D. in psychology (1956) at the University of California, Los Angeles, where he was a clinical psychology trainee (1954–1957). He was assistant to associate professor and coordinator, clinical trainee, University of North Dakota, Grand Forks (1957–1962) and visiting associate professor, Ohio State University, Columbus (1960–1961). At Harvard University, Cambridge, Massachusetts, Rosenthal was lecturer, clinical psychology (1962–1967); professor of social psychology (1967–1995); chair, Department of Psychology (1992–1995); Edgar Pierce Professor of Psychology (1995–1999); Edgar Pierce professor emeritus (since 1999); and distinguished professor, University of California, Riverside (since 1999).

His awards and honors include Professor of the Year Award (2000–2001); James McKeen Cattell Award, American Psychological Society (APA) (2001); Distinguished Scientific Award for Applications of Psychology, APA (2002); Distinguished Scientific Contributions Award, Evaluation, Measurement, and Statistics, APA Division 5 (2002); Gold Medal Award for Life Achievement in the Science of Psychology of the American Psychological Foundation (2003); and co-chair of the Task Force on Statistical Inference of the American Psychological Association.

Major Contributions

Rosenthal's research has centered for over 40 years on the role of self-fulfilling prophecy in everyday life and in laboratory situations. His special interests include the effects of teacher's expectations on students' academic and physical performance, the effects of experimenters' expectations on the results of their research, and the effects of clinicians' expectations on their patients' mental and physical health. He has studied the role of nonverbal communication in interpersonal relationships; the relationship between members of small work groups and small social groups; and teacher-student, doctor-patient, manager-employee, judge-jury, and psychotherapist-client interaction.

In the realm of data analysis, his special interests are in experimental design and analysis, contrast analysis, and meta-analysis. The sociologist Robert Merton (1910–2003) was the first to describe the phenomenon of self-fulfilling prophecy. When teachers have been led to expect better intellectual performance from their students they tend to get it; when behavioral researchers are led to expect certain responses from their research participants they tend to get those responses — the Pygmalion effect. Interpersonal expectations tend to influence behavior, positively or negatively. To silence his critics over his methodology, Rosenthal developed the "meta-analysis" statistical technique that has become the dominant method within psychology for summarizing the results of multiple studies.

Major Literature

Rosenthal, Robert, Ralph L. Rosnow, and Donald B. Rubin. *Contrasts and Effect Sizes in Behavioral Research: A Correlational Approach*. New York: Cambridge University Press, 1999.

Rosenthal, Robert, and L. Jacobson. *Pygmalion in the Classroom: Teacher Expectation and Pupils' Intellectual Development*. New York: Rinehart and Winston, 1968. Bancyfelin Carmarthen, South Wales: Crown House Publishing, 2002.

Rosnow, Ralph L., and Robert Rosenthal. *Beginning Behavioral Research: A Conceptional Primer*. New Jersey: Prentice-Hall, 2004.

Harrigan, Jinni, Robert Rosenthal, and Klaus Scherer. *The New Handbook of Methods in Nonverbal Behavior and Research*. New York: Oxford University Press Inc., 2005.

Rotter, Julian B. (1916–)
SOCIAL LEARNING THEORY

Born in Brooklyn, New York, Julian B. Rotter gained a B.A. in chemistry (1937) from Brooklyn College, his M.A. in psychology from the University of Iowa, Ames (1938), and a Ph.D. in psychology (1941) from Indiana University, Bloomington. After serving in both the Army and Air Force during World War II, he took an academic position at Ohio State University. In 1963, Rotter left Ohio State to become the director of the clinical psychology training program at the University of Connecticut, Storrs. He has served as president of the American Psychological Association's divisions of Social and Personality Psychology and Clinical Psychology. In 1989, he was given the American Psychological Association's Distinguished Scientific Contribution Award.

Major Contributions

Rotter believes that personality is an interaction of the individual with his or her environment. To understand behavior, one must take into account the individual (i.e., his or her life history of learning and experiences) and the environment (i.e., those stimuli of which the person is aware and responding to).

Rotter is also known for his locus of control theory, which describes the ways in which we attribute responsibility for events that occur in our lives. They may be factors within ourselves and within our control, which include abilities, efforts, achievements, and self-direction. Or they may be factors outside ourselves and outside our control, which include fate, luck, chance, and the influence of powerful people. *Externals* are people who believe they have little or no control or influence over what happens to them. *Internals* are people who believe that they do have an influence over the direction their lives take. People can be classified along a continuum from very *internal* to very *external*. People have elements of both in their personalities.

Rotter is opposed to the medical model idea of mental disorders as being diseases or illnesses. Rather, he views psychological problems as maladaptive behavior brought about by faulty or inadequate learning experiences: symptoms of pathology, like all behavior, are learned. Treatment should be considered a learning situation where adaptive behaviors and cognitions are taught, and the therapist-client relationship is viewed as being similar to a teacher-student relationship. Much of current cognitive-behavioral treatment has its roots in Rotter's social learning theory.

Major Literature

Rotter, Julian B., and J.E. Rafferty. *The Rotter Incomplete Sentences Blank Manual: College Form.* New York: Psychological Corporation, 1950.

Rotter, Julian B. *Social Learning and Clinical Psychology.* New York: Prentice-Hall, 1954.

Rotter, Julian B. "Some Implications of a Social Learning Theory for the Practice of Psychotherapy." In D. Levis (Ed.), *Learning Approaches to Therapeutic Behavior Change.* Chicago: Aldine Press, 1970.

___, J.E. Chance, and E.J. Phares. *Applications of a Social Learning Theory of Personality.* New York: Holt, Rinehart and Winston, 1972.

Rotter, Julian B. "Internal Versus External Control of Reinforcement: A Case History of a Variable." *American Psychologist* 45 (1989): 489–493.

Rush, Benjamin (1745–1813)
FATHER OF AMERICAN PSYCHIATRY

Born in Byberry, near Philadelphia, Pennsylvania, Benjamin Rush graduated from the College of New Jersey (now Princeton) in 1760. He studied for six years in the office of a Philadelphia physician, graduated in medicine from the University of Edinburgh, Scotland (1768), and worked in London and Paris hospitals. He returned to Philadelphia in 1769, when he was appointed professor of chemistry in the College of Philadelphia. His *Syllabus of a Course of Lectures on Chemistry* (1770) was the first chemistry textbook published in the United States.

Major Contributions

He was an early advocate of preventive medicine. In particular, he pointed out that decayed teeth were a source of systemic disease. He promoted inoculation and vaccination against smallpox. In 1793, Rush was credited with curing the epidemic of yellow fever in Philadelphia. The king of Prussia, the queen of Etruria, and the emperor of Russia honored him for his replies to their questions on yellow fever; however, his cures, it is reported, were more dreaded by some than the disease.

A pioneer in the study and treatment of mental illness, Rush insisted that the insane had a right to be treated with respect. He protested at the inhuman accommodation and treatment of the insane at Pennsylvania Hospital. When he received an inadequate response to his complaints from the hospital's board of managers, Rush took his case to the public at large. In 1792 he was successful in getting state funding for a ward for the insane.

He constructed a typology of insanity that is strikingly similar to the modern categorization of mental illness and studied factors such as heredity, age, marital status, wealth, and climate that he thought predisposed people to madness.

His *Medical Inquiries and Observations upon the Diseases of the Mind* (1812) was the first American treatise on psychiatry. In 1791 Rush organized the medical school at the University of Pennsylvania. He was a member of the Continental Congress and a signer of the Declaration of Independence (1776). During 1777 and 1778, Rush served as surgeon general with the Continental Army and was present at the battles of Trenton (1776) Princeton (1777) Brandywine (1777), Germantown (1777) and at Valley Forge (1777). He resigned because of differences with General Washington's military tactics, and because of certain injustices done to the soldiers.

He began lecturing at the University of Pennsylvania in 1780 and took up his medical practice again. He was a founder of Dickinson College, Carlisle, Pennsylvania, and the Philadelphia dispensary. In 1797 President John Adams named him treasurer of the United States Mint, a position Rush retained until his death in Philadelphia. Rush was also a social reformer; his pamphlets attacked slavery, capital punishment, alcohol, tobacco, and war; he promoted free public schools, the education of women, and a national university.

Major Literature

Rush, Benjamin. *An Account of the Manners of the German Inhabitants of* Pennsylvania. 1789. Reprint 1910, with a new introduction by William T. Parsons. Collegeville: Institute on Pennsylvania Dutch Studies, 1974.

____. *An Address on the Slavery of the Negroes in America. Address to the Inhabitants of the British Settlements in America* . New York: Arno Press, 1969.

____. *Benjamin Rush's Lectures on the Mind.* Edited, annotated, and introduced by Eric T. Carlson, Jeffrey L. Wollock, and Patricia S. Noel. Philadelphia: American Philosophical Society, 1981.

____. *A Plan for the Punishment of Crime; Two Essays.* Edited by Negley K. Teeters. Philadelphia: Pennsylvania Prison Society, 1954.

Rutter, Sir Michael Llewellyn (1933–)

CHILD PSYCHIATRY

Born in Brummanna, Lebanon, Michael Llewellyn Rutter moved to England in 1936 and spent 1940–1944 in the United States. He graduated with (1955) M.B. and Ch.B. degrees from the University of Birmingham Medical School. After postgraduate posts in neurology, pediatrics and cardiology, he gained his academic diploma in psychological medicine at the University of London (1962) at the Maudsley Hospital, London. He spent a year on a research fellowship at Albert Einstein College of Medicine in New York and on his return, joined the Medical Research Council (MRC) Social Psychiatry Unit and was appointed as senior lecturer at the Institute of Psychiatry in London (1966). In 1973 he was appointed professor of child psychiatry and head of the Department of Child and Adolescent Psychiatry.

From 1984 to 1998 he was honorary director of the MRC Child Psychiatry Research Unit and from 1994 to 1998 he was also honorary director of the Social, Genetic and Developmental Psychiatry Research Centre, both of which he set up at the Institute of Psychiatry. Since 1998 he has been professor of developmental psychopathology, and emeritus professor of Developmental Psychopathology, University of London, Institute of Psychiatry. He was a founding member of both the Academia Europaea and the Academy of Medical Sciences, both based in London). He is a foreign member of the U.S. Institute of Medicine and currently president of the Society for Research into Child Development.

Major Contributions

Professor Rutter's research has covered epidemiology, long-term longitudinal studies, investigations of school effectiveness, tests of psychosocial risk mediation, studies of interviewing techniques, and quantitative and molecular genetics. His clinical research has focused on the genetics of autism, neuropsychiatric disorders, depression, antisocial behavior, the study of both school and family influences on children's behavior, reading difficulties, deprivation syndromes and hyperkinetic disorder, the links between mental disorders in childhood and adult life, epidemiological approaches to test causal hypotheses, and gene-environment interplay. He has published some 38 books and over 400 scientific papers and chapters. His studies influenced the 1989 Children Act. In his approach to understanding development, he challenges the assumption that development ceases at adolescence. In his study of Romanian orphans, he found that severe deprivation did not necessarily result in life-long intelligence deficit. People are much more resilient than John Bowlby (of whom Rutter is a critic) would give credit for.

Major Literature

Rutter, Michael Llewellyn, and Marjorie Rutter. *Developing Minds: Challenge and Continuity Across The Lifespan*. London: Penguin Books Ltd., 1993.

Moffitt, Terrie E., Avshalom Caspi, Michael Llewellyn Rutter, and Phil A. Silva. *Sex Differences in Antisocial Behaviour: Conduct Disorder, Delinquency, and Violence in the Dunedin Longitudinal Study*. Cambridge, England: Cambridge University Press, 2001.

Rutter, Michael Llewellyn, and Beate Hermelin. *Bright Splinters of the Mind: A Personal Story of Research with Autistic Savants*. London, England: Jessica Kingsley Publishers, 2001.

Rutter, Michael Llewellyn. *Genes and Behavior: Nature-Nurture Interplay Explained*. Oxford, England: Blackwell Publishing, 2005.

___, and Eric Taylor. *Child and Adolescent Psychiatry*. Oxford, England: Blackwell Science, 2005.

Sakel, Manfred Joshua (1900–1957)

INSULIN SHOCK THERAPY

Born in Nadvorna, Austria-Hungary (now Nadvirna, Ukraine), Manfred Joshua Sakel studied neurology and neuropsychiatry and qualified as a doctor of medicine at the University of Vienna in 1925, then practiced in both Vienna and Berlin. He became a research associate at the University Neuropsychiatric Clinic in Vienna in 1933, and in 1936, fled to the United States. In the U.S., he became an attending physician and researcher at the Harlem Valley State Hospital.

Major Contributions

Sakel is most remembered for his discovery of the use of insulin shock therapy in the treatment of schizophrenia and other psychotic conditions. Sakel had used insulin to tranquilize morphine addicts undergoing withdrawal, and in 1927 one addict accidentally received an overdose of insulin and went into a coma. After the patient recovered from the overdose, Sakel noted an improvement in the patient's mental state, and hypothesized that inducing convulsions with insulin could have similar effects in schizophrenics. His initial studies found the treatment effective in 88 percent of his patients, and the method was applied widely for a brief period. Follow-up studies showed the long-term results to be less satisfactory, and insulin-shock treatment was largely replaced by the discovery of other tranquilizing drugs. Sakel completed his work at the Harlem Valley State Hospital and published his findings in *The Pharmacological Shock Treatment of Schizophrenia* (New York: Nervous and Mental Disease Publishing Co., 1938).

With insulin shock treatment, the patient is given increasingly large doses of insulin, which reduce the sugar content of the blood and bring on a state of coma. Usually the comatose condition is allowed to persist for about an hour, at which time it is terminated by administering warm salt solution via stomach tube or by intravenous injection of glucose. Insulin shock had its greatest effectiveness with schizophrenic patients whose illness had lasted less than two years (the rate of spontaneous recovery from schizophrenia also is highest in the first two years of the illness). Insulin-shock therapy also had more value in the treatment of paranoid and catatonic schizophrenia than in the hebephrenic (simple) types. By 1937 this therapy had already been known worldwide and continued for more than twenty years. Sakel's achievement furnished proof that psychoses were treatable and was one of the factors leading to a changed approach toward mental illness. Sakel died in New York.

Over the years there have been three major shock therapies: insulin therapy; malarial therapy and electroconvulsive therapy (ECT). Although they have been severely criticized as barbaric, they were used to improve the life of severely disturbed patients. There were reformers who brought humanity to the prison-like conditions of the mentally ill sufferers and psychosis did not prove amenable to psychoanalysis, so the advent of shock therapy brought hope and a new era of treatment was ushered in.

Major Literature

Sakel, Manfred. *Schizophrenia*. London, England: Peter Owen Publishers, 1959.

Satir, Virginia (1916–1988)

FAMILY THERAPY

Born in Neillsville, Wisconsin, Virginia Satir gained a B.A. in education (1936) at the University of Wisconsin–Milwaukee, and an M.A. (1948) at the University of Chicago School of Social Service Administration. In 1969 she founded the International Human Learning Resources Network, and in 1977, the Avanta Network, an international training and membership organization.

In 1976 she was awarded the Gold Medal of Outstanding and Consistent Service to Mankind by the University of Chicago. In 1982 she was voted by the West German government as one of the twelve most influential leaders in the world. She was awarded honorary doctorates from University of Wisconsin (1978) and from the Professional School of Psychological Studies (1986). In 1987 she was made an honorary member of the Czechoslovakian Medical Society.

One of Satir's major themes was what she could contribute to world peace; to this end she established professional training groups in the Satir Model in the Middle East, the Orient, Western and Eastern Europe, Central and Latin America, and Russia. Her philosophy could be summed up in her universal mantra: peace within, peace between, peace among.

Major Contributions

Virginia Satir's main contribution was in family therapy. In 1959, with psychiatrist Donald Jackson (see entry), she co-founded the Mental Research Institute, Menlo Park, California, to train family therapists. In her book *Peoplemaking*, she identifies four universal patterns of responses we use to get around the threat of rejection. We feel and react to the threat but, because we do not want to reveal "weakness," we attempt to conceal our feelings. A fifth mode — the Leveler — is positive and genuine. The five communication modes:

1. **Placaters.** Are frightened that people will get angry, go away and never return. However, they don't dare admit this.
2. **Blamers.** Feel that nobody cares about them; they react to this with verbal behavior intended to demonstrate who is in charge, the boss, the one with power.
3. **Computers.** Are terrified that someone will find out that they have feelings. *Star Trek*'s Mr. Spock — except for the troublesome human side of him that makes him so interesting — is a classic Computer type.
4. **Distracters.** Shift rapidly between the other modes, yet never stay long in any one of them. The underlying feeling is of panic. The surface behavior is a chaotic mix.
5. **Levellers.** Levellers do what the term implies — level with you. What Levellers say is what Levellers feel. The Leveller verbal message is congruent with the body language. The aim is single, straight messages.

Major Literature

Satir, Virginia. *Peoplemaking*. London, England: Souvenir Press Ltd., 1972.Palo Alto, California: Science and Behavior Books, 1990.
___. *Conjoint Family Therapy: A Guide to Therapy and*

Technique. London, England: Souvenir Press Ltd., 1991.
___. *The Satir Model: Family Therapy and Beyond*. Palo Alto, California: Science and Behavior Books, 1991.
___. *Meditations of Virginia Satir: Peace Within, Peace Between, Peace Among*. Palo Alto, California: Science and Behavior Books, 1991.
___. *Self Esteem*. Berkeley, California: Celestial Arts Publishing Company, 2001.

Scarr, Sandra Wood (1936–)
CHILD DEVELOPMENT

Sandra Wood was born in Washington, D.C., and in 1961 married Harry Scarr. She gained an A.B. in sociology at Vassar College in New York (1958), and an A.M. (1963) and Ph.D. in behavior genetics (1965) at Harvard University, Cambridge, Massachusetts. Scarr was associate professor, Graduate School of Education, University of Pennsylvania, Philadelphia (1970–1971); professor of child psychology, University of Minnesota, Minneapolis (1973–1977); professor of psychology, Yale University, New Haven, Connecticut (1977–1983); Commonwealth professor of psychology, University of Virginia, Charlottesville (1983–until retirement); and chief executive officer of Kinder-Care Learning Centers (1994–1997).

She was president of the Behavior Genetics Association (1985–1986); founding member, American Psychological Society (1988); fellow, American Academy of Arts and Sciences (1989); president, American Psychological Society (1996–1997); associate editor, *American Psychologist* (1976–1980); editor, *Developmental Psychology* (1980–1986); and co-editor, *Current Directions in Psychological* Science (1991–1995). Her awards and honors include Distinguished Contributions to Research in Public Policy, American Psychological Association (APA) (1988), and James McKeen Cattell Award for Distinguished Contributions to Applied Research, APA (1993).

Major Contributions

After graduating from Vassar, Scarr worked at a social service agency for one year, where she was exposed to members of ethnic minority groups and people from lower socioeconomic status. Scarr believed that the agency's treatment of clients was unsatisfactory because she thought the emphasis was more economical than psychological. After a year, Scarr moved on to work as a research assistant in the Laboratory of Socio-Environmental Studies at the National Institute of Mental Health, where she helped work on studies of hospitalized schizophrenics, gaining more knowledge about research methodology.

In the 1960s, she studied identical and fraternal twins' aptitude and school achievement scores. The study revealed that intellectual development was heavily influenced by genetic ability, especially among disadvantaged children. It also showed that on average, black children demonstrated less genetic and more environmental influence on their intelligence than white children.

Scarr also collaborated with Margaret Williams on a clinical study which demonstrated that premature birth infants who receive stimulation gain weight faster and recover faster than babies left in isolation (the practice at that time). Scarr, rejecting the traditional nature-nurture split, combined the two, incorporating her background in sociology and anthropology into her research. She was a signer of a collective statement, "Mainstream Science on Intelligence," written by Linda Gottfredson (see entry) and wrote a favorable review of *The Bell Curve*.

Major Literature

Scarr, Sandra. *Genetic Effects on Human Behavior: Recent Family Studies (Master Lectures on Brain-Behavior Relationships)*. Washington, D.C.: American Psychological Association, 1977.

___. *I.Q., Race, Social Class and Individual Differences*. Hillsdale, New Jersey: Erlbaum Associates, Inc., 1981.

___. *Understanding Development*. New York: Harcourt, Brace and Company, 1986.

___. *Understanding Psychology*. 5th edition. New York: Random House Inc., 1987.

___. *Mother Care/Other Care: Child Care Dilemma for Women and Children*. New York: Penguin Group, Inc., 1987.

Lande Jeffrey S., and Sandra Scarr. *Caring for Children: Challenge to America*. Hillsdale, New Jersey: Erlbaum, Associates Inc., 1989.

Schachter, Stanley (1922–1997)

ATTRIBUTION OF EMOTIONS

Born in Flushing, New York, Stanley Schachter gained a B.S. in (1942) and an M.A. in psychology (1944) from Yale University, New Haven, Connecticut. He served for a short while in the Biophysics Division of the Aero-Medical Laboratory, U.S. Air Force, at Wright-Patterson Air Force Base in Ohio working on visual problems. In 1946, he went to the Massachusetts Institute of Technology (MIT) in Cambridge to work with Kurt Lewin (see entry), who had just set up his Research Center for Group Dynamics for the theoretical and applied study of social issues, studying social issues. When Lewin died, the research center moved to the University of Michigan, where it became part of the Institute for Social Research, from where Schachter gained his Ph.D. in 1949.

He became an assistant professor at the University of Minnesota, Minneapolis, then associate professor (1954) and full professor (1958). In 1961 Schachter moved to the Department of Psychology, Columbia State University, New York, as Robert Johnston Nivens Professor of Social Psychology. He received the Distinguished Scientific Contributions Award of American Psychological Association in 1968 and was elected to the National Academy of Sciences in 1983.

Major Contributions

In 1956, Schachter co-authored *When Prophecy Fails*, which described what happened to a millennial group that had predicted the end of the world on a certain date. The appointed hour came and went, but the group's adherents did not give up their beliefs. On the contrary, they decided their faith had saved the world and began to proselytize for converts. The book and its subject gave rise to much interesting social psychology, including Leon Festinger's cognitive dissonance theory (see entry), and played a key role in showing Schachter how powerful social influence could be.

In a 1968 study of obesity, widely reported in the press, Schachter found that obese people are prompted to eat by "external" cues unrelated to physical hunger, such as the immediate presence of food, surroundings, time of day and strong emotions, for example. And in a 1978 study, he showed that cigarette smokers are physiologically addicted to nicotine, and that when they switch to lower-nicotine brands, they smoke more to prevent symptoms of nicotine withdrawal.

Schachter formulated the two-factor theory of emotion, which states that any emotional state requires two conditions: physiological arousal and situational cues. The limitation of the theory is that it ignores other cues, such as facial expressions. Schachter also worked on group affiliation; when a situation is ambiguous but potentially threatening, people seem to require knowledge of other people's emotional states to help them decipher their own.

Major Literature

Schachter, Stanley, L. Festinger, and H. Riecken. *When Prophecy Fails*. Minneapolis: University of Minnesota Press, 1956.

Schachter, Stanley. *The Psychology of Affiliation*. Stanford: Stanford University Press, 1959.

___. *Emotion, Obesity and Crime*. Burlington Massachusetts: Academic Press Inc., 1971.

___. *Psychology of Affiliation: Experimental Studies of the Sources of Gregariousness*. Palo Alto, California: Stanford University Press, 1972.

Schaie, K. Warner (1928–)
ADULT DEVELOPMENT
AND AGING

Born in Stettin, Germany (now part of Poland), K. Warner Schaie gained a B.A. in psychology from the University of California, Berkeley (1952), and an M.S. (1953) and Ph.D. in psychology (1956) at the University of Washington, Seattle. He was assistant to associate professor of psychology, University of Nebraska, Lincoln (1957–1964); associate to professor of psychology at West Virginia University, Morgantown, the University of Southern California, Los Angles, and Pennsylvania State University, Philadelphia (1964–1986); Evan Pugh Professor of Human Development and Psychology, Pennsylvania State University (1986–1992); affiliate professor of psychiatry and behavioral science, University of Washington, Seattle; director of the Gerontology Research Center, Pennsylvania State University (1992); visiting scientist, Lund Gerontology Center, Sweden (1995); and visiting scientist, University of Geneva, Switzerland (2002).

His awards and honors include the Distinguished Contribution Award, American Psychological Association (APA) Division 20 (1982); honorary doctorate, Friedrich Schiller University of Jena, Germany (1997); elected member, Akademie für gemeinnützige Wissenschaften zu Erfurt (Academy of Sciences in the Public Interest, Erfurt, Germany) (1997); Lifetime Career Award, Mensa Research Foundation (2000); and honorary Sci.D. from West Virginia University, Morgantown (2002).

Major Contributions

Schaie's work has been focused primarily on the study of cognitive development from young adulthood to advanced old age as exemplified by the ongoing Seattle Longitudinal Study (SLS), which has been conducted in seven-year intervals: 1956, 1963, 1970, 1977, 1984, 1991, 1998, and 2005. The purpose of the research is to study various aspects of psychological development during the adult years of 500 people. The study investigates health, demographic, personality, and environmental factors that influence individual differences in successful cognitive aging. It has also investigated family similarity in cognition, environmental factors, and health behaviors, and has included the long-term follow-up of cognitive training effects in older adults.

Most recently the study has collected neuropsychological and genetic data that may be relevant to the early detection of dementia. The families in the studies are now being extended to a third generation. The SLS is considered to be one of the most extensive psychological research studies of how people develop and change through adulthood. Professor Schaie's contributions to the testing literature include the Test of Behavioral Rigidity and the Schaie-Thurstone Test of Adult Mental Abilities.

Major Literature

Schaie, K. Warner. *Methodological Issues in Aging Research*. New York: Springer-Verlag, 1988.

___, and Jon Hendricks. *The Evolution of the Aging Self: The Societal Impact on the Aging Process*. New York: Springer-Verlag, 2000.

___. *Developmental Influences on Adult Intelligence: The Seattle Longitudinal Study*. New York: Oxford University Press, Inc., 2005.

Birren, James E., and K. Warner Schaie. *Handbook of the Psychology of Aging*. Burlington, Massachusetts: Academic Press, Inc., 2006.

Scott, John Paul (1909–2000)
COMPARATIVE PSYCHOLOGY

Born in Kansas City, Missouri, John Paul Scott gained a B.A. (1930) in zoology, English and psychology from the University of Wyoming, Laramie, a B.A. (1932) in natural science at Oxford University, England, and a Ph.D. in zoology (1935) at the University of Chicago, Illinois, with his dissertation on the embryology of guinea pigs. Following graduation, he was chair of the Department of Zoology of Wabash College, Crawfordsville, Indiana. From 1945 to 1965 he was at Jackson Laboratory in Bar Harbor, Maine, where he founded a new division of behavior studies. He returned to academic work at Bowling Green State University, Ohio, as director of graduate studies in psychology, as research professor, and later as Ohio Regents Professor.

At Bowling Green, Scott established a center for the study of social behavior. He retired in 1980 as a Regents Professor Emeritus of Psychology. He was a fellow of the Center for Advanced Study in the Behavioral Sciences at Stanford, California, during 1963–1964 and a research professor at Tufts University, Medford, Massachusetts, during 1981–1982. In 1990, the Animal Behavior Society honored Scott as the first recipient of its Distinguished Animal Behaviorist Award. He received many other awards and was a member of several distinguished societies, including both Phi Beta Kappa and Sigma Xi. Bowling Green has named its new research center the J.P. Scott Center for Neuroscience, Mind, and Behavior.

Major Contributions

Scott's primary interests were in behavior genetics, development, and social behavior. His early research included a 1942 study of social behavior in inbred house mice, studies of leadership and dominance in goats, and a study of social behavior and organization in sheep. He studied aggression in mice and came to believe that aggression was the product of complex interactions between genetic and environmental factors.

An extensive series of studies on genetics and development led to Scott and John L. Fuller's classic *Genetics and the Social Behavior of the Dog* (Chicago, Illinois: University of Chicago Press, 1965), which helped to establish the field of behavior genetics. The dog research influenced human development in various capacities. As a practical consequence of his "critical period" concept, Scott was able to recommend the period of approximately 8 to 12 weeks of age as the ideal time to move puppies from their mothers to human homes. Scott was the prime mover in the formation of the Animal Behavior Society.

Major Literature

Scott, John Paul. *Animal Behavior*. Chicago, Illinois: University of Chicago Press, 1958, 1972.
___. *Aggression*. Chicago, Illinois: University of Chicago Press, 1958, 1972.
Eleftheriou, B.E., and John Paul Scott. *Physiology of Aggression and Defeat*. New York: Plenum Publishing Corporation, 1971.
Scott, John Paul, and John L Fuller. *Dog Behavior: The Genetic Basis*. Chicago, Illinois: University of Chicago Press, 1974.
Scott, John Paul. *Critical Periods*. Stroudsburg, Pennsylvania: Dowden, Hutchinson and Ross, 1978.
___. *The Evolution of Social Systems*. Gordon and Breach Science Publishers Ltd., 1989.

Scott, Walter Dill (1869–1955)
PSYCHOLOGY OF ADVERTISING

Born in Cooksville, Illinois, in 1895, Walter Scott gained a B.A. from Northwestern University, Evanston, Illinois, and a B.D. (1898) from McCormick Theological Seminary, Chicago. Unable to secure the post he desired as a missionary in China, Scott went to Europe to do postgraduate work with Professor Wilhelm Wundt (see entry) at the University of Leipzig, from which he received his Ph.D. in 1900.

Soon after returning from Germany, while he was teaching at Northwestern University, he was approached by an advertising executive looking for ideas to make advertising more effective. Scott was one of the first applied psychologists. In 1909, he was appointed professor of applied psychology and director of the bureau of salesmanship research at Pittsburgh Carnegie Technical University. During World War I Scott helped apply psychological principles to personnel selection, for which he was awarded the Distinguished Service Medal.

After the war, Scott formed the Scott Company, providing consulting services to help corporations with problems of personal selection and worker efficiency. When considering advertising, Scott argued that consumers do not act rationally, and therefore they can be easily influenced; emotion, sympathy, and sentimentality are all factors that increase consumer suggestibility. Applying his laws of suggestibility, he recommended that companies use direct commands to sell their products, and that they use return coupons because they required consumers to take direct action. His techniques were used by advertisers and by 1910 were used all over the country.

Scott came up with a rating scale and group test to measure characteristics of people who were already successful as sales people, business executives, and military personal. He also questioned army officers and business managers, asking them to rank the importance of appearance, demeanor, and character. Scott then ranked job applicants on the qualities found for effective job performance.

He also developed psychological tests to measure intelligence and other abilities, but instead of an individual test he made tests that could be given to groups of people. Scott was not only measuring general intelligence but he was also interested how a person applies intelligence. He defined intelligence in practical terms such as judgment, quickness, and accuracy. He compared applicants' test scores with scores of employees who were successful, and was not concerned about what those test scores would say about the person's mental problems.

From 1920 to 1939 he was president of Northwestern University, and Scott Hall at Northwestern is named for Walter and his wife Anna Miller Scott.

Major Literature

Scott, Walter Dill. *The Theory and Practice of Advertising*. Boston, Massachusetts: Small, Maynard and Company, 1903.

___. *Psychology of Public Speaking*. Boston, Massachusetts: Small, Maynard and Company, 1907.

___. *Influencing Men in Business*. Whitefish, Montana: R.A. Kessinger Publishing Co., 1911, 2003.

___. *Increasing Human Efficiency in Business*. Macmillan, 1994. Whitefish, Montana: R.A. Kessinger Publishing Co., 1914.

___. *The Psychology of Advertising*. Boston, Massachusetts: Small, Maynard and Company, 1921. Manchester, New Hampshire: Ayer Co. Publishers, 1978.

Sears, Pauline Snedden (1908–1993)

CHILD DEVELOPMENT

Pauline (Pat as she was called) Snedden was born in Fairlee, Vermont, gained a B.A. (1930) in psychology from Stanford University, California, and an M.A. in clinical child psychology from Teachers College, Columbia University, New York (1931). She married Robert Sears (see entry) in 1932, and they formed a life-long partnership for research in the psychology of child development. She received her Ph.D. in psychology at Yale University, New Haven, Connecticut (1939). Her dissertation examined the effects of success and failure on school children's level of aspiration. The couple worked at the Universities of Iowa, Ames, and Harvard University, Cambridge, Massachusetts, then in 1953 they joined the faculty at Stanford University, California. Sears was promoted to assistant professor in 1955, associate professor in 1958, and full professor in 1966, and retired in 1973 as emeritus professor.

She was elected president of the Division of Developmental Psychology of the American Psychological Association (1959), and in 1968 was named a fellow of the Center for Advanced Study in the Behavioral Sciences, Stanford. She was also a member of Sigma Xi, the American Educational Research Association, and the Society for Research in Child Development, and was a fellow of the American Board of Examiners in Professional Psychology. In 1980, Pauline and Robert Sears together received the American Psychological Association Gold Medal Award.

Major Contributions

Sears was a national expert on child develop-

ment, known particularly for her research on self-esteem, motivation and personality development in young children. At Stanford, in the early 1960s, she pioneered the systematic observation of teachers' classroom teaching styles to assess their impact on the motivation and achievement of children with different initial aptitudes. She was among the first to raise questions concerning whether classroom atmospheres might be biased in favor of boys. Her research subjects included the classroom effects of computer assisted instruction, development of creativity, and teaching strategies for effective reinforcement of culturally different children.

She was one of the first psychologists to serve in the Stanford School of Education, and her teaching and research in child development became part of the doctoral program in psychological studies in education. She was also one of the founding members of the Stanford Center for Research and Development in Teaching.

In later years, she participated in the Stanford Center for the Study of Families, Children, and Youth. One of her important studies was of the "Terman girls"—671 "gifted" women who were part of a 50-year longitudinal study initiated by the late psychology Professor Lewis M. Terman (see entry) in 1922. Her report on these gifted women as they reached retirement showed that they were far more likely than their age-mates to have achieved higher educational degrees and also to report higher satisfaction with their lives.

Major Literature

Sears, Pauline Snedden. *In Pursuit of Self-Esteem*. Belmont, California: Wadsworth, 1964.

___. *Intellectual Development*. New Jersey: John Wiley and Sons, Inc., 1971.

Sears, Robert Richardson (1908–1989)

ADULT DEVELOPMENT AND AGING

Born in Palo Alto, California, Robert Sears gained a B.A. at Stanford University, California (1929) and a Ph.D. at Yale University, New Haven, Connecticut (1932). He married Pauline Snedden in 1932. He was instructor in psychology, University of Illinois, Urbana, Champaign (1932–1936); moved through the ranks to associate professor of psychology at Yale (1936–1942); was professor of child psychology and director of the Child Welfare Research Station, University of Iowa, Ames

(1942–1949); professor at Harvard (1949–1953) with an honorary an M.A. (1950); professor of psychology and chair of the Department of Psychology, dean of the School of Humanities and Sciences, Stanford (1953); trustee of the Center for the Advanced Study in the Behavioral Sciences, Stanford (1953–1975); organizer and first head of the Boys' Town Center for Youth Development, now known as the Center for the Study of Children, Youth and Families (1961–1970); David Starr Jordan Professor of Social Sciences in Psychology (emeritus), Stanford (1970–1975).

Sears was: president, American Psychological Association (APA) (1951); president, Western Psychological Association and APA Division 7 (1963); president, Society for Research in Child Development (SRCD) (1970); and member, American Academy of Arts and Sciences. His awards and honors include the G. Stanley Hall Award (1963); Distinguished Scientific Contribution Award, APA (1975); Gold Medal Award, American Psychological Foundation (with Pauline S. Sears) (1980); Distinguished Scientific Contribution Award, SRCD (1983); editor, *Monographs of Society for Research in Child Development*, published by Blackwell Publishing, Ames (1970–1975).

Major Contributions

Although Sears started off in experimental psychology, at Illinois, he became interested in the psychology of personality. His wife suggested psychoanalysis as a framework for his lectures, but he was more drawn to the motivational aspect of psychoanalysis than to its structured mental approach. He became the leading figure in the effort to bring psychoanalytic concepts into the mainstream of psychology by subjecting them to the rigors of operational definition and empirical test.

At the Iowa Child Welfare Station he focused on the personality patterns children acquired. He believed that the root of personality differences could be found in how children were reared and in the kinds of socialization pressures families applied. He devised family interaction situations where the children's own parents carry out standardized socialization procedures under laboratory conditions. He founded the Bing Nursery School at Stanford as a model preschool and research facility. When Lewis M. Terman (see entry) died in 1956, he named Robert Sears as his scientific executor, and the husband and wife team carried on Terman's work.

Major Literature

Sears, Robert Richardson. *Survey of Objective Studies of Psychoanalytic Concepts*. Westport, Connecticut: Greenwood Press, 1943. New York: Social Science Research Council, 1979.

___. Macoby, E. E. and H. Levin. *Patterns of Child Rearing*. New York: Row Peterson, 1957.

Sears, Robert Richardson, L. Rau, and R. Alpert. *Identification and Child Rearing*. Palo Alto, California: Stanford University Press, 1965.

Holahan, Carole K., Robert Richardson Sears, and Lee J. Cronbach. *The Gifted Group in Later Maturity*. Palo Alto, California: Stanford University Press, 1995.

Seashore (Sjöstrand), Carl Emil (1866–1949)
PSYCHOLOGY OF MUSIC AND ART

Born in Morlunda, Sweden, Carl Emil Seashore immigrated with his family to the United States in 1869 and settled in Boone County, Iowa. Seashore graduated from Gustavus Adolphus College, St. Peter, Minnesota (1891), having studied mathematics, music, and classical languages and literature, and paying for his tuition as the organist and choir director of a Swedish-Lutheran church. He studied at the new psychology department at Yale University, New Haven, Connecticut, under George Trumbull Ladd (see entry) and was awarded the school's first Ph.D. (1895) in psychology for his dissertation on the role of inhibition in learning.

He spent from 1897 to his retirement in 1937 at the University of Iowa; he was professor (1905) and then chairman of the department of psychology, dean of the Graduate School (1908) and director of the Psychological Laboratory. He was recalled as dean pro tempore of the Graduate School in 1942 and finally retired for the second time in 1946. He was president of the American Psychology Association (1911) and of the American Psychological Association (APA) (1947). Seashore's list of publications covering the years 1893 to 1949 includes 237 books and articles.

Major Contributions

Seashore was particularly interested in audiology, the psychology of music, the psychology of speech and stuttering, the psychology of the graphic arts and measuring motivation and scholastic aptitude. He devised the Seashore Tests of Musical Ability (1919), which tests five kinds of musical ability: discrimination of pitches, dissonance, rhythmical figures, and intensity, as well as an ability to remember melodies. A version of the test is still used in United States schools.

In his role as dean of the Graduate School, he founded and shaped what was to become an outstanding speech and hearing department at the University of Iowa, now the University's Department of Speech Pathology and Audiology, offering a full range of degrees up to Ph.D. He also established the Iowa Psychological Clinic, Psychopathic Hospital, Iowa Institute for Mental Hygiene, Gifted Student Project, and the Iowa Child Welfare Research Station (see also, Sears, Robert). His interests in the fine arts led to a joint effort with Professor Norman Meier and the publication of the Meier-Seashore Art Judgment Test in 1929.

Major Literature

Seashore, Carl Emil. *The Psychology of Musical Talent.* New York: Silver, Burdett and Company, 1919. Chapel Hill, North Carolina: Best Books Company, 2001.
___. *A Survey of Musical Talent in the Public Schools.* Iowa City: University of Iowa, 1924. Chapel Hill, North Carolina: Best Books Company, 2001.
___. *Psychology of Music.* New York: McGraw-Hill Companies, Inc. 1938. Mineola, New York: Dover Publications, Inc., 1967.
___. *In Search of Beauty in Music.* New York: Ronald Press, 1947. Westport, Connecticut: Greenwood Press, 1981.
___. *Measures of Musical Talents Manual.* New York: Psychological Corporation, 1956 (revised edition).

Seligman, Martin E.P. (1942–)
LEARNED HELPLESSNESS

Born in Albany, New York, Martin E.P. Seligman gained an A.B. in philosophy from Princeton University, New Jersey (1964), and a Ph.D. in psychology at the University of Pennsylvania, Philadelphia (1967). Seligman's awards and honors include the Distinguished Scientific Contribution Award, American Psychological Association (APA) (1976); Distinguished Scientific Contribution Award, APA, Division 12 (1986); honorary Ph.D., Uppsala University, Sweden (1989); Distinguished Scientific/Professional Contribution Award, Pennsylvania Psychological Association (1995); Distinguished Contribution Award for Basic Research with Applied Relevance, American Association of Applied and Preventive Psychology (1992); honorary doctor of humane letters, Massachusetts College of Professional Psychology (1997); Presidential Citation for Lifetime Achievement, APA (2002); Theodore Roosevelt Fellow and American Academy of Political and Social

Science Lifetime Achievement Award, California Psychological Association (2002); honorary Ph.D., Complutense University, Madrid (2004); Distinguished Scientific Achievement Award, Division 12 (Clinical), APA (2005); honorary doctor of science, University of East London, England (2006); and Distinguished Scientific Achievement Award, APA (2006).

Seligman is Fox Leadership Professor of Psychology in the Department of Psychology at the University of Pennsylvania, Philadelphia, and director of the Positive Psychology Center, also at Philadelphia. He is a best-selling author and is well known in academic and clinical circles. His bibliography includes twenty books and 200 articles on motivation and personality. He works on positive psychology, learned helplessness, depression, and on optimism and pessimism. His research on preventing depression received the Merit Award of the National Institute of Mental Health (1991). He is the network director of the Positive Psychology Network and scientific director of the Classification of Strengths and Virtues Project of the Mayerson Foundation.

Major Contributions

The name of Martin Seligman is synonymous with the concept of learned helplessness, a term he coined in 1968 (*Journal of Abnormal Psychology* 73, 256–262). From his experiments he noted that when animals are restrained from escaping a noxious stimulus they learn to be helpless, and will remain inert even if the noxious stimulus is repeated when restraints are removed. Learned helplessness has been also demonstrated in humans; Seligman and his colleagues believe that learned helplessness reduces the motivation to solve problems, interferes with the ability to learn from experience, and produces depression.

The Positive Psychology Center promotes research, training, education, and the dissemination of positive psychology. This field is founded on the belief that people want to lead meaningful and fulfilling lives, to cultivate what is best within themselves, and to enhance their experiences of love, work, and play.

Major Literature

Seligman, Martin E.P. *Learned Optimism.* New York: Free Press, 1990, 1998.
Peterson, Christopher, Steven F. Maier, and Martin E.P. Seligman. *Learned Helplessness: A Theory for the Age of Personal Control.* New York: Oxford University Press, Inc., 1996.

Seligman, Martin. E.P., K. Reivich, L. Jaycox, and J. Gillham. *The Optimistic Child*. New York: Harper Collins, 1996.

___. *Authentic Happiness: Using the New Positive Psychology to Realize Your Potential for Lasting Fulfillment*. New York: Free Press, 2002.

Selye, Hans Hugo Bruno (1907–1982)

STRESS MANAGEMENT

Born in Vienna of Austrian-Hungarian parents, Hans Hugo Bruno Selye gained an M.D. (1929) and a Ph.D. (1931) from the German University of Prague, Czechoslovakia. In 1931 he was appointed a research fellow at Johns Hopkins University, Baltimore, Maryland. In 1932 he moved to McGill University, Montreal, Canada, where he taught biochemistry and conducted his pioneering studies on stress. He was later president of the International Institute of Stress at the University of Montreal. Between 1945 and 1976 he was professor at the Montreal Medical University and simultaneously served as the general surgical advisor to the American Army.

In addition to being awarded honorary doctorates from 18 universities, and being a member of the Canadian Academy of Sciences, he was a member of 43 scientific associations, the honorary citizen of a number of cities and countries, and holds several prestigious awards. Ten times he was nominated for the Nobel Prize. He was Companion of the Order of Canada. He wrote 38 books and more than 1600 technical articles.

Major Contributions

Selye, "the father of stress," first detected the effects of stress in 1936 when working with rats. When he injected ovarian hormones into the glandular system of laboratory rats, he found that the hormone stimulated the outer tissue of the adrenal glands of the rats, caused deterioration of the thymus gland, and produced ulcers and finally death. He eventually determined that these effects could be produced by administering virtually any toxic substance, by physical injury, or by environmental stress. He extended his theory to humans, demonstrating that a stress-induced breakdown of the hormonal system could lead to conditions such as heart disease and high blood pressure, which he called "diseases of adaptation." He formulated General Adaptation Syndrome (GAS), which has three stages:

* *Alarm.* When we are surprised or threatened, we have an immediate physical reaction, often called the fight-or-flight reaction.
* *Resistance.* As we become used to the stress levels, the body's immune system fights to keep up with demands and expectations.
* *Exhaustion.* Eventually reality kicks in, parts of the body literally start to break down and we become very unwell. If we continue to fight this situation, we may even die.

His famous and revolutionary concept of stress opened countless avenues of treatment through the discovery that hormones participate in the development of many degenerative diseases, including coronary thrombosis, brain hemorrhage, hardening of the arteries, high blood pressure and kidney failure, arthritis, peptic ulcers and even cancer. The Canadian Institute of Stress (CIS), Toronto, Ontario, was founded in 1979 by Drs. Hans Selye and Richard Earle.

Major Literature

Selye, Hans. "The General Adaptation Syndrome and the Diseases of Adaptation." *Journal of Clinical Endocrinology* 6 (1946): 117–230.

___. *The Story of the Adaptation Syndrome*. Montreal, Quebec, Canada: Acta Inc., 1952.

___. *Stress Without Distress*. New York: Signet Books, 1974, 1991.

___. *The Stress of Life*. New York: McGraw-Hill, 1956, 1978.

Shakow, David (1901–1981)

SCHIZOPHRENIA

Born in New York City, David Shakow received both his bachelor's and master's degrees in science from Harvard University, Cambridge, Massachusetts. His Ph.D. studies were interrupted by his need to earn money to support his family, so from 1932 to 1949 he worked at Worcester State Hospital, Massachusetts, He completed his Ph.D. in 1946, and in 1949 he became professor in the psychiatry department and head of the Medical School at the University of Illinois, and in 1951 he was appointed professor of psychology at the University of Chicago; he held both positions concurrently.

From 1954 to 1966 he worked for the National Institute of Mental Health, serving as the first head of the Laboratory of Psychology in NIMH's Intramural Research Program. He was awarded both the Distinguished Scientific Contribution Award and the Distinguished Professional Contribution Award of the American Psychological

Association. Rochester University, New York, awarded him a D.Sc. in 1976, and he was awarded the Salmon Deal medal for Distinguished Service in Psychiatry.

Major Contributions

Shakow's dissertation, "The Nature of Deterioration in Schizophrenia," was recognized as a classic study on the psychology of the condition. In his long career Shakow conducted research that led to a vastly improved understanding of schizophrenia, one of the most complex mental disorders. His research covered all aspects of the disease, but in particular he focused on the mental deterioration that accompanied its progression. He was a strong advocate for patients of schizophrenia, which helped lessen the stigma that so often accompanies them. Through his work with patients, Shakow made clear that, whatever their condition, they were still human beings and needed to be treated compassionately.

In his time at Worcester, Shakow chaired a committee of the American Psychiatric Association charged with defining the standards of education and training of the developing field of clinical psychology. The results of the report set the agenda for the famous Boulder Conference of 1949 in Boulder, Colorado. In his time with the NIMH, the laboratory developed special sections to study not only schizophrenia, but also perception, aging, childhood development, and personality. The laboratory published more than 500 articles highlighting its research during those years.

Shakow retired from his position in 1966 but stayed on as senior research psychologist. During the 1970s he and his staff continued to do important research on schizophrenia. One of his important findings in the area of dysfunction of attention in schizophrenia, was to make a clear distinction between mental deterioration (which is irreversible) and deficit (which has never been present).

Major Literature

Shakow, David. *Clinical Psychology as Science and Profession.* Los Angeles: Aldine Books, 1959, 2006.
Shakow, David, and David Rapaport. *The Influence of Freud on American Psychology.* New York: International Universities Press, Inc., 1964, 1998.
Shakow, David. *Schizophrenia: Selected Papers.* New York: International Universities Press, Inc., 1977, 1998.
___. *Adaptation in Schizophrenia: Theory of Segmental Set.* New Jersey: John Wiley and Sons, Inc., 1979.

Sheldon, William Herbert
(1898–1977)
BODY TYPES

Born in Warwick, Rhode Island, William Herbert Sheldon served in the Army as an officer during World War I. He gained an A.B. degree in 1919. He was an oil field scout, was a wolf hunter in New Mexico, then was a high school teacher. He gained his master's degree at the University of Colorado, Boulder, and a Ph.D. in psychology at the University of Chicago, Illinois (1925). From 1925 to 1933, he taught psychology at the University of Texas in Austin, the University of Chicago, and the University of Wisconsin, Madison. He gained an M.D. at the University of Chicago (1933), then studied psychiatry with Carl Jung (see entry) in Zurich, Switzerland.

Sheldon was professor of psychology, University of Chicago (1936); worked with Smith Stevens (see entry) in experimental psychology, Harvard University, Cambridge, Massachusetts (1938); was a lieutenant colonel during the World War II, and in 1946, was director of the Constitution Clinic and Laboratory at Columbia University College of Physicians and Surgeons, New York, where he began examining the relationships between physical attributes and disease. From 1951 to 1970 he was clinical professor of medicine, University of Oregon Medical School, Portland, and rose to be distinguished professor of medicine and, from 1970, emeritus professor, University of Oregon.

Major Contributions

Sheldon developed "constitutional psychology," the theory associating physique, personality, and delinquency (see also, Kretschmer, Ernest). He was convinced that the psychological makeup of humans had biological foundations. To describe physical build, Sheldon studied thousands of photographs (he was the first to use standardized photography for studying physical traits) and developed a rating system for three major components. He constructed a classification system that associated physiology and psychology, which classified people according to three body types:

- endomorphs, who are rounded and soft, were said to have a tendency toward a "viscerotonic" personality (i.e., relaxed, comfortable, extroverted)
- mesomorphs, who are square and muscular, were said to have a tendency toward a "somotonic" personality (i.e., active, dynamic, assertive, aggressive)

- ectomorphs, who are thin and fine-boned, were said to have a tendency toward a "cerebrotonic" personality (i.e., introverted, thoughtful, inhibited, sensitive).

He later used this classification system to explain delinquent behavior, finding that delinquents were likely to be high in mesomorphy and low in ectomorphy and arguing that mesomorphy's associated temperaments (active and aggressive but lacking sensitivity and inhibition) tended to cause delinquency and criminal behavior. Although his research was pioneering, it was criticized on the grounds that his samples were not representative and that he mistook correlation for causation. Sheldon's correlations remain unproven. In 1995, it was revealed that many of the photographs Sheldon studied were obtained by requiring students at universities to be photographed naked and without informed consent as to how the pictures might be used.

Major Literature

Sheldon, William H. *Psychology and the Promethean Will*. Montana: R.A. Kessinger Publishing Co., 1936, 2003.
___. *The Varieties of Human Physique: An Introduction to Constitutional Psychology*. New York: Harper and Brothers, 1940.
___. *Atlas of Men*. New York: Macmillan Publishing Co., 1970.
___. *Prometheus Revisited*. Rochester, Vermont: Schenkman Books, Inc., 1974.

Sherif, Muzafer (1906–1988)

PREJUDICE IN SOCIAL GROUPS

Born in Odemis, Izmir, Turkey, Muzafer Serif Basoglu later changed his name to Muzafer Sherif. He gained a B.A. at American International College, Izmir (1927); an M.A. at the University of Instanbul (1929); an M.A., Harvard University, Cambridge, Massachusetts (1932), and Ph.D. at Columbia University, New York (1935). His thesis was "Some Social Factors in Perception." Sherif was assistant professor of psychology at the Gaza Institute, Ankara, Turkey (1937). In 1944 he was jailed for four months in Turkey for outspoken opposition to the Nazi movement.

He immigrated to the USA was made a fellow of the U.S. State Department, Princeton University, New Jersey. He was resident fellow in psychology, Yale University, New Haven, Connecticut (1947); professor, University of Oklahoma, Norman (1949); visiting professor, University of Texas, Austin (1958); professor of research and the

Ford Visiting Professor at the University of Washington, Seattle (1960); distinguished visiting professor at Pennsylvania State University, Philadelphia (1965); and professor of sociology and director of Psycho-Social Studies Program (emeritus), Pennsylvania State (1972). He was fellow and council member of the American Psychological Association (1963) and distinguished visiting professor at Pennsylvania State University, Philadelphia (1965). He received the Kurt Lewin Memorial Award (1967).

Major Contributions

Throughout his distinguished academic career, Sherif focused mainly on understanding group processes and succeeded in making significant contributions to the field of social psychology. He was the first ever to receive the Cooley-Mead Award for Contributions to Social Psychology from the American Sociological Society (1980). He published some 24 books and 60 articles.

Much of his research was jointly conducted with his wife, Carolyn. Sherif's "realistic conflict theory" accounts for inner group conflict, negative prejudices, and stereotypes as a result of competition between groups for desired resources.

Sherif validated his theory in one his most famous experiments, "The Robber's Cave," set in a remote summer camp in Oklahoma, Robbers Cave State Park. In this experiment, 22 white, fifth grade, 11 year old boys with similar background and education were split into two groups — the Eagles and the Rattlers; neither group was aware of the other. After a week of close bonding, the groups were brought together, and set a series of competitions, with medals and camping knives promised to the winners. Competition quickly turned to aggressive acts. The only way harmony could be achieved was work toward a common goal, one of which was to restore to the camp the supply of drinking water, which had been sabotaged by the researchers.

Major Literature

Sherif Muzafer. *The Psychology of Social Norms*. New York: Harper and Row, 1936.
___. *Intergroup Conflict and Cooperation: The Robber's Cave Experiment*. Institute of Group Relations, 1961. Middletown, Connecticut: Wesleyan University Press, 1988.
Sherif, Carolyn Wood, and Muzafer Sherif. *Reference Groups: An Exploration of Conformity and Deviance of Adolescence*. New York: Harper and Row, 1964.
Sherif, Muzafer. *Social Interaction: Process and Products*. Los Angeles: Aldine Books, 1967, 2005.

Sherif, Carolyn Wood, and Muzafer Sherif. *Attitude, Ego-Involvement and Change*. Westport, Connecticut: Greenwood Press, 1976.

Sherrington, Sir Charles Scott (1857–1952)

EXPERIMENTAL PSYCHOLOGY

Born in Islington, London, England, Charles Scott Sherrington gained a B.A. (1883) from Gonville and Caius College, Cambridge University, England, and qualified in medicine (1885) from St. Thomas' Hospital Medical School, London. From 1886 to 1887 he studied at the University of Berlin under Robert Koch (1843–1910), the discoverer of the cholera bacillus (1883). After serving as a lecturer at St. Thomas' Hospital, he was successively a professor of physiology at the universities of London (1891–1895), Liverpool (1895–1913), and Oxford (1913–1935). He was made a fellow of the Royal Society in 1893 and was president (1920–1925).

He received the Knight Grand Cross of the British Empire in 1922 and the Order of Merit in 1924. With Edgar Adrian (1889–1977) he shared the Nobel Prize (1932) for Physiology or Medicine, for their discoveries regarding the function of the neuron. Sherrington Crater (lunar) was named after him by the International Astronomical Union, as is one of the University of Liverpool's medical buildings. A stained glass window in the dining hall of Caius College, Cambridge, commemorates C.S. Sherrington.

Major Contributions

Although Sherrington was a physiologist, he has made considerable contributions to the field of psychology, and many of the terms he coined are part and parcel of the language of psychology — for example, neuron and synapse to denote the nerve cell and the point at which the nervous impulse is transmitted from one nerve cell to another, respectively.

In his classic work *The Integrative Action of the Nervous System* (New York: Charles Scribner's Sons, 1906), he distinguished three main groups of sense organs: exteroceptive, such as those that detect light, sound, odor, and tactile stimuli; interoceptive, exemplified by taste receptors; and proprioceptive, or those receptors that detect events occurring in the interior of the organism. He found — especially in his study of the maintenance of posture as a reflex activity — that the muscles' proprioceptors and their nerve trunks play an important role in reflex action, maintaining the animal's upright stance against the force of gravity, despite the removal of the cerebrum and the severing of the tactile sensory nerves of the skin.

As a physician, he did important work in the study of cholera in Spain and of diphtheria and tetanus antitoxins, and played an important role in the improvement of health and safety conditions in British factories during World War I. He also contributed to the understanding of vision and challenged William James's (see entry) hypothesis that the emotions derive from bodily changes (i.e. visceral sensations). Sherrington demonstrated that visceral sensations reinforce emotions but do not initiate them.

Major Literature

Sherrington, Charles Scott. *Mammalian Physiology*. Oxford, England: Clarendon Press, 1919, rev. ed. 1929.
___. *The Reflex Activity of the Spinal Cord*. Oxford, England: Clarendon Press, 1932.
___. *The Brain and its Mechanism*. Cambridge, England, Cambridge University Press, 1933.
___. *Man On His Nature*. Cambridge, England: Cambridge University Press, 1940, 2d ed. 1952.

Sidis, Boris (1867–1923)

PSYCHOPATHOLOGY

Born in Berditchev, Russia, Boris Sidis was imprisoned as a political prisoner for teaching peasants to read, which was against Czarist law (1884). He escaped to the U.S. in 1887 and gained an A.B. (1894) and an A.M. (1895); he was assistant in Aristotelianlogic (1896) and gained a Ph.D. (1897) and an M.D. (1908) at Harvard University, Cambridge, Massachusetts. He was associate psychologist and psychopathologist, Pathology Institute, New York State Hospitals (1896–1901); established (on endowment) the Psychopathological Hospital and Psychopathic Laboratory at the New York Infirmary for Women and Children (1901); started private psychotherapy in Brookline, Massachusetts (1904), and in 1908, founded the Criminology Institute of Chicago University.

In 1909, Sidis was given an estate in Portsmouth, New Hampshire, and founded the Sidis Psychotherapeutic Institute for the treatment of nervous disorders. He was editor, *Archives of Neurology and Psychopathology*; and editor, *Journal of Abnormal Psychology*, founded for him by Morton Prince (see entry). He was secretary of the American Psychopathological Society and a member of the American Institute of Criminal Law and Criminology.

Major Contributions

Sidis was one of the first to undertake really scientific exploration of the subconscious region of the mind. He demonstrated the value of hypnosis as a means of gaining access to the subconscious and effecting impressive cures in cases of functional nervous and mental disorder. In *Multiple Personality* (1904), Sidis describes the restoration of memory by hypnosis of the Reverend Mr. Hanna, who suffered from so severe a case of amnesia that a secondary personality was considered. He also demonstrated the over-development of the fear instinct in the causation of psychopathic disorders. His study of sleep verified Édouard Claparède's (see entry) theory of sleep as being protective rather than recuperative. Boris and Sarah Sidis's son was child prodigy and mathematics genius William James Sidis (1898–1944), who could read at 18 months, taught himself Latin at the age of 2, and wrote a treatise on anatomy at the age of 4. By age 8 he had written four books and knew eight languages. At the age of 11 Sidis entered Harvard University; his IQ was estimated to be between 250 and 300.

Major Literature

Sidis, Boris. *The Psychology of Suggestion: A Research Into the Subconscious Nature of Man and Society.* New York: D. Appleton and Co., 1898. Manchester, New Hampshire: Ayer Co. Publishers, 1973.

___, William Alanson White, and George M. Parker. *Psychopathological Researches: Studies in Mental Dissociation.* London, England: W. Rider and Son, 1902.

Sidis, Boris, and Simon P. Goodhart. *Multiple Personality: An Experimental Investigation Into the Nature of Individuality.* New York: D. Appleton, 1904.

___. *An Inquiry Into the Nature of Hallucinations.* New York: Macmillan, 1904.

___. *The Doctrine of Primary and Secondary Sensory Elements.* Lancaster, Pennsylvania: The Review Publishing Company, 1908.

___. *An Experimental Study of Sleep.* Boston: Badger, 1900.

___. *Hypnoidal Psychotherapy in the Treatment of Functional Nervous Diseases.* New York: Moffat, Yard, 1910.

___. *The Psychology of Laughter.* New York: D. Appleton, 1913, 1919, 1923.

___. *The Foundations of Normal and Abnormal Psychology.* London, England: Duckworth, 1915.

Simon, Herbert Alexander (1916–2001)

COGNITIVE PSYCHOLOGY

Born in Milwaukee, Wisconsin, Herbert Alexander Simon gained a B.A. (1936) and a Ph.D. (1943) from the University of Chicago, Illinois. He was professor, Carnegie Mellon University, Pittsburgh (1949), and served at the following universities: Case Institute of Technology, Cleveland, Ohio (1963); McGill University, Montreal, Quebec, Canada (1970); University of Michigan, Ann Arbor (1978); University of Pittsburgh, Pennsylvania (1979); Marquette University, Milwaukee, Wisconsin (1981); Columbia University, New York (1983); and Gustavus Adolphus College, St. Peter, Minnesota (1984). He was Richard King Mellon University Professor of Computer Science and Psychology, Department of Psychology at Carnegie-Mellon University, Pittsburgh, Pennsylvania.

Simon's awards and honors include an honorary D.Sc., Yale University, New Haven, Connecticut (1963); honorary LL.D., University of Chicago (1964); member, National Academy of Sciences (1967); honorary doctorate, Lund University, Wakefield, Massachusetts (1968); American Psychological Association Scientific Contribution Award (1969); doctor of economic science, Erasmus University, Rotterdam, Netherlands (1973); A.M. Turing Award of the Association for Computing Memory (1975); Nobel Prize in economic science (1978); docteur, University of Paul Valery, Montpellier, France (1984); American Political Science Association's James Madison Award (1984); and National Medal of Science (1986).

Major Contributions

Simon was a researcher in the fields of cognitive psychology, computer science, public administration, economic sociology, and philosophy. His Turing Award (with Allen Newell) was given for making "basic contributions to artificial intelligence, the psychology of human cognition, and list processing." The Nobel Prize was "for his pioneering research into the decision-making process within economic organizations." He coined the terms "bounded rationality" (a central theme in behavioral economics, concerned with the ways in which the actual decision-making process influences decisions), and "satisficing" (seeking or achieving a satisfactory outcome, rather than the best possible). At Carnegie Mellon he helped form the Graduate School of Industrial Administration and the School of Computer Science.

He was best known for a theory of corporate decision, and the framework he suggested provided a more satisfactory theoretical approach where decision-making units were large enough for each one to have significant effects on prices and outputs. Crucial to this theory was the concept of satisfying behavior as contrasted with the traditional emphasis on the achievement of maximum profits as the primary motivating factor. He thus attempted to consider the psychological factors involved in decision-making.

Around 1954 Simon determined that the best way to study human problem-solving was to simulate it with computer programs, which led to his interest in computer simulation of human cognition. He became increasingly involved in an attempt to create artificial intelligence by computer technology.

Major Literature

Simon, Herbert Alexander. *Models of Man*. New Jersey: John Wiley and Sons, Inc., 1957. Pennsylvania, Philadelphia: Taylor and Francis Books Ltd., 1987.
___. *Administrative Behavior*. New York: Macmillan, 1976.
___. *The New Science of Management Decision*. New Jersey: Prentice-Hall, 1977.
___. *Models of My Life* (autobiography). Jackson, Tennessee: Basic Books, 1991.
___. *An Empirically Based Microeconomics*. New York: Cambridge University Press, 1997.

Skinner, Burrhus Frederic (1904–1990)

OPERANT CONDITIONING

Born in Susquehanna, Pennsylvania, B.F. Skinner gained a B.A. at English, Hamilton College, New York (1926). At Harvard University, Cambridge, Massachusetts, he earned an M.A. (1930) and Ph.D. in psychology (1931); was a junior fellow, Harvard Society of Fellows (1933–1936); professor (1948–1957); Edgar Pierce Professor of Psychology (1958–1974); and professor emeritus (1975–1990). From 1936 to 1937 Skinner was instructor in psychology, University of Minnesota, Minneapolis. At Indiana University, Bloomington, he was assistant professor (1937–1939), associate professor (1939–45) and professor of psychology (1945–1948).

He was a member of the American Philosophical Society (1949). He received a citation for Lifetime Contribution to Psychology, American Psychological Association (1990), was awarded more twenty-five honorary doctorates, and was a member of Lambda Chi Alpha fraternity. Skinner died of leukemia after becoming perhaps the most celebrated psychologist since Sigmund Freud.

Major Contributions

Skinner was attracted to psychology through the work of Ivan Pavlov (see entry) on conditioned reflexes, the ideas of John B. Watson (see entry), the founder of behaviorism, and the writings of Bertrand Russell (1872–1970). Skinner became the leading exponent of behaviorism, and like other behaviorists, he rejected theories of he mind, for example, psychoanalysis, concerning himself only with patterns of responses to rewards and stimuli. Skinner maintained that learning occurred as a result of the organism responding to, or operating on, its environment. He coined the term "operant conditioning" to describe this phenomenon. He did extensive research with animals, notably rats and pigeons, and invented the famous Skinner box (operant conditioning chamber) in which an animal learns to press a lever in order to obtain food.

At Indiana University, Skinner gained some public attention through his invention of the Air Crib baby tender — a large, soundproof, germ-free, mechanical, air-conditioned box designed to provide an optimal environment for child growth during the first two years of life. In 1948 he published one of his most controversial works, *Walden Two* (republished in 2005 by Hackett Publishing, Indianapolis, Indiana), a novel on life in a utopian community modeled on his own principles of social engineering.

At Harvard he trained laboratory animals to perform complex and sometimes quite exceptional actions; one example was his pigeons that learned to play table tennis. He developed the idea of programmed learning, which he envisioned to be accomplished through the use of so-called teaching machines.

Major Literature

Skinner, Burrhus Frederic. *The Behavior of Organisms*. New Jersey: Appleton-Century-Crofts, 1938. Acton, Massachusetts: Copley Publishing Group, 1991.
___. *Verbal Behavior*. New Jersey: Appleton-Century-Crofts, 1957. Acton, Massachusetts: Copley Publishing Group, 1991.
___, and J.G. Holland. *The Analysis of Behavior*. Columbus, Ohio: McGraw-Hill, 1961.
Skinner, Burrhus Frederic. *Beyond Freedom and Dignity*. New York: Knopf, 1971. Indianapolis, Indiana: Hackett Publishing Co., Inc., 2002.
___. *Particulars of My Life*. New York: Knopf, 1976.
___. *A Matter of Consequences*. New York: Knopf, 1983.
___. *The Shaping of a Behaviorist*. New York University Press, 1985.
___. *Recent Issues in the Analysis of Behavior*. Columbus, Ohio: Charles Merrill Co., 1989.

Socarides, Charles W.
(1922–2005)
SEXUALITY

Born in Brockton, Massachusetts, Charles W. Socarides graduated from Harvard College, Cambridge, Massachusetts (1952), and gained his certificate in psychoanalytic medicine from Columbia University, New York (1954). Until his death he taught psychiatry at Columbia University and the State University of New York Downstate Medical Center. From 1978 to 1996 he was clinical professor of psychiatry at the Albert Einstein College of Medicine, New York City. In 1992 he co-founded NARTH, the National Association for Research and Therapy of Homosexuality.

His awards and honors include the Sigmund Freud Award given by the American Society of Psychoanalytic Physicians in recognition of distinguished service to psychiatry and psychoanalytic research; Distinguished Psychoanalyst, Association of Psychoanalytic Psychologists, British National Health Service, London, England; Sigmund Freud Lectureship Award, New York Center for Psychoanalytic Training, New York City; and Physicians' Recognition Award of the American Medical Association.

Major Contributions

Much of Socarides' career was devoted to studying how homosexuality develops and how it could be cured. Following the psychoanalytic tradition, he maintained that male homosexuality develops in the first two years of the boy's life, during the pre-oedipal stage of personality formation. It is caused by a controlling mother who prevents her son from separating from her, and a weak or rejecting father who does not serve as a role model for his son and does not support what Socarides perceived as a son's effort to escape from the mother.

He reported that he cured roughly 30 percent of his patients and that after treatment they led heterosexual lives. Critics of "reparative therapy," as it is called, put forward the view that all he achieved was repression of feelings, with all the personality consequences of that. In 1973 he fought against the decision by the American Psychiatric Association (which maintains there is no substantial evidence that reparative therapy works) to remove homosexuality from its list of mental disorders, saying the association was bowing to pressure from the gay lobby. Further, the American Psychiatric Association points to the medical dictum to "first, do no harm."

Socarides had an openly gay son, Richard, who served as a White House advisor on gay and lesbian rights in the Clinton Administration. Socarides made a show of "willingly" taking some of the blame for his son's homosexuality, saying that he had "failed" his son by not seeing him enough after divorcing his first wife.

Major Contributions

Socarides, Charles W. *The Overt Homosexual.* Lanham, Maryland: Rowman and Littlefield Publishers, Inc., Jason Aronson, 1968.
___. *Beyond Sexual Freedom.* New York: Times/Quadrangle Books, 1975.
___. *Homosexuality.* Lanham, Maryland: Rowman and Littlefield Publishers, Inc., Jason Aronson, 1978.
___. *Preoedipal Origin and Psychoanalytic Therapy of Sexual Perversions.* Madison, Connecticut: International Universities Press, Inc., 1988.
Volkan, Vamik D., and Charles W. Socarides. *The Homosexualities: Reality, Fantasy, and the Arts.* Madison, Connecticut: International Universities Press, Inc., 1990.
Socarides, Charles W., and Abraham Freedman. *Objects of Desire: The Sexual Deviations.* Madison, Connecticut: International Universities Press, Inc., 2002.

Spearman, Charles Edward
(1863–1945)
HUMAN INTELLIGENCE

Born in London, England, Charles Edward Spearman served as Army officer, mainly in India (1883–1897). He studied experimental psychology under Wilhelm Wundt (see entry) at the University of Leipzig (1897–1906), and was recalled during the South African War as deputy assistant adjutant-general in Guernsey. He gained a Ph.D. in Leipzig (1906) and was reader in experimental psychology, University College London (1907–1911). He was Grote Professor of Mind and Logic, University College London (1911–1928), replacing William McDougall (see entry), who had recommended Spearman for the position.

During World War I, Spearman served on the general staff of Tyne defenses (North of England). From 1928 to 1931 he was professor of psychology of the newly created separate Department of Psychology, University College London, and emeritus professor (1931). He was fellow of the Royal Society (1924) and president of the Psychology Section, British Association for the Advancement of Science (1925). He received an honorary LL.D., University of Wittenberg, Germany (1929), and was an honorary member of the British Psychological Society (1934) and honorary member of several foreign academies of science and psychological societies.

Major Contributions

Spearman noticed that people who did well on one mental ability test tended to do well on the others. He devised a technique for statistical analysis, which he called "factor analysis," that examines patterns of individual differences in test scores and is said to provide an analysis of the underlying sources of these individual differences. His attempt to establish general, fundamental laws of psychology was reflected in his 1904 paper.

Spearman's factor analyses of test data suggested to him that just two kinds of factors underlie all individual differences in test scores. The first and more important factor he labeled the "general factor," or *g*, which is said to pervade performance on all tasks requiring intelligence. In other words, regardless of the task, if it requires intelligence, it requires *g*. The second factor is specifically related to each particular test. By 1912 he had developed an order of correlation coefficients separating various performances into the general factor, *g*, and varying specific factors, s_1, s_2, and so on. In 1927, Spearman proposed that the general factor might be something he called "mental energy."

Spearman taught at Colombia University, New York, the Catholic University of America, Washington, D.C., and at Chicago, Illinois, as well as at the University of Cairo, Egypt. Spearman regarded his statistical work as subordinate to his quest for the fundamental laws of psychology.

Major Literature

Spearman, Charles Edward. "The Proof and Measurement of Association Between Two Things." *American Journal of Psychology* 15 (1904): 72–101.

___. *The Nature of "Intelligence" and the Principles of Cognition*. London: Macmillan, 1923. Manchester, New Hampshire: Ayer Co. Publishers, 1973.

___. *The Abilities of Man: Their Nature and Measurement*. London: Macmillan, 1927. New York: Ams Press Inc., 1970.

___. *Psychology Down the Ages*, 2 vols. London: Macmillan, 1937.

___. *Human Ability: A Continuation of "The Abilities of Man."* London: Macmillan, 1950.

Spence, Kenneth Wartenbee (1907–1967)

THEORY OF LEARNING

Born in Chicago, Illinois, Kenneth Wartenbee Spence grew up in Montreal, Quebec, Canada. At McGill University, Montreal, he gained a B.A. (1929) and an M.A. (1930); he won the Wales Gold Medal in Mental Sciences (1929) and the Governor-General's Medal for Research (1930). He gained a Ph.D. at Yale University, New Haven, Connecticut (1933). Spence was National Research Council fellow and research assistant, working with chimpanzees at the Yale Laboratories of Primate Biology in Orange Park, Florida (1933); assistant professor of psychology, University of Virginia, Charlottesville (1937); associate professor, State University of Iowa (now the University of Iowa) in Iowa City (1938); and professor and head of the psychology department at Iowa (1942).

He was head of the psychology department, University of Texas in Austin (1964) and also served on the U.S. Air Force Committee on Human Resources and the Army Scientific Advisory Panel. He was a fellow of the American Association for the Advancement of Science, and of the American Psychological Association (APA), and a member, National Academy of Sciences. He received the Howard Crosby Warren Medal of the Society of Experimental Psychologists (1953) and the first Distinguished Scientific Contribution Award of the APA (1956).

Major Contributions

Spence's contributions fall into three major categories: learning and motivation theory, the experimental psychology of learning and motivation, and methodology and philosophy of science. At Yale, Spence studied with Robert M. Yerkes and with Clark L. Hull (see entries), where his early work was concerned with discrimination learning and conditioning in animals. At Iowa he extended the research and theories of Hull in an attempt to establish a precise, mathematical formulation to describe the acquisition of learned behavior. He tried to measure simple learned behaviors such as salivating in anticipation of eating.

Much of his research focused on classically conditioned, easily measured, eye-blinking behavior in relation to anxiety and other factors. He measured anxiety using the Taylor Manifest Anxiety Scale. He believed in "latent learning," and although reinforcement was not necessary for learning to occur, for him it was a strong motivator for performance. Collectively, this work eventually became known as the Hull-Spence theory of conditioning and learning. Together with Kurt Lewin (see entry) at the Child Welfare Research Station,

Spence made the University of Iowa into a major center of theoretical psychology, with the goal of transforming psychology into an advanced natural science.

Major Literature

Spence, Kenneth Wartenbee. "The Nature of Discrimination Learning in Animals." *Psychological Review* 43 (1936): 427–49.

___. and G. Bergmann. "Operationism and Theory in Psychology." *Psychological Review* 48 (1941): 1–14.

Spence, Kenneth Wartenbee. *Behavior Theory and Conditioning.* New Jersey: Prentice-Hall, 1956. Westport, Connecticut: Greenwood Press, 1978.

___. *Behavior Theory and Learning: Selected Papers.* New Jersey: Prentice-Hall, 1960.

___. and Janet Taylor Spence. *Psychology of Learning and Motivation: Advances in Research and Theory* (2 vols.). Burlington, Massachusetts: Academic Press, Inc., 1967.

Sperry, Roger Wolcott (1913–1994)

BRAIN FUNCTIONING

Born in West Hartford, Connecticut, Roger Wolcott Sperry gained a B.A. in English (1935) and an M.A. in psychology (1937) from Oberlin College, Ohio. His Ph.D. was from the University of Chicago, Illinois (1941). He did post-doctoral research with Karl Lashley (see entry) at Harvard University, Cambridge, Massachusetts (1941), then worked at the Yerkes Laboratories of Primate Biology in Atlanta, Georgia (then a part of Harvard University) (1942–1946).

Sperry was assistant professor and later associate professor, University of Chicago (1946–1952); section chief of Neurological Diseases and Blindness at the National Institutes of Health (1952–1954); and Hixon Professor of Psychobiology, California Institute of Technology (Caltech), Pasadena, California (1954–1994). Sperry's awards and honors include an honorary doctor of science, the Rockefeller University (1980); American Academy of Achievement Golden Plate Award (1980) and in 1981; and a shared the Nobel Prize in Medicine with David Hunter Hubel and Torsten Nils Wiesel, for his work with split-brain research.

Major Contributions

Before Sperry's experiments, some research evidence seemed to indicate that areas of the brain were largely undifferentiated and interchangeable. In his early experiments Sperry challenged this view by showing that after early development, circuits of the brain are largely hardwired, in the sense that each nerve cell is tagged with its own chemical individuality early in embryonic development; once this happens, the function of the cell is fixed and is not modifiable thereafter.

In his Nobel-winning work, Sperry separated the corpus callosum — the area of the brain used to transfer signals between the right and left hemispheres — to treat epileptics. Sperry and his colleagues then tested these patients with tasks that were known to be dependent on specific hemispheres of the brain and demonstrated that the two halves of the brain may each contain consciousness. The left hemisphere is the one with speech, and it is dominant in all activities involving language, arithmetic, and analysis. The right hemisphere is superior to the left hemisphere in, among other things, spatial comprehension — in understanding maps, for example, or recognizing faces. This research contributed greatly to understanding the lateralization of brain function. Further, Sperry concluded, both hemispheres may be conscious simultaneously in different, even in mutually conflicting, mental experiences that run along in parallel.

Major Literature

Sperry, Roger Wolcott. "The Problem of Central Nervous Reorganization After Nerve Regeneration and Muscle Transposition." *Quarterly Review Biology,* 20 (1945): 311–369.

___. "Regulative Factors in the Orderly Growth of Neural Circuits." *Growth Symposium* 10 (1951): 63–67.

___. "Cerebral Organization and Behavior." *Science* 133 (1961): 1749–1757.

___. "Lateral Specialization in the Surgically Separated Hemispheres." In F. Schmitt and F. Worden (Eds.), *Neurosciences Third Study Program.* Cambridge, Massachusetts: MIT Press, 1974.

___. "Mind-Brain Interaction: Mentalism, Yes; Dualism, No." *Neuroscience,* 5 (1980): 195–206. Reprinted in A.D. Smith, R. Llanas, and P.G. Kostyuk (Eds.), *Commentaries in the Neurosciences.* Oxford: Pergamon Press, pp. 651–662, 1980.

___. *Science and Moral Priority: Merging Mind, Brain and Human Values.* New York: Columbia University Press, 1982.

Spitz, Rene Arpad (1887–1974)

SENSORY DEPRIVATION IN CHILDREN

Born in Austria, Rene Arpad Spitz spent most of his childhood in Hungary. He qualified as a physician (1910) from Budapest University. During the First World War, he served in the army as a military physician. He underwent a training analysis with Sigmund Freud (see entry), and between 1924 and 1928, participated in the Vienna Psychoanalytic Society and, subsequently, worked in Berlin and was a member of the German Psychoanalytic Society (DPG). From 1932 to 1938 he taught psychoanalysis and child development at the elite École Normale Supérieure, Paris.

He fled the Nazis to the United States and worked at the University of Denver, Colorado. Spitz was another pioneer (see also, entries for Bowlby, John, and Harlow, Harry) in the effort to document the value of human contact. In 1945 he compared two sets of children, one in a typical orphanage, the other in a chaotic prison nursery. In the orphanage — a don't touch sort of place — cribs were separated from each other by hung sheets, a form of solitary confinement, to stave off infection. In the prison nursery, children shared a common room filled with noise and toys and germs. Mothers (convicts) were allowed to spend as much time with their children as possible, and most did.

During Spitz's investigation, the orphanage cared for 88 children; more than a third died. Twenty-one were still living in institutions after 40 years, most of whom were physically, mentally, and socially retarded. The prison nursery, on the other hand, cared for 90 children, and none died during his study. Spitz went on to film a handful of children in the orphanage. His film presented happy, precocious children transformed into emotionless zombies after mere weeks of isolation. He closed his film with a silent-movie cue card, which read: "The cure: Give Mother Back to Baby."

Spitz took his films around medical society meetings in New York in the late 1940s and it is reported that critics shredded the film as being emotionally overwrought and non-scientific. Spitz's work went a long way toward changing adoption policies. Early adoption is now universally recognized as the best option for orphans and unwanted babies. These findings presented by Bowlby and Spitz almost 40 years ago are corroborated by recent neurobiological research. The studies in question suggest that the absence of loving physical contact between child and parent will cause certain areas of the brain, notably those responsible for the emotions, to remain underdeveloped. Spitz died in died in Denver, Colorado.

Major Literature

Spitz, Rene Arpad. *Genetic Field Theory of Ego Formation: Its Implications for Pathology.* New York: International Universities Press, Inc., 1962.

Spitz, Rene Arpad, and Godfrey R. Cobline. *The First Year of Life: Psychoanalytic Study of Normal and Deviant Development of Object Relations.* New York: International Universities Press Inc., 1965, 2006.

Spitz, Rene Arpad. *No and Yes: On the Genesis of Human Communication.* New York: International Universities Press, Inc., 1966.

Sternberg, Robert J. (1949–)
HIGHER MENTAL FUNCTIONS

Born in Maplewood, Jew Jersey, Robert J. Sternberg gained a B.A. in psychology from Yale University, New Haven, Connecticut (1972), and a Ph.D. in psychology at Stanford University, California (1975). Sternberg is listed as one of the 100 top young scientists in the U.S. by *Science Digest* (1986), also in the *Esquire Register* recognizing the achievements of outstanding American men and women under 40, and is listed as one of the "Top 100 Psychologists of the 20th Century" by the American Psychological Association (APA) *Monitor.*

Sternberg is a past-president of the American Psychological Association, dormer IBM Professor of Psychology and Education, Yale, and is currently dean, School of Arts and Sciences, Tufts University, Medford, Massachusetts. He is a fellow of five distinguished associations and societies, the author of many books and articles, and has won roughly two dozen awards for his scholarship. His research has taken him to five different continents, where he has studied the relationship between culture and competence. Six universities have awarded him honorary doctorates.

Major Contributions

Sternberg is at pains to state that his work is very much a team effort, dedicated to doing multicultural and cross-cultural research. Sternberg views intelligence as a form of developing competencies, as forms of developing expertise. In other words, intelligence is modifiable rather than fixed and can be defined as competencies. *Metacompetencies* plan, monitor, and evaluate problem-solving strategies. *Performance competencies* execute the instructions from the metacompetencies and provide feedback to them. *Knowledge-acquisition competencies* learn how to solve the problems in the first place.

Sternberg classifies his work into:

1. *Higher mental functions*, a triarchic theory which includes intelligence, creativity, and wisdom

2. *Styles of thinking*, a theory of mental self-government, which is a theory of thinking styles
3. *Cognitive modifiability*, a theory of change, both for organizations and people
4. *Leadership*; much of his work on leadership has been concerned with what one needs to know to adjust to an environment that is not usually verbalized and that often is even concealed
5. *Love and Hate*; the components of his theory of love are intimacy, passion, and commitment, which are negated by hate.

Major Literature

Sternberg, Robert J. *Beyond IQ: A Triarchic Theory of Human Intelligence*. New York: Cambridge University Press, 1985.

___. "Construct Validation of a Triangular Love Scale." *European Journal of Social Psychology* 27 (1997), 313–335.

___. "A Balance Theory of Wisdom." *Review of General Psychology* 2 (1998): 347–365.

___. *Thinking Styles*. New York: Cambridge University Press, 1999.

___, and V.H. Vroom. "The Person Versus the Situation in Leadership." *Leadership Quarterly*, 13 (2002): 301–323.

Sternberg, Robert J., J.C. Kaufman, and J.E. Pretz. *The Creativity Conundrum: A Propulsion Model of Creative Contributions*. New York: Psychology Press, 2002.

Sternberg, Robert J. "A Duplex Theory of Hate: Development and Application to Terrorism, Massacres, and Genocide." *Review of General Psychology* 7 (3) (2003): 299–328.

Stevens, Stanley Smith (1906–1973)

PSYCHOPHYSICS

Born in Ogden, Utah, Stanley Smith Stevens gained a B.A. at Stanford University, California (1931), and a Ph.D. in the (1933) Department of Philosophy at Harvard University, Cambridge, Massachusetts, from which the Psychology Department emerged in 1934. He remained Harvard at for the rest of his career; he was instructor in experimental psychology (1936–1938), assistant professor (1938), associate professor (1944), professor of psychology (1946), and professor of psychophysics (1962). His awards and honors include the National Research Council Fellowship (1934–1935); Rockefeller Foundation Fellow (1935–1936); Warren Medal, Society of Experimental Psychologists (1943); Distinguished Scientific Contribution Award, American Psychological Association (1960); Beltone Institute Award (1966); and Rayleigh Gold Medal Award, British Acoustical Society (1972).

Major Contributions

From 1923 to 1926, Stevens was a Mormon missionary in Belgium and later in France, then did a variety of courses at University of Utah, Salt Lake City, before gradating from Stanford. At Utah, Stevens discovered comparative psychology and shocked the fundamentalist Mormons with his support of J.B. Watson's view on the force of nurture (environment) over nature (heredity). Later, however, Stevens became a firm advocate of heredity over environment.

When working on his Ph.D. at Harvard he studied advanced statistics and physiology, two subjects that were to form the foundation of his future work. Stevens studied perception under E.G. Boring (see entry) and from 1932 to 1935 he was an assistant in psychology to Boring. Stevens started research on tonal volume, which became the topic of his Ph.D. dissertation. He audited courses on mathematics and physics before settling for psychology in 1936.

As America prepared for war in 1940, with funding from the U.S. Army Air Corps, Stevens established and was the director of the Psycho-Acoustical Laboratory at Harvard. By 1945 the laboratory was employing some fifty research workers, all of whom made important contributions to psychoacoustics and beyond. It was at Harvard that he met B.F. Skinner (see entry), who introduced him to power functions in his experiments with rats. Stevens introduced the Stevens power law (1953), which concerns the relation between the strength of some form of energy, such as the sound pressure level of a tone, and the magnitude of the corresponding sensory experience, loudness in this example. He also made important contributions to the study of hearing and to an understanding of measurement theory and its role in psychology.

Major Literature

Stevens, Stanley Smith, and H. Davis. *Hearing: Its Psychology and Physiology*. New Jersey: John Wiley and Sons, Inc., 1938.

___. "Psychology and the Science of Science." *Psychological Bulletin* 36 (1939): 221–63.

___. "On the Theory of Scales of Measurement." *Science* 103 (1946).

___ (Ed.). *Handbook of Experimental Psychology*. New Jersey: John Wiley and Sons, Inc., 1951, 2004.

___. "On the Psychophysical Law." *Psychological Review* 64 (1957): 153–81.

___. *Psychophysics: Introduction to Its Perceptual, Neural, and Social Prospects.* New Jersey: John Wiley and Sons, Inc., 1975.

Stumpf, Carl (1848–1936)

PSYCHOLOGY OF SOUND AND MUSIC

Born in Wiesentheid, Lower Franconia, Germany, Carl Stumpf studied philosophy and theology with Franz Brentano (see entry) at Würzburg University in 1865, then studied philosophy and natural sciences at Göttingen University, where he gained a D.Phil. in 1868. Stumpf was privatdozent, Gottingen (1870–1873); professor of philosophy, University of Wurzburg (1873–1879); professor of philosophy, Prague University, Czechoslovakia (1879–1883); professor of philosophy, University of Halle, Germany (1884–1889); professor of philosophy, University of Munich, Germany (1889–1894); and professor of philosophy and director of the Institute of Experimental Psychology, Friedrich-Wilhelm University of Berlin. He founded the Berlin School of Experimental Psychology (1894–1922); he was joint president, 3rd International Congress of Psychology, Munich (1896); and rector, University of Berlin, Germany (1907–1908). He was awarded the Prussian Order of Merit.

Major Contributions

A talented musician, Stumpf learned to play six instruments and taught himself harmony and counterpoint. He is most noted for his research on the psychology of music and tone. When taking up his position at Berlin (1894), Stumpf transformed a small psychological laboratory founded by Hermann Ebbinghaus (see entry) into the *Psychologisches Institut,* which rivaled the psychological laboratory founded by Wilhelm Wundt (see entry) at the University of Leipzig. Continuing his research on tone psychology, he founded the journal *Beiträge zur Akustik und Musikwissenschaft* (*Contributions to Acoustics and Musicology*) in 1898, and in 1900 established an archive of primitive music. He was also a co-founder of the Berlin Society for Child Psychology (1900), and co-founder of the *Phonographic Archiv,* a collection of over 10,000 records of primitive music gathered by missionaries and travelers. He was director of a commission set up by the Ministry of Education to collect recordings of native dialects and songs from prisoners of war. In 1901 Stumpf and Otto Abraham recorded a visiting Siamese orchestra on wax cylinders.

In two important papers of 1907 Stumpf stressed that the experimental study of sensory and imaginal experience (e.g., images, sounds, colors) comes before the study of mental functions (e.g., perceiving, willing, desiring). Thus he drew into psychology his own version of phenomenology — the philosophy that concentrates on the examination of conscious phenomena.

Until Stumpf's retirement from Berlin in 1922 his institute had numerous famous students, for example Edmund Husserl (1859–1938) (founder of phenomenology); also Max Wertheimer, Wolfgang Köhler and Kurt Koffka (see entries). Stumpf also formed a panel (1907) of 13 eminent scientists, known as the Hans Commission, to study the claims that a horse named Clever Hans could count. Psychologist Oskar Pfungst eventually proved that the horse could not really count.

Major Literature

Stumpf, Carl. *Tonpsychologie* (2 vols). Leipzig: Hirzel, 1890.

___. *Erscheinungen und psychische Funktionen* (*Presentations and Mental States*). Hildesheim: Reimer, 1907.

___. *Zur Einteilung der Wissenschaften* (*On the Classification of Scientific Disciplines*). Hildesheim; Reimer, 1907.

Sullivan, Harry Stack (1892–1949)

INTERPERSONAL THEORY OF PSYCHIATRY

Born in Norwich, New York, Harry Stack Sullivan graduated in medicine (1917) from Chicago College of Medicine and Surgery. After working at St. Elizabeth's Hospital in Washington, D.C., and doing clinical research at Sheppard and Enoch Pratt Mental Hospital in Baltimore, Maryland (1925–1930), he was appointed to in the University of Maryland's School of Medicine. Sullivan helped to found the William Alanson White Psychiatric Foundation in 1933 and the Washington (D.C.) School of Psychiatry in 1936.

After World War II he helped establish the World Federation for Mental Health. In later life, he served as professor and head of the department of psychiatry in Georgetown University Medical School, Washington, D.C. He was editor of *Psychiatry* and chairman of the Council of Fellows of the Washington School of Psychiatry. Sullivan died in Paris and was buried in Arlington National Cemetery, Virginia.

Major Contributions

Sullivan developed a theory of psychiatry based on interpersonal relationships. He believed that anxiety and other psychiatric symptoms result from fundamental conflicts between the individual and his human environment and that personality development also takes place by a series of interactions with other people. While working at Sheppard and Enoch Pratt Hospital, Sullivan became acquainted with Adolf Meyer (see entry), whose practical psychotherapy emphasized psychological and social factors rather than neuropathology as the basis for psychiatric disorders.

Sullivan showed that, with sufficient contact, it is possible to understand schizophrenic patients, no matter how bizarre their behavior. He interpreted schizophrenia as the result of disturbed interpersonal relationships in early childhood; by appropriate psychotherapy, Sullivan believed, these sources of behavioral disturbance could be identified and eliminated. He extended his ideas to include group work with schizophrenics.

Sullivan differed from Sigmund Freud (see entry) in viewing the significance of the early parent-child relationship as being not primarily sexual but, rather, as an early quest for security by the child. Sullivan objected to studying mental illness in people isolated from society. Personality characteristics were, he considered, determined by the relationship between each individual and the people in his environment. Sullivan believed that personality can develop past adolescence and even well into adulthood. He called the seven stages in his developmental theory *epochs* (see also Erikson, Erik).

Major Literature

Sullivan, Harry Stack. *Conceptions of Modern Psychiatry.* New York: W.W. Norton, 1953. Montana: R.A. Kessinger Publishing Co., 2006.

___. *The Interpersonal Theory of Psychiatry.* New York: W.W. Norton, 1953, 1980.

___, Helen Swick Perry, and Mary Ladd Gawel. *The Psychiatric Interview.* New York: W.W. Norton, 1954, 1980.

Sullivan, Harry Stack. *Clinical Studies in Psychiatry.* New York: W.W. Norton, 1956, 1980.

___. *Schizophrenia as a Human Process.* New York: W.W. Norton, 1962, 1980.

___. *The Fusion pf Psychiatry and Social Sciences.* New York: W.W. Norton, 1964, 1980.

___. *Personal Psychopathology.* New York: W.W. Norton, 1972.

Sumner, Francis Cecil (1895–1954)
AFRICAN-AMERICAN PIONEER

Born in Pine Bluff, Arkansas, Francis Cecil Sumner gained a B.A. at Lincoln University in Jefferson City, Missouri (1915), a B.A. in English at Clark University, Worcester, Massachusetts (1916), and an M.A. at the University of Nebraska, Lincoln (1917). He saw military service (1918–1919) and then gained a Ph.D. in psychology at Clark University (1920). He was the first black man to receive a Ph.D; his dissertation was "Psychoanalysis of Freud and Adler." Sumner was professor of philosophy and psychology, Wilberforce University, Wilberforce, Ohio, and Southern University, Louisiana (1920–1921); instructor of psychology and philosophy, West Virginia Collegiate Institute, Charleston (now West Virginia State College) (1921); and professor and head of the Psychology Department, Howard University, Washington, D.C. (1928). Sumner was a member of the American Psychological Association, the American Association for the Advancement of Science, American Educational Research Association, Eastern Psychological Association, Southern Society for Philosophy and Psychology, and District of Columbia Psychological Association.

Major Contributions

Sumner was self-educated with the help of his parents, and his early education consisted of intense reading and writing assignments given to him by his father who, too, had been self-educated. Sumner enrolled at Lincoln University at the age of 15 and passed a written exam to be accepted because he did not have a high school diploma.

At Lincoln, two of the most important relationships he formed were with the president of Clark University, G. Stanley Hall (see entry), and with James P. Porter, dean of Clark University and professor of psychology. It was largely his regard for Hall that influenced Sumner's decision to focus on psychology, and Hall supported him in what he was doing for the advancement of many African-Americans at Clark and in the field of psychology. Throughout his career, Sumner was interested in psychological topics dealing with race and religion and did research in these areas, including a study to look at the "attitudes of blacks and whites toward the administration of social justice."

At Howard University — where one of his students was Kenneth Bancroft Clark (see entry) —

he pushed for and achieved an independent department of psychology. At the West Virginia Collegiate Institute, Sumner created a prestigious award that was given to a psychology student with the most outstanding essay on a particular topic. Sumner was a creator of abstracts for both the *Journal of Social Psychology* and the *Psychological Bulletin*. He was a member of Psi Chi, Pi Gamma Mu, and Kappa Alpha Psi.

Related Literature

Guthrie, Robert V. *Even The Rat Was White: A Historical View of Psychology* (2nd ed.). Boston: Allyn and Bacon, 1998.

Sawyer, Thomas. F. "Francis Cecil Sumner: His Views and Influence on African American Higher Education." *History of Psychology,* 3(2) (2000): 122–141.

Szasz, Thomas (1920)
ANTI-PSYCHIATRY

Born in Budapest, Hungary, Thomas Szasz gained an A.B. with honors in physics (1941) and an M.D. (1944) at the University of Cincinnati, Ohio. He was medical resident, Cincinnati General Hospital (1945–1946) and psychiatric resident, University of Chicago Clinics, Illinois (1946–1948). He worked at the Institute for Juvenile Research, Chicago (1949), had psychoanalytic training, Chicago Institute for Psychoanalysis (1947–1950), and gained his diploma, Chicago Institute for Psychoanalysis (1950), diplomate, National Board of Medical Examiners (1947–1950), and diplomate in psychiatry, American Board of Psychiatry and Neurology (1951).

He was staff member, Chicago Institute for Psychoanalysis (1951–1956); professor of psychiatry, State University of New York Health Science Center, Syracuse, New York (1956–1990); visiting professor, Department of Psychiatry, University of Wisconsin, Madison (1962); visiting professor, Marquette University School of Medicine, Milwaukee, Wisconsin (1968); co-founder, the Citizens Commission of Human Rights (1969); and visiting professor, New Mexico State University, Las Cruces, New Mexico (1981).

Szasz has been honored with many awards in America, Great Britain, Australia, and Guatemala. He has been listed in *Guide to America's Top Physicians*, Consumers' Research Council of America, 2003, and in "35 Heroes of Freedom," by *Reason* in December 2003. He is distinguished life fellow, American Psychiatric Association; life member, American Psychoanalytic Association; International Psychoanalytic Association; and fellow, International Academy of Forensic Psychology.

Major Contributions

A controversial figure for over four decades, Szasz is professor of psychiatry emeritus at the State University of New York Health Science Center in Syracuse, New York, and adjunct scholar at the Cato Institute, Washington, D.C. Szasz is a critic of the moral and scientific foundations of psychiatry and of the social control aims of medicine in modern society, as well as of scientism.

He argues that labeling people as, for example, schizophrenics, is dehumanizing, and that mental disorders are social and ethical judgments, not matters of medical facts. He is not opposed to the practice of psychiatry but maintains that psychiatry should be a contractual service between consenting adults with no state involvement. He favors the abolition of involuntary hospitalization for mental illness. While people behave and think in ways that are very disturbing, this does not mean they have a disease. According to Szasz, disease can only be found on the autopsy table. For Szasz, psychiatry has become the secular state religion.

Major Literature

Szasz, Thomas. *The Myth of Mental Illness.* New York: Paul B. Hoeber, Inc., 1961. Harper and Row, 1984.

___. *Law, Liberty, and Psychiatry.* New York: Macmillan, 1963. Syracuse, New York: Syracuse University Press, 1989.

___. *The Ethics of Psychoanalysis.* New York: Basic Books, 1965. Syracuse, New York: Syracuse University Press, 1989.

___. *Ceremonial Chemistry.* Garden City, New York: Doubleday Anchor, 1974. Syracuse, New York: Syracuse University Press, 2003.

___. *The Myth of Psychotherapy.* Garden City, New York: Doubleday Anchor, 1978. Syracuse, New York: Syracuse University Press, 1988.

___. *Our Right to Drugs.* Syracuse, New York: Syracuse University Press, 1996.

___. *The Manufacture of Madness.* New York: Harper Collins Publishers, Inc., 1997.

___. *The Meaning of Mind.* Syracuse, New York: Syracuse University Press, 2002.

Tajfel, Henri (1919–1982)
SOCIAL PSYCHOLOGY

Born in Wloclawek, Poland, of Polish-Jewish parentage, at the outbreak of the Second World War, Henri Tajfel was studying chemistry at the Sorbonne, Paris. While serving in the French army he was captured by the Germans. He kept his Jewish identity hidden and survived a series of prisoner of war camps, but his whole family was wiped out. After the war, Tajfel worked with a number of organizations, including the U.N. Refugee Organization, to help rebuild the lives of orphans and concentration camp survivors. He immigrated to Britain in 1946 and gained his B.A. and Ph.D. in psychology from Birkbeck College, London University, and from 1967 to 1982 he was professor in social psychology at Bristol.

He was also supernumerary fellow, Linacre College, Oxford; fellow, Centre for Advanced Studies in the Behavioral Sciences; president, European Association of Experimental Social Psychology, 1969–72; professor extraordinarius, University of Leiden, Netherlands; co-editor, *European Journal of Social Psychology*; editor, *European Social Psychology Monographs*; editorial board, *European Studies in Social Psychology*.

Major Contributions

Tajfel's early social psychology work was part of the so-called "new look," concerned with processes of perceptual overestimation. He was critical of psychologists who were indifferent to human society. At Bristol he conducted "minimal group experiments." These studies led Tajfel and John Turner (professor of psychology and Australian Professorial Fellow) to develop social identity theory (SIT).

The idea behind SIT is that people define ourselves in terms of the categories of which they are members and then, in order to achieve a positive self-definition, seek to advantage the ingroup over comparison out-groups. The questions Tajfel asks are: if people seek positive social identities, what do they do if they are defined negatively in an unequal social world, as Jews in an anti–Semitic world, blacks in a racist world, women in a sexist world? When do they act collectively to challenge such inequalities? In other words, social identity theory is more a theory of social change than social discrimination and the concept of social identity is primarily intended as a mediating concept in the explanation of social change.

Tajfel more than anyone else brought European social psychology into being. To honor Tajfel, in 1982, an Henri Tajfel Lecture was founded by the European Association of Experimental Social Psychology. The address is normally published in a subsequent issue of the *European Journal of Social Psychology*.

Major Literature

Tajfel, Henri, and J.L.M. Dawson. *Disappointed Guests*. Oxford, England: Oxford University Press, 1965.

Tajfel, Henri. *The Social Psychology of Minorities*. London, England: Minority Rights Group International, 1978.

___, and J.C. Turner. "The Social Identity Theory of Intergroup Behavior." In W.G. Austin and S. Worchel (Eds.), *The Social Psychology of Intergroup Relations* (pp. 7–24). Chicago, Illinois: Nelson-Hall, 1979.

Tajfel, Henri. *Human Groups and Social Categories: Studies in Social Psychology*. Cambridge, England: Cambridge University Press, 1982.

Tajfel, Henri (Ed.). *The Social Dimension: European Developments in Social Psychology* (2 volumes). Cambridge, England: Cambridge University Press, 1984.

Terman, Lewis Madison (1877–1956)
INTELLIGENCE TESTING

Born in Johnson County, Indiana, Lewis Madison Terman gained a B.A. and an M.A. at Indiana University, Bloomington (1903), and a Ph.D. in psychology at Clark University, Worcester, Massachusetts (1905). He was school principal, San Bernardino, California (1905) and professor, Los Angeles Normal School (1907). He was at Stanford University, California, from 1910 to 1945, serving as professor of education (1916), professor of cognitive psychology (1922), and chairman of the psychology department (1922–1945).

Major Contributions

During World War I, Terman served in the United States military, contributing to developing the first notable mass-group intelligence testing in the U.S. In 1916 he published the *Stanford Revision of the Binet-Simon Scale*, based on previous work by Alfred Binet (see entry) and Theodore de Simon of France. The sample covered in the current revised edition (1986) is larger and more diverse, which minimizes the gender and racial inequities that had been criticized in earlier versions.

Unlike Binet and Simon, whose goal was to identify less able school children in order to aid them with the required care, Terman adopted William Stern's suggestion of IQ as a measure of general intelligence. Terman proposed using IQ tests to classify children and put them on the appropriate job track. He believed IQ was inherited and was the strongest predictor of one's ultimate success in life.

In 1921 he launched a comprehensive long-term program for the study of 1,528 California gifted children with IQs exceeding 140 (see also, Pauline Sears and Robert Sears). He found that gifted children — colloquially referred to as "Termites"— were generally taller, in better health, better developed physically, and better adapted socially than other children. By the age of 35, 80 percent of the gifted children had posts in the highest occupational groups (semi-professional or higher business) as contrasted with 14 percent of the ordinary population; 20 percent were already mentioned in *Who's Who in America* or *American Men of Science,* and some had achieved international reputations.

One of the most significant differences, according to Terman, was the greater drive to achieve and the greater mental and social adjustment of the gifted group as compared with the non-gifted. Terman later joined the Human Betterment Foundation, a Pasadena-based eugenics group founded by E.S. Gosney in 1928 that had as part of its agenda the promotion and enforcement of compulsory sterilization laws in California.

Major Literature

Terman, Lewis Madison. *The Measurement of Intelligence.* Boston, Massachusetts: Houghton Mifflin, 1916.
___. *The Use of Intelligence Tests.* Boston, Massachusetts: Houghton Mifflin, 1916.
___. *The Intelligence of School Children.* Boston, Massachusetts: Houghton Mifflin, 1919.
___. *Genetic Studies of Genius.* Palo Alto, California: Stanford University Press, 1925, 1947, 1959.
___. *Mental and Physical Traits of a Thousand Gifted Children.* Palo Alto, California: Stanford University Press, 1926, 1981.
___. *Psychological Factors in Marital Happiness.* Columbus, Ohio: McGraw-Hill, 1938.

Thompson, Clara Mabel (1893–1958)

PSYCHOLOGY OF WOMEN

Born in Providence, Rhode Island, Clara Mabel Thompson gained an M.D. from Johns Hopkins University in Baltimore, Maryland (1920), and it was at Hopkins where her interest in psychiatry and psychoanalysis was fostered. After an internship at the New York Infirmary for Women and Children, she started a three year residency at the Phipps Clinic, Hopkins University, under Adolf Meyer (see entry), where she also formed a friendship with Harry Stack Sullivan (see entry).

She left Johns Hopkins in 1925, established a private practice in Baltimore, and began teaching mental hygiene at Vassar College, New York. In 1930 Stack Sullivan organized the Washington-Baltimore Psychoanalytic Society and Thompson was elected as its first president. In 1931 she left for Budapest to undergo psychoanalysis with Sandor Ferenczi (see entry). Her analysis, which had actually started with Ferenczi in 1927 when Ferenczi lived in America, ended in 1933 when Ferenczi died.

On her return to America, Thompson set up practice in New York where, through her friendship with Karen Horney (see entry), she lectured on psychoanalysis at the New York Psychoanalytic Institute until Horney was forced to resign because of her unorthodox approach to analysis. Thompson, with others, resigned in protest and joined Horney in setting up the American Association for the Advancement of Psychoanalysis. When Eric Fromm (see entry) was ousted from the association, on account of lack of a medical degree, Thompson resigned in protest, taking her students with her. From 1943 to 1958 she was director of the William Alanson White Psychiatric Foundation School in New York, where she developed a liberal academic and holistic approach of psychoanalytic concepts, anthropology and social psychology.

In her paper "Towards a Psychology of Women" (1953), Thompson identifies many of the major issues facing women at that time, focusing mainly on childbirth, menopause, and women's roles in sex. In focusing on women's issues and recognizing the influence of cultural factors, she broke with mainline Freudian psychoanalysis. She also points out the conflict between women's social role as the self-sacrificing caretaker and the drive for success as women become more educated and begin to take their place in the professional world. Also present in this paper is a critique of Freud's theory, which she believes was biased toward the superiority of men. She also challenges Freud's theory of women and their sexual role by attempting to define a more positive aspect to women's sexuality.

Major Literature

Thompson, Clara Mabel. *Psychoanalysis: Evolution and Development.* New York: Thomas Nelson and Sons, 1950.
___. "Towards a Psychology of Women." *Pastoral Psychology* 4 (34) (1953): 29–38.
___. "The Different Schools of Psychoanalysis." *American Journal of Nursing* 57 (1957): 1304–1307.
___, and M.R. Green. *Interpersonal Psychoanalysis.* Jackson, Tennessee: Basic Books, 1964.
Thompson, Clara Mabel. *Interpersonal Psychoanalysis: The*

Selected Papers of Clara M. Thompson. Jackson, Tennessee: Basic Books, 1964.

Thorndike, Edward Lee
(1874–1949)
OPERANT CONDITIONING

Born in Williamsburg, Massachusetts, Thorndike gained an A.B. in English at Wesleyan University, Middletown, Connecticut (1895). He studied at Harvard University, Cambridge, Massachusetts, under William James (see entry), but earned his Ph.D. in psychology at Columbia University, New York, under the guidance of James McKeen Cattell (see entry) (1898).

He was assistant professor of pedagogy at Case Western Reserve University, Cleveland, Ohio (1898). At Teachers College, Columbia University, he was lecturer (1899–1901); adjunct professor of educational psychology (1901 to 1904); professor of psychology (1904–1940); professor emeritus (1941–1949); and director of the psychology division at the Institute of Educational Research (1922–1940). He was William James Lecturer, Harvard University (1942–1943).

Thorndike was president of the American Psychological Association (1912), president of American Association for the Advancement of Science (1934) and was awarded seven honorary degrees from universities in America, Scotland and Greece.

Major Contributions

Thorndike's Ph.D. thesis, "Animal Intelligence: An Experimental Study of the Associative Processes in Animals," in which he concluded that an experimental approach is the only way to understand learning, was published in 1911 (New York: Macmillan and Cosmo Publications, India, 2003). His thesis showed that cats learn through a gradual process of trial and error. Such trial and error methods in learning leads to the "stamping in" of correct responses. In his thesis he established his famous "Law of Effect." Thorndike went on to be the most prolific of writers in the various divisions of psychology. Thorndike:

- introduced the use of animals and humans in controlled settings to test and prove (or disprove) theories that predicted behavior;
- emphasized the consequences of behaviors as key determiners of what is learned and what is not;
- made the study of child development into an objective science;
- established the use of tests and statistical models in education and psychology;
- wrote dictionaries for various age groups of children and for teachers; and
- paved the way for the behaviorism of B.F. Skinner and John B. Watson (see entries).

Major Literature
(books still in print)

Thorndike, Edward Lee. *First Dictionary*. London: University of London Press, 1964.
___. *Human Learning*. Cambridge, Massachusetts: MIT Press, 1966.
___. *Fundamentals of Learning*. New York: Ams Press Inc., 1972.
___. *Human Nature and the Social Order*. Cambridge, Massachusetts: MIT Press, 1974.
___. *Teacher's Word Book of the Twenty Thousand Words Found Most Frequently and Widely in General Reading*. Farmington Hills, Minnesota: Gale Group, 1975.
___. *Psychology of Wants, Interests and Attitudes*. New York: Johnson Reprint Corporation, 1988.
___. *Classics in Psychology: An Introduction to the Theory of Mental and Social Measurements* Vol. 38. 1904. London, England: Continuum International Publishing Group Ltd., Thoemmes, 1998.

Thurstone, Louis Leon
(1887–1955)
PSYCHOMETRICS AND PSYCHOPHYSICS

Born in Chicago, Illinois, Louis Leon Thurstone gained a master of engineering degree at Cornell University, Ithaca, New York (1912), and was assistant to Thomas A. Edison (1912). Thurstone taught descriptive geometry and drafting at the College of Engineering, University of Minnesota (1912–1914). He was assistant, Division of Applied Psychology at the Carnegie Institute of Technology (1915–1917) and gained a Ph.D. in psychology at the University of Chicago, Illinois (1917).

He was professor, Carnegie Institute of Technology, Pittsburgh, Pennsylvania (1917–1923), then worked at the Institute for Government Research, Washington, D.C. (1923); was professor, University of Chicago, where he established the Psychometric Laboratory (1924–1952); and professor of psychology and director, Psychometric Laboratory, University of North Carolina at Chapel Hill (1952–1955), renamed the L.L. Thurstone Psychometric Laboratory.

Thurstone was president of American Psychological Association (1932) and founder and first president of the American Psychometric Society (1936). He received numerous awards, including Best Article, American Psychological Association

(1949); Centennial Award, Northwestern University, Evanston, Illinois (1951); and honorary doctorate, University of Göteborg, Sweden (1954).

Major Contributions

Thurstone was instrumental in the development of psychometrics — the science that measures mental functions. With his wife, Thelma Gwinn Thurstone (see entry), he developed statistical techniques for analyzing multiple factors of performance on psychological tests. He attacked the concept of an ideal "mental age," which was commonly used in intelligence testing at that time, advocating instead the use of percentile rankings to compare performance. Challenging Charles Spearman's (see entry) emphasis on general (g) intelligence, and using his new approach to factor analysis, Thurstone found that intelligent behavior does not arise from a general factor, but rather emerges from seven independent factors that he called *primary abilities*: word fluency, verbal comprehension, spatial visualization, number facility, associative memory, reasoning, and perceptual speed.

Thurstone developed the Primary Mental Abilities Test (1938), which measured these variables. He also developed a rating scale for locating individual attitudes and opinions along a continuum between extremes. Further tests revealed that the seven primary abilities were not entirely separate; he did find evidence of g. The final version of his theory was a compromise that accounted for the presence of both a general factor and the seven specific abilities. This compromise helped lay the groundwork for future researchers who proposed hierarchical theories and theories of multiple intelligences. He is also responsible for the standardized mean and standard deviation of IQ scores used today, as opposed to the Intelligence Test system originally used by Alfred Binet (see entry). Thurstone was an environmentalist, and suggested an early system for generating hydroelectric power from rivers and waterfalls.

Major Literature

Thurstone, Louis Leon. *The Nature of Intelligence*. London: Taylor and Francis Books Ltd., Routledge, 1924 and 1999.
___. "Multiple-Factor Analysis." *Psychological Review* 38 (1931): 406–27.
___. "The Vectors of the Mind." *Psychological Review* 41 (1934): 1–32.
___. *Primary Mental Abilities*. Chicago: University of Chicago Press, 1938 and 1969.

___, and T.G. Thurstone. *Factorial Studies of Intelligence*. Chicago: University of Chicago Press, 1941.
Thurstone, Louis Leon. *Multiple-Factor Analysis*. Chicago: University of Chicago Press, 1947.

Thurstone, Thelma Gwinn (1897–1993)
INTELLIGENCE TESTING

Thelma Gwinn was born in Hume, Missouri. She earned a B.A. (1917) and B.S. in education (1920) at the University of Missouri, St. Louis, an M.A. in psychology at Carnegie Institute of Technology, Pittsburgh, Pennsylvania (1923), and a Ph.D. in psychology at the University of Chicago, Illinois (1926). She was mental tester and statistician, American Council of Education (1924–1948); instructor in psychology, Teachers College, Chicago (1938–1942); research associate, University of Chicago (1942–1952); director, Division of Child Study, Chicago Public Schools (1948–1952); professor of education, University of North Carolina, Chapel Hill (1952–1970); and director, Psychometric Laboratory, University of North Carolina (1955–1957).

Major Contributions

Thelma Thurstone's work in creating and improving ability and achievement tests started in 1923 and continued over a 60-year period. During 1923 and 1924, L.L. Thurstone (see entry) and Thelma Gwinn both were employed in the foundation-supported Institute for Government Research in Washington, D.C., with responsibility for suggesting improvements in the quality of civil service examinations. They married in 1924, and set up a lifetime partnership in designing psychological tests.

Her dissertation was a pioneering effort to establish a basic relation in test theory between item difficulty and the discriminating power of a test. Using real data — responses from 100 sixth-grade students to 1,000 spelling items — she generated results for sets of 50-item spelling tests. Each test contained items of uniform difficulty, but at different levels of difficulty from test to test.

From 1923 onward, the husband and wife team developed many different tests, which were applied to schools and colleges and were continually updated. In 1946, with the support of the Thurstones, the Science Research Associates (SRA) was formed as a vehicle for publishing the Primary Mental Abilities Tests. Thelma Thurstone was the sole author of curricular materials and achievement tests for use in elementary classrooms — the *Learning to Think* series, and *Reading for Understanding*. The former was described as teaching children to perceive identities, similarities, and differences; to increase vocabulary; to reason in cause-effect and genus-species terms; to reason quantitatively; and to improve eye-hand coordination. The latter emphasized teaching reading comprehension from primary to college levels, and required students to find implied answers using inferential comprehension.

Major Literature

Thurstone, Thelma Gwinn. *Learning to Think*. Columbus, Ohio: McGraw-Hill Education, 1941, 1950, 1957, 1961.
___. *Reading for Understanding*. Columbus, Ohio: McGraw-Hill Education, 1958, 1963, 1965, 1978, 1980.
___. *Teacher's Handbook*. Bloomington, Illinois: Schools Publishing Co., 2001.
___. *Reading for Understanding Teacher's Handbook for Levels B and C*. Columbus, Ohio: McGraw-Hill Education, 2001.

Titchener, Edward Bradford (1867–1927)
PSYCHOLOGY OF CONSCIOUSNESS

Born in Chichester, West Sussex, England, he gained a B.A. at Oxford University, England (1890), a Ph.D. at Leipzig University, Germany (1892), and studied at under Wilhelm Wundt (see entry). At Cornell University in Ithaca, New York, Titchener was head of the psychology department (1892–1927); full professor of psychology (1895); founded the first psychology laboratory in the United States; was a charter member of the American Psychological Association (1892); and founded the Society of Experimental Psychologists (1904). He was editor, *Studies from the Department of Psychology of Cornell University* (1894–1927); American editor, *Mind* (1894–1917); and editor, *American Journal of Psychology* (1895–1927).

Major Contributions

Titchener brought "new psychology" — the experimental psychology of Wundt and others — to the United States, changing the discipline from mental philosophy to psychology as it is currently practiced. Titchener attempted to classify the structures of the mind in much the same way as a chemist breaks down chemicals into their component parts — water into hydrogen and oxygen, for example. Just as hydrogen and oxygen are structures of a chemical compound, so sensations

and thoughts are structures of the mind. He became the acknowledged leader of the school of structuralism — a study of the elemental structures of consciousness based on introspection — which was born at Cornell.

Titchener refused to consider applied psychology as being valid; he had no interest in studying animals, children, abnormal behavior, or individual differences. For Titchener, psychology was the study of experience from the point of view of the experiencing individual. All elements must exist in the consciousness. He marginalized habit, action, instinct, and any Freudian mechanism. For him the characteristics of mental processes were quality, intensity, duration, clearness, and extensity.

In 1923, he initiated change in his system, abandoning the elemental approach and considering a phenomenological approach to the study of consciousness. He was criticized as being a misogynist because he excluded women. He translated 11 German works, including titles by Wilhelm Wundt and Oswald Külpe. He himself wrote eight works, many of which went through several revised editions and were translated into a number of languages.

Major Literature

Titchener, Edward Bradford. *Experimental Psychology* (two student manuals and two teachers' manuals). New York: Macmillan, 1901–1905.
___. *Lectures on the Elementary Psychology of Feeling and Attention*. New York: Macmillan, 1908. Manchester, New Hampshire: Ayer Co. Publishers, 1973.
___. *A Textbook of Psychology*. New York: Macmillan, 1910.
___. *Systematic Psychology: Prolegomena*. New York: Macmillan, 1929. New York: Cornell University Press, 1972.
Meyer, Adolf, and Edward Bradford Titchener. *Defining American Psychology: The Correspondence Between Adolf Meyer and Edward Bradford Titchener*. Baltimore: Johns Hopkins University Press, 1990.

Tizard, Jack (1919–1979)
LEARNING DIFFICULTIES

Born in Stratford, New Zealand, Tizard gained an M.A., in New Zealand in psychology and philosophy under Karl Popper (1940). During World War II, he served in an ambulance unit, mainly in North Africa; he was at the battle of El Alamein. He was awarded a scholarship to study in Britain; he spent some time with Karl Popper at the London School of Economics teaching logic and was a lecturer in psychology at St. Andrews

University, Scotland. In 1948 he worked under Sir Aubrey Lewis at the Social Psychiatry Research Unit, Institute of Psychiatry, London. He gained a B.Litt. at the University of Oxford (1948) and a Ph.D. from the University of London (1951).

Tizard was chairman, Association of Child Psychology and Psychiatry (1964–1965); chairman, Education Research Board, Social Science Research Council (1973); and president, British Psychological Society (1975–1976). His awards and honors include the Research Award, American Association on Mental Deficiency (1969–1971); Kennedy International Scientific Award (1968); Commander of the British Empire (1973); honorary member, British Pediatric Association; and member of the Society for Social Medicine.

Major Contributions

Tizard's work with people with severe learning difficulties led his appointment by the World Health Organization to visit various countries in the world to report on policy and provision, especially for disabled children. In Russia he was a guest of the famous neuropsychologist Alexander Luria (see entry). At the time, thousands of people lived in large institutions, where their treatment and their compulsory detention were administered in a way that was often inhumane and under outdated legislation. He became involved with the National Council for Civil Liberties, and following a Royal Commission on the issue, a new Mental Health Act was passed in 1959 involving a major switch from compulsory to voluntary residence for people living in institutions. In one experiment Tizard demonstrated the improvement in language development and behavior that followed the transfer of severely retarded children from a large hospital to a small residential nursery school.

In 1973 Tizard founded the Thomas Coram Research Unit as part of the Institute of Education, University of London. Its principal function is to carry out policy-relevant research within a changing world. The focus of its research is children and young people both within and outside their families. The Jack Tizard School, South Africa Road, London, is now a day school for pupils age 2–19 years with a range of severe learning difficulties, including profound and multiple learning difficulties. The school's goal is to enable each pupil to develop to his or her full potential. The ethos of the school is founded on the principle of respect for all regardless of gender, race, sexuality, social background, ability, nationality or religion.

Major Literature

Tizard, Jack. *Mentally Handicapped and Their Families: A Social Survey*. Oxford, England: Oxford University Press, 1961.

___. *Community Services for the Mentally Handicapped*. Oxford, England: Oxford University Press, 1964.

___. *Integration of the Handicapped in Society*. London: Edutext Publications, 1966.

___. *All Our Children: Pre-School Services in a Changing Society*. London, England: Temple Smith, 1976.

Tolman, Edward Chace (1886–1959)
COGNITIVE APPROACH TO LEARNING

Born in Newton, Massachusetts, Edward Chace Tolman gained a B.Sc. in electrochemistry (1911) and an M.A. (1912) at the Massachusetts Institute of Technology, and a Ph.D. with a dissertation on retroactive inhibition (1915) at Harvard University, Cambridge, Massachusetts. He was instructor in psychology at Northwestern University, Evanston, Illinois (1915). At the University of California, Berkeley, he was instructor (1918–1920); assistant professor (1920–1922); associate professor (1923–1928); professor 1928–1954); and professor emeritus from 1954.

He was president of the American Psychological Association (APA) (1937) and chairman of Lewin's Society for the Psychological Study of Social Issues (1940). He received the Distinguished Scientific Contributions Award, APA (1957) and an honorary LL.D., University of California (1959).

Major Contributions

In 1912, Tolman studied Gestalt at Giessen, Germany. Then at Harvard he studied nonsense syllable learning under Hugo Munsterberg (see entry) and Herbert Langfeld (1879–1958). Raised in a Quaker family, Tolman was twice in conflict with the authorities: he was dismissed from Northwestern University (1918) for a pacifist contribution to a student publication, and in 1949 when he refused to sign the loyalty oath as imposed by the University of California, Berkeley.

Tolman developed purposive, or molar, behaviorism, which attempts to explore the entire action of the total organism and is often considered the bridge between behaviorism and cognitive theory. "Purposive" means that behavior is regulated in accordance with objectively determinable ends; "molar" comes from Gestalt and means that it is holistic and cannot be broken down. Around

1922 he began to assert that the stimulus-response behaviorism of John B. Watson was too limited; it was molecular and did not acknowledge the problems of goal-seeking behavior. Although remaining a behaviorist, Tolman suggested that behavior is goal-directed, organized around the purposes served and guided by cognitive processes.

One of his most well known studies examined the role that reinforcement plays in the way that rats learn their way through complex mazes, and led to the theory of latent learning, which describes learning that occurs in the absence of an obvious reward. His idea of cognitive maps is one of his theories that is still used today. Cognitive maps were the precursor to concepts of spatial memory and spatial thinking.

In 1963, the University of California, Berkeley, named its newly constructed education and psychology faculty building Tolman Hall in his honor.

Major Literature

Tolman, Edward Chase. "A New Formula for Behaviorism." *Psychological Review* 29 (1922): 44–53.
___. *Purposive Behavior in Animals and Men.* New York: Appleton-Century-Crofts, 1932.
___. "The Determinants of Behavior at a Choice Point." *Psychological Review* 45 (1938): 1–41.
___. *Drives Towards War.* New York: Appleton-Century-Crofts, 1942.
___, B.F. Ritchie, and D. Kalish. "Studies in Spatial Learning: II. Place Learning Versus Response Learning." *Journal of Experimental Psychology* 37 (1946): 385–392.
Tolman, Edward Chase. "Cognitive Maps in Rats and Men." *Psychological Review* 55 (1948): 189–208.
___. "Principles of Performance." *Psychological Review* 62 (1955): 315–326.

Torrance, Ellis Paul
(1915–2003)
CREATIVITY

Born in Milledgeville, Georgia, Ellis Paul Torrance gained a B.A. at Mercer University, Atlanta, Georgia (1940); an M.S. at the University of Minnesota, Minneapolis (1944); and a Ph.D. at the University of Michigan, Ann Arbor (1951). At Minneapolis he was associate professor of educational research, Bureau of Educational Research and General Education (1957), and director (1958–1966). At University of Georgia, Athens, he was professor of educational psychology (1967–1984) and professor emeritus (1984).

His awards and honors include the Distinguished Contributions Award, the Association for the Gifted Council for Exceptional Children (1973); National Association for Gifted Children, Distinguished Scholar (1974); Creative Education Foundation Founder's Medal (1979); fellow, National Academy of Physical Education (1979); National Affiliation of Arts Educators Award for contributions to art education (1980); Arthur Lipper Award for contributions to human creativity (1982); and Hall of Fame, National Association of Creative Children and Adults (1985). He was on the editorial board of nine educational journals, including *Journal of Group Psychotherapy.*

Major Contributions

Torrance is known as "the Father of Creativity," or "the Creativity Man." He developed the benchmark method for quantifying creativity and invented the Torrance Tests of Creative Thinking (TTCT) (1966), which proved that the IQ test was not the only way to measure intelligence. He created the Future Problem Solving Program International (FPSPI) based in Melbourne, Florida. FPSPI engages students in creative problem solving, stimulates critical and creative thinking skills and encourages students to develop a vision for the future. In 1984, the University of Georgia established the Torrance Center for Creative Studies. Because of the work of this one man, children and adults all over the world have been given the opportunity and wherewithal to develop their creative talent.

Manifesto for Children, a film documenting Torrance's life and work, was broadcast on Georgia Public Television in the fall of 2000. The documentary focused on the 40-year longitudinal study that followed 215 young adults who attended two elementary schools in Minnesota from 1958 to 1964. The students were given creativity tests each year and were followed up with a questionnaire in 1980. The *Manifesto* was developed to describe their ongoing struggle to maintain their creativity and use their strengths to create their careers and provide guidance to children. In 1998, the participants were followed up to get a picture of their creative achievements and to validate the manifesto. Some of the 101 respondents had attained eminence, while others had attained only mediocre careers.

Torrance authored of over 2,000 books, monographs, articles, reports, tests, manuals and instruction materials.

Major Literature

Torrance, Ellis Paul. *Education and the Creative Potential.* Minneapolis: Minnesota University Press, 1963.

___. *Rewarding Creative Behavior: Experiments in Classroom Creativity*. New Jersey: Prentice-Hall, 1965.

___. *Mental Health and Achievement: Increasing Potential and Reducing School Dropout*. New Jersey: John Wiley and Sons, Inc., 1965.

___. *Gifted Children in the Classroom*. New York: Collier-Macmillan, 1965.

___. *Creativity in the Classroom*. Washington, D.C.: National Education Association, 1977.

Torrey, Edwin Fuller (1937–)
TREATMENT OF SCHIZOPHRENIA

Born in Utica, New York, Torrey earned a bachelor's degree, with great honor, from Princeton University, New Jersey; he received a medical doctor's degree from the McGill University School of Medicine, Montreal, Quebec, Canada, and a master's degree in anthropology from Stanford University, California. He trained in psychiatry at Stanford University School of Medicine.

He practiced general medicine for two years as a Peace Corps physician in Ethiopia, in the South Bronx, New York, and in Alaska in the Indian Health Service. From 1970 to 1975, he was a special assistant to the director, National Institute of Mental Health.

In March 2006, The *Washington Post* referred to Torrey as "the most famous psychiatrist in America." He is president of the board of the Treatment Advocacy Center (TAC) in Arlington, Virginia, a national nonprofit advocacy organization dedicated to eliminating legal and clinical barriers to treatment of severe mental illnesses. TAC supports involuntary treatment when deemed appropriate by a judge (at the urging of the patient's psychiatrist and family members).

He is the associate director for laboratory research of the Stanley Medical Research Institute in Chevy Chase, Maryland, the largest private provider of research on schizophrenia and bipolar disorder in the U.S. The institute also maintains a collection of postmortem brain tissue from individuals with schizophrenia, bipolar disorder, and major depression and from unaffected controls, which are made available to researchers without charge. The institute has been sued for allegedly taking brains for use in research without proper consent; one lawsuit (2005) was settled out of court.

Torrey opposes the views of Thomas Szasz and R.D. Laing (see entries) and is also opposed by those who criticize involuntary detention, including the Scientologists (see Szasz). When Torrey first became a psychiatrist, it was commonly thought schizophrenia was caused by bad parenting. That his sister, Rhoda, had schizophrenia and Torrey himself did not led him to question evidence for this theory. Although there is a belief that schizophrenia is a biologically based illness, there is still no biological diagnostic test for schizophrenia. In searching for a cure, Torrey has studied whether a parasite in cat droppings causes schizophrenia. He is testing antibiotics against the feline parasite *Toxoplasma gondii* to treat people with the disorder.

In 1999, Torrey received a research award from the International Congress of Schizophrenia. In 2005, a tribute to Torrey was included in the National Alliance on Mental Illness 25th Anniversary Celebratory Donor Wall.

Major Literature

Torrey, Edwin Fuller. *Schizophrenia and Civilization*. Lanham, Maryland: Rowman and Littlefield Publishers, Inc., Jason Aronson, 1980.

Torrey, Edwin Fuller. *Surviving Schizophrenia*. New York: Harper Collins Publishers, Inc., (1983, 2001).

___. *The Mind Game: Witchdoctors and Psychiatrists*. Lanham, Maryland: Rowman and Littlefield Publishers, Inc., 1986.

___, and Judy Miller. *The Invisible Plague: The Rise of Mental Illness from 1750 to the Present*. Piscataway, New Jersey: Rutgers University Press, 2002.

Treisman, Anne (1935)
VISUAL ATTENTION AND MEMORY

Anne (Taylor) Treisman was born in Wakefield, England, and gained a B.A. at the University of Cambridge, England, and a D.Phil. at Oxford, England (1962); her doctoral thesis was titled "Selective Attention and Speech Perception." She was research assistant to professor R.C. Oldfield, Department of Experimental Psychology, University of Oxford (1961–1963). From 1961 onward, she was on the faculties of Trinity College in Cambridge, University of Oxford, University of British Columbia in Vancouver, and the University of California at Berkeley. She was a member of Medical Research Council, Psycholinguistics Research Unit, Department of Experimental Psychology, University of Cambridge (1963–1966); visiting research scientist, Behavioral Sciences Department, Bell Telephone Laboratories, Murray Hill, New Jersey (1966–1967); and visiting scholar, Russell Sage Foundation, New York (1991–1992).

Her honors include the Spearman Medal of the British Psychological Society for Experimental Research (1963); James McKeen Cattell Sabbatical Award (1982); fellow of the Royal Society, London (1989); Distinguished Scientific Contribution Award of the American Psychological Association (1990); the William James Fellow Award (2002); and honorary professor in Institute of Psychology, Chinese Academy of Sciences (2004).

Major Contributions

Currently professor of psychology at Princeton University, New Jersey, Treisman's areas of research are visual attention, object perception, memory, "binding problem," patients with brain damage, object perception, global attention, perception of statistical properties, conscious awareness, and visual working memory. One of her most influential works is the feature integration theory (FIT) of attention, first published in 1986.

Feature integration, which has had a broad impact both within and outside psychology, is still an essential theory in the field of visual attention, although it is not without its critics. Her studies demonstrated that early vision encodes features such as color, form, orientation, and others, in separate "feature maps" and that without spatial attention these features can bind randomly to form illusory conjunctions and deficits in selection. This work has formed the basis for thousands of experiments in cognitive psychology, vision sciences, cognitive science, neuropsychology and cognitive neuroscience.

At about the same time as FIT was proposed, neuroscientists were working out how "binding" occurred — how the visual system recombines luminance, color, shape, size, motion, and so on. By testing patients with selective attention problems, Treisman and her students and colleagues first demonstrated that the binding problem could be a real problem in everyday life and that one solution required spatial attention.

Major Literature

Humphreys, Glyn, John Duncan, and Anne Treisman. *Attention, Space and Action: Studies in Cognitive Neuroscience.* Oxford, England: Oxford University Press, 1999.

Schendel, Krista L., L.C. Robertson, and Anne Treisman. "Objects and Their Locations in Exogenous Cueing." *Perception and Psychophysics* 63 (2001): 577–594.

Wheeler, M.E., and Anne Treisman. "Binding in Short-Term Visual Memory." *Journal of Experimental Psychology*, General 131 (2002): 48–64.

Chong, S.C., and Anne Treisman. "Representation of Statistical Properties." *Vision Research* 43 (2003): 393–404.

___, and Anne Treisman. "Attentional Spread in the Statistical Processing of Visual Displays." *Perception and Psychophysics* 66 (2004): 1282–1294.

Tversky, Amos (1937–1996)
PROSPECT THEORY

Amos Tversky was born in Haifa, Israel, to parents who emigrated from Poland to Russia. His father, Yosef, put his medical training to use as a veterinarian and his mother, Genia, served in the Knesset (the Israeli Parliament) from its establishment in 1948 until her death in 1964. Tversky was an officer in a paratrooper unit of the Israeli army and fought during the 1956, 1967 and 1973 wars, winning honors for bravery in 1956 when he saved the life of a fellow soldier who was setting an explosive charge. He was himself wounded and earned Israel's highest military decoration.

He gained a B.A. at Hebrew University, Jerusalem (1961) and a Ph.D. at the University of Michigan, Ann Arbor (1965). From 1966 to 1978 he was at Hebrew University, Jerusalem. He was a fellow at the Center for Advanced Study in the Behavioral Sciences, Stanford, California (1970); Davis Brack Professor of Behavioral Sciences, Department of Psychology, Stanford University (1978–1996); affiliated with the Hebrew University from 1984 to 1985; and with Tel Aviv University as a visiting professor of economics and psychology.

His awards and honors include the American Academy of Arts and Sciences (1980); member, American Association for the Advancement of Science (1982); Distinguished Scientific Contribution Award, American Psychological Association (with Daniel Kahneman) (1982); Society of Experimental Psychologists (1983); MacArthur and Guggenheim Fellowships (1984); and foreign associate, National Academy of Science (1985). He received honorary doctorates from the University of Chicago, Yale University, the University of Goteborg in Sweden, and the State University of New York at Buffalo. Tversky and Kahneman jointly won the 2003 Grawemeyer Award for Psychology. He was on the editorial boards of the *Journal of Mathematical Psychology*, *Journal of Economic Behavior and Organization*, and *Synthese*.

Major Contributions

In his twelve-year stay at the Hebrew University, he formed a long working relationship with Daniel Kahneman (see entry). Tversky's work focused on how people make decisions during conditions of uncertainty and showed that such choices can be predicted. He was a pioneer of cognitive science and a key figure in the discovery of systematic human cognitive bias and handling of risk.

With Kahneman, he originated prospect theory — how individuals evaluate losses and gains to explain irrational economic choices. He was a co-founder of what is now the Stanford Center on International Conflict and Negotiation. He made *Major Contributions* to many areas of psychology, from the foundations of measurement to the nature of similarity assessment and the misperception of randomness or chance. He died of melanoma.

Major Literature

Kahneman, Daniel, Paul Slovic, and Amos Tversky (Eds.). *Judgment Under Uncertainty: Heuristics and Biases*. New York: Cambridge University Press, 1982.

Bell, David E., Howard Raiffa, and Amos Tversky (Eds.). *Decision Making: Descriptive, Normative, and Prescriptive Interactions*. New York: Cambridge University Press, 1988.

Kahneman, Daniel, and Amos Tversky (Eds.). *Choices, Values, and Frames*. New York: Cambridge University Press, 2000.

Tversky, Amos, and Eldar Shafir. *Preference, Belief, and Similarity: Selected Writings*. New York: Cambridge University Press, 2003.

Tyler, Leona Elizabeth (1906–1993)

VOCATIONAL GUIDANCE AND COUNSELING

Born in Chetek, Wisconsin, Leona Elizabeth Tyler gained a B.A. in English (1925), an M.S. (1939) and a Ph.D. (1941) from the University of Minnesota, Minneapolis. She was teacher of English and literature (1925–1938) and spent her sabbatical at the Maudsley Hospital in London, England, working with Hans Eysenck (see entry) (1951–1952). She was professor at the University of Minnesota (from 1955) and dean of the Graduate School from 1965 until she retired in 1971; president, Oregon Psychological Association (1956–1957); president, Western Psychological Association (1957–1958); and president of the American Psychological Association (APA) Division 17 (1959–1960).

She spent her Fulbright sabbatical in Amsterdam, Holland (1962–1963). She was on the board of directors (1966–1970), and the eighty-first president (1972–1973) of the APA. She was awarded an honorary doctor of humane letters from Linfield College, McMinnville, Oregon (1979). Other awards and honors include Distinguished Contributions to Psychology, American Psychological Foundation; associate editor, *Journal of Counseling Psychology* (1966); editor, *Personal Guidance Journal* (1956–1962); editorial board member, *Intelligence* (1977–1984).

Major Contributions

Although her first degree was in English, Tyler also attended chemistry classes, but it was in psychology (though much later) that she found the ideal channel for her orderly, mathematical mind. Her professional career as a psychologist was based at the University of Oregon, where she began as an instructor in 1940 and ended as professor and dean emeritus in 1993. During the faculty shortage in World War II, she headed up the Personnel Research Bureau and taught mathematics.

Her lifelong interest in peace-making issues was reflected in her counseling of conscientious objectors during that period, and she was active in Amnesty International, Common Cause. After World War II, she established the University Counseling Center for the veterans of the war. Throughout her career, Tyler continued to counsel students on their vocational and personal concerns and was at pains to draw a distinction between what she did and psychotherapy.

During her years in teaching she started to focus on individual differences and individuality, which was to become her life work. She developed the choice pattern technique that required people to indicate their constructs of occupations and free-time activities, which she tested in Holland, India and Australia, and was expanded to take in values, daily activities, and future time-perspectives in adolescents. Tyler sought to hold together the ideas of cognitive structure and projective techniques for studying personality. The three editions of *The Work of the Counselor* were perhaps the leading influence on the development of the counseling profession in their day.

Major Literature

Tyler, Leona Elizabeth. *Psychology of Human Differences*. New Jersey: Appleton-Century-Crofts, 1947. New Jersey: Prentice-Hall, 1965.

___. "Toward a Workable Psychology of Individuality." *American Psychologist* 13 (1959): 75–81.

Goodenough, Florence Laura, and Leona Elizabeth Tyler. *Developmental Psychology: An Introduction to the Study of Human Behavior*. New York: Irvington Publishers, 1959.

Tyler, Leona Elizabeth. *Work of the Counselor*. New Jersey: Prentice-Hall, 1969.

___. *Individuality*. New Jersey: John Wiley and Sons Inc.: Jossey Bass Wiley, 1978.

___. *Thinking Creatively*. New Jersey: John Wiley and Sons, Inc., Jossey Bass Wiley, 1984.

Viteles, Morris Simon (1902–1996)

INDUSTRIAL PSYCHOLOGY

Born in Zvanstz, Russia, Morris Simon Viteles moved to Philadelphia in 1904. At the University of Pennsylvania, Philadelphia, he received a B.A. (1918), an M.A. (1919) and a Ph.D. (1921), then set up a vocational guidance section of the Psychological Clinic. From 1922 to 1923, he was on an American Field Service fellowship in Europe. Also at Pennsylvania, he was assistant professor of psychology (1925); associate professor (1935); full professor (1940); dean of the Graduate School of Education (1963 to 1967); and emeritus professor (1968).

Viteles was research fellow, Soviet Union (1934–1935); president, International Association of Applied Psychology (1958–1968); chair of the Consulting Division of the American Psychological Association; president of the Pennsylvania Psychological Association; president, International Council of Applied Psychology; honorary member of the Italian Society of Scientific Psychology; the Spanish Psychological Society; the Psychological Society of France. He was also a member of the National Institute of Industrial Psychology of Great Britain, and was active in the American Association for the Advancement of Science, the Industrial Relations Research Association, and Training Directors of America. He received honorary LL.D. from the University of Pennsylvania and the Psychological Professional Gold Medal Award, American Psychological Foundation (1988).

Major Contributions

As an industrial psychologist, Viteles had a long list of consulting roles. He was consultant for the Yellow Cab Company (1924–1961). At the Philadelphia Electric Company (1927–1964), he served as part-time director of selection and training. In the 1930s and 1940s he was on the technical board of the U.S. Employment Service, where he helped develop a system of job classification.

From 1942 to 1951 he chaired the National Research Council Committee on Aviation Psychology, where, among other activities, he monitored a series of studies on pilot training and helped develop the standard flights for pilot evaluation, su-pervised research projects for the National Defense Research Committee, and was a consultant to the War Manpower Commission, the U.S. Navy, and the U.S. Air Force, as well as serving as the chairman of the committee supporting a wide range of research relevant to the war effort.

At Bell Telephone Co. of Philadelphia (1951–1984), he sponsored a management development program based on the need for "humanistic education" of managers. During the 1950s, nearly 140 members of the managerial staffs of Bell System companies spent a full year at Penn devoted entirely to the humanities, including history, science, philosophy, and the arts.

Major Literature

Viteles, Morris Simon. "Test in Industry." *Journal of Applied Psychology* 6 (1921): 392–401.

___. "Psychology in Industry." *Psychological Bulletin* 23 (1926): 638–88.

___. *Industrial Psychology*. New York: W.W. Norton and Co. Ltd., 1934.

___. *The Science of Work*. New York: W.W. Norton and Co. Ltd., 1945.

___. *Motivation and Morale in Industry*. New York: W.W. Norton and Co. Ltd., 1953.

___. "The Aircraft Pilot: Five Years of Research; A Survey of Outcomes." *Psychological Bulletin* 42 (1953): 489–526.

___. "Psychology Today, Fact and Fiction." *American Psychologist* 27 (1972): 601–605.

Vroom, Victor H. (1932–)

EXPECTANCY THEORY OF MOTIVATION

Born in Montreal, Quebec, Canada, Victor H. Vroom gained a B.Sc. (1953) and an M.Sc. (1955) in psychology from McGill University, Montreal, and his a Ph.D. in psychology (1958), then was instructor in the Department of Psychology (1958) and lecturer (1959) at the University of Michigan, Ann Arbor.

Vroom was assistant professor, Department of Psychology, University of Pennsylvania, Philadelphia (1960–1963); associate professor, Graduate School of Industrial Administration, Carnegie Institute of Technology, Pittsburgh, Pennsylvania (1963–1966); and professor of psychology and industrial administration, Graduate School of Industrial Administration, Carnegie-Mellon University, Pittsburgh, Pennsylvania (1966–1972). At Yale University in New Haven, Connecticut, he was professor of administrative sciences and of psychology (1972–1973); chairman, Department of Administrative Sciences; associate director, Institute of Social and Policy Sciences (1972–1975);

John G. Searle Professor of Organization and Management; and professor of psychology (since 1973).

Vroom's awards and honors include the Ford Foundation doctoral dissertation competition winner (1958–1959); Ford Foundation faculty fellowship (1961–1962); McKinsey Foundation research design competition winner (1967); Fulbright lecturer in United Kingdom (1967–1968); James McKeen Cattell Award, American Psychological Association (1970); president, Society of Industrial-Organizational Psychology (1980–1981); and Distinguished Scientific Contribution Award, Society for Industrial and Organizational Psychology (1998).

Major Contributions

Vroom is an authority and an international expert on the psychological analysis of behavior in organizations, particularly on leadership and decision making, and has been consultant to over 100 major corporations in the United States and abroad, including Bell Laboratories, GlobeTel Communications Corporation (GTE), American Express, and General Electric.

He is renowned for his work on the "expectancy theory of motivation," in which he examines why people choose to follow a particular course of action. Vroom's theory assumes that behavior results from conscious choices among alternatives whose purpose it is to maximize pleasure and minimize pain. He suggested that an employee's performance is based on individual factors such as personality, skills, knowledge, experience and abilities.

When the Yale School of Management was founded in 1976, Vroom was named to its original board of permanent officers. In 1973 he began his famous work on leadership with the publication of *Leadership and Decision Making*, written with Philip Yetton. His work has influenced organizational psychology worldwide and his books have been translated into many different languages. His ideas have stimulated many research studies by scholars and may be found in virtually every textbook on management and leadership published since.

Major Literature

Vroom, Victor H. *Work and Motivation*. New Jersey: John Wiley and Sons, Inc., 1964.

___, and Edward H. Deci. *Management and Motivation*. New York: Penguin Group, Inc., 1970, 1992.

Vroom, Victor H., and Phillip Yetton. *Leadership and Decision Making*. Pittsburgh, Pennsylvania: University of Pittsburgh Press, 1973.

Vroom, Victor H. *Some Personality Determinants of The Effects of Participation*. Pennsylvania, Philadelphia: Taylor and Francis Books Ltd., Garland, 1987.

___, and Arthur G. Jago. *The New Leadership: Managing Participation in Organizations*. New Jersey: Prentice-Hall, 1988.

Vygotsky, Lev Semeonovich (1896–1934)
SOCIAL DEVELOPMENT THEORY

Born into a prosperous Jewish family from Belarus (then Russian Empire), Lev Semeonovich Vygotsky gained a law degree (1917) and a Ph.D. (1925) from Moscow University, and from 1924 to 1934 he worked at the Institute of Psychology, Moscow.

Major Contributions

Vygotsky was one of the significant post-revolutionary Soviet psychologists, and his contributions are influential within the fields of developmental psychology, education, and child development. He argued for the inclusion within psychology of the study of consciousness, but rejected introspection as a method. A study of the mind, as opposed to just behavior, was necessary to distinguish human beings from lower animals. Vygotsky contended that what separates humans from animals is humans' capacity to alter the environment for their own purposes. His theory suggests that social interaction leads to continuous step-by-step changes in children's thought and behavior that can vary greatly from culture to culture, and that the intellectual development of children is dependent on interaction with other humans.

Vygotsky's work can be grouped under the following headings:

1. *Zone of proximal development and scaffolding.* The zone of proximal development (ZPD) refers to the gap or difference between a child's existing abilities and what she or he can learn with the guidance of a more knowledgeable adult or a more capable peer. ZPD is known as scaffolding, developed by Jerome Bruner (see entry) as instructional scaffolding. Four basic principles underlying the Vygotskian framework of development are:

   • Children construct their knowledge
   • Development cannot be separated from its social context

- Learning can lead to development
- Language plays a central role in mental development.

2. *Thought and language.* Vygotsky stresses the inter-relationship of language development and thought; it is through inner (silent) speech and oral language that thoughts and mental constructs are formed. Speech and thought develop through interaction.

3. *Psychology of play.* Vygotsky believed that play contains all developmental levels in a condensed form. Therefore, play is akin to imagination where a child extends himself to the next level of his normal behavior, thereby creating a zone of proximal development for himself. In essence, Vygotsky believed play to be the source of development.

4. *Cultural mediation and internalization.* Culture and community play a huge role in early development of thought, language, reasoning processes and mental functions, developed through social interactions with significant people in a child's life, particularly parents and other adults. The specific knowledge gained by a child through these interactions and shared knowledge of a culture is known as internalization.

Major Literature

Vygotsky, Lev Semeonovich. "The Problem of the Cultural Development of the Child." *Journal of Genetic Psychology* 36 (1929): 415–34.

___. "Imagination and Creativity in Childhood." *Soviet Psychology* 28 (1990): 84–96 (1st pub., 1930).

___. "Play and Its Role in the Mental Development of the Child." In J. Bruner, et al. (Eds.). *Play: Its Role in Development and Evolution.* London: Penguin Books Ltd., 1976 (1st pub., 1933).

___. "The Development of Higher Psychological Functions." *Soviet Psychology* 15 (1977): 60–73.

Wagner-Jauregg, Julius Von (1857–1940)

PATHOLOGY OF THE NERVOUS SYSTEM

Born in Wels, Austria, Julius von Wagner-Jauregg studied medicine at the Institute of General and Experimental Pathology, Vienna University. In 1876–1877 he spent his (then compulsory) one year medical service in the Navy at Garrison Hospital No. 1 in Vienna and graduated in 1880. He began his academic career as an assistant in the First Psychiatric University Clinic in Vienna in 1883, and in 1885 qualified in neurology, then in psychiatry in 1887. In 1889 he was appointed extraordinary professor at the Medical Faculty of the University of Graz, Austria, and director of the Neuro-Psychiatric Clinic as successor to Richard von Krafft-Ebing (see entry). It was there that he started his investigations on the connections between goiter and cretinism; on his advice, the government, some time later, started selling salt to which iodine had been added, in the areas (hill districts) most affected by goiter.

From 1893–1928 he was extraordinary professor of psychiatry and nervous diseases and director of the First Clinic. In recognition of his services to forensic medicine he was awarded the diploma of doctor of law.

Major Contributions

In 1917, Wagner-Jauregg started using malaria therapy in patients suffering from general paralysis of the insane (GPI), caused by syphilis (3rd stage) with dramatically successful results; it was the first example of shock therapy. The method brought a previously incurable fatal disease under medical control and earned him the Nobel Prize for Physiology or Medicine in 1927, the first psychiatrist to be so recognized.

His work led to the development of fever therapy and shock therapy for a number of mental disorders. The patient was injected with serum from patients infected with Plasmodium vivax (malaria parasite). Then followed paroxysms of high fever and intense rigors; usually 10–12 repetitions were given. Quinine was then given to break the cycle. Although malaria therapy was later replaced largely by administration of antibiotics, it was still in use well into the late 1940s, and is currently being investigated for the treatment of AIDS. One of the disadvantages is that caring for a patient undergoing malarial therapy is time-consuming and labor intensive.

In later years it has come to light that Wagner-Jauregg was a national socialist (Nazi) and backed Hitler's program of racial hygiene (sterilization). This shocked Austria, where schools, roads and hospitals were named in his honor.

Related Literature

Eissler, Kurt R. *Freud as an Expert Witness: The Discussion of War Neuroses Between Freud and Wagner-Jauregg.* Madison, Massachusetts: International Universities Press, Inc., 1986.

Whitrow, M. *Julius Wagner-Jauregg (1857–1940).* London, England: Smith-Gordon and Co. Ltd, 1993.

Wallach, Hans (1904–1998)
VISUAL AND AUDITORY PERCEPTION

Born in Berlin, Germany, Hans Wallach gained a Ph.D. at the University of Berlin (1934). Being Jewish, he was advised to leave Germany. He joined Swarthmore College, Swarthmore, Pennsylvania, where he spent the remainder of his career. He was research associate (1936–1942); instructor (1942); assistant professor (1944); visiting professor at the New School for Social Research, New York (1947–1957, 1968); associate professor (1948); professor (1953); and chair of the psychology department (1957–1966). He retired in 1975 but continued his work as a research associate until 1987.

Wallach's awards and honors include a Guggenheim Fellowship (1949–1950); member of the Institute for Advanced Study, Princeton University, New Jersey (1954–1955); named Centennial Professor of Psychology (1971); Distinguished Scientific Contribution Award, American Psychological Association (1983); elected to the National Academy of Science (1986); and winner of the Howard Cosby Warren Medal of the Society of Experimental Psychologists (1987).

Major Contributions

At age 22, Wallach joined the University of Berlin's Institute of Psychology — then the center of Gestalt psychology — as a research assistant to Wolfgang Köhler (see entry) for a year, a relationship which continued on his arrival at Swarthmore. Wallach's research on perceptual adaptation advanced the field's understanding of the role of learning in the perceptual process. His early work was on sound localization, and he demonstrated how sound is localized. He also discovered the precedence effect, which underlies stereophonic reproduction. Precedence effect is the ability of the auditory system to process sound that reaches the ears directly from a source even when significant reflected sounds reach the ears shortly afterward.

Research on lightness constancy followed, and he was known for his study of the nature of neutral colors. He spent some years on measuring the processes that compensate for stimulation caused by the relative motions that result from one's own head movements and one's locomotion. Wallach has also published important work in other areas of perception such as size, shape and stereoscopic depth constancy.

Wallach published more than 100 papers in his career. In 1991, a fellowship was established in Wallach's honor to support a summer research project in psychology by a Swarthmore student. Many of his colleagues and former students contributed to the creation of the prize. Although known primarily for his work in perception, Wallach thought the subject had been explored enough. So he began to study memory.

Major Literature

Wallach, Hans. "On Memory Modalities." *American Journal of Psychology* 68 (1955); 249–257 (with E. Averbach).
___. "The Constancy of Stereoscopic Depth." *American Journal of Psychology* 76 (1963): 404–412 (with Z.C. Zuckerman).
___. *On Perception.* New York: Henry Holt and Company, Inc., Times Books, 1975.
___. "Two Kinds of Adaptation in the Constancy of Visual Direction and Their Different Effects on the Perception of Shape and Visual Direction." *Perception and Psychophysics* 21 (1977): 227–242 (with J. Bacon).
___. "Learned Stimulation in Space and Motion." *American Psychologist,* 40 (1985): 399–404.

Wallin, John Edward Wallace (1878–1969)
EXPERIMENTAL PSYCHOLOGY

Wallin gained a Ph.D. at Yale University, New Haven, Connecticut (1901), and from 1901 to 1902 worked on a Carnegie Foundation research grant at Clark University, Worcester, Massachusetts. He was assistant professor, experimental psychology, University of Michigan, Ann Arbor (1902–1903); experimental psychology teacher, Princeton University, New Jersey, (1903–1906); head of the department of psychology and education and vice-president of East Stroudsburg State Teachers College, Stroudsburg, Pennsylvania (1906–1909); head of the department of psychology and education, Cleveland School of Education, Cleveland, Ohio (1909–1910); and professor of Clinical Psychology and director of the Bureau of Special Education and of the Psycho-Educational Clinic, Miami University in Oxford, Ohio (1921–1928). Between 1914 and 1954, Wallin served on the faculties of twenty universities from North Carolina to Florida.

Major Contributions

At Yale, Wallin studied educational, physiological and experimental psychology, phonetics, the psychology of expression, and abnormal psychology with George Trumbull Ladd (see entry). At Clark he attended lectures by Adolf Meyer (see entry) on the psychobiological system of mental disorders, and did research with Granville S. Hall (see entry) on how students understand clouds. In 1910 he visited Vineland Training School where he served as H.H. Goddard's (see entry) substitute while Goddard spent the year on tour in Europe.

It was from Vineland and from his visits to Lightner Witmer (1867–1956) at the University of Pennsylvania that Wallin developed his interest in developmentally disabled people. He founded in 1910 the Village for Epileptics in Skillman, New Jersey, where he established a laboratory for clinical psychology — the first of its kind associated with an institution for epileptics. There he tested the intelligence, physical abilities, physical attributes (height, weight, lung capacity, grip strength, etc.) of the residents and published many of his results. In all, Wallin opened eight psycho-educational and mental hygiene clinics and six special education departments.

Among his concerns were the Stanford Binet intelligence test. He maintained that teachers should not be giving the test; the administration should be in the hands of expert psychologists located in psycho-educational clinics offering a wide range of diagnostic services. He also believed that it should not be used as the only measure of intelligence. Wallin asserted that the notion of "fixed intelligence" had unfortunately deprived those with mental deficiency of their right to a good education and to good treatment.

Major Literature

Wallin, John Edward. *Experimental Studies of Mental Defectives: A Critique of the Binet Simon Tests and a Contribution to the Psychology of Epilepsy.* Educational Psychology Monographs 7. Baltimore: Warwick and York, 1912.
___. "A Census of Speech Defects." *School and Society* 3 (1916): 203–216.
___. "Theories of Stuttering." *Journal of Applied Psychology* 1 (1917): 349–367.
___. *Children with Mental and Physical Handicaps.* New York: Prentice Hall, 1949.
___. *Education of Mentally Handicapped Children.* New York: Harper, 1955.
___. "Training of the Severely Retarded, Viewed in Historical Perspective." *Journal of General Psychology* 74 (1966): 107–127.

Warr, Peter Bryan (1937–)
INDUSTRIAL PSYCHOLOGY

Born in Birkenhead, Merseyside, England, Peter Bryan Warr gained a B.A. (1960) and an M.A. (1963) at the University of Cambridge. His Ph.D. (1963) was from the University of Sheffield in England, where he became research professor (now emeritus professor) and director of the Institute of Work Psychology, Applied Social Psychology Unit (since 1973). He was on the Manpower Services Commission's Training Research Advisory Committee (1973–1980); Ministry of Defense, Flying Personnel Research Committee (1975–1980); Industry and Employment Committee, Economic and Social Research Council (ESRC) (1984); and Medical Research Council, Neurosciences and Mental Health Board (since 1984).

In 2004 Warr and two other distinguished academics were appointed as independent advisors to the board of SHL, an employee assessment company, on research and the latest developments in academia.

His awards and honors include the Spearman Medal for Distinguished Research (1969). He received the British Psychological Society's President's Award, for outstanding contributions to psychological knowledge (1982). He is on the editorial board of *Leadership and Organization Development* and *Current Psychological Research and Reviews.* His memberships and fellowships include fellow of the British Psychological Society, International Association of Applied Psychology, European Association of Work and Organizational Psychology, Society for Industrial and Organizational Psychology, and foreign affiliate of the American Psychological Association.

Major Contributions

Warr's main interests are attitudes and well-being; personality and behavior; learning, training and development; age differences in employment settings; happiness and unhappiness at work; processes and outcomes of work meetings; and factors influencing personality-behavior links. Warr argues that the harmful features of some jobs are also those that cause deterioration during unemployment, and the factors that are beneficial can also enhance mental health during unemployment.

The large- and small-scale studies Warr carried out within nine countries have shown that continuing joblessness affects people of all ages, particularly middle-aged people. Helpful counteracting factors are the amount of time since job loss, employment commitment, social relationships, gender, ethnic-group membership, social class, local unemployment rate, and personal vulnerability. Warr suggests that the impact on mental health of opportunity for control, physical security and valued social position, and how individual differences can moderate environmental features, is analogous to the influence of vitamins on physical health.

Warr has developed the Job Aspiration Questionnaire, the Job Competence Questionnaire and the Corporate Culture Questionnaire, which have been used in a large number of studies throughout the world.

Major Literature

Warr, Peter Bryan. *Training for Managers*. London, England: Institute of Management, 1992.
___. "Age and Personality in the British Population Between 16 and 64 Years." *Journal of Occupational and Organizational Psychology* 74 (2001): 165–199 (with Anthony Miles and Conall Platts).
___. "Age and Work Behaviour: Physical Attributes, Cognitive Abilities, Knowledge, Personality Traits and Motives." In C. L. Cooper and I.T. Robertson (Eds.). *International Review of Industrial and Organizational Psychology*, pp. 1–36. London: Chichester, West Sussex, England. Wiley, Europe Ltd., 2001.
___(Ed.). *Psychology at Work*. 5th ed. London: Penguin Books Ltd., 2002.

Washburn, Margaret Floy (1871–1939)

ANIMAL BEHAVIOR

Margaret Floy Washburn was born in Harlem, New York City. At Vassar College, Poughkeepsie, New York, she received a B.A. (1891) and an M.A. (1893). At Vassar she was associate professor of philosophy (1903); professor of psychology (1908–1937); professor emeritus of psychology (1937); she also set up an independent department of psychology (1908). She was the first woman a Ph.D. in psychology, Cornell University, Ithaca, New York (1894).

She also served as professor of psychology, philosophy, and ethics at Wells College, Aurora, New York (1894–1900); Warden of Sage (women's) College, New York (1900–1902); University of Cincinnati, Ohio (1902–1903); representative of psychology, Division of Psychology and Anthropology, National Research Council (1919–1920 and 1925–1928); first woman president, American Psychological Association (APA) (1921); chairman, Section 1, vice-president, American Association for the Advancement of Science (1927); president, New York Branch, APA (1931); chairman, Society of Experimental Psychologists (1931); and U.S. delegate, International Congress of Psychology, Copenhagen, Denmark (1932).

In 1928, Washburn established a scholarship to aid students of psychology. She was elected to the Society of Experimental Psychologists (1929); was a fellow of the National Academy of Sciences (second woman to receive that honor) (1931); and was editor, advisory editor, associate editor or cooperating editor for six prestigious journals, including *American Journal of Psychology*. She received an honorary D.Sc. from Wittenberg College, Springfield, Ohio (1927). In 1903, Washburn was included in James McKeen Cattell's list of 1000 most important "men of science."

Major Contributions

Washburn was known primarily for her work in animal psychology. *The Animal Mind* (1908) was the first book by an American in this field and remained the standard comparative psychology textbook for the next 25 years. In *Movement and Mental Imagery* she presented her motor theory of consciousness, in which she attempted to reconcile the structuralist, or "introspective" tradition of Wilhelm Wundt and Edward B. Titchener (see entries), and the opposing behaviorist view. Her theory — which has gone out of fashion — explored the ways in which thoughts and perceptions produce motor reaction.

Between 1905 and 1938, she published sixty-eight studies from the Vassar Psychological Laboratory, with 117 students as joint authors. In 1921, she was awarded a prize of $500 by the Edison Phonograph Company for the best research on the effects of music — a study titled "The Emotional Effects of Instrumental Music" in collaboration with a colleague in the Department of Music at Vassar. Washburn published over 200 scientific articles and reviews, and translated Wundt's *Ethical Systems* (1897).

Major Literature

Washburn, Margaret Floy. *The Animal Mind*. New York: Macmillan, 1908. New York: Thoemmes Continuum, 1998.
___. *Movement and Mental Imagery*. Boston, Massachusetts: Houghton Mifflin, 1916. New York: Arno Press, 1978.
___. "Some Recollections." In C. Murchison (Ed.), *A History of Psychology in Autobiography* (Vol. 2, pp. 333–358). Worcester, Massachusetts: Clark University Press, 1932.
___. "The Comparative Efficiency of Intensity, Perspective and the Stereoscopic Factor in Producing the Perception of Depth." *American Journal of Psychology* 51 (1938); 151–155 (with C. Wright).

Watson, John Broadus (1878–1958)

BEHAVIORISM

Born in Greenville, South Carolina, John B. Watson gained an M.A. at Furman University in Greenville, South Carolina (1899). At the University of Chicago, Illinois, he gained a Ph.D. in psychology (1903) and was instructor (1906). At Johns Hopkins University, Baltimore, Maryland, he was associate professor of psychology (1907) and professor (1908). He was president of the American Psychological Association in 1915.

Major Contributions

Watson's dissertation, "Animal Education: An Experimental Study on the Psychical Development of the White Rat, Correlated with the Growth of its Nervous System," is the first modern scientific book on rat behavior, a classic of developmental psychobiology. His early major work was a series of ethological studies of sea birds done in the Dry Tortugas Islands in Florida, where he studied all aspects of the birds' behavior—imprinting, homing, mating and nesting habits, feeding, and chick-rearing.

In *Psychology as the Behaviorist Views It*—sometimes called "The Behaviorist Manifesto"—Watson outlined the major features of his new philosophy of psychology, called "behaviorism." The Watsonian school of behaviorism, which became the dominant psychology in the United States during the 1920s and '30s, asserted that psychology is the science of human behavior, which, like animal behavior, should be studied under exacting laboratory conditions. Watson's behaviorism is typically considered a historical descendent of British empiricism, and particularly the views of philosopher John Locke (1632–1704).

Watson claimed (possibly facetiously) that he could take any 12 healthy infants and, by applying behavioral techniques, create whatever kind of person he desired. He also conducted the controversial "Little Albert" experiment. Later he went on from psychology to become a popular author on child rearing. He argued forcefully for the use of animal subjects in psychological study and described instinct as a series of reflexes activated by heredity.

He also promoted conditioned responses as the ideal experimental tool. In 1920, in the wake of a sexual affair with Rosalie Rayner, a graduate student, and the divorce from his first wife, Watson was forced to resign from Johns Hopkins. In 1921 he began a successful second career in the advertising business, and from 1924 to 1945 he was vice president of J. Walter Thompson Agency.

Watsonian psychology can be summed up thus:

1. Observation of behavior replacing introspection
2. Prediction and control replacing theoretical understanding
3. Avoidance of "mind" terms
4. An atomistic, stimulus-response view of behavior.

Major Literature

Watson, John Broadus. "Psychology as the Behaviorist Views It." *Psychological Review* 20 (1913): 158–177.
___. *Behavior: An Introduction to Comparative Psychology*. New York: Henry Holt and Company, Inc., 1914.
___. *Psychology from the Standpoint of a Behaviorist*. New York: Palgrave Macmillan, 1919. New York: Lippincott, 1984.
___. *Behaviorism*. New York: W.W. Norton and Co. Ltd., 1925, 1980.
___. *The Ways of Behaviorism*. New York: Harper and Brothers Publishers, 1928.
___. "John Broadus Watson" [Autobiography]. In C. Murchison (Ed.), *A History of Psychology in Autobiography* (Vol. 3, pp. 271–81). Worcester, Massachusetts: Clark University Press, 1936.

Wechsler, David (1896–1981)

INTELLIGENCE SCALE FOR CHILDREN

David Wechsler was born in Lespedi, Romania, and immigrated with his family to New York in 1902. Wechsler gained an A.B. at City University of New York (1916); an M.A. at Columbia University, New York (1917), and was then an Army psychologist at Long Island, New York, and Camp Logan, Texas. In 1918 he was sent by the Army to the University of London to work with Charles Spearman (see entry) and the mathematician Karl Pearson (1857–1936). From 1919 to 1922 he held a experimental psychology research fellowship at the University of Paris.

He was clinical psychologist, Bureau of Child Guidance, New York City (1922–1925), and gained a Ph.D. in experimental psychology at Columbia in 1925. From 1925 to 1932 he was in clinical psychology private practice and from 1932 to 1967, chief psychologist at Bellevue Psychiatric Hospital in New York and professor at New York University College of Medicine. He received the Distinguished Contribution to Psychology Award, American Psychological Association (APA) (1960); APA Division of School Psychology Tribute (1973);

and APA Distinguished Professional Contribution Award (1973).

Major Contributions

In 1939, Wechsler produced a battery of intelligence tests known as the Wechsler-Bellevue Intelligence Scale. The original battery was geared specifically to the measurement of adult intelligence, for clinical use. He rejected the idea that there is an ideal mental age against which individual performance can be measured, and he defined normal intelligence as the mean test score for all members of an age group; the mean could then be represented by 100 on a standard scale. In 1942 Wechsler issued his first revision. The Wechsler Intelligence Scale for Children was published in 1949 and updated in 1974.

In 1955 Wechsler developed the Wechsler Adult Intelligence Scale (WAIS), with the same structure as his earlier scale but standardized with a different population, including 10 percent nonwhites, to reflect the U.S. population. (The earlier test had been standardized for an all-white population.) He contributed to the revision of the WAIS in 1981 shortly before his death. The last of his intelligence tests, the Wechsler Preschool and Primary Scale of Intelligence, was issued in 1967 as an adaptation of the children's scale, for use with very young children.

His intelligence tests continue to be updated for contemporary use. Wechsler is also notable for his use of the deviation quotient (DQ), a technical innovation that replaced the use of mental ages in computing IQ scores. This greatly improved the utility of normative comparisons when intelligence tests are used with adult examinees. He also developed the Army Wechsler (1942).

Major Literature

Wechsler, David. *The Measurement of Adult Intelligence*. Baltimore: Williams and Wilkins, 1939.

___. "Non-Intellective Factors in General Intelligence." *Psychological Bulletin* 37 (1940): 444–445.

___. *Manual for the Wechsler Intelligence Scale for Children*. New York: The Psychological Corporation, 1949.

___. *Manual for the Wechsler Adult Intelligence Scale*. New York: The Psychological Corporation, 1955 (2nd ed.).

___. *Manual for the Wechsler Preschool and Primary Scale of Intelligence*. New York: Psychological Corporation, 1967.

___. *Wechsler Intelligence Scale for Children* (WISC-IV, fourth edition). London, England: Harcourt Assessment, 2003.

Wernicke, Karl (1848–1905)
BRAIN TRAUMA AND SPEECH

Born in Tarnowitz, Poland, Karl Wernicke's family moved to Germany, where he received all his education. He qualified in medicine in 1884 at the University of Breslau (now Wroclow) and was conferred a doctor of medicine at Breslau in 1870 before undergoing specialist training in psychiatry at the Allerheiligenhospital, Breslau. He was habilitated for psychiatry at Breslau (1875) and at Berlin (1876).

From 1876 to 1878 he was assistant in the clinic for psychiatry and nervous diseases at the Berlin Charité. From 1878 to 1885, Wernicke practiced as a private neuropsychiatrist in Berlin; from 1885 to 1890 he was associate professor of neurology and psychiatry at Breslau. In 1890 he obtained the chair at Breslau and in 1904 he was professor at Halle, Germany. He died from injuries received in an accident while riding a bicycle in the Thuringian forest, in the German state of Thuringia.

Major Contributions

Shortly after the French physician Paul Pierre Broca (1824–1880) published his findings on language deficits caused by damage to what is now referred to as Broca's area (situated in left the frontal lobe of the cerebral cortex), Wernicke discovered that damage to the left posterior superior temporal gyrus (ridge) of the cerebral cortex affected language comprehension. This region is now referred to as Wernicke's area, and the associated syndrome is known as Wernicke's aphasia. In *The Aphasic Syndrome* (1874) he described what later became known as sensory aphasia (defects in, or loss of, speech and expression) as distinct from motor aphasia, first described by Broca. Wernicke used the distinguishing clinical features of the two aphasias to formulate a general theory of the neural bases of language.

Some of Wernicke's other discoveries that bear his name are:

- *Wernicke's Disease*: a form of degeneration of the brain induced by thiamine (Vitamin B$_1$) deficiency.
- *Wernicke's cramp*: a form of painful muscle cramp precipitated by anxiety or fear.
- *Wernicke's dementia* (or syndrome): a frequent condition of old age marked by defective memory, loss of sense of location, and disorientation with confabulation (a fictitious account of an event).
- *Wernicke's pupillary reaction*: the absence of

direct reaction to light in the blind part of the retina.

- *Wernicke-Korsakoff disease*: a combination of Korsakoff's dementia and Wernicke's encephalopathy, a severe syndrome characterized by loss of short-term memory (see entry, Korsakoff, Sergei).
- *Wernicke-Mann hemiplegia*: a posture anomaly with partial hemiplegia (paralysis) of the extremities characterized by typical posture and gait disorders.

In psychiatry, Wernicke did not believe in specific psychiatric diseases, and he was an ardent adversary of Emil Kraepelin (see entry), considering the latter's classification as not being sufficiently scientific. Wernicke aimed at a natural system for the classification of mental disorders, chiefly based on the anatomy and pathology of the nervous system. Between 1897 and 1903, he and four collaborators published the three-part *Atlas of the Brain*.

Major Literature

All of Wernicke's works are in German.

Wertham, Fredric (1895–1981)
SEDUCTION OF MASS MEDIA

Born in Munich, Germany, Wertham graduated with an M.D. (1921) from the University of Würzburg, Germany, then was appointed to Munich's Kraepelin Clinic. He settled in the United States in 1922 and was appointed to the Phipps Psychiatric Clinic, John Hopkins University medical school, New York City; he became a U.S. citizen in 1927. His book *The Brain as an Organ* (Macmillan, 1926) — one of the most widely used psychology books of the time — earned him the honor of being the first psychiatrist ever awarded with a National Research Council grant.

In 1932 he was appointed senior psychiatrist for Bellevue Hospital, New York, where he focused on criminal behavior linked with mental health and environment. During the thirties he advised the City of New York on the first psychiatric hospital for convicted criminals. *Dark Legend* (New York: Duell, Sloan and Pearce, 1941) — made into a play — was the true story of a 17 year old New York City teenager who, in the late thirties, killed his mother. Wertham believed that the boy's interests in movies, radio and comic books led him to live in a fantasy world, and finally to the crime itself.

In 1948, an article in *Reader's Digest* magazine reinforced the idea that comics were directly linked to increasing violence in American children. *Show of Violence* (Gollancz, 1949) continued the attack on comics, movies and other forms of media entertainment. The Senate Subcommittee on Juvenile Delinquency was convened during the early 1950s to investigate the influence on youth by violence and sex in mass media and, in particular, comic books. Major cities in some states banned comic books. Laws were introduced in 18 states restricting the sale of comics. Large-scale protests were staged in front of stores and newsstands that sold comics, and magazine distributors were deluged with complaints. *Seduction of the Innocent* recounted examples of sex and violence, dope, sadism, and rape. By the end of 1954 almost three quarters of the comics publishing industry was gutted, one reason being the adoption of the Comics Code (the Comics Code Authority [CCA] was created in 1954.)

On two other fronts, Wertham's writings about the effects of racial segregation were used as evidence in the landmark Supreme Court case *Brown v. Board of Education*, and part of *A Sign for Cain* dealt with the involvement of medical professionals in the Holocaust. In the 1970s he did a U-turn and said that certain science fiction publications were healthy and creative, but his turnabout did not convince his critics. He was booed out of a conference and gave up writing.

Major Literature

Wertham, Fredric, *Seduction of the Innocent*. Mattituck, New York: Amereon Ltd., 1954.
___. *The Circle of Guilt*. New York: Springer-Verlag, Dobson, 1958.
___. *A Sign for Cain: An Exploration of Human Violence*. London, England: Robert Hale Ltd., 1968.
___. *The World of Fanzines: A Special Form of Communication*. Southern Illinois University Press, 1973.

Wertheimer, Max (1880–1943)
GESTALT PSYCHOLOGY

Born in Prague, Czechoslovakia, Max Wertheimer gained a Ph.D. in psychology at the University of Würzburg, Germany (1904). He was private instructor, Frankfurt University and the Friedrich-Wilhelm University, Berlin (1912–1922). He was assistant professor of psychology, Berlin (1922–1929), and professor of psychology, University of Frankfurt, directing research in social and experimental psychology (1929–1933). He fled Germany to the United States via Czechoslovakia (1933) and was faculty member of the New

School for Social Research, New York (1933–1943). Wertheimer co-founded the journal *Psychological Research* (1921).

Major Contributions

Wertheimer's original intention was to become a musician; in his youth he played the violin and composed symphonic and chamber music. In 1900 he began to study law at Charles University in Prague but the following year he left Prague to study psychology at Berlin under Carl Stumpf (see entry). At Würzburg, as part of his dissertation, he developed a lie detector for the objective study of courtroom testimony and devised a method of word association — a test for assessing personality traits and conflicts in which the subject responds to a given word with the first word that comes to mind or with a predetermined type of word, such as an antonym. Between 1905 and 1912 he carried out research at psychology institutes in Prague, Berlin, and Vienna, where he focused on the perception of complex and ambiguous structures.

In 1912 he published his influential paper "Experimental Studies of the Perception of Movement." Wertheimer discovered that children with low IQs can solve problems when they can grasp the overall structures involved, and he began to formulate the ideas that would later take root in Gestalt psychology. His demonstration (1910–1912) of the phi phenomenon — the optical illusion of movement — became a basis for Gestalt psychology. Convinced that the atomistic approach of most psychologists to the study of human behavior was inadequate, Wertheimer, Wolfgang Köhler, and Kurt Koffka (see entries) formed the new Gestalt school. The basic Gestalt belief is that an examination of the whole is vitally important in order to understand the individual parts.

Major Literature

Wertheimer, Max. "On Truth." *Social Research* 1 (1934): 135–146. Reprinted in M. Henle (Ed.), *Documents of Gestalt Psychology*. Berkeley: University of California Press, 1961.

___. "Some Problems in the Theory of Ethics." *Social Research* 2 (1935): 353–367. Reprinted in M. Henle, (Ed.), *Documents of Gestalt Psychology*. Berkeley: University of California Press, 1961.

___. "Gestalt Theory." [English translation of "Über Gestalttheorie" 1924–1925]. *Social Research* 11 (1944): 78–99.

___. *Productive Thinking*. New York: Harper and Row, 1945. London, England: Tavistock Publications, 1966.

___. *Readings in Perception*. New York: Van Nostrand Reinhold, 1958.

Scherer, G.A.C., and Max Wertheimer. *Psycholinguistic Experiment in Foreign-Language Teaching*. Columbus, Ohio: McGraw-Hill Education, 1964.

Winnicott, Donald Woods (1896–1971)
CHILD PSYCHIATRY

Donald Woods Winnicott was born in Plymouth, Devon, England, the son of a successful hardware merchant who eventually became mayor and was knighted. After studying biology at Cambridge University and medicine, and seeing service on a destroyer during World War I, Winnicott worked St. Bartholomew's Hospital, then in pediatric hospitals, and started a private pediatric practice. Interested in psychoanalysis, he was in training analysis with James Strachey (1887–1967) from 1923 to 1933.

Winnicott was one of the first candidates in the British Psychoanalytic Institute in 1927 and graduated from the institute in 1935, after which he was supervised by Melanie Klein and at the same time analyzed her son. From 1936 to 1941, he had a second analysis and, in the same year, began working with Clare Britton, a pioneering social worker (and future analyst) working with evacuee children in Oxfordshire. Winnicott was divorced from his first wife and married Britton in late 1951. Winnicott traveled to America several times to give lectures, and on a trip to New York in 1969, he suffered a serious cardiac crisis after a bout of the flu. He died just over a year afterward.

Major Contributions

Some of Winnicott's important concepts as a pediatrician and psychoanalyst are:

- transitional phenomena and transitional objects, what we know as the "comfort blanket"
- the essential role of the mother in infancy; the infant is an equal partner in the mother-child relationship
- the good enough mother and the good enough environment
- the holding environment for children and for relatively sick, needy, dependent patients
- true self versus false self
- the invention and use of the powerful therapeutic tool of "squiggles" — engaging children in drawing to express their feelings. The Squiggle Foundation — a charity — is based in London, England.

Winnicott is considered one of the "middle

group" of psychoanalysts, sitting between Anna Freud and Melanie Klein. However, because of his refusal to ally himself with either, in many ways he was shunned by both major British camps for much of his life. Much of his large output of work lives on and remains useful, stimulating, and much discussed within and well beyond the field of psychoanalysis.

Major Literature

Winnicott, Donald Woods. "Hate in the Counter-Transference." *International Journal of Psychoanalysis* 30 (1949): 69–74.

___. "Transitional Objects and Transitional Phenomena." *International Journal of Psychoanalysis* 34 (1953): 89–97.

___. *Mother and Child: A Primer of First Relationships.* New York: Basic Books, Inc., 1957.

___. *Collected Papers: Through Paediatrics to Psycho-Analysis.* London: Tavistock Publications. New York: Basic Books, 1958. London: Hogarth Press and the Institute of Psychoanalysis, 1975. London: Karnac Books, 1992.

___. *The Family and Individual Development.* London: Tavistock Publications, 1965.

___. *Playing and Reality.* London: Tavistock Publications, 1971.

Related Literature

Bertolini, Mario, Andreas Giannakoulas, and Max Hernandez (with Anthony Molino). *Squiggles and Spaces: Revisiting the Work of D. W. Winnicott* Volume 2. New Jersey: John Wiley and Sons, Inc., 2001.

Wolpe, Joseph (1915–1997)

SYSTEMATIC DESENSITIZATION

Born in Johannesburg, South Africa, Joseph Wolpe gained his basic medical degree from the University of Witwatersrand, Johannesburg (1939), and an M.D. (equivalent to an American a Ph.D.) (1948). During the Second World War he was a South African Army medical officer in a military psychiatric hospital, where he worked with soldiers suffering from what would today be called "post–traumatic stress disorder." Wolpe and his colleagues first tried to treat the problem with drug therapy, but the results were not encouraging, so he decided to find more something more effective. After the war he worked at the University of Witwatersrand and at some stage underwent a training psychoanalysis.

From 1965 to 1988 Wolpe was professor of psychiatry at Temple University Medical School, Philadelphia, during which time he also served as director of the behavior therapy unit at nearby Eastern Pennsylvania Psychiatric Institute. He served as the second president of the Association for the Advancement of Behavior Therapy, from which he received a lifetime achievement award. Although Wolpe retired in 1988 and moved to California, he lectured at Pepperdine University, Malibu, California, until a month before his death.

Major Contributions

Dissatisfied with lack of progress in treating patients, Wolpe began to devise "systematic desensitization" as a form of behavior therapy. His reasoning was that behavior therapy was as much an applied science as any other aspect of medicine, and if much of behavior, both good and bad, is learned, so it could not be unlearned? Gradual exposure to the object of fear can help to desensitize the sufferer of crippling fears and phobias to those fears. Modern desensitization techniques include teaching patients relaxation techniques and gradually rehearsing stressful situations, until the patient is finally able to handle the fear-inducing objects.

Wolpe's research also led to assertiveness training, which, with desensitization, requires a gradual move into new behaviors. People who have trouble asserting themselves are very much like sufferers from phobias in that they fear confrontation and conflict, anger in others, and rejection. Assertiveness training gives them the framework to build their confidence, relax in formerly stressful situations, and conquer their fear.

Desensitization was originally criticized as a therapeutic process only useful in cases that have a single symptom, whereas with more complex problems, it was alleged that "the deep causes" of neuroses were left untouched. However, there is no real proof that any such "deep causes" exist. Both phobias and more complex neuroses develop as a result of the learning process going astray, so desensitization aims to enable people to "relearn."

Major Literature

Wolpe, Joseph. *Psychotherapy by Reciprocal Inhibition.* Palo Alto, California: Stanford University Press, 1958.

___. *The Practice of Behavior Therapy.* London: Reed Elsevier Group, Pergamon, 1969.

___, and Leo Reyna. *Behaviour Therapy in Psychiatric Practice.* London: Reed Elsevier Group, 1976.

Wolpe, Joseph. *Theme and Variations: Behaviour Therapy Casebook.* London: Reed Elsevier Group, 1976.

___, and David Wolpe. *Life Without Fear.* Oakland, California: New Harbinger Publications, 1988.

Woodworth, Robert Sessions (1869–1962)

EXPERIMENTAL PSYCHOLOGY

Born in Belchertown, Massachusetts, Robert Sessions Woodworth gained a B.A. in philosophy at Amherst College, Massachusetts (1891). He earned a B.A. (1896) and M.A. in philosophy (1897) Harvard University, Cambridge, Massachusetts. At Columbia University, New York City, he was awarded a Ph.D. in psychology (1899); he was also instructor in physiology under Raymond Cattell (1901–1909); professor (1909); head of department (1918–1927).

Woodworth served in the posts of vice-president, American Association for the Advancement of Science (1909, 1929), president American Psychological Association (APA) (1914), and president, Psychological Corporation (1929). He received the Gold Medal from the American Psychological Foundation (1956) and was awarded five honorary degrees. He was editor, *Archives of Psychology* (1906–1945).

Major Contributions

In 1902, Woodworth spent a one-year postdoctoral fellowship at University of Liverpool, England, studying physiology under Charles Scott Sherrington (see entry). Woodworth and Edward L. Thorndike (see entry) demonstrated that training could not be transferred; learning one subject did not produce an overall improvement in learning ability. Woodworth believed that behavior was a function of both environmental stimuli and the makeup of the organism.

One of Woodworth's early tasks at Columbia was collecting data from some eleven hundred subjects for psychometric testing at the World's Fair in St. Louis, Missouri (1904). He made the standard physical anthropological measurements, testing also muscular strength, speed and accuracy, vision and hearing, and intelligence. Woodworth designed the first questionnaire to detect and measure abnormal behavior; it served as a rough screening device for behavioral disorders. His presidential address for the APA, "A Revision of Imageless Thought" (published in 1915), was an attempt to resolve the ongoing battle between two former Wundt students — Oswald Külpe (a German psychologist from the Würzburg school) and Edward B. Titchener (see entry).

During World War I, Woodworth was commissioned by the APA to prepare a test for emotional stability that might be used in the evaluation of recruits. The result was Woodworth's Personal Data Sheet (a "yes or no" questionnaire), but it was produced too late to be thoroughly tested on recruits. It was, however, subsequently revised and used by others in the field of personality measurement.

Woodworth considered physiological and experimental psychology as his basic courses but also taught various other courses, including introductory, abnormal, social, tests and statistics, history and survey of contemporary psychology, until his retirement in 1942. His *Psychology* (1921) became a standard textbook. His *Experimental Psychology*— sometimes known as the "Columbia Bible"— replaced Titchener's laboratory manuals as the standard technical guide for the succeeding generation of experimental psychologists.

Major Literature

Woodworth, Robert Sessions. "Racial Differences in Mental Traits." *Science* 31 (788) (1910): 171–186.
___. *Psychology*. New York: Holt, 1921, 1929, 1934, 1940.
___. "Dynamic Psychology." In C. Murchison (Ed.), *The Psychologies of 1925* (pp. 111–126). Worcester, Massachusetts: Clark University Press, 1926.
___. *Experimental Psychology*. New York: Holt, 1938.
___. *Dynamics of Behavior*. New York: Holt, Rinehart and Winston, 1958.
___, and M. Sheehan. *Contemporary Schools of Psychology*. New York: Ronald Press, 1964 (3rd. ed.).

Woolley, Helen Bradford Thompson (1874–1947)

SEX DIFFERENCES

Helen Bradford Thompson was born in Chicago, Illinois; she graduated (1897) and gained a Ph.D. in neurology and philosophy (1900) from the University of Chicago. She was awarded a fellowship from the Association of Collegiate Alumnae (now the American Association of University Women) to study in Paris and Berlin (1901–1902). She was professor of psychology and director of the psychological laboratory Mount Holycke College, South Hadley, Massachusetts (1902). In 1905 she married Dr. Paul Gerhardt Woolley; they moved to the Philippines, where he was director of the Serum Laboratory in Manila. She was as an experimental psychologist for the Philippines Bureau of Education, then chief inspector of Health, Bangkok (1907).

In 1908, the couple moved to Nebraska, then to Cincinnati, Ohio. She was instructor of philosophy, University of Cincinnati (1909–1911) and director of the Bureau for the Investigation of Working Children, Ohio (1911). In 1921 she worked at the Merrill-Palmer school in Detroit and in 1922 became associate director and organized one of the first nursery schools in the country for the study of child development and the training of teachers.

She was president of the National Vocational Guidance Association (1921); professor of education, Columbia University's Teacher's College (1924), and director of the Institute of Child Welfare Research, both in New York. Because of ill health she was asked to resign from Columbia University in (1930).

Major Contributions

For her doctoral research, Woolley tested the Darwinian assumption that women were biologically inferior to men. Results of a series of tests given to 25 males and 25 females to measure motor abilities, sensory threshold, intellectual abilities, and personality traits showed no sex differences in emotional functioning and only small, non-significant differences in intellectual abilities, and that women were slightly superior to men when it came to abilities such as memory and sensory perception.

Woolley attributed these differences to social and environmental factors, the differences in child-rearing practices and expectations for boys and girls, rather than to biological factors. Her research on the effects of child labor led to changes in the state labor laws. She was also instrumental in designing early performance tests, the beginnings of what would become the Merrill-Palmer Scale of Mental Tests. Woolley was a women's rights activist and a member and chairperson at one point of the Ohio Woman Suffrage Association. She died of cardiovascular disease.

Major Literature

Woolley, Helen Bradford Thompson. *The Mental Traits of Sex: An Experimental Investigation of the Normal Mind in Men and Women.* Chicago: The University of Chicago Press, 1903.

___. "The Validity of Standard of Mental Measurement in Young Childhood." *School and Society* 21 (1925): 476–482.

___. *David: A Study of the Experience of a Nursery School in Training a Child Adopted From an Institution.* Child Welfare League of America, Case Studies, No. 2, 1925.

___. *An Experimental Study of Children: At Work and in School Between the Ages of Fourteen and Eighteen Years.* New York: The Macmillan Company, 1926.

Wundt, Wilhelm Max
(1832–1920)
EXPERIMENTAL PSYCHOLOGY

Born at Neckarau/Mannheim, Germany, Wilhelm Max Wundt studied medicine from 1851 to 1855 at Tübingen and Heidelberg Universities, Germany, and was medical assistant at a Heidelberg clinic (1855) and gained a Ph.D. and an M.D. at Heidelberg (1856). He was habilitated as *Dozent* in physiology; *Privatdozent*, Physiological Institute, Heidelberg (1857–1864); *Ausserordentlicher* (assistant) *Professor* (1864); Army doctor, Franco-Prussian War (1870–1871); professor in inductive philosophy, Zürich, Switzerland (1874); professor of philosophy, Leipzig, Germany (1875); rector of Leipzig University (1889–1890); and emeritus professor (1915). Wundt founded the *Institut für Experimentelle Psychologie* (Leipzig, 1879) and the journal *Philosophische Studien* (1879).

Major Contributions

Wundt is generally acknowledged as the "father of experimental psychology" and the "founder of modern psychology." He is less commonly recognized as a founding figure of social psychology. His later years were spent working on *Völkerpsychologie* (people's psychology), which he understood as a study into the social basis of higher mental functioning.

At Heidelberg (1862) Wundt offered the first course ever taught in scientific psychology, as distinct from philosophy. Wundt perceived psychology as part of an elaborate philosophy where mind is seen as an activity, not a substance. Wundt established at Leipzig the first laboratory in the world dedicated to experimental psychology. This laboratory became a focus for those with a serious interest in psychology, first for German philosophers and psychology students, then for American and British students as well. All subsequent psychological laboratories were closely modeled in their early years on the Wundt model. (In 1882 the laboratory was renamed the Institute for Experimental Psychology.)

Wundt stressed the use of experimental methods drawn from the natural sciences. His *Principles of Physiological Psychology* is probably one of the most important in the history of psychology. In it he expounded on a system of psychology that sought to investigate the immediate experiences of consciousness, including sensations, feelings, volitions, and ideas; it also contained the concept of apperception, or conscious perception. The methodology prescribed was introspection, or conscious examination of conscious experience.

His publications include articles on animal and human physiology, poisons, vision, spiritualism, hypnotism, history, and politics; textbooks and handbooks of medical physics and human physiology; and encyclopedic tomes on linguistics, logic, ethics, religion, and a system of philosophy. Throughout his work, Wundt sought to associate the physiological with the psychological, to integrate the body-mind complex that is the human being.

Major Literature

Although many of Wundt's publications were translated into English, only recent editions have been included.

Wundt, Wilhelm Max. *Lectures on Human and Animal Psychology* (Significant Contributions to the History of Psychology 1750–). Westport, Connecticut: University Publications of America, 1977.

___. *Elements of Folk Psychology: Outlines of Psychological History of the Development of Mankind.* Westport, Connecticut: University Publications of America, 1983.

___. *Outlines of Psychology.* New York: Scholarly Press, 1999.

___. *Ethics: The Facts of Moral Life.* New York: Cosimo Inc, 2006.

___, and Thomas A. Sebeok (Eds.). *Language of Gestures.* Berlin: Walter de Gruyter, 2006.

Yerkes, Robert Mearns (1876–1956)

INTELLIGENCE TESTING

Born, Breadysville, Pennsylvania, Robert Mearns Yerkes gained an A.B. at Ursinus College, Collegeville, Pennsylvania (1897). At Harvard University, Cambridge, Massachusetts, he received an A.B. (1898) and Ph.D. (1902), then became instructor and assistant professor in Comparative Psychology (1902–1917). He was director, Psychological Services and Research, Boston Psychopathic Hospital (1913–1917); chief, Division of Psychology, office of the Surgeon General (1917–1919); chairman, Research Information Service, National Research Council (NRC) (1919–1924); professor of psychobiology, Yale University, New Haven, Connecticut (1924–1944). In 1929 Yerkes founded and directed the Yale Laboratories of Primate Biology until 1941 (the first non-human primate research laboratory in the United States, renamed the Yerkes National Primate Research Center 1941; it is in Atlanta, Georgia, at Emory University).

He was president, American Psychological Association (1917); president, American Philosophical Society (1936); president, American Society of Naturalists (1938); member, American Physiological Society, and fellow, American Academy of Arts and Sciences. His awards and honors include an honorary LL.D., Ursinus College (1923); honorary D.Sc., Wesleyan University, Middletown, Connecticut (1923); honorary M.A., Yale (1931); and Gold Medal, New York Zoological Society (1954).

Major Contributions

Robert Yerkes is most famous for his comparative psychology work with apes and chimpanzees. His writings emphasized that the cognitive differences between below-human primates and humans is often simply a matter of degree. Further, he believed that the study of primates would be a profitable route to discovering more about humans. He believed in eugenics and argued that humankind could benefit from intentional, selective interbreeding, though his ideas were not carried through.

Part of his work during World War I was as chairman, Committee on the Psychological Examination of Recruits, helping to develop group intelligence test that could identify recruits with low intelligence and allow the Army to recognize men who were particularly well-suited for special assignments and officers' training schools. The final forms of the Army Alpha and Beta tests were published in January 1919, and by the end of the war they had been administered to approximately two million men. His work as chairman of the National Research Council's Committee for Research in Problems of Sex helped Yerkes establish close relationships with officers from Rockefeller philanthropic foundations, relationships that later helped him to solicit substantial funds for his chimpanzee projects.

Major Literature

Yerkes, Robert Mearns, and Fanny Stevenson. *The Dancing Mouse: A Study in Animal Behavior.* New York: Macmillan, 1907. Manchester, New Hampshire: Ayer Co. Publishers, 1926.

___. *The Mental Life of Monkeys and Apes: A Study of Ideational Behavior.* Delmar, New York: Scholars' Facsimiles and Reprints, 1916/1979.

___ (Ed.). "Psychological Examining in the United States Army." *Memoirs of the National Academy of Sciences* 15 (1921): 1–890.

___, and A.W. Yerkes. *The Great Apes: A Study of Anthropoid Life.* New Haven: Yale University Press, 1929.

___. "Man-Power and Military Effectiveness: The Case for Human Engineering." *Journal of Consulting Psychology* 5 (1941): 205–209.

Zigler, Edward (1930–)
DEVELOPMENTAL PSYCHOLOGY

Born in Kansas City, Edward Zigler gained a B.S. at the University of Missouri, Kansas City (1954), and a Ph.D. in developmental psychology at the University of Texas, Austin (1958). Zigler was named by President Richard Nixon as the first director of the office of Child Development (now the Administration on Children, Youth and Families) and chief of the U.S. Children's Bureau, Washington (1970). His awards and honors include an honorary M.A., Yale University, New Haven, Connecticut (1967); honorary commissioner, National Commission on the International Year of the Child (1979); honorary doctorate, Boston College, Boston, Massachusetts (1985); B. Sarason Seymour Award, American Psychological Association (1993); Graduate School Distinguished Alumnus Award, University of Texas, Austin (2000); the Connecticut Higher Education Lifetime Achievement Community Service Award (2001); Lifetime Achievement Award, Connecticut Voices for Children (2002); and National Head Start Association, in honor of four decades of pioneering work in early childhood education (2003).

Major Contributions

Zigler is widely regarded as the "father" of Head Start and the nation's leading researcher of programs and policies for children and families. His main thrust is child development and family functioning, which encompasses mental retardation, psychopathology, intervention programs for economically disadvantaged children, and the effects of out-of-home care on the children of working parents. He is currently Seeling Professor of Psychology, emeritus, Yale University, and director emeritus, Edward Zigler Center in Child Development and Social Policy (until 2005, the Bush Center in Child Development and Social Policy). The center, which is at Yale, is one of the nation's oldest centers for child and family policy research, founded by Zigler in 1978 with funding from the Bush Foundation of Minnesota. His investigation into infant care in America inspired the Family and Medical Leave Act of 1993.

Zigler is frequently called as an expert witness before congressional committees and to comment on social policy issues that concern children and families in the United States. He has also chaired numerous conferences concerned with children. Zigler served on the President's Committee on Mental Retardation (1966) and was requested by President Gerald Ford to chair the Vietnamese Children's Resettlement Advisory Group (1970). In 1980, at President Jimmy Carter's request, he chaired the fifteenth anniversary Head Start Committee. This committee was charged with planning future policy for this government-run intervention program.

He is the author or editor of 32 books and has written over 600 scholarly articles. He is a member of the editorial boards of over 10 professional journals.

Major Literature

Kagan, Sharon Lynn, and Edward Zigler (Eds.). *Early Schooling: The National Debate*. New Haven, Connecticut: Yale University Press, 1969.

Zigler, Edward, Jacob A. Burack, and Robert M. Hodapp. *Handbook of Mental Retardation and Development*. New York: Cambridge University Press, 1998.

Zigler, Edward, and Dianne Bennett-Gates (Eds.). *Personality Development in Individuals With Mental Retardation*. New York: Cambridge University Press, 1999.

Zigler, Edward, and Susan Muenchow. *Head Start: The Inside Story of America's Most Successful Educational Experiment*. Jackson, Tennessee: Basic Books, 1999.

Timeline

Dates	Name *Area of Interest*
1734–1815	Mesmer, Franz Anton *Forerunner of Modern Hypnotism*
1745–1826	Pinel, Philippe *Reformer of Asylums*
1745–1813	Rush, Benjamin *Father of American Psychiatry*
1772–1850	Esquirol, Jean Etienne Dominique *Asylum Reform*
1794–1866	Conolly, John *Asylum Reform*
1801–1887	Fechner, Gustav Theodor *Psychophysics*
1809–1873	Morel, Bénédict Augustin *Dementia Praecox (Schizophrenia)*
1815–1890	Baillarger, Jules-Gabriel-François *Manic-Depression*
1818–1903	Bain, Alexander *Pragmatism and Empiricism*
1822–1884	Mendel, Gregor Johann *Genetics*
1824–1886	Gudden, Von Johann Bernhard Aloys *Neuropsychiatry*
1832–1920	Wundt, Wilhelm Max *Experimental Psychology*
1833–1944	Jastrow, Joseph *Optical Illusions*
1935–1911	Jackson, John Hughlings *Clinical Neurology*
1835–1909	Lombroso, Cesare *Criminal Anthropology*
1837–1902	Bucke, Richard Maurice *Stages of Consciousness*
1838–1917	Brentano, Franz Clemens *Founder of Act Psychology*
1839–1916	Ribot, Theodule-Armand *Pioneering Work on Memory Loss*
1840–1902	Krafft-Ebing, Richard von *Sexual Perversion*
1842–1925	Breuer, Josef *Forerunner of Psychoanalysis*
1842–1910	James, William *Pragmatism and Functionalism*
1842–1921	Ladd, George Trumbull *Experimental Psychology*
1844–1924	Hall, Granville Stanley *Child and Educational Psychology*
1847–1930	Ladd-Franklin, Christine ͺ*Color Vision*
1848–1931	Forel, Auguste-Henri *Neuroanatomy*
1848–1894	Romanes, George J. *Comparative Psychology*
1848–1936	Stumpf, Carl *Psychology of Sound and Music*
1848–1905	Wernicke, Karl *Brain Trauma and Speech*
1850–1934	Müller, Georg Elias *Experimental Psychology*
1850–1909	Ebbinghaus, Hermann *Study of Memory*
1851–1943	Martin, Lillien Jane *Gerontological Psychology*
1852–1936	Morgan, Conwy Lloyd *Comparative Psychology*
1853–1900	Korsakoff, Sergei *Amnestic Disorders*
1854–1929	Prince, Morton Henry *Multiple Personality*
1856–1931	Dercum, Francis Xavier *Psychobiology*
1856–1939	Freud, Sigmund *Founder of Psychoanalysis*
1856–1926	Kraepelin, Emil *Classification of Mental Illness*
1857–1911	Binet, Alfred *Measurement of Intelligence*
1857–1939	Bleuler, Eugen *Studies of Schizophrenics*

1857–1924	Clarke, Charles Kirk *Canadian National Committee for Mental Hygiene*
1857–1952	Sherrington, Sir Charles Scott *Experimental Psychology*
1857–1940	Wagner-Jauregg, Julius *Pathology of the Nervous System*
1859–1952	Dewey, John *Pragmatism*
1859–1939	Ellis, Henry Havelock *Human Sexual Behavior*
1859–1947	Janet, Pierre *Pathological Psychology*
1860–1949	Angell, James Rowland *Functional Psychology*
1860–1955	Bryan, William Lowe *Learning and Experimental Psychology*
1860–1944	Cattell, James McKeen *Psychological Testing*
1861–1934	Baldwin, James Mark *Educational Psychology*
1863–1930	Calkins, Mary Whiton *Self-psychology*
1863–1945	Delabarre, Edmund B. *Mental Imagery*
1863–1916	Munsterberg, Hugo *Psychology of Business*
1863–1945	Spearman, Charles Edward *Human Intelligence*
1864–1915	Alzheimer Aloysius "Alois" *Senile Dementia*
1864–1922	Rivers, William Halse *Mental Functioning*
1866–1950	Meyer, Adolf *Psychobiology*
1866–1949	Seashore, Carl Emil *Psychology of Music and Art*
1867–1923	Sidis, Boris *Psychopathology*
1867–1927	Titchener Edward Bradford *Psychology of Consciousness*
1869–1955	Scott, Walter Dill *Psychology of Advertising*
1869–1962	Woodworth, Robert Sessions *Experimental Psychology*
1870–1937	Adler, Alfred *Individual Psychology*
1870–1952	Montessori, Maria *Developmental Psychology*
1871–1938	McDougall, William *Experimental Psychology*
1871–1939	Washburn, Margaret Floy *Animal Behavior*
1872–1940	Claparède, Édouard *Child Psychology*
1872–1950	Howes, Ethel Dench Puffer *Sexual Equality*
1873–1954	Carr, Harvey A. *Functionalism*
1873–1933	Ferenczi, Sandor *Active Analytic Techniques*
1874–1933	Franz, Shepherd Ivory *Brain Functioning*
1874–1953	Hinkle, Beatrice Moses *Jungian Analyst*
1874–1955	Moniz, António Caetano de Abreu Freire Egas *Founder of Modern Psychosurgery*
1874–1949	Thorndike, Edward Lee *Operant Conditioning*
1874–1947	Wooley, Helen Bradford Thompson *Sex Differences*
1875–1893	Charcot, Jean-Martin *Hypnosis*
1875–1932	Downey, June Etta *Personality*
1875–1949	Dunlap, Knight *Behaviorism*
1875–1961	Jung, Carl Gustav *Analytical Psychology*
1875–1973	Kent, Grace *Clinical Psychology*
1876–1943	Beers, Clifford *Mental Health Education*
1876–1956	Yerkes, Robert Mearns *Intelligence Testing*
1877–1963	Cerletti, Ugo *Neuropsychiatry*
1877–1956	Terman, Lewis Madison *Intelligence Testing*
1877–1925	Abraham, Karl *Infant Sexuality*
1877–1943	Hamilton, Gilbert Van Tassel *Objective Psychopathology*
1878–1949	Aichhorn, August *Psychological Criminology*
1878–1972	Gilbreth, Lillian Moller *Industrial Psychology*
1878–1969	Wallin, John Edward Wallace *Experimental Psychology*
1878–1958	Watson, John Broadus *Behaviorism*
1879–1963	Bühler, Karl *Thought Process*
1879–1958	Jones, Ernest *Applied Psychoanalysis*
1880–1955	Ames, Adelbert Jr. *Visual Perception*
1880–1952	Bingham, Walter Van Dyke *Industrial Psychology*

1880–1961	Gesell, Arnold Lucius *Child Development*
1880–1943	Wertheimer, Max *Gestalt Psychology*
1881–1966	Binswanger, Ludwig *Existential Psychotherapy*
1882–1962	Bonaparte, Princess Marie *Founded the French Institute of Psychoanalysis*
1882–1960	Klein, Melanie *Analytical Play Therapy*
1883–1971	Burt, Sir Cyril Ludowic *Educational Psychology*
1883–1969	Jaspers, Karl Theodor *Existentialist Psychotherapy*
1883–1972	Porteus, Stanley David *Race Psychology*
1884–1982	Deutsch, Helene *Psychology of Women*
1884–1952	Hull, Clark Leonard *Drive Reduction Theory*
1884–1939	Rank, Otto *Will Therapy*
1884–1922	Rorschach, Hermann *Projective Diagnostic Test*
1885–1952	Horney, Karen *Personality Disorders*
1886–1969	Bartlett, Sir Frederic Charles *Cognitive Psychology*
1886–1968	Boring, Edwin Garrigues *History of Psychology*
1866–1957	Goddard, Henry Herbert *Eugenics*
1886–1959	Goodenough, Florence Laura *Intelligence Testing*
1886–1959	Guthrie, Edwin Ray *Theory of Learning*
1886– 1939	Hollingworth, Leta Stetter *Developmental Psychology*
1886–1941	Koffka, Kurt *Gestalt Psychology*
1886–1959	Tolman, Edward Chace *Cognitive Approach to Learning*
1887–1967	Köhler, Wolfgang *Experimental Psychology*
1887–1974	Spitz, Rene Arpad *Sensory Deprivation in Children*
1887–1955	Thurstone, Louis Leon *Psychometrics and Psychophysics*
1888–1974	Assagioli, Roberto *Psychosynthesis*
1889–1957	Fromm, Frieda *Psychodynamic Psychotherapy*
1888–1971	Harding, Mary Esther *First American Jungian Analyst*
1888–1964	Kretschmer, Ernest *Body Types and Mental Illness*
1889–1964	Fairbairn, W.R.D. *Object Relations*
1889–1974	Moreno, Jacob Levy *Psychodrama*
1889–1972	Bekesy, Georg von *Industrial Psychology*
1890–1978	Allport, Floyd Henry *Experimental Social Psychology*
1890–1958	Lashley, Karl Spencer *Behaviorism*
1890–1947	Lewin, Kurt *Gestalt Psychology*
1891–1964	Alexander, Franz Gabriel *Psychosomatic Medicine*
1891–1953	Roheim, Geza *Psychoanalytic Anthropology*
1892–1949	Sullivan, Harry Stack *Interpersonal Theory of Psychiatry*
1893–1974	Buhler, Charlotte Malachowski *Life Span Development*
1893–1989	Cattell, Psyche *Measurement of Intelligence in Children*
1893–1990	Menninger, Karl Augustus *The Menninger Clinic*
1893–1988	Murray, Henry Alexander *Psychological Testing*
1893–1970	Perls, Fritz *Gestalt Therapy*
1893–1958	Thompson, Clara Mabel *Psychology of Women*
1894–1970	Hartmann, Heinz *Ego Psychology*
1894–1981	Kanner, Leo *Infant Autism*
1894–1936	Pavlov, Ivan *Classical Conditioning*
1895–1982	Freud, Anna *Child Psychoanalysis*
1895–1980	Rhine, Joseph Banks *Psychical Research*
1895–1954	Sumner, Francis Cecil *First African American Pioneer in Psychology*
1895–1981	Wertham, Fredric *Seduction of Mass Media*
1896–1970	Balint, Michael *The Basic Fault*
1896–1988	Heider, Fritz *Balance Theory*
1896–1987	Jones, Mary Cover *Behavior Therapy*
1896–1980	Piaget, Jean *Cognitive Development Theory*

1896–1964	von Meduna, Ladislas *Convulsive Therapy*
1896–1934	Vygotsky, Lev Semeonovich *Social Development Theory*
1896–1981	Wechsler, David *Intelligence Scale for Children*
1897–1967	Allport, Gordon Willard *Theory of Personality*
1896–1971	Winnicott, Donald Woods *Child Psychiatry*
1897–1987	Bender, Lauretta *Child Psychiatry*
1897–1979	Bion, Wilfred Ruprecht *Group Psychotherapy*
1897–1979	Briggs Myers, Isabel *Personality Typing*
1897–1946	Brunswick, Ruth Mack *Emotional Development*
1897–1972	Dreikurs, Rudolf *Family Psychology*
1897–1987	Guilford, Joy Paul *Psychophysics*
1897–1979	Kluver, Heinrich *Animal Experiments*
1897–1985	Mahler, Margaret Schoenberger *Separation of Infant from Mother*
1897–1957	Reich, Wilhelm *Character Analysis, Orgone Therapy*
1897–1993	Thurstone, Thelma Gwinn *Intelligence Testing*
1898–1973	Carmichael, Leonard *Military and Child Psychology*
1898–1976	Foulkes, Sigmund Heinrich *Group Analytic Therapy*
1898–1974	Moreno, Jacob *Psychodrama*
1898–1972	Penrose, Lionel Sharples *Genetics of Learning Disability*
1898–1977	Sheldon, William Herbert *Body Types*
1899–1994	Bayley, Nancy *Infant Development*
1899–1996	Keller, Fred *Experimental Psychology*
1899–1992	Klineberg, Otto *Personality and Social Psychology*
1899–1988	McGraw, Myrtle Byram *Child Development*
1900–1980	Dollard, John *Race Relations*
1900–1980	Fromm, Erich Pinchas *Interactive Psychology*
1900–1991	Havighurst, Robert James *Adult Development and Aging*
1900–1997	Howard, Ruth Winifred *Developmental Psychology*
1900–1957	Sakel, Manfred Joshua *Insulin Shock Therapy*
1901–2002	Allen, Doris Twitchell *Psychodrama*
1901–1981	Lacan, Jacques *Language of the Unconscious*
1901–1994	May, Rollo *Existential Psychotherapy*
1901–1981	Shakow, David *Schizophrenia*
1902–1982	Buxbaum, Edith *Child Development*
1902–1980	Dąbrowski, Kazimierz *Positive Disintegration*
1902–1959	Dunbar, Helen Flanders *Psychosomatic Medicine*
1902–1987	Rogers, Carl Ransom *Person-Centred Therapy*
1902–1996	Viteles, Morris Simon *Industrial Psychology*
1902–1980	Erickson, Milton *Paradoxical and Strategic Therapy*
1902–1994	Erikson, Erik Homburger *Lifespan Development*
1902–1977	Luria, Alexander Romanovich *Neuropsychology*
1902–2003	Murphy, Lois Barclay *Child/Social Psychology*
1903–1990	Bettelheim, Bruno *Emotionally Disturbed Children*
1903–1990	Boss, Medard *Daseinsanalysis*
1903–1955	Brunswik, Egon *Cognitive Psychology*
1903–1996	Gulliksen, Harold Oliver *Mathematical Psychology*
1904–?	Arnheim, Rudolph *Visual Perception*
1904–1980	Bateson, Gregory *Double-bind*
1904–1979	Gibson, James Jerome *Visual Perception*
1904–1985	Hebb, Donald Olding *Neuropsychology*
1904–2001	Hilgard, Ernest Ropiequet *Hypnosis*
1904–1993	Niederland, William Guglielmo *Survivor Syndrome*
1904–1990	Skinner, Burrhus Frederic *Operant Conditioning*
1904–1998	Wallach, Hans *Visual and Auditory Perception*

1905–1975	Carpenter, Clarence Ray *Animal Behavior*
1905–1998	Cattell, Raymond B. *Personality Testing*
1905–1997	Frankl, Viktor *Logotherapy*
1905–1981	Harlow, Harry Frederick *Study of Affection in Primates*
1905–1967	Kelly, George Alexander *Personal Construct Theory*
1905–1960	Neumann, Erich *Developmental Psychology*
1906–1991	Hunt, Joseph McVicker *Developmental Psychology*
1906–1988	Sherif, Muzafer *Prejudice in Social Groups*
1906–1973	Stevens, Stanley Smith *Psychophysics*
1906–1993	Tyler, Leona Elizabeth *Vocational Guidance and Counselling*
1907–1996	Asch, Solomon Elliot *Gestalt Psychology*
1907–1990	Bowlby, John *Attachment Theory*
1907–1987	Delay, Jean *Psychopharmacology*
1907–1996	Hooker, Evelyn *Male Sexuality*
1907–1982	Selye, Hans Hugo Bruno *Stress Management*
1907–1967	Spence, Kenneth Wartenbee *Theory of Learning*
1908–1971	Ackerman, Nathan Ward *Family Therapy*
1908–2001	Anastasi, Anne *Intelligence Testing*
1908–1970	Maslow, Abraham H. *Needs Hierarchy*
1908–1993	Sears, Pauline Snedden *Child Development*
1908–1989	Sears, Robert Richardson *Child Development*
1909–2005	Frank, Jerome David *Classification of Psychotherapies*
1909–2002	Miller, Neal Elgar *Theory of Motivation*
1909–2000	Scott, John Paul *Comparative Psychology*
1910–1970	Berne, Eric *Transactional Analysis*
1910–2002	Gibson, Eleanor Jack *Developmental Psychology*
1911–1988	Beach, Frank Ambrose *Behavioral Endocrinology*
1912–1980	Cade, John Frederick Joseph *Bipolar Disorder*
1912–1977	Crutchfield, Richard Stanley *Personality Assessment*
1912–1988	Hamilton, Max *Psychopharmacology*
1912–1961	Hovland, Carl Ivor *Persuasion*
1913–1999	Ainsworth, Mary Dinsmore Salter *Early Emotional Attachment*
1913–	Ellis, Albert *Rational Emotive Therapy*
1913–1997	Inhelder, Barbel *Human Intelligence*
1913–1981	Kohut, Heniz *Self-psychology*
1913–1994	Sperry, Roger Wolcott *Brain Functioning*
1914–2005	Clark, Kenneth Bancroft *Social Psychology*
1915–	Bruner, Jerome Seymour *Cognitive Learning Theory in Education*
1915–2000	Kety, Seymour *Psychiatric Genetics*
1915–2003	Torrance, Ellis Paul *Creativity*
1915–1997	Wolpe, Joseph *Systematic Desensitization*
1916–2004	Bales, Robert Freed *Evaluation and Measurement*
1916–1996	Campbell, Donald Thomas *Evolutionary Epistemology*
1916–2001	Cronbach, Lee Joseph *Educational Psychology*
1916–1997	Eysenck, Hans Jurgen *Behavior Therapy*
1916–2002	Gagné, Robert Mills *Conditions of Learning*
1916–2001	Neugarten, Bernice Levin *Adult Development and Aging*
1916–1991	Osgood, Charles Egerton *Semantic Differential*
1916–	Rotter, Julian B. *Social Learning Theory*
1916–1988	Satir, Virginia *Family Therapy*
1916–2001	Simon, Herbert Alexander *Cognitive Psychology*
1917–2005	Bronfenbrenner, Urie *Head Start Program*
1917–2002	Chapanis, Alphonse *Father of Ergonomics*
1917–1983	Clark, Mamie Phipps *Psychology of Self-esteem*

1917–	Hoffer, Abram *Orthomolecular Psychiatry*
1917–1996	Koch, Sigmund *Human Mentality and Functioning*
1917–1998	McClelland, David Clarence *Achievement Motivation*
1917–	Maccoby, Eleanor Emmons *Psychology of Sex-differences*
1918–1989	Himmelweit, Hilde Therese *Cognitive Psychology*
1918–1990	Janis, Irving Lester *Groupthink*
1918–	Loevinger, Jane *Developmental Psychology*
1918–	Milner, Brenda *Clinical Neuropsychology*
1918–1988	Rokeach, Milton *Open-mindedness*
1919–	Estes, William Kaye *Mathematial Psychology*
1919–1989	Festinger, Leon *Cognitive Dissonance Theory*
1919–2005	Gerbner, George *Cultivation Theory*
1919–1999	Ratliff, Floyd *Neuropsychology*
1919–1982	Tajfel, Henri *Prejudice*
1919–1979	Tizard, Jack *Learning Difficulties*
1920–2001	Bailey, Marian Breland *Operant Conditioning*
1920–	Deutsch, Morton *Conflict Resolution*
1920–1968	Jackson, Donald De Avila *Conjoint Family Therapy*
1920–1997	Jaynes, Julian *The Origin of Consciousness*
1920–2002	Lazarus, Richard S. *Stress Appraisal*
1920–	Szasz, Thomas *Anti-Psychiatry*
1921–	Beck, Aaron T. *Cognitive Therapy*
1921–1988	Bejerot, Nils *Stockholm Syndrome*
1921–1999	Carterette, Edward Calvin Hayes *Auditory Perception*
1921–	Culbertson, Frances Mitchell *Gender and Depression*
1921–2003	Kelley, Harold Harding *Attribution Theory*
1921–1998	Progoff, Ira *Intensive Journal Method*
1921–2003	Singer, Margaret Thaler *Brainwashing and Cults*
1922–1911	Galton, Sir Francis *Intelligence*
1922–1997	Schachter, Stanley *Attribution of Emotions*
1922–2005	Socarides, Charles W. *Sexuality*
1923–	Argyris, Chris *Industrial Psychology*
1923–2003	Gerard, Harold *Experimental Social Psychology*
1923–	Gregory, Richard Langton *Perception*
1923–	Hinde, Robert Aubrey *Comparative and Physiological Psychology*
1923–1981	Humphrey, Jeanne Block *Ego Development*
1923–	Jensen, Arthur Robert *Developmental Psychology*
1923–	Michie, Donald *Artificial Intelligence*
1924–1976	Berlyne, Daniel Ellis *Comparative Psychology*
1924–	Cummings, Nicholas Andrew *Behavioral Health*
1924–	Goodnow, Jacqueline Jarrett *Influence of Culture On Thinking*
1924–	Janov, Arthur *Primal Therapy*
1924–	Laplanche, Jean *Psychosexual Development*
1925–2002	Argyle, John Michael *Non-verbal Language*
1925–	Bandura, Albert *Social Learning Theory*
1925–1997	Brown, Roger William *Language Development*
1925–1961	Fanon, Frantz Omar *Effects of Discrimination*
1925–	Glasser, William *Reality Therapy*
1925–	Moscovici, Serge *Group Psychology*
1925–	Paivio, Allan Urho *Imagery, Language and Memory*
1925–2001	Payton, Carolyn Robertson *Psychotherapy*
1926–	Berkowitz, Leonard *Human Aggression*
1926–1993	Broadbent, Donald Eric *Experimental Psychology*
1926–	Dunnette, Marvin D. *Counselling Psychology*

1926–2006	Lambert, Nadine M. *Developmental Psychology*
1926–	Lifton, Robert Jay *Psychohistory*
1926–2004	Kübler-Ross, Elisabeth *Death, Dying and Bereavement*
1926–	Patterson, Gerald R. *Antisocial Behavior*
1927–2005	Barber, Theodore Xenophon *Hypnosis*
1927–	Baumrind, Diana Blumberg *Family Socialization*
1927–	Green, André *Psychoanalytic Criticism*
1927–	Kamin, Leon J. *Intelligence*
1927–1987	Kohlberg, Laurence *Theory of Moral Development*
1927–1989	Laing, Robert David *Family Psychology*
1927–2006	Miller, Jean Baker *Psychology of Women*
1927–	Minsky, Marvin Lee *Artificial Intelligence*
1927–2000	Orne, Martin Theodore *Hypnosis*
1928–	Chomsky, Noam *Linguistics*
1928–	Kernberg, Otto F. *Borderline Personality Disorder*
1928–	Schaie, K. Warner *Adult Development and Aging*
1929–	Kagan, Jerome *Physiology in Psychological Development*
1930–	Altman, Irwin *Close Relationships*
1930–	Branden, Nathaniel *Self-esteem*
1930–	Irigaray, Luce *Feminism*
1930–	Lynn, Richard *Intelligence*
1930–	Mischel, Walter *Personality Structure*
1930–	Zigler, Edward *Developmental Psychology*
1931–2001	Bernal, Martha *Racism and Sexism*
1931–	Denmark, Florence Harriet Levin *Psychology of Women*
1931–	De Mause, Lloyd *Psychohistory*
1931–	Elkind, David *Child Development*
1931–	Grof, Stanislav *Transpersonal Psychology*
1931–1981	Mayo, Clara Alexandria Weiss *Social Psychology*
1932–	Aronson, Elliot *Media Psychology*
1932–	Haber, Ralph Norman *Experimental Psychology*
1932–	Lazarus, Arnold Allan *Multi-modal Therapy*
1932–	Vroom, Victor H. *Expectancy Theory of Motivation*
1933–	Kimura, Doreen *Clinical Neuropsychology*
1933–1984	Milgram, Stanley *Obedience and Authority*
1933–	Rosenthal, Robert *Self-fulfilling Prophecy*
1933–	Rutter, Sir Michael Llewellyn *Child Psychiatry*
1934–	Csikszentmihalyi, Mihaly *Flow Theory*
1934–	Ekman, Paul *Facial Expressions*
1934–	Kahneman, Daniel *Behavioral Finance*
1935–	Craik, Fergus I.M. *Adult Development and Aging*
1935–	Treisman, Anne *Visual Attention and Memory*
1936–	Entwistle, Noel J. *Educational Psychology*
1936–	Feigenbaum, Edward A. *Artificial Intelligence*
1936–	Gilligan, Carol *Psychology of Women*
1936–	Goodwin, Frederick K *Bipolar Disorder*
1936–2005	Peck, M. Scott *Psychiatry and Religion*
1936–	Scarr, Sandra Wood *Child Development*
1937–	Lewis, Michael *Developmental Psychology*
1937–	Latané, Bibb *Social Impact Theory*
1937–	Torrey, Edwin Fuller *Treatment of Schizophrenia*
1937–1996	Tversky, Amos *Prospect Theory*
1937–	Warr, Peter Bryan *Industrial Psychology*
1938–	Bem, Daryl J. *Self-perception*

1938–   Parke, Ross D.   *Child Development*
1939–   Apter, Michael John   *Reversal Theory*
1939–   Baltes, Paul   *Lifespan Development*
1939–   Gazzaniga, Michael S.   *Neuropsychology*
1940–   Cooper, Cary Lynn   *Stress Management*
1940–   Fowler, James W.   *Stages of Growth in Faith*
1940–   Grinder, John   *Neurolinguistic Programming*
1940–   Hackman, J. Richard   *Industrial Psychology*
1941–   Deaux, Kay   *Psychology of Women*
1941–   Kleinman, Arthur   *Psychiatric Anthropology*
1942–   Ajzen, Icek   *Consumer Health*
1942–   Clark, Eve Vivienne   *Linguistics*
1942–   Morris, Robert Lyle   *Parapsychology*
1942–   Seligman, Martin E.P.   *Learned Helplessness*
1943–   Gardner, Howard Earl   *Multiple Intelligences*
1944–   Appelle, Stuart   *Sensory Perception*
1944–   Bem, Sandra Lipsitz   *Bem Sex Role Inventory*
1944–   Coles, Michael G.H.   *Psychophysiology*
1944–   Farrington, David Philip   *Criminology*
1944–   Kaufman, Alan S.   *Intelligence Testing*
1944–   Loftus, Elizabeth F.   *Study of Memory*
1945–   Bickhard, Mark H.   *Developmental Psychology*
1945–   Cialdini, Robert Beno   *Persuasion*
1945–   Kaufman, Nadeen L.   *Intelligence Testing*
1946–   Bar-Tal, Daniel   *Developmental Psychology*
1946–   Brooks-Gunn, Jeanne   *Child Development*
1946–   Jamison, Kay Redfield   *Bipolar Disorder*
1947–   Anderson, John Robert   *Artificial Intelligence*
1947–   Gottfredson, Linda Susanne   *Educational Psychology*
1947–   Langer, Ellen J.   *Adult Development and Aging*
1948–   Plomin, Robert   *Behavioral Genetics*
1949–   Allik, Jüri   *Visual Psychophysics*
1949–   Golden, Charles Joshua   *Neuropsychology*
1949–   Sternberg, Robert J.   *Higher Mental Functions*
1950–   Bandler, Richard   *Neurolinguistic Programming*
1952–   Brown, Laura S.   *Feminist Therapy*
1954–   Pinker, Steven Arthur   *Language Development*
1956–   Bentall, Richard P.   *Forensic Clinical Psychology*
1957–   Cosmides, Leda   *Evolutionary Psychology*
1967–   Bowden, Blake Sperry   *Study of Adolescents*

Psychologists, Psychiatrists and Psychotherapists Listed by Discipline

PSYCHOLOGY

Aichhorn, August
Ainsworth, Mary Dinsmore Salter
Ajzen, Icek
Allen, Doris Twitchell
Allik, Jüri
Allport, Floyd Henry
Allport, Gordon Willard
Altman, Irwin
Ames, Adelbert, Jr.
Anastasi, Anne
Anderson, John Robert
Angell, James Rowland
Appelle, Stuart
Apter, Michael John
Argyle, John Michael
Argyris, Chris
Arnheim, Rudolph
Aronson, Elliot
Asch Solomon Elliot
Bailey, Marian Breland
Bain, Alexander
Baldwin, James Mark
Bales, Robert Freed
Baltes, Paul
Bandler, Robert
Bandura, Albert
Barber, Theodore Xenophon
Bar-Tal, Daniel
Bartlett, Sir Frederic Charles
Bateson, Gregory
Baumrind, Diana Blumberg
Bayley, Nancy
Beach, Frank Ambrose

Bekesy, Georg von
Bem, Daryl J.
Bem, Sandra Lipsitz
Bentall, Richard P.
Berkowitz, Leonard
Berlyne, Daniel Ellis
Bernal, Martha
Bettelheim, Bruno
Bickhard, Mark H.
Binet, Alfred
Bingham, Walter Van Dyke
Boring, Edwin Garrigues
Bowden, Blake Sperry
Branden, Nathaniel
Brentano, Franz Clemens
Briggs Myers, Isabel
Broadbent, Donald Eric
Bronfenbrenner Urie
Brooks-Gunn, Jeanne
Brown, Laura S
Brown, Roger William
Bruner Jerome Seymour
Brunswik, Egon
Bryan, William Lowe
Bühler, Charlotte Mala-chowski
Bühler, Karl
Burt, Sir Cyril Ludowic
Calkins, Mary Whiton
Campbell, Donald Thomas
Carmichael, Leonard
Carpenter, Clarence Ray
Carr, Harvey A.

Carterette, Edward Calvin Hayes
Cattell, James Mckeen
Cattell, Psyche
Cattell, Raymond B.
Chapanis, Alphonse
Chomsky, Noam
Cialdini, Robert Beno
Claparède, Édouard
Clark, Eve Vivienne
Clark, Kenneth Bancroft
Clark, Mamie Phipps
Coles, Michael G. H.
Cooper, Cary Lynn
Cosmides, Leda
Craik, Fergus I. M.
Cronbach, Lee Joseph
Crutchfield, Richard Stanley
Csikszentmihalyi, Mihaly
Culbertson, Frances Mitchell
Cummings, Nicholas Andrew
Deaux, Kay
Delabarre, Edmund Burke
Denmark, Florence Harriet Levin
Deutsch, Morton Henry
Dewey, John
Dollard, John
Downey, June Etta
Dunlap, Knight
Ebbinghaus, Hermann
Ekman, Paul
Elkind, David
Ellis, Henry Havelock

303

Entwistle, Noel J.
Erikson, Erik Homburger
Estes, William Kaye
Eysenck, Hans Jurgen
Farrington, David Philip
Fechner, Gustav Theodor
Feigenbaum, Edward A.
Festinger, Leon
Fowler, James W.
Franz, Shepherd Ivory
Gagné, Robert Mills
Galton, Sir Francis
Gardner Howard Earl
Gazzaniga, Micheal S.
Gerard, Harold
Gerbner, George
Gesell, Arnold Lucius
Gibson, Eleanor Jack
Gibson, James Jerome
Gilbreth, Lillian Moller
Gilligan, Carol
Goddard, Henry Herbert
Golden, Charles Joshua
Goodenough, Florence Laura
Goodnow, Jacqueline Jarrett
Gottfredson, Linda Susanne
Gregory, Richard Langton
Grinder, John
Grof, Stanislav
Guilford, Joy Paul
Gulliksen Harold Oliver
Guthrie, Edwin Ray
Haber, Ralph Norman
Hackman, J. Richard
Hall, Granville Stanley
Harlow, Harry Frederick
Havighurst, Robert James
Hebb, Donald Olding
Heider, Fritz
Hilgard, Ernest Ropiequet
Himmelweit, Hilde Therese
Hinde, Robert Aubrey
Hollingworth, Leta Stetter
Hooker, Evelyn
Hovland, Carl
Howes, Ethel Dench Puffer
Hull, Clark Leonard
Humphrey, Jeanne Block
Hunt, Joseph McVicker
Inhelder, Barbel
James, William
Jamison, Kay Redfield
Janis, Irving Lester
Jastrow, Joseph
Jaynes Julian
Jensen, Arthur Robert

Jones, Mary Cover
Kagan, Jerome
Kahneman, Daniel
Kamin, Leon J.
Kaufman, Alan S.
Kaufman, Nadeen L.
Keller, Fred
Kelley, Harold Harding
Kent, Grace
Kimura, Doreen
Klineberg, Otto
Kluver, Heinrich
Koch, Sigmund
Koffka, Kurt
Kohlberg, Laurence
Köhler, Wolfgang
Kohut, Heniz
Krech, David
Ladd, George Trumbull
Ladd-Franklin, Christine
Lambert, Nadine M.
Langer, Ellen J.
Lashley, Karl Spencer
Latané, Bibb
Lazarus, Arnold Allan
Lazarus, Richard S.
Lewin, Kurt
Lewis, Michael
Loevinger, Jane
Loftus, Elizabeth F.
Luria, Alexander Romanovich
Lynn, Richard
Maccoby, Eleanor Emmons
Martin, Lillien Jane
Maslow, Abraham H.
Mayo, Clara Alexandria Weiss
McClelland, David Clarence
McDougall, William
McGraw, Myrtle Byram
Mendel, Gregor Johann
Milgram, Stanley
Miller, Neal Elgar
Milner, Brenda
Minsky, Marvin Lee
Mischel, Walter
Montessori, Maria
Morgan, Conwy Lloyd
Morris, Robert Lyle
Moscovici, Serge
Müller, Georg Elias
Munsterberg, Hugo
Murphy, Lois Barclay
Murray, Henry Alexander
Neugarten, Bernice Levin
Osgood, Charles Egerton
Paivio, Allan Urho

Parke, Ross D.
Patterson, Gerald R.
Pavlov, Ivan Petrovich
Penrose, Lionel Sharples
Perls, Fritz
Piaget, Jean
Pinker, Steven Arthur
Porteus, Stanley David
Ratliff, Floyd
Rhine, Joseph Banks
Ribot, Theodule-Armand
Rokeach, Milton
Romanes, George J.
Rosenthal, Robert
Rotter, Julian B.
Scarr, Sandra Wood
Schachter, Stanley
Schaie, K. Warner
Scott, John Paul
Scott, Walter Dill
Sears, Pauline Snedden
Sears, Robert Richardson
Seashore, Carl Emil
Seligman, Martin E. P.
Selye, Hans Hugo
Sheldon, William Herbert
Sherif, Muzafer
Sherrington, Sir Charles Scott
Simon, Herbert Alexander
Skinner, Burrhus
Spearman, Charles Edward
Spence, Kenneth Wartenbee
Sperry, Roger Wolcott
Sternberg, Robert J.
Stevens, Stanley Smith
Stumpf, Carl
Sumner, Francis Cecil
Tajfel, Henri
Terman, Lewis Madison
Thorndike, Edward, Lee
Thurstone, Louis Leon
Thurstone, Thelma Gwinn
Titchener Edward Bradford
Tizard, Jack
Tolman, Edward Chace
Torrance, Ellis Paul
Treisman, Anne
Tversky, Amos
Tyler, Leona Elizabeth
Viteles, Morris Simon
Vroom, Victor H.
Vygotsky, Lev Semeonovich
Wallach, Hans
Wallin, John Edward Wallace
Warr, Peter Bryan
Washburn, Margaret Floy

Watson, John Broadus
Wechsler, David
Wertheimer, Max
Wolpe, Joseph

Woodworth, Robert Sessions
Wooley, Helen Bradford
    Thompson
Wundt, Wilhelm Max

Yerkes, Robert Mearns
Zigler, Edward

PSYCHIATRY

Adler, Alfred
Alzheimer, Aloysius "Alois"
Assagioli, Roberto
Baillarger, Jules-Gabriel-
    François
Beck, Aaron T.
Beers, Clifford, Whittington
Bejerot, Nils
Bender, Lauretta
Bleuler, Eugen
Bowlby, John
Bucke, Richard Maurice
Cade, John Frederick Joseph
Cerletti, Ugo
Charcot, Jean-Martin
Clarke, Charles Kirk
Conolly, John
Dąbrowski. Kazimierz
Delay, Jean
Dercum, Francis Xavier
Deutsch, Helene
Dunbar, Helen Flanders
Erikson, Milton
Esquirol, Jean Etienne
    Dominique
Fanon, Frantz Omar

Forel, Auguste-Henri
Frank, Jerome David
Glasser, William
Goodwin, Frederick K
Hamilton, Gilbert Van Tassel
Hamilton, Max
Hoffer, Abram
Horney, Karen
Janet, Pierre
Jaspers, Karl Theodor
Kanner, Leo
Kety, Seymour
Kleinman, Arthur
Korsakoff, Sergei
Kraepelin, Emil
Krafft-Ebing, Richard von
Kretschmer, Ernest
Kübler-Ross, Elisabeth
Laing, Robert David
Lifton, Robert Jay
Lombroso, Cesare
Menninger, Karl Augustus
Mesmer, Franz Anton
Meyer, Adolf
Moniz, António Caetano de
    Abreu Freire Egas

Morel, Bénédict Augustin
Orne, Martin Theodore
Peck, M Scott
Pinel, Philippe
Plomin, Robert
Prince, Morton
Reich, Wilhelm
Rivers, William Halse Rivers
Rorschach, Hermann
Rush, Benjamin
Rutter, Sir Michael Llewellyn
Sakel, Manfred Joshua
Shakow, David
Sidis, Boris
Socarides, Charles W.
Spitz, Rene Arpad
Sullivan, Harry Stack
Szasz, Thomas
Thompson, Clara Mabel
Torrey, Edwin Fuller
Wagner-Jauregg, Julius Von
Wernicke, Karl
Wertham, Fredric
Winnicott, Donald Woods
Wolpe, Joseph

PSYCHOTHERAPIES

Abraham, Karl
Ackerman, Nathan Ward
Alexander, Franz Gabriel
Balint, Michael
Berne, Eric
Binswanger, Ludwig
Bion, Wilfred Ruprecht
Bonaparte, Princess Marie
Boss, Medard
Breuer, Josef
Brunswick, Ruth Mack
Buxbaum, Edith
De Mause, Lloyd
Dreikurs, Rudolf
Dunnette, Marvin D.
Egan, Gerard

Ellis, Albert
Fairbairn, W. R. D.
Ferenczi, Sandor
Foulkes, Sigmund, Heinrich
Frankl, Viktor
Freud, Anna
Freud, Sigmund
Fromm, Erich Pinchas
Fromm, Frieda
Green, André
Gudden, Von Johann
    Bernhard Aloys
Harding, Mary Esther
Hartmann, Heinz
Hinkle, Beatrice Moses
Irigaray, Luce

Jackson, Donald De Avila
Janov, Arthur
Jones, Ernest
Jung, Carl Gustav
Kelly, George, Alexander
Kernberg, Otto F.
Klein, Melanie
Lacan, Jacques
Laplanche, Jean
Mahler, Margaret Schoenberger
May, Rollo
Miller, Jean Baker
Moreno, Jacob
Neumann, Erich
Niederland, William
    Guglielmo

Index